Contemporary Political Ideologies

Edited by JOSEPH S. ROUCEK

About the Book

THIS SYMPOSIUM of original studies by 21 leading American specialists is headed by such authorities as Professor Carle C. Zimmerman of Harvard University, Anthony T. Bouscaren of Le Moyne College, Stanley Rothman of Smith College, Heinz Eulau of Stanford University, Chancellor Williams of Harvard University.

It presents penetrating analyses of the main ideological cross currents in the world today, under such headings as Ideological Movements and Social Change, Variations in Marxism and Neo-Marxism, Soviet Russia's Reluctant Satellites, Remnants of Socialism, New Nationalism and Pan-Movements, Colonialism at the Crossroads, Zionism, Latin America, New Democracies (Germany's Reconstruction, Rejuvenated Italy, Japan's Reforms, India's Gandhism), and The American Welfare State.

LITTLEFIELD, ADAMS & CO.

Paterson, New Jersey

T0352409

LITTLEFIELD QUALITY PAPERBACKS
A. W. LITTLEFIELD, General Editor

ACCOUNTING, COST
ACCOUNTING (CPA EXAMS)
ACCOUNTING, ELEMENTARY
ADMINISTRATION, BASIC
ADMINISTRATION, PUBLIC
ADVERTISING, Principles
ALGEBRA, COLLEGE
ANATOMY, HUMAN, ATLAS
ANTHROPOLOGY, DICTIONARY*
ASTRONOMY and ASTRONAUTICS, DICT.*
BENTHAM'S FICTIONS, THEORY†
BIOLOGY, General
BUSINESS COMMUNICATION
BUSINESS ORGANIZATION
CALCULUS
CHEMISTRY, Elementary
CHEMISTRY, General*
CHILD'S CONCEPTION of Phys. Causality†
CHILD'S CONCEPTION OF WORLD†
CHILD, JUDGMENT, REASONING†
CITIZENSHIP, Tools for Good
COMMUNICATION FOR NURSES N
CONSTITUTION, ANALYZED
CONSTITUTION, LEADING CASES
CONSTITUTIONS, MODERN
CORPORATE FINANCE
CREDITS AND COLLECTIONS
DISASTER NURSING N
DOCUMENTS, BASIC AMERICAN
ECONOMIC HISTORY OF U. S.*
ECONOMICS, Principles
ECONOMICS, DICTIONARY
ECONOMIC DOCTRINES, R'D'GS, Vol. I
ECONOMIC DOCTRINES, R'D'GS, Vol. II
EDUCATION, PHILOSOPHY OF*
EDUCATORS, SOCIAL IDEAS, AMER.*
ENGINEERING MECHANICS
ENGLISH ESSENTIALS
ETHICAL RELATIVITY†
ETHICAL THEORY, FIVE TYPES†
FICTION, MODERN WORLD
FIGURES THAT COUNT (Math. for Nurses) N
FOREIGN POLICY, AMER.*
FRENCH LITERATURE, DICT.*
GOVERNMENT, AMERICAN
GOVERNMENT, AMER., DICT.*
GOVERNMENT, COMPARATIVE*
GOVERNMENT, U. S. (Visual) *
GRAMMAR, AMER., DICT.*
HISTORY, AMER., DICT.*
HISTORY, AMER., to 1865*
HISTORY, AMER., Since 1865*
HISTORY, AMERICAN, Before 1877
HISTORY, AMERICAN, After 1865
HISTORY, ANCIENT*
HISTORY, CIVILIZATION, Before 1648
HISTORY, CIVILIZATION, After 1500
HISTORY OF ENGLAND
HISTORY, EUROPE, 1500-1848
HISTORY, EUROPE, After 1815
HISTORY, FAR EAST
HISTORY, MEDIEVAL*
HISTORY, U. S. DIPLOMATIC
INDUCTION AND PROBABILITY†
INSURANCE, DICTIONARY

INSURANCE, General Principles
INTELLIGENCE, NATURE OF†
INTELLIGENCE, PSYCHOLOGY OF†
LANGUAGE, LOGICAL SYNTAX†
LAW AND CONTEMPORARY NURSING N
LITERATURE, AMERICAN
LITERATURE, AMERICAN, DICT.*
LITERATURE, ENGLISH, Vol. I
LITERATURE, ENGLISH, Vol. II
LITERATURE, RECENT AMERICAN
LITERATURE, RUSSIAN, DICTIONARY*
LITERATURE, TREAS. OF WORLD*
LITERATURE, SPANISH, HISTORY
LITERATURE, WORLD, DICTIONARY*
MARKETING
MATERNAL AND CHILD HEALTH N
MATHEMATICS, FOUNDATIONS OF†
MATHEMATICS, NATURE OF†
MATHEMATICS TABLES
MATHEMATICS, UNDERSTANDING
MIND, GROWTH OF THE†
MIND, ITS PLACE IN NATURE†
MONEY AND BANKING
PHARMACOLOLGY FOR NURSES N
PHILOSOPHICAL STUDIES†
PHILOSOPHICAL SYSTEMS*
PHILOSOPHY*
PHILOSOPHY, AMERICAN
PHILOSOPHY, DICTIONARY OF*
PHILOSOPHY, LIVING SCHOOLS*
PHILOSOPHY, WORLD TREASURY*
PLATO'S WORKS, ABRIDGED*
POLITICAL SCIENCE
POSITIVISM, LOGICAL, AN EXAM. OF†
PSYCHIATRIC NURSING N
PSYCHOLOGICAL TERMS, HANDBOOK
PSYCHOLOGY, ABNORMAL*
PSYCHOLOGY, ABNORMAL, R'D'GS
PSYCHOLOGY, EDUC.
PSYCHOLOGY, EDUC., R'D'GS
PSYCHOLOGY, GENERAL
PSYCHOLOGY, INDIVIDUAL†
PSYCHOLOGY, REVIEW
PSYCHOLOGY, MODERN
READING, RAPID
RELIGION OF THE OCCIDENT*
RELIGION, ENCYCLOPEDIA*
RELIGIONS, LIVING SCHOOLS*
SALESMANSHIP
SAVAGE SOCIETY, CRIME, CUSTOM†
SHAKESPEARE'S PLAYS, SYNOPSES
SCIENCE, DICTIONARY*
SLIDE RULE, UNDERSTANDING THE
SCIENTIFIC METHODS†
SOCIOLOGY, An Introduction
SOCIOLOGY, DICTIONARY OF*
STATISTICAL PRESENTATION
SYNONYMS, AMERICAN, DICT.*
THERMODYNAMICS, ENGINEERING
THESES, TYPED MSS., PREP.
THESIS WRITING
THOUGHT, SCIENTIFIC†
WESTERN CIVILIZATION, READINGS
WORD ORIGINS, DICTIONARY OF*

* Asterisk indicates titles in the new Students Outline Series.
† Dagger indicates titles in the International Library of Psychology, Philosophy and Scientific Method.
N Indicates Nurses Handbook Series.
All others are Littlefield College Outlines.

Contemporary Political Ideologies

Edited by

JOSEPH S. ROUCEK

ROWMAN & LITTLEFIELD PUBLISHERS, INC.
Lanham • *Chicago* • *New York* • *Toronto* • *Plymouth, UK*

Published by Rowman & Littlefield Publishers, Inc.
4501 Forbes Boulevard, Suite 200, Lanham, Maryland 20706
www.rowman.com

10 Thornbury Road, Plymouth PL6 7PP, United Kingdom

Originally published by Philosophical Library
Copyright © 1961 by PHILOSOPHICAL LIBRARY, INC.
First Rowman & Littlefield paperback edition 2014

British Library Cataloguing in Publication Information Available

Library of Congress Cataloging-in-Publication Data Available

ISBN: 978-1-4422-3390-4 (pbk. : alk paper)
ISBN: 978-1-4422-3391-1 (electronic)

♾™ The paper used in this publication meets the minimum requirements of
American National Standard for Information Sciences—Permanence of Paper
for Printed Library Materials, ANSI/NISO Z39.48-1992.

Printed in the United States of America

CONTENTS

CHAPTER   PAGE

PREFACE   ix
JOSEPH S. ROUCEK, *University of Bridgeport*

THE FRAMEWORK

1. IDEOLOGICAL MOVEMENTS AND SOCIAL CHANGE   3
CARLE C. ZIMMERMAN, *Harvard University*

VARIATIONS IN MARXISM AND NEO-MARXISM

2. SOVIETISM   31
ANTHONY T. BOUSCAREN, *Le Moyne College*

3. CHINESE COMMUNISM   47
THEODORE HSI-EN CHEN, *University of Southern California*

4. SOVIET RUSSIA'S RELUCTANT SATELLITES   65
EDWARD TABORSKY, *University of Texas*

5. TITOISM   88
DAN N. JACOBS, *Miami University*

REMNANTS OF SOCIALISM

6. SOCIALIST INTERNATIONALS AND CONTINENTAL SOCIALISM   111
GERARD BRAUNTHAL, *University of Massachusetts*

7. BRITISH SOCIALISM   137
STANLEY ROTHMAN, *Smith College*

NEW NATIONALISM, COLONIALISM AND PAN-MOVEMENTS

8. COLONIALISM AT THE CROSSROADS   161
WALLACE SOKOLSKY, *New York University*

9. ZIONISM   177
SIDNEY J. KAPLAN and LEON ZOLONDEK,
University of Kentucky

CONTENTS (continued)

CHAPTER   PAGE

10. RACIAL THEORIES OF SOUTH AFRICA   194
COLIN RHYS LOVELL, *University of Southern California*

11. PAN-ASIATIC AND PAN-AFRICAN MOVEMENTS   212
CHANCELLOR WILLIAMS, *Howard University*

12. LATIN AMERICA   241
STEPHEN S. GOODSPEED, *University of California*

NEW DEMOCRACIES

13. FRANCE'S FIFTH REPUBLIC: "UNITY, TRUTH, AUSTERITY"   265
JOHN T. EVERETT, JR.,*Texas Christian University*

14. GERMANY'S RECONSTRUCTION   281
ERIC WALDMAN, *Marquette University*

15. REJUVENATED ITALY   319
TIBOR KEREKES, *Georgetown University*

16. AUSTRIA'S SURVIVAL   345
HERBERT P. SECHER, *Western Reserve University*

17. JAPAN'S REFORMS   379
DAVID HENRY KORNHAUSER, *State University Teachers College* (New Paltz, N. Y.)

18. INDIA'S GANDHISM   397
HOWARD BOONE JACOBSON, *University of Bridgeport* and DANA RAPHAEL, *Columbia University*

CROSS CURRENTS

19. THE AMERICAN WELFARE STATE: NEITHER IDEOLOGY NOR UTOPIA   415
HEINZ EULAU, *Stanford University*

NOTES   433

INDEX   467

CONTEMPORARY POLITICAL IDEOLOGIES

PREFACE

"Thought control" is one of the most important weapons of modern declared and undeclared wars, and much is being said these days—and properly so—concerning the war of ideologies. It is true that the history of mankind is also the history of wars of ideologies, exemplified, for instance, by the Crusades, the bloody struggle between Catholicism and Protestantism in the sixteenth century, and the consequences of the French Revolution. But present-day conflicts differ from any in the past. Our modern era has given birth to a class of intellectuals trained in the use of ideologies for social control purposes and able to carry on the warfare of ideas on a level never matched before. In addition, the amazing advances in mass communications in recent years have challenged innumerable traditions, upset many fixed beliefs, and introduced a unique ideological aspect into the intellectual struggle, so that today there is not a single system of thought which is not influenced by the present conflict of ideologies.

It can be, in fact, safely said that, for the most part, men live within the framework of institutions whose architecture is not of their own choosing, and they are periodically asked, even at the price of their lives, to preserve or destroy these institutions. Aggressive and conflicting ideologies have already set the armies of the world marching in two world wars. These hidden forces also penetrate all aspects of social life and form a spiritual basis for every social struggle. As powerful dynamic forces of contemporary social life, they give seemingly logical meaning to our politics and social efforts.

Yet the problem of ideologies as the supreme influence on purposive thinking in social life has been, until recently, ignored by social scientists in America, although since Kant there has been a growing recognition that the basic aims of philosophical criticism belong not to "science" in the usual sense of that term, but to the area for which there is no other word but "ideology."

A notable eccentricity of our age of specialization is the attempt of one author to be panoramic, for the flood of materials in every field is so great that even specialists find it difficult to keep abreast of their own specialties. Hence the editor is grateful to the distinguished group of co-authors who have made this significant volume possible. Also, special thanks and appreciation are due Dr. Dagobert D. Runes, Director of Philosophical Library, for conceiving the basic idea of this volume and for assisting the editor to bring it to fruition.

JOSEPH S. ROUCEK

University of Bridgeport

The Framework

CHAPTER ONE

IDEOLOGICAL MOVEMENTS AND SOCIAL CHANGE

CARLE C. ZIMMERMAN
Harvard University

Part A

SOCIOLOGICAL NATURE OF THE TWENTIETH CENTURY

In the second decade of this twentieth century the United States of America entered a world war more or less under the influence of the ideological slogan of Mr. Woodrow Wilson, "To save the world for democracy." In the next decade, that of the twenties, one ideological event stands out. The inflation and stock market gambling of that time had as its leading slogan "The new era has come." In the early thirties, a decade unknown to many readers, two ideological slogans captured the minds of the people. In the South the ideological scheme of Governor Huey Long of Louisiana arose under the banner of "Every man a king." On the national scene was President Franklin D. Roosevelt, who captivated the world with his ideals embodied in three words, "The Four Freedoms."

These expressions differ from the comforting ideas of the beginning of the century such as the pithy statements from Ben Franklin's POOR RICHARD'S ALMANAC, the moral adornments of the McGuffey series of reading books for the children of the United States, or even the famous one of the world empire of that time, "The sun never rises and sets on the British Empire."

While it is generally held that the current ideological movement of importance is one connected with the territorial control or change of management by an economic, a religious, a new governmental, a cultural or an ethnic group, it is correct to recognize that the two current classes of ideological movements are closely related. The conditions of society and of culture which make one possible also make the other feasible and probable. The techniques of one and the other may differ slightly but not fundamentally. If one believes, one does do, or at least one remains passive while others do. Consequently in the following discussion of the relation between ideological movements and social change the writer will not always discriminate carefully between the backgrounds of the internal and external types of movements. They are intermixed as to application to either type of event—the internal change of a given segment of culture (e.g., The Four Freedoms) for any reason whatsoever or the external changes for religious, political, ethnic or cultural purposes (e.g., Communism or Pan-Arabism). As a matter of fact, many of the larger ideological movements have been of both types. The Hitler movement was a small internal affair at first and gradually moved onto the world scene. Communism started as a slogan in a small German revolution and later became a world program. In a sense, while Pan-Arabism is inherent in the memories of the earlier Mohammedan empire with its center at Bagdad, it took its rebirth largely through a smaller internal movement beginning in Egypt through which Nasser came into control and then began to expand.

IDEOLOGICAL MOVEMENTS NOT NECESSARILY BAD

Nor is it necessary to say that all ideological movements are either good or bad *per se*. One can study the ideological movement in Mexico which is referred to there as "the revolution." This movement took shape about 1912 and is still virile. Apparently it has not harmed the country materially. Mexico has changed from a country once beset by many political and social difficulties to one which now proudly boasts that it has become the *hermano mayor* of the Caribbean world. A *hermano mayor* in Spanish is an older son or brother who takes care of all the members of the family and keeps them out of trouble, acting almost as a parent until the real parents are deceased and all the children are mature. Until that time he is apt to work more for his close relatives than for himself.

We have here the problem which Aristotle studied in detail, that any human trait can be either bad or good according to its use. For instance, the old Inca state of South America was probably as much dictatorial as are some of the Communist states of today, and certainly as much or more socialistic. However, considering the humanism in

4

the Inca regimes, and its century-long attempts to appease, please and improve the Indians under its dominion, one could hardly say it was bad for them. The Indians certainly did not fare so well for centuries after the Incas as they did under that benevolent rule.

Finally it should be pointed out that there are distinct differences between the ideological slogans of the twentieth century mentioned above, and the older nineteenth-century pithy phrases of Franklin, McGuffey and John Bull. The older ones sought to incite people to order and to self-improvement. The new ones, no matter what else they hope to achieve, incite to social change, to mass unit movements and to what seems to be a distinctly new type of world. They have in many cases incited groups to collective violence against many types of persons and under many varied circumstances. An outstanding example was the persecution and killings of Moslems by Hindus and of Hindus by Moslems in Greater India when the British government left. Roughly it is estimated that twenty millions of persons died.

All of this prelude introduces the idea that social change and ideological movements, particulary of the dominant types which now clutter the world about us, are birds of the same nest, if not exactly of the same feather.

IDEOLOGICAL MOVEMENTS AND SOCIAL CHANGES ARE RELATED

Ideological movements and social change are related closely to each other. Unless one understands this principle he can not think validly about many of the problems of the twentieth century. The more there is of social change, either actual, immanent, imminent or impending, the more there is of ideological movements. This is a principle the modern student of society should understand.

Perhaps other ways of stating this principle will make it more clear. *In those periods when social change is greatest, or the needs for it are greatest, then we have the most numbers and the most vocal and strange ideological movements.* Once a great change occurs within a social system, or a group of interrelated ones, such as is the characteristic of the whole modern world of the Space Age, then further changes and their associated ideological movements become inherent. Thus an ideological movement is a proposed new plan for the integration or reintegration of a social system.

The appearance of many ideological movements within one period

5

of time or within one related social system means that many persons have variant views as to the reorganization of the system or systems. *Cold wars* are thus conflicts between or among ideological movements. Capitalism fights Communism or vice versa. Nationalism fights disunity. Pan-nationalism fights nationalism of a smaller scale. Local freedom fights the proponents of pan-unionism. Every ideological movement thus tries to surmount its competitors.

CENTURIES HAVE SOCIOLOGICAL NATURES

The previous remarks have the purpose of showing that periods of three or four generations, or what may be called "centuries," may be viewed from the combined points of view of ideological movements and social change. We should look at them in such a combined fashion in order to understand them. All centuries known to man have been associated with some social change. We may say that the beginnings of a century period have never been like their endings and endings are always different from the beginnings.

This may be illustrated by taking the period in Europe from 1500 to 1600. At the onset of January 1, 1500, Martin Luther was but seventeen years of age, Niccolo Machiavelli thirty-one, Desiderius Erasmus thirty-four. and Henry VIII of England was at least eight years from conception. At the end of the century the Catholic Church, almost supreme social and governing body of Europe theretofore, was broken to pieces. The followers of Luther ruled the religious life of northern Europe and Elizabeth, the Protestant, ruled England. The rule of family law and marriage conduct by the priesthood, so savagely attacked by Erasmus in his PRAISE OF FOLLY, was now broken in many countries beyond repair. The followers of Machiavelli's ideological movement for social change, as enunciated in THE PRINCE and his DISCOURSES, had gone so far that Francis Bacon was even beginning to deny the validity of Aristotelian and Scholastic logic.

Not only that, but Bacon was using the ideas of Machiavelli as taken in their worst and unintended (by Machiavelli) sense from THE PRINCE in his personal ideological crusade for what he called THE ADVANCEMENT OF LEARNING. The Council of Trent (1545-1563) had modernized the Catholic Church but had failed to reunite the dissident Protestants with it. Sir Isaac Newton was fifty-eight years of age by 1600 and the modern world of Baconian empiricism and Newtonian physics was under way.

All of this is an example only of how the endings of centuries can be remarkably unlike the beginnings. Not all centuries are like the sixteenth or our present one called the twentieth. All centuries we know about show change. Some change more slowly than others. Some change in different directions from others. Some maximize small trends seen at the beginning and minimize other, grander currents. Civilizations, dynasties, forms of government, business methods and enterprises, ideal types of men, even whole cultures are subject to these changes.

For instance, the continents of the Americas had at the onset of 1500 three of the less than thirty-five great cultures of the world known to history, as recognized by the combined studies of W. E. Flinders-Petrie, O. Spengler, A. Toynbee and P. A. Sorokin. These were those of the Aztecs of Mexico, the Mayans of Yucatan and the Incas of Northwest South America. By the end of the century these three great cultures were almost completely destroyed and their people enslaved. Not only were the cultures and the people destroyed but the records of there even having been such cultures were almost obliterated. Bishop Landa read the documents of the Mayans, wrote a book about them, and then burned them all. (Three small ones have since been found.) Then Landa's manuscript itself was hidden away and lost in Europe for several centuries. It was not rediscovered until the twentieth. In Incaland the *Quipus,* on which they kept their records, were destroyed and even the people who could read the *Quipus* were killed.

Using the common characteristic of social change, which applies to all such periods, we may put all centuries into four classes.

A. Centuries of slow change;
B. Centuries of rapid change;
C. Centuries which during their course maximize trends present at the opening;
D. Centuries of revolutionary and almost incomprehensible change.

THE SOCIOLOGICAL NATURE OF THE
TWENTIETH CENTURY

As indicated above, we now know enough of broad general history to classify centuries according to their types of social change. For instance, with the onset of the modern world, after that catastrophic sixteenth, described above, the seventeenth changed slowly, but on the same pathway of the trends at the end of the sixteenth. The eighteenth changed more rapidly, but in the path of the trends in evidence at the end of the seventeenth. The nineteenth century of industrialism and city-dwelling changed even more rapidly yet, but still in the Baconian and Newtonian patterns. Then came the twentieth, our century, the one of violent change of a revolutionary nature like the sixteenth. Thus our century belongs with the fifth, twelfth and sixteenth in the class of unrecognizability. They are also together in the class of the Greater Ideological Centuries.

In the fifth century the Roman Empire fell to pieces. At about the beginning of the century the philosopher Jerome told the people this was going to take place but no one believed him. Shortly after this long period Gregory of Tours (538-593), who lived in a part of that old empire, could not even get Roman law enforced to settle the dispute of the clan vendetta type between the Sichaire and Ausregisil families. This old Roman region had lost its comprehension of former basic social control.

The twelfth was the century of the real renewal of Western life after the Dark Age. John of Salisbury (1120-1180) was so conscious of the former greatness of Western peoples before the Dark Age, as compared with their then poverty-stricken state, that he went everywhere proclaiming his ideological slogan—"WE ARE BUT DWARFS ON THE SHOULDERS OF GIANTS." By this he meant that Europe of 1100 was a feeble culture compared with Europe at the height of the Roman Empire. By the end of the twelfth century things had changed so much for the good that Europe's civilized law code, the old Roman law of the *Corpus Juris Civilis,* was being taught and used in the courts. For five centuries up to that time the codes had been forgotten and neglected.

The twentieth century is one of those centuries like the fifth, twelfth and sixteenth. All had seen such revolutionary change (and associated ideological movements) that *people at the beginning could not believe what would take place* and *people at the end could not understand what had taken place.*

That is the sociological nature of the twentieth century. That is why we have such profuse and drastic ideological movements now. That is why we are so confused with our times. That is why we must

8

understand. Only by understanding this can we see the dawn of hope of a reformed culture and gather courage to march more rapidly and directly toward it.

Part B

THE MAJOR SOCIAL CHANGES OF THE TWENTIETH CENTURY

When a social system changes in a major sense, then all of its parts have to readjust. An earthquake is a major slippage in the earth crust which is followed by minor readjustments over extended areas and periods. After these comes a longer period of stability until the conditions are ripe for another major slippage.

Using the above figure of speech for clarification, we may speak of four major social earthquakes as being characteristic of the twentieth century. All these four have been associated with our high number of ideological movements. Ideological movements have partly brought them about and have helped to spread the influence and significance of each. For illustration take the case of the changing history of the ideological movement *Communism* in Russia. It started after the Kerensky revolution. Then in time it grew from a Russian movement to a bid for world power. First Russia, then the satellites, then China, etc.

Most of the mechanical changes of our century, such as the atomic discoveries and the moon shots, are sideline effects of the major social changes. That is, we got into wars and other troubles on account of the success of some of our major ideological changes. Then we started to explore the use of rockets and atom bombs as ultimate war weapons. Out of this came moon shots and earth satellites. Then realizing that we stood a good chance of exterminating ourselves if we used the atom bombs against each other, we have entered upon a "moon-race" for prestige. Russia and the United States are each trying to prove its superiority by economic methods, by ideological propaganda or by sending manned space ships aloft. Out of this situation arises a general world of vastly increased change, unrest, ideological movements and unsettlement.

The four major basic changes of the twentieth may be noted in the following fields: (1) Vast shifts have taken place in territorial power control. (2) Internally there have been drastic changes in the social classes and in the power exercised by the various social classes. (3)

9

Physical space as a factor in isolation and protection of groups and cultures, and their insulation and safety from each other, has practically disappeared in the Space Age. (4) In the whole world all peoples have developed the feeling that *"We are but dwarfs standing on the shoulders of giants."*

In the following pages we will illustrate the significance of these four basic changes. Then we will show some of the major sociological problems raised by them.

SHIFTS IN TERRITORIAL CONTROL

Every century has seen some changes in the government of given pieces of territory. The sixteenth century was the one in which the colonial system had its major expansion. From about 1500 to 1600 the three great empires of the new world (Aztec, Mayan and Inca) were put under the control of European countries. Some of this colonial growth was still being carried out even in the nineteenth century. But by that time most of the world was already under the colonial system so that this type of growth was largely on the fringes and in the less desirable lands from the then commercial point of view.

Further, by then colonialism had changed in two other aspects. One of these was the development of what were called mere "zones of influence." This meant that a given European country did not necessarily claim the new territory .as a colony but it claimed the right to insist upon the country being managed so as to give the major commercial rights in the territory to the European power claiming a "zone of influence." In the first case—colonialism—trade followed the flag. In the second case—the zone of influence—the flag followed trade.

This meant often that the advisers to the government of the "zone of influence dominated country" would be nationals of that European country which claimed the zone of influence. For instance, Indochina was under the French either as colonies or as a zone of influence. Across Siam, Malay and Burma were two British colonies. Siam (Thailand), which separated the two colonial zones of government and influence, was supposed to be free. But traditionally certain of the ministers in Siam had British advisers, and certain others French. In later years the odd ones were given to Americans.

The second change in the colonial governing system during the latter nineteenth century was the yielding of rights to the territories among European countries as the results of wars, trades or agreements. This continued into the twentieth century and was particularly active as a result of the treaties made after World War I.

Thus it was that early in this twentieth century the world was very much under territorial rule. The largest aggregation was the British Empire. In a considerable degree it held the majority of the people of the world under it. Even China with its British trade ports, such as Hong Kong, was largely British dominated and ruled. South America, through the Monroe doctrine, was fairly independent in most areas. However, partly in South America but elsewhere many European countries governed areas ten or twenty times larger than themselves and that many times more populous.

For instance, the Netherlands with a population of about ten million in Europe and an area of 12,850 square miles, had among its colonies one, Indonesia, with an area of 735,000 square miles and a population of eighty-five million. In 1958 it was claimed that there were only 46,000 Dutch citizens in Indonesia. In addition the Netherlands had other colonies scattered over the world.

Now nearly all of this is broken up. India, Burma, French Indochina, and Indonesia, to name only a few regions with almost a billion population, are decolonized and have the job now of self-government.

The shifts in territorial power control in the twentieth century affect nearly the whole world. The British, French, Dutch, Belgian, German and Italian colonies are largely broken from the colonial system or in revolution against it. The European countries concerned have themselves been affected by new adjustments, as for instance the losses of the Dutch in Indonesia or the financial and blood cost of the various colonial crises through which France has gone. Needless to say, each of these minor changes has fanned the flame of various ideological movements.

Within Europe itself the territorial changes have been vast. Germany expanded under Hitler and then contracted. Russia contracted after 1919 and then expanded after World War II. The various smaller countries affected by these movements have been influenced by a different ideological movement about once every decade during the century.

CHANGES IN THE POWER OF SOCIAL CLASSES

A second major type of change in the twentieth century has been the internal shifting of political, social and economic power among

11

the older social classes. In many cases new classes have risen to power and older ones have disappeared entirely. Every country has seen a great deal of this. Russian aristocrats were exterminated during the Revolution and the Communist Party took over. Within the party there has been a constant struggle for power among the various segments so that first one, and then the other, has been purged and replaced. The whole peasant class in Russia has been reshuffled juridically and locationally. Workers of an urban skilled type have risen to prominence. In 1935 a committee at Harvard was seeking to nominate a social scientist from Russia for the three hundredth celebration in 1936. This was a long process of repeated nominations because the earlier named persons were always purged before the Tercentenary and new ones had to be named constantly.

This shifting of power among classes is marked in the United States of America by the almost total disappearance of common labor as a commodity and its replacement by machines and skilled labor. In 1900 almost 80 per cent of American workers were manual. Now less than 10 per cent are. The farmer class is rapidly disappearing in numbers and in political significance in favor of factories in the fields. We now have less than two million farms, only one million of which are important. At one time we had nearly eight millions. The class of household servants has almost disappeared. Now the "household servant" is a service-skilled worker or a salesman of automatic washers, driers or refrigerators. He either sells you a new washing or cleaning machine, which you must operate yourself by pushing buttons, or he is there to repair the ones you have so they will continue serviceable.

Organized labor with its bosses has risen into great power in the U.S.A. In many sections of the country these labor bosses have become even more powerful than the elected governments. The illiterate in the country have been replaced by the literate. We no longer count our illiterates because they are such a small percentage. The teaching profession has increased in its social power and in its influence. Scientists have come more to the forefront. In the early days the scientists who took public positions were called derisive names such as "brain-trusters" and "egg-headers." Now they have assumed a more important role and are not the subject of epithets. The scientific associations have risen in numbers, in strength and in influence. Many of these persons are given government positions for their scientific knowledge alone just by the sides of cabinet members. Large amounts of money are spent each year to promote scientists and science. The aim is to promote scientific discovery. Many lengthy discussions are held and scientific books and papers are written on the best methods of doing this. Questions are constantly raised as to whether this scientific promotion is being done better in the United States than in Russia.

Since the defeat of Germany in World War II, the conquering nations, particularly Russia and the United States, have been wooing the scientists of the old Germany trying to get them to move to Russia or America to spread their ideas and techniques. We have even tried to develop translating machines so that the findings of science reported in other languages may be made available mechanically in English with the least of human effort and loss of time.

The change of power of social classes, particularly of skilled labor and management, has been marked by a number of books which seek to point this out. Earlier in the century Thorstein Veblen made a critique of the decline of the business class in his work entitled THE THEORY OF THE LEISURE CLASS. He wrote another work showing the rising importance of technicians in THE ENGINEER AND THE PRICE SYSTEM. Now we have such works as THE ORGANIZATION MAN and THE MAN IN THE GRAY FLANNEL SUIT. These describe the new position of technicians and managers.

Similar changes have taken place in the European countries. In the former colonial countries, the natives who once were largely merely errand boys for the colonial administrators have replaced their former bosses. In China the feudal war lords have now consolidated and risen to national power through the military bureaucracies which control the Communist state. In Russia the scientist, doctor of philosophy and the "stakhanovite" (or unusually skilled worker) are now given preference in living conditions and material comforts.

THE DECLINE OF SPACE

Physical space has declined as a factor for the safety, the isolation and the insulation of peoples and cultures from others. News and new ideas get everywhere and at once through the press, radio and television. Men everywhere (if not behind the Iron and Bamboo Curtains) hear all that seems important in the whole world each day and before that day ends. In one or two days at the most men and machines in the free world at least can and do move from any one section of the

13

globe to another. A little room is now left for provincialism, ignorance of events or privacy from public affairs.

Associated with this extreme proximity of men and events, of nations and cultures, now with one another, is the problem of the newer weapons of war. Everyone has a feeling and is given to understand that the weapons of one section of the world are but a few moments away from their targets in any other part of the world's domain.

Also there is the immense possible coverage in terms of space and the long-lasting effects of each weapon. An atom bomb is said to contaminate a large area and its effects held to continue to carry out destruction over a long period. These effects have become so massive that we daily monitor our air for "fall-out." We study the bodies of samples of our dead corpses to see if contamination is increasing. And these precautions are merely taken to find if the practice of use of these newer weapons has contaminated the surface of the globe to a dangerous level. We want to know if these poisons are getting to humans through consuming the animals which eat the grass grown in the contaminated earth.

No longer in any section of the globe is there much left of pastoral isolation or insulation from the mighty forces loose in the world. All of this gives rise to tremendous new fears and more ideological movements. Further, it makes the possible audiences for any ideological movement vaster in numbers and more easily swayed. The psychological resistance levels of people to ideological movements has been lowered. Statements warning of the possible contamination of the earth by atom bombs like that by Albert Schweitzer are printed everywhere.

This century has witnessed the capacity of some ideological groups to completely pervert and overthrow long-established and traditional moral values and human character traits, at least for a time. Several countries — in fact, a number of large areas — have seen these reversions. Peoples who have lived in a friendly fashion side by side for countless generations have been turned into mobs, killing each other allegedly because of ethnic, color, economic or religious differences.

Three illustrations point this out. Hindu and Moslem have lived together fairly peacefully in greater India for some centuries. Jew and Arab have been side by side in the Middle East for some thousands of years. Gentile and Jew have resided as neighbors in Europe since the Roman Empire. During this century each of these groups has turned violently at times against the other. The former friendships of peoples have been turned into lusts for wholesale extermination.

"WE ARE BUT DWARFS"

The fourth great social change of this century has been the universal rise among nearly all peoples of the idea that we are but dwarfs standing on the shoulders of giants. Most of the regions of the world, outside of Russia, the U.S.A. and Canada, southeast South America and Australia and possibly a part of Africa, are peopled by the descendants of ancient cultures which have at least once or several times been more powerful and successful economically and socially than they were in the first third of the present century or are now. These are called "the fellaheen peoples" in Oswald Spengler's significant book THE DECLINE OF THE WEST. This term as used in that book, published about 1920, has a peculiar significance.

The word "fellaheen" is used in the Middle East to signify the class of peasants who are illiterate, who barely make a living by agriculture, who know little of their history and of their background, but who till their small pieces of land near the remains of great ruins which their forefathers once built. A typical example is the poverty-stricken Nile peasant who does not know much about his previous great cultures during which the pyramids were built.

Spengler did not believe that history was continuous because he thought when a given civilization fell into long decay the memory of that civilization also vanished, and the people there entered into a quiescent or resting state. In this condition they are completely ignorant of their former greatness. They become mere fellaheen according to Spengler.

Whether or not this is as true as Spengler thought it was, it is obvious that at the beginning of the twentieth century most all of the peoples of the world, with the few exceptions in the areas mentioned above, were living rather ignorantly among the ruins of their former greatness. The mention of a few such areas other than Egypt will demonstrate this. India, China, Southeast Asia, Indonesia, all the Arab world in the Middle East and North Africa are illustrations of these types of people on the older continents. In the Americas we have the Aztec, Mayan and Inca ruins. These cover all of present Mexico, Central America, and the northwest third of South America. The poor

15

Mayan, with his *milpa* or corn plot on streets of a ruined former city, did not know much about his former greatness.

The "we are but dwarfs on the shoulders of giants" idea is one which inspired Western Europe during the Renaissance of the twelfth century. At that time the peoples of Europe had begun to find out that in the days of the Roman Empire they had been much more cultured and civilized than they were in the present. So leaders like John of Salisbury and others went about Europe proclaiming their former greatness. This dwarf idea was used as a challenge, and inspiration, to get the then European "fellaheen" to rise again toward their former greatness.

The point of importance is that now all the "fellaheen" peoples in the world have become aware to a considerable extent of their former greatness. They want to rise again. This has inspired many ideological movements. Pan-Arabism is an example. The inspiration of this ideological Arab movement lies in the hopes of recreating the great former Arabic civilization which, with its capital at Damascus, was so powerful during those centuries (sixth to twelfth) of the Western Dark Age.

Ideas such as this stir people to attempt to rise to creativity again and the ideologies become slogans or banners or new "collective representations." They are now spreading everywhere in the twentieth century.

The idea that "we are but dwarfs" is also not now limited to the present "fellaheen"-like countries. Russia and the United States, for example, have taken up this idea, even though in their territories are no vast ruins of former greatness. The peoples of these two great cultures are fairly recent migrants — the Americans mostly from many countries of Europe and the Russians from out of Asia. All this happened mostly in the past few centuries for both Russia and the U.S.A. But still they have picked up this idea of a possible greatness better than their present greatness. In a large sense they got this "we are but dwarfs" idea from other than historical sources.

How did Russia and the United States get this "dwarf idea." They reached it by science. In each civilization there was a vast demographic and cultural transformation arising out of the recent events of their existence. In the U.S.A. it was the settlement of the country by diverse European groups none of which had any great understanding of their native cultures. The American people, no matter from whence they came, were distinctly unlearned, mostly peasants from their former countries. They did not ordinarily speak their own pure languages, such as German, Italian or what not, but dialects. They united here under one tradition — the Mayflower one — and under one language — American English. Growing rapidly, they met the challenge of the twentieth century and developed scientific ideas imported from Europe. Once they started, they began their own science. Their own science gave them a vision of creativity. So now, although there are no great ruins in the United States of previous cultures, other than the mounds of New Mexico, the Americans have the vision of being dwarfs on the shoulders of giants. Thus America itself is one gigantic ideological movement. It is a fact, and also a challenge to creativity on an unprecedented scale.

Russia is also a country with the synthetic widespread development of the idea of being dwarfs. How this came about due to the terror and destruction of the Revolution, the challenge and the rebuilding, is a story that is evident, but not clearly understood. But Russia is one vast ideological movement in itself. The Russians are shooting at the moon just to prove to the world that they are no longer satisfied to remain dwarfs in a world when giants can emerge.

Thus we see that no matter how we interpret ideological movements in this century, there are four great social changes behind them. Among these changes the psychological one of hope that man can better himself and no longer remain the *fellah* he once was is by all means the most substantial.

Part C

MAJOR SOCIOLOGICAL PROBLEMS RAISED BY THE TWENTIETH CENTURY IDEOLOGICAL MOVEMENTS

Social problems may be classified as to their relative importance. In the remainder of our century four great problems will be outstanding in their significance. The first is that new sources of leaders and of leadership and new classes of leaders are arising all over the world and will continue to rise rapidly to power. Secondly, most of these new leaders and leadership groups come from classes of persons who, in their previous experience, have had little or no training in large-scale leadership and its responsibilities. They now have to lead and they do not know how or what to do.

17

Thirdly, our present century has some of the greatest possibilities to offer mankind and yet some of the greatest dangers and difficulties. The twentieth century already is mankind's hardest or most difficult period to date. The amateur leadership which is now coming to power nearly everywhere all at once faces the greatest challenges that any class of leaders has faced since the dawn of history.

Fourthly, for the above reasons we need a sophisticated social science for guidance of the new leadership. They have to transmit it to the led. We need an academic group in the social sciences which is more sophisticated and understanding than any this world has seen to this time. However, in spite of this vaster need in the social sciences several giant road blocks stand in our way. One is that the perplexed and frightened world is so confused that mankind now tends to trust plausible slogans and ideologies rather than more thoughtful social science principles. Another phase of this is the failure of much of our academic leadership so far to face the main issues and seek answers.

These four great social problems — new leaders, amateur leaders, increased difficulties of leadership, and lack of a sophisticated social science — are the major difficulties of the twentieth century. Compared with these, all others are minor.

For instance, look at these situations. What should have been done about Berlin and divided Germany at the end of the Second World War? By having done what we did, what can we do now?

Should we have dropped the atomic bomb on two of Japan's cities? By having done so, what can we do now? It is contended that the abrupt cessation of the war between the United States and Japan on account of the two bombs saved several millions of lives of American soldiers. Did it save human lives or merely postpone misery for a possible greater slaughter by atomic weapons?

Should England have given greater India a distinguished position in the commonwealth in 1919 or allowed it later freedom after massive resistance? Having taken this last course of rather forced freedom, we now witness the dismemberment of that great territory into three or four distrusting and suspicious states.

What can be done now in Indonesia? In the Middle East? In the African colonies and territories of greater France? In the Central African territories south of the Sahara? In Laos and in former French Indochina?

Everywhere the world is now in a precarious position subject to

18

both good and evil ideological movements. The whole world is now like a great lava bed which is beginning to erupt again. First here, then there, but always somewhere.

NEWNESS IN LEADERSHIP

This century has witnessed the demise of the colonial system, the rise of the U.S.A. and Russia as two new world powers, and the changing of the situations in which the older knowledge of the former European leaders could function world-wisely as it once did. This means that everywhere new leaders have come into power. In the former colonies throughout the world the people now have the job of governing themselves.

This may be illustrated in the case of India. Here for several centuries the British governed. Railroads were built, health measures were taken, commerce flourished, and industry began. Local law prevailed in most private affairs but British law was available for public affairs. The civil servants all had the same chance at the examinations for positions because English became the governing language. The universities could use English texts, so the problem of scientific books in a native language was not critical.

Now the Indians have the job of governing themselves. Several hundred local languages or dialects are used in India but the great masses use fourteen. Since modern free India does not wish to continue to use English as a common public language their problem is which of the popular languages should be substituted. The argument runs like this. If we accept Hindi as the common language, even though 50 per cent of the people speak it, then the other 50 per cent who speak mainly thirteen other languages will be handicapped in the examinations for positions because they will be examined in a strange tongue. Although they have now accepted Hindi as the main public language (with English as a second), still a half of the people feel disfranchised by this selection.

Thus India has the problem of teaching Hindi to two hundred millions of persons in order that common public knowledge can pass easily from one part of the population to the other.

Before now very few in India faced this problem of national unity. It is one of a common language, of common laws and practices, and of a converging national culture. This illustrates for that large section of the world's population one of the aspects of newness in leadership.

19

Then study the case of Indonesia. This is a new republic of 85 millions on three thousand islands off the southeast coast of Asia. In 1953, 52 millions of the 85 lived on Java and 12 on Sumatra, the main islands. After several centuries of occupation by the Dutch, this former colonial dependency became self-governing about a decade ago. Now it has a problem somewhat comparable to that of India, that of creating a national self-governing culture. It has two things in its favor. Nearly all of the people use a form of the Malay language and the characters of the language are Latin letters. Nevertheless it is a tremendous task to make modern culture in all its aspects available to the Indonesians in their own tongue. It is one which few in Indonesia have had any experience with so far in their history.

But the problem of newness in leadership is not entirely one of the rise of the former colonies of Europe to self-government, even though this involves approximately two-thirds of the world's population. The emergence of Russia and the United States as world powers brings entirely new leadership to the forefront. Decisions in world affairs made in Washington and Moscow have replaced in importance those formerly made in London, Paris and Berlin. In each case — Washington and Moscow—the decisions are made by persons whose background has been largely that of a new people hardly prepared for dealing with the great problems of a world of diverse cultures.

Take the case of the American Presidents since 1912, when the new world began to emerge. All of these men from Woodrow Wilson on have had the best of intentions regarding the responsibilities of world leadership. But they and their advisers have never been sure what was the best course of action. If we tried open public "convenants between nations," which was Mr. Wilson's ideal, then we had trouble when we found the European nations had made secret covenants contradictory to the open covenants they disclosed to the United States. If we tried secret covenants, as some later Presidents did, then we found our good faith was met by bad faith. We lived up to our agreements but others did not.

In each case — Russia or the United States — the ultimate decision is one that has to be one of public opinion. In the United States this public opinion expresses itself in a major sense in the biennial elections to Congress. And every four years the President and the whole executive branch of the government has to stand before the bar of public opinion.

While conditions are different in Russia in the sense that free elections are never held, still there is the bar of public opinion. A monolithic state such as Russia expresses its public opinion through the constant purges of leaders. About every five years they have a grand purge. Even though the Russians exercise thought control by force, still the feelings of the more than two hundred millions of direct subjects to the Kremlin have to be given some consideration.

Newness in leadership is also reflected by the new social groups coming to the forefront. Take for instance the composition of the Communist Party in Russia which rules that country. Whatever its membership may be it is certainly different and less experienced in world affairs than the older internationally trained aristocracy under the last-century regimes in that country.

In the United States this is seen notably in two questions raised upon each important issue. These are: What does labor think? What do the Catholics think? Other questions are asked but these two are illustrative of new groups in power.

No one can deny the tremendous influence of the Catholic Church in world affairs. While it suffered a setback in the Reformation and the more rapid industrialization after that of the Protestant countries, it has lately begun to emerge toward a more powerful position. One of the major characteristics of human affairs is *social change*. Things which are up can always go down, and things down are always striving to recreate themselves. Now in the United States, once largely a Protestant country, there are about forty millions of Catholics. This group is concentrated very largely in our cities in the northeastern part of the United States. There they constitute a deciding influence in our national elections and hence in our long-time national policies. Further, they are more wealthy, sophisticated and devout compared with most other Catholic groups in the world. As such, what these people think is of great importance to Rome, and what Rome does is of fundamental significance to them.

This group of Catholics mainly descended from four ethnic groups who migrated in the last seventy-five years to the United States. Most of them are only first and second-generation native-born of Irish, Italian, French-Canadian and Polish extraction. In each case they came from relatively unsophisticated basic environments — the bogs of Ireland, the small farms of eastern Canada, the hillsides of Italy and the marginal poor agricultural lands of Poland. Now their feelings, whether experienced or not, are a tremendous influence in world affairs.

In America there is a story that in one of the wartime conferences between President Roosevelt and Premier Stalin Roosevelt asked Stalin if a representative of the Papacy might not be invited to attend. Stalin is reported to have sneered and said, "How many divisions of troops does the Pope command?" The above explanation shows that whereas the Church has no divisions of troops, it has a number of divisions of extremely powerful influence in world affairs. In a somewhat similar way Mohammedan influences are re-emerging in world affairs.

All these three factors — the resurgence of colonials, the rise of entirely new world powers and the emergence to power of new social and economic groups — inevitably means almost a complete newness in leadership in world affairs.

THE NEW LEADERS IN WORLD AFFAIRS ARE AMATEURS

These new groups (or old ones re-emerging) have had relatively little recent experience in leadership of this nature. Some of them had this governing experience before and did it well. For instance, the Inca people had power in South America five centuries ago and did a good job. But now the emerging power of these peoples brings to the forefront a group which has to learn again the difficulties and dangers and the proper use of social power. What is said now for the old Inca lands can also be said for almost the whole world. New people have risen or are rising to power in the world's most difficult century. They have to learn to lead us in our perilous atomic and space age world but their backgrounds for centuries have isolated them from the experiences of leadership.

This does not mean necessarily that we would be any better guided if the older nineteenth-century groups remained in power. The world of the past has moved out from under us and we all have to learn anew.

For instance: one of the main expressions of the older now gone period was that attributed to the Prussian General von Clausewitz (1790-1831). He defined war as political science in action. Essentially he said that "war is the political aims carried out to the field of battle." By this he meant that war had a legitimate place in the activities of nations. Now that can no longer be true. Now we have the absolute weapons. They will destroy both vanquished and victor alike. Many nations of the world, including numerous of the less powerful ones, have access to uranium, to mining techniques and to the know-how of the crude but extremely disastrous atomic bombs. War is no longer in agreement with man's occupation of this planet.

As a result the newness of leadership in the world today has a certain good side. The new leaders have everything to learn and nothing to forget.

Nevertheless, we are bound to make many mistakes on account of our newness of leadership until we learn the new system of government and international relations which will work in a world in which physical space has disappeared between peoples and cultures.

A NEW SOCIAL SCIENCE NEEDED

We have moved so rapidly into this new age that we are confused. A new social science is needed for the guidance of the cultures of the world and for the inspiration and stimulation of the new leadership. We need a social science and an academic group with a larger and more adequate view of the human problems now impinging upon us. We have moved into the new era so rapidly and so quickly that we as yet do not even have the vision to see it nor the vocabulary to talk about it.

The question might be raised as to why we do not have such a social science now. What have our social scientists been doing during this century. The answer to that is relatively simple — *almost nothing of importance.*

Up to 1920 social science, where studied, was carrying out methodically the outdated ideas of the past century. Sociology was broken into two schools — the theoretical and the practical. The theoretical sociologists were still teaching the instinctivist and evolutionary doctrine which had taken over all Western social science since Auguste Comte and G. W. F. Hegel. The right wing of the theorists were teaching mainly Spencerism, after the conservative evolutionary British sociologist Herbert Spencer (1820-1903). The left-wing sociologists were teaching about the same doctrines with a thinly hidden Marxian overcast.

The practical sociologists were promoting measures for the reform of our morals and standards of living in the city and the country with particular reference to housing, sanitation, overcrowding, misuse of sex and alcohol. While there were differences in various countries, the situation was about the same in the various countries of Europe as in America. The other countries of the globe—in South America, Asia and Africa — either had no sociology or theirs were copies of the European and American. One does not have to read Japanese to know what was in their texts because the references are in European languages and they are about the same as in the Euro-American texts. Chinese sociology, where it existed, was almost all plagiaristic of American and other texts.

Since 1920 sociology has had some interesting experiences. Most of the time it has been (and still is) illegal to study, write about or even to discuss the subject in Russia, which is a sixth of the globe.

During most of the same time it has been submerged or frowned upon in most of the other European countries. During the war period, which with reconstruction lasted almost the last twenty years, no one had time or energy to think of anything other than immediate necessities. Prior to that time the totalitarian movements in various European countries prohibited any sociology of importance and before that the inflation in Central Europe had the same effect. In other words, except in minor details there has been practically no sociological thinking at all in most of Europe since 1914. Just now it is beginning again.

This leaves sociology in the United States as about the only place free to develop such thinking. But, in general, sociology in the United States has degenerated, rather than grown, during this period. In other words, it has developed into a mess of confused abstruse and useless hypotheses and theories which have no relation to reality. The names of its three major schools show this exactly — formalism, functionalism and social actionism.

Formalism was the name for the dominant theoretical system in our sociology from about 1920 to 1935. This was the school of sociology brought over from prewar Germany by certain professors at the University of Chicago, the leading sociological center during those years. It merely studied and classified the *forms* of social relations not to find principles but used them like shelves in a storeroom so that any new study could be put on its proper shelf or shelves. It was a sort of useless game with no reference to the main problems of sociology — social change and what to do or not to do in case of social change. It did not guide people anywhere. It even denied that sociology should have an ethical or metaphysical background of guidance.

24

The writer has lived through this and disclaimed it. In a book published in 1935 the preface began with these words quoted from Aristotle: "Every art, and every science reduced to a teachable form, and likewise every action and moral choice, aims, it is thought, at some good." These thoughts however were a minority.[1]

The two other dominant schools which have followed since, *Functionalism* and *Social Actionism*, are, if anything, even more useless and unimportant than *Formalism* of the Simmel variety. All they have accomplished is to set up a framework in which a social system can be described, and only described. It is like saying that a chair is made of wood, and has four legs, and functions to be sat upon, and is dysfunctional if one can't sit on it. It leaves the meaning out of the social system. Values are only "integrative" and the intelligibility of society is simply lost or neglected. It has nothing to do with social change nor can it be used as any guide to decisions which we have to make now.

We have to make ethical decisions whether we wish to or not. Even the fluoridization of water or the use of DDT is an ethical decision. If we kill the malarial-bearing mosquito we make a decision to allow more people to live longer and then we have to make other ethical decisions as to how they should be fed.[2] Why? Well, that is an ethical decision itself!

NATURE OF THE NEW SOCIAL SCIENCE

During this period in the United States, practical sociology has changed too. It has grown some in a few fields like criminology and race relations. In others it has probably deteriorated. Space does not allow us to go into this matter. Helpful influences have arisen in two sources. One of these is the rising to influence of men outside the strict field of sociology but whose views take the place of older sociology. A couple of good examples are the books of Oswald Spengler and Arnold Toynbee. Neither of these practiced sociology but both pre-empted the minds of the kinds of people who once read Herbert Spencer, Auguste Comte and the older sociologists.

A second influence of importance has arisen in the field of foreign travel for scholars, notably in the Fulbright visiting professorships made available to many American and other professors each year. Many countries needed our left-over war supplies but did not have the foreign exchange to purchase these with. Senator Fulbright of Arkansas sponsored a bill to let these countries purchase the goods in their own currencies and then use the credits to support the exchanges of students and professors between the U.S.A. and other lands. In this way, to 1959 more than 37,000 academicians have been exchanged between the United States and other lands. Among these 37,000 are many who have begun to understand the new world in which we are embarked.

Slowly but surely we are now beginning to create a new social science. What it will be like we do not yet know. However, several things are certain. First, it will have to have *a respect for humanity of all kinds*. We know that in all groups of men there are those who possess creativity which can be challenged and developed. Secondly, it will emphasize a study of the *processes of social change* in order that we understand the human being as he actually is, a being always in motion, individually and collectively. Third, it will have to have *a new ethics*, a realization that most change is the result of an ethical evaluation by someone and the new situation always leads to further ethical evaluation. We want freedom; we get freedom; now of many alternative actions, what do we do? We want science; we get science; now what do we do with the atom power? Fourthly, and most important of all, the new social science will *take man out of the category of nature*, where he has rested since the Renaissance, and put him in the category of sacred things. We can no longer afford to consider man as expendable. A continuation of thought and action along this line means the end of our occupation of this planet.

These four principles should be carefully appraised in relation to the future of ideological movements and of man himself.

SELECTED BIBLIOGRAPHY

This chapter is a summary of a large work on THE SOCIOLOGY OF CHANGE, which the author, with the collaboration of Professor Joseph B. Ford of San Fernando State College, is preparing to publish shortly. Consequently a short bibliography is impossible and an adequate one would cover hundreds of volumes. However, if one is interested, he should turn to all the works of three authors — Pitirim A. Sorokin, Arnold Toynbee and the late Oswald Spengler.

The main writers on social change the past 1,500 years since the decay of the Roman Empire have been:

Zosimus (wrote c. 400 A.D.); Jerome (340?-420 A.D.) ; Augustine (354-430 A.D.); P. Orosius (wrote c. 415); Salvian (wrote c. 440); Justinian

(483-565); Theodora (503-548); Pseudo-Isidorean writers (wrote c. 850); Salisbury, John of (1120-1180); Aquinas (1225-1274); Dante (1265-1321); Chaucer (1340-1400); Langland (*Piers Plowman*) (1330-1400); Machiavelli (1469-1527); Erasmus (1466-1536); Luther (1483-1546); Francis Bacon (1561-1626); Bodin (1530-1596); Milton (1608-1674); Hobbes (1598-1679); Locke (1632-1704); Vico (1668-1744); Montesquieu (1689-1755); Turgot (1727-1781); Voltaire (1694-1778); Rousseau (1712-1778); Paine (1737-1809); Hegel (1770-1831); Marx (1818-1883); Durkheim (1858-1917); Tönnies (1855-1936); Max Weber (1864-1920); Spengler (1880-1936); Sorokin (1889-   ); Toynbee (1889-   ).

CURRICULUM VITAE

CARLE C. ZIMMERMAN (1897-   ) was born a son of a schoolteacher in Cass County, Missouri; took his Ph.D. in Sociology and Economics at Minnesota in 1925 after attending the Universities of Missouri, North Carolina State, and Chicago; has carried on extensive field sociological investigations in four American states, in Siam, Cuba, Canada, England, Germany and Italy; taught sociology at Minnesota from 1923-30 and at Harvard since 1931, when he returned from a year as adviser to the Royal Government of Siam. In addition to service in two wars he served on commissions for the United States government and for Cuba and Canada. His books and monographs were in the field of Rural Sociology to 1934. After that they were in studies of standards of living and community studies until 1940. Since then he has published a number on family sociology, including FAMILY AND CIVILIZATION (New York: Harper, 1948) and part of MARRIAGE AND THE FAMILY (Chicago: Regnery, 1956); his most recent work is in the field of Social Change and Social Theory.

In 1954-55 he was Visiting Research Professor at the University of Rome. He is a Fellow of the AAAS and a Councilor of the American Academy of Arts and Sciences. His position on sociological development is one that sees theory of no value unless followed by empirical study and empiricism as of no value unless growing out of theory. Consequently he is, always has been, and will remain impatient with anything else that claims to be sociology.

He is Secretary for the United States and Canada for the International Institute de Sociologie. His latest book (1959) is SUCCESSFUL FAMILIES, (New York: Pageant Press, 1960). In 1959 he was Visiting Professor at the Universities in Lima, Arequipa and Trujillo, Peru. He is director of the Center for Studies of Family Creativity which is at present studying the family backgrounds of college, university and professional men.

He has an M.A. (*honoris causa*) from Harvard and a Doctor of Science (*honoris causa*) from North Carolina State.

Variations in Marxism and Neo-Marxism

CHAPTER TWO

SOVIETISM

Anthony T. Bouscaren

Le Moyne College

Sovietism can best be defined as the system of government by the soviets.[1] A soviet is the primary unit in the political organization of the Union of Soviet Socialist Republics. The term in itself has no political implication, being simply the Russian word for council, and there were soviets of various kinds in Russia long before the Russian Revolution.

The theoretical relationship between the Communist Party on the one hand and the dictatorship of the proletariat and the Soviets on the other is not easy to define. In his PROBLEMS OF LENINISM, Stalin quotes Lenin as saying that the dictatorship is exercised by the proletariat which is organized into soviets and is led by the party. He declares that "the Party exercises the dictatorship of the proletariat," and that "the dictatorship is in *essence* the dictatorship of its vanguard, the Party," although he insists that this does not mean that the party *is* the dictatorship, because things which are *"in essence the same"* are not thereby identical. On the other hand, he defines the soviets as "the direct expression of the dictatorship of the proletariat," although he admits with Lenin that "not a single important political or organizational question is decided by our Soviet without guiding directions from our Party."[2]

HISTORICAL EVOLUTION

In the modern political meaning of the word, the first soviets were revolutionary committees organized by the Russian Socialists in the Revolution of 1905 among striking factory workers. The Bolsheviks were at first extremely cool toward the whole idea of the 1905 Soviet of Workingmen's Deputies as a spontaneous organization of factory labor delegates which had sprung up during the 1905 Revolution without visible leadership from the Bolshevik faction. It appeared to be a potentially dangerous competitor. The local Bolshevik leaders in St. Petersburg at first boycotted the Soviet and then confronted it with an ultimatum that it recognize their program and "join" the party; but Lenin, writing from Stockholm, rebuked the local leaders with these words:

> Comrade Radin . . . is wrong to pose the question: 'Soviet of Workingmen's Deputies or the Party'. It seems to me the solution ought to be: Both the Soviet of Workingmen's Deputies and the Party.[3]

Impressed by the mass support which the Soviet rallied, Lenin saw in it both a field of activity for the expansion of Bolshevik influence and "the germ of a provisional revolutionary government." Actually, the Mensheviks and especially Trotsky played a far more active role in the life of the soviets than the Bolsheviks. The latter found it much more difficult to make a quick adjustment from underground existence to open political activity.

THE 1917 SUCCESS

For Lenin, the lesson of this experience was not to boycott the soviets, but to intensify Bolshevik activity within them in order to establish control. This principle Lenin applied more successfully in 1917 than he did in 1905. The experience with the soviets of 1905 had captured the imagination of the revolutionaries, and when the February Revolution of 1917 occurred, it was only natural that Soviets of Workers' and Soldiers' Deputies be formed throughout the country.

Upon his return to Russia in April 1917, Lenin denounced the parliamentary form of government and said:

> The Soviet of Workers' Deputies is the only *possible* form of revolutionary government . . . to return to a parliamentary republic from the Soviet of Workers Deputies would be a retrograde step. [There must be] not a parliamentary republic . . . but a republic of soviets of Workers', Agricultural Laborers' or Peasants' Deputies throughout the country from top to bottom.[4]

The slogan of the Communists was to be "All Power to the Soviets." The Bolsheviks (who later changed their name to Communists) knew that they could not win control of a popularly elected parliament, but they thought that they could win control of the soviets, which were composed predominantly of the urban working class where the Bolsheviks had their greatest strength.

At the first All Russian Soviet Congress (1917) the Socialist Revolutionaries had 285 deputies, the Mensheviks 248 and the Bolsheviks only 105. The soviets, rather than the provisional government of Kerensky, represented the real power in Russia, and when the Bolsheviks under Lenin succeeded in capturing the most important soviets in Petrograd (Leningrad), in Moscow and in the armed forces, their success was assured.

Their example was imitated in other countries, notably in Germany and Hungary between 1918 and 1920, where workers', peasants', and soldiers' councils were also formed, but with less success. A Soviet republic in Bavaria was short-lived, and the regime of Béla Kun in Hungary was put down. The soviets in the Baltics similarly failed.

With respect to the colonial areas of Asia, one of the theses of the Second Congress of the Communist International read as follows:

> . . . the proletarian parties must carry-on vigorous and systematic propaganda of the Soviet idea, and organize the peasants', and workers' soviets as soon as possible. These soviets will work in cooperation with the Soviet Republics in the advanced capitalist countries for the ultimate overthrow of the capitalist order throughout the world.[5]

By the time of the October Revolution the Bolsheviks actually succeeded in winning control of the All-Russian Congress of Workers' and Soldiers' Deputies, and by insisting that only the soviets could govern, Lenin, in effect, insisted that only Communists could govern. The soviets were hailed by Lenin for drawing

> . . . in the freest, proudest, and most energetic manner, all the masses into the work of the government. . . . It is a power that is open to all—that does everything in sight of the masses—that is accessible to the masses, that springs directly from the masses; it is the direct organ of the masses and of their will.[6]

CENTRALIZATION OF CONTROL

Actually power within the soviets came to be exercised by executive committees rather than by the members of the soviets as a whole. The Eighth Party Congress in 1919 decreed that party fractions under

33

strict party discipline should be set up within each soviet with the aim of unifying and subordinating the whole structure of the soviets to the single will of the party. The Congress declared:

> The Russian Communist Party must win for itself undivided political mastery in the Soviet and practical control over all their work.[7]

The concentration of power within the party matched a similar process in the organs of state. The same men directed the affairs of party and of state; the same incessant crises and the same uninterrupted pressure of events weighed equally between 1917 and 1921 on party and on Soviet institutions. In spite of a resolution of the Eighth Party Congress in 1919 deploring the tendency to relegate important decisions from soviets to executive committees, the process continued unchecked, effective power passing from the congresses of soviets to the executive committees elected by them.

One of the theses of the Second Congress of the Communist International (1920) read:

> The origin of the Soviets as an historically basic form of the dictatorship of the proletariat, in no way lessens the guiding role of the Communist Party in the proletarian revolution. The assertions made by the 'left' Communists of Germany . . . that the party must always adapt itself to the idea of Soviets and assume a proletarian character, is nothing but a hazy expression of the opinion that the Communist Party should dissolve itself into the Soviets, that the Soviets can replace the Communist Party. This idea is essentially mistaken and reactionary.
>
> There was a period in the history of the Russian Revolution when the Soviets were acting in opposition to the party, and supported the policy of the agents of the bourgeoisie. The same has happened in Germany, and may take place in other countries.
>
> In order that the Soviets may perform their historic mission, a strong Communist Party is necessary which should not merely adapt itself to the Soviets, but on the contrary should take care that the Soviets do not adapt themselves to the bourgeoisie, and to the white guard Social Democracy; that with the aid of the Communist factions in the Soviets the latter be brought under the banner of the Communist Party.[8]

Centralization of control led directly to a loss of mass support for the soviets as was made clear by the Kronstadt rebellion of 1921. The soviets never regained their initial position as popular agencies. The soviets became, to a degree, an extension of the party administrative structure. Though mass participation was one of the major purposes of the structure of the soviets there were formal limitations upon it in the higher soviets until 1936. Election to the All-Union Congress of Soviets, "the Supreme Authority of the USSR," was indirect and the electoral districts were unequal. Voting was public by a show of hands — "class enemies" were not allowed to vote.

Additionally, the Congress of Soviets met only for a few days every two or more years leaving little opportunity for continuous and effective participation in government, even by those indirectly chosen as representatives of the masses. In the long intervals of the meetings of the Congress, power was delegated to a Central Executive Committee which had two chambers: a Union Council and a Council of Nationalities. This body was supposed to meet three times in the intervals between Congresses.

THE 1936 CONSTITUTION

Under the 1936 Constitution, legislative power was separated from administrative, the former (technically) exercised by the Supreme Soviet, the latter by the Council of Ministers. The same distinction is made in the case of the union republics and it is only on the lowest levels of government organs that the soviets of working peoples' deputies (theoretically) have administrative and executive responsibilities, largely through being themselves activists in the tasks of the Soviet state. The 1923 Constitution had described the Congress of Soviets and the Central Executive Committee as "The Supreme Authority of the USSR," combining legislative, executive and administrative authority. According to the 1936 Constitution a Supreme Soviet is elected for four years, both houses at the same time. The Soviet of the Union has one member for 300,000 of the population; the Soviet of Nationalities has 25 for each union republic, 11 for each autonomous republic and 5 for each autonomous region and 1 for each national area. The total number of deputies in 1954 was 1,347 (708 in the Soviet of the Union and 639 in the Soviet of Nationalities).

One of the obvious reasons for the meetings of the Supreme Soviet is to inspire the delegates and to educate both them and their constituents. Technically, the thirty-three man Presidium, which is elected by the Supreme Soviet, may exercise all the powers of the Supreme Soviet. Indeed, far more is put into effect through the edicts and

35

decrees of the Presidium than through the relatively small number of laws passed so perfunctorily by the Supreme Soviet; but, of course, not only the Presidium and Supreme Soviet, but also the Constitution are clearly subordinate to the ruling power of the party. The soviets are merely the facade behind which the party exercises absolute authority.

LOCAL SOVIETS

Soviet local government does not aim at autonomy in local affairs, but exists to provide the central organs of the state with machinery to implement their own policy. The local soviets have a term of office of only two years (Article 95 of the Constitution). The hierarchy of local soviets, which begins at the provincial level — the territorial or regional soviets — includes other subdivisions from district (county) and city soviets to the smallest rural or village soviets.

All the local soviets are elected by the inhabitants of each area and by such soviet citizens as may be present in a particular constituency on election day. Only candidates of the Communist Party or those approved by the party may stand for election. Therefore, the local soviets are just as docile as the various supreme soviets. M. A. Arzhanov, of the Institute of Law of the Academy of Sciences of the USSR, writing in 1949 in the Institute's Journal, describes the Communist domination of the soviets in these words:

> The composition of the soviets is completely uniform politically in accordance with the social structure of the population of the USSR and the moral and political unity of the Soviet society. All the soviet deputies are elected as representatives of the Communists — non-Party Bloc.[9]

According to the Soviet writer S. S. Studenikin:

> Not one important question is decided without instructions by the Party organs which formulate them in the light in their own rich and practical experience.[10]

The party members who happen to be deputies of the local soviets or members of the local executive committee carry out the policy of the corresponding party organs, while their non-party colleagues on the soviet or executive committee unanimously support their efforts.

The attainment of unanimity within the local soviets is encouraged by the following rule: "Questions are decided in an open vote by simple majority."[11] The open vote always results in that unanimity which is the pride of the Soviet regime.

According to "democratic centralism" the acts of the lower soviets can be squashed by the higher soviets. All Soviet roads lead to the same center of power. The Council of Ministers of the USSR has an inner ring called the Presidium, which is composed of persons who are also members of the Presidium of the Central Committee of the Communist Party. Thus the whole structure of thousands of soviets forms a pyramid controlled by and directed from the top — the Presidium of the Central Committee acting through the Council of Ministers.

THE POWER STRUGGLE WITHIN CONTEMPORARY SOVIETISM

In October, 1952, the first party Congress since 1939 was convened in Moscow. At this time Stalin's heir-apparent was Georgy Malenkov, increasingly prominent in the top echelons of the Soviet system ever since the death in 1948 of another of Stalin's favorites — Andrei A. Zhdanov. At this Congress, Malenkov was entrusted with the delivery of the main report, the first time since Stalin's power had been consolidated that anyone but he had given it. The Congress announced the replacement both of the Politburo and the Orgburo by a Presidium of the Party Central Committee. There were twenty-five full members of the new Presidium, as contrasted to the eleven in the old Politburo. In January, 1953, PRAVDA announced that nine doctors, six of them Jewish, had been charged with assassinating, through medical mistreatment, a number of prominent Soviet figures, including Andrei Zhdanov. The epithets "cosmopolitanism and Zionism" were employed in the discussion of the case, while similar phrases were used in the simultaneous trial in Prague of the Czechoslovak Party's General Secretary, Rudolph Slansky. At the same time, the MVD, led by Laurenty D. Beria, was accused of insufficient vigilance in failing to detect the "doctors' plot."

On March 5, 1953, Stalin died. Immediately thereafter, persons close to Stalin who might have been in a position to challenge either the power of Malenkov or Beria, such as Alexander Poskrebyshev, Chief of Stalin's Personal Secretariat, were purged. For ten days after Stalin's death, Malenkov held both of the important posts of the Soviet system — Senior Party Secretary, and Chairman of the Council of Ministers, but then he released the more important post of Senior Party Secretary to Nikita Khrushchev.

In the Presidium as reconstituted after Stalin's death, the new roster of full members was reduced from twenty-five to ten, and the Party Secretariat was reduced from ten to five.

On April 3, 1953, Beria announced that "the doctors' plot" which had been "exposed" during Stalin's last days had been a hoax. This was apparently an effort on Beria's part to strengthen his position and clear his name.

By June, 1953, the post-Stalin changes in leadership had created a public impression of indecision and weakness. In the satellites, as well as the USSR, several demonstrations of unrest occurred within a few weeks of each other. On June 1, there were strikes in several Czechoslovak cities, occasioned by a financial "reform" which brought much hardship to the industrial workers. In Poznan the strikers held a political demonstration, seized the City Hall and demanded free elections, before Secret Police intervened. On June 16, an increase of labor "norms" in East Germany provoked a protest which rapidly turned into a revolutionary general strike in Berlin and other East German cities. Soviet troops were brought in, and the strike was crushed.

On July 10, Beria was arrested and shortly thereafter shot. Wilhelm Zaisser, Beria's appointee as East German Police Chief, and other Beria henchmen were also purged. In some ways the most astonishing of the first series of post-Stalin demonstrations occurred in the Soviet Union itself a few days after Beria's arrest. In the concentration camp complex at Vorkuta, in the Pechora Basin of Northeast European Russia, there developed a mass strike of prisoners who voiced political demands. After initial hesitation, the strike was put down with mass executions.

Khrushchev's rise to power stemmed from his appointment as First Secretary of the Communist Party. In November and December, 1954, his signature appeared alone on certain decrees and he became more prominent in the Soviet press than any other Soviet leader. On February 8, 1955, Georgy Malenkov resigned as Chairman of the Council of Ministers, making an unprecedented statement in which he referred to his "inexperience," took on himself the "guilt" for what was admitted to be "the most unsatisfactory state of affairs in agriculture," and declared that the policy of founding the economy on heavy industry was the "only correct" one. On Khrushchev's motion, the Supreme Soviet promptly elected Nicholas A. Bulganin as the new Prime Minister. Marshal Georgy K. Zhukov replaced Bulganin as Minister of Defense.

At the Twentieth Congress of the Communist Party of the Soviet Union, held in February, 1956, in Moscow, Khrushchev dominated the proceedings as expected. Khrushchev delivered a "secret speech" on the night of February 24, itemized a good many of Stalin's crimes, chief among them being the murder of party leaders loyal to him, and leveled other accusations against Stalin such as responsibility for the break with Tito. It seemed that Khrushchev was trying to exorcise the incubus of his dead master, whom he had loyally served so long, because of the massive unpopularity of all he stood for among the Soviet people, yet he wished to avoid calling into question the structure of the whole regime or opening the way to public queries about the role of the leaders of 1956 during the commission of the crimes which he detailed. Despite the attack on Stalin, Khrushchev declared that the "whole tragedy" lay in the fact that Stalin's errors were not "the deeds of a giddy despot," but that he "doubtlessly performed great services to the Party, to the working class and to the international workers' movement." The task of the party was to restore "the victorious banner of our Party — Leninism!" and under this slogan to eradicate the "cult of personality," strengthen "collective leadership" and criticism and self-criticism on all levels of the party, and restore "the Leninist principles of Soviet socialist democracy" as expressed in the Constitution.

Following the Congress, there were several public rehabilitations about party leaders long dead, including some in the satellite countries.

Khrushchev's criticisms of Stalin and revelations of his crimes created disturbances in the Georgian capital of Tbilisi in which hundreds were killed. On June 28, 1956, factory workers in Poznan, Poland, organized a demonstration which developed into armed clashes with the police, resulting in the killing of about one hundred people. Prime Minister Cyrankiewicz rushed to the scene denouncing "imperialistic agents," and warned that anyone who dared "raise his hand against the people's rule" would "have his hand chopped off by the authorities." Nevertheless, the Poznan rioters who were given public trial received unexpectedly mild sentences, and criticism continued more and more openly, especially from the Polish writers. In August,

Wladyslaw Gomulka, who had been Poland's chief alleged Titoist, was reinstated in the party, and on October 19 the Central Committee of the Polish United Workers' (Communist) Party elected him First Secretary and took his strong stand for further internal changes. Previously (in July), Khrushchev had effected a rapprochement with Tito. In July, perhaps in consequence of Tito's visit to Moscow, the Hungarian leader, Rakosi, was forced out and replaced by Erno Gero as First Secretary. For some time public criticism had been sharpening in Hungary, especially in the "Petofi circle" of Hungarian writers. On October 6, the reburial of Laszlo Rajk (executed in 1949 as a Titoist) turned into a silent mass demonstration, and a week later Imre Nagy was publicly restored to party membership. On October 23, a demonstration of university students led to a general uprising of the Hungarian people against Sovietism. In an effort to appease the crowds, the government was reorganized on October 27, to include non-Communists, and Soviet forces withdrew from Budapest. However, after a few heady days of freedom, Soviet troops suddenly swept into Budapest. On the same day Janos Kadar, who defected from the increasingly popular government of Imre Nagy, was installed by Soviet troops as Prime Minister of a new regime.

The whole world was shocked by the Soviet repression in Hungary and many fellow travelers, particularly in Europe, as well as some Communist leaders, repudiated the Soviet action. Indeed there were public meetings among university students in the Soviet Union itself, and angry questions about the Hungarian events were asked. In October, a full-fledged strike was reported in the Kaganovich Ball Bearing Works in Moscow, the first such manifestation by Soviet workers in decades. In the summer of 1957, the Chinese Communists admitted the occurrence of sizable student riots which ended in fighting in certain cities, and even judging by official reports, there was considerable resistance in China.

The Soviet system, however, managed to weather the storm. In June, 1957, Khrushchev obtained the dismissal from the Presidium of Malenkov, Kaganovich, Molotov and the candidate member Shepilov. The Presidium was now raised to fifteen full members. There is some evidence that Marshal Zhukov supported Khrushchev in the downgrading of Khrushchev's chief potential opponents, and for a time Zhukov's name was prominently mentioned as Khrushchev's chief ally. However, Zhukov's pre-eminence lasted only a few months.

In October he was dismissed from the Defense Ministry and shortly afterward from the Presidium and from the Central Committee.

KHRUSHCHEV SUPREME

Khrushchev had more power than any one man had had since Stalin's death, and when he deposed Bulganin and himself assumed the office of Premier in March, 1958, he demonstrated that he had attained something like the undisputed primacy in both the party and the government that Stalin had held.

Meantime, in Poland, Gomulka gradually withdrew minor concessions he had made in the direction of freedom of the press and religious freedom, and drew closer and closer to Moscow. In Hungary, the Kadar regime shot Imre Nagy and the freedom fighter General Pal Malater. Meantime, the subservience of the Chinese Communists to the Soviet Union remained unchanged. Mao Tse-tung and Chou En-lai, on the thirty-seventh anniversary of the October Revolution in 1954, extended hearty congratulations to the Soviet leaders with the claim that "progressive humanity throughout the world . . . regards the great Soviet Union as the beacon lighting the path of advance." In similar language, the Central Committee of the Communist Party of China sent its fraternal salute:

> The Soviet State, like a beacon, illuminates the road to progress for the exploited people and oppressed nations of the entire world. The brilliant achievements have inspired all progressive mankind to an untiring struggle for a fine future.[12]

CONCLUSION

The structure and operation of the Soviet regime remain as they were during Stalin's lifetime, as evidenced by the abundant current Soviet pronouncements and official publications. Any flat predictions on the Soviet regime and its present leaders would properly belong in the realm of fortune-telling. According to W. W. Kulski:

> Undue hope should not be entertained that a totalitarian regime could peacefully evolve into a democratic one. Such a peaceful revolution could eventually endanger the position of the present leaders who have attained their power through their former association with Stalin, and not through free elections.
> Caution is also recommended to those incorrigible optimists who have been anticipating a violent revolution in the USSR since 1917. As long as the rigid control of all information and

education media and strict police supervision are maintained, they will continue to constitute psychological as well as physical blocks to any "popular" uprising. Moreover, the governmental monopoly of powerful modern weapons of coercion precludes the success of a spontaneous 19th-century style revolution. Finally, the vested interests in the regime of the upper class should not be forgotten.

Those who envision a military coup should be reminded that the military leaders are also important and influential Party members. Their own stake in the regime may be greater than the temptation to indulge in an Army plot which would open the gate to an unknown future.[13]

Sovietism, in the broad sense of the word, encompasses the international Communist apparatus which is based on the doctrine of Marxism-Leninism. The Declaration and Manifesto of the Communist and Workers' Parties adopted in Moscow, November 14-16, 1957, states:

> The theory of Marxism-Leninism derives from dialectical materialism. This world outlook reflects the universal law of development of nature, society and human thinking. It is valid for the past, the present, and the future.[14]

Sovietism, then, as an international system, is a dynamic force which is in a constant state of evolution. This evolution begins with the establishment of the dictatorship of the proletariat (or more precisely of the Communist Party) in one country (the establishment of Bolshevik power in Russia in 1917). Just as the Communist Party is the vanguard of the proletariat, so is the Soviet Union the vanguard of the international Communist movement. Through war and diplomacy, the Soviet system of government has been established in the countries of East Central Europe, mainland China, North Korea, North Viet-Nam and Tibet. Soviet leaders describe the regime now prevailing in the Soviet Union as socialism. The satellite regimes are "building socialism." Thus the Soviet Union has already achieved socialism, and the satellites are striving to achieve it. But in neither case is this the end of the process. It is inevitable that ultimately *all* states will fall under the control of the dictatorship of the Communist Party, leading to the establishment of socialism throughout the world. At this juncture, and only at this juncture, can the transition be made from the imperfect state of socialism to the perfect state of Communism. Thus Sovietism has as its final and supreme objective and end result the achievement of Communism.

Lenin taught that force and violence would be required without exception in order to establish the dictatorship of the Communist Party in all countries. Khrushchev, at the Twentieth Party Congress of the Communist Party of the USSR, suggested that in some countries (presumably countries like France and Italy where the Communist Parties are strong) the dictatorship of the party could come about through relatively peaceful means. But, according to the resolution of the Central Committee of the Communist Party of the USSR in 1956, force and violence would still be required to overthrow leading industrialist states and particularly the United States. Indeed this resolution stresses the difference between Western socialist parties, which seek to establish their version of socialism through evolutionary means and reform, and the Communist Parties of the world, led by the Soviet Union, which remain devoted to the Marxist-Leninist conception of revolution. The Central Committee emphasized that force and violence will have to be applied by the Soviet Union, the satellites and the Communist Parties within the free world in order to overthrow the last remnants of resisting capitalism. The Central Committee pointed out that the "ruling classes" never relinquish power voluntarily, and that power therefore can only be taken away from them by force. The Declaration and Manifesto of the Communist and Workers' Parties, adopted in Moscow in 1957, puts it this way:

> In the event of the ruling classes resorting to violence against people, the possibility of non-peaceful transition to socialism should be borne in mind. Lenin teaches and experience confirms that the ruling classes never relinquish power voluntarily.[15]

At the Twenty-first Congress of the Communist party of the Soviet Union, Khrushchev reiterated the *possibility* of a peaceful transition to world Communism. But he talked only about a possibility, not a probability. What he meant, and he spelled this out clearly, is not that the Communists should desist from their plans of world conquest, nor that they expect to win by democratic processes. What he is betting on is that the democracies will be so weakened by subversion, and frightened by the possibility of nuclear war, that they will not dare resist continuing expansionism by the Communist movement. This "possibility" mentioned by Khrushchev is not a point of Com-

43

munist doctrine, but an estimate of Western internal security and moral courage. Khrushchev's junior partner in Sovietism, Mao Tse-tung, in Volume II of his SELECTED WORKS, published by International Publishers in New York in 1954, stresses that "political power grows out of the barrel of a gun." He stated:

> Communists should prove themselves the most clear-headed leaders in the war. Every communist must grasp the truth: "Political power grows out of the barrel of a gun." Our principle is that the party commands the gun, and the gun will never be allowed to command the party. But it is also true that with guns at our disposal we can really build up the party organizations, and the Eighth Route Army has built up a powerful party organization in North China. We can also rear cadres and create schools, culture and mass movements. Everything in Yenan has been built up by means of the gun. Anything can grow out of the barrel of a gun. According to the Marxist theory of the state, the army is the chief component of the political power of a state. Whoever wants to seize the political power of the state and to maintain it must have a strong army. Some people have ridiculed us as advocates of the "omnipotence of war"; yes, we are, we are the advocates of the omnipotence of the revolutionary war, which is not bad at all, but is good and is Marxist. With the help of guns the Russian communists brought about socialism. We are to bring about a democratic republic. Experience in the class struggle of the era of imperialism teaches us that the working class and the toiling masses cannot defeat the armed bourgeoisie and landlords except by the power of the gun; in this sense we can even say that the whole world can be remoulded only with the gun. As we are advocates of the abolition of war, we do not desire war; but war can only be abolished through war — in order to get rid of the gun, we must first grasp it in our hand.[16]

Moreover, two entire paragraphs which appear in the second volume of Mao's SELECTED WORKS, page 505 of the Chinese 1952 edition, were left out of both the 1954 and 1958 English editions. The key sentence which is omitted from the English text reads as follows: "The central task and the supreme form of a revolution is the seizure of political power by force of arms and the solution of problems by war."[17]

This statement of Mao's also occurs in the 1953 Russian edition of his works, ISBRANNIE SOCHINENIYA, Volume 2, page 379. The following sentence of Mao's also appears in this same Russian edition of his works: "This principle of Marxism-Leninism holds true holds true everywhere; this principle is absolutely true for China as well as for other states."[18]

SELECTED BIBLIOGRAPHY

Two useful volumes providing insight into the doctrine of Sovietism are: R. N. Carew Hunt, THE THEORY AND PRACTICE OF COMMUNISM (New York: The Macmillan Co., 1951), and Philip Selznick, THE ORGANIZATIONAL WEAPON (New York: McGraw-Hill Book Co., 1952).

For the early period of Sovietism, the works of three authors are indispensable: William Henry Chamberlin, THE RUSSIAN REVOLUTION 1917-21, 2 vols. (New York: The Macmillan Co., 1952); Edward Hallett Carr, A HISTORY OF SOVIET RUSSIA; THE BOLSHEVIK REVOLUTION 1917-23, 3 vols. (London: Macmillan & Co., Ltd. 1950-53); George F. Kennan, SOVIET-AMERICAN RELATIONS 1917-20, Vol. I, RUSSIA LEAVES THE WAR (Princeton: Princeton University Press, 1956).

Among the leading textbooks on the Soviet system are: Merle Fainsod, HOW RUSSIA IS RULED (Cambridge: Harvard University Press, 1953); David Dallin, THE CHANGING WORLD OF SOVIET RUSSIA (New Haven: Yale University Press, 1956); and M. W. Kulski, THE SOVIET REGIME (Syracuse: Syracuse University Press, 1959). The Kulski volume is a massive and extremely well-documented source book.

Among the most valuable volumes relating chronologically to the evolution of Sovietism and its expansionism are: Stefan T. Possony, A CENTURY OF CONFLICT (Chicago: Regnery, 1953); Hugh Seton-Watson, FROM LENIN TO MALENKOV (New York: Frederick A. Praeger, 1953); and Donald W. Treadgold, 20TH CENTURY RUSSIA (Chicago: Rand McNally & Co., 1959).

An excellent study of the important events that took place at the Twentieth Party Congress is Bertram D. Wolfe's KHRUSHCHEV AND STALIN'S GHOST (New York: Frederick A. Praeger, 1957).

CURRICULUM VITAE

ANTHONY T. BOUSCAREN, Associate Professor of Political Science, Le Moyne College, Syracuse, New York. Formerly member of the faculty, University of San Francisco, Marquette University, The National War College, Washington, D.C., The National Strategy Seminar (The National War College). A.B., Yale University; M.A. and Ph.D., University of California (Berkeley). Author: SOVIET

EXPANSION AND THE WEST (1949); IMPERIAL COMMU-
NISM (1953); AMERICA FACES WORLD COMMUNISM (1954);
A GUIDE TO ANTI-COMMUNIST ACTION (1958); SECURITY
ASPECTS OF IMMIGRATION WORK (1959); Co-author, with
Robert C. Hartnett: THE STATE AND RELIGIOUS EDUCATION
(1952). Contributor to: BACKGROUND TO EUROPEAN GOV-
ERNMENTS (1951), THE GREAT PRETENSE (1956), and
WHAT IS BEHIND SOVIET PROPOSALS FOR A SUMMIT CON-
FERENCE (1958), Consultation with the Committee on Un-American
Activities. Editorial Adviser, FREE WORLD FORUM. Contributor to
WESTERN POLITICAL QUARTERLY, CATHOLIC WORLD,
CURRENT HISTORY, JOURNAL OF POLITICS, AMERICAN
MERCURY, SPADEA SYNDICATE, SOCIAL ORDER, U.S. NEWS
AND WORLD REPORT, SATURDAY EVENING POST, WORLD
AFFAIRS, MODERN AGE, etc. Recipient: Christopher Award
(1953); Freedom's Foundation Citation, 1953; Freedom's Foundation
Award (1958). *Member*: American Political Science Association,
Catholic Commission for Intellectual and Cultural Affairs, Mid-West
Conference of Political Scientists, Educational Projects Committee,
National Military Industrial Conference.

CHAPTER THREE

CHINESE COMMUNISM

THEODORE HSI-EN CHEN
University of Southern California

The Chinese call themselves faithful disciples of Marxism-Leninism. They believe that no revolution can succeed without correct ideological guidance and the Communist revolution is destined to succeed because the Chinese Communist Party is "a party with discipline, armed with the theories of Marx, Engels, Lenin, and Stalin."[1] Said Mao Tse-tung at the threshold of national victory in 1949:

> Our Party has passed through 28 years. As everyone knows, these have been difficult years. We had to fight against enemies within the country and abroad, and within and outside the Party. Our thanks are due to Marx, Engels, Lenin, and Stalin for having given us weapons. These weapons are not machine guns but Marxism-Leninism.[2]

The Communists take their ideology seriously. They believe that wrong action stems from wrong ideological thinking and that the best corrective for wrong action lies in proper ideological orientation. Whenever teachers prove inefficient in their teaching or workers fall behind in production schedule or engineers commit errors in construction, the chief source of difficulty is always found to be "bourgeois ideology" and the most effective cure is believed to be a heavier dose of ideological indoctrination. Mao wrote in 1942:

> In the study of Marxism-Leninism, we must use as our main text the *History of the Communist Party of the Soviet Union*, all other material being supplementary in nature. *The History of the Communist Party of the Soviet Union* constitutes the highest synthesis and summation of the world Communist movement in the last hundred years. It is the model of the union of theory and practice and it is the only perfect model in the world. By observing how Lenin and Stalin inter-linked the universal truth of

Marxism-Leninism with the concrete practice of Soviet revolution and in this way developed Marxism, we shall know how to carry on our work in China.[3]

Two points in the above quotation deserve careful notice. First, the Chinese Communists look to the Soviet Union for guidance in ideological matters and in actual revolutionary experience. Secondly, they believe that Marxism-Leninism contains "universal truth" which holds good for all countries but must be applied and adapted to the "concrete practice" of each country. A cliché the Chinese Communists love to repeat is: "Marxism is not a dogma, but a guide to revolutionary action." They claim that the very method of Marxist dialectics dictates that theory must be integrated with action and that action must be planned in the light of the "objective conditions" that obtain at a given place or time. Just as Lenin and Stalin "inter-linked" the "universal truth" of Marxism to Russian conditions, so the challenge in China is to apply the sound principles of Marxism-Leninism to the concrete situation in China. The goals of the socialist-proletarian revolution are the same for all countries but the exact course of the revolution and the detailed methods must vary according to "objective conditions."

IDEOLOGY EXPRESSED IN THE PATTERN OF GOVERNMENT ORGANIZATION

Two Stages of the Revolution. The Chinese Communists say that Communism cannot be achieved overnight and it is necessary to provide for a transitional stage preparing for the advent of Communism. This stage is called the New Democracy. When he wrote his treatise ON THE NEW DEMOCRACY, Mao Tse-tung said that the transitional stage "is by no means short" and should not be hurried. The New Democracy would be both capitalistic and socialistic; it must encourage certain forms of capitalism and build up the industries, but it must also move in the direction of increasing socialism.

In terms of ideology, the New Democracy was to be guided by the "minimum program" of Communism, with its "maximum program" as a goal for the future. It was this "minimum program" of Communism that formed the basis of the Common Program with which the regime began on October 1, 1949.

Democratic Dictatorship. Proceeding from the statement in the Communist Manifesto to the effect that "political power, properly so-called, is merely the organized power of one class for oppressing another," the Chinese Communists say that the state is an organ of class domination and has the duty of suppressing those who are opposed to the interests of the people, especially the working class. The New Democracy, they argue, is democratic and dictatorial at the same time: it is democratic because it serves the interests of "the people"; it is dictatorial in dealing with the counter-revolutionaries and the enemies of the people, and it does not hesitate to adopt harsh measures to suppress these enemies.

The New Democracy must be on guard against ultra-democratism. It must preclude any possibility of counter-revolutionary elements taking advantage of "freedom" to pursue their own ends. Freedom and democracy must be reserved for those who heartily support the people's democracy. Even then, freedom and democracy can not be unrestrained. They must be under central guidance and supervision. This is the essence of "democratic centralism." Democracy in the form of broad participation by the many on basic levels of party and government is not only desirable but necessary. At the same time, all the work of lower levels must be subject to the approval and control of higher levels so that democracy always functions under centralized guidance and is not permitted to get out of hand.

Joint Dictatorship of Revolutionary Classes. In unindustrialized China, the proletariat is yet too weak to assume dictatorship. In the present transitional stage of the revolution, the Communists maintain that it is necessary for the proletariat to seek the alliance of non-proletarian classes sympathetic to the proletarian cause. These classes are all "revolutionary" in character because they are all opposed to feudal and imperialistic domination. They exercise a "joint dictatorship" at a stage when conditions are not yet ripe for a dictatorship of the proletariat.

Four of these "revolutionary classes" are recognized in China today. They are the workers, the peasants, the petty bourgeoisie, and the national bourgeoisie. At the center is the working class; its chief and fundamental ally is the peasant class; around the worker-peasant alliance rally the other revolutionary classes; and in all cases, the leadership of the Communist Party, as the vanguard of the working class, is absolutely indispensable.

The presence of non-proletarian classes in transitional society is reflected in the existence of non-proletarian political parties along with

49

the Communist Party. There are a number of "democratic parties" in Communist China, such as the Democratic League, the Chiu San Society, the Democratic National Construction Association, and several others. These are, in the main, the parties of the petty bourgeoisie and the national bourgeoisie, and they recruit their members from these classes. Just as all the "revolutionary classes" exercising joint dictatorship must function under the leadership of the working class, so all the "democratic parties" must accept the leadership and guidance of the Communist Party. As long as there continue to exist non-proletarian classes in society, these non-proletarian political parties must also be tolerated. One of their chief tasks, however, is to "remold" their members politically and ideologically by a constant program of "political education" in Marxism-Leninism. Their function, in other words, is to assist the Communist Party and to organize their membership for active support of the program of the Communist Party. Their platform is in essence the platform of the Communist Party.

IDEOLOGY AS EXPRESSED IN THE PATTERN OF ECONOMIC DEVELOPMENT

The Common Program of 1949 did not stress socialism; it promised the protection of the private economy. By 1954, however, the Chinese Communists were pushing toward socialism and the new emphasis was clearly reflected in the Constitution of 1954. The Constitution issued a call for the socialist industrialization of the country and "the socialist transformation of agriculture, handicrafts, and capitalist industry and commerce." This process of "socialist transformation" is guided on the one hand by the clear goal of socialism-Communism and, on the other, by the principle of gradual transition. It is characterized by a number of intermediate stages each representing a further advance than the preceding stage in the direction of full socialism.

Socialist Transformation of Agriculture. Take, for example, the socialist transformation of agriculture. When the agrarian reform was introduced in 1949-50, the Communists gave land to peasants and guaranteed the right of private ownership. In 1951, they began to appeal to the peasants to "get organized." Co-operativization was recommended as the best way to "get organized." The most elementary form of co-operativization was the mutual-aid team, in which peasants of several households were brought together to help one another in farmwork. Some of the teams were temporary or seasonal arrangements; others functioned throughout the whole year. The essential characteristics of private farming were unchanged: each household owned and managed its own land, planted its own crops, and took care of the entire farming process; and peasants were paid for work done on other people's land.

After some experience with mutual-aid teams, peasants were urged to advance into the next higher stage of co-operation, namely, the agricultural producers' co-operative. The co-operative has many "socialist features" that the mutual-aid team does not have. Land of the participating households is pooled together and placed under unified management. Crops are planted according to need and all plans are co-ordinated with state planning. Individual farming disappears, and there is more division of labor instead of having each household doing the same work on an individual basis. Unified management is extended to manpower as well as farm implements and animals. A part of the animals and implements is collectively owned by the co-operative, and a definite portion of the income is set aside for communal savings.

On the other hand, the ordinary agriculture producers co-operative can only be considered as semi-socialist, because certain characteristics of private farming still remain. Although land is pooled together for unified use, the legal title still belongs to individual owners. Profit is divided according to land and labor so that the land owner receives remuneration for the use of his land.

These "unsocialist characteristics" are eliminated in the next stage of co-operativization, viz., the collective, or what the Chinese Communists prefer to call "higher-level agricultural producers' co-operative." Now, private land ownership is abolished; all land becomes the property of the co-operative. Agriculture is thus completely socialized. Until 1958, Communist planning did not go beyond these stages of socialist transformation. Since the spring of 1958, however, the Communists have introduced an even more advanced form of socialism than the collectives or "higher-level co-operatives." The new form is the commune.

The Commune. The communes go far beyond the collective farms in abolishing the vestiges of private farming and private ownership. The units are much larger than the collectives; while a collective takes in a few hundred households, a commune covers a whole geographical

51

area and organizes thousands of peasant households into one unit. The control of manpower is more complete; the commune has the authority to assign any person, regardless of age or sex, to any job considered important to the collective group. Common mess halls, common tailor shops, and nurseries for children mean a much more advanced stage of collective living.

The commune is more than a stage in the collectivization of agriculture. It is the collectivization of the entire range of social, economic and political life of the rural population. It is not merely concerned with farming; it is a basic unit of social organization. The activities of the individual family are greatly reduced; food, child care, mending-sewing, as well as economic and educational activities are all taken over by the commune. As far as private ownership is concerned, the Chinese Communists claim that the commune makes it possible to advance from "ownership by the collective" to "ownership by the people." When the latter is achieved, socialism will have entered the era of Communism.

The commune is hailed as a big and important step in the direction of a Communist society. It combines agriculture with industry and wipes out the distinctions between workers and peasants. Indeed, agriculture, industry, trade, education and military affairs are merged, and a citizen is at once a peasant, a worker, a trader, a student and a member of the militia. Moreover, the administrative committees of the communes will gradually take over the functions of local government so that eventually there will be no need of separate government agencies and the state will have withered away as far as domestic affairs are concerned; the function of the state will then be confined to external relations and protection against external enemies.[4] By that time, the communes will have moved from the socialist system of "from each according to his ability, to each according to his work" to the Communist system of "from each according to his ability, to each according to his needs."

The enthusiam for the communes reached a high peak in the autumn of 1958. The Chinese Communists saw the possibility of extending the commune system to the entire country and the authoritative JEN MIN JIH PAO (PEOPLE'S DAILY) optimistically predicted that the advance from socialism to Communism might take place in five or six years.[5] Since that time, partly on account of opposition at home and partly because of a desire to iron out possible ideological differences with the Soviet Union, the Chinese Communists have trimmed down their hopes and ambitions and adopted the policy of slower development. By December, 1958, the Chinese Communist Party had taken the official position that the development of communes should be interpreted as a transition from socialism to Communism, not as the actual approach of Communism, and that even the advance from "socialist collective ownership" to "ownership by the whole people" would not necessarily mean the arrival of the era of Communism.[6] Thus the views of the Chinese Communist Party in regard to socialism and Communism became essentially the same as those expressed by Khrushchev in the Twenty-first Congress of the Communist Party of the Soviet Union in January-February, 1959.

State Capitalism. Intermediate stages of transition from private enterprise to socialism have also been prescribed for private industry and commerce, and for the handicrafts. The Constitution of 1954 states that "the policy of the state toward capitalist industry and commerce is to use, restrict, and transform them." It is unnecessary for our purpose to relate the various stages of transition and the various forms of state capitalism. The principles involved are not greatly different from those illustrated by the socialist transformation of agriculture. In all cases, the goal is the complete liquidation of private ownership and private enterprise, and the process is marked by a number of transitional stages each representing a further advance toward the goal.[7]

IDEOLOGY AS EXPRESSED IN THE PATTERN OF FOREIGN POLICY

Opposition to Imperialism. The Communists attach great importance to anti-imperialism because (1) it is politically expedient, and (2) it is a basic concept in their ideology. Anti-imperialism is a good way to win popularity because nationalism is one of the most powerful forces in Asia and to many Asians nationalism is practically synonymous with anti-imperialism. By posing as the leaders in the struggle against imperialism, the Communists have linked themselves with the powerful force of nationalism and in this way captured extensive support from the patriots and nationalists of Asia.

To the nationalism-minded patriots of Asia, anti-imperialism is a necessary phase of the struggle for national independence, but to the ideology-minded Communists, opposition to imperialism is a phase of the struggle against capitalism and a prelude to the establishment of socialism. Mao Tse-tung declared many years ago that the "twin-enemies" of the Chinese revolution are imperialism and feudalism, and of the two the first is by far the more deadly enemy.[8] In fighting imperialism, the Chinese Communists constantly quote Lenin to the effect that capitalism inevitably leads to imperialism and imperialism is the outgrowth of capitalism. To destroy imperialism, therefore, is to strike at the heart of capitalism.

World Revolution. The Chinese Communists consider their revolution in China as inseparable from the world-wide proletarian-socialist revolution. The struggle against imperialism, said Mao Tse-tung in his NEW DEMOCRACY, is a part of a world-wide struggle against the international bourgeoisie. Consequently, the Chinese Communists consider it their duty not only to bring about socialism within China, but also to work for the socialist proletarian revolution in other countries. It is absolutely necessary to unite with all the other socialist states and "people's democracies."

Liu Shao-ch'i is even more emphatic in regard to China's role in the world revolution. He decried as "bourgeois nationalism" any tendency to remain satisfied with the success of the revolution within one country. He said:

> Communists will be betraying the proletariat and Communism . . . if, after their own nation has been freed from imperialist oppression, they descend to the position of bourgeois nationalism, carrying out a policy of national selfishness and sacrificing the common international interests of the working people and the proletarian masses of all the nations throughout the world . . . or if they adopt the policy of national seclusion and chauvinism to oppose proletarian internationalism, to reject the international unity of the proletariat and the working people and to oppose the Socialist Soviet Union.[9]

The Two-Camp View. The concept that national revolution cannot be isolated from the world revolution is related to the two-camp view of the world. In the view of the Communists, the nations of the world fall into two opposing camps guided by opposing ideologies, the camp of the socialist states and the camp of the capitalist states. This view has been clearly and repeatedly expressed by Chinese Communist leaders. Liu Shao-ch'i wrote as follows:

> The world today has been divided into mutually antagonistic camps: on the one hand, the world imperialistic camp, composed

54

of the American imperialists and their accomplices — the reactionaries of all countries of the world; on the other hand, the world anti-imperialist camp composed of the Soviet Union and the New Democracies of Eastern Europe, and the national liberation movements in China, Southeast Asia and Greece, plus the people's democratic forces of all the countries of the world. American imperialism has become the bastion of all the reactionary forces of the world, while the Soviet Union has become the bastion of all progressive forces.[10]

That the two-camp view is based on Communist ideology rather than the result of international politics is attested by the fact that as early as 1940 Mao Tse-tung had already expressed it in no uncertain terms. He said:

> The contest between the socialist Soviet Union and the imperialist England and America is being sharpened step by step. If China does not stand on one side, she will have to stand on the other. This is inevitable. Does anyone think it is possible to be neutral? This is just sheer fantasy. The whole world is going to be embroiled in a war between these two camps.[11]

This two-camp view is at the root of the "lean-to-one-side policy" that Mao Tse-tung pronounced in 1945. You either lean to the side of imperialism or to the side of socialism, he said; there could not possibly be a third road.[12] China, he emphatically declared, must lean to the side of socialism and unite with the Soviet Union.

Was there a contradiction between Mao's 1940 statement on two opposing camps and the fact that the Soviet Union was at that time fighting on the side of the Western allies and the Chinese Communists themselves were supposed to be co-operating with the Kuomintang in a united front against Japan? From the Communist point of view, there was no inconsistency at all. Mao explained the so-called united front as follows:

> An important part of the political line of the Chinese Communist Party is to unite with as well as to struggle against the bourgeoisie. An important part of the building of the Chinese Communist Party is that the Party develop and steel itself in the cause of both uniting with the bourgeoisie and struggling against it. Unity here means the united front with the bourgeoisie. Struggle means the "peaceful" and "bloodless" struggle waged along ideological, political, and organizational lines when we unite with the bourgeoisie, a struggle which will turn into an armed struggle when we are forced to split with the bourgeoise.[13]

55

This candid statement throws a good deal of light on the Communist conception of co-operation between allies or between parties in a united front. Such co-operation can not be wholehearted, for at the very time of co-operation the Communists are engaged in a "struggle against" the bourgeoisie they are co-operating with. The methods used at this time are "peaceful" non-violent methods, but struggle goes on just the same. The "peaceful" methods of struggle, however, are only temporary; in time, co-operation must end and the peaceful struggle must "turn into an armed struggle when we are forced to split with the bourgeoisie." Thus, even in the course of outward co-operation, the Communists anticipate the eventual split and armed struggle. The two camps may temporarily co-operate or they may "peacefully co-exist" for a given period of time, but the basic antagonism of the two camps remains.

Soviet Union and Tito. The two-camp view of the world is not only basic to the "lean-to-one-side" foreign policy but also to the continuing emphasis on the solidarity of the socialist bloc headed by the Soviet Union. Despite reports of Chinese disappointment with Soviet aid and rumors of Peking-Moscow friction, the Chinese Communists have seized every opportunity to pledge anew their allegiance to international Communism and their support of the Soviet Union as the leader of world Communism.

The Chinese Communists have been severe in their condemnation of Tito. Tito's offenses have been detailed in editorials and resolutions. Two charges have been especially emphasized: first, Tito rejects the leadership of the Soviet Union; second, Tito fails to appreciate the impassable gulf between the two camps of the world. The JEN MIN JIH PAO declared that Tito's objection to dividing the world into two camps made him a traitor to the socialist cause, because to deny the existence of the two camps is tantamount to a denial of the existence of classes in society. This fundamental error, said the editorial, led Tito to eulogize U.S. aid.[14]

It is, then, no wonder that the Chinese Communists have time and again reaffirmed their support of "socialist solidarity" under Soviet leadership. The preamble of the Constitution of the People's Republic of China specifically stipulates "an indestructible friendship with the great Union of Soviet Socialist Republics and the People's Democracies." In the same spirit, it is stated in the General Program of the Constitution of the Chinese Communist Party (adopted in 1956) that

56

the party should "endeavor to develop and strengthen China's friendship with all other countries in the camp of peace, democracy, and socialism headed by the Soviet Union, to strengthen the internationalist solidarity of the proletariat, and to learn from the experiences of the world Communist movement."

"East Wind" and *"West Wind."* The ideology of the Chinese Communists leads them to believe that capitalism will eventually collapse and socialism will eventually triumph all over the world. They see nothing but a dark future for the capitalist countries; on the other hand, they firmly believe that the socialist states will steadily grow in strength and prosperity. The United States and other capitalist countries are constantly being depicted as decadent societies paralyzed by grave economic crises and unable to solve the serious problems of unemployment and class antagonisms. They are likened to the "paper tiger," seemingly ferocious in look but utterly lacking in real strength or durability.

As early as 1950, the Communists were introducing into the primary schools of China, among children's books designed to inculcate a new outlook compatible with proletarian society, a little book titled *Two Worlds.* It presents a sharp contrast between the capitalist world as represented by the United States and the socialist world as represented by the Soviet Union. A dark picture is painted of capitalist America: cruel exploitation of the workers and the common people, poor people living in slums while the privileged few enjoy extravagant luxuries, a land which is "paradise for the rich but hell for the poor." In contrast, the Soviet Union is portrayed as a land where workers enjoy all sorts of privileges and luxuries, where everything is done for the benefit of the people, rather than the profit of a few. Eventually, concludes the book, the capitalist world will disappear and the whole world will then become one — the socialist world.

In 1958, Chinese Communist propaganda made a renewed effort to publicize Mao Tse-tung's statement that the decadent capitalist countries are as frail and easily destructible as a paper tiger. The PEKING PEOPLE'S DAILY, official organ of the Chinese Communist Party, published on October 31, 1958 a collection of Mao's writings on the central theme that "imperialism and all reactionaries are paper tigers." It was said that the collection of writings ranged over a period of twenty years, thus showing that the concept had been an important part of the Communist ideology, and did not consist merely of off-hand reactions to contemporary events. From 1940, when he said in his NEW DEMOCRACY that the capitalist system was outmoded and sinking fast like a dying person, to September, 1958, when he declared in a speech at the Supreme State Conference that the general trend of world affairs is that the east wind prevails over the west wind, Mao was steadily expressing his Marxist conviction that capitalism is bound to collapse and socialism destined to prevail.

Following Mao's lead, writers and speakers have tried to draw detailed contrasts between the rapidly declining capitalist countries and the flourishing socialist states. They dwell on the advances made by Soviet science and technology far outdistancing the achievements of capitalist science, the great strides in industrialization in China, the economic progress and increased production output of North Korea, Viet Minh, Mongolia, and the "people's democracies" in Eastern Europe. One long article devoted to this theme concluded: "In 1958, in a word, the East wind further prevailed over the West wind; it was a year in which, as Chairman Mao Tse-tung recently said, 'the enemy rots with every passing day, while for us things are getting better daily.' "[15]

IDEOLOGY AS EXPRESSED IN THE PATTERN OF EDUCATION AND CULTURE

The Socialist Man. The Communists consider the cultural phase of their revolution as important as the economic and the political. They have undertaken to build a new society and the new society calls for new men with new minds, new attitudes, new loyalties. The Common Program adopted in 1949 states that the "public spirit of all nationals" should be manifested in the "five loves," namely, "love of the fatherland, love of the people, love of labor, love of science, and love of public property."

The new man in the proletarian-socialist society must be thoroughly imbued with the Marxist-Leninist ideology, in which the love of labor and the development of the "scientific" viewpoint are important elements. Besides, he must discard the outmoded loyalties of the feudal-bourgeois society and adopt the loyalties of the proletarian-socialist man. He must learn to live as a member of the collective group and to subordinate his personal interests to those of the group.

The Chinese Communists lay a good deal of stress on "Communist morality." They say that the development of "Communist morality" is one of the major tasks of education in schools, in the youth organizations, and in other groups. The most succinct definition of "Communist morality" was made by Liu Shao-ch'i in his HOW TO BE A GOOD COMMUNIST (1934). He said: To sacrifice one's personal interests and even one's life without the slightest hesitation and even with a feeling of happiness, for the cause of the Party, for class and national liberation and for the emancipation of mankind is the highest manifestation of Communist morality." He further elucidated as follows:

> At all times and on all questions, a Communist Party member should take into account the interests of the Party as a whole, and place the Party's interests above his personal problems and interests. It is the highest principle of our Party members that the Party's interests are supreme. Every Party member should firmly build up this conception in his ideology. This is what we have often spoken of as "Party spirit," "Party conception" or "'organizational' conception." He should have only the Party and the Party's interests uppermost in his mind and not considerations of a personal character.

The "Organizational" Spirit. Now that they are engaged in transforming the entire Chinese society, the Communists have set out to remold the entire population according to the "organizational" model. The word "organization" carries immense weight in China today. It sometimes refers to the collective group in the school or in the factory or in a government office; usually, it means the party. Non-Communists as well as Communists are told that they must look to the "organization" for guidance on all matters. No matter whether it is a question of public policy or ideological orientation, or whether it is a purely personal problem, the ruling of the "organization" must be accepted without question. When young people are about to fall in love, they must consult the "organization" to find out whether the romance and the anticipated marriage will be compatible with the revolutionary cause. When they have problems of adjustment in family relations, they must ask for the advice of the "organization," in order to know whether to oppose a "reactionary" parent or to seek a divorce. Even in the selection of friends, they must seek the wisdom of the "organization" in order to make sure that the interests of the "revolution" would benefit from the association.

59

The effort to break down the traditional family loyalties fits into the concept of the party or "the revolution" above all else. Members of the Young Pioneers youth organization have been rewarded with medals and honors because they have denounced their "reactionary" parents and exposed the "counter-revolutionary" activities of family members. Young people graduating from secondary schools or higher institutions are sent to serve in areas far away from home; since the "organization" is supreme, the jobs assigned to each person must be accepted without question.

The Public-Spirited Citizen. An interesting application of the "public-spirit" that the Communists are striving to develop is the attempt to introduce various forms of "honor system services." As early as 1951, the Communists gave wide publicity to a self-service bookstore in Peking where customers helped themselves and left payment according to marked prices, without the supervision of a storekeeper; and to a few other experiments such as a self-service motion picture ticket station in the city of Kweilin, and "self-paying" water stations in Peking and Canton, all of which were publicized to show that the new citizens were so mindful of public welfare that they would not seek personal benefit at public expense.

More recently, an experiment with "conductorless buses" was reported in Shantung province. Passengers paid their fare either to a fellow passenger volunteering to serve as collector or dropped their money in a box. It was reported that at the end of the first month of the experiment there was only an error of twenty *yuan* in the total receipts of fifteen thousand *yuan*.[16]

The Chinese Communist press has boastfully publicized an experiment in "eight no" conducted by a factory in the Manchurian province of Heilungkiang. The experiment consists of eight forms of honor system. The dining hall has no attendants, and workers help themselves to food and leave their payment. The wages are paid by the honor system: money for all the workers is left in a place without any person to watch it, and workers come and take what is their due and sign their names and amount taken. The stockroom is open all the time, and every worker is free to take what he needs and returns the tools after use. Other services with no attendants are a library, a games and recreation room, a receptacle for dues to be paid by workers, a motion theater without a ticket booth or inspector of tickets, and a bathhouse where workers pay for its use by the honor system.[17] Such, the Communists say, is the public spirit of the socialist man.

Educating the New Man. In the task of producing the new socialist man, education of all forms and on all levels is concerned with two major objectives, namely, to raise the political or ideological consciousness of the individual and to increase his ability for production. The Communists maintain that there are only two kinds of worthwhile knowledge, knowledge pertaining to the class struggle and knowledge pertaining to production. Said Mao Tse-tung:

> What is knowledge? Ever since the existence of class society there have been in the world only two kinds of knowledge, that which concerns the struggle for production and that which concerns the class struggle. The natural and social sciences are the crystallizations of these two kinds of knowledge, and philosophy is the generalization and summary of the knowledge of both nature and society.[18]

Exclusive concern with these two kinds of knowledge is reflected in the Communist policy in regard to the promotion of students and their admission into higher institutions of learning. "Advanced workers" with good production records and of proven political "reliability" are given priority over students of much higher academic qualifications; in fact, many of them have been admitted into "colleges" and "universities" with very inadequate academic preparation. When questioned about academic standards, the Communists fall back on their cliché that there are only two kinds of knowledge worth any attention; as long as a person is politically sound and adept in production he must be considered as highly qualified, though he may be judged deficient by false "bourgeois" standards.

The desired product of education is a "Red expert." An oft-repeated slogan is that an educated person must be "both Red and expert." No scholar, no expert, no scientist can be of any real value unless he is at the same time "Red," i.e., ideologically and politically sound and "reliable." To supply the need for Red experts, numerous "Red-and-Expert Universities" have been established. While the studies are closely linked with actual problems of production in farms and factories, the slogan in these new "universities" is: "Let politics take command." The entire educational program, in other words, must be designed to serve the cause of the proletarian-socialist revolution.

A Proletarian Intelligentsia. The old type intellectuals, products of bourgeois society, are criticized for their aloofness from politics and their non-participation in production. The new society calls for a new "proletarian intelligentsia" who come from the working and peasant classes, who are firmly rooted in proletarian ideology, and who are free from the shortcomings of the bourgeois intellectuals. The students in the "Red-and-Expert Universities" are peasants and workers engaged in production and in active "revolutionary work." The Communists claim that they are in this way not only bringing up a new generation and a new type of "proletarian intelligentsia," but are quickly wiping out the distinctions between the manual worker and the mental worker.

The "professors" in the new "universities" are experienced farmers and workers most of whom have had little formal schooling. The old type academicians take a back seat. They are ridiculed for their useless bookish knowledge divorced from politics and production. They not only must undergo thorough "ideological remolding" to replace their old bourgeois ideology with the proletarian ideology; they must sit at the feet of the new "proletarian intelligentsia" and learn the new knowledge closely linked with politics and production. They must participate in labor and engage in production.

The demand that education be closely integrated with productive labor has resulted in a new emphasis on "work-study" programs which combine education with productive labor. Schools of all levels have been ordered to make specific provision for labor and production activities as integral part of the regular schedule. Schools and universities have established farms, factories, and other production units which accept orders and produce goods just as regular productive enterprises do. Classroom work is closely integrated with production work and study is designed to help solve production programs. Schools thus become centers of production as well as centers of learning and the gap between theory and practice is supposed to have disappeared.

The Communists claim that this emphasis on productive labor is in line with the teachings of Marx and Engels. They quote from the writings of Marx and Engels to show that Marxist theory calls not only for the elimination of distinctions between mental work and manual labor and the distinctions between workers and peasants, but also for "fully developed human beings" who are able to switch from one branch of production to another.[19] By making old-type intellectuals engage in labor, by elevating workers and peasants to the position of "new-type intellectuals," by combining agriculture with industry in the communes, and by developing "all-round persons" versatile enough to shift from one branch of production to another whenever necessary, the Chinese Communists declare that they are moving steadily toward Communism and about to fulfill all the ten measures Marx and Engels specified in the Communist Manifesto as steps toward the establishment of Communist society.[20]

SELECTED BIBLIOGRAPHY

CHUNG KUO CH'ING NIEN (CHINESE YOUTH) and other Chinese Communist periodicals.

HONGQI (RED FLAG), a fortnightly publication dealing with ideological questions.

HSUEH HSI (STUDY), a fortnightly journal discussing ideological problems.

JEN MIN JIH PAO (PEOPLE'S DAILY), a daily newspaper published by the Central Committee of the Chinese Communist Party.

Liu Shao-ch'i, INTERNATIONALISM AND NATIONALISM (Peking: Foreign Languages Press, no date). Written to support the 1948 resolution of the Cominform condemning the Communist Party of Yugoslavia; a strong statement of the position of "proletarian internationalism" as opposed to "narrow bourgeois nationalism."

Liu Shao-ch'i, HOW TO BE A GOOD COMMUNIST (Peking: Foreign Languages Press, no date). A series of lectures delivered in 1939 and giving specific instructions concerning the ideological cultivation of party members and the maintenance of discipline in the party.

Mao Tse-tung, SELECTED WORKS, Vols. I to IV (New York: International Publishers, 1954-56). Treatises of especial significance to the present study are THE CHINESE COMMUNIST PARTY AND THE CHINESE REVOLUTION, ON THE NEW DEMOCRACY, ON COALITION GOVERNMENT, ON PEOPLE'S DEMOCRATIC DICTATORSHIP.

PEKING REVIEW. A fortnightly English periodical published in Peking. The 1958-1959 issues contain a number of articles stating the "two-camp" view and elaborating on the theme that "East wind prevails over West wind."

CURRICULUM VITAE

THEODORE HSI-EN CHEN has been on the faculty of the University of Southern California since 1938. He is Professor and head of the Department of Asiatic Studies. He was formerly Dean and,

63

later on, President of Fukien Christian University in China. In 1954, he went to Formosa as a representative of the United Board for Christian Higher Education in Asia to help establish Tunghai University. He is the author of DEVELOPING PATTERNS OF THE COLLEGE CURRICULUM IN THE UNITED STATES (1940), ELEMENTARY CHINESE READER AND GRAMMAR (1945), CHINESE COMMUNISM AND THE PROLETARIAN-SOCIALIST REVOLUTION (1955), THOUGHT REFORM OF THE CHINESE INTELLECTUALS (1960), and numerous articles appearing in the ANNALS of the American Academy of Political and Social Science, FAR EASTERN SURVEY, PACIFIC AFFAIRS, AMERICAN JOURNAL OF SOCIOLOGY, SOCIOLOGY AND SOCIAL RE-SEARCH, CURRENT HISTORY, THE NEW LEADER, JOURNAL OF HIGHER EDUCATION and other periodicals. He is also a contributor to COMPARATIVE EDUCATION (edited by A. H. Moehlman and J. S. Roucek, Dryden Press, 1952), the ENCYCLOPAEDIA BRITANNICA, WORLD BOOK ENCYCLOPEDIA, ENCYCLOPEDIA OF MODERN EDUCATION, AND ENCYCLOPEDIA OF VOCATIONAL GUIDANCE.

CHAPTER FOUR

SOVIET RUSSIA'S RELUCTANT SATELLITES

EDWARD TABORSKY

University of Texas

UNDER THE LIFE OF ENFORCED CONFORMISM — A BREEDING PLACE OF "PERNICIOUS ISMS"

Three major streams may be distinguished in the present ideological flux within the Soviet satellite orbit: (1) the Kremlin-interpreted Marxism-Leninism which continues, in spite of the turmoils and ferment of the post-Stalin era, to be the only permissible official doctrine of each and every satellite, including Gomulka's Poland; (2) the revisionism which seeks to reform and streamline Marxism-Leninism rather than discard it, and which thus constitutes a challenge from within the Marxist-Leninist camp itself; (3) the anti-Communism which embraces all those "isms" aiming at the elimination of Marxism-Leninism and even Marxism as such.

Naturally, these three categories are not separated by airtight barriers. Overlapping is of frequent occurrence and local varieties are plentiful. It is often hard to say nowadays where a permissible adaptation of Marxism-Leninism to specific local or historical conditions ends and a revisionist "heresy" begins; or where a revisionist effort to redeem Marxism by ridding it of the Stalinist "distortions" slides into anti-Communism. The tactics of orthodox Marxist-Leninists to denounce all revisionists as working actually for the return of "bourgeois capitalism" add further to the confusion. So do the understandable endeavors of many an inveterate opponent of Marxism-Leninism to hide his ultimate anti-Communist aims by posing as a mere reformer operating within the framework of "creative" Marxism. Nonetheless, with these limitations, the above threefold classification does reflect the major ideological trends on the satellite scene and is helpful as an orientation marker through the ideological ferment characteristic of the Soviet orbit today.

I. ORTHODOX MARXISM-LENINISM

First to consider is, of course, the official doctrine of Marxism-Leninism which alone is supposed to guide the satellite regimes in all their activities. How, if at all, has it been affected by the spectacular developments which have been taking place within the Soviet world since the death of Joseph Stalin? Does satellite Marxism-Leninism differ from its Soviet version? Or, if it does not and the Soviet version is binding upon them, can the satellite leaders share in its interpretation and adaptation? Are there some variations from one satellite to another?

The answers to these questions are essentially in the negative. While differences in local conditions and developmental stages were allowed to bear in varying degrees on the satellite practice of Marxism-Leninism even at the height of Stalinism, and this has been substantially more noticeable since Stalin's death, in respect to ideology the satellites were and are afforded nothing but a Hobson's choice, Stalin or no Stalin. Contrary to outward appearances, this is true also of the one satellite country which undoubtedly is most unorthodox of them all in the practical application of Marxism-Leninism, Gomulka's Poland.

That a rigid ideological uniformity dominated the satellite scene throughout the Stalin era need not be elaborated. However prominent the various satellite Communists may have been in their own bailiwicks, none of them could depart one inch from the Marxist-Leninist dogma as defined by Stalin. Loyalty to Stalin, which was then the supreme test of good Communism, implied unquestioning acceptance of the Master's *ex-cathedra* edicts in the realm of Communist ideology. Not only was it unthinkable to display publicly anything but enthusiasm about any one of Stalin's interpretations, but even a strictly private expression of the slightest doubt was fraught with heavy risks. As learned the hard way by such high-ranking satellite communists as Rajk of Hungary, Kostov of Bulgaria, Slánsky and Clementis of Czechoslovakia, any departure from the Kremlin-prescribed orthodoxy, or even a trumped-up accusation thereof, amounted to a capital offense. Thus, whether it was Stalin's well-known thesis on the sharpening of the class struggle during the construction of socialism, his

66

views on genetics or his intervention in philology, all such ideological dicta of the Muscovite pontiff were invariably hailed by all the leading satellite Communists as brilliant enrichments of Marxism-Leninism. This ideological prostration reached its climax at the time of the Nineteenth Congress of the Soviet Communist Party in October, 1952, when all the satellite leaders from Bierut and Gottwald to Rakosi went heels over heads in chanting hosannas to Stalin's sterile pamphlet on the *Economic Problems of Socialism in the USSR,* which merely rehashes a few shopworn Marxist-Leninist tenets without adding anything new.

Stalin's death and subsequent downgrading deprived the Communist world of the untouchable symbol of unity, vacated the position of the exclusive interpreter of Marxism-Leninism and *ipso facto* nullified the validity of loyalty to Stalin as the supreme test of good Communism. Khrushchev's 1955 reconciliation with Tito, the only Communist ruler who dared to oppose Stalin and get away with it, his pronouncement in favor of different roads to socialism and his condemnation of Stalin's "distortions" of Marxism-Leninism in 1956 could not but further loosen the straitjacket of rigid Stalinist orthodoxy. What had once been the worst of Communism's heresies seemed to have suddenly become at least tolerable; and it looked as if specific people's democratic roads to socialism ceased being damnable "counterrevolutionary concepts." Thus an exceptionally favorable confluence of circumstances occurred within the Soviet orbit for the sprouting, if not of "one hundred flowers" of thought, then at least of a few alternative shoots of Marxism-Leninism besides the strictly Muscovite variety.

However, paradoxically though not at all surprisingly, none of the topmost satellite Communists seized the rare opportunity of streamlining the antiquated doctrine and thus making a bid for a posthumous place among the "classics of Marxism-Leninism." While a lively ideological ferment soon erupted among the *lesser* Communists, especially in Poland and Hungary, the satellite rulers and their lieutenants continued to cling to the Kremlin's ideological coat-tails as tenaciously as ever. As throughout the Stalin era, they made no move beyond the habitual routine until they could discern the signals on the Kremlin switchboard. A careful check of the post-Stalin behavior of the satellite regimes on the ideological front and, in particular, the timing of their actions and pronouncements, reveals

67

as complete a dependence on Soviet guidance as in the days of Stalin.

The Kremlin's public censure of the "cult of the individual" shortly after Stalin's death and the elevation of the neo-old deity of "collective leadership" as "the highest principle of Party leadership" found prompt echoes on the satellite level.[1] Although the satellite leaders were caught completely off guard and were obviously dismayed by Khrushchev's sudden head-on attack on Stalin in February, 1956, they nevertheless swallowed their evil forebodings and assumed with customary obedience the none too pleasant duty of explaining the "results and lessons of the Twentieth Congress" to their subjects.[2] And when the unpredictable Khrushchev reversed himself once more and proclaimed Stalin to have actually been a "model Bolshevik," his satellite lieutenants hurriedly jumped on the neo-Stalinist bandwagon, hardly concealing their pleasure at seeing their own Stalinist past vindicated.[3]

A similar dependence on the Kremlin characterizes the satellite attitude toward Tito. None of the specters haunting the orthodox Stalinists in the last years of the Stalin era had been exorcized more ferociously and fought more vigorously than "Titoism." To be labeled a "Titoist" meant not only political disgrace but often criminal prosecution. Hence, the abrupt Soviet reversal, dramatized by Khrushchev's Canossa-like journey to Belgrade in the spring of 1955 and the Soviet leader's unprecedented apology to the one-time "Judas of Communism" and "lackey of capitalism" confronted the East European Communists with a most ticklish problem. What to do about the thousands of "Titoists" languishing in Communist jails? Worst still, what to do about those who could no longer be resuscitated? Nevertheless, however hard it was for them, the satellite rulers swallowed the bitter pill, although it took them several months before they utttered their own sour and halfhearted apologies.[4] However, hardly had the satellite regimes caught up with the new Soviet line when relations between Tito and Khrushchev took a turn for the worse following the suppression of the Hungarian uprising; and the Yugoslav leader became once more the leading villain in the Marxist-Leninist gallery of rogues. Again, and this time with much more alacrity, the satellite leaders rallied behind the newly unfolded anti-Tito banner and have since then wasted no suitable opportunity of lashing out at Tito's "distortion and falsification" of the Marxist-Leninist teaching.[5]

68

The same deference to Soviet ideological *fiats* is reflected by satellite official attitudes in all other instances concerning the Marxist-Leninist theories in the post-Stalin era. Thus, only after Moscow had modified the rigid "Zhdanov line" on culture did the satellite art censors adopt a somewhat more lenient interpretation of "socialist realism"; and the gradual return to more repressive measures since 1957 has also paralleled the tightening of cultural reins in the Soviet Union. Again, only after Khrushchev and Mikoyan, pursuing their new line of professed modesty, had publicly urged the Soviet people to pay more attention to the achievements of other nations, especially the people's democracies, did the satellite leaders decree that the previous excessive praise of everything Soviet be toned down somewhat. Similar parrot-like behavior could be observed in foreign relations, where the satellite regimes have in turn smiled, frowned and rattled their sabers in conditioned reflex to corresponding Soviet attitudes; in foreign trade matters, where trading with the capitalists ceased once again to be incompatible with the status of a good Marxist-Leninist; in carefully guided "fraternization" with the West, which was stricken off the roll of Communist must-nots; etc. In like manner, Khrushchev's ideological dicta enunciated at the Twentieth and Twenty-First Congresses of the Soviet Communist Party were hailed and accepted without questioning or dissent throughout the satellite world as the only universally binding interpretation of Marxism-Leninism, just as Stalin's bulls had been in the past.[6]

But what about Imre Nagy of Hungary and Wladyslaw Gomulka of Poland? Had they not deviated from the official doctrine of Marxism-Leninism as interpreted by the Kremlin? Although the first impression seems to suggest an affirmative answer, a closer look reveals that what the two foremost anti-Stalinist rebels stood for, and Gomulka still stands for today, *in the realm of ideology* was and is well within the framework of the Soviet version of Marxist-Leninist teaching.

As for Nagy, his political convictions are amply revealed in a dissertation which he wrote in his defense in 1955 and 1956 after having been relieved of premiership in 1955. This lengthy exposé, addressed to the Central Committee of the Hungarian Communist Party, couched in strictly Marxist terms and replete with quotations from Marx, Lenin and Stalin, shows Nagy to have been a dedicated Marxist-Leninist.[7] In it the one-time Hungarian Premier spoke of his battle for "the purity of Marxism-Leninism" and warned not only against "leftist, sectarian anti-Marxist views," but also against "the dangers of rightist deviation." He stressed that "one must fight, with all possible means pertaining to an ideological battle, for the eradication of these deviations and against the petit bourgeois frame of mind and the influence exerted by the lower middle class upon the workers." He defended his 1953-1955 "New Course" as a correct "application of Marxism-Leninism to the concrete Hungarian situation" and as necessary to uphold "the power of the proletariat" which was "the basic and indispensable requirement needed to build Socialism." He accused his opponents of attempts "to cover their own deviation by hypocritically alluding to Marxism" and of endangering the dictatorship of the proletariat by weakening the worker-peasant alliance. Moreover, he reminded his critics that each and every item of his "New Course" had been approved in Moscow; and that this was true even of the most radical part of the Hungarian "New Course" — the permission granted to the peasants to leave collective farms.

The "Marxist-Leninist faith" which Nagy sought to prove by his dissertation stayed with him also when he became again Premier of Hungary after the outbreak of the revolution on October 24, 1956. That is at least the conclusion which the present writer has reached on the basis of all the accessible evidence concerning Nagy's behavior during the hectic days of the Hungarian uprising in the fall of 1956.[8] As long as he cherished a hope that he might be able to put down the uprising Nagy evidently strove to preserve intact the party's dictatorship. While he undoubtedly wished to meet what he considered to be just grievances by a return to his earlier "New Course" policies, he most certainly did not want, if he could help it, to yield on any of the major tenets of Marxism-Leninism, least of all to give up the party's monopoly of power. In his very first speech upon the assumption of the premiership on October 24, 1956, he excoriated the "hostile elements" who "turned against the People's Democracy, against the power of the people" and called upon the workers to "line up behind the Party."[9] The following day he still threatened that he would "apply the full severity of the law" to those who continued armed attacks. He also insisted that it was merely "a small group of counter-revolutionary provocateurs" who "launched an armed attack against the order of our People's Republic" and who were supported only by "a part of the workers of Budapest," and this only because of their "bitterness" over "the political and economic mistakes of the past."

It was his cabinet which announced on October 25, 1956, rather prematurely, that "the Army, the State Security forces and armed workers guards have liquidated, *with the help of Soviet troops,* the attempt at a counter-revolutionary coup d'etat on the night of October 24-25."[10] Although Nagy subsequently claimed (on October 31) that the aid of Soviet troops had been requested without his knowledge, in his radio address of October 25 he did speak approvingly of the presence of the "Soviet forces whose intervention in the fighting had been made necessary by the vital interests of our Socialist order" and he promised their withdrawal only "after the restoration of peace and order."[11] His intention to keep Communist control intact was borne out also by the fact that his new cabinet, constituted on October 27, 1956, the fourth day of the revolution, consisted of twenty-one Communists, holding all the key positions, as against six members of former non-Communist parties.

Only when the revolutionaries were winning the upper hand and the Soviets seemed to waver in their armed aid did Nagy begin to change the line. In a speech on October 28 he conceded that the revolutionaries constituted "a great national and democratic movement embracing and unifying all our people," although he still suggested that "this movement was exploited by criminal . . . and reactionary, counter-revolutionary elements . . . with the aim of overthrowing the people's democratic regime." On October 30 he announced his government's intention to negotiate with the Soviet Union on the withdrawal of Soviet troops from Hungary. He also proclaimed the abolition of the one-party system and a return "to a system of government based on the democratic co-operation of the coalition parties as they had existed in 1945." Although these were clearly retrograde steps from the standpoint of Marxism-Leninism, they still amounted *per se* to a break neither with the doctrine nor with the Soviet Union. For Janos Kadar, who had publicly thrown his support behind Nagy on behalf of the above-mentioned program, could still subsequently be approved as the Kremlin's lieutenant in Hungary. Nor did Nagy's program of internal reforms contain anything else that ran afoul of the theoretical precepts of Marxism-Leninism. Such promises as "revision of norms and salaries," the "implementation of higher family allowances," "the extension of democracy in the enterprises" or "putting an end to the serious illegalities committed in the collective farm movement" were either

71

ideologically irrevelant or so broadly phrased that they could mean anything.

Thus it was only when Nagy announced the Hungarian withdrawal from the Warsaw Pact on October 31 and November 1, 1956, and subsequently appealed to the United Nations for protection against Soviet troops, that he violated the Soviet version of Marxism-Leninism, in particular its tenet of proletarian internationalism. Nevertheless, it seems that even thereafter Nagy continued to consider himself to be a Marxist-Leninist. Although no positive proof is possible, at least some indication thereof may perhaps be seen in the fact that, when his regime had collapsed, Nagy sought refuge in the embassy of a country officially committed to Marxism-Leninism, though not its current Soviet variety, rather than in the diplomatic mission of a Western democratic country.

While the quick Soviet suppression of the Hungarian revolution had relegated forever to the realm of hypotheses the question whether Nagy would or could have developed any new version of Marxism-Leninism in Hungary, his fellow rebel in Poland has been more fortunate. Not only has Gomulka stayed alive and in power, but he has managed to gain a certain amount of internal autonomy unequaled in any other part of the satellite world. Pushed by the explosive inner pressures that culminated in the Polish "October Revolution" and intent on preserving the Communist power in Poland, Gomulka has conceded a notable measure of unorthodoxy in actual practice, such as the disbandment of collective farms, religious instruction in schools, substantial authority of workers' councils, at least some choice of candidates in parliamentary elections, and literary freedom going beyond anything allowed elsewhere behind the Iron Curtain. But he has never faltered in his adherence to all the major tenets of Marxism-Leninism; not even at the height of the Polish revolt. This is clearly apparent from his various pronouncements since his accession to power in October, 1956, which also amply document his gradual ideological stiffening once he felt more firmly in the saddle.

His very first address delivered at the epoch-making Eighth Plenum of the Party's Central Committee in October, 1956, after he had assumed again the leadership of the party did contain certain passages which could not have sounded well to orthodox Communist ears.[12] He scored "the clumsy attempt to present the painful Poznan tragedy as the work of imperialist agents and provocateurs." He emphasized the voluntary character of collective farms and suggested that those bringing only economic loss should be allowed to dissolve. He dwelled upon the desirability of different roads to socialism adapted to the "varying circumstances of time and place." He conceded that even "the forms of socialism" could vary and mentioned alongside the Soviet model also the Yugoslav variety. While proclaiming that the mutual relations between the parties and states of the socialist camp should be based on the principle of international solidarity of the working class, on mutual trust, equal rights and mutual assistance, he stressed also that "within the framework of such relations each country should have full independence" and that "the rights of each nation to a sovereign government in an independent country should be fully and mutually respected."

However disagreeable a public discussion of such matters might have been to the Soviet rulers, especially at that particular time, none of Gomulka's statements could truly be said to constitute an ideological heresy. After all, insofar as theory was concerned, they held close to the 1955-1956 Soviet version of Marxism-Leninism as interpreted by its new chief interpreter, N. S. Khrushchev, on a number of occasions, such as his visit in Belgrade in 1955 and the Twentieth Congress of the Soviet Communist Party in 1956. Moreover, Gomulka made it amply clear that the Communist monopoly of power must remain and that the party must be guided by "all the Leninist principles of Party life;" and he served an ominous warning on those who wanted to use the "democratization process to undermine socialism" as well as on those who believed that they could "nurture anti-Soviet moods."

If any doubts still persisted about Gomulka's ideological leanings they were fully dispelled by his lengthy report to the Ninth Plenum of the Party's Central Committee in May, 1957.[13] While he continued to defend the doctrine of different roads to socialism and considered it as "neither necessary nor entirely suitable" for nations with different historical conditions to follow the Soviet road, he recognized the "general validity of the universal principles derived from the experience in the construction of socialism in the Soviet Union" and accused those who undervalued these principles of "national revisionism." He reiterated his acceptance of such basic Marxist-Leninist precepts as the dictatorship of the proletariat, democratic centralism, socialization of all means of production, proletarian internationalism and "the unity of socialist countries and forces against the imperialist aggression and for the protection of peace." He lay great emphasis on the necessity of class struggle, the paramount importance of the leadership of the "Marxist-Leninist Party of the working class," and its role of "preventing the bourgeoisie and the reaction from abusing democratic freedoms to the detriment of socialism and the interests of the working class." He stressed that any discussions resulting from differences of opinions as between Communist parties should be conducted "on the basis of ideological togetherness, acceptance of common rules valid for all the Parties and used for the struggle to overthrow the capitalist order and to build a socialist order."

Taking a very substantial departure from the original Polish appraisal of the events in Hungary, he referred to "the help of the Soviet Army in the suppression of the counter-revolution" as "a regrettable but unavoidable necessity for the maintenance of peace and security of all the socialist countries." In yet another significant gesture of subservience to the Kremlin he conceded that the strength of people's democratic Poland, the future of her socialist construction, as well as her "independence and sovereignty," were "based on the unity of all socialist countries and especially on the Polish-Soviet alliance."

Gomulka also went a long way toward placing in a proper ideological perspective, and narrowing substantially, the several concessions which had been granted during the "October Revolution" and which constituted the main ingredients of the "Polish way toward socialism." Thus he scored various "harmful tendencies" and "false concepts" concerning the workers' councils, asked for the removal from the councils of "ideologically alien elements which emerged on the crest of the October wave" and denied the councils the character of "the organs of political power of the working class." Similarly, he dashed the wishful thoughts of those who hoped that the party's new First Secretary had tacitly given up the idea of eventual collectivization of Polish agriculture. Although he restated that no compulsion should be used, he gave vent to the belief that "the peasants would sooner or later become convinced that the Party, which supports the production co-operatives, does not harm them but only wants their best." Nor did Gomulka retreat one inch from the Marxist-Leninist ideology with regard to party-church relations. On the contrary, he made it quite clear that the current co-existence between the church and the party in Poland was only a temporary, although fairly long-term, arrangement which, moreover, "did not exclude certain ideological struggles."

But the most ominous part of Gomulka's speech was his scathing attack on Polish revisionism. He branded it as a "distortion of Marxism through interlacing into it false and mistaken theses," "an ideology of capitulation before the difficulties of the construction of socialism and before the class enemy" stemming from "the same bourgeois ideology which had also fathered the social democratic ideology." In particular, he strongly condemned L. Kolakowski, the leading Polish revisionist, and denounced him and his associates as "ideologically confused comrades and men who had already turned their back on socialism and had no longer anything in common with it, except their Party membership cards which they had not yet turned in and that the Party had not yet reclaimed."

This last-mentioned omission was quickly remedied by the Tenth Plenum of the Central Committee in October, 1957, which issued directives for a thorough "verification" of the entire membership of the party. In response to Gomulka's call that the party "should strike first of all at the basic source of its weakness, revisionism and liquidationism," the brunt of the purge fell, by an ironic twist of fortunes, on those who had mainly helped Gomulka to stage his come-back in October, 1956.[14]

Having thus purged the party of most of his one-time revisionist allies as well as some of his "dogmatist" rivals, Gomulka summoned in March, 1959, the Third Party Congress, the first such congress to be held since his accession to power. In a six-hour-long report to the assembled delegates the Polish party chief reaffirmed his Marxist-Leninist orthodoxy and full conformity with the current Soviet line.[15] Once again, he cast the revisionists in the role of the main villains and blamed them not only for their own heresies, but also for "pushing many honest but ideologically weak comrades into the embraces of dogmatists. While still insisting · on "the voluntary principle" in matters of agricultural collectivization, he underscored his conviction that "the socialist reconstruction of the countryside is in the best interests of the working peasantry" and promised peasants the party's help in setting up collective farms. He served a stern warning on the church, advising it "to stop provoking the people's authority because it will do the church no good." He called for a "rapid overcoming of the excessive liberalism expressed in the light treatment of activities directed against the people's State."

More than in any previous speech Gomulka inveighed against the relative freedom conceded the Poles in the fields of literature and science since 1956. He demanded that "lectures bearing on outlook or general ideology . . . be conducted exclusively in a spirit of Marxism." While promising not to "intervene administratively in normal scientific arguments," he ruled that "publication of pseudo-scientific works written from points of view hostile to Socialism" would be disallowed. He bade writers to apply the precepts of "Socialist realism," although he expressed willingness to allow also publication of "artistically valuable work of modern and contemporary artists who, without standing on a Marxist platform, serve by their work the cause of man's liberation." But he barred most emphatically the publication of what he called "a black literature proclaiming man's despair and helplessness in his social endeavors" because such works "are not works of art but a weapon of political propaganda for anti-Socialist forces."

Also, more than any other of his public utterances since he had resumed the leadership of the party, Gomulka's presentation at the Third Party Congress displayed his growing servility vis-à-vis the Kremlin. He parrotted Khrushchev's favorite we-will-bury-them slogan and denounced capitalism as "a dying system condemned by historical development to leave the arena of human history." He echoed the standard Soviet line on "Western imperialism." In contrast to his 1956-57 moderation regarding America he used the occasion to cast direct aspersions on the United States. He dutifully censured the Yugoslav Communists for having broken away from the united socialist camp. He went out of his way to please Soviet ears by stressing that the eastern territories "had been justly returned to their mother Soviet republics," even though he knew perfectly well how offensive such statements were for the strongly national Poles. Finally, in a spectacular double-talk reminiscent of Orwell's famed dictum about all animals being equal but some of them being more equal than others, he humbly conceded the Soviet claim to primacy. Having restated the principle of equality and independence of all the Communist parties, he hurried to deny his own words by stressing that "one of them, the Communist Party of the Soviet Union, enjoys in this group of equal parties special authority and occupies a leading position," is "the central nerve of the world Socialist system" and "the mainstay of all Socialist countries."

What makes the satellite rulers, including even such men as Gomulka, cling so tenaciously to Marxist-Leninist orthodoxy? What makes them bow so obediently to the Kremlin's ideological *ukases* despite a number of objective factors which should have lessened their dependence on Moscow in the post-Stalin era?

One reason lies undoubtedly in doctrinal loyalty. The men who stand today at the helm of satellite Communism are mostly devout Marxist-Leninists. They joined the movement because of strong beliefs in its cause. They have worked and fought for Communism their whole lives and staked their personal and political fortunes on its victory. They are fully aware of the importance of iron discipline and the political value of the movement's unity; and they know how much Communism's strength and effectiveness depends on the might of the Soviet Union. Thus, even though they may from time to time have some doubts about one or another matter of secondary ideological importance, they have no wish to turn their backs on their lifelong Marxist-Leninist convictions.

However, doctrinal loyalty alone provides only a partial answer. As documented by many actual cases of recent years, not even the most dedicated Marxist-Leninists are immune against the loss of faith in their dogma or against the desire to give priority to their own interpretations of Marxism-Leninism over those of Moscow. Gomulka himself is a living example of the latter tendency. While he had never lost faith in Marxism-Leninism, there is no doubt that he genuinely strove for more independence of Moscow, disagreed with some of the Soviet interpretations of the dogma and accepted them only with reluctance.[16] Thus the basic and truly decisive reason for the ideological subservience of the satellite Communist leaders to the Kremlin appears to be their weakness vis-à-vis their own peoples. Through their ruthless behavior during the Stalin era and their failure to fulfill so many of their rosy promises of yesteryears the satellite rulers embittered the broad masses of their hapless subjects as well as the majority of their own Communist rank-and-file. In so doing, they succeeded in putting Marxism-Leninism into such disrepute that it would be overwhelmingly rejected if the satellite peoples could freely decide. Hence, the advent of true democracy after which their subjects strive would inevitably spell the political, and in many instances even physical, end of those ruling in the name of the discredited dogma. This applies not only to the neo-Stalinist regimes predominant in the satellite orbit, but to Gomulkaism as well. This being so, the instinct of self-preservation itself pushes the satellite leaders, including Gomulka, inexorably under the Kremlin's political and ideological control, no matter what their private convictions might be.

II. REVISIONISM

While the satellite leaders and their henchmen rely strictly on the Kremlin's *fiats* in setting their ideological course, the rank-and-file of their parties has come in recent years under the spell of what the Communist rulers now label officially as revisionism. Having been first used to denounce the anti-Stalinist Polish Communists who pressed for further advances on the reformist road initiated by Poland's "October Revolution" of 1956, revisionism was placed formally on the index of proscribed heresies by the Moscow Declaration of November, 1957.[17] Although borrowed from the attic of the Marxian past and thus lacking in originality, this old-new label is nevertheless a more fitting description of present day Communism's main malaise than any other of the variety of pernicious "isms" that Communist rulers pin on the inner-party opposition. What the revisionists want is, indeed, such a full-scale revision of Marxism-Leninism that it would cut out its totalitarian core, release it from the Muscovite bondage and convert it into a rather benign variety of democratic or quasi-democratic socialism.

Revisionism has assumed its most radical form and most explosive character in Poland and, prior to the suppression of the 1956 uprising, in Hungary. Thanks to the relative leniency of Gomulka's regime, especially in the realm of the press, Poland's revisionists could develop their theses and publicize them much more thoroughly and for a longer time than their colleagues elsewhere in the Soviet orbit. Taking full advantage of this rare opportunity for a "free competition of ideas", such men as Kolakowski, Zimand, Woroszylski, Wazyk, Kott, Chalasinski and many others have flooded the Polish press with articles attacking the very substance of Marxism-Leninism.[18] They have rejected its "fetishist" belief in historical determinism. They scoff at its "irrational tendencies" and proclaim the "eternal ethical values" as the only proper guide. They have taken stand against such crucial concepts of Marxism-Leninism as the class struggle, the dictatorship of the proletariat and democratic centralism. They insist that Marxism "be submitted to the same methods of scientific verification and con-

78

trol as any other discipline." Some of them even question the very pivot and condition *sine qua non* of the Marxist-Leninist system, namely the desirability of the party's monopoly of political power.

Although revisionism elsewhere behind the Iron Curtain has been less vociferous and more cautious in its critique of Marxist-Leninist orthodoxy than its Polish variety, no satellite has escaped its profound impact. Like a fast-spreading epidemic, it has swept across the satellite orbit in all directions, from the Baltic to the Adriatic and from the Elbe to the Black Sea. Whenever and wherever it has found an opportunity to do so, revisionism has pushed its way to the surface in the form of articles questioning, directly or obliquely, the validity of the current official interpretation of various Marxist-Leninist tenets. Since newspapers and periodicals managed directly by the party are vigilantly guarded against revisionist heresies, they have been appearing mostly in literary journals and magazines devoted to questions of history, philosophy, and similar disciplines where they can also be better disguised under a scholarly garb. Whenever repression and outright public advocacy of revisionism becomes too risky, it hides below the surface where it continues to gnaw at the very foundations of the Marxist-Leninist teaching as subterranean termites eating out the basic structure of an outwardly undisturbed house.

The presence and the seriousness of this revisionist menace is documented by many sources. In spite of the stepped-up efforts of the satellite regimes to deny revisionism access to any kind of publicity, it nevertheless keeps on breaking into the open, especially in the field of fiction and poetry which seems to have become the main refuge of revisionist thought.[19] Information which reaches the outside world through underground channels and escapees from behind the Iron Curtain points in the same direction. So does the mammoth anti-revisionist campaign unleased throughout the Soviet orbit in 1957-1958.[20] Following obediently the directives of the Moscow Declaration of 1957, which labels revisionism as the main danger confronting the Communist movement today, the satellite rulers have proclaimed the struggle against "the vicious poison" of revisionism to be the principal task of the "revolutionary workers' movement." Party congresses, conferences and even local meetings have been made an occasion for vitriolic tirades against revisionism. Press, radio, and all the other media of indoctrination have been mobilized to combat that "black plague." As shown above, even Gomulka has been drafted as one of the chief anti-revisionist crusaders. Editors and publication directors who had allowed publication of objectionable articles and books were replaced in a number of instances by persons likely to abide better by the supreme duty of Communist vigilance. Even total suppression was resorted to in extreme instances, such as the case of the Polish review *Po Prostu.*

What makes the struggle against revisionism especially complicated are two closely related factors. Firstly, even devout Communists realize that some of Marxist-Leninist theories in their present form are outdated and require streamlining. Although they would not go as far as some of the more radical revisionists, they nevertheless recognize the desirability of an ideological inquiry and, if need be, of a revision as such. Thus they unwittingly help the revisionists' cause. Secondly, unlike the case of some other "pernicious isms," the Communist rulers are unable to pin on revisionism their favorite label of bourgeois origin. Not that they have not tried. Parroting the Soviet cliché, their propagandists have done their utmost to portray revisionism as a creation of "American imperialism," "a class weapon of the bourgeoisie," "a survival of bourgeois and petty-bourgeois thinking," and the like. But such assertions are too absurd to believe even by Communist standards. They are belied by the presence, among the ranks of the revisionists, of many men of long-standing and meritorious service to the Communist cause. Moreover, there is every indication that they, rather than their neo-Stalinist mentors, are endowed with that ideological zeal and spirit of sacrifice that characterized the earlier disciples of the Communist creed when allegiance to the teaching of Karl Marx meant privation instead of the executive swivel chairs bestowed upon today's orthodox Communists with clean "cadre reports." RUDE PRAVO, the main daily of the Czechoslovak Communists, hit the nail on the head when it lamented that "the fight against revisionism is a complicated matter because revisionism appears misleadingly under the title of creative development of Marxism while its ideas are formulated with particular care in the people's democratic countries where the revisionists cannot take the anti-Party line quite so openly."[21]

III. ANTI-COMMUNISM

Despite the stigma of treason which the orthodox Communists attempt to affix to their revisionist comrades, genuine revisionists continue to think of themselves as Communists. "We are communists," wrote the foremost Polish revisionist, Leszek Kolakowski, "not because we have accepted communism as a historical necessity. We are communists because we are on the side of the oppressed against the oppressors, on the side of the poor against their masters, on the side of the persecuted against their persecutors. We are moved to action not by regards for theory but by moral impulses."[22] Indeed, the *genuine* revisionists consider themselves to be better Communists than their orthodox comrades, for their work is supposed to redeem Marxism by purging it of its fossilized deposits and fetishist beliefs. However, it is undoubtedly true that many of the so-called revisionists are not that at all, but in reality belong to one or another category of anti-Communists who constitute, by all the indications, an overwhelming majority in every satellite country. They simply hope to get away with their critique of Marxism-Leninism by pretending that they only wish to improve the teaching.

Since advocacy of anti-Communism of any kind anywhere behind the Iron Curtain is tantamount to treason, there exist no published materials which could be scanned and from which one could extract knowledge of anti-Communist ideologies present within the Soviet orbit. Nor do the ubiquitous police controls of a totalitarian system leave much opportunity for unorganized private groups to meet and formulate anti-Communist programs. The few prominent anti-Communists of pre-Communist days who managed to stay out of jail are closely guarded. Recent information reaching the free world does mention the emergence of various circles of younger intellectuals meeting in private homes in small groups for the purpose of reading and discussing banned literature and preparing reports on cultural, philosophical and ideological trends in the Western world.[23] But these groups, which arise spontaneously out of intellectual curiosity seeking to break out of the narrow confines prescribed by satellite censors, have mostly no contacts with one another and can seldom risk circularizing their reports beyond a narrow circle of trusted friends.

Thus information on anti-Communist thought behind the Iron Curtain can be drawn mainly from two sources: (1) political programs and other evidences of ideological relevance smuggled out by anti-Communist opposition; (2) Communist revelations contained in published records of political trials of members of various anti-Communist groups and recurrent attacks on these groups in the Communist press.

Neither of these two main sources provides an adequate basis for dependable evaluation. Many of the anti-Communist groups which had been quite active in the first years of the Communist rule have meanwhile been liquidated. Others have had to scatter and to sink deeper into the underground. Their contacts with the outside world have also become scarcer. Moreover, with the passage of time it is increasingly difficult to estimate to what extent the political attitudes expressed by such groups are representative of major trends and to what extent they mirror only personal opinions of a few individuals. As for the Communist press and trial records, it is always extremely difficult to separate the grain of truth from the chaff of propaganda and distortion. Nevertheless, in spite of their glaring inadequacies, these sources allow at least a rudimentary insight into the broad trends characteristic of present-day anti-Communism in the satellite system.

Perhaps the most general of these trends is *nationalism*. Fresh memories of national oppression have imbued the peoples of Central and Southeastern Europe with very strong nationalistic feelings. Hence, it is no wonder that such feelings have turned sharply against the new oppressor from the East even in countries which had previously been known for pro-Russian sentiments, such as Czechoslovakia and Bulgaria. Indeed, of all the "pernicious isms" tossed around by the Communist rulers none has been exorcized more persistently than so-called "bourgeois nationalism." Yet, no matter what methods have been used to combat it, nationalism has displayed the vitality of the Lernaean Hydra and has assumed a pronounced anti-Russian character. Aided unwittingly by the leaders' crude and mostly self-defeating methods of extolling Soviet superiority and, above all, by the naked facts of Soviet domination, it seems to have yielded no ground to the "proletarian internationalism" with which Communist leaders would like to replace it.

Next to "bourgeois nationalism" the most widespread trend of anti-Communist ideologies appears to be *"social democratism,"* sometimes dubbed also "social democratic sectarianism," "social democratic opportunism" or "anarcho-syndicalism." As revealed by various Communist indictments leveled at persons accused of this particular heresy, "social democratism" implies the following basic beliefs:

a. that the present economic system in the satellite orbit is state capitalism rather than socialism;

b. that, as originally promised, workers ought to participate in the management of nationalized enterprises;

c. that the trade unions should plead for the right of the workers instead of being a pliable tool in the enforcement of "socialist labor discipline";

d. that there should be free collective bargaining and at least a tacit acceptance of the strike as a last line of workers' defense;

e. that the differentiation of wages and bonuses should not be so sharp.

Aimed at the very heart of the Marxist-Leninist economic system, "social democratism" is all the more dangerous to the Communist rulers as its main habitat is in the industrial proletariat. Since its most efficient carriers thus belong to the working class which is supposedly the backbone of Communism, it is extremely hard to pin on the "social democratism" the all too much abused epithet of "bourgeois" and "reactionary."

That is not the case with *"religious obscurantism,"* yet another of the major "pernicious isms" troubling the satellite rulers. While many an element of "social democratism" sounds plausible to a true Marxist, his doctrine clearly condemns any spreading of the religious "opiate of the people" and automatically labels any church as reactionary and as a sworn enemy of Marxism-Leninism. However, the factual circumstances at the time of the Communist take-over, viewed against the earlier Soviet experience, have forced upon the satellite regimes a temporary *modus vivendi* with the church and a grudging tolerance of religious worship. A potent non-Marxist factor has thus been allowed to operate, even though with severe restrictions, in the bosom of the Marxist-Leninist system. As a result, unlike many other "harmful manifestation of bourgeois ideologies," "religious obscurantism" has been conceded a legitimate, though precarious, basis from which to compete with Marxism-Leninism. Since today's Christianity is not only a religion but a whole way of life from which politics cannot be arbitrarily cut out, this necessarily entails competition in the arena of political ideologies. As bared by reports from underground sources and corroborated by persistent Communist attacks on "religious obscurantism," a Christian concept, not dissimilar to the Western European Christian democratism, thus figures prominently among the anti-Communist ideologies with which the satellite regimes have to cope.

These, then, seem to be the main trends of anti-Communist thought in the satellite world: nationalism, with its sharpest edge aimed at the

Russian overlordship; social democratism, which is an Eastern counterpart of Western European democratic socialism and which can be said to embrace also the substantial portion of revisionism seeking to "revise" Marxism-Leninism by doing away with it; and Christian democratism which looks much like a leftist variety of a similar movement of Western Europe.

IV. SUMMARY

Thus the satellite ideological scene presents today the following basic pattern: The Muscovite version of Marxism-Leninism continues to be the only permissible official doctrine and the Kremlin retains the exclusive right of amendment. The initial hopes that Gomulkaism would develop into a distinctive westernized variety of Marxism have fizzled out. On the other hand, revisionism has been gaining ground steadily among the party's rank-and-file everywhere in the satellite orbit and it has been growing the more radical the sharper it is denounced. As had been the case with religious reformers of the past, the stubborn intransigence and ideological inflexibility of their orthodox superiors drives the would-be reformers of present-day Communism further than many of them originally meant to go. Thus the ideological gap between orthodox Marxism-Leninism and revisionism grows wider and that between revisionism and the leftist varieties of anti-Communism, such as "social democratism," tends to become ever narrower. As the Hungarian revolt and the Polish "October Revolution" have shown, it is this rapprochement of the two sworn enemies of Marxist-Leninist orthodoxy that poses the gravest ideological and political dilemma for the satellite rulers.

SELECTED BIBLIOGRAPHY

The two richest sources of information in the English language on matters pertinent to this chapter are the periodicals EAST EUROPE (formerly THE NEWS FROM BEHIND THE IRON CURTAIN), a monthly published by the Free Europe Committee, New York, and PROBLEMS OF COMMUNISM, a bimonthly published by the United States Information Agency, Washington, D.C. Both cover regularly and thoroughly all the major aspects of current developments in satellite Europe. Some scattered references to ideological trends in the respective satellite countries may also be gleaned from the series EAST-CENTRAL EUROPE UNDER THE COMMUNISTS prepared by the Mid-European Studies Center of the Free

Europe Committee and published by Frederick A. Praeger, New York.

L. B., "Revisionist Poland," THE WORLD TODAY, XIV, (June, 1958), 247-259. A succinct review and interpretation of political and ideological developments in Poland since Gomulka's accession to power.

Robert Finlay Delaney, Ed., THIS IS COMMUNIST HUNGARY (Chicago, Ill.: H. Regnery, 1958). A symposium of articles by exiled Hungarians; prefaced with a story of the 1956 revolt by the late *New York Times* correspondent, John MacCormac.

Francois Fejto, BEHIND THE RAPE OF HUNGARY (New York: David McKay, 1957). An account of the Hungarian revolution of 1956, its prelude and its motivations, written by a Hungarian political exile who had taken an active part in the intellectual ferment preceding the revolution; preface by Jean-Paul Sartre.

John H. Hallowell, Ed., SOVIET SATELLITE NATIONS: A STUDY OF THE NEW IMPERIALISM (Gainsville, Florida: Kalman Publishing Co., 1958). A symposium of nine articles by American scholars dealing with Communist policies and ideology in the Soviet satellites and elsewhere, with special emphasis on the post-Stalin era.

Siegfried Kracauer and Paul L. Berkman, SATELLITE MENTALITY: POLITICAL ATTITUDES AND PROPAGANDA SUSCEPTIBILITIES OF NON-COMMUNISTS IN HUNGARY, POLAND AND CZECHOSLOVAKIA (New York: Frederick A. Praeger, 1956). A study of political attitudes based on interviews conducted in 1951-1952 with several hundred escapees from behind the Iron Curtain; foreword by Henry L. Roberts.

Melvin J. Lasky, Ed., THE HUNGARIAN REVOLUTION: A WHITE BOOK, (New York: Frederick A. Praeger, 1957). A day-to-day chronology of the Hungarian revolution, containing various official and unofficial documentary materials.

Flora Lewis, A CASE HISTORY OF HOPE, (New York: Doubleday, 1958). A thorough review of political developments in Poland since the death of Stalin to Gomulka's return to power, written by the wife of the *New York Times* correspondent in Poland and based mainly on the author's personal observations and interviews with key figures of the period.

Pawel Majewski, Ed., THE BROKEN MIRROR: A COLLECTION OF WRITINGS FROM CONTEMPORARY POLAND (New York: Random House, 1958). A collection of stories, essays and philosophical works by seven Polish writers belonging to the revisionist wing, among them scathing criticisms of the orthodox version of Marxism-Leninism by the prominent Polish revisionists Kolakowski, Woroszylski and Strzelecki.

Imre Nagy, IMRE NAGY ON COMMUNISM: IN DEFENSE OF THE "NEW COURSE" (New York: Frederick A. Praeger, 1957). A complete text of the "dissertation" with which the Hungarian Premier of 1953-1955, ousted from the premiership and expelled from the Central Committee of the Hungarian Communist Party, sought to justify his post-Stalin "New Course" policies and prove that he was a loyal party member.

Konrad Syrop, SPRING IN OCTOBER: THE POLISH REVOLUTION OF 1956 (New York: Frederick A. Praeger, 1958). An account of the Polish "October Revolution" by an analyst of the British Broadcasting Corporation.

Edward Taborsky, CONFORMITY UNDER COMMUNISM, (Washington, D.C.: Public Affairs Press, 1958). A short study of Communist indoctrination efforts in satellite Europe and an interim evaluation of their results.

Edward Taborsky, "The Revolt of the Communist Intellectuals," THE REVIEW OF POLITICS, XIX, 3, (July, 1957), 308-329. A review and analysis of the post-Stalin intellectual ferment within the Soviet orbit.

THE REVOLT IN HUNGARY: A DOCUMENTARY CHRONOLOGY OF EVENTS (New York: Free Europe Press, 1956). A day-to-day collection of monitored broadcasts of the Hungarian radio stations between October 23, 1956, and November 4, 1956, including government proclamations and speeches by Imre Nagy and other figures of the Hungarian revolution of 1956.

George Urban, THE NINETEEN DAYS (London: W. Heinemann, 1957). A factual account of the Hungarian uprising of 1956 by a reporter of the British Broadcasting Corporation.

Paul Zinner, Ed., NATIONAL COMMUNISM AND POPULAR REVOLUTION IN EASTERN EUROPE, (New York: Columbia University Press, 1957). A collection of documentary materials (speeches, party resolutions, editorials, etc.) reflecting mainly the vicissitudes of Polish and Hungarian Communism since the Twentieth Congress of the Soviet Comunist Party.

CURRICULUM VITAE

EDWARD TABORSKY, Associate Professor of the Department of Government in the University of Texas, was born in Praha, Czechoslovakia (1910). He received the degree of Doctor of Laws and Political Science from Charles University, Praha, Czechoslovakia, in 1934. After postdoctoral studies and research at Charles University he joined the Czechoslovak Foreign Service in 1937 and served successively as Secretary to the Czechoslovak Foreign Minister (1937-1938), Personal Aide to the President of Czechoslovakia, Eduard Benes, in exile in England and in postwar Czechoslovakia (1939-1945), and as Envoy Extraordinary and Minister Plenipotentiary of Czechoslovakia in Sweden (1945-1948). He accompanied President Benes to his wartime conferences with President F. D. Roosevelt, Premier Stalin,

General De Gaulle, the Shah of Iran, etc. He resigned from the Czechoslovak diplomatic service after the Communists had seized power in Czechoslovakia in 1948 and settled in the United States in 1949.

Dr. Taborsky's previous academic career includes a lectureship in international law at Charles University, Praha, Czechoslovakia, a lectureship in political science at the University of Stockholm, Sweden, and visiting professorships in political science at the Ohio State University and the University of Tennessee. He is the author of seven books, two of them written in English, in the field of comparative government, international law and relations. He is a contributor to FOREIGN AFFAIRS, AMERICAN POLITICAL SCIENCE REVIEW, AMERICAN SLAVIC AND EAST EUROPEAN REVIEW, JOURNAL OF CENTRAL EUROPEAN AFFAIRS, PROBLEMS OF COMMUNISM, REVIEW OF POLITICS, NEW LEADER, MODERN LAW REVIEW, WORLD AFFAIRS INTERPRETER, SOUTHWESTERN SOCIAL SCIENCE QUARTERLY, THE ANNALS OF THE AMERICAN ACADEMY OF POLITICAL AND SOCIAL SCIENCE and other journals. Dr. Taborsky is a member of the American Political Science Association, Southern Political Science Association, Southwestern Social Science Association, Associate of the Institute of Ethnic Studies of Georgetown University. He is recipient of a 1959 Guggenheim Fellowship for the study of the Communist experiment in Czechoslovakia.

CHAPTER FIVE

TITOISM

Dan N. Jacobs
Miami University

INTERNATIONAL COMMUNISM NATIONALIZED

The international Communist movement has been dominated by "National Communism" for the past forty years. That the socialist movement was no longer "international" was demonstrated by the vast majority of socialists who became "social patriots" during World War I. And Bolshevism followed suit co-opting for "National Communism" on November 7, 1917, although this was not acknowledged until 1924 when Stalin proclaimed the possibility of achieving "socialism in one country."

In the first few months after October, Lenin, Trotsky and their fellow revolutionaries waited anxiously for the Revolution to spread to the highly industrialized countries of the West. This failing, they hoped that their regime would at least be able to survive the seventy-one days of the Paris commune. As it grew apparent that the fledgling government was not going to be submerged, the defense and cultivation of their unique and fragile creation became paramount. The protection of the RSFSR, "the first Communist nation in the world," held precedence over the welfare of any other Communist grouping. The first principle of international Communism became the defense of the national Communist entity against "capitalist encirclement" in all its myriad forms. The Soviet Union came first. The possibility of establishing Communism in any other country was secondary to the existence of Communism in the USSR.

Of course, the Communist Party never frankly conceded that the principle of "socialism in one country" was a repudiation of international Communism. It repeatedly branded such allegations as "calumnies" and "fabrications." Communism, by definition, is international and can be no other, said the CPSU. And what was good for the Soviet Union, the only Communist country in the world, was good for international Communism.

So long as the USSR was the only Communist country in the world, the CPSU had little difficulty in keeping the interests of all Communists synonymous with its own. In addition to making full utilization of the natural inclination of the uninitiate to defer to those who have achieved success and power, it employed patronage, politics and force, wherever necessary, to insure international Communist unity. But after World War II a number of new Communist states came into being. For the most part these Communist regimes were created by Soviet arms. Their native leadership had been trained in the USSR, had fled and remained there during the Nazi occupation of their own countries, and had returned only in the wake of the Russian victory. To maintain their position in the new People's Democratic Republics they relied upon Soviet weapons and Soviet manpower. They rode to power on the wings of Russian victory and they could remain in power only through the continuing sustenance of Russian power.

For the Rakosis, the Dimitrovs and the Hoxhas, there was no alternative to the acceptance and endorsement of Soviet primacy, even if they had desired one. Whatever and however the USSR proposed and disposed, this was, again by definition, in the best interests of the Communists and the working class of Hungary, Bulgaria and Albania.

THE YUGOSLAV BACKGROUND

Only in one country in the Soviet bloc was there the possibility of resisting the claims of Soviet hegemony, if there was the will to do so. In Yugoslavia, the Communist Party leadership had not fled to Moscow following the overrunning of the country by the Germans. It remained behind to organize the struggle against both the Nazis and Mihailovich's Chetniks. In its efforts, little help was received from the USSR. A Soviet mission was not dispatched to Tito until February, 1944, almost two years after the first Allied mission had reached him. Actually, Tito became a nationalist at the behest of Stalin, who urged him to moderate his Communist stand in order to attract the widest popular support and avoid antagonizing Great Britain and the United States — "advice" which the Yugoslav leader was to take to heart particularly at a much later date.

Out of military success, there developed for Broz, Djilas, Pijade

89

and their followers, confidence in their own abilities. Their victories, it seemed to them, were achieved through their own efforts, not through Soviet might. The final onslaught of the Soviet forces in 1944 was but the *coup de grâce* in a victory that had already been assured by the native Yugoslav Communist organization.

After the war, when the Politburo tried to treat the CPY with the same condescension as its lackeys in the other satellites and to extract the same pound of flesh from Yugoslavia as from Rumania, Hungary and Bulgaria, Tito was not nearly so pliant as his opposite numbers in the other Communist countries. In the cause of liberating Yugoslavia, Tito, for the most part, had acted as a free agent, unfettered by Muscovite commands and demands. He had built up his own organization, loyal to himself and not to Stalin, though undoubtedly this was the consequence of circumstances rather than design. Success built the egos of the Yugoslav Communists and gave them confidence to think that they knew what was best for the Yugoslav Communist Party and the country, even though this might differ from the decisions of the Soviet Politburo. These factors, plus the absence of Soviet troops from Yugoslavia, and the country's geographical situation, bordering nowhere directly on the territory of the USSR, further tended to nurture Yugoslav independence.

CUT OFF FROM THE SOURCE

It will long be a matter for discussion as to whether Stalin could and would have modified his conduct toward the Yugoslav comrades, had he foreseen the result of Soviet behaviour. Stalin's pathological demands for homogeneity, compounding those of Communism itself, may have precluded any other action. But insofar as Tito and his men were concerned they certainly wanted no break with Moscow. Whatever their quarrels with the CPSU, they were strong party men, accustomed for decades past to obeying unhesitatingly party orders. The emotional attachment of the party member for the party must never be underestimated. "I owe to our Party every achievement I have made," said Tito. "I was an ignorant young man and the Party took me, educated me, made me a man. I owe it everything."[1] The party of which Tito spoke was, of course, the CPSU. As reams of pages from the pens of defected party members have attested, it is never a simple matter to break with the symbol from which seemingly so much has been derived and to which all has been given.

The Yugoslav Communists didn't want the break, but as the vitriol flowed back and forth between Moscow and Belgrade it became apparent to the Yugoslav Politburo that there was no possibility of reconciliation, short of complete capitulation. And experience indicated that in that circumstance the very least that they could expect for their previous assertions was political annihilation. Therefore, for Tito and his cohorts there was no real alternative to continued defiance. The TsK of the CPY accepted the break in June, 1948. However, as late as May 1, 1949, portraits of Stalin were prominently displayed among the May Day decorations in Belgrade. Regardless of what the Yugoslav Communists considered as the correctness of their position and the unavoidability of their action, there was an inevitable reluctance and regret at being cut off from the "Motherland of the working class of all countries" — and a smidgeon of hope that it was not really so.

ACCOMMODATION — EXTERNAL

But it was so. And the Yugoslav Communists had to take stock of their position. Internationally, they were completely isolated. In a world that was becoming increasingly bipolar, they were anathema to both protagonists. They had been drummed out of the Communist world, but their dialectic and recent associations certainly did not make them at home in the West. From the first they had to try to hold fast to the pendulum that swings between East and West, fleeing to one side when the other seems too threatening, perhaps being attracted more to the Red pole, but always wary of being devoured. It is their own position, cut off from both of the power points, that leads the Communists of Yugoslavia to inveigh against blocs of any sort. Active coexistence, they aver, is possible only between countries, not between blocs. Blocs provide reactionaries — East and West — with the excuse for suppressing "internal progress under the pretext of external danger."[2] The Yugoslavs have been in the forefront of the development of the "Third Force" and have labored strenuously to strengthen relations among countries that wish to belong neither to the capitalist nor to the Communist camp.

ACCOMMODATION — INTERNAL

When it came to an assessment of the internal situation, the CPY leadership had to acknowledge that the success of their defiance depended upon the support which they could elicit both from the party rank-and-file and from the country at large. As far as the party itself was concerned, its apparatus was completely in the hands of the Yugoslavs. The only direct contact possible between the CPSU and the members of the CPY was through the CPY at its upper levels. Thus the Soviets could not use the Yugoslav party machinery to turn party members against their own leadership.

The Yugoslav Politburo recognized that there was considerable internal opposition to their regime. The Soviet-inspired programs of industrialization and collectivization had done much to alienate the Yugoslav people. It was of the essence that those features of the system most resented — particularly by the peasants, who still made up the larger part of the Yugoslav populace — be changed. Compulsory deliveries and sowing were abolished and beginning in 1953 decollectivization was permitted. The peasants were not told to "enrich" themselves, as Bukharin had suggested (the amount of land that can be owned by one family being limited), but the peasant was told to "feel secure on his land, that his land [is] protected by law."[3] It is conceded that private holdings do interfere with advancement toward socialism. Communists will block all tendencies toward capitalism in the countryside, but Yugoslavia will not again make the mistake of attempting to enforce "the Soviet Union's system of collective farming."[4] The peasants will be turned toward large-scale socialist agriculture through contacts with the socialist section of the economy and through increasing dependence on the social means of production. But in the meantime the policy of the Yugoslav Communists "consists in gradual socialization of agricultural production by developing the means of production within the framework of the existing socialist agricultural organizations and other forms that may come up in the process — without forcible interference with individual ownership of [the] land."[5]

Clearly contemporary Soviet-brand Communism as practiced in Yugoslavia after World War II was not a symbol that could be used successfully to engender mass support. But what the Yugoslav Communists did have working for them was the national character of their party and its leadership: the fact that both had been forged in the throes of war and had successfully led the people against a dread national enemy. It was that the Yugoslav Communists were Yugoslavs as well as Communists that accounted in large part for their difficulties with the Russians and for their support among their own people. Tito has never ceased to recognize the importance of his position as national hero to the Yugoslav Communist cause. When he speaks, it is almost always as a national leader. Party and ideological matters are left to Kardelj and others of lesser stature. Tito is the chief manipulator of the national symbols. When he returned from his protracted trip among the Afro-Asian countries in early 1959, he addressed the Yugoslav people not on the subject of his journey nor on the progress and acceptance of socialism that he had witnessed — as any Soviet or Soviet-oriented Communist would assuredly have done — but on the fierce pride of the Yugoslav people and on the evils of the Yugoslav *bête noir*, the USSR.

Tito has made the most of the enmity between the Yugoslav and Soviet Communist parties by posing as the knight-defender of his beleaguered nation against the mighty Soviet behemoth. South Slav history and folklore is dominated by tales of the heroism of the suffering and oppressed against the cruel wielders of power, usually Turkish and infidel. It has merely been necessary to substitute the Russians for the Turks and to put Tito at the head of the defending forces.

Having set the Russians up as whipping boys, all the evils in the country from 1945 to 1949 and the difficulty in effecting changes since that time have been ascribed to them. The USSR is described as having a totalitarian government approaching fascism. While the intensity of the attacks directed at the Soviet Union has varied from time to time, their persistence and opportuneness suggests their popularity.

ACCOMMODATION — IDEOLOGICAL

However, the USSR and its system are lambasted not only because it is thought that the exercise unites the masses behind the attackers, but for ideological reasons as well. The Yugoslav party leadership saw that it was not enough to wave the flag of nationalism if the support, or at least, tolerance of the masses was to be won. It was also essential that the features of the local version of the Soviet way most unpalatable to the people of Yugoslavia be substantially altered. To make the kind of changes demanded would be a wrenching experience for any system, but particularly so for a Bolshevik-styled one, where all moves require ideological justification. If the changes to be made went contrary to the Russian model, then it had to be shown that the Russian model was in error and that the Yugoslav alterations

93

were designed to rectify those errors. If the Soviet model was based on a correct analysis and if it was operated correctly in accord with that analysis, then there was no need for the Yugoslav changes. Thus the diagnosticians of the CYP were put to work developing a theoretical rationale for the practical alterations which Yugoslavia's perilous position dictated.

In the years immediately following World War II the CPY was a loyal cadre of the CPSU. The Yugoslav Communists no less than the members of any non-Russian Communist party were convinced that the fate of their own party was dependent upon the fortunes of the CPSU. If they were at all conscious of "errors" in the conduct of the CPSU, the demand for international working class solidarity in the face of the imperialist threat constantly being depicted by the USSR explained these away. The crude behavior and excesses of the Soviet power were either denied as being figments of bourgeois imagination, or were tossed aside as being caused by the exigencies of defense against capitalist encirclement. But when the Communists of Yugoslavia awoke to find themselves tossed bodily out of the socialist camp, their previously unconscious, denied or minimized perceptions of Soviet error were released. No longer was there any reason to suppress criticisms of what were now obvious shortcomings. The fate of the Yugoslav Communists and their movement was no longer seemingly linked inextricably with that of the Soviet party and state. Moreover, their situation seemed to require, not only that these Soviet faults be allowed to rise to the surface, but that they be broadcast far and wide to justify what had been done and was being done in Yugoslavia.

The Yugoslav Communists make it clear that had it not been for the deliberate forcing of a break by the CPSU, the Communist Party of Yugoslavia might never have been roused from its slavish following of the Soviet path. "We escaped . . . thanks only to our revolutionary spirit, the ethical quality of our cadres, the patriotism of our people, and — why should I not mention it — the brutal tactlessness and rudeness of Soviet policy."[6] Thus the Soviet Union literally forced Yugoslavia into the situation out of which came the damning indictment of Soviet Communism.

THE ERROR OF THE SOVIET WAY

Yugoslav theoreticians, regardless of the state of relations with the USSR at the time they write, acknowledge the debt of all socialists to the October Revolution. The Bolshevik triumph in 1917 facilitated the realization of socialism elsewhere. But since that time, and particularly since the death of Lenin, the CPSU has strayed far from the path of Marxism-Leninism. True, economic backwardness, foreign intervention, civil war, capitalist encirclement help to explain Soviet aberrations. But all of these — including capitalist encirclement — represent dangers and problems already overcome, and still the USSR maintains the forms that could, at the best, be justified only by prior threats. Dedijer contends that "no one in modern times has so much betrayed the noble ideas of socialism and Communism, for the development of which all peoples of the world have contributed so much, as has the Soviet Union."[7]

The Soviet Union today reflects the complete degeneration of the October Revolution. This is "the result of [the] despotism of the administrative apparatus over the social initiative of the workers, the result of the victory of bureaucracy over the proletarian revolution."[8] Bureaucratism and its twin, centralism, are the two snares in which the USSR has become entangled. The early crises in which the Soviet Union found itself required that organization be concentrated in the hands of the party and the state. However, this concentration did not end but continued, increased and ultimately became institutionalized in the Soviet forms of bureaucratism and centralism. With these two in control, the state apparatus succumbed to self-aggrandizement and the links between the party and the working class are imperiled.

From bureaucratism and centralism stem most of the evils of the Soviet state: indifference to the individual, the solving of tasks by rote, the belief that everything can be settled by decrees and formula, self-complacency, egotism, and the assumption of personal indispensability. "In such a system people know much more about chickens and about varieties of potatoes and corn than they know about relations among men."[9] It seems to the bureaucrat that all that is required is to build factories, plants and dams without surcease, to make investments as sizable and uninterruptedly as possible. But there is neither knowledge of nor concern for what goes on among the people. "In Yugoslavia," says Tito, "the man means everything; . . . in the USSR a man is a number."[10] The happiness of the individual is the highest goal of socialism, therefore it cannot be subordinated to some higher good.[11] The needs of the individual, material and political, must be satisfied in the present state of social development. The reward for

95

yesterday's and today's effort cannot be endlessly postponed, but must be realized by the individual in his own generation. It is completely unrealistic to expect him to respond indefinitely to a regimen of deferred consumption.

The Yugoslav Communists contend that in their country the tendency toward bureaucratism and centralism has been contained, although constant vigilance must be maintained against new outbreaks. This is not to imply that these evils have been completely removed. They cannot be extirpated "overnight," but progress has been made against them and, as the educational level of the masses rises, they will be eliminated increasingly.

The Yugoslavs were not, of course, the first to see that Bolshevism had succumbed to bureaucratism. Trotsky noted it but considered it to be only a passing phenomenon, due to the proclivities of the men then directing the USSR. His solution was a "palace revolution," to throw the rascals out and set the Revolution back on the tracks. Djilas, who was the chief Yugoslav ideologist immediately following the break with the Soviet Union, regards bureaucratism as ineradicable from the Communist system. It is the inevitable concomitant of Communism and so long as the system persists, bureaucratism and its accompanying disregard for the individual will persist.[12] This is one of Djilas' major ideological points of contention with Tito, for the latter, like Trotsky, believes that bureaucratism can be eradicated, and will be as the result of the growing self-discipline of the masses.

THE YUGOSLAV SOLUTION — THE WITHERING AWAY OF THE STATE

But the reduction of the forces of bureaucratism and centralism cannot await the full development of this self-discipline. It must begin immediately. As power becomes and remains concentrated in the state apparatus, bureaucratism and centralism flourish. These are evils which must be restrained, and eventually wiped out. Since they are direct functions of the power of the state, they can be removed only by curtailing the power of the state.

According to Marx, the power of the state must be at a maximum during the dictatorship of the proletariat. However, he intended for the dictatorship to continue only long enough for the expropriators to be expropriated and for the means of production to be concentrated in the hands of the working class. As soon as this had been accomplished the state would begin to wither away. Developments within the Russian Revolution, however, caused Lenin and then Stalin to extend the period of the dictatorship indefinitely. And Stalin came to hold that the state, instead of withering away, would grow from strength to strength until, at some time in the future, it seemingly would suddenly disappear simultaneous with the realization of Communism. This the Yugoslav Communists hold to be a fatal departure from Marxism. On the other hand, they assert that they themselves, in holding for the immediate commencement of the withering away of the state, are returning to the true principles of Marx-Engels. The state, they say, is "a factor of stagnation and the obstruction of social development." It prevents the evolving of new instruments to further the growth of socialism; therefore socialism must undertake to begin the withering away of the state as soon as the power of the working class has been consolidated.[13]

The withering away of the state must begin where the "real strength of the state is to be found, that is in the national economy, in its management, in the right which the state has assumed to decide exclusively how to distribute the product of social labor."[14] In keeping with this formulation, the withering away of the state in Yugoslavia theoretically was begun with the establishment in each factory[15] of a workers' council which is elected by all the workers in the plant and which in turn elects a managing board, including a manager in whose selection the state plays a part and who actually runs the plant. The workers' council approves the actions and plans of the managing board, studies reports, distributes the disposable part of the plant profits and establishes wage rates in co-operation with the trade-union organization. In addition there is a national workers' council in each industry elected by the workers of that industry, and also a national board of managers. However, the board of managers, at this stage of socialist development, is headed by a manager appointed by the Federal Republic or by the central government if the industry extends beyond a single republic. The state continues to draw up the master plan, but within industries and within plants the manner of complying with the state's demands is left to local determination. Thus, while the state retains full control at the top, it allows greater leeway at the bottom.

In the Yugoslav system, the factory, by and large, must be self-supporting. It cannot depend on the state to bail it out if it gets into trouble. It establishes the market prices of the commodities produced, though the state still determines the cost of raw materials. It must meet competition. If the factory prices its product out of the market or if, as is so often the case in the USSR, quantity holds precedence over quality, then the products will not sell, and all the workers in the plant will suffer since there are no profits to be distributed. If the plant cannot meet its payroll according to the government-established minimum-wage rate, it must borrow, the loan to be repaid from future earnings. Again it is the plant and its workers that will suffer from disregard of consumer desires, inefficiency, and so forth — and will gain from concern and efficiency. This is the "market socialism" that Soviet Communists view with such alarm and anathematize as a complete denial of socialism.

It is the cornerstone of dialectical materialism that the material productive forces and relationships of a society set the pattern for that society, all other relationships — juridical, political and cultural — flowing from them: economic factors determine everything. Thus it follows that from changes in the economic sphere, other changes are to be expected elsewhere. So it has happened that, from the institution of workers' control, the decentralization of planning and the inauguration of "market socialism," have come new developments in other areas of society. Just as in the economic sphere, the withering away of the state is indicated by the transmission of power into the hands of the workers, so elsewhere there is an increase of popular control. The direct relationship between economic and political institutions and the influence of the former upon the latter is shown in the development of the Producers' Councils. The workers' council, belonging to the economic sphere, came first, being announced in January, 1950. Two years later, Producers' Councils, elected by workers and employees actively producing in private or nationalized industries — political institutions, but clearly economically based — were introduced on the local level, becoming the second house of the erstwhile unicameral People's Council. By 1953 the Producers' Council, in one more step in the direction of the withering away of the state, was brought up to the republic and federal status with representation based on the proportionate contribution of agriculturists, workers and handicraftsmen, as groups, to "the total social product of the Federal People's Republic of Yugoslavia."[16]

Every increase of worker control is a blow against bureaucratization and centralization and for the withering away of the state. To effect workers' control, Yugoslavia, in addition to the institution of the workers' councils and producers' Councils, claims to have introduced the nomination of candidates to public office at all levels by open meeting, actively granted the right of non-party candidates to appear on ballots, secured secret elections and the recall of elected officers through the use of the referendum. No longer are the deputies of the people isolated from the people and oblivious to them. They must be responsive to the people or they will be removed by them. Similarly there is no longer a cabinet which is separated from the National Assembly. In its stead there is an Executive Council which is elected by the National Assembly from its members and which administers whatever state business has not been taken over by direct worker control.

The Yugoslav goal is for the extension of direct worker control or "social self-management" to all spheres. Already it has taken over in the socialist sector, in housing, education, science and culture. But again self-management has "self-discipline" as a prerequisite. It can work only if there is a high sense of responsibility. In the future, control will be exercised by "certain formally non-obligatory norms which will nevertheless to a greater or less extent carry a moral and political obligation. Such social norms will gradually be able to replace many legal or administrative provisions and measures, even in those fields where today these provisions appear to be not replaceable."[17] But, as desirable as complete self-government may be, it is at present unfeasible. For the time being, the state is still necessary within a certain framework. There are aspects of planning, control, co-ordination and regulation where its participation is indispensable. The withering away of the state is the ultimate aim, but let no one confuse this aim with a lack of determination and purpose. The old will never be allowed to reinstate itself, nor will anarchy be permitted to take over. There must always be control and if it is not administered by the individual over himself then it must be enforced by the state.

THE YUGOSLAV SOLUTION — THE WITHERING AWAY OF THE PARTY

It follows from the withering away of the state, that the party necessarily withers away with it. The function of the party as the vanguard of the working class ceases once the revolution has been achieved and the means of production safely installed in the hands of the workers. The party belongs to a certain stage in history, and like the multi-party system, once its purpose has been fulfilled it will gradually cease to exist.[18] Always the working class is the propelling force of society, but today the working class operates less and less through the party and increasingly through organs of self-management. As socialist democracy grows stronger, as social antagonisms lose their force, the leading political role of the party fades away. Djilas claims that the party should disband since it no longer has any part to play. But the Yugoslav Communists state that in the present stage of development, the party is still required to serve as inspirer, champion, exemplar and educator. The party must not "dragoon" citizens, but must set an example. It must cajole, not order; it must urge, not command.

Should the party refuse to heed the objective social laws calling for its changed function, as is the case in the USSR, then "it will play the role of a brake on socialist development."[19] The role of the party is a function of time; the party's concept of itself and its role must change as democratic socialism develops. As evidence that the Yugoslav Communists are not opposing the march of history is the fact that they have changed the name of their organization from the Communist Party of Yugoslavia to the League of Communists of Yugoslavia, that republic Communist congresses now have new authority, that Communist organizations hold open meetings to which non-members are invited. But again let no one imagine that this means that the Communists are relaxing their vigilance for they "will continue the struggle for keeping key positions of state authority in firm revolutionary hands."[20]

THE HIGH ROAD (S) TO SOCIALISM

The Yugoslav Communists state that they are headed away from the swampland of bureaucratism and centralism and toward increased worker self-management, socialist democracy and the withering away of the state. They do not claim to know the precise course that will be followed in bringing these to complete realization other than that it must be one of probing experimentation with new ideas and new institutions. Their aim is what Galbraith terms "a kind of pragmatic Marxism."[21] "The development in Yugoslavia [does] not proceed in a straight line nor along a trodden path. In our search for a most suitable way we sometimes [have] to take a roundabout way, wander about, sometimes advancing quickly, sometimes feeling our way in order to find the right direction."[22] Mistakes have been made and will be made in this continuing process, but it is far better to make mistakes than to hinder the socialist development of society and to cling stubbornly to outlived forms and methods.

The Yugoslav Communists hold that since the development of workable institutions is the function of experience, each country will develop different institutions according to its own experience. "Men build socialism consciously, but in different countries they do it under very different conditions."[23] Everywhere socialism seeks the same goals, but socialism will be achieved through varying paths. The value of the experience of others is not denied, but the "truths" derived from one nation's struggle for socialism do not necessarily hold for other nations, as well.

It is this Yugoslav contention that there are "many paths" to socialism, that has generated most of the heat in the Yugoslav-Soviet feud. Fundamentally, the issue between the two has been simply whether or not Yugoslavia would continue to recognize the Soviet Union as being the primary Communist country and its experiences and institutions as being definitive. In the early correspondence between the TsKs of the CPSU and the CPY ideological matters were of no consequence. Only when it became obvious that the differences were not going to be readily settled, that the Yugoslav Communists would not yield their position, did ideology enter the conflict, as though to contest on the ideological field of battle what, for one reason or another, was not being settled by military force.

Obviously, Stalin would not willingly surrender the controlling position that he had painstakingly built up for the Soviet Union in the Communist world. The problem of maintaining power, the Russian passion for unanimity, reinforced by the similar totalitarian-Bolshevik demand for unity and fear of dissolution, meant that Stalin would oppose Yugoslav assertions of independence. By 1955, Khrushchev apparently had concluded that the wisest thing to do was to admit the bankruptcy of the Stalinist position and to attempt to arrange a reconciliation with Tito. This he proceeded to do, granting that there were many possible roads to socialism, until the Polish and Hungarian situations raised the old problem of whether liberalizing tendencies undertaken by totalitarian regimes are not innately destructive of those regimes, the taste of freedom only whetting the appetite of the masses for larger and larger portions. At the time of the Fortieth Anniversary of October, Khrushchev seemingly made the demand that Yugoslavia ascribe to what has come to be known as the Twelve Nations Declaration, which emphasized loyalty to the USSR, and asserted that the development of all countries proceeds according to common "basic laws," and played down the idea of "many paths." This Tito refused to do, and the ideological epithets once more bounced back and forth between Moscow and Belgrade. At Party Congress XXI Khrushchev, in a slightly more mellow mood, conceded that every country has its own features of Communist development. "But this does not mean that we can advance to socialism by some other road, one that is to the side of the general path indicated by Marxism-Leninism." There is only one road to socialism, but it is a diversified one, a "broad highway."[24]

The Yugoslav Communists have steadfastly refused to admit the ideological primacy of the USSR. The argument based on the tremendous obstacles overcome by the USSR is of no value in proving the universal applicability of Soviet experience, nor do the opinions of other Communist parties, still under Soviet hegemonist pressures, indicate the falseness of Yugoslav theory. "The correctness and progressive character of an ideology or of certain forms of socialist construction depend exclusively on their vitality and verification by practice, not on the approval [of] some international forum."[25]

THE STRUGGLE FOR DISCIPLESHIP

The Soviet Communists identify this "new" Titoism with the older, proscribed revisionism of Bernstein, Kautsky, Trotsky, Bukharin, *et al.* They are particularly hostile to the Yugoslav ideas which speak of the simultaneous withering away of the party with the state; of the impossibility of approaching socialism without gradual changes in party function; of relentless opposition to all blocs regardless of their political orientation and the concomitant identification of Soviet international behavior with that of the imperialist nations. To the charge that Titoism is just a new name for revisionism the Yugoslavs reply that Titoism is no new ideology, but the application of Marxism to contemporary conditions. It is, on the contrary, Stalin who is the Revisionist. "It is he who has wandered from the Marxist road."[26] Radio Belgrade, as proof of its orthodoxy, has identified itself with the first two bars of the *"International."* Just before the opening of

102

Party Congress XXI, the Yugoslavs, again as though to indicate their ideological steadfastness, put through a meaningless piece of legislation ordering the nationalization of building lots for the "perfection of socialist social relations."[27] On the attack, the Chinese communes have been assailed by Vukmanovic-Tempo as being "terrible Revisionism."[28] And Kardelj asserts that the Soviet system is not only "not a necessary form of socialism, but that it is not socialism at all."[29]

As much as the Yugoslav Communists are against the "dogmatism," "bureaucratism," "opportunism concealed by leftist slogans" and so forth of Soviet revisionism, they are no less against that revisionism which is characterized by "bourgeois ideology," "opportunism," "declassé anarchism" and "pseudo-liberal slogans." They cannot accept the "socialism" of the CPSU, but this does not mean that they are any more open to the "reformism" of the older school of revisionism. This type of revisionism, too, is conducive to the development of bureaucratism, because it strengthens anti-socialist forces, thus sharpening inner contradictions and leading to the augmentation of the forces of bureaucratism. It is in this camp that the Yugoslavs place Djilas.

THE FUTURE — REVOLUTION, EVOLUTION

Despite the seemingly endless gauntlet of perils through which socialism must pass on its way to fulfillment, the Yugoslav Communists, ideologically speaking, have no more doubts than do the Soviet Communists that the future belongs to socialism and Communism throughout the world. World capitalism, in deepening crises, is inevitably doomed. The events of the past forty years — notably the October Revolution, the Great Depression, World War II, the victories of socialism and the dissolution of colonial empires — make this more certain than ever. Under the influence of these events and constantly increasing working class pressure, changes in the direction of socialism have been and are being induced throughout the world. "More and more, socialism is becoming a matter of practice of all nations. More and more it is becoming one world process and a world system."[30] But this does not mean that the need for revolution is thus obviated. Repeatedly it has been demonstrated that socialist parties that come to power by parliamentary means cannot quickly and effectively introduce the needed alterations in the economic structure. Moreover, such parties do, without a revolution, merely lay the way open for the return to power of the forces of the bourgeoisie. But such a revolution

103

need not necessarily be bloody and protracted. For the movement in the direction of socialism is today so pronounced and definite as to offer "the working class more prospects than before of becoming, in certain countries and under certain conditions, the leading force in society by means of a relatively peaceful political struggle."[31] The Yugoslav Communists thus concede, as Marx did, the possibility of socialism being achieved in the most advanced capitalist countries without the turmoil represented by 1848 or 1917. They do not say that the chances of this occurring are "good," but they are "better" than before. The impression is given, however, that the League of Communists of Yugoslavia is quite convinced of the strong possibility of the "relatively peaceful," i. e., evolutionary, revolution, but that it guards its words carefully against the dread accusation of revisionism.

ANALYSIS

This is, of course, not the only place in the Yugoslav Communist analysis where considered reflection has had to give way before the necessity of appearing orthodox and Marxian. For the Communists of Yugoslavia — no less than for the purge trial accused who confessed crimes that they could not have committed in order to perform one last service for the party and thus affirm that their lives had not been lived in vain — there is the necessity to assert the correctness of the Marxism for which they have struggled all their years. They still cling tenaciously to the Marxian concept of human nature, of the infinite perfectibility of man — that man is hostile and selfish only because he has never had a "chance," See that he never suffers economic want and that he is properly educated, and there will no longer be any need for the coercive apparatus of the state.

The Marxian concept of man's nature was in accord with the nineteenth-century belief in the possibility of infinite progress, *per aspera ad astra*. Today, our less optimistic dispositions have been reinforced by the conclusions of modern psychology to indicate that the aggressiveness of man is only in very small part, if at all, due to his economic situation and far more to the human one. But the theory of the withering away of the state is in doubt not at this point alone. The state has not only a coercive function but also an organizing one. The more highly developed industrial society becomes, the more organization it requires. The task of organizing society in all its proliferating aspects cannot be left up to local workers' councils, no matter how full the workers' bellies may be or how "educated" their minds. The recent necessity of the central authority in Yugoslavia to limit the functions of the workers' councils and to institute trade-union control indicates that, as yet, the Marxian contention of human perfectibility, upon which the withering away of the state must rest, remains unproved.

Of course, the theory of the withering away of the state was a very convenient one to have around to help in explaining the concessions that the exposed position of the CPY forced it to make. It was so compatible to the changes in the direction of worker control that seemed to be required. Changes that were virtual apostasies to Soviet Communism were thinly explained as being in accordance with Marx, and actually designating Yugoslav Communism as being far more orthodox than the Russian brand.

The Yugoslav Communists are in the situation of constantly trying to balance themselves, as they stagger back and forth on a whole series of interconnecting tightropes. To secure the support of the masses they have had to modify some of the acerbity of Soviet Communism, but not so much as to be linked with the revisionists, "pseudo-liberals," etc. They cannot retain Stalinism, but they will not permit "Djilasism." In international relations they are no longer in the Soviet camp, but they will not be in the Western one, either. Circumstances compel them to proclaim the withering away of the party, but they will not allow any other political force to appear. They seemingly abjure power for themselves, but they permit it to no others. They say that the party should exist only for discussion, not discipline, but they have not the slightest intention of allowing themselves to be voted out of office.

The Program of the League of the Yugoslav Communists holds that the "Yugoslav Communists must not, nor do they wish to, become a power through the use of the state apparatus."[32] But it does not say that they do not or will not maintain power through that apparatus. The changes made in Yugoslavia in the direction of the "further development of socialist democracy" have been concessions granted by the regime, that can be withdrawn at its discretion. In practice, worker control is still hedged about by the organized presence and expressed opinion of the party apparatus at all levels. In effect, the workers of Yugoslavia have freedom of choice only to the extent that their choice is the party's choice.

Never has a totalitarian party in power voluntarily surrendered its authority. Even if the Yugoslav Communists today are convinced of the necessity for the withering away of the state and party, they have not yet, all assertions to the contrary notwithstanding, relinquished the instruments of control, and it does not seem likely to expect that they will soon do so.

SELECTED BIBLIOGRAPHY

Thad Paul Alton, "Postwar Changes in the Yugoslav Economic System and Methods of Planning," AMERICAN ECONOMIC REVIEW PAPERS AND PROCEDURES, XLVI (May, 1956), 380-388.

Hamilton Fish Armstrong, TITO AND GOLIATH (New York: Macmillan, 1957). A first-rate, popular account of the break between Stalin and Tito. Particular attention is paid to repercussions of "Titoism" beyond the Yugoslav frontier, but the information is dated.

Robert Bass and Elizabeth Marbury, Eds., THE SOVIET-YUGOSLAV CONTROVERSY, 1948-1958: A DOCUMENTARY RECORD (New York: Prospect Books, 1959). A collection of significant letters, speeches, newspaper articles, etc., connected with the development and vacillations of the Soviet-Yugoslav dispute, ably placed in the context of events by the editors.

Vladimir Dedijer, TITO (New York: Simon and Schuster, 1953). The life of the President of the Federal Executive Council of the FPRY, by a leading Yugoslav journalist, later purged for his Djilas sympathies and now partially rehabilitated. Valuable for the reports of conversations with Tito.

Milovan Djilas, THE NEW CLASS (New York: Frederick A. Praeger, 1957). An analysis and critique of Communism by one of its adherents, who became a Titoist and is now imprisoned by the Yugoslav government for having gone beyond "Titoism" to develop "pseudo-liberal" sympathies. The importance of the book lies chiefly in the former position of its author.

Milovan Djilas, "Yugoslav-Soviet Relations," INTERNATIONAL AFFAIRS, XXVII (April, 1951), 167-175. The one-time Number 2 man of the Yugoslav Communists, while still at his zenith, describes the rethinking of Marx then at work in Yugoslavia.

Alfred Joachim Fischer, "Heresey in Yugoslavia," WORLD AFFAIRS, III (January, 1949), 55-63.

Joseph Frankel, "Federalism in Yugoslavia," AMERICAN POLITICAL SCIENCE REVIEW, XLIX (June, 1955), 416-430. An analysis of the nationalities problem—still very real in multi-national Yugoslavia—but currently overshadowed by the Soviet-Yugoslav dispute.

Thomas Taylor Hammond, "Yugoslav Elections," POLITICAL SCIENCE QUARTERLY, LXX (March, 1955), 57-74. A description of the first Yugoslav elections held under THE NEW FUNDAMEN-

TAL LAW. How the Yugoslav Communists attempt to get the old results with new machinery.

Richard Lowenthal, "The Djilas Case," TWENTIETH CENTURY, CLV (April, 1954), 316-326. A long-time observer of the Yugoslav scene fits the Djilas "heresy" into the picture of contemporary Yugoslav political ideology. A number of interesting questions about the future of "Titoism" are raised—and left unanswered.

Fitzroy MacLean, ESCAPE TO ADVENTURE (Boston: Little, Brown, 1950). The exciting story of the Tito struggle against the Nazis and the Chetniks. By a dashing Englishman who was parachuted into Yugoslavia and attached to the Tito forces early in the conflict.

Fitzroy MacLean, THE HERETIC: THE LIFE AND TIMES OF JOSIP BROZ TITO (New York: Harper, 1958).

Bernard Morris, "Soviet Policy Toward National Communism: The Limits of Diversity," AMERICAN POLITICAL SCIENCE REVIEW, LIII (March, 1959), 128-137. A résumé of and comment on the Russian Communist position on "nationalist tendencies" from their Party Congress I (1898) through Party Congress VII (1958) of the LCY.

Fred Warner Neal, "Reforms in Yugoslavia," AMERICAN SLAVIC AND EAST EUROPEAN REVIEW, XIII (April, 1954) 227-244.

NEW FUNDAMENTAL LAW OF YUGOSLAVIA, intro. by Edvard Kardelj (Belgrade, Union of Jurists' Associations of Yugoslavia, 1953). The 1953 changes in the Stalin-inspired Constitution of 1946, with a commentary by the Vice-President of the Federal Executive Council of the FPRY. Helpful for its exposition of the Titoist line at that point.

Adam Bruno Ulam, "Background of the Soviet-Yugoslav Dispute," REVIEW OF POLITICS, XIII (January, 1951), 39-63.

Adam Bruno Ulam, TITOISM AND THE COMMINFORM (Cambridge, Massachusetts, Harvard University Press, 1952). An early but still useful study of the Yugoslav-Soviet breach, by a leading authority.

Radivo Uvailic, "Management of Undertakings by Workers in Yugoslavia," INTERNATIONAL LABOR REVIEW, LXIX (March, 1954), 235-254.

Vladimir Velibit, "Yugoslavia on Her Way Toward a Socialist Democracy," INTERNATIONAL AFFAIRS, XXX (April, 1954), 156-165. A Yugoslav diplomat presents, for an English-speaking democratically oriented audience, the argument that "real" democracy is rapidly being achieved in the Yugoslav metamorphosis.

WHITE BOOK ON AGGRESSIVE ACTIVITIES BY THE GOVERNMENTS OF THE USSR, POLAND, CZECHOSLOVAKIA, HUNGARY, RUMANIA, BULGARIA AND ALBANIA TOWARDS YUGOSLAVIA (Belgrade: The Ministry of Foreign Affairs of the Federal People's Republic of Yugoslavia, 1951). An official Yugoslav compilation of incidents and situations involving economic, political and military coercion perpetrated by the USSR and its satellites against the FPRY in the years immediately following the Yugoslav-Soviet split.

Robert Lee Wolff, THE BALKANS IN OUR TIME (Cambridge, Massachusetts: Harvard University Press, 1956). An up-to-date examination of the geography, economics, history and politics of the Balkan nations. Well-written and valuable as background.

YUGOSLAVIA'S WAY: THE PROGRAM OF THE LEAGUE OF COMMUNISTS OF YUGOSLAVIA, Stoyan Pribechevich, Trans. (New York: All Nations Press, 1958). Marx brought up-to-date: Yugoslav version. Roundly lambasted by the CPSU. The basic document of "Titoism."

CURRICULUM VITAE

DAN N. JACOBS is a graduate of Harvard College, 1949, and holds the M.A. from Yale University, the Certificate of the Russian Institute and the Ph.D. from Columbia University. Currently Assistant Professor of Government at Miami University, Oxford, Ohio, he has previously taught on the Political Science Faculty at Hunter College. Mr. Jacobs has written for THE AMERICAN SLAVIC AND EAST EUROPEAN REVIEW, THE NEW LEADER and other scholarly and popular journals. At the present time he is preparing a volume on the May and October slogans of the Central Committee of the CPSU for publication.

Remnants of Socialism

CHAPTER SIX

SOCIALIST INTERNATIONALS AND CONTINENTAL SOCIALISM

GERARD BRAUNTHAL
University of Massachusetts

In this age of "isms," democratic socialism must compete with other powerful ideologies for the allegiance of the masses. Despite pockets of weakness, it still has a significant impact on diverse political cultures and societies, and exerts an attraction to those seeking a new economic order, humanistic faith, or chimerical utopia. Its historical development is marked by remarkable strength in some nations and a plethora of crises, schisms, revisions and external assaults upon it in others. Western Europe has witnessed the conception and flowering of socialism, but new adherents have been gained on other continents who, emerging from colonialism and achieving independence, seek an alternative to the credos of capitalism and the Soviet Union's version of Communism. In a cross-fertilization process, non-European socialist leaders are now adapting the original socialist tenets to the maturing political and economic institutions in their own countries.

In the meantime, what is happening to democratic socialism on the continent of Europe? Have its doctrines met the challenge of climactic twentieth-century developments — world wars, Fascism, Communism, nationalism and the atomic age? Have its doctrines in the postwar era been cast in an orthodox or revisionist mold? To suggest some answers, the focus of attention in this chapter will center on the development of the Socialist Internationals, and on some of the more important European continental socialist movements that have traditionally reflected the various roots of socialist thought.

Of an impressive number of architects who blueprinted the ideological foundations of socialism a century ago, none achieved more fame than Karl Marx. He and Friedrich Engels constructed an imposing scientific edifice which still stands today, although it is less solid than it once was and has needed major replastering and redecorating. The economic and social doctrines were drafted in the midst of the industrial revolution and the consequent exploitation of the emerging working classes. Briefly summarized, they concern themselves with the Hegelian rhythm of history in which the economic way of life conditions the political and the social processes. In the nineteenth century the constant contradictions in the social system are reflected in the relationship of the capitalists to the oppressed proletariat. The latter, more and more conscious of its purpose and power, would seize control of the capitalist state and of the means of production, suppress the bourgeoisie, and establish a temporary dictatorship of the proletariat. This transition period of socialism would be followed by the final epoch of communism in which the classes and the state would gradually wither away.

I. THE SOCIALIST INTERNATIONALS

Not only interested in abstract theorizing, Marx actively supported the establishment of the First International (International Workingmen's Association) in London, in 1864. As one of five corresponding secretaries, he drafted the Inaugural Address, and in later years penned numerous resolutions defining the attitude of the organization toward crucial events, such as the Paris Commune uprising. The British and French workers and the exiles from the continent, who founded the International, envisaged its role primarily as an organizational and educational nucleus for the development of nascent working class parties and the sowing of socialist seeds. These potentially dangerous activities evoked a gamut of negative reactions in bourgeois ruling circles. A typical attitude is revealed in an incident noted by a delegate to the last Congress (1872) of the First International, held at the Hague:

> The Hague, being the place of Royal residence and the seat of the government of the country, may be safely trusted to possess a considerable number of enemies of the Revolution. Indeed, so strong is the feeling in some quarters against the Society (the International) that the children of the town have been warned not to go into the streets with jewelry or articles of value upon them, as "The International is coming and will steal them."[1]

The early death of the International was caused partially by external circumstances, such as the failure of the Commune uprising,

112

the era of reaction after the Franco-Prussian War, and the mounting hostility of governments to the working class organizations; but, more important, it was plagued by grave internal weaknesses of an organizational and ideological character. As the emerging working class movements were too engrossed in their own affairs to vigorously support the International, the organization consisted only of isolated national sections loosely bound to its executive organ, the General Council. Financial resources were limited. And finally, fundamental schisms relating to theory and tactics between the feuding adherents of Marx, Blanc, Bakunin and Proudhon caused exciting verbal fireworks but resulted in a serious sapping of strength. Unable to surmount these formidable obstacles, the Hague Congress in 1872 decided to transfer its headquarters to New York, where no requiem was sung at its unheralded end four years later.

The meteoric rise of socialist and labor movements in England and on the continent made it inevitable that, despite the continued hostility of governments to socialism as exemplified by Chancellor Bismarck's anti-socialist laws in Germany, a new body would be created in due time. The Second International was formed at a Paris Congress in 1889. Organizationally stronger than its predecessor, it served as a federal grouping of the primarily European constituent national parties. Although the parties were fraternally allied and confident of their growing strength, the congresses, in the mode of early socialism, were arenas of rigorous debates concerning the tactics and aims of the movement. Marxist theory could only serve as a blueprint; a host of problems still had to be thrashed out: attitudes toward the capitalist state, bourgeois governments and non-socialist parties, colonialism, militarism and pacifism. Yet, a consensus was reached on some of these problems, such as the need to prevent war at all costs, to end a war quickly if it were to erupt, and to use the revolutionary situation in order to speed up the demise of capitalism. But when the German Social Democratic Party, the ideological front-runner in the International, experienced a fateful three-way schism, other national parties and the International itself experienced similar convulsions.

All groups claimed Marx and Engels as their apostles. The left wing, led by Rosa Luxemburg and Wilhelm Liebknecht, formed the nucleus of what later became the revolutionary Communist parties. The center, led by August Bebel and Karl Kautsky, remained faithful to the original Marxist theories. The right wing, led by Eduard

Bernstein, Jean Jaurès, and Emile Vandervelde, pressed for revisions to meet partially unforeseen developments. Not prophesying an imminent collapse of the capitalist system, the right wing renounced the theory of revolution, and stressed instead the evolutionary road to socialism. In countries with a firm democratic heritage, the attempt would be made to extend the franchise, gain power in parliament, and make reforms within the capitalist system which would eventually lead to socialism. Marx had been proven wrong, so argued the right wing, in forecasting an increasing pauperization of the workers. On the contrary, their rising living standards would neither necessitate a revolution to achieve greater social justice and equality nor require a class dictatorship to consolidate the power gained.[2]

Of these three wings, the center had majority support at the congresses of the International and imposed a doctrinal uniformity upon its policies. A classic illustration of this steamroller tactic occurred at the Amsterdam Congress of 1904 when the French complied reluctantly with a resolution asking socialists not to participate in coalition governments with bourgeois parties.[3]

The International made unsuccessful attempts to avert the Armageddon of 1914. Its survival was doomed when the constituent parties abandoned their internationalist creed and for diverse reasons supported the war efforts of their own governments. As a result of these patriotic actions new schisms arose which wartime conferences could not heal. A wave of radicalism among the masses, especially those of the Central powers, the Russian Revolution of 1917, and the subsequent establishment of Communist parties, all combined to create the necessary prerequisites for a permanent fissure in the international movement.

Moscow created the famed Communist International (Comintern or Third International) in 1919, which was to serve as a controlling agency of the revolutionary proletariat and the pliant tool of Soviet policy. Its Declaration (1919) provided the theoretical framework and the magnetic slogans in the style of "Proletarians of the world, unite" and "Long live the International Republic of the Workers' Soviets." Despite the significant impact it had upon leftists, it was unable to clasp any social democratic parties "to its bosom" for a long span of time.

Such reform socialist parties as the British, the German, and a few others, obviously would not associate with the Communist International, and, after some preparatory conferences, resuscitated the Second International (Berne-Geneva International) in July, 1920.[4] In the middle of this political spectrum stood the International Working Union of Socialist Parties (Vienna Union or the "Second-and-a-Half" International), founded in 1921 by Austrian, French, German Independents, Swiss and other parties of the center and left. When its ambitious objective to restore socialist unity in an all-inclusive international failed, it merged with the reformist Second International in May, 1923. The new association, known as the Labor and Socialist International (LSI), was more homogeneous than its prewar counterpart. It claimed a not inconsiderable strength of thirty-five parties, which had six million members and polled twenty-five million votes. Revisionist in principle, the LSI devoted much time, as did the League of Nations, to methods of seeking peace and disarmament. But, primarily, it served as a liaison and information center and not as an agency of political leadership.[5] The LSI too had to face formidable obstacles, such as the power of the Communist International, the rigors of the Great Depression, the rise of Fascism, and finally Hitler's military onslaughts, which sealed its fate in March, 1940.

At the conclusion of hostilities, the prospects for socialism seemed bright again on the continent. Old or newly reconstituted parties gained or shared power in nearly all countries. But the wounds of war had not yet healed sufficiently to create a new International, including the socialist parties of ex-enemy countries. British and Scandinavian parties were also opposed to an immediate reconstitution in view of the divergencies that had developed before the war between the LSI and socialist-led governments.[6] Thus, the Committee of the International Socialist Conference (COMISCO) was not founded until November, 1947, and the new Socialist International not until July, 1951, when its first Congress convened in Frankfort, Germany.[7]

The Socialist International still represents primarily the coordinating agency of European socialist movements, although parties in the western hemisphere and some in Asia have joined its ranks. Most Asian socialist parties, still sensitive to European colonialism and its occasional support by a few European socialist parties, have decided not to join the Socialist International and to form instead an autonomous Asian Socialist Conference, only loosely associated with the International. Nevertheless, the International is supported by thirty-seven parties with a claimed membership of ten million and a vote of sixty-five million in recent general elections.

The Frankfort Congress adopted a Declaration of basic principles, *Aims and Tasks of Democratic Socialism*,[8] which faithfully reflects a synthesis of the revisionist point of view and eliminates much of the sterile dogmatism from socialist thought. In view of the Communist and Fascist experiments, socialists had to re-examine the relationship of democracy and freedom to socialism. The Declaration thus speaks of the incompatibility of totalitarianism with democratic socialism. But the Communists are now singled out as enemy number one, for having set back the realization of socialism in many countries for decades and for having "built up a rigid theology which is incompatible with the critical spirit of Marxism." The Declaration categorically denounces Communism as "the instrument of a new imperialism" which destroys freedom or the chance of gaining freedom. Instead, the concepts of freedom and democracy, including civil and political rights, are given primary stress: "Without freedom there can be no Socialism. Socialism can be achieved only through democracy."

In its economic section, the Declaration reflects the fraternal liaison of many socialist parties with organized labor. There are references to full employment, higher production, a rising standard of living, social security, and a fair distribution of income and property. Naturally, socialist planning and the transformation of private property into public ownership are not forgotten. However, "Socialist planning does not presuppose public ownership of all the means of production. It is compatible with the existence of private ownership in important fields, for instance in agriculture, handicraft, retail trade and middle-sized industries." The structure of the country concerned must determine the extent of public ownership. Such ownership is not to be an end in itself, but a means of controlling basic industries and services, of rationalizing inefficient industries, or of preventing private monopolies from exploiting the public. Economic power is to be decentralized by adopting multiple forms of public ownership, such as public concerns, municipal or regional enterprises, consumers' or producers' co-operatives. An analysis of these important policy statements follows in later pages.

Concomitant with the new approach to economic problems, the Declaration emphasizes the need to develop humanism, a flowering of culture and the individual personality if economic and social progress

116

is to have any moral meaning. Here an acknowledgment to the libertarian and ethical tributary of democratic socialism is implicit. But other tributaries are not rejected:

> Socialism is an international movement which does not demand a rigid uniformity of approach. Whether Socialists build their faith on Marxist or other methods of analyzing society, whether they are inspired by religious or humanitarian principles, they all strive for the same goal—a system of social justice, better living, freedom and world peace.

The revisionists not only abandoned much of the Marxist jargon in the Declaration, and thus the semantic lag in which theory lost out to reality, but they made, as we have observed, substantive changes in the Marxist dogma. This fact is well illustrated in one clause: "The achievement of Socialism is not inevitable." Probably the delegates had the haunting specter of twentieth-century totalitarianism in mind, which serves to disprove Marx's theory of the inevitability of a socialist society.

We have dealt at length with the ideological texture of the Socialist International because it reflects so faithfully, as we shall see, the doctrines of the member parties, although in some the magnetic pull of Marxism still is strong. But despite this apparent unity in ideology, programmatic differences have plagued the organization. For instance, at the December, 1956 Congress, British Labour Party chief Hugh Gaitskell insisted on introducing a resolution condemning the Anglo-French invasion of Egypt in 1956. The Socialist International Bureau vainly attempted not to put the organization on record, in order to save the French party, which had supported the invasion, from embarrassment. Guy Mollet, head of the French party, was highly critical of the resolution, but failed to receive any backing. Unity of the Socialist International was precariously maintained after 1956, especially in view of Mollet's support of French colonial policy in Algeria. The issue of West German rearmament caused further dissension. These instances serve to illustrate the fact that the parties tend to represent first their often divergent national interests and only secondarily their international interests. On the other hand, it is equally true that on some issues, such as the opposition to Soviet Communism, there is a wide measure of agreement. A sentimental attachment to pacifism by some socialist parties has dimmed, now that the principle of collective defense against Communism has been

117

approved. As a matter of fact, in the light of the Soviet menace, the Marxist version of wars being caused by capitalist states had to be revised. The causes of war and imperialism are now deemed much more complex than ever before.

From these observations of the ideological development of the Socialist Internationals we may conclude that the cyclical renewal of the organization after the catastrophic wars of recent decades has given rise to successive revisions of Marxism and, concurrently, to an acknowledgment of the validity of many principles of Marx and other oracles of socialism. We turn to a survey of key socialist parties on the continent: more specifically, to their ideological growth in Germany, Austria, Italy, France and the Scandinavian countries.[9] Here too there has been much continuity and change, uniformity and diversity, and a good deal of cross-fertilization not only between the parties, but also between them and the Socialist Internationals. After all, no organization lives in a vacuum.

II. GERMANY

National upheavals leading to fateful international crises have characterized the course of German history. The German Social Democratic Party (SPD), however, has been able to weather the turbulent storms and to maintain its venerable aura of tradition, prestige and respectability, despite its suppression on two occasions. Its legacy of Marx and Engels, its leadership steeped in theory, and its mass membership and organizational apparatus, catapulted the party into prominence in the international socialist arena, especially before World War I.

The beginning was more modest. The party was founded at Gotha in 1875 in an amalgamation of two major groups: the "General Workingmen's Association" organized by Ferdinand Lassalle in 1863, and the Marxist "Eisenach" bloc formed by August Bebel and Wilhelm Liebknecht in 1869. A repressive era followed from 1878 to 1890, in which Bismarck outlawed the new party, fearing its potential strength. The policy was ill-conceived because the party, deprived of its status as an opposition party, adopted a radical Marxist program, and once it achieved legality attracted millions of followers in any case.

The previously cited three-way split in the party had important repercussions in the nation and abroad. Bebel, the party leader, and

118

Karl Kautsky, the theoretician, steered the majority on a faithful Marxist course, and debated the theory of revolution and the general strike with the left wing (Luxemburg and Liebknecht) and the right wing (Bernstein). More interested in practical reforms, Bernstein was able, however, to convince the party to support such measures as an extension of the suffrage, a democratization of the state, and an improvement of working conditions.

The SPD could not surmount this internal dissension during World War I. The failure of the party initially to oppose the war, on the ground that Czarism had to be defeated, proved shocking to many. More so was the party's continued patriotic support of the war effort, which led to wholesale defections of left wing and other elements, and the formation of the Independent Socialist Party (USPD) and the more radical Spartacist group. The end of the war carried Friedrich Ebert and other majority socialists into power, but, unprepared for a socialist transformation of society, they refused to engage in any radical experiments, especially after they failed to receive an absolute majority of votes in a national election. Thus the disillusionment with their mild policies and their insistence on strict parliamentarism strengthened the ranks of the newly established Communist Party, formed by Spartacists and the left wing of the USPD.

The minority of the USPD (Kautsky, Rudolph Hilferding) rejoined the SPD in 1922 and demanded the adoption of a more Marxist program. Three years later these efforts were crowned with success as the party assented to the Heidelberg Program replete with Marxist jargon. But once again the revolutionary statements clashed with the party's pragmatic efforts to wring social improvements out of the capitalist economic order. Unfortunately, not enough efforts were made to strengthen sufficiently the democratic fibers of the Weimar Republic, and the Nazi juggernaut doomed the SPD in the nightmare era of terror from 1933 to 1945.

After 1945, reformist elements of Social Democrats, made up of those who had been either in exile, where many had been influenced by British Fabianism, in jail, or in the "inner" emigration, asked themselves critically what had gone wrong, and how could the errors of the past be avoided in the future. But this heterogeneous group could not cope with the strongly entrenched cadre men who longed emotionally for the good old days and who desired no rejuvenation of the party organization or its ideas. The traditionalists did not want to face up to the problem of how the SPD could crash the maximum 30 per cent electoral barrier and seek support from strata of society other than the industrial proletariat. This class, after all, was assuming less numerical importance in the face of the rising middle class, not to speak of a downgrading of the class conflict itself.

According to Kurt Schumacher, the dynamic party chairman who died in 1952, the surest method to accomplish "an opening to the right" is to dilute the party's goals by revising Marxist dogma and adopting a new nationalist line. During the Weimar era, Schumacher contended, the SPD had shied away from nationalism, a position which Hitler cleverly exploited. Thus, after 1945, it was imperative to exploit the growing nationalistic feeling. Schumacher consequently demanded an independent and united Germany, and assailed the Christian Democratic Union's plans for limited European integration plans, calling the Council of Europe "conservative, clerical and capitalistic-cartel" dominated. But the new pitch failed to attract new voters because it smacked too much of opportunism, and of a desire to oppose the administration policy without presenting a convincing alternative.

As to a dilution of Marxism, the concentration on influencing the domestic and foreign policies left the leaders little time to draft a new theoretical charter to supplant the Heidelberg Program. Eventually one will be accepted which will shed some of the original Marxist theories.[10] But a new program will also, as did Schumacher at the 1946 party convention, express the great debt which the SPD owes Marxism as a tool of analysis of the economic and social system.

That a new look cannot be adopted too readily in the SPD is evidenced by the recurring factional disputes and programmatic differences. The "conservative" leadership under party chairman Erich Ollenhauer. an able administrator but not as colorful a figure as his predecessor, represents to a great extent the tradition-bound center wing.

A reform group opened a frontal assault on the leadership after the 1953 electoral defeat, by demanding a spiritual renewal of the party, but drew the counterfire not only of the center, but of the Marxist left wing. Between 1954 and 1956, however, the left wing sniped at the center, which suddenly supported a German defense force and the European Economic Community. The left, led by Heinz Seeger, head of the Wood Workers Union, and Professor Wolfgang

Abendroth, close to the trade unions, insisted on an orientation diametrically opposed to that of Chancellor Adenauer in order to differentiate the aims of the Christian Democrats and the Social Democrats. Faced by the enmity of left and right, the leadership steered the party on a neutral course up to the 1957 election—a compromise which did not pay off either.

The Christian Democratic Union victory caused a renewed discussion concerning organization, tactics and goals throughout the Social Democratic Party. Nearly all elements saw the necessity of a change at the 1958 party convention, and agreed first of all on an overhaul of the organizational structure which will weaken the cadre element and the dominance of the center. The reform wing is moving into the saddle. Ollenhauer remains as party chairman, but he will be assisted by two deputy chairmen: Waldemar von Knoeringen, "a pure idealist of irreproachable character and many ideas, but soft and not aggressive," and Herbert Wehner, a former Communist "whose political past and flaring temper have made him a bogeyman to the German bourgeoisie."[11]

From Heinrich Deist, the expert on economic affairs, the delegates heard the details of a revisionist and non-dogmatic economic program which provides for public controls, limited nationalization, community properties, but also a maximum freedom of the economy. The program, approved at the convention despite cries of "Why are we afraid to be regarded as a socialist?" was discussed at local levels and then adopted at the 1959 convention.

In the realms of foreign affairs and defense no new formulas were adopted. Thus, on balance, there has been no complete breakthrough yet toward the reformists' goal of making the SPD a "people's party" rather than a "workers' party," and no decision on the course the party would take if it were to become the governing rather than the permanent opposition party at the federal level.

III. AUSTRIA

Austria is now a small country, but its Socialists have played a large role in the ideological direction of modern socialism within and outside of its borders. Austrian Socialist leaders were both theoreticians and practitioners, active in the debates rocking the councils of the International, but also responsible for many domestic reforms in the nation. In Austria, as elsewhere, a moderate reform wing was pitted

121

against a radical wing in the latter part of the nineteenth century. The ideological differences became less important after the Hainfeld Congress of 1889, at which the eminent leader Victor Adler was able to achieve an organizational unity of the party.

In the following years, the contribution of the Austrian Socialists was the development of the Austro-Marxist school of socialist thought. It included the application of the Marxist method of analysis to current problems, i.e., the question of Austrian nationalism as developed by two leading figures, Otto Bauer and Karl Renner, and the theory of banking capital (Rudolph Hilferding). The Austro-Marxists succeeded in reducing the strength of the Austrian Communists to negligible proportions by speaking in the language of dialectical materialism and a classless society, while simultaneously endeavoring to make social reforms. Bauer even spoke of a temporary dictatorship of the proletariat, but conceived of it as merely a weapon of defense should the bourgeoisie attempt to destroy democracy. On the other hand, Renner, supported by a wing of the party and some trade unions, attempted to bring about a reconciliation between the Socialists and the clerical camp, because a democratic order could not be maintained in any other fashion.

Although these differences should not be minimized, they were minor in comparison with those between the Socialists and the conservatives. The tensions produced by the economic depression and the arming of rival political militias exploded in the short civil war of February, 1934, which resulted in the end of the democratic order and the suppression of the Socialist Party by the Dollfuss regime.

During the First Republic era (1918-1934), the ideological contribution of the Socialists was matched by their practical reforms, especially in their stronghold of "Red Vienna," in the fields of social welfare and labor legislation, assistance to trade unions and co-operatives, and public housing. Hanusch and Breitner, more pragmatic than Marxist, were responsible for these gains. And yet a fear among the bourgeoisie that a socialist majority in parliament someday would try to accomplish more and wipe out the capitalist system also led to the conservatives launching the civil war.

In the next eleven years a heroic struggle against the reactionary forces of Dollfuss, Schuschnigg and the Nazis was inaugurated by the sub-rosa Revolutionary Socialists inside, and by the leaders of the party in exile outside, the country. Dissension among the movements sapped their strength. But they united after 1945 in a reborn party with a new name, *Sozialistische Partei Oesterreichs* (SPO).

The second largest party in the country in terms of parliamentary seats, it gained respectability and even strength in hitherto enemy strongholds, the rural areas. Learning a lesson from the past, the SPO has participated since 1945 in a coalition government with the conservative People's Party. The theoretical image of the SPO consequently has changed. No longer identified with Austro-Marxism, it has adopted a pragmatic and less doctrinaire stance. The explanation for this shift in ideology lies in many factors. These include: a general devaluation of dogmatism among socialist parties; an acknowledgment that the theories of Marx need overhauling; a product of the now strong reformist, right-wing leadership in the party, which became totally disillusioned with the Soviet version of Communism and ousted the extreme left wing; a realization of the improved status of the workers in the social hierarchy; a fear of being branded pro-Communist; and finally, a "bourgeoisization" in the party as a result of sharing responsibility in governing the country with a conservative party.[12] Hence, the SPO has devoted more time to an empirical discussion of current problems than to theoretical discussions about the long-range future of socialism.

Articles appearing in DIE ZUKUNFT, the monthly theoretical organ of the party, and discussions at congresses indicate, however, a failure to agree on programs and goals. The great majority, to be sure, espouses the current conciliatory attitude toward other political parties, the church and religion, and the state. "Socialism is no unrealizable dream . . . [it] has lost its utopian character and the transformation of society succeeds very unromantically," wrote one leader.[13] A minority, however, dreams of the emotionally charged era of Austro-Marxism and provides a radical undercurrent to current party politics. One of its leaders advances this argument: the élan against a capitalism fettered by economic crises can only be maintained if Marxism, instead of being debased, serves as a foundation against capitalism. A sharing of power with a non-socialist party is not in the interest of the party. Nor should any concessions be made to the Catholic Church, given its clerical policy and refusal to make counter-concessions to the SPO.[14]

Obviously, majority and minority views were still far apart from one another, and were aired in 1958 at 7,000 party meetings attended by more than 300,000 members called to discuss the draft of a new

123

basic program. A special party conference in May, 1958, adopted the program, reformist in nature and basically in rapport with the Socialist International Frankfort Declaration of 1951. The radical views were effectively squashed as most speakers proceeded to emphasize the need for a more pragmatic and humanist socialism and the desirability of minimizing the appeal of messianic slogans.

Thus the Austrian Socialist Party, too, as it matures has a mellower outlook on life, which, as the 1959 election indicated, will appeal to more voters in the future.

IV. ITALY

Italian socialism is marked by schisms, clashing ideologies, few successes and many failures since the birth of the party in 1892. Even then it included adherents of nearly all leftist factions on the continent from anarchists and syndicalists to Marxist revisionists. Powerful were the Maximalists, who were orthodox Marxists, and the revisionists, with both alternating in power. The ideological ferment in the party, however, hardly affected the masses to the same extent as it did its leaders. The movement was weakened by constant splits due to several factors. As one writer put it: "The first [factor] is the overmeticulous clarity of the Latin mind, expressing itself in politics by a passion for detailed and logical analysis of its position and a consequent inability to stay in a party with those who have other views," and the second factor is proportional representation, for "there is only one way of breaking the vicious circle, that is to abolish proportional representation, since national temperaments cannot be abolished."[15]

Be that as it may, in the long run equally fateful was the refusal of the party to enter any bourgeois coalition governments in two eras, 1903-1912 and 1919-1921, when it had the opportunity to share in the responsibility of governing and to strengthen the forces of moderation. In the second period, the party led by the Maximalists voted in 1919 to adhere to the Communist International, but two years later balked at the twenty-one demands, in which Moscow insisted on strict obeisance to its dictates, and subsequently left the International. As a result, the radical left seceded and formed the Communist Party. This period was truly one of turmoil. A revolutionary wave of plant seizures, strikes and intimidations of employers following the war finally spent itself by 1920. Then the Fascists adopted equally violent measures to challenge the legitimate government and the Socialists, which both

124

were incapable of meeting. Indeed, the reformists feared that any revolution would lead to an anti-working class reaction, and were finally ready to accept ministerial appointments to strengthen the government. The Maximalists could not countenance such a move, and in 1922 expelled the reformists, who thereupon promptly formed a new Workers' Socialist Party.

The political crisis in the nation resulted in Mussolini's march on Rome in 1922, and his assumption and consolidation of power. As in Germany and Austria, the Socialists chose to go into exile or the underground. It was impossible to maintain any effective organization, and therefore the leaders were able to carry on only "tadpole" politics (all head and no tail, or the politics of leaders without followers).[16] Pietro Nenni, newspaper editor and Maximalist empiricist, and Giuseppe Saragat, theoretician and reformist, the leaders of the now rival Socialist parties, were in exile together, and read and discussed political theory at length. In 1930 Italian Maximalists and reformists joined forces officially, and in 1934 concluded (in France) a popular front pact with the Italian Communists, a harbinger of the French Popular Front. The pact was reaffirmed in 1944 by a Pact of Alliance signed by Nenni, head of the Italian Socialist Party (PSI) and Palmiro Togliatti, head of the Communist Party. Nenni reasoned that many ills of the nation had been caused by the socialist splits, and favored united action for political rather than ideological reasons. This unity was enhanced by the co-operation of anti-Fascist parties in the immediate postwar coalition cabinets and by the East-West honeymoon.

The Cold War led to dissatisfaction with the Pact of Alliance on the part of Saragat, heading a right wing within the PSI. He seceded in January, 1947, to form the Italian Socialist Workers' Party, and in 1951 the Italian Social Democratic Party (PSDI). In the meantime, COMISCO, the forerunner of the Socialist International, expelled Nenni's PSI for collaborating with the Communists, and admitted instead the Saragat party.[17]

Why have the Communists and Nenni's Socialists, despite many defections, been able to attract so many more voters than Saragat's Social Democrats? Or, to put it quantitatively, why did the Communists in the 1958 national election receive nearly 7 million votes, the PSI 4.2 million, (or a combined total of 37 per cent of the popular vote), and the PSDI only 1.5 million? It is easy to say that people have traditionally adopted extreme positions in politics and would

125

prefer not to support center parties. But the explanations are more complex. Certainly there is a correlation between a relatively low standard of living and a high vote for the extremists. The government is blamed, quite correctly, for the slow pace in enacting economic and social reform measures. Sharing in the blame is the PSDI, since it became a satellite in Christian-Democratic-led governments; hence the high vote for the left, not because of any deep doctrinal commitment but as a measure of protest.

Then too the PSDI's posture of moderate reformism and gradualism — it speaks of political, economic and social democracy on the British Fabian model — has not fired the imagination of the electorate. Compared to the PSI, few workers have rallied to its banners; the party has had to rely instead on white-collar groups, artisans, shopkeepers and intellectuals for membership and voter support.

Nevertheless, the alliance between the Communists and the PSI has not stood the test of time, and Nenni has become interested instead in a "socialist alternative," as a third force between Christian Democracy and Communism. To accomplish this he seeks to win back the Social Democrats, although the pro-Communist elements in his party are opposed. Nenni's inability to win the support of all wings in his party for a unification program, his espousal of a mildly neutralist program, and his continued collaboration with the Communists at city and town government level, in the co-operatives and the trade unions, are factors which make Saragat wary of joining hands with Nenni. Said Saragat: "For years I have been waiting for him to take the democratic path, and I have the impression that I will have to wait a while longer."[18] In other words, Saragat will not accept a merger unless the PSI firmly commits itself to the tenets of democracy in advance.

This position has not been shared by all in the PSDI. A strong left wing, headed by Matteo Matteotti, claiming to represent 25 per cent of the party, seceded in February, 1959, to form an autonomous organization, "Socialist Initiative," dedicated to an immedite unification of the entire socialist movement. Whether the new three-way split can be healed in the near future is now more doubtful than ever.

There have been few opportunities for socialist ideologists to devote time to developing theories; instead, they have been immersed in practical politics. They still must study the relationship of a socialist party to the Church and the state.[19] But the most important question

126

to be resolved from an ideological as well as organizational and strategic point of view is how to extricate the masses of workers from the Communist spider web. There is a challenge in this problem. Will the Socialists meet it?

V. FRANCE

The birth of the Fifth French Republic has not signaled a lusty revival of the moribund Socialist Party (SFIO). A diagnosis of its past behavior may unravel the mystery of what is ailing the party today and perhaps provide the clues for a speedy recovery of the patient.

Certainly the party never lacked inspirational guidance from its numerous mentors. These men, such as Babeuf, Fourier, Proudhon, Blanc and others, also had a profound influence on Marx and Engels, who, in turn, left their imprint on the party. This rich heritage of clashing ideologies naturally led to the now familiar schism. The party itself was not founded until 1905 as an amalgamation of groups led by Jules Guesde (Marxist), Jean Jaurès (center) and Edouard Vaillant (Blanquist). Jaurès was able to synthesize the views of the extremist groups and to put the party on a footing of moderate reformism. That the party communicated its message in Marxist parlance was not too paradoxical, given the French revolutionary tradition and the inability of the non-political trade unions to curb the radical theorists.[20]

The tragic assassination of Jaurès in 1914 left a void in the party leadership. The crisis was accentuated by the growing sympathy of the masses for the Soviet Revolution. At Tours, in 1920, a majority split off from the SFIO and formed the Communist Party. Although the workers still formed an important segment of the SFIO clientele in addition to many minor government officials and civil servants, most workers cast their vote for the revolutionary Communist Party.

Therefore, during the interwar years, Léon Blum, SFIO chairman, and a reformist in attitude, had to face the problem of winning back the workers to the party. There were the Marxist slogans and there was the refusal to shore up the capitalist system by sharing ministerial responsibility in bourgeois cabinets. But Blum was not that dogmatic, for he acknowledged the principle that Socialists should head a coalition government if they have a cabinet majority and can make economic and social reforms. This became an actuality in 1936 when, as the strongest party, they formed a Popular Front government. Yes,

127

the principle had paid off, but France for a number of tragic reasons did not remain long a republic.

The war years left an imprint on the ideological position of the party. Resistance to Nazi and Vichy totalitarian rule demonstrated to SFIO supporters the necessity to fight extremist parties more vigorously. One way in which this could be done was to participate in center cabinets regardless of the party's minority status. Thus, since World War II there have been few years in which the SFIO has been in opposition. It has become a question of tactics whether one would gain or lose by sharing the responsibility of governing. A member of the Third Force against the extremist bloc, the SFIO supported the democratic regime but, paradoxically, as one coalition partner among many, had consistently to compromise its program with a consequential loss of potential support from the left.

Blum's tenacious faith in human dignity and social justice, in the light of his war-time incarceration, was indeed remarkable. The legacy he left to his party and the International was to reaffirm the synthesis of Marxism and humanism stressed earlier by his mentor, Jaurès. How did he envision the road to Socialism? Not by a class struggle as Marx had predicted, but by class action, which to Blum meant the peaceful assumption of governmental power within a capitalist system. Then major economic and social reforms would take place, which would alter the system itself and lead to a socialist society, based on the creeds of democracy and human brotherhood.[21]

After Blum's death in 1950, a doctrinaire wing, led by the present chairman, Guy Mollet, gained power. In theory, Mollet wanted to base the party on the industrial workers, and not broaden it to include more bourgeois elements. Moreover, he did not want the party to pose as the center of anti-Communism, because in France such a position implies a hostility to the working class.[22] However, when he headed a coalition government from February, 1956 to May, 1957, surely a peak longevity performance in recent French parliamentary history, Mollet became less doctrinaire. In the tradition of the French Republic, his rule was marked by a lack of significant domestic reforms and by the failure to solve the explosive Algerian issue.

What are the problems facing the SFIO? Why has there been a relentless drop in membership and electoral figures since the war? A lack of a real doctrine or a comprehensive program undoubtedly hampers the party's growth. In a land of revolutionary tradition, it does not want to abandon the Marxist heritage entirely and become more conservative. Yet when the party shares the reins of government it cannot assume a radical posture. Caught on the horns of this dilemma, the party has not been able to extricate itself to face the future with more confidence.[23]

At the root of this dilemma lies the shifting social and geographical basis of the party. Its working class membership (13 per cent) is small as compared to the bloc of civil servants and employees (50 per cent), and other categories. Moreover, its concentrated strength in small towns and rural areas, rather than in industrial centers, gives a rather conservative ideological coloration to the party and constitutes a source of conflict with the more militant leaders.[24] As in Italy, the party's growth is assured only if it can increase its working class support. The odds are against it at this time, because the powerful Communist Party persuasively rallies the workers to its banners of protest against the *status quo.*

Finally, the lack of a doctrine and little opportunity to rise to the top has alienated potential backing from intellectual circles and from youth respectively. Thus the image of the party as a tired and old organization run by firmly entrenched "Organization men," who are worried mostly by day-to-day problems, haunts those who would like to see a revival of the socialist movement. A dissident group led by Edward Depreux and André Philip seceded in 1958 to form the Autonomous Socialist Party, thereby weakening Mollet's party even further. The schism was accentuated after the May, 1958 crisis, when Mollet, fearing a civil war, saw no effective alternative but to back General de Gaulle. The Depreux-Philip party, however, urged a "no" vote on the new constitution, and now has adhered to the Union of Democratic Forces, an organization of anti-Gaullist groups led by Pierre Mendès-France, and to the Socialist Left Party, an organization hostile to both the Communist and Socialist parties.

How difficult it is to achieve real unity among adherents of the left has been demonstrated again in the context of the colorful French political scene. Were the Socialists able to meet the Communist and anti-colonial challenge with more imagination and vigor, then, perhaps, they could serve as a rallying point for those who do not share the essentially conservative outlook of the de Gaullist movement.

VI. THE SCANDINAVIAN COUNTRIES

An analysis of continental socialism today would be incomplete if one of the citadels of democratic socialism, the Scandinavian countries, were omitted. In this region, the socialist parties have dominated the political arena for decades, largely by a successful blending of ideology with a receptive native environment.

Much of the ideological impact came from Marx and the German Socialists, since Scandinavian theorists were scarce, and theory played no significant role. The explanation for these facts lies in Norway, for instance, in a lack of of a long political tradition, a struggle for national independence, a stress on pragmatism, and a lack of conservative business philosophy which could have spurred on socialist theorists.[25]

A further glance at Norway reveals that, characteristically for the Scandinavian countries, the Norwegian party, founded in 1887, in turn created the trade unions a decade later. A fraternal bond developed, which paid off in voter support. However, a speedy industrialization at the turn of the century precipitated a radicalism among the young workers. Fueled by the failure of social democracy in 1914, the war, inflation and the Russian Revolution, the Labor Party joined the Communist International in 1920, thereupon a reformist wing seceded to form the Social Democratic Labor Party in 1921. Refusing to submit to Moscow dictates, the Labor Party in turn seceded from the International in 1923. Nevertheless, the party remained attached to Marxist dogma in its program, even after its merger with the reformists in 1927. As a result of the Great Depression, however, the united party abandoned much of the Marxist core and called for a gradual introduction of a planned economy combined with immediate measures to combat the crisis. Testimony to the success of this program lies in the election results since 1935, in which the part consistently has made the strongest showing and held the reins of government.[26]

The Danish party, founded in 1871, was influenced by Kautsky, but soon pursued a reformist line. Heretics in the party seceded after World War I to form a small and ineffective Communist Party. More important to the Socialists was the question of participation in a non-socialist government. The party rejected such a move, although it allied itself in Parliament with liberal parties after 1900. By 1924 it had enough strength to form the first all-Socialist cabinet. Since then it has been a coalition partner in governments, and, mirroring public opinion, has been responsible for much reform legislation and the pursuit of a disarmament policy until World War II.[27]

130

The Swedish party, founded in 1889, followed the same course as its Danish counterpart, although it became the most important party as early as 1914. Highly reformist, it too has participated in cabinets ever since World War I. Its efforts in the realm of social welfare met with success, so that in 1959 the Socialist prime minister, Tage Erlander, could announce proudly the winding up of the major goals, including a sweeping compulsory health insurance scheme, old age pensions and maternity benefits.[28]

The Scandinavian parties have achieved a great measure of success because of their evolutionary principles: their respected and stable leadership; their excellent organization and press; their wide membership basis which encompasses not only industrial workers, but an increasing number of the middle class, the youth, the intellectuals and the farmers (the party supports small holdings, and not collective farms) ; and their ties to the trade unions and the co-operatives. Then too, when they did assume government responsibility, they moderated their programs in order to perpetuate their rule. Unlike the French, they did not have to fear the growth of a Communist movement, because the workers benefited greatly from the higher standard of living and reform policies initiated by the Labor governments. And who can deny that success breeds success?

The basic programs of the Scandinavian parties parallel that of the Socialist International. There is a stress on humanism and a pluralist approach to economic democracy. In Norway, for example, only 20 per cent of the economy is in the public sector. But the government has been able to level class differences and redistribute economic power, so that the income of, say, lumberjacks and fishermen has increased at the expense of the wealthier class without a major change in the ownership pattern. Government planning agencies, controlling prices, profits and investments, and trade unions, have been primarily responsible for this development. But the Norwegian experience has shown, according to a Socialist writer, that Socialist government leaders must be concerned not only with problems of ownership and the workers' standard of living, but equally with problems of increased productivity and efficient management.[29] He feels that Socialism can be achieved more with public controls and some publicly run enterprises than with a wholesale nationalization program. The danger of the latter is a "bureaucratization" of the state machine. To achieve a balance between centralization, necessary for planning, and decentralization, necessary for freedom, is a most important and difficult task facing such leaders. One solution he advances is to provide for maximum voluntary controls and positive incentives instead of a set of compulsions and prohibitions. Finally, the enrichment of democracy demands that the worker not be alienated from his job and that he participate in community affairs and cultural pursuits in order to provide for the full development of his personality.

Of course, not only Scandinavian socialists are concerned with these problems, but socialists and non-socialists elsewhere. What makes their discussion especially significant in Scandinavia is the degree to which the welfare state has become a *fait accompli* and answers are sought to questions transcending the bread-and-butter demands of the workers. We shall presently come back to this subject.

VII. CONCLUSION

This necessarily cursory survey of the ideological development of the Socialist Internationals and the German, Austrian, Italian, French and Scandinavian Social Democratic parties indicates a swing in the pendulum from a deep doctrinal attachment to socialism to a devaluation of ideology. The shift in position has served to underline the dilemma facing a movement which is not quite sure of its basic philosophy in an age of transition.

The dilemma is encountered in countries, such as Scandinavia, Austria and Great Britain, where the Social Democrats poll more than 40 per cent of the popular vote, as well as in France and Italy, where they must compete with the magnetic appeal of powerful Communist and left-wing Socialist parties and trade unions. In these areas of political, economic and social discontent socialism is likely to improve only if there is a corresponding decline of Communism. Frequently in many of the countries analyzed the crisis is aggravated by a failure of leadership, by damaging internal schisms, by youth's wariness in politics, and by a softening of the rigid class stratification.

What then is the nature of the dilemma? It is a matter of searching for new goals once those of earlier decades have been achieved. After all, the extension of the suffrage, the establishment of regulatory bodies, the recognition of trade unions, the introduction and growth of social insurance schemes, and limited nationalization of industry are now accepted by nearly all elements of European society. As Raymond Aron aptly observes: "Socialism has ceased in the West to be a myth because it has become part of reality."[30]

Socialists will be the first to admit that everywhere the millennium has not been achieved in reaching these targets. Much more has to be done in Europe where democracy sometimes rests on a weak foundation and where the capitalist order lacks a social conscience. This is even more true in areas of extreme nationalist ferment. Indeed, the spotlight will increasingly focus in the decades to come on Asia and Africa where socialism may become a major ideological force.

In Europe, the search for new goals has meant a re-evaluation of the content and meaning of socialism. A none too philosophic discussion among intellectuals, the leaders and the rank-and-file seeks to find an answer to the question of how to fill the vacuum created by the scrapping of outdated Marxist theories. No longer are Socialists concerned with their role as gravediggers or physicians of capitalism; no longer are they prone to speak in Marxist terminology and act otherwise; rather they are worried about assuming a highly pragmatic, eclectic and opportunistic stance which lacks ideological depth. That such an approach holds the advantage of drawing new classes into socialist ranks remains beyond doubt, but as the French Socialist leader Paul Ramadier put it, "a Socialism without doctrine becomes diluted and loses its vigor."[31]

How can this dilemma be resolved? Socialists insist that some Marxist theories still provide the necessary basis for a rationalization of their program and the necessary ideological foundation. Superimposed upon the theories of the Socialist International and of some of the Socialist parties are programmatic declarations stressing the need to strengthen democratic regimes, individual freedoms, and economic and social equality. But some Socialists are asking themselves how such programs differ fundamentally from those of a neo-capitalistic welfare state. To sharpen the differences and to serve as a source of inspiration for their adherents, Socialists are now engaged in retracing the deeper roots of their earlier doctrines. Their emphasis is on flexibility, on a diversity of approaches incorporating not only the Marxist, but also moral, ethical, humanitarian and religious modes of thinking. Will these new theoretical principles and concepts provide the necessary mystique and appeal to the electorate? Are they sufficiently different from the approaches of other political groups? Or will Socialism and capitalism in the forthcoming dialectics of history draw ever closer together in the philosophy of the welfare state until the "isms" disappear?[32] It is too early to tell.

133

SELECTED BIBLIOGRAPHY

F. R. Allemann, "German Socialists Reorganize," THE NEW LEADER, XLI (June 16, 1958), 18-19. A brief commentary about the 1958 party convention.

Léon Blum, FOR ALL MANKIND (New York, New York: The Viking Press), 1946. An important contribution.

Julius Braunthal, "The Socialist International in World Affairs." A lecture sponsored by the Social Science Foundation, University of Denver, Denver, Colo., November 18, 1958 (mimeographed), 1-12. A survey by the retired General Secretary of the Socialist International.

————. Ed., YEARBOOK OF THE INTERNATIONAL SOCIALIST LABOUR MOVEMENT, 1956-1957 (London: Lincoln-Prager International Yearbook Publishing Co., Ltd., 1956). An indispensable reference work of the postwar Socialist International. Statistics. Documents, including programs of member parties.

Ernst Christianson, "The Ideological Development of Democratic Socialism in Denmark," THE SOCIALIST INTERNATIONAL INFORMATION, VIII (January 4, 1958), 1-16. This is one of several excellent articles on the ideologies of Socialist parties which appeared in the organ of the Socialist International.

G. D. H. Cole, A HISTORY OF SOCIAL THOUGHT, 4 vols. (London: Macmillan and Co., Ltd., 1955-1958). The most outstanding and comprehensive survey so far of the Socialist movement in the nineteenth and twentieth centuries.

C. A. R. Crosland, "Socialist Parties of the Future," CONFLUENCE, VII (Summer, 1956), 159-172. A British Socialist examines the tasks ahead.

Karl Czernetz, "Nur keine Selbstzufriedenheit!," DIE ZUKUNFT, Nos. 5/6 (May-June, 1956) 128-131. An Austrian reformist view.

Maurice Duverger, "S.F.I.O.: Mort ou Transfiguration?," LES TEMPS MODERNES, X (May, 1955), 1863-1885. A pessimistic report by a French political scientist.

Henry W. Ehrmann, "The Decline of the Socialist Party," Chapter 11, 181-199, in Edward M. Earle, Ed., MODERN FRANCE: PROBLEMS OF THE THIRD AND FOURTH REPUBLICS (Princeton, N. J.: Princeton University Press, 1951). A balanced critique.

Torolf Elster, "The Ideological Development of Democratic Socialism in Norway," SOCIALIST INTERNATIONAL INFORMATION, V (November 5, 1955), mimeographed reprint, 1-27. A brilliant analysis.

Hans Gerth, THE FIRST INTERNATIONAL: MINUTES OF THE HAGUE CONGRESS OF 1872 WITH RELATED DOCUMENTS (Madison, Wis.: The University of Wisconsin Press, 1958). A fascinating account.

E. Drexel Godfrey, Jr., THE FATE OF THE FRENCH NON-COMMUNIST LEFT (Garden City, New York: Doubleday and Co.,

1955). A short but incisive history of the party and the trade unions.

Walter F. Hahn, "The Socialist Party of Austria, Retreat from Marx," JOURNAL OF CENTRAL EUROPEAN AFFAIRS, XV (July, 1955), 115-133. A sound, scholarly report.

W. Hilton-Young, THE ITALIAN LEFT: A SHORT HISTORY OF POLITICAL SOCIALISM IN ITALY (London: Longmans, Green and Co., 1949). Highly useful and informative.

Josef Hindels, "Kann der Sozialismus den Mensch ändern?," DIE ZUKUNFT, Nos. 5/6 (May-June, 1956), 123-127. An Austrian Marxist point of view.

James Joll, THE SECOND INTERNATIONAL 1889-1914 (New York: Praeger, 1956). One of the best volumes about the organization.

Paul Ramadier, "Socialist Ideas—Theory and Practice," SOCIAL-IST INTERNATIONAL INFORMATION, VIII (May 24, 1958), 324-327. A thoughtful critique.

Dankwart A. Rüstow, "Scandinavia: Working Multiparty Systems," Chapter V, 169-193, in Sigmund Neumann, Ed., MODERN POLITICAL PARTIES (Chicago, The University of Chicago Press, 1956). Norway, Sweden and Denmark are treated in this comparative analysis.

Giuseppe Saragat, "Italy's New Government," THE NEW LEADER, XLI (August 18-25, 1958), 17-18. A brief commentary.

Klaus-Peter Schulz, OPPOSITION ALS POLITISCHES SCHICK-SAL? (Köln Verlag für Politik und Wirtschaft, 1958). A highly critical but constructive analysis.

Klaus Schütz, "Die Sozialdemokratie im Nachkriegsdeutschland," Section II, 157-271, in PARTEIEN IN DER BUNDESREPUBLIK (Stuttgart: Ring Verlag, 1955). The most comprehensive treatment of the SPD in the postwar era.

Adolf Sturmthal, "Democratic Socialism in Europe," WORLD POLITICS, III (October, 1950), 88-113. An important contribution to the comparative study of parties.

Leo Valiani, "Die ideologische Entwicklung des demokratischen Sozialismus in Italien," Chapter X, 161-181, in Julius Braunthal, Ed., SOZIALISTISCHE WELTSTIMMEN (Berlin and Hannover: J. H. W. Dietz, 1958). An illuminating treatment by a participant in the Italian Socialist movement.

Adam Wandriszka, "Das sozialistische Lager," Section II, Chapter V, 422-479 in Heinrich Benedikt, Ed., GESCHICHTE DER REPUB-LIK OSTERREICH (München: Oldenbourg, 1954). An incisive and full analysis of the Austrian Republic.

Philip Williams, POLITICS IN POST-WAR FRANCE: PARTIES AND THE CONSTITUTION IN THE FOURTH REPUBLIC (London: Longmans, Green and Co., 1954). An excellent and well-documented study.

Raphael Zariski, "Problems and Prospects of Democratic Socialism

135

in France and Italy," JOURNAL OF POLITICS, XVIII (May, 1956),
254-280. A fine, scholarly appraisal.

CURRICULUM VITAE

GERARD BRAUNTHAL, Assistant Professor of Government,
University of Massachusetts, received his B.A. degree from Queens
College (1947), M.A. degree from University of Michigan (1948),
and his Ph.D. from Columbia University (1953). He served in the U.S.
Army (1943-1946), and as civilian in the U.S. Army Air Force Intelli-
gence (1950-1952); Research Assistant, National Bureau of Economic
Research (1953-1954); Lecturer, Brooklyn College (summer, 1954);
Instructor (since 1954) and Assistant Professor (since 1957) at the
University of Massachusetts; Visiting Instructor, Mt. Holyoke College
(fall, 1957); Visiting Fulbright Professor, University of Frankfurt, Ger-
many (1959-1960). Has authored such studies as "The German Free
Trade Unions During the Rise of Nazism," JOURNAL OF CENTRAL
EUROPEAN AFFAIRS (January, 1956, reprinted in THE NAZI
REVOLUTION, PROBLEMS OF EUROPEAN CIVILIZATION,
Boston: D. C. Heath, 1959); "The German Trade Unions and Dis-
armament," POLITICAL SCIENCE QUARTERLY, (March, 1958);
and "A Conflict Between Direct and Representative Democracy:
Atomic Armament in West Germany," CANADIAN JOURNAL OF
ECONOMICS AND POLITICAL SCIENCE (August, 1959).

CHAPTER SEVEN

BRITISH SOCIALISM

STANLEY ROTHMAN

Smith College

An understanding of British[1] Socialism, in both thought and action, requires examining it in the general context of European development. The emergence of Socialist movements in all the major countries of Europe at about the same time, while none of any size developed in, for example, the United States, certainly leads one to suspect that the British were partaking in a development which was related to that of the rest of the continent.

Once this is said, however, it becomes equally obvious that an understanding of British Socialism requires that the movements be placed in its peculiarly British context. The British Labour movement, after all, is uniquely British in its orientations and its action. To fail to relate the movement to its home environment, then, would be a serious omission from any study.

Finally, it is clear that whatever continuities one finds, 1945, and the coming to power of a majority Labour government for the first time, marked one of those crucial dividing points in the history of the party. This is true not only because Labour was able to put its "immediate" program into effect and to learn from this, but also because of the profound alterations which have occurred since then (at an ever-increasing rate) in England's position in the world and in the internal structure of English society as well.

This essay, then, will consist of two major sections: one tracing the development of the movement until the conquest of power, and the other dealing with developments since 1945. In both sections, although more in the former than in the latter, an attempt will be made to place the development of the movement in a broader context.

THE ORIGINS AND DEVELOPMENT OF BRITISH SOCIALISM

The development of British politics, like that of other European countries, has been shaped by the fact that she emerged as a nation out of a traditional society which was both feudal and Catholic.[2] The importance of the feudal element lies in the fact that the source of class divisions in nineteenth and twentieth century England is to be found in the class divisions of feudal society. And, of course, the continuing class structure of English society was responsible for the class consciousness of the British working class. In addition the feudal heritage provided a traditional base from which to criticize the development of Liberal Capitalism in terms of an alternate set of social values (those of collective community responsibility, among others).

But if this is true it is also true that modern industrial Capitalism and the Liberal outlook associated with it were also native British growths. That is, unlike most other countries in the world, the normative orientations necessary to the emergence of a Capitalist society developed naturally out of the ideas and values which preceded them, and were not introduced (as in France, Germany or Russia) from the outside.[3] Thus, as against these other countries, the break with traditional society was never so sharp, never so violent, and it did not produce the continuing ideological and physical upheavals which have characterized the modern world. English history, then, has been characterized by that constant interplay of the old and the new so that, in a sense, the more the social patterns of the country change, the more they seem to remain the same.

In any event, by the early part of the eighteenth century (and really as far back as the Tudor monarchy) England had been taking the form of a modern nation. She was ruled by a king *in* a Parliament which was dominated by a gentry-aristocracy and she boasted a relatively unified system of common law. But while the modern state had replaced the earlier congeries of feudal authorities, the structure of society still retained significant elements of its feudal past. The aristocracy was not only responsible for the well-being of those attached to its manors but it was also responsible for actively governing the realm. In fact all of the estates of the realm were bound to each other by sets of mutual rights and obligations and, in a sense, the greater the rights and prerogatives, the greater the duties. I don't mean to paint an idyllic picture, but the contrast to France, for example, is interesting. In England the aristocracy played an active role in Parliament and also was responsible for local government and affairs. This meant more than dispensing justice. It meant carrying the burden of the "poor rates" which were designed to insure that no member of the parish should be left entirely destitute, and it also meant accepting and enforcing measures designed to insure both just prices and just conditions of employment.

This society was not static and even as it had developed out of a more purely feudal past so it was itself in the process of change. The sources of change were twofold: the agricultural and industrial revolutions and the rise of Liberal Capitalism.

Of the changes brought in by the rapid industrialization of the country little need be said. The improvements in agriculture, the development of modern machinery, the history of the enclosures, and the remarkably rapid transition of England from an agricultural to an industrial society—the first in the world—have been described over and over again.[4]

Liberal Capitalism as a system of ideas and institutions calls for, just a bit more extended treatment. The development of these ideas and institutions was part of a single pattern and was not unrelated to the industrialization which has just been mentioned. As a system of ideas it fused both economic and political doctrines, and is most sharply developed in the writings of the English Utilitarians. Briefly, both its political and economic outlooks were in direct antithesis to the premises of the society from which it emerged. For natural inequality it substituted natural equality, each man counting as one. For a view of history which was pessimistic, or at least a view which saw history as a straight line, it substituted a conception of history as a story of progress in which men would become ever more moral and ever more happy as they achieved increasing control over nature. For reliance upon the traditional ways of doing things it substituted the method of reason and the standard of utility.[5]

Its economic thought idealized the free market and it attacked all limitations upon the free working of economic laws whether these were in the form of tariffs, guilds, the regulation of wages or the poor rates. And it sought to eliminate these in the name of progress. To be sure, the premises of the new creed were not nearly as radical in form as in France, but, in terms of the society it was striving to replace, they were radical enough.

Of course, the nineteenth century witnessed the triumph of these premises, but only in part. Only in part because as one examines developments during the century they make most sense when seen as the result not of a purely Liberal triumph, but, rather, as an interplay between Liberalism as a set of ideas and the Conservative thinking which emerged to defend the old way of doing things. Nor were these two points of view associated that clearly with a single party or, more importantly, with a single social class.

The triumphs of the Liberal idea are easily traced: the gradual equalization of the suffrage through the great reform bills; the establishment of free trade, the repeal of the Corn Laws, the new Poor Law of 1834. Politically the effect was to create a society which was more and more democratic, with consequent shifts in the distribution of power. Economically, the effect was to create a society which, for a short time approached the model of "laissez faire." But only for a short time and never completely. For at the same time that a new "economic" Poor Law was being introduced, so were factory acts (acts designed to regulate the hours and conditions of work). And the pace of enactment of social reform measures increased as the century wore on, to culminate in the great Reform Act of 1911, providing for universal unemployment insurance, old age protection and a very extensive system of free medical care. By this time, of course, England was a fully industrialized society, and a new era was just opening during which both her industrial and commercial supremacy would rapidly become a thing of the past.[6]

Again, it should be emphasized that the history of reform cannot be associated with a single party. The Conservatives, or at least many of them, accepted significant portions of the new politics and the new economics. And the Whigs, then Liberals, accepted much of the idea of social responsibility despite the arguments of the classical economists. After all, it was a Conservative government that extended suffrage to the skilled workers of the cities and a Liberal government which instituted the reforms of 1911.

In part the transformation of the commercial classes to a sense of responsibility was undoubtedly related to the new evangelicalism sparked by Methodism. In part, however, it was produced by the acceptance of aristocratic orientations. Thus the commercial classes accepted the continuation of a monarch, a quasi-feudal House of Lords, and all the paraphernalia of tradition. They also accepted a class system which was rigid enough to separate them from the lower orders as a group, but fluid enough to permit entrance into the aristocracy itself. And if the acceptance of a status society helps explain the

140

emergence of British Socialism, so the acceptance of the responsibilities which went with it may help explain the peaceful character of this Socialism.

An English Socialist tradition can be traced back to John Ball and the peasant upheavals of the twelfth and thirteenth centuries, through the Diggers of the English Civil Wars. In its modern variant, however, it is a post-Liberal-Capitalist phenomenon, and the content of modern Socialist thought clearly indicates this. In all its forms, whether the militant quasi-Marxism of the Social Democratic Federation or the emotional militancy of Owen or Keir Hardie, or the cautious quasi-Utilitarianism which marked the Fabian Society, the Socialist orientation does not strike one as completely new. It seems related to what has gone before. In fact, it seems to represent a revolt against the individualistic premises of Liberal Capitalism and the uprooting caused by the Industrial Revolution at the same time that it represents a desire to achieve the aspirations which Liberal Capitalism had promised to satisfy, i.e., a rich productive society and equality.

In their criticisms of Liberal Capitalism, Socialists are at one with the Conservative reaction. They attack the ugliness and inhumanity of the new industrial society, but whereas the Conservatives want to return to a past of sharply defined classes and estates the Socialists see a future where all men, as brothers, are equal.

From the very beginning Socialist economics takes as its starting point Liberal economic theory. The idea that labor is the source of all value is borrowed from Locke, Smith and Ricardo; and the argument that Capitalism involves inherent contradictions finds its inspiration in Ricardo and Malthus, but uses their analyses as the basis of a critique of Capitalism itself. The problem, or so these pre-Marxist Socialists argued, anticipating Marx, was one of an improper relationship between production and consumption. When the worker received all of the product that was his due, then productivity would increase by leaps and bounds and there would be enough for all.[7]

None of the critics whose thought I have been summarizing were first-rank thinkers, and since Marx they have been relegated to the ranks of the utopians. The relegation stems from the fact that most of them were greatly influenced by the one among them whose name is still remembered, Robert Owen. For the most part they agreed with Owen in arguing that the way to bring about a transformation was, on the one hand, to convince people of the correctness of the idea of Socialism, and, on the other, to encourage the setting up, by the workers, of various types of co-operative communities. Needless to say, attempts to accomplish this latter aim, primarily associated with Owen, failed.

However, despite the failures and the label utopian, it can be legitimately argued that the pre-Marxist Socialists won the day in the end. Marx himself had relatively little influence on English Socialist ideas, despite the fact that he spent most of his later years in England. His major English disciple, H. M. Hyndman, did set up an organization, the Social Democratic Federation, to propagate the faith. However, while the S. D. F. included as members at one time or another many of the young men who were later to play important roles in the trade union movement, it does not seem that any of these ever really understood Marxism and they left the organization, which always remained very small, with their first successes in the trade union field.[8]

Far more than Hyndman, Keir Hardie and the Independent Labour Party represent the ethos of the early Labour Party. Hardie's emotional Socialism drew to him people as varied as G. D. H. Cole, Ramsay MacDonald and Hugh Dalton. And, in the last analysis, these people agreed with both Hardie and the utopians that Socialism as an idea would carry the day as the community as a whole became convinced of its superior morality.[9]

Two other streams of thought played a role in the foundations of modern Socialist ideas and the Labour Party. At the turn of the century, some working class, and a good many middle class, intellectuals came under the influence of the idealism of T. H. Green and, more importantly, the influence of the Fabians.[10] It is difficult to summarize the thinking of the latter group in detail because they held to no single line. People like George Bernard Shaw, the Webbs and H. G. Wells differed considerably among themselves. Most generally, however, they used the arguments of the Liberals — the utilitarianism of Bentham — to prove that the greatest good of the greatest number required collectivism, and they drew their economic theory from the classical English tradition, supplemented by some of Henry George.

Again, they were convinced that Socialism could come by peaceful methods and that the road to Socialism simply required developing community consciousness as to the real problems which existed. They refused, of course, to accept the Marxian argument that Capitalism could not be gradually reformed since one had either to operate according to its law or to create a society governed by a whole new set of laws. Rather they felt that Capitalism could almost imperceptibly give way to an efficient Socialist society. Thus, while they supported the idea of a Labour Party which would be Socialist, much of their activity, in the early years at least, was directed to permeating the other parties; to convincing them that certain practical measures of social reform were necessary.

English craft unions, like those on the rest of the continent, are direct descendants of the medieval guilds. In fact the transformation from guild to union was so gradual that it is hard to point to a clear dividing line. By the first quarter of the nineteenth century, however, it was pretty clear that the artisans of preindustrial England had been transformed into a modern working class and that their associations were taking on all the functions of modern trade unions.[11]

This, however, was not the complete story, for the new industry did not draw only upon skilled craftsmen. More and more, it drew ex-peasants, yeomen and agricultural workers, as well as women and, for a long time, children, into the cities to work at non-skilled jobs.

To the employers of this labor, some of whom had but recently emerged from the working class themselves, workers were simply commodities, like any other, to be bought cheaply and used with efficiency.[12] That the state should play a role in regulating conditions of work and wages defied the natural economic laws, and that men should combine to artificially raise the cost of their labor did likewise. Thus the old statutes regulating wages and conditions of work were gradually repealed or fell into disuse, and new provisions outlawing combinations of either men or masters were placed on the books. This legislation, of course, was pushed by the same men who were fighting for improved sanitation in the cities, the ending of slavery, and extension of the suffrage.[13]

Yet the new theories which justified these actions did not hold ground for very long. In part the pressure of the working class helped bring about their downfall in practice, but, in part, so did the conscience of the community. There was no reason, many argued, that working class men should not be allowed to combine for mutual assistance or to defend their legitimate interests.[14] As Englishmen they were entitled to this right. Thus, in 1824-5 the Combination Acts were repealed and although the trade unions continued to operate under some limitations until the last quarter of the century, their legality was assured.

This did not mean the immediate development of a large-scale trade union movement. Many employers remained very hostile and, for the most part, the mass of unskilled workers had not developed the self-discipline necessary for such organization. In fact, the activities of those workers who were aroused to action were largely spent in the futility of destroying new machines or in ephemeral attempts to establish grand national organizations whose aim was to remake the social order.

By the middle of the nineteenth century, however, the organization of unions among the skilled workers, at least, was proceeding with some rapidity, and by the last quarter of the century they were an accepted part of the English scene. In fact, many of the craft unions had become so strong that employer's associations were just a little horrified. One noted with alarm in 1873 that:

> ... They have through their command of money, the imposing aspect of their organization, and partly, also from the humanitarian aspirations of a certain number of literary men of good standing, a large army of literary talent. . . . They have a standing Parliamentary Committee and a programme; and active members of Parliament are energetic in their service. They have the attentive ear of the ministry of the day.[15]

If craft unions were accepted by the rest of the community it was in part because they were moderate in their demands and leadership. They preferred letters to the TIMES to (as in the case of French workers) storming the barricades, and they turned to strikes only as a last resort. In general they accepted the virtues of English middle-class society, the need for self-discipline, restraint and moral uprightness. The bond that tied them to "bourgeois" England was, in part, that of religion. The same evangelical fervor that was so responsible for the development of Victorian middle-class culture played no small part in disciplining workers to the requirements of an industrial society.[16]

But if they differed from the French working class in this respect, they also differed from their American counterparts. Unlike Americans, they considered themselves as a separate class rather than as members of a huge undifferentiated middle class. The British worker, in other

144

words, was conscious of class. He expected, by and large, to rise with his class, not out of it.

These, however, were the skilled workers. Until the end of the century the situation of the growing millions of the unskilled remained unchanged in terms of industrial organization. In the 1880's and 90's, however, the *crise de conscience* of middle-class intellectuals, who went among the workers to teach and save them, began to bear fruit. The unskilled began to clamor for a larger share of the economic pie. Beginning with the success of the Match Girls' strike in 1889, thousands rushed into newly formed industrial and general unions of the unskilled. Dockers, transport workers, and others hitherto untouched by organization of any kind, now began to form themselves into battalions. In 1892 total trade union membership in Great Britain was about 1,530,000. By 1914 the figure had risen to something like four million. As of 1895 the big unions were still to be found among the skilled workers. By 1913 the majority of British organized workers were in the industrial or general unions of the unskilled, and henceforth these were to dominate the trade union movement.[17]

And, of course, by this time, too, these latter unions had become an accepted part of the British scene. When the National Insurance Act of 1911 was passed, for example, a provision was included stipulating that funds be administered by friendly societies, i.e., the trade unions, including the new general and industrial unions. Within two years after the passage of the bill trade union membership had risen by a million.

To those who saw these new unions as militant forces which would transform British society, this provision of the Act was a way in which the bourgeoisie had bought off the trade unions, a plot to conservatize them — to draw off their revolutionary élan.[18] As an explanation of motives the statement contains no more than a grain of truth, but as a guide to future trade union development it tells us quite a bit.

The organizers of the new unions had, unlike those who organized the skilled, been militants committed (or at least so they thought) not only to unionism but to revolutionary change. With their success, however, the picture changed. Either they turned conservative, e.g., Ernest Bevin, or else they found themselves on the periphery of the union movement, e.g., Tom Mann. More and more the requirement for leadership was skill at the conference table rather than at the mass rally.[19] And, of course, in the next generation the leadership of these

145

unions was to be largely a bureaucratic leadership which had come up through the paid ranks of the unions. This was a leadership with all the inherent conservative tendencies of any bureaucracy. It was unwilling to risk union money in strikes which could not succeed and it was more interested in conserving strength than in expending it. Further, meeting employers around a conference table meant a reduction in social distance and social tension. It also meant that one had been able to rise with one's class and rise above it. All of these factors tended to result in a decline in the militancy of union leadership. For the great mass of workers, of course, trade union success meant that their interests were and would be protected. Thus a new element was added which bound them to existing institutional arrangements, or at least cushioned their dissatisfaction.

It is little wonder then that in the 1930's, when the intellectuals and constituency party militants in the Labour Party were turning to the left and calling for popular fronts and an end to reformism, the most conservative elements in the party were to be found in the mass unions of the unskilled. The leadership, at least, was committed to the Labour Party and to Socialism, but their conception of Socialism was something which would come in good time and through peaceful change. In the meantime such was their position in the society that they were willing to work for more limited goals within the framework of a Capitalist society,[20] And to the rank and file of trade union members who were Socialists, and not all of them were in any real sense, Socialism meant equality, security, the chance to have one's own home with a plot of grass around it and lots more time to do what one wanted. Beyond that, except for a relatively small group of activists, it is doubtful that thoughts traveled.

The more immediate origins of a political labor movement in England go back to the founding of the Independent Labour Party (I. L. P.) at Bradford in 1893. Keir Hardie presided at the initial meeting, and the delegates decided upon an organization with a federal structure so as to permit the affiliation of trade unions. For, it was felt, the success of any party which spoke for the working man would depend upon trade union support.[21]

Despite this decision, however, the I. L. P. attracted neither trade unions nor voters, in 1900 its paid membership was only some 4,000, organized into 51 branches; not a single M. P. bearing its label was sitting in Parliament, and in the 1895 general election it had only received some 45,000 votes.[22] To a considerable extent its failure stemmed from the fact that at a time when most trade unionists were unwilling to take this step it unabashedly announced that it was a Socialist Party.

It was, in fact, some seven years after the formation of the I. L. P., in 1900, that the trade unions took their first step toward independent political action. Following a recommendation by the Trades Union Congress (T. U. C.) the year before, representatives from the I. L. P., the Social Democratic Federation, the Fabian Society and some of the newer trade unions gathered together to establish a "Labour Representation Committee" (L. R. C.).

The T. U. C. resolution had not called for a Socialist Party. Rather the function of the L. R. C. was merely to be that of devising ways and means of securing the election of an increased number of working men to Parliament. Working men, it was felt by many of those who supported the resolution, could much better represent the interest of the working class.

But even given the moderate terms of the resolution and the moderate aims of the organization which stemmed from it, the L. R. C. did not meet with overwhelming initial success. At first the only unions which affiliated were the new unions, those of the unskilled. The even larger and better-organized unions of the skilled workers still seemed to feel that the L. R. C. had about it a taint of un-English radicalism. It was only after the Taff Vale decision of 1901 that they began to change their attitudes.

Briefly, the decision seemed to imply that trade unions could be sued for damages suffered by employers in the normal course of a strike. The anger and dismay felt by trade unionists at the ruling of the House of Lords translated itself into a rush to join the L. R. C., which, by 1906, had become the Labour Party.

Initially, both trade unionists and Labour Party leadership continued to support the Liberals in Parliament and to arrange electoral bargains with them on the outside. In fact it almost seemed as if the party regarded itself as something like a pressure group rather than a political organization whose ultimate aim was control of the mechanisms of the state. The eventual split with the Liberal Party developed, fundamentally, because the Liberals were unable or unwilling to make the kind of concessions that the Labour Party demanded. But this was

147

in part due to the fact that the nature of the concessions demanded was changing.

Doctrines urging that the whole structure of British society was unjust were becoming increasingly respectable. It was here, of course, that both the Fabians and the I. L. P. played their most effective role. The latter group, especially, not only served as a constituency organization for the new Labour Party but as that organization where young middle-class intellectuals, who could not belong to unions, could work for the cause of a more just England. As G. D. H. Cole has put it:

> So when I wanted to become actively connected with the political Labour movement, I joined the I.L.P. Over a large part of the country to all intents and purposes, the I. L. P. was the Labour Party, and had in its hands almost the entire work of political propaganda on the Party's behalf.[23]

These men served to educate the working class, to make them self-aware, and to heighten the level of their aspirations.

It was not until 1918, however, that the party formally committed itself to Socialism. In that year it adopted a statement largely composed by Sidney Webb and entitled *Labour and the New Social Order*. The statement announced the ultimate aim of the movement as the "common ownership of the means of production." To be sure, the program did not outline in detail how this was to be achieved, and its proposals for immediate action were much more moderate, but the promise was there.

At the same time that the party adopted its new program it also provided itself with a new constitution which, for the first time, envisaged the formation of regular party constituency organizations. Eventually this decision was to mean the destruction of the Independent Labour Party, which was left without any real function to perform. During the 1920's the I. L. P. dwindled gradually in importance, and as it did so, it came under the control of a more radical leadership. Led by such men as James Maxton, John Paton and Fenner Brockway it kept up a running fight with the leadership of the party. Its desire was for "Socialism in our time," and it violently criticized what it considered to be the weak quality of the Labour Party's program and, just as importantly, the weakness of its one-time hero Ramsay MacDonald.[24]

During the middle twenties some of its criticisms found a sympathetic echo among many trade unionists who were, at this time, still to the left of party leadership. MacDonald himself was committed to a gradual, almost imperceptible, transition to Socialism, and as he grew older became somewhat more touchy with regard to criticisms directed against him by those urging more radical measures. Until 1931, however, such was his prestige among the rank and file that his leadership remained unchallenged, despite the fact that as the head of two minority Labour governments (1924 and 1929-31) he had revealed an amazing capacity for doing very little.

Nineteen thirty-one was the year of the great betrayal which has become part of party mythology. The party had taken office in 1929 as a minority government despite the warnings of the left, primarily the I. L. P., that as a minority government they would not be in a position to accomplish anything, and in fact would be forced to accept responsibility for the inevitable Capitalist depression. By 1930 the predictions of the I. L. P. seemed to be coming true. England had entered a period of increasing unemployment, as the depression which had begun in the United States spread throughout Europe. As the year wore on, unemployment, which had stood at some 10 per cent of the working population through the 1920's, continued to rise until it approached the 20 per cent level.

Both MacDonald and his Chancellor of the Exchequer, Philip Snowden, were convinced that as governors of a Capitalist society they must accept Capitalist economic laws, and they attempted to handle the problem by reduced government services and a balanced budget. They were pushed still further in this direction by indications from New York banking firms that loans would not be forthcoming unless sound economic policies were followed.

The upshot of the whole affair was a sharp split between Mac-Donald and the rank and file of the party, and his subsequent desertion of the party. With Snowden and some others, MacDonald joined in coalition with the Conservative Party and a portion of the Liberal Party to form a "national government." In the election which followed the vote of the Labour Party dropped from 8.4 million to 6.6 million, and its parliamentary representation from 288 to 46.

The depression, MacDonald's "treason" and, just a bit later, the rise of National Socialism in Germany, all came as profound shocks to Labour Party members and, especially, to those middle-class and activist working class elements who constituted the core of its constituency organization. The result was a rapid shift in opinion. To a good

149

many, Marxism, in its revolutionary form, seemed a very plausible description of the way in which the world operated. Capitalist Society could not be reformed from within. The next time it came to office, a Socialist party must be prepared to offer a total Socialist program which it must be prepared to implement.[25] And, given the experience of Nazi Germany, it must be prepared to expect violent resistance frim the Capitalist class. As Aneurin Bevan put it:

> Were they to assume that their opponents loved democracy more than they loved their property? If their property was threatened because of democracy would they abandon their property because they loved democracy?[26]

In 1932, 1933 and 1934, then, the Labour Party engaged in a rewriting of its program. This rewriting was to make it clear to the electorate that:

> The choice before the nation is either a vain attempt to patch up the superstructure of a capitalist society in decay at its very foundations, or a rapid advance to a socialist reconstruction of the national life. There is no half way house between a society based on private ownership of the means of production . . . and a society where public ownership of those means enables the resources of the nation to be deliberately planned for attaining the maximum of general well being.[27]

But when the actual program of the party executive came to the floor of the annual conferences it revealed certain peculiar characteristics. To be sure, it called for the nationalization of a number of industries, and warned that obstructionism, on the part of the House of Lords especially, would be dealt with. But was this indeed a program which provided for a Socialist society? And was this the program of a militant working class party?

As the left pointed out at several conferences, even if the whole of the announced program were adopted England would still remain an economy in which the private sphere was predominant. At most the program called for a mixed economy. The left's argument may have been logical, given the stated premises of the leaders who drew up the program, but it did not sway them or the party. The Labour Party might be Socialist, but it was still gradualist, and it still believed in democratic processes and full compensation.

Actually, during the latter part of the 1930's social reform took second place to international politics as the rise of Nazi Germany and the collapse of collective security threatened world peace. The Labour

Party had a long pacifist tradition. In part this stemmed from the conviction that war was simply bad, and, in part, especially during the interwar period, it stemmed from the feeling that war itself was merely the result of Capitalist rivalries.

This latter feeling had been re-enforced by the aftermath of World War I. Despite their protestations, so Labour Party members felt, the victorious allies had clearly seen the war as a means of bettering their economic position. In the view of Labour Party members, then, to put arms in the hands of a Capitalist government was only to encourage them in imperialist adventures.[28]

With the rise of National Socialism and the aggressive action of the dictators, Labour's policy of pacifism and disarmament was subject to severe strain. By 1937 party leaders felt forced to reverse themselves. The League of Nations was effectively dead and England had to rearm. Responding to the urging of people like Hugh Dalton and Ernest Bevin, the party decided to vote for the arms estimates.[29] In 1938 and 1939 they constantly urged a vigorous British policy against Nazi Germany and also protested the tendency of the government to ignore the Soviet Union, toward which most members of the party still felt a considerable sympathy, even while rejecting the activities of domestic Communists.[30]

When war finally came, the party initially refused to join a coalition government. The refusal had little to do with a Socialist analysis of the wickedness of collaborating with Capitalist governments. Rather the party simply distrusted Chamberlain as the father of appeasement.[31] Thus when he stepped down in favor of Churchill the party readily changed its mind, despite the latter's "reactionary" views.

With Attlee as deputy premier and a number of other members of the party and the trade union movement in important political and economic posts, Labour gained important experience in the running of government. More importantly, from the point of view of their own programs, they gained experience in running what was essentially a planned economy.

As the war drew to an end in Europe the party became restive in coalition and finally withdrew preparatory to another electoral contest. The platform was substantially that developed in the prewar years, widespread social reform, specific programs of nationalization, and a movement toward general equality. All of this the first stage on the road to a Socialist commonwealth.

151

The election was held in July of 1945 and the British people elected their first majority Labour Government.

AFTER THE REVOLUTION

During its approximately six years in office the Labour Party fulfilled all specific pre-election pledges. It nationalized the coal industry, transport, the Bank of England, steel, gas and electricity. In addition it set up a program for the development of new planned communities; expanded educational opportunities, established a free health service; and developed a tax program designed to equalize wealth, the heaviest burden falling upon unearned income. Finally, it engaged in a program of national economic planning, using both physical and financial controls, to ensure that resources flowed in the right directions.[32]

Actually all of this was not as radical as seems at first glance. The coal industry had been coming under ever tighter government control even before the war, as had gas and electricity, and the Bank of England had always operated under very substantial public regulation. When all is said and done only the nationalization of steel provided a really radical break with trends which had been developing for some time, and, even with the nationalization of steel, the British economy was still one characterized predominantly by private ownership.

Further the Conservative-dominated wartime coalition government had already suggested extensive expansion of educational opportunity after the war, and Labour's action in this sphere constituted, basically, only an extension of original Conservative proposals. As for the national health service, the British working man had long been provided with free medical care. What the program did, essentially, was to extend this to the entire population, thus removing the taint of charity, and provide for national planning of the utilization of the nation's medical resources.[33]

Finally, any postwar government would have had to continue extensive control over the economy, for a while at least. And, in fact, as the initial postwar crises drew to an end, the Labour Government relied less and less upon direct controls and more and more upon the kind of financial controls which the Conservatives had, by now, come to accept.

In the last analysis, then, the English people had been gradually abandoning the idea of laissez faire for a long time (if they had ever accepted it whole), and were moving in the direction of social as well as political equality. The advent of a Labour Government pushed the process a little further and a little faster, but represented no sharp break with the past. And, incidentally, while it further cut down the delaying power of the House of Lords, Labour exhibited no real desire to eliminate it, the monarchy, or other aspects of that tradition which had become so firmly associated with the British Community.

In one sense the evidence of the relative moderateness of the change is to be found in the ready acceptance of it by most of the community and, especially, by the Conservative Party. Upon coming to office the Conservatives did denationalize steel and part of transport; did move more rapidly to ending direct economic controls, and did revise tax laws so as to allow money to "fructify in the pockets of the people." But the rest of Labour's work remained untouched except in details.[34]

In another area, too, the Labour Government revealed its continuity with the British past, that of foreign policy. Initially, at least some had felt that the party, representing a Socialist orientation, would find it easier to get along with the Soviet Union than a Conservative government. This proved untrue. Almost from the very beginning Labour found itself at one with the United States on most of the crucial issues of foreign policy. And, under the leadership of Ernest Bevin. Great Britain supported the United States in almost every action, from the development of N. A. T. O. to the rearmament of Germany.[35]

This is not to say that the actions of the Labour Government in both the domestic and foreign policy spheres went unchallenged. In both areas a vocal minority, varying in size on different issues, called for a more consistent and militant Socialist policy. Associated through the late 1940's and most of the fifties with the name of Aneurin Bevan, the left wing of the party called for promises of still more nationalization, more extensive taxes, and, in general, a dedicated attempt to achieve a future Socialist society.[36]

In the field of foreign affairs they condemned what they considered the blind following of the American lead; argued, for a while at least, that America was just as responsible for the cold war as the Soviet Union; opposed rearmament and the arming of Germany; and, more recently, urged not only the ending of nuclear tests but the abandonment by England of atomic weapons and the elimination of American bases from British soil.[37]

In the area of domestic policy the protests of this left wing have, with some exceptions, not resulted in substantial policy modifications. The turn of the party program as a whole has been away from a completely socialized economy. In the area of foreign policy, however, they have commanded more support, and, in a number of instances, party policy has accommodated itself to their views.[38] It is hard, however, to speak of some of these issues in purely left-right terms. Opposition to German rearmament commanded the support of those who, as a result of the experience of the 1930's and 1940's, still felt a powerful antagonism toward and distrust of the Germans. Disagreement with respect to America's China policies has crossed party lines and is partly related to Britain's desire, as a trading nation, to make the best of a *fait accompli*. Finally attitudes toward the H-Bomb stem at least partially from England's position as a small island, and her experience with bombing. These issues, too, cross party lines somewhat.

As the 1945-50 Labour Government drew to an end, there appeared signs of a malaise in the party. Except for the left, which still argued that the revolution had yet to be consummated, the party seemed to have lost its sense of direction as well as its enthusiasm. The confusion continued through the 1951 and 1955 defeats, and was blamed by many for these defeats. The party as a whole seemed to have drifted from its ideological moorings but did not seem to be going anywhere. One sign of this was its decreasing appeal to youth.

Since 1955 there has been a rethinking of Labour Party policy on the part of the center and right wings. And this rethinking has been embodied in a series of policy statements which were adopted at the 1957 and 1958 conferences. The statements indicate that, whatever its slogans, the party has dropped a good part of its Socialist rhetoric. It still conceives of itself as essentially a Socialist Party for the long run, but it emphasizes a mixed rather than a fully socialized economy and it refuses to commit itself to extensive future programs of nationalization.

Further, it argues that Capitalism, in the modern welfare state, has had most of its fangs pulled. Large-scale concentrations of wealth are coming to an end, as are concentrations of Capitalist economic power. Further it is now possible to mitigate the worst effects of economic cycles.

As a Socialist Party, then, Labour now conceives its job as a gradual push toward a less competitive and more egalitarian society, emphasizing, especially, the need to eliminate the class snobbery which is still quite characteristic of British society. It points out, however, the continuing need for incentives and that, for raising living standards, increasing national productivity must constitute a primary goal. Nor does it argue that Socialism will provide a panacea for all present ills or eliminate all future problems. In an even more Socialist society the problem of controlling power will remain, as will problems of increasing productivity, and resolving conflicts among sections of the community.[39]

The change in orientation is the result of many factors, the relative weight of which it is difficult to measure. The experience of the party in creating and running nationalized industries had been sobering. For one thing, the attitude of workers toward their work did not change appreciably, and problems of efficiency were not automatically solved.

Further, the British electorate has shown signs that it is not interested in further nationalization, and this has certainly affected a party leadership which desires to obtain the rewards of office. But, of course, the changing attitudes of the population are partly the result of continuing changes in British society itself. Despite the effects of a more relaxed Conservative tax policy, there is little question that British society is more mobile and egalitarian than it was before. Further, the old class system is eroding at an ever more rapid rate. No longer do working men and middle-class men dress that differently or walk that differently or speak that differently. As G. D. H. Cole put it:

> To one who can look back over more than sixty years, it is remarkable how conditions in Great Britain have changed.
> Nowadays . . . it is often impossible to tell by looking at a man —or woman—and by hearing them talk, to what class they belong. . . . It is still, no doubt, possible to pick out some persons, at sight, as members of the upper middle class or as manual workers from their dress and ways of holding themselves and moving their limbs; but there are many more who carry no such evident signs about them.[40]

These changes are only partly the result of post-World War II social policies. The increasing growth of mass production in England as in the United States has resulted in a standardization of products which masks income inequalities, and the increasingly pervasive influ-

155

ence of television as well as that of geographic mobility has had an important impact on language. In many ways unrelated to political decisions, England is in the midst of a continuing and important social revolution which is likely to accelerate in tempo.[41]

Insofar as this revolution or evolution has reduced the area of ideological conflict which sprang up in the nineteenth century with the development of an industrial Capitalist society, it is all to the good, as is the fact that England, today, is probably a more just and humane society than it was one hundred or even twenty years ago. However, the picture is not without its negative elements. Democratization has tended to result in a general lowering of cultural standards even as cultural opportunities have been broadened. And this has at least something to do with the fact that standards are more and more coming to be set by mass tastes.

The new mass culture with its greater emphasis on violence and the satisfaction of rather narrow material impulses is not entirely attractive.[42] Further, the social characteristics historically part of the behavior pattern of the British upper and middle classes are coming under even more sustained and bitter attack as their real power declines. The new generation of "angry young men," the literary lions of today, seem to feel that civilized social living is all "cant." The only alternative which they offer is a kind of amoral struggle to get to the top.[43]

While it is true that old England contained many injustices, and that the dominant elites were both stuffy and blind in many ways, these qualities were at least partially balanced by a sense of independence, duty and restraint which was not without its virtues.

It may be that having achieved their goals, those who wanted a more democratic and just England will find that both their aims and the general patterns of social life developing in the twentieth century have resulted in the loss of the baby with the bath water.

SELECTED BIBLIOGRAPHY

Clement R. Attlee, THE LABOR PARTY IN PERSPECTIVE— AND TWELVE YEARS LATER (London: Longmans, Green and Co., 1949). A statement of Labour Party history, policy and structure as viewed by the first majority Labour Prime Minister. The book was originally written in 1937.

————, AS IT HAPPENED (London: William Heinemann

156

Ltd., 1954). An autobiography which also covers party history. Objective and modest, but a little dull.

M. Beer, A HISTORY OF BRITISH SOCIALISM (one volume edition; London: George Allen and Unwin Ltd., 1940). A classic study by a German scholar.

Fenner A. Brockway, INSIDE THE LEFT: THIRTY YEARS OF PLATFORM, PRESS, PRISON AND PARLIAMENT (London: Allen and Unwin, 1947). An autobiography which also describes the course of left wing Labour politics in the 1920's and 1930's.

G. D. H. Cole, A HISTORY OF THE LABOUR PARTY FROM 1914 (London: Routledge and Kegan Paul Ltd., 1948). A history of the party by one of its elder statesmen; a scholar who had been active in the Labour movement all his life. Presents moderate left wing point of view.

————, BRITISH WORKING CLASS POLITICS, 1832-1914 (London: Routledge and Kegan Paul Ltd., 1941). Covers the earlier period of Labour politics

C. A. R. Crosland, THE FUTURE OF SOCIALISM (London: Jonathan Cape Ltd., 1956). A postwar revisionist analysis of Socialism by a leading young Labour Party economist and M. P.

Richard H. S. Crossman, Ed., NEW FABIAN ESSAYS (New York: Frederick A. Praeger, Inc., 1952). A collection of essays by leading members of the Labour Party which discuss the future of the party.

Leon D. Epstein, GREAT BRITAIN: UNEASY ALLY (Chicago: University of Chicago Press, 1954). A discussion of British foreign policy in the postwar period, with several chapters on the Labour Party.

Gerard Lowenberg, "The Transformation of British Labour Party Policy Since 1945," THE JOURNAL OF POLITICS, 21 (May, 1959), 234-258. A summary and analysis of the rethinking of Labour Party policy in the postwar years.

R. T. McKenzie, BRITISH POLITICAL PARTIES: THE DISTRIBUTION OF POWER WITHIN THE CONSERVATIVE AND LABOUR PARTIES (London: William Heinemann Ltd., 1955). An outstanding study by a British political scientist which makes the point that in terms of power structure the two parties are more alike than different.

J. F. Milburn, "The Fabian Society and the British Labour Party," THE WESTERN POLITICAL QUARTERLY, XI (June, 1958), 319-39. A history of the activities of the Fabian Society since 1920.

Edward R. Pease, A HISTORY OF THE FABIAN SOCIETY (New York: E. P. Dutton & Co., 1916). A classic study of the early years of the society by its secretary.

Henry Pelling, THE ORIGINS OF THE LABOUR PARTY (London: Macmillan and Co. Ltd., 1954).

————and Frank Bealey, LABOUR AND POLITICS (London:

Macmillan and Co. Ltd, 1958). Two detailed scholarly studies which carry the history of the party from its origins to 1910.

Raymond Postgate, THE LIFE OF GEORGE LANSBURY (London: Longmans, Green and Co., 1952). The biography of one of the most beloved figures in the Labour Party.

Adam Ulam, THE PHILOSOPHICAL FOUNDATIONS OF BRITISH SOCIALISM (Harvard: Cambridge University Press, 1952). A discussion of the idealist contribution to Labour Party thought.

Beatrice Webb, OUR PARTNERSHIP (London: Longmans, Green and Co., 1948). An autobiography of two of the most eminent Fabians.

Sidney and Beatrice Webb, A HISTORY OF TRADE UNIONISM, 2nd Edition (London: Longmans, Green and Co., 1920). The definitive study of the trade union movement to 1920.

Francis Williams, FIFTY YEARS MARCH: THE RISE OF THE LABOUR PARTY (London: Odhams Press Limited, 1949). A popular history of the Labour Party by a well known Labour journalist.

———— MAGNIFICENT JOURNEY: THE RISE OF THE TRADE UNIONS (London: Odhams Press, 1954). A popular history of the trade union movement.

CURRICULUM VITAE

STANLEY ROTHMAN, Assistant Professor of Government, Smith College (1959—), received his B.S.S. degree from the City College of New York (1949), M.A. from Brown University (1951)and Ph.D. from Harvard University (1958). He was the recipient of the Teaching Fellowship in Government and General Education, Harvard University (1952-6) and the Harvard Traveling Fellowship (summer, 1955), and served as Instructor in Government, Harvard Summer School, summers of 1957 and 1958) and as Instructor in Government, Smith College (1956-59). RADICALISM VERSUS REFORM IN BRITISH LABOUR: THE PREWAR DECADE was his dissertation and he has published studies and reviews in EXPLORATIONS IN ENTRE-PRENEURIAL BEHAVIOR, THE AMERICAN SOCIOLOGICAL REVIEW, and other scholarly journals.

New Nationalism, Colonialism and Pan-Movements

CHAPTER EIGHT

COLONIALISM AT THE CROSSROADS

WALLACE SOKOLSKY

New York University

In 1945, when asked what he thought future historians would consider to be the most important event of the twentieth century, Arnold Toynbee is reputed to have said that it would be the impact of European civilization upon the rest of the world and the reaction to that impact.

Anyone who has lived through the past fourteen years and followed world events with even a casual interest must have been struck by the almost bewildering variety of places calling for, fighting for, achieving and facing the problems of independence. It takes little genius to realize that we have witnessed a revolution of the first magnitude — the passing of European colonialism with its resultant shift in the world balance of power! Scarcely a day has passed without mention of Algeria, Indonesia, Indochina, Malaya, Kenya, Ghana, Cyprus, India, Iraq, Suez, Morocco, Nyasaland, etc. In fact, we have become surfeited with the names and problems. The consequent danger in our analysis of the issues involved is that observers, both laymen and serious students, have tended to get bogged down in the intricacies of special situations, losing sight of the forest, or have cavalierly dismissed complex events with bland platitudes. However much one's interest may at times be jaded by the sheer weight of rapidly moving political changes in the non-Western world, it is obviously pure folly for either the layman or those with professional interests in the social sciences to remain ignorant of these world-wide changes. To phrase Toynbee's "challenge and response" in a somewhat different manner, and quote H. G. Wells, it may still be a "race between education and catastrophe."

How can one put these kaleidoscopic events into perspective? Can one properly assess them at the present time? At the outset, let it be said that I am of the conviction that too many historians and political analysts are primarily modern antiquarians who survive by unnecessarily obfuscating and then "clarifying" issues. As this relates to questions of imperialism, I believe that, despite the myriad of events and their subtleties, it *is* possible to see the fundamental forces that bear on them in a reasonably meaningful context. Furthermore, we have arrived at a time when such evaluation is necessary. The following schema, making due allowance for limitations of space, has that aim.

HISTORICAL BACKGROUND

The "old colonial system" reared by England, France, Spain, Portugal and Holland as a consequence of their mercantile expansion during the sixteenth through the eighteenth centuries came to a symbolic end in 1776. Why go to the expense of securing colonies, thought the advocates of laissez faire, if they were only to gain their independence? Significantly enough, the trade of the new United States with Great Britain increased during the nineteenth century. Spokesmen of an anti-imperialist bent increasingly were able to persuade this most powerful of colonial and industrial nations that her future did not lie in possessing extensive domains. For almost a century such acquisitions of territory as were taken ran against the tide of British anti-imperialism.

During the decade of the 1870's, however, a renewed interest in imperialism burst forth into a "mad scramble" for overseas territories. Within two generations almost all of Africa was partitioned, China carved into spheres of influence and most of the rest of Asia and the Middle East placed under various forms of European control. Why? What caused the West to shoulder "the white man's burden"? (It is noteworthy that E. D. Morel titled a book of his THE BLACK MAN'S BURDEN.) Lenin's explanation and definition in his book IMPERIALISM (1916), that imperialism is the last stage of monopolistic, finance capitalism is much too facile a generalization. As a definition it leaves much to be desired in its arbitrariness. Adhering to it would mean that the investment of Swiss money in Holland would have to be defined as an imperial relationship. Lenin's view is as arbitrary as the "labor theory of value." But Seeley's observation that the British Empire was acquired in "a fit of absence of mind" is just as glib. The reasons for the revival of expansionism during the last quarter of the nineteenth century are complex and interwoven. Admittedly the

162

economic factors are extremely important, in many cases crucial. One wonders though, whether they could have or did operate as the prime determinants in all cases. And within the category of economic factors there is no conclusive evidence that investment overseas was more important than the desire for markets, raw materials or emigration. The inextricable tangle of jingoistic nationalism, missionary activity, search for strategic bases, diversion by politicians of discontent at home toward attention abroad, greater knowledge of tropical medicine, the search for adventure in exotic lands, the opening of the Suez Canal in 1869, the sense of cultural "mission," the pervasive influence of the Darwinian "survival of the fittest," and what George Kennan has called "contingent necessity" — or get there before others do — all these and others operated together to bring on the revival of imperialism. While E. M. Winslow in "THE PATTERN OF IM-PERIALISM" underplays the economic factor as a cause for this renewal and Joseph Schumpeter in "IMPERIALISM AND SOCIAL CLASSES[1] overplays the atavistic element in it, they correctly provide the necessary antidote to the exclusive economic interpretations. The hey-day of this modern imperialism continued, very roughly, down to World War I. It was the era of Rhodes, Chamberlain and Kipling, and one during which one did not apologize for being an imperialist.

The second stage of modern imperialism may be termed the period of anti-imperialism. Gathering momentum during the twentieth century, it reached a climax in the post-World War II world. Its process is too intricate to describe here, but symbolic highlights of the transition to independence include the following: the victory of the Japanese over the Russians in 1905, Woodrow Wilson's "self-determination" of peoples, the mandate system, the Bolshevik call for the overthrow of imperialism, India's struggle for self-rule under Gandhi's leadership, the British Statute of Westminster, the Atlantic Charter (which non-Western peoples took seriously), the defeat of France, Holland, England and the United States in the Pacific, and the attainment of independence by countries such as India, thus em-boldening others to strive for the same.

The roster of those countries gaining self-government since World War II includes: Indonesia, the Philippines, Korea, Indochina, Malaya, Burma, India, Pakistan, Ceylon, Syria, Lebanon, Jordan, Israel, Libya, the Sudan, Tunisia, Morocco, Guinea, Ghana, Cyprus, British West Indies. In 1960, Nigeria, Togoland, the Cameroons,

Somaliland and the Central African Federation are scheduled to get self-government. In addition, twelve French African "republics" have been formed with greater control over their destinies than they previously had. Under pressure of riots in the Congo, the Belgian King in 1959 announced the intention of granting self-government to the Congolese "in the future." In short, imperialism has been on the wane. Its last stronghold is in central and eastern Africa where it is increasingly under attack. Exulting in their new status, the Asians and Africans desire to keep their freedom despite the many pitfalls that some people in the West are only too anxious to note. The guiding spirit of revolution has been exemplified by Sun Yat-sen's "three principles": (1) drive out the foreign devils; (2) drive out the domestic devils; (3) people's livelihood. The latter, rather nebulous, has been claimed by Communists and moderate socialists.

As this phase of the West's expansion draws to a close (though imperialism continues to exist in Algeria and other parts of Africa and in the Guianas in Latin America) evaluations of its impact have poured forth.

CONFLICTING EVALUATIONS OF IMPERIALISM

Though there are still a few die-hards of the Colonel Blimp variety who think that Europe's rule is inherently justified, more numerous are the occasionally sophisticated rationalizations of present-day and past colonialism. They focus on the introduction of peace, good government, sanitation, hospitals, industrial products and the general influx of "civilization." They claim that the professed aim of their policy is one of "trusteeship" and self-government "when the colonies are ready for it." They point to the step-by-step progress toward self-government in places such as Ghana and India. Some actually have talked themselves into believing the sincerity of their sanctimonious pronouncements. In a statement at the Seventh Session of the United Nations on November 10, 1952 Belgian Minister of Foreign Affairs Van Zeeland said,

> I hope that no one in this Assembly will confuse colonialism as thus defined [the old exploitive type] with a different and indeed contrary activity, based on the highest motives and entirely consistent with the provisions of the Charter. In saying this I am thinking of the systematic exertions made by a highly developed people with the object of helping the backward indige-

nous peoples under its administration in their efforts towards political, economic, social and educational advancement. The Charter itself regards this action as a "sacred trust."[1]

What is not mentioned in the above is that steps in the direction of greater political self-rule in the Congo were not granted until *pressure* was exerted for them, and the economic gains of the Congolese were largely *tangential* to Belgian interests. The truth is that India was not "granted" independence in 1947. And it is a myth that passive resistance won freedom for India. The use of and the threat of the use of force more accurately explains why the Labour government withdrew in 1947. Making a *virtue of necessity*, the British with diplomatic skill have "given" self-government to their possessions. That is not to say that there were no benefits, economic, political and social bestowed upon the "backward" areas. Very real and substantial advances (in terms of Western culture) were made under the *Pax Britannica*. It would, nevertheless, be hypocritical to believe that the primary object of colonial policy has been its abdication. Undoubtedly many persons and groups within the colonizing countries have been sincerely concerned with the welfare of subject peoples. It is hard to doubt the sincerity of Professor Eric Walker when he says, "A lively sense of trusteeship makes it easier for a colonizing people to regard Colonials as ends in themselves and not as means to their own ends."[2] But the goals of these men have been "used" by other imperialists. Just as the Russian Communists when it suits their purposes may quote Lenin on the inevitability of conflict between capitalist and Communist worlds or Khrushchev on the possibility of peaceful coexistence, so too, when pressure for self-government mounts, do the apologists of imperialism refer to the liberal aims of some of their countrymen as their own. Their stand is analogous to those critics of the New Deal during the thirties who now praise the healthy state of American capitalism by pointing to its advances in social security, etc., policies they scarcely supported in the past.

Defenders of imperial control also justify their role by pointing to the possibility of chaos at their withdrawal. They cite the cases of Moslem-Hindu friction in 1947-8, of strongman rule in Pakistan and now in Burma and Indonesia and note the putting down of uprisings in the latter. They question the skill of these former colonials in governing themselves in today's modern world. In reply, the anti-imperials say that if the above is so, it is due to the delay in the

165

training of leaders and the populace for self-rule. They observe too that many European countries themselves have resorted to strongman government. While acknowledging that they are not paragons of democratic virtue, they claim that the best way to learn how to govern is to do so. As Prime Minister Kwame Nkrumah of Ghana puts it,

> We in Ghana believe—and in this we are in the happy company of most of the enlightened world—that the government which can do the most for the peoples of Africa is of the type which exercises complete and independent sovereignty over its territory, and which subscribes to the principles of democracy. This is so because the maximum welfare of any people can never be achieved unless they have the right to decide, in full freedom, the nature of their needs and how they can best be satisfied. The welfare of one people cannot be given in trust indefinitely to another people, no matter how benevolent the governing power may be. . . . The idea of freedom is so enshrined in the philosophy of the Western world that it is not even necessary to enlarge upon this. However, the champions of the western democracy very often fail to realize that the idea of democracy cannot be confined to themselves in their own states, but has to be a universal principle whose application must be consistent and worldwide.[3]

Still another reason offered for thinking twice about letting colonies go is the fear by some that they may turn to communism. In an article entitled "Colonial Problems in Perspective"[4] Stephan T. Possony attacks the "flimsy ideology of extreme anticolonialism." His article bristles with attacks on the movement toward self-government and by the intemperateness of his assertions invites a brief comment. "Anti-colonialism is the concern of small but noisy minorities, as are all radical political movements. Consequently, the democratic argument that government must rest on the consent of the governed does not seem to apply to the colonial problem."[5] And: "The Communists are making every effort to exploit the colonial problem to advance their world revolution, yet the deliberate dissolution of colonial structures, far from disproving Communist propaganda and crippling their political warfare operations, would actually strengthen the Communists and bring them closer to their world revolution."[6] Obsessed with the *idée fixe* that all the world's problems are caused by Communism, Possony says, "This one-sided 'anticolonialism' advances solutions which would—as they are deliberately designed to do—enhance Soviet power. Such policies are precisely the ones which the Communists want the democratic nations to adopt: the unilateral dismantling of Western positions of strength."[7] His incredible assumption that the West can be secure in areas where the populations are antagonistic to foreign control is amazing. Furthermore, Communism has *not* taken over most of the former colonies. The success of Ho Chih Minh in Indochina was precisely due to his being able to pose as the national champion against the French. Nasser is not a Communist and uses the Soviet as much as he is used. True, most of these states are socialistically oriented (at least in theory), but their foreign policy is opposed to *all* forms of colonial control. India, Ceylon, Pakistan, Ghana and others have been sufficiently impressed by the desirable aspects of Western rule to remain within the Commonwealth. Oddly enough, Possony and Lenin seem to agree that the ending of Western control will enhance the Communist position. Both, in my view are wrong. (Lenin's views will be examined later.) The charge that the withdrawal of Western control does not guarantee that the new or old domestic leadership will be enlightened may well be true. It would be foolish to gloss over it. One may take some comfort, though, in the thought that in recent years Latin-American countries have been moving away from palace-type revolutions. Given time these other underdeveloped areas probably will too.

Some defenders of empire paradoxically point to budding imperialisms of former colonies as a reason for resisting their independence. For example, it may well be that Nasser's aspirations to unite the Arab world would mask his desire for Sudanese territory and Iraq's oil. Surely the West has no monopoly on imperialism. The solution, however, is to oppose imperialism when it appears, not maintain another form of it. On still another basis do some defenders of the imperial connection take their stand. The technologically backward areas need the "mother" country for capital to develop themselves economically. As E. W. Evans puts it in the derisively titled THE BRITISH YOKE, ". . . The peoples of Europe can justify the economic crusade which they have successfully carried all the world over, partly by colonisation, but by many other methods as well, by a clearly demonstrable claim to have raised the general level of material well-being not only for themselves but for the peoples who have submitted to their economic initiative."[8] And: "If British self-interest first brought British rule to tropical Africa, African self-interest, judged by material standards, seems to demand its prolongation."[9] A discussion of economic questions will follow, but at this point, while certainly agreeing that there is a need for capital, the nationalists would say that political freedom gives them maneuverability in securing better terms. Independent Morocco is not necessarily tied to French capital.

Yet another criticism talked of by those wary of the new political freedom of technologically backward areas is that by the creation of new national entities they are furthering an anachronism. Nation-states, they say, are passé. The new nationalists answer that they have often been told that what they need technologically is not elaborate farm machinery but more rudimentary, intermediate-type tools. And similarly, they claim that until the world at large arrives at closer political compacts, they are justified in their nationalism.

By way of summary the opinions of Sir Alan Burns, a long-time colonial civil servant and member of the Trusteeship Council, may be cited:

> There is, however, a much wider and more insidious attack on British colonial policy, coupled with a defeatist attitude among some people in the United Kingdom who tend to accept as valid the condemnation of "colonialism." Such people have been led to believe that the possession of colonies is inherently wrong, and something to be ashamed of, and they credit all foreign critics with a sincere interest in the welfare of colonial peoples. They overlook the undoubted achievements of their country in the colonial field. They forget that in large areas of the world *Pax Britannica* established order where formerly there had been nothing but chaos. They ignore the slavery, the human sacrifices, the cannibalism, and the gross tyrannies which prevailed in various lands before these lands became British colonies or protectorates. They forget the former poverty and misery of peoples who today are gathering the fruits of British work in the development of natural resources and transport facilities, and of medical and educational advances. They do not appreciate the amount of patient work which has led to the establishment of democratic institutions in so many colonial territories. They fail to compare the conditions existing in neighboring independent countries. They refuse to recognize the danger of collapse into chaos if British control of dependent territories is too hastily removed.[10]

And:

> . . . these facts . . . should . . . justify our pride in the achievements of British colonial policy, which, with all its mistakes, has set a

168

high standard in the world. . . . Our policy as regards colonial territories has been clearly and repeatedly stated by representatives of successive governments, both Socialist and Conservative. It is to help the people of these territories to self-government and independence, and we can be trusted to implement this policy in the future as we have implemented it in the past.[11]

Further on he says,

"We should use our own judgment in the timing of constitutional advance in the colonies and ignore the advice, sometimes well-meaning and sometimes mischievous—but almost invariably ill-informed—of the nationals of other countries who do not share our responsibility."[12]

According to Sir Alan, " 'Colonialism,' in the form in which it is supposed to exist would indeed be an evil, but in fact it is sometimes very different from the bogey that has been built up in the world's imagination."[13]

While the main anti-colonialist attitudes have been cited above, it may be well to note their response to this stance. First, it is worthy of mention that there is a widely acknowledged recognition of the perhaps more beneficial rule of the British in comparison with other colonial powers. And, too, one may observe that Sir Alan Burns is representative of the more responsible type of colonial official. As seen by this school of thought, in the grand perspective of history, what we are witnessing is the Europeanization of the world, a process which they imply is inexorable. Centuries from now it is believed that one will no more blame the West for its expansion than one does the Arabs of the Middle Ages for theirs. This Hegelian-like view, seeing the mission of history in the Westernization of the world, is often speciously used as a rationalization for a multitude of sins. The anti-imperialist answers by saying that there is no more necessity for accepting imperialism in the process of industrialization than one has to accept war as the only method for securing technical advances. The two do not have to be in one package. And the anti-imperialist wants the right to separate the wheat from the chaff by himself.

THE LENINIST VIEW OF IMPERIALISM

How have the Marxists viewed imperialism? Lenin has provided the Communists with the source of most of their arguments on the

169

subject. His writings are still considered gospel, and the following definition is often quoted:

> If it were necessary to give the briefest possible definition of imperialism, it would be defined as the monopoly stage of capitalism. . . . Imperialism is capitalism in that phase of its development in which the domination of monopolies and finance-capital has established itself; in which the export of capitalism has acquired very great importance; in which the division of the world among the big international trusts has begun; in which the partition of all the territories of the earth amongst the great capitalist powers has been completed.[14]

This imperialism was "fully developed in the period 1898-1914."[15] The present era must be seen as one of conflict amongst the imperial powers which ultimately will lead to the break-up of empire and capitalism and the triumph of socialism. As the hoped-for and even expected world revolution did not result from the First World War, Lenin and his followers looked for the victory of world Communism in the undermining of the West's imperial structures. The back door to Europe lay in China. But this presupposed that capitalism *had* to become imperialistic or die. Lenin thought that the emergence of a rentier class that lived by cutting coupons from overseas investment indicated that the capitalistic nations were vitally dependent upon these investments for survival. Hence, the support given by the Leninists to the bourgeois, national liberation movements. As Demetrio Boersner, however, says of Marx and Engels in his THE BOLSHEVIKS AND THE NATIONAL AND COLONIAL QUESTION, (1917-28):

> The two founders of "scientific socialism" attached an immense importance to the struggles carried on by nations desirous of independence and consolidation. They considered national liberation and unification movements as expressions of the bourgeois revolution against feudalism and patriarchalism. Evaluating these bourgeois-national phenomena in a relativist and dialectical spirit, they never looked at them as ends in themselves, but merely as a passing historical phase which could—but need not necessarily—further the overall march of mankind toward socialism.[16]

So too does Lenin express his pragmatic approach to the national question:

> This state of affairs confronts the proletariat of Russia with a twofold or rather, a two-sided task: to combat all nationalism and,

above all, Great-Russian nationalism; to recognize not only complete equality of rights for all nations in general, but also equality of rights as regards statehood, i.e., the right of nations to self-determination, to secession. And at the same time, precisely in the interest of the successful struggle against the nationalism of all nations in any form, preserving the unity of the proletarian struggle and of the proletarian organizations, amalgamating these organizations into a closeknit international association, in spite of the bourgeois strivings for national segregation.

Complete equality of rights for all nations; the right of nations to self-determination; the amalgamation of the workers of all nations—this is the national program that Marxism, the experience of the whole world, and the experience of Russia, teaches the workers.[17]

In other words, Lenin's policy was one of permitting self-determination to take place so long as the workers themselves were in control and united their efforts.

In fact, though, while the imperial structures of the capitalist powers have fast declined, the economies of these Western powers have *not* collapsed as Lenin anticipated. In a "new deal" form they continue to exist. And if one retorts that much of the investment abroad continues if the political control does not, a counter-reply may be that there is no proof that these nations are anywhere as economically dependent upon overseas investments as Lenin stated. True the capitalists *desired* to increase their earnings by investing abroad. There is no proof that they were or are crucially dependent upon it. According to figures of the Department of Commerce as reported in the New York Times, private United States investments abroad at the end of 1957 totaled almost $37,000,000,000. Earnings on foreign investments rose to $3,700,000,000.[18] Of this, 33 per cent has gone to Canada, 35 per cent to Latin America, 16 per cent to Western Europe, and 16 per cent to Asia, the Middle East and Africa. As substantial as is the $3.7 billion, it still only constitutes a very small percentage of toal personal income in the United States, just a little over one per cent. This does not mean that trade as distinct from investment is not important to the American economy, but it does show that the glib assumption that the capitalistic, imperialistic countries would fall with the overthrow of imperialism was more of a hope of the Leninists than a complete actuality. While hurt financially and psychologically by the loss of colonies, the European countries have not embraced socialism. There is a distinct difference between having one's industry controlled by government and owned by government. The once-colonial powers' economies are regulated, and there is no reason to believe that this is merely a transitional stage to socialism and not an end in itself. The above thoughts are not to be construed as meaning that imperialism did not pay. It did, quite handsomely for some capitalists—and workers. But its importance has at times been exaggerated. Worthy of notice also is the fact that investment *in* the United States from overseas was almost equal to that sent to other countries. In any case, to assume that investment *per se* is exploitive is only a definition. Ironically, the Soviet Union, while charging less than the capitalist powers, does assess an interest rate of circa $2\frac{1}{2}$ per cent on its loans abroad. To say that its capital is "non-exploitive" pushes the question of the accumulation of capital far back into the nebulous reaches of history. The final irony is to be found in the report that in early 1959, Mikoyan is supposed to have invited some American capital to invest *in* the Soviet Union.

THE POST-COLONIAL ERA

If imperialism may be defined arbitrarily as political control of one country over another without the latter's consent (obviously this leaves much to be desired, but other definitions are even more lacking), then imperialism has passed through the two stages of entrenchment and decline. We have entered the period of post-colonialism. What questions remain? Aside from the basic questions of cultural change, urbanization, "racial" relations and which political system to adopt or retain, it would seem that the *key problem* facing these technologically backward, former colonies is how to get the capital to benefit from the potential fruits of modern industrialism. Many were misled into believing that the mere onset of freedom would bring forth a cornucopia of abundance. It was thought that poverty was solely due to past exploitation. But the intelligent and responsible leaders of the new nations know that poverty of resources, ignorance of technical know-how, lack of capital and archaic social systems were all hindrances to industrial advance. The dilemma they face is how to break out of the circle of poverty. As Gunnar Myrdal points out in RICH LANDS AND POOR there has been no closing of the gap in the postwar world between the underdeveloped and developed countries. In fact it is increasing. How can the circle be broken in the face of the simultaneous obstacles of:

172

(1) insufficiency of capital within the country; (2) rising populations; (3) a desire for heavy industry and consumer goods; (4) a desire for social welfare services; (5) a lack, in some cases, of economic resources; (6) a lack of trained personnel; (7) in some cases an outmoded feudal system; (8) tribal or racial conflict within the country? Is there any solution? Or must these countries follow the path of Communist China?

What sources of capital are available to them?

The International Bank for Reconstruction and Development (*World Bank*) as of June, 1958, had loans of $3.8 billion outstanding. Its main drawback is that its loans are made on sound banking principles precluding the situations of risk that exist in most areas. It is highly respected. The *Export-Import Bank* in its twenty-five years of existence, had by 1959 disbursed over $6.6 billion in loans. This quasi-U. S. Government organization has as its aim the stimulation of U. S. trade. Most of its loans have been to Latin America, and it too takes no unnecessary risks. The *United Nations Technical Assistance Administration* established in 1949 has done excellent work with its limited resources, having been limited to a budget of about $25 million a year. The United Nations *Special Fund* inaugurated on January 1 of this year will have a first-year budget of $26.8 million. In terms of the needs of the Asian, African and Latin-American countries, these latter sums are notably small. The Colombo Plan, established in 1950 for countries in Southeastern Asia and under British guidance, has provided for $3.5 billion in assistance, of which $3 billion has been provided by the United States from 1950 to 1957. As to United States aid under the successive agencies *"Point Four," Mutual Security Agency, Foreign Operations Administration* and *International Cooperation Administration,* it has been given in the form of grants and loans over the past decade to fifty-five lesser-developed countries and amounts to $16 billion. As of January 1, 1958, a *Development Loan Fund* has been in operation and committed to $570 million in loans in ten months of its existence.

Considering the deep and widespread needs of the technologically backward areas, though the above amounts plus British, French, Belgian and Dutch government grants and private investment have helped, there is a crying demand for vastly increased aid to enable these countries to do more than just patchwork. When members of the United States Congress annually think of paring the foreign aid budget, they ought to realize that the seemingly large amounts are trifling in terms of the benefits they bring to other lands and to the United States itself. Far from spending too much on foreign aid, the American people are spending too little really to get excited about. If one assumes that there will not be another major war, then the greatest challenge facing the West is how, with two strikes against it for the sins of past colonialism, it can help these former colonies to get the greatest assets of western civilization, namely, industrial skills and liberalism. What is called for is a dynamic new program of greatly increased aid, intelligently administered, which respects the new nations' sentiments. In turn, these countries have to understand that independence demands reciprocal concessions, and that in a nation-state world, the world does not "owe them a living." The Soviet Union knows full well that the stakes are high. Since 1954 its loans have totaled $1,728,000,000. If coexistence of sorts is the prospect for the foreseeable future, the main problem of foreign policy will be how to win the hearts of the vast third of the world as yet uncommitted. This can be done by treating people with respect and dignity and sympathy and assisting them financially. And if somehow a *modus vivendi* can be worked out that would permit disarmament to occur, the world might truly face an era of abundance that people previously thought of only in dreams.

We are indeed at a turning point in the history of modern imperialism!

August, 1959

SELECTED BIBLIOGRAPHY

Joseph S. Berliner, SOVIET ECONOMIC AID (New York: Frederick A. Praeger, Inc., 1958). A fine survey of the pertinent questions.

Demetrio Boersner, THE BOLSHEVIKS AND THE NATIONAL AND COLONIAL QUESTION (Geneva: Librairie E. Droz, 1957). Traces the ideas and policies of the Communists on these matters from 1917-28. Useful for the scholar.

Sir Alan Burns, IN DEFENCE OF COLONIES, (London: George Allen and Unwin, 1957). An apologia by a longtime civil servant of the Crown and author of works on Nigeria and the West Indies. An intelligent statement of the pro-colonial attitude.

Vera Micheles Dean, THE NATURE OF THE NON-WESTERN WORLD, (New York: Mentor Books, 1957). An excellent general introduction and survey of the problem. Thoughtful and stimulating. Well worth fifty cents.

Kumar Goshal, PEOPLE IN COLONIES (New York: Sheridan House, 1948). A survey of the history of the acquisition, control and prospects of colonies from the point of view of a determined anti-imperialist.

J. A. Hobson, IMPERIALISM (London: George Allen and Unwin, fourth impression, 1948). Classic statement by an anti-imperialist of a liberal persuasion; much admired by Lenin. First published in 1902.

Robert Strausz-Hupé and Harry W. Hazard, ed., THE IDEA OF COLONIALISM (New York: Frederick A. Praeger, Inc., 1958). A series of fifteen essays on various aspects of colonialism, some quite thoughtful and useful.

William L. Langer, THE DIPLOMACY OF IMPERIALISM. 1890-1902 (New York: Alfred A. Knopf, 1951). An excellent example of scholarship, written in 1935. Chapter III on the triumph of imperialism a thoughtful, brief survey of the causes of the renewal of imperialism.

Nikolai Lenin, IMPERIALISM (New York: The Vanguard Press, 1929). The indispensable statement of the Communist position. Written in 1916.

Rita Hinden, EMPIRE AND AFTER (London: Essential Books, Ltd., 1949). The Labourite view of the past and future of colonies written by a close student of the problems.

Max F. Millikan and W. W. Rostow, A PROPOSAL: KEY TO AN EFFECTIVE FOREIGN POLICY (New York: Harper and Brothers, 1957). A call for an increase in foreign aid by two professors of economics at M.I.T.

Parker T. Moon, IMPERIALISM AND WORLD POLITICS (New York: The Macmillan Company, 1926). The best over-all introduction and survey of the history of modern imperialism. Needs to be brought up to date by someone of great knowledge and fortitude.

Jawaharlal Nehru, INDEPENDENCE AND AFTER (New York: The John Day Company, 1950). A collection of speeches by the Indian Prime Minister and probably the foremost living symbol and spokesman of the anti-imperialist revolution. Charming and intelligent.

Joseph Schumpeter, IMPERIALISM AND SOCIAL CLASSES (New York: Meridian Books, 1955). An essay trying to show how the pre-capitalist elements of social life affected imperialism.

Eric A. Walker, COLONIES (Cambridge: Cambridge University Press, 1944). A wartime essay by an English professor discoursing on comparative colonial policies and speculating on the postwar situation.

E. M. Winslow, THE PATTERN OF IMPERIALISM (New York: Columbia University Press, 1948). The only study of the theories of imperialism in English. Useful. Overstates his case at times.

CURRICULUM VITAE

WALLACE SOKOLSKY, Intructor in History, New York University (1955-), was formerly Lecturer in History, City College of New York (1949-1957), and Sometime Lecturer, New School for Social Research; is the author of articles on "Empire," "The Algeciras Conference," and "The Truman Doctrine" for the forthcoming edition of the ENCYCLOPAEDIA BRITANNICA, and co-author of CONTEMPORARY CIVILIZATION (Chicago: Scott, Foresman & Co., 1959). For several years, he has conducted an elective history course entitled "Modern Imperialism" at the City College of New York and does so now at the New School for Social Research.

CHAPTER NINE

ZIONISM

SIDNEY J. KAPLAN and LEON ZOLONDEK

University of Kentucky

In 1948 the aspirations of world Zionism were largely realized. Israel as a modern political state came into being—an ideological tour de force whose roots extended deeply not only into the character of historical and contemporary Jewry but into the historical sweep of Eastern and Western civilizations as well.

From the time of their ancient appearance in the Middle East the attachment of the Jews for Palestine had profound religious significance. Following the Babylonian and Roman conquests this spiritual attachment took on even greater significance as the Jews gave continual expression to their longing for return to Palestine in lamentation, ritual and prayer. During generations of dispersion in Africa, Asia and Europe this hope for restoration helped to sustain them. And fostered by an intolerant and persecuting medieval Europe, the yearning for Palestine took on new meaning with the development of the modern nation-state.

At the end of the nineteenth century the movement known as Political Zionism emerged. Nurtured for centuries by religious yearning and Christian intolerance it took shape in the context of Western nationalism and a resurgent anti-Semitism. Inchoate, finding both support and opposition among Jews, the movement gathered momentum and was in the first few years of the twentieth century institutionalized through the efforts of a zealous and articulate leadership. From an idea involving a handful of zealous Jews having feeble financial backing, political Zionism expanded in fifty years to become a movement embracing much of world Jewry and a budget of millions of dollars.[1]

Is should be added however that Zionists have never represented world Jewry in any formal sense, although pretensions to that effect

177

have sometimes been made. Actually considerable Jewish opposition to Zionism developed, an opposition which still exists. But even though many Jews disclaim Zionist identification, being non-Zionists perhaps, only a small segment is anti-Zionist. Zionism for most Jews is not so much a matter of commitment to a systematic ideology as it is an expression of identity with Jewish history and religion, philanthropic endeavor, and a reaction to the mass extermination of Jews by the Nazis. Of the latter it may be said that more than any other force the annihilation of millions of Jews mobilized overwhelming support for Zionism as it concomitantly squelched the development of anti-Zionism among Jews.

Ideologically Zionism represents a system of beliefs which has elicited ardent commitment from a small collectivity of Jews as it has elicited sympathetic support from the bulk of Jews. Ardent commitment on the one hand has varied from formal affiliation with a Zionist organization to actual migration to Israel while on the other hand sympathetic support has varied from expressions of concern and identity to systematic philanthropic aid. Supporters, moreover, whether merely sympathetic or ideologically committed, have been drawn, with some few exceptions, from the full range of political, economic and religious spectrums.

In a very real sense Parson's characterization of an ideology is manifest in Zionism.[2] As a system of beliefs it has functioned to provide an evaluative integration for Jews by giving meaning to successive Jewish life-situations in terms of the historical circumstances through which Jews have passed and the goals to which they are oriented. The fact that many Jews do not subscribe to Zionism, finding an evaluative integration of their existence in some other belief system, is of small moment. Whether it is acknowledged or not, the bulk of world Jewry in lesser or greater degree has been affected by the historical continuity of Zionism and the creation of the state of Israel. What may be anticipated, now that the aims of political Zionism have been achieved, is a reassessment and recrystallization of the Zionist belief system in terms of contemporary and future world situations.

THE IDEOLOGICAL CONTINUITY OF ZIONISM

According to a well-known student of Zionism,

The essence of the Zionist idea, the re-establishment of the

Jews as a nation in Palestine, instinctively came into being immediately after the destruction of Judaea by the Romans. No sooner had the Jews lost their independence, which had lasted for over 1,200 years, than they began to pray for its revival. The belief in the restoration of Zion acquired the position of a cardinal principle of the Jewish faith and became an all-pervasive element in Jewish life.[3]

This characterization though adequate from the viewpoint of the political history of the Jews, is incomplete in that Zionism, with its attachment to Palestine, has an older history. Moreover, such a characterization restricted to the political and national aspects of Zionism would posit the end of the Zionist movement after the state of Israel came into being in 1948. That Zionism is still alive today would suggest that Cohen's definition of the "essence of the Zionist idea" is incomplete. A complete understanding of Zionism would necessitate a broader examination of the Zionist idea, an idea which is historically far older and ideologically far more comprehensive than that which is conveyed by either Cohen in his definition above or by the term "Zionist" coined in the nineteenth century.

According to the Bible, the relationship between the Jew and Palestine is derived from the covenant between God and Abraham:

> In the same day the Lord made a covenant with Abram, saying, Unto thy seed have I given this land, from the river of Egypt unto the great river, the river Euphrates.[4]

This covenant with Abraham is restated several times in the Bible; in Ezekial, for example, the following lines appear:

> Son of man, they that inhabit those wastes of the land of Israel speak, saying, Abraham was one, and he inherited the land: but we are many; the land is given us for inheritance.[5]

While the dates of the several books of the Bible are problematic, it seems likely that the above ideas expressed in the Bible are of an earlier date than the destruction of the second Temple in 70 A.D.

Similarly derivable from the Biblical period and expressed as well in the Talmudic era was the belief in the cosmological role of Israel, namely, that from "Zion shall go forth the law, and the word of the Lord from Jerusalem,"[6] and "from Zion was the beauty of the world perfected."[7] This viewpoint, it may be added, was also of earlier origin than the destruction of the second Temple.

Attaching to this cosmological viewpoint was the profound relationship of Israel to the Resurrection, conveyed, for example, by the following Talmudic words:

> There are those who will inherit the world to come, viz.: he who dwells in Eretz Yisrael; and he who brings up his sons to the study of the Torah. . . .[8]

> Whoever walks a distance of four cubits in the land of Israel is assured of a place in the world to come.[9]

Thus there was an anticipation that the Resurrection would take place in Palestine, some scholars making the claim that only those interred in the Holy Land would enjoy the future world. So intense was this belief that many devout Jews went so far as to arrange to have their bodies brought to Palestine to prevent the "Gilgul," that is, the mystical transmission of their corporeal remains to the Holy Land by transfer through the ground. In short, for the union of body and soul, the body had to be in the Holy Land.[10]

From the foregoing characterization of Biblical and Talmudic writings there may be abstracted three ideas which taken together provide a framework for understanding Zionism. This trilogy, if it may be termed such, consists of Zion, Israel and Torah, i.e., the land, the people and the "message." Each element of the trilogy is interrelated with the others and imbued as the Jews have viewed it with a special relationship to God. Zionism, then, if it is to be understood in its ideologically most comprehensive form must be appraised to terms of this trilogy of elements.

The pertinence of this ideological framework for an understanding of Zionism is further exhibited in the experience of medieval Jewry. The Jew, living in his segregated community, was isolated by the larger society in which he lived. As a consequence of the many political and social restrictions under which he maintained his day-to-day existence, he drew upon his traditional origins for spiritual as well as mundane sustenance. His main reservoir of psychological strength, his physical security being assured by Gentile sufferance or bribe, rested upon the belief that God was testing him preparatory to rewarding him for the torment of his earthly existence. This hope for a reward was expressed not only in eschatological terms but also in terms of a reconstituted Israel in the Holy Land.

> Take pity, Adonoi, our God on us
> and on Israel, thy folk

and on Jerusalem, thy city,
and on Mount Zion, thy Glory's habitation,
and on the grand and holy house,
over which thy name is called.[11]

And the kingship of the house of David, thine anointed,
return to its place
speedily in our days.[12]

Throughout the history of the medieval Jew the theme of "return" was constantly reaffirmed. This recurrent theme was sometimes expressed in terms of a desire for the re-establishment of the Davidic House, sometimes expressed in terms of a return of the body to the Holy Land, and sometimes and most generally expressed in a hope for a restoration of the proper harmonious relationship of the elements of Zion, Israel and Torah.

Even though the theme of return functioned mainly to provide a source of hope and sustenance for the historic Jew, it nonetheless added a latent motive power to the Zionistic ideology. Thus the concept of movement was deeply imbedded within the Zionist trilogy. Zionism, it may be argued, was never merely an ideal; only the proper circumstances were necessary for its practical expression.

That this theme of return was more than a religious ideal was exhibited time and again by the response made to various pseudo Messiahs during the medieval and early modern eras. Moreover, additional impetus to the Zionistic return was given by the influence of the Christian Millenarians in the seventeenth century who both ideologically and practically encouraged Zionistic aspirations.

In the nineteenth century the Zionist dream was given additional momentum by the rise of nationalism, the development and communication of ideas concerning personal liberty, the general social enlightenment attendant upon the industrial revolution, the emergence of utopian and socialistic ideas, philanthropic endeavor, and a resurgent anti-Semitism. All these factors played their part in molding the ideas expressed in the "classical" Zionist literature of the nineteenth century.

Among those who gave expression to Zionist aspirations in the nineteenth century was the orthodox leader at Thorn in East Prussia, Rabbi Zebi Hirsch Kalischer (1795-1874). A student of the Talmud and the Pentateuch, he provided a religious rationale for active participation in the return to Zion. In his influential work, THE QUEST OF ZION, Jewry with its latent aspiration for reconstitution in the

Holy Land received religious sanction for practical participation in the achievement of this hope.[13] Heretofore much of world Jewry believed that the return to the Holy Land would occur with the appearance of a Messiah, and as a consequence Zionism had not been an active or "practical" movement. But with Kalischer's reinterpretation of the mission of Israel, Zionism was divested of theological barriers to its practical attainment. Jews were urged to participate in their own redemption before the appearance of the Messiah. To realize this and the colonization of Palestine was called for by Kalischer.

In 1862 another contribution to classical Zionist literature was made with the publication of Moses Hess' ROME AND JERU-SALEM.[14] In this work Hess (1812-1875) offered a characterization of the Jewish situation and a recommendation for its solution, namely, a Jewish return to Palestine. Hess' appraisal of Zionism is of considerable sociological significance since it was a response to the revolutionary influences of the mid-nineteenth century and a reassertion of Hess' Jewish identification. Moreover it was a response to the aspirations of the assimilationists and believers in emancipation — ideas which were current in Western Europe, and particularly in Germany as expressed in the Mendelssohnian movement. Written in an era of nationalistic striving and the development of socialistic ideas, Hess' writings combine these two influences in his approach to the solution of the "Jewish Problem." Hess felt that the restoration of the Jewish homeland would not only solve the problem of Jewish rootlessness but would make possible as well the establishment of a society based upon a more humane socialistic ideal. Hess' assessment of the Jewish situation led him to maintain that the Jew was essentially rootless, and in European nations would be permanently estranged; that the Jew, historically indestructible, would never lose his group consciousness; and that personal and social fulfillment was only possible in an independent and Jewish Palestine. For the Jew, then, restoration of Zion was the only permanent solution to his anomalous social role.

Hess' analysis evoked little response. Hess' solution to the Jewish problem, confronted as it was by the momentum of emancipation, made no impress upon his intellectual contemporaries. For many Western Jews a solution to the Jewish problem lay in emancipation or assimilation rather than escape to some chimerical ideal. Moreover, it was felt by some that embracing the goal of return would compromise their own national loyalties and for that reason was inimical to their aspirations for complete acceptance in the Gentile world.

From the viewpoint of the trilogy of Zionism Hess' thought is significant in that it was focused chiefly on the return to Palestine although it combined Messianic elements as well. Hess' ideas, in short, embodied Zion, Israel and Torah. Furthermore it may be submitted that Hess' aspirations for the good society in Palestine fits well within the concept of Torah. Essentially though, Hess' statement was non-religious. His solution to the Jewish situation was primarily sociological.

Paralleling the Mendelssohnian movement of emancipation in Western Europe was the activity of the Haskalah (Enlightenment) movement[15] in Russia. Like their Western counterparts the leaders of the Haskalah rejected their traditional Judaic culture and sought to incorporate as fully as possible the culture of their Russian compatriots. This they felt would hasten emancipation and put them on an equal social footing with their non-Jewish brethren. The movement, eliciting enthusiastic response from the Jewish intelligentsia, made considerable progress when in the 1880's its momentum was checked by the pogroms following the assassination of Czar Alexander II. The terror of the pogroms disillusioned many intellectuals who had regarded the Haskalah as the answer to the problem of anti-Semitism. Made aware that they could not entrust their security to the humane impulses of non-Jewish political leaders, they sought for an answer elsewhere.

The pogroms led the former leaders of the Haskalah to seek another solution to the Jewish problem. The most compelling solution was offered by Dr. Leon Pinsker (1821-1891). This work, also one of the "classics" of Zionist literature, was entitled AUTO-EMANCIPA-TION.[16] Pinsker, who before 1882 was instrumental in propagating the emancipationist viewpoint in Russia, characterized the Jewish problem in terms of the Jewish lack of self-respect and the Judeophobia of the Gentiles. The odium Judaica, Pinsker asserted, would permanently persist and be manifest in the future, as in the past, by Gentile degradation of the Jew. Only by the development of a Jewish nationality, only by auto-emancipation by the Jews on a soil of their own, would this historical malady be cured.

Everywhere estranged, the Jew's presence was suffered by his non-Jewish countrymen. Even the effects of humanitarianism and emancipation would not elevate the Jew to a position of permanent respect. These were the conclusions drawn by Pinsker. And the only sound remedy for the Jew, Pinsker further maintained, was the creation of a Jewish center. If the Jews were ever to achieve permanent security they would have to have a land of their own. To achieve a homeland Pinsker recommended that a conference of distinguished Jews be held to implement his plans. In his recommendations — and in this regard he anticipated the World Zionist Congress established by Herzl — Pinsker proposed the establishment of several agencies to draw up plans for raising money, selecting a site for the homeland, and supporting Jewish resettlement.[17]

Hess' and Pinsker's ideas, it may be observed, were influenced by similar social conditions. National autonomy, a dominant European ideal was adopted as solution to anti-Semitism and the rootlessness of the "exile." Disillusionment with the results of assimilation and the failure of the Haskalah, and the continued persecution of the Jews led these former assimilationists to reaffirm, in different terms, two aspects of the trilogy of Zionism, namely, Zion, the land, and Israel, the people. Though writing in terms of the nineteenth century and deriving their rationale from contemporaneous experiences, their expression is but a reassertion of part of the basic trilogy rooted in the Biblical period.

Largely as a result of the disillusionment with the fruits of emancipation there developed in Russia, and subsequently expanded to other countries, a movement known as Hoveve Zion, "Lovers of Zion." This movement concerned with the revival of Jewish culture and the colonization of Palestine gave impetus to the organization of the BILU, a movement to settle Palestine with dedicated Pioneers.[18] Members of the BILU (House of David, Come Let Us Go) made their way to Palestine and after some feeble gropings established a small group at Rishon le Zion. Subsequently other pioneers settled elsewhere in Palestine, but unprepared for the rigors of pioneering effort, were largely ineffectual in their pioneering endeavors. Despite the apparent failure of the BILU, however, as Samuel puts it, it "was to modern Zionism what Wycliffe was to the reformation — a morning star which was eclipsed before the full flood of daylight washed over the horizon."[19]

Among those writers who were critical of the early colonization efforts in Palestine was Asher Ginsberg (1856-1927). Under his pen name of Ahad Ha-Am, Ginsberg became an articulate advocate of what has been known as "Cultural Zionism."[20] For Ahad Ha-Am the major problem was that of a spiritual and cultural renaissance of Judaism. While he acknowledged the desirability of a Jewish homeland he felt that it would be more feasible once Judaic culture was rejuvenated. His concern, then, while it did embrace the physical well-being of the Jew, transcended it, and focused on the development of a spiritual center which would serve as a fountainhead for worldwide Jewish influence. In short, Ahad Ha-Am reasserted the hope that "Out of Zion shall go forth the law and the word of the Lord from Jerusalem." In effect, the third element of the Zionist trilogy was reaffirmed, namely, Torah or "message." Though the substance of Ahad Ha-Am's Zionism may be variously interpreted, the important point is that the affirmation of the cultural content of Zionism led the contemporaneous Zionist movement back to its Judaic roots, and by so doing provided a broad philosophical rationale for its continued existence.

Thus, with Ahad Ha-Am's Cultural Zionism being joined to what may be termed Political Zionism, the trilogy of Zionism, though formulated in terms of the experiences of the nineteenth century, was reincorporated into Jewish history.

In 1896 new vigor was given the Zionist cause by Dr. Theodor Herzl (1860-1904). Herzl, an Austrian journalist, having little knowledge of the Zionist writers who had preceded him, and having limited contact with traditional Judaism, provided at one and the same time a coherent plan for the realization of a Jewish homeland and an intense, zealous leadership. Due largely to his efforts the varied strands of Zionism were drawn together and given effective international expression.

Herzl was drawn to the problem as a consequence of the growth of anti-Semitism in Austria and his experience with the Dreyfus case which he had observed in France. Having been raised in an assimilationist milieu, Herzl was disturbed by the persecution of Dreyfus and the anti-Semitism which echoed throughout France. That anti-Semitism could be manifest so openly in a liberal France was for Herzl an indication that nowhere would the Jew be secure.

Publishing his recommendations in DER JUDENSTAAT Herzl re-emphasized ideas which had been previously offered by Hess and Pinsker.[21] Again the assertion was made that the answer to the Jewish problem was the creation of a Jewish homeland. Herzl's contribution, however, lay in the fact that he elevated the Jewish problem to the international level. In his unceasing efforts to enlist the backing of world powers to grant the Jews autonomy in a land of their own, Herzl made Zionism a world issue. In this regard it is noteworthy that Herzl, like Pinsker, did not commit himself to a particular territory, but proposed both Argentina and Palestine, and later entertained the possibility of a territory in Eastern Africa.

Mustering international support among Jews, Herzl convened a Congress at Basle, Switzerland in 1897 which in addition to establishing the world Zionist Organization adopted a series of Zionist principles. These principles were enunciated in the following form:

> The aim of Zionism is to create for the Jewish people a home in Palestine secured by public law. The Congress contemplates the following means to the attainment of this end.
>
> 1. The promotion, on suitable lines, of the colonization of Palestine by Jewish agricultural and industrial workers.
>
> 2. The organization and binding together of the whole of Jewry by means of appropriate institutions, local and international, in accordance with the laws of each country.
>
> 3. The strengthening and fostering of Jewish national sentiment and consciousness.
>
> 4. Preparatory steps towards obtaining Government consent, where necessary, to the attainment of the aim of Zionism.[22]

The Basle Congress was a peak in Zionist history. Simultaneously, the centuries-old aspiration of a return to Zion was given formal utterance, and an agency — the world Zionist Organization — was established to achieve that aspiration. Thus was the Zionist ideology institutionalized.

In the years that followed, the Zionist Organization expanded. It established a bank, several agencies to purchase land in Palestine and settle colonists, and other administrative units to co-ordinate both Palestinian and various world-wide activities. Development, however, did not proceed smoothly. Dissension within the ranks of Zionists and opposition from non-Zionist and anti-Zionist Jews threatened the destruction of the Zionist movement.

The rivalry between the "Politicals" and the "Practicals," that is, those concerned with obtaining legal recognition immediately as opposed to those who urged that major efforts should be expended in colonization and developing Palestine, was finally resolved with the passage of time, ideological differences being ultimately breached with the development of what has been termed synthetic Zionism. Similiarly, heated controversy concerning the possibility of colonizing an area other than Palestine terminated with a rejection of such a possibility. The force of Jewish history was apparently too great to be denied and Palestine was affirmed as the only conceivable homeland.

On the international level there was continual Zionist effort concerning the enlisting of support for the Zionist cause. Herzl, and the Zionist leaders who followed him, particularly Chaim Weizmann (1874-1952), utilized every diplomatic means to obtain a legally constituted Jewish Palestine. All those sovereign powers who might have been of aid were turned to but it was not until 1917 that the international maneuvering of the Zionists bore fruit in the issuance of the Balfour Declaration.

For a variety of strategic and humanitarian reasons, some obscure, many controversial, the British Government, through the office of Arthur James Balfour, Secretary of State for Foreign Agairs, made known its official position on the matter of a Jewish Palestine. The Balfour Declaration, its full meaning to arouse endless debate later, was issued in the following form:

> His Majesty's Government view with favor the establishment in Palestine of a National Home for the Jewish People, and will use their best endeavors to facilitate the achievement of this object, it being clearly understood that nothing shall be done which may prejudice the civil and religious rights of existing non-Jewish communities in Palestine, or the rights and political status enjoyed by Jews in any other country.[23]

Despite the phrase "National Home" and its equivocal meaning, the Zionists were enthusiastic and anticipated the restitution, as they viewed it, of Zion under the aegis of a sympathetic British Government. Unfortunately for the Zionists, however, the Balfour Declaration had specified the safeguarding of the civil and religious rights of Palestinian non-Jews; moreover, the Jews were a small minority in Palestine. As a consequence of these very real factors, opposition to the Zionists developed among the Arabs of Palestine, an opposition that led in the following thirty years to riots, endless British reassessments, and finally to open suspicion and antagonism among all the parties concerned. Ultimately, with the ending of the Second World War, the antagonisms led to systematic strife and terrorism, all of this

187

culminating in the United Nations partition plan, the withdrawal of a hard-pressed and hapless Britain, a war between the Jews and Arabs, and the establishment of the state of Israel in 1948.

As Palestinian history unraveled, the context in which the above events were conditioned changed. The interwar period gave way to the holocaust of the Second World War, the extermination of millions of Jews by the Nazis, and the plight of thousands of Jewish refugees. In turn, the aftermath of the war gave rise to revolutionary and nationalistic strivings in Africa and Asia. And the Arabs, stirred also by world changes, sought for a more meaningful existence and identity in a revived nationalism. All of these factors conditioned the Zionist ideology, as it too, in Palestine and in the Diaspora, underwent its own peculiar changes.

Subsequent to the Balfour Declaration and the incorporation of its provisions in the British mandate over Palestine, the Zionist movement sought to enlist the aid of world-wide Jewry, particularly American Jewry, in its cause. To that end the Jewish Agency was expanded, despite the objection of fervent nationalistic Zionists, to include representatives from non-Zionist organizations.[24] Thus the Zionist movement was given a broader population and financial base.

Later with the onset of Nazism in Germany and the systematic annihilation of European Jews, Palestine as a place of refuge and a Jewish homeland took on an immediate meaning for world Jewry. Jews who had heretofore been antagonistic, indifferent, or merely sympathetic lent their support in increasing numbers. Their support was only to a limited extent an ideological commitment to Political Zionism; it arose rather out of their sense of Jewish identity and a profound concern for their European co-religionists. Thousands of Jews needed an immediate refuge. Palestine seemed to provide just such a refuge.

In 1942 the World War, the annihilation of millions of Jews, the problem of refugees, all serving as a backdrop, a conference of World Zionists and Zionist sympathizers was held at New York's Biltmore Hotel.[25] The deliberations of this conference led to the enunciation of several principles, the most significant declaring that Palestine be established as a Jewish state. Thus the quest for a Jewish home became, formally acknowledged and formally subscribed to, a quest for a Jewish state. Admittedly this was no change for committed Zionists. But the Biltmore program lent a new world-wide prestige to Zionist

188

aspirations. The goal of immediate statehood was given formal and unequivocal expression as it was simultaneously given unequivocal support by the bulk of world Jewry.

Six eventful years later Israel was established as a nation among other nations. The political goal of Zionism was achieved.

ZIONIST IDEOLOGY AFTER THE ESTABLISHMENT OF ISRAEL

Since 1948 Zionists around the world — Israel included — have engaged in prolonged soul-searching. With the establishment of Israel the compelling ideal of the Zionist movement disappeared. And similarly departed, at least for non-Israeli Zionists, are the agitation, fervor and dedication, all becoming attenuated with the founding of Israel.

The motive power of the Zionist ideology is not entirely diminished however. Israel is still in her early and problematic years of development. Internally there are economic, political and social problems yet to be solved. Externally a hostile Arab world surrounds them. Zionists outside of Israel will still make their contribution in the form of moral, political and finanical support. But that the tremendous Zionist apparatus outside of Israel can be sustained by these means is from the long-range point of view more than doubtful. Similarly, within Israel, problems once Zionistic are now Israeli. Energies previously devoted to Zionism, its ideology, its effectiveness as a movement, are now dedicated to the upbuilding of a new political state. In what sense, then, is Zionism a viable ideology now that Israel has been attained?

Three crucial questions emerge from this ideological dilemma. What meaning does Zionism have for Israelis? What meaning does Zionism have for Jews — Zionist and Zionist sympathizers — elsewhere in the world? And finally, what overarching meaning does Zionism hold in common for both Israelis and non-Israeli Jews?

The most realistic and certainly the most hard-headed viewpoint has been persuasively expressed by David Ben Gurion (1886-   ), the prime minister of Israel. For him, "classical Zionism," that is, that of the nineteenth century, is dead for both Israelis and Diaspora Zionists.

> When about eight years ago, the Jewish State was established, the whole of the Zionist ideology, as it took shape at the end of the nineteenth century and was fostered till the rise of the State, found the ground cut away from under its feet.[26]

189

Interpreted from within the framework of the nineteenth century, Zionist ideology is indeed dead. Few Zionists outside of Israel feel a "personal need" for a Jewish homeland. For these Zionists there is a homeland, namely, England, the United States, or wherever else they may be living. In what sense are these Jews inspired by the ideal of Return? Similarly for Zionists in Israel, the monumental task is that of developing a new nation under difficult conditions. In what sense would they, already in Zion, be nourished or inspired by the ideal of Return?

For Ben Gurion, Zionism if conceived broadly has, if it is to be viable at all, a twofold task, applicable to both Israel and the Diaspora. In the first place the ingathering of the Jews to Israel, insofar as it is possible, will be continued. "The Ingathering of the Exiles is both the precondition and the complementary process to our national and social redemption and liberation."[27] Secondly, Ben Gurion argues that there is need to heighten world-wide Jewish consciousness, a consciousness of identity based upon "the great spiritual heritage of the people, the common destiny that unites all parts of the Jewish people, and the vision of the redemption of Jewry and humanity."[28]

Ben Gurion, thus, addresses himself to all three parts of what in this paper has been termed the Zionist trilogy, Torah, or as Ben Gurion puts it, the Messianic vision, being currently the most significant element. Zion is obtained; the ingathering continues. The Messianic tradition, then, takes on pre-eminent importance as an ideal for Jewish fulfillment, an ideal partaking of the prophetic vision of "justice, fraternity, peace, and mercy."[29]

> Only the Messianic vision which is derived from the Bible, will implant in the hearts of our youth the consciousness in the historic partnership between them and the Diaspora, in spite of the wide gap of language, place, and atmosphere.[30]

Zionism, seen in terms of its historical continuity, is in this fashion made meaningful, both in and out of Israel. Like the "classical" writers of the nineteenth century Ben Gurion has rationalized Zionism for his contemporaries. As an ideologist and perhaps most significantly, as a political leader of a nation, Ben Gurion has drawn upon the Bible (as he also has upon his Socialistic background) for a new motive force to replace the motive force of the Return, the *élan vital* of the nineteenth-century ideologists. There still remains a return, but return not to Zion, but return rather to the "message of the prophets and their vision of the Latter Days"[31] as these are understood in terms of the contemporary social and political context. What Ben Gurion is doing, in effect, is endowing Zionism with a new, and yet old, *élan vital*.

The Messianic vision is not incompatible with the understanding of the realities of the Jewish and International scene; on the contrary it shapes and moulds the reality through powerful moral forces and bold pioneering creative efforts.[32]

But what of Zionism in the Diaspora? Doubtless as time goes on the program of world-wide Zionism will undergo changes as will some of its functions be taken over by other Jewish agencies. This in some measure has already taken place. Zionists in the Diaspora will continue to lend support of various kinds to Israel, particularly financial. Moreover, it may be anticipated that some Diaspora Zionists will go to Israel, a handful as emigrants, the bulk as tourists.

That the establishment of Israel will enhance a world-wide sense of Jewish consciousness may be taken for granted. But that Israel will become a spiritual and cultural fountainhead for the rejuvenation of world-wide Judaism is problematic. Indeed, given the weight of the Jews in the Diaspora, particularly those in the United States, it is entirely possible that the "fountainhead" will be nourished by the Diaspora. Acculturation, may it be observed, works both ways.

That there has been a revival of Jewishness and Judaism in the Diaspora as a consequence of Israel cannot be denied. But that this is due exclusively to Israel is questionable. The Diaspora, like Israel itself, has been caught up in the stream of Western civilization. If there has indeed been a spiritual revival among Jews it may be attributed also to the same forces which have apparently called up a spiritual resurgence in Christianity be they mid-century conservatism, world disenchantment, or a generalized fear engendered by the Atomic Age.

SELECTED BIBLIOGRAPHY

Elmer Berger, THE JEWISH DILEMMA (New York: The Devin-Adair Co., 1945). A vigorous statement by a protagonist of the American Council for Judaism who opposes Zionism as he affirms the desirability of emancipation and the integration of Jews in the countries in which they live.

191

Israel Cohen, A SHORT HISTORY OF ZIONISM (London: Frederic Muller Ltd., 1951). A concise yet comprehensive history of the Zionist movement by an active participant who for over fifty years was intimately connected with its development.

Abba Eban, VOICE OF ISRAEL (New York: Horizon Press, 1957). A series of speeches by the former Israeli Ambassador to the United States made to the U.N. and to Jewish organizations and educational institutions. Provides several very cogent assessments of contemporary Middle East problems from an Israeli viewpoint.

FORUM FOR THE PROBLEMS OF ZIONISM, WORLD JEWRY AND THE STATE OF ISRAEL (Jerusalem: World Zionist Organization, August, 1957). A symposium on the problems of world-wide Zionism. Provides a many-sided treatment of the role of Zionism in Israel and outside of Israel in the contemporary period.

Will Herberg, JUDAISM AND MODERN MAN (New York: Farrar Straus and Young, 1951). An assessment of the Biblical-rabbinic tradition of Judaism with commentary on its relationship to Zionism in which the author sees the development of Israel as running counter to divine purpose.

Theodor Herzl, THE JEWISH STATE, trans. by Sylvia D'Avigdor (New York: Scopus Publishing Co., 1943). One of the writings of Zionist "classical literature" by the "founder" of the world-wide Political Zionist movement. Presents one of the major rationales for a Jewish State.

Moses Hess, ROME AND JERUSALEM, trans. by Meyer Waxman (New York: Block Publishing Co., 1943). A Zionist nineteenth-century "classic." Provides a rationale for the development of a Jewish homeland deriving from Socialistic, Biblical and nationalistic sources.

Rufus Learsi, FULFILLMENT (Cleveland: World Publishing Co., 1951). Subtitled the "Epic Story of Zionism," it is a knowledgeable account of the development of Zionism. Concisely put, it is nonetheless comprehensive in its scope. Avowedly partisan in its presentation.

Alfred M. Lilienthal, WHAT PRICE ISRAEL (Chicago: Henry Regnery Company, 1953). A point of view in opposition to Zionism in which the author, an American Jew, discusses the problem of dual allegiance and the political background of the development of Israel.

Leon Pinsker, AUTO-EMANCIPATION, trans. by D. S. Blondheim (New York: Zionist Organization of America, 1944). One of the major Zionist writings. A discussion of the role of the Jew and the solution to his problem of world estrangement in the form of a Jewish homeland.

Frank C. Sakran, PALESTINE DILEMMA (Washington: Public Affairs Press, 1948). Written by a Christian Arab born in Palestine, it provides what the author regards as a well-rounded picture of the chief events leading to the development of Israel. Actually written from the Arab point of view.

Maurice Samuel, HARVEST IN THE DESERT (Philadelphia: The Jewish Publication Society of America, 1948). A rapturous and somewhat romantic account of the development of Israel by an essayist and novelist profoundly dedicated to the cause of Zionism.

Leon Simon (trans.), AHAD HA-AM (London: East and West Library, 1946). Essays, letters and memoirs of the exponent of "Cultural Zionism." A comprehensive selection of the writings of Asher Ginzberg setting forth his views on spiritual and cultural aspects of Judaism and Zionism.

Nahum Sokolow, HISTORY OF ZIONISM 1600-1918 (London: Longmans, Green and Co., 1919). A "classical" account of the evolution of Zionism up to the Balfour Declaration. Provides a wealth of information pertaining to the world-wide development and ramifications of the Zionist idea.

Alan R. Taylor, PRELUDE TO ISRAEL (New York: Philosophical Library, 1959). An analysis of Zionist diplomacy between 1897 and 1947. Ostensibly a "candid" and "objective" appraisal, it is actually a one-sided and questionable interpretation of the Zionist position.

CURRICULUM VITAE

SIDNEY J. KAPLAN, Assistant Professor of Sociology at the University of Kentucky, received his Ph.D. in 1953 at the State College of Washington. His major publications and research have been in the areas of collective behavior and criminology. During the early 1940's Dr. Kaplan was an active participant in the Zionist movement, being for two years president of the Boston chapter of Masada, a Zionist youth organization, and a representative to the New England Zionist Youth Commission.

LEON ZOLONDEK, Instructor of Semitics at the University of Kentucky, received his Ph.D. in Islamic Culture in 1957 at the University of Chicago. He was a Fulbright Fellow in Egypt, 1955-1956, and a Smith-Mundt Research Scholar at the University of Leiden in Holland, 1957. Dr. Zolondek is presently engaged in a study of the modern Islamic renaissance and its relationship to contemporary Judaism.

CHAPTER TEN

RACIAL THEORIES OF SOUTH AFRICA

Colin Rhys Lovell

*University of Southern
California*

The complex ethnic-cultural composition of the Union of South Africa is a natural breeding ground for racial theories. Only 21 per cent of its 14,200,000 population is white, or European, by South African terminology; although this figure represents the largest European settlement in any major political division of Africa. Another 9 per cent is of mixed ethnic strains, or Colored, including the Moslem Cape Malays of East Indian descent. Approximately 3 per cent of the population is Indian, about equally divided between Hindu and Islamic groups and concentrated in Natal, although there is also a bloc along the Rand in the Transvaal. The largest group, 67 per cent of the Union's population, is the Bantu, a term actually denoting a general language, not an ethnic group. Within this last element there are four major ethnic-cultural divisions and numerous subdivisions. Conventionally, but erroneously, termed "natives," in that they entered South Africa from the north at the same time the whites were penetrating from the south, the Bantu thus have wide variations in cultural and social levels.[1] For all of these people in their relations with other groups, and for their attitudes about their own group, there is the fact that all are descendants from immigrants into South Africa, which now they all know as their only home.

Until the twentieth century racial attitudes were largely pragmatic and rested on the obvious technological superiority of Europeans over non-whites with much lower living standards. Occasionally there crept into these pragmatic values the phrase, "Christian trusteeship," which implied a set of paternalistic attitudes by European toward non-Europeans, and caught up an elaborate complex of superior-subordinate relationships.

This easy pragmatism began to break down under the pressures generated by economic and social results produced by the rapid industrialization of South Africa after World War I, and particularly during and after World War II, which left the Union with a nearly self-sufficient economy, including a large secondary industry producing consumer goods on a mass production basis.

For Europeans these results have included an 80 per cent urbanization of their number, but also a large influx of Bantu into industry to swell the traditionally urban Colored and Indian communities.[2] These non-white elements have been obviously experiencing an increase of living standards by virtue of industrial employment and more consumer goods. Although few could be said to have reached European living standards as yet, the trend has been clearly pointing to a time when a large number of non-whites will be approaching the European level. There thus has arisen the question as to what position the white minority will then enjoy, and, whether, indeed, it will be able to maintain its group identity.

LITERAL APARTHEID

From these considerations, joined with the strong emotional connotations attached to previous South African racial attitudes, has come the theory of "apartheid." Literally meaning "separation," the word has received considerable elaboration since its appearance in the Afrikaans language in the late 1940's. On a theoretical level links can be seen between apartheid in its literal meaning and the rigid predestination of the strong Calvinism enunciated by the Synod of Dort in 1619 and carried by Dutch settlers to the Cape Colony in 1651. Three centuries later the Federal Council of the Dutch Reformed Church in South Africa, the largest of the three Afrikaans denominations in the Union,[3] has applied this seventeenth-century Calvinism to the modern state and the position of people within it. Through this statement of approval for apartheid runs the implication that divine will has favored some people more than others on this earth, although such earthly advantage has no relation with future eternal reward or punishment. However, divine arrangements are naturally beyond human question, and certainly human interference.[4] From here it is a very short distance to the view that men who are of the elect by divine will have the duty, and right, to govern others, albeit in a Christian manner.

The intimate connection between the Dutch Reformed Church

and Afrikaner nationalism makes the former's support of apartheid of real utility to the latter. However, as a theory apartheid has only a limited degree of superior-subordinate relationships implied within it. Instead, the theory emphasizes that within its particular region each people has full rights and that others have only those which the first group chooses to give them. This is to shift the theological view of Calvinism, although it still presupposes that the supreme interest of every ethnic group is its group cohesion and separateness.

These premises generate two arguments in favor of literal apartheid — physical, territorial separation of races — as the best policy for a multi-ethnic-cultural country such as South Africa; and these arguments have great appeal for certain intellectuals in their precision and their satisfaction of ethical sensibilities. The first is that the greater technological knowledge of the European community, its enormously larger capital resources, and its educational background give to the white person an unfair advantage in any competitive situation over the non-European, who is thus doomed to a perpetually inferior status, naturally galling to him and creating bitter resentments toward his white competitor. Therefore, equity and good race relations require the removal of this unfair advantage by removing Europeans and non-Europeans from each other into distinct areas so that the non-European may compete on equal terms with his fellows in every area of life, with the promise that he will rise to the highest level his abilities will carry him.[5]

From this first argument for literal apartheid flows the second, which tacitly presumes and accepts mutual hostility among racial groups. This view holds that in a mixed ethnic situation European fear of any evidence of improvement in status by non-Europeans will cause white resentment and a determination to keep non-whites at low socioeconomic levels, by whatever means, legal or illegal. Such an attitude by Europeans, say supporters of literal apartheid, is immoral and fraught with peril for both whites and non-whites. The only way to avoid the immorality and the danger, say proponents of literal apartheid, who thus assume the permanency of racial animosity, is to ensure the physical separation of non-Europeans from whites, who then will not resent, but will actively assist, their rise in the certainty that whites will not have to compete with them.[6]

These two arguments for literal apartheid have been urged as "official" policy in South Africa since the Nationalist victory in 1948,[7] and they have been elaborated by the South African Bureau of Racial Affairs (Suid-Afrikaanse Buro van Rasse Aangeleenthede), better known as SABRA. Although largely Afrikaner in membership and Nationalist in political orientation, with close connections with the Afrikaans cultural center of the University of Stellenbosch, SABRA welcomes membership from all interested persons. Among its founders in 1947 was Colonel Charles Frampton Stallard, leader of the strongly anti-Nationalist, "English" Dominion Party, but also, significantly, from Natal, with its heavy Bantu and Indian concentrations. SABRA does not claim to have originated the theory of apartheid, which is generally credited to Professor R. F. Hoernlé,[8] who proposed this solution to white—non-white relationships a full two years before the founding of SABRA.[9] SABRA, however, in its elaboration of the idea in its numerous publications, some of them giving extremely detailed plans, has always accepted his fundamental premise that continued Bantu-European economic contact, especially in an urban situation, could lead only to the ultimate disappearance of the white minority into the Bantu mass.[10] Probably it is concern for European group identity, typical of minority groups, which is the basic interest of SABRA, which thereby reflects the attitude of most South African whites.

In its official pronouncements on literal apartheid and its plans for their implementation, SABRA has not disguised the heavy sacrifices which they entail for Europeans. More of the limited arable land of the Union, much of it already in native reserves,[11] will have to go to the Bantu, who will no longer be available as labor in, and as consumers of, European industry. Some of the more zealous members of SABRA have toyed with the idea of an outright independent Bantu state, but most members do not support this "Bantustan" plan and instead presume ultimate European control of native life. Below this ultimate, however, their blueprints for apartheid call for large native direction of many aspects of life in these native territories, which will be closed to Europeans. Taken together, these SABRA plans fully support the society's warning that they call for sacrifice by Europeans, who will either accept such sacrifice or the alternative one of their own disappearance.

FUNCTIONAL APARTHEID

It is precisely at this point that literal apartheid clashes with the meaning of apartheid for most South African Europeans, who have strong emotions about it. When the average white speaks of apartheid, he has no reference to the literal sort, and instead makes the term embody the traditional attitudes of South African whites toward non-whites. This definition of apartheid might be called its functional one and was summed up neatly, if somewhat bluntly, by Prime Minister J. G. Strijdom in the 1955 Parliamentary session as "baaskap." Functional apartheid has clashed with literal apartheid from the first days of white settlement in South Africa in its demanding the presence among Europeans of non-Europeans to perform labor. Early Dutch settlers found Biblical support for this attitude in the curse of Ham.[12] Historically, however, this attitude is a product of forces typical of any frontier, except that in South Africa whites and non-whites were essentially competing immigrants. The victory of the whites left non-whites as their employees. Historically, every government in South Africa has tried to adhere to literal apartheid, only to have to accept the functional, frontier type by virtue of the monopoly of political life by Europeans.[13]

These attitudes of functional apartheid belong equally to the Afrikaner and English sections in South Africa. The earlier participation by Afrikaners in the frontier tradition caused them to accept its racial views first, but the later appearance by the English on the frontier produced the same racial attitudes among them. It is notable that those Afrikaners who remained in the Cape Colony after the Great Trek, and who were always a majority of that colony's white population, were willing to have a more liberal racial policy than were the other portions of South Africa. British Natal and the two Boer republics differed little in their attitudes toward non-whites.[14] The discovery of gold on the Rand made the Transvaal, with the functional apartheid of the frontier, the dominant portion of South Africa; and the association of the various colonies in the Union of South Africa after 1910 meant that this functional apartheid came to govern official policy, particularly in its industrial aspects.

All government attempts to set aside more land for exclusive native occupancy and use have encountered European opposition, from the futile Native Land Act of 1913[15] through the Native Trust Act of 1936[16] This last measure provided for systematic purchase by the government of European land for subsequent sole native use. Initially, purchases were fairly large, but the outbreak of World War II nearly

198

ended them. In contrast, the Mines and Works Act of 1926 guaranteed skilled and semi-skilled jobs as monopolies for Europeans[17] and was the product of the Nationalist (Afrikaner)-Labor (English) Pact Ministry, which had swept into power on the flood tide of white urban labor fury about the dabbling by the Smuts government in job equality,[18] a policy which had produced the violent Rand Rebellion of 1922.

Nearly all legislation of functional apartheid enacted since 1948 has antecedents prior to the Nationalist victory, and it is doubtful that were the opposition parties returned to power they would repeal, or even substantially modify, it. The United Party has racial attitudes resting squarely on functional apartheid. The Labor Party, with a nodding recognition toward a mild Fabian socialism, owes its birth and its being to its real principle of "good jobs for whites" — at European rates of pay. In view of general European attitudes, for these parties to hold any other views would be political suicide.

The vast majority of Europeans see little reason why they should accept literal apartheid, and even less reason for dropping their traditional racial views. Beyond the strong emotions contained in these views, there is the argument that although a numerical minority, Europeans are the vast majority in terms of education, professional training, capital investment, and industrial development. Europeans regard themselves as the reason for the three-century advance of South Africa to the position of being the most advanced country on the continent. They point out that if they are not indigenous to the country, neither are any of the non-whites, who have no longer rights of possession than Europeans, and in the case of the Indians considerably less. European industry may depend upon non-white labor, but equally, only European capital and technology have offered an opportunity for industrial employment to non-whites, and so their resultant rise in living standard. The few non-whites who have raised themselves to European levels loom so large that they obscure the vast mass of non-Europeans, particularly the Bantu, who remain far below European standards and retain cultures at complete variance with European values and with aspects of them often repellent to civilized peoples.

It is thus easy for these Europeans to argue that the failure of non-Europeans to adopt European ways of life and manner of thinking, even after coming into contact with modern technology and industry, and despite heroic efforts by missionaries and government to have them change their basic values,[19] is proof of their inherent racial inferiority. Thus, concludes the argument or functional apartheid, although Europeans have the solemn duty of treating non-whites justly, they owe them no obligation to treat them as equals and that to do so would mean the destruction of modern South Africa, and even of these non-Europeans, who would be hurled back into barbarism without the whites, either by virtue of the latter's departure or of their disappearance into the mass of non-whites.

THE CLASH OF APARTHEIDS

The Union government since 1948, even while making literal apartheid its official policy, in terms of the source of its votes, like all Union governments has had to honor functional apartheid. Supporters of the literal sort have not been happy about the choice and argue that the facts indicate the steady *rise* of non-whites toward, and inevitably to, the European level. At this point there will be the time of terrible retribution for Europeans who have vainly been seeking to thwart that rise.

Much of the legislation since 1948 has been admittedly illiberal and even repressive. Although such measures voice conventional white attitudes, the question inevitably arises as to why these attitudes require statutory reinforcement. The most outstanding examples of such legislative expressions of white racial opinion are the Mixed Marriages Act of 1949[20] and the Immorality Act of the next year,[21] the latter strengthening similar legislation of 1927.[22] These laws forbid, under heavy penalties, sexual contacts between Europeans and non-whites, either within or outside of marriage. The stern disapproval by white South Africans of miscegenation thus receives reflection in these acts, but their very presence seems to indicate that social disapproval alone is insufficient to prevent such contacts.[23]

Although the Nationalists naturally reflect the general racial views of white South Africans, they rely less upon apartheid of either type to maintain themselves in power, than upon their appeal to the powerful emotion of Afrikaner solidarity. Nationalist identification with this desire has paid increasing political dividends in three successive elections, although enough Afrikaners identify themselves with the English so that on the all-Union level the opposition parties together have a slight popular majority.[24] Within constituencies Nationalist success in identification of the party with Afrikanerism has permitted the party to ignore the elaborate plans of SABRA for true apartheid; and it must be admitted that any serious effort by the government to implement these plans to any extent would alienate its supporters.

Initially, SABRA had hopes for such an implementation. In 1948 one of its charter members, Dr. Ernest George Jansen, sometime Minister of Native Affairs, again assumed this post. Simultaneously, Professor Werner Eiselen, another founder and the son of a Dutch Reformed missionary, became permanent Secretary of the department.[25] Two years later upon Jansen's appointment as Governor-General, another charter member, Dr. Henrik Verwoerd, succeeded him as Minister; and in 1958 Verwoerd became Prime Minister.

SABRA has thus had important links into the government, and all of them, but especially Eiselen and Verwoerd, at one time spoke favorably for true apartheid and launched large welfare schemes for Bantu development. At the opening of his tenure, Eiselen declared that once there was territorial separation, non-Europeans would have "complete development in every sphere and will be able to develop their own institutions and social services whereby the forces of the progressive non-Europeans can be harnessed for their own national development."[26] By 1954, however, he had shifted ground to declare that the Bible taught the basic inequality of peoples.[27] Behind the shift lay the inexorable facts of South African politics as the monopoly of Europeans except for a small and ineffectual representation by Europeans of non-whites in Parliament.[28] Nationalist supporters could see only limited utility in large welfare and educational plans for Bantu, when their cost was to be met from tax revenues, overwhelmingly paid by whites. Critics of Nationalist policy denounced these schemes as frauds.

Both sides thus turned on the Bantu Education Act of 1953,[29] which transferred elementary native education from either public or private (usually missionary) auspices to the Department of Native Affairs, which received broad control over the curriculum. The immediate direction of native education, however, would be by locally elected Bantu school boards. Critics of the law, which included leaders of churches other than those of the Dutch Reformed Church, which supported the act, denounced it as a plan to give Bantu inferior education and to condition them to accept an inferior status. Defenders of the law said that it would increase the already high per capita figure for Bantu education[30] and make the Bantu responsible for their own development. During the passage of the measure Verwoerd's remarks about the "wrong kind" of education for natives lent weight to the criticisms, but the actual curriculum drafted by the Department of Native Affairs received the endorsement of the South African Institute of Race Relations (SAIRR), older and more liberal than SABRA.[31]

SABRA, meanwhile, had to accept a middle type of apartheid in the Group Areas Act of 1950,[32] in turn resting on a law of 1923,[33] which aimed at residential racial segregation in urban areas. The actual operation of the law proved too expensive for any consistent application of it. Simultaneously, the Population Registration Act,[34] requiring all persons to carry identity cards indicating their race, seemed to indicate further segregation in this manner, but not true territorial apartheid.

THE TOMLINSON REPORT

SABRA idealists, concerned about the apparent government policy of keeping natives permanently in urban-industrial areas, emphasized that such a policy was not true apartheid and would end only in the ruin of Europeans. Pressure by these idealists and concern by other whites that government policy was not solving racial problems, but if anything was exacerbating them, resulted in the appointment of a commission in 1952 "to conduct an exhaustive inquiry into and to report on a comprehensive scheme for the rehabilitation of the Native Areas with a view to developing within them a social structure in keeping with the culture of the Natives and based on effective socio-economic planning."[35] Although this was to ignore the Indian and Colored groups, the commission began its work under the chairmanship of Professor F. R. Tomlinson of the University of Pretoria, who gave his name to the commission and its subsequent report. The commission was largely Afrikaner and generally sympathetic to SABRA attitudes. After two years of intensive work and receiving masses of evidence, the commission reported in October, 1954. The government delayed a year before publishing the report, and then only in abridged form on the grounds of the expense of printing the full version.[36]

Discussion of this abridged report came against the background of the statement by Prime Minister Strijdom early in the 1956 Parliamentary session that the government recognized full racial separation as a noble ideal, toward which all efforts should ever be directed — but impossible of complete achievement. The Tomlinson Report admitted the same thing. After considering all possible additions to the Bantu territories, and the fullest possible development of these enlarged regions over a twenty-five to thirty year period, the commission found that they could not take care of more than 8,000,000 natives, leaving 2,000,000 still in European areas. The threat by the commission that without such planned development, there would be 17,000,000 Bantu in European territories[37] did not soften the fact that total separation was impossible.

The report did not hide the fact that even this incomplete separation of Bantu and Europeans would require heavy expenditures, largely from European taxes. The cost for the first ten years of native territorial development would be £104,000,000, with a subsequent tapering off as the enlarged native territories became more economically self-sufficient. The repetition in the report of the Hoernlé forecast that anything less would mean the eventual submergence of whites into a black sea[38] did not move Europeans, when they considered the implications for their industry in the commission's recommendation for the development of secondary industry in the native territories. Finally, there was the opinion of Tomlinson, himself, that even assuming the full implementation of the commission's report (which did not include this opinion), by the year 2000 an entirely new approach to the Bantu problem would be demanded.[39]

With these facts of the report, no major South African party, dependent upon white votes, could make its findings into a party platform. The report, the result of two years hard work, received three days of perfunctory debate in the 1956 session of Parliament, and then went to gather dust alongside the many previous ones on native affairs.

With the debacle of the Tomlinson report, the government has operated more frankly in terms of traditional functional apartheid. This policy, in response to traditional white attitudes, at first glance seems to serve the interests of Europeans well. A closer analysis raises large questions about the utility to whites of functional apartheid as operating since 1948.

THE RESULTS OF FUNCTIONAL APARTHEID

Of the various ethnic groups in the Union, the one which has benefitted the most from government policy of the past decade has been the Bantu. Despite repressive legislation, none of it of direct concern to the mass of natives, government activity has meant an increase in the material standard of living for Bantu, particularly the large number engaged in industry. Although the government is not happy about their presence there and has thrown out hints about removing some from urban factories, or at least not permitting any more to enter industrial work, the facts of an expanding South African industrial plan and its need for consumers demand Bantu industrial workers. Government welfare schemes for urban natives, although admittedly incomplete, have vastly improved health and sanitation for Bantu. Under the Bantu Education Act, the next generation of natives will be completely literate. In addition, a severe shortage of white labor has meant that Bantu are performing semi-skilled industrial labor in defiance of the formal law.

Few benefits have come from functional apartheid to the Indian minority, disliked by other ethnic groups in the Union. The government has been frank in its desire to see Indians take advantage of a plan of 1927, whereby the Union pays Indians to emigrate to India, and has increased the bonus rate. The intervention by the Republic of India on behalf of South African Indians has heightened this desire. Such Indian "repatriation," however, is unlikely in that the Indians in South Africa are at least third generation, and the few who have gone to India have made great efforts to return to the Union with its better living conditions.

Definitely hurt by the application of functional apartheid has been the Colored population. Living in a European manner, usually with Afrikaans as a home language, this group prior to 1956 had nearly the same political rights as Europeans in the Cape Province, in whose Western portion most were concentrated. It was the hope of the Nationalist leader, General J. B. M. Hertzog, Prime Minister from 1924 to 1939, that this political status could be extended to the few Colored people in the other three provinces. This hope proved illusory against the attitudes of frontier apartheid, and since 1948 the government has moved in the opposite direction to make Coloreds a separate legal community. As part of this policy Cape Colored men were removed from the general to a separate election register for the purpose of communal representation (by Europeans) in Parliament. The effort succeeded in 1956 after producing the most serious and continuous constitutional crisis in the Union's history, from 1951 to 1956. In the course of the crisis there was brought into question the status of

Parliament, the issue of judicial review of its legation; the appellate court was enlarged, and finally the Senate was nearly doubled and the method of its election changed so that the ministry could get the legislation passed by a two-thirds majority of the membership of a joint session of Parliament, as required by the constitution and insisted upon by the courts.[40]

Perhaps more serious to individual Colored persons has been the actual operation of the Population Registration Act, which has permitted local boards, with no special qualifications, to reclassify Coloreds as natives, with resultant lower standards of living. Such reclassifications have divided members of the same family and have resulted in deep individual tragedies.

But by far the most seriously injured by the devices of functional apartheid has been the European minority, itself divided in a 60-40 ratio between Afrikaners and English. Neither of these groups has a tradition of political authoritarianism, although Afrikaners generally prefer the presidential, and the English the parliamentary expression of representative government. However, both groups in their anxiety about the position of the white minority have accepted legal devices to control and even to stifle dissident opinion among non-whites, only to discover that these devices are capable of application within the European community. Initially, this extension of illiberal laws to white persons has been to the obviously extreme critics of government racial policy, but there are signs that milder critics are feeling at least the threat of these techniques.

The best example of such an extension has been the treason trials, in progress since 1957, in which the government has sought — so far unsuccessfully — to broaden the definition of treason to dangerous lengths.

The Suppression of Communism Act,[41] dissolving the feckless party of that name, gives the Minister of Justice wide powers to order individuals to give up offices in organizations and to restrict their freedom of movement. The vague terminology of the act would also seem to give him considerable control over the press. Although passed to deal with Communism among the non-white majority, the most prominent persons dealt with under the law have been Europeans. Most Europeans are not happy about these ministerial powers, but accept them as unfortunate necessities in the South African situation.

The considerations underlie government censorship, and white acceptance of it, of movies and books. Since all non-Europeans can see the former and will soon be able to read the latter — with many already capable of doing so—the "wrong" kind of movies and books are "dangerous" for non-whites, so that Europeans must also forego them.

Much more serious, however, for the European minority in its long-term effects is the demonstrated capacity of apartheid as a theory to become ever more refined in application. Its initial stage of simple differentiation between white and non-white has passed, and the sense of "difference" is now being applied between the two sections of the white minority, who at best have only a tradition of uneasy co-operation, and at worst one of active suspicion and hostility. Apartheid as applied within the European group has pressed its two sections ever further away from each other since 1948. The last decade has seen a strong Afrikanerism, which, despite official denials, does not hide too well its desire to eradicate, or at least dominate, the English and English ideas. The draft constitution for a republic in 1940 frankly had this aim, and among its signers were all the Prime Ministers of the Union since 1948. Although since that date official Nationalist pronouncements have deprecated the idea of any English subordination, still less ejection, the all-Afrikaner character of ministries since 1948 and their personnel links into strong Afrikaans cultural and business organizations have not eased English fears. Each of the white groups increasingly is aiming at group self-sufficiency for itself in language, intellectual values, business, banking and industry.[42] Each group tends to regard those of its members who do reach toward members of the other side as "disloyal."

The government has assisted this trend toward isolation between the two white groups by requiring separate Afrikaans and English medium schools below the university level, with parents required to send their children to the school with the medium used in the home.[43] Although the other language is taught in these separate medium schools, it is increasingly as a "foreign" language. Students continuing into university work invariably attend an Afrikaans or an English one depending upon which type of elementary school they attended. Although such educational separation is to Nationalist political advantage, it denies to the European sections knowledge and understanding of each other. If this fragmentation of the European minority, the only place where literal apartheid is actually operative, continues, it

206

could, however impossible it might seem, drive the losers in this inter-necine white struggle over to the leadership of the non-white majority.

THE DISSENTERS

The serious results of apartheid of either type in their ultimate have caused a small segment of Europeans to diverge sharply from traditional white racial attitudes. This group has been influential in the South African Institute of Race Relations, whose existence was one reason for the establishment of SABRA as a counterpoise to its "libera-listic" tendencies. After the 1953 elections these people left the United Party in protest against its racial attitudes, differing little from those of their victorious Nationalist opponents, to form the Liberal Party.

Essentially, the Liberal Party, whose most prominent members have an Afrikaner background,[44] urges a return to the old Cape Colony tradition, expressed by Cecil Rhodes as being "equal rights for all civilized men." The few Liberals point out that even with the severity of legislation supporting functional apartheid (the Liberals dismissing the literal type as impossible in South Africa), non-Europeans are rising in economic status and technical knowledge toward equality with Europeans, who will then reap the reward of their present racial attitudes. Meanwhile, whites are accepting limitations upon their intellectual horizons and industrial expansion out of support for a functional apartheid, which in the end will only destroy them.

Liberals thus call for a complete reversal of South African white attitudes on race in urging that the full political and civil rights of Europeans be given to civilized non-Europeans. The party's program calls for the repeal of all laws denying such rights, many of them antedating the Nationalist accession to power in 1948.[45] The Liberal Party, however, has found it difficult to determine criteria for civiliza-tion, and significantly, does not represent a single European constitu-ency in Parliament. The strong probability of the abolition in the near future of Bantu Parliamentary representation (by Europeans) will leave the Liberal Party without Parliamentary means of expres-sion.[46]

Nevertheless, there have been signs recently of a slight shift in general European attitudes, albeit in a very halting manner, toward the Liberal position. Although this shift as yet is not on the level of political action, should it continue, it would inevitably move to this level. The intervention by India at the UN on behalf of South African

Indians was bitterly resented by all whites, and was thus of actual benefit to the government, particularly since it was ineffective. The fact of such intervention, however, makes the emergence of African national states of deep significance to the South African white minority. In startling departure from the previous orientation of the Dutch Reformed Church, the retired head of the Stellenbosch Seminary, which supplies most of its clergy, has declared the illogicality and immorality of a color test as the criterion for civilization. The government's plan to require apartheid in public worship (where it has generally existed) in 1957 produced not only the expected objections from "English" churches — which was of no concern to the government — but also the unexpected opposition of the Dutch Reformed Church — which was of deep concern to the ministry. The objections by the latter that the proposed legislation struck at the independence of the Church caused the government to modify the bill considerably before its enactment.

Perhaps even more startling was the statement by the Secretary of SABRA, and its real force, Professor N. J. J. Olivier of Stellenbosch, at its 1958 meeting to the effect that some bridge had to be found between Europeans and non-Europeans, and that to this end there should be joint meetings between SABRA and Bantu leaders. Although this proposal did not open the society's membership to natives, and the meeting took no formal action on the suggestion, it elicited sympathetic interest[47] and was the more significant for its being made even as the government was planning legislation forbidding all interracial meetings. Prime Minister Verwoerd almost immediately resigned from SABRA, but his son remained a member with his approval.

These scattered events and personalities are insufficient to support a statement that Europeans as a whole are making a reappraisal of their traditional racial attitudes. But should these isolated opinions begin to coalesce, they might create a climate of opinion conducive to such a reappraisal.

SELECTED BIBLIOGRAPHY

The amount of material on racial theories and policies in South Africa is enormous so that no more than representative selections of the various views are presented here. Because of the nature of most readers of this volume, only English items are listed here. However, a full understanding of racial attitudes and issues in the Union requires the reading of the numerous Afrikaans works on these subjects.

African National Congress and South African Indian Congress, DISABILITIES OF NON-WHITE PEOPLES OF SOUTH AFRICA (Johannesburg: Joint Congresses, 1952). Listing of various discriminatory legislation and administrative regulations.

Edgar H. Brookes and J. B. Macaulay, CIVIL LIBERTIES IN SOUTH AFRICA (Cape Town: Oxford Univ. Press, 1958). Native affairs expert and barrister join in discussing wide powers of government over individual.

G. H. Calpin, THERE ARE NO SOUTH AFRICANS (London: Thomas Nelson and Sons, 1941). Emphasizes separate group loyalties in Union.

Gwendolen M. Carter, THE POLITICS OF INEQUALITY (New York: Praeger, 1958). Excellent discussion of theory and operation of apartheid since 1948.

L. J. du Plessis, PROBLEMS OF RACE AND NATIONALITY IN SOUTH AFRICA (London: Diplomatic Press, 1949). Stresses multiplicity of cultural values and loyalties.

United Party, PROGRAM AND PRINCIPLES OF THE UNITED SOUTH AFRICAN NATIONAL PARTY (Johannesburg: United Party, 1946). Reveals haziness by party on racial matters.

Eric A. Walker, A HISTORY OF SOUTHERN AFRICA (London: Longmans, Green and Co., 1957). Far and away the best general history of South Africa, with a wealth of information.

Quintin Whyte, THE SOUTH AFRICAN INSTITUTE OF RACE RELATION'S APPROACH TO RACIAL PROBLEMS (Johannesburg: South African Institute of Race Relations, 1952). Both an apologia for the Institute and a plea for a more liberal racial policy by the former director of the Institute.

Wentzel du Plessis, HIGHWAY TO HARMONY (New York: Union of South Africa Government Information Office, 1958). Ambassadorial explanation of apartheid in glowing terms.

D. D. T. Jabavu, NATIVE DISABILITIES IN SOUTH AFRICA (Lovedale, Cape Province: Lovedale Press, 1932). Bitter account by Bantu intellectual.

G. H. Hiemstrow, THE GROUP AREAS ACT (Cape Town: Juta, 1953), Critical account of theory and operation of urban segregation.

A. W. Hoernlé, REPORT ON WORKING OF BANTU EDUCATION ACT (Johannesburg: South African Institute of Race Relations, 1955). Favorable report from unlikely source.

R. F. Hoernle, SOUTH AFRICAN NATIVE POLICY AND THE LIBERAL SPIRIT (Johannesburg: Witwatersrand University Press, 1945). Suggested source of idea of territorial apartheid, proposed here as a measure to reduce European illiberal attitudes.

Labour Party, NON-EUROPEAN POLICY OF THE LABOUR PARTY (Johannesburg: South African Labour Party, 1946). Reveals basic concern with having only whites in skilled work.

209

Liberal Party, THE POLICIES OF THE LIBERAL PARTY OF SOUTH AFRICA (Rondebosch: South African Liberal Party, 1955). Calls for complete reversal of recent South African policy.

I. D. MacCrone, RACE ATTITUDES IN SOUTH AFRICA (London: Oxford University Press, 1937). Excellent historical and psychological treatment.

Johannes S. Marais, THE CAPE COLOURED PEOPLE (Johannesburg: Witwatersrand University Press, 1939; reprinted 1956). Best account of this South African ethnic group.

Leo Marquard, THE PEOPLES AND POLICIES OF SOUTH AFRICA (London: Oxford University Press, 1952). Excellent brief analysis of racial issues in the Union.

National Party, DR. MALAN'S POLICY FOR SOUTH AFRICA'S MIXED POPULATION (No place: National Party of South Africa, 1948). Leader of National Party and subsequently Prime Minister formally adopts literal apartheid as party policy in this 1948 election pamphlet.

L. E. Neame, WHITE MAN'S AFRICA: THE PROBLEM OF A WHITE NATION IN A BLACK CONTINENT (Cape Town: Stewart, 1952). Moderate account by journalist of practical problems for South African Europeans in race relations.

N. J. J. Olivier, APARTHEID — A SLOGAN OR A SOLUTION (Stellenbosch: South African Bureau for Racial Affairs, 1954). Best brief explanation of apartheid by the real force in the organization urging this solution.

SUMMARY OF THE REPORT OF THE COMMISSION FOR THE SOCIO-ECONOMIC DEVELOPMENT OF THE BANTU AREAS WITHIN THE UNION OF SOUTH AFRICA, U.G. 61/55 (Pretoria: Government Printer, 1941). Abridgement of full report by Tomlinson Commission, but contains much valuable information on native life and problems.

TREATMENT OF INDIANS IN SOUTH AFRICA: RECENT DEVELOPMENTS (New Delhi: Government Printer, n.d.). Indian indictment of Union's Indian policy at United Nations; extremely bitter. Subject matter would make publication about 1954.

CURRICULUM VITAE

COLIN RHYS LOVELL, Associate Professor of the Department of History in the University of Southern California (Los Angeles, California), was born in Fairmount, Minnesota (1917). He received the A.B., *summa cum laude* from the University of Minnesota in 1939; the A.M. in 1941 from the University of Wisconsin, and the Ph.D. from that University in 1947. His graduate work in history had a particular emphasis on South Africa, with the Ph.D. dissertation on General J. B. M. Hertzog and the National Party. In the course of research on this project he learned Afrikaans in order to be able to read, write and speak it. During the year of 1955 Dr. Lovell held a Fulbright lecturership in the Union of South Africa, and traveled widely there for a year, giving lectures in English and Afrikaans, and meeting prominent people of widely differing opinions on race relations.

Dr. Lovell is a contributor to CURRENT HISTORY, CANADIAN HISTORICAL REVIEW, AMERICAN HISTORICAL REVIEW, JOURNAL OF AGRICULTURAL HISTORY, WESTERN POLITICAL SCIENCE QUARTERLY, WEST INDIAN HISTORICAL REVIEW.

Dr. Lovell is a member of Phi Beta Kappa (Univ. of Minn.), American Historical Association, Canadian Historical Association, Canadian Political Science Association, Fellow of the African Studies Association.

CHAPTER ELEVEN

PAN-ASIATIC AND PAN-AFRICAN MOVEMENTS

CHANCELLOR WILLIAMS
Howard University

PAN-ASIA AND THE QUESTION OF UNDERSTANDING

The significance of the Pan-Asian and Pan-African movements seems not to be fully understood in the Western world. This moderate way of putting matters of great import often glosses over the essential fact that "misunderstanding" may not be misunderstanding at all, but a refusal to accept what one understand perfectly well. On the international level, the United States and the Soviet Union are good examples. The trouble, it is generally declared, is that the two countries do not understand each other and that "Summit Talks," cultural exchanges, etc. will bring about the desired understanding. Now nothing would seem to be more obvious than that the United States understands the Soviet Union well enough and that the Soviet Union likewise fully understands the principles and policies of the United States. What is involved, very simply, is not misunderstanding, but a refusal of each other to accept some of the most fundamental principles, policies and practices of the other. Even if ten million Americans spread over the Soviet Union every month and the same number of Russians toured the United States, the most they would discover is what they already know: that people are friendly and basically the same everywhere.

The ideological factors underlying Pan-Afro-Asian aspirations, therefore, may clash so sharply with Western preconceptions about the yellow, brown and black peoples of the two continents that, while understood, they are not at all acceptable. This, we think, is the crux of the matter. Tragic errors of judgment have been made in the past because of this, and are still being made—errors which may have serious consequences for the whole human family.

THE DEVELOPMENT OF THE PAN-ASIAN SPIRIT

Pan-Asianism is not a twentieth century social phenomenon. To trace its origin it would be necessary to go far back into the centuries when the Crusades had an impact on the Orient far different from that of earlier Hellenism. Saladin fired the spirit of the East in his brilliant opposition to this invasion from the West, and his series of victories, particularly the rout of the Christian armies at Tiberias and Jerusalem in 1187, made him an unforgotten symbol of the equal dignity and worth of Eastern man.

Pan-Asianism developed as a reaction of the Asian peoples to the ordering of their lives and the imposition of Western ideals and practices on their homeland. It was, and is, a spiritual-moral reaction that is tied in inseparably with the idea of race; and the idea of race involves the idea of equal worth and equal dignity—the point around which the whole non-white world today revolves.

The revolution is around this point, we say, and it will be a continuing and most serious error to think that what goes on as nationalism in Asia (and Africa) is nothing more than an attempt by backward peoples to imitate their erstwhile masters, an undertaking for which they are woefully unprepared (and by European racial concepts most of them never will be) ; that the West is to be blamed for carrying its enlightened ideals of freedom and equality to such people, who would have never of themselves had these high aspirations; or that the two world wars are solely responsible for arousing an otherwise docile and easily dominated people.

History tells a different story. For a hundred years Pan Asia has, with characteristic Oriental patience, been moving toward today. The trend toward solidarity became manifest when Europeans and Americans began to force their way into different Asiatic countries, "opening them up," as they called it.[1] There were, of course, voices of protest and warning in the West. Kelly of Australia, for example, warned of the grievous error of "forcing ourselves upon the Asiatic races" and "our craze for imposing our forms of religion, morals and industrialism upon them."[2]

Asia is the homeland of the yellow and brown peoples, the former occupying the Far East, the latter the Middle, Near East and North Africa, embracing a land area of nearly 12,000,000 square miles and a population of over 1,220,000,000 souls. Nine-tenths of all of this land and all of these people came under the control of a relatively few white men. This fact alone should have caused a serious, soul-searching pause, and a radical change of attitude, policies and practices by a West that, assuredly, was not deaf, dumb and blind.

The white man's penetration of the continent was not bad. What was bad was the racial ideology, now becoming more and more deeply rooted, that made the pause just referred to impossible, and the Christianity he preached a great hypocrisy in Eastern eyes. It was this idea about race, more than any other single factor, that was to spell damnation to Western rule and even make its wonderful medical services, vast, continent-wide economic and social improvements appear not to be appreciated by the Asians. The West had taken over an Eastern religion as its very own, had lost its substance in material progress, and it was now unable to understand the overriding and deathless power of a great spiritual-moral idea.

How could it? Had not its Christian Church given moral sanction by equating colonialism with Christianization and a civilizing mission? Were not missionaries of the various Christian creeds allies in the field? What else could Darwinian science mean but the superiority of European man and his corresponding right of overlordship of the earth? No further proof seems to be needed, but if there was, the system of siphoning the wealth of the world from peoples who apparently even did not have sense enough to use it, and the phenomenal industrial triumphs through science and technology should be the final answer.

A host of racist writers had taken the field for further education of the West—Gobineau, Carlyle, Alfred Schutz, Madison Grant, Lothrop Stoddard, Garcia-Colderon, *et al.* That their racist doctrines were being carefully studied by Asian thinkers also seemed to be a matter of no concern. Yet these ideas, and the attitudes and practices that developed from them, were to become as giant rocks against which the colonial power was to be dashed.

By the turn of the century the white race had made its purpose to rule the entire globe clear to Asians beyond all peradventure of doubt. Practically the whole African continent had been seized in a wild scramble for power by competing European nations and its peoples, including those of Asiatic origin who occupied the northern portion, were brought under colonial rule. Stoddard noted that anyone who looked at a political map of the world in 1914 would be struck by the "overwhelming preponderance of the white race in ordering the world's affairs" and that "the white man towered the undisputed master of the planet."[3]

214

And after the turn of the century, Asians began to react in more positive ways. Japan led off with its crushing victory over a great white power—the Russian empire. The electrifying effect of this victory was immediate not only in Asia but in Africa also, where a "wireless telegraph" system carries news as certainly as anywhere—and there was rejoicing.[4] The quick intervention of the American President, Theodore Roosevelt, to soften the peace terms for Russia[5] was regarded by many Asians as an attempt to save the day for the West by breaking the impact of the victory of a non-white people over a white. If this was a controlling motive behind the Treaty of Portsmouth, it failed.

Asians became more articulate than ever. An Afghan scholar warned that the West itself was promoting a Pan-Islam and a Pan-Asia by its "racial prejudice, that cowardly, wretched caste-mark of the European and the American the world over."[6] Professor Nagai of Japan declared that the "World was not made for the white races [alone], but for other races as well";[7] and he went on to point out that the ruling powers had vast tracts of unoccupied territory awaiting settlement in their own countries, "and although citizens of the ruling powers refuse to take up the land, no yellow people are allowed to enter." Another writer Yone Noguchi, wrote about the sadness of the Orientals' deception in believing that Western civilization was higher and on a sounder footing than their own. "We are sorry," he said, "that we somehow overestimated its happy possibility and were deceived and cheated by its superficial glory."[8] The writer concluded that his travels in the West convinced him that the so-called dynamic Western civilization was opposed to Asiatic beliefs, and that resistance was inevitable, active or silent.

All European and American thinkers, of course, were not racists. Many students of Oriental affairs kept up a steady stream of warnings in articles and books. They were widely read. Some, such as Townsend's ASIA AND EUROPE,[9] required edition after edition. Townsend pointed out that for two hundred years all European countries had been involved in a great effort to conquer Asia, that Asians would now resist, that, like the Europeans, they had the same spirit of unity among the respective countries, and that the idea of Asia for Asians was just as real as the similar idea, such as the Monroe Doctrine, that the white world reserves as its own special prerogative.

These were as voices crying in the wilderness, for the Madison Grants had the field, and this fact, allied as it was in support of the drive for economic gain and power, drowned out reason among the powers embarked on economic dominance, and made reflective thinking on the part of the leaders impossible. Granting that this could not be universally true, and that some of the most uncompromising imperialists fully realized the possibility of future danger, the results were the same. They could not stop even if such had been their wish. The siren song of empire with its vision of riches charmed them on.

Furthermore, how could effective solidarity among Asians or Africans, who were always warring among themselves, be possible? Panism was possible only among the superior races, was it not? Much was therefore banked on the proposition that division and mutual hostility were characteristic of these inferior peoples, and the real basis of the whites' successful rule over them. It was convenient to forget European history, its tribal past or even its current division and mutual hostility.

THE JAPANESE LEADERSHIP

The significance of Japan and its attempted leadership role was never appreciated fully. One may doubt whether it was even understood. It was easier to dismiss Japan simply as an imperialist nation that, having quickly become modern, was trying to imitate the West. To fight Russia was out of line with the expected—truly a phenomenon, but to fight China was so much in line with traditional expectations that few saw that Pan-Asia, rather than Japanese imperialism, was the underlying force in the Japanese invasions of China.

China, which even at the turn of the century had over one-fourth of the population of the world, was one of the most disorganized and, therefore, weakest of countries. The long rule of the Manchu emperors was characterized by disunity, corruption, oppression and poverty beyond the human imagination. There were countless rebellions during the eighteenth and nineteenth centuries—China trying to find itself. The greatest of these was the fifteen-year Taiping Rebellion which began in 1851. The tremendous loss in lives, estimated by some historians as being as high as forty million, left only the ideal of brotherhood as a social goal, community of property,[10] and equality. The vast empire was weaker and even more disorganized and ripe for further European and American exploitation.

The Boxer uprisings, 1898-1900, and the Revolution of 1911 were strivings toward the same end. In fact, the Revolution of 1911 checked

European plans to partition China just as Africa had been partitioned. The new Republic, nevertheless, found itself bound to Europe and America with economic ties; and while Chinese leaders knew better than anyone the extent to which they were being both degraded and exploited, there were in all this certain very real economic advantages that they were unbale to forego. The Treaty Ports, for example, had become a most important factor in the economic life of the country, notwithstanding the indignity of the unequal treaties. China, therefore, by being thus forced to acquiesce in Western domination, became the sore spot in Pan-Asianism and the chief obstacle to its realization. And this is one of the most important reasons for its conflicts with Japan.[11]

Japan had become the determined leader of Pan-Asia and, since her victory over Russia, had apparently been accepted by the other dominated Asian countries not only as their leader but also the symbol of their hopes. Japan's chief aim was to break the hold of foreign power on Asia—all Asia. China, the closest to her both territorially and in ties of blood, was the one great stumbling-block to the aspirations of all other Asians. Japan was resolved to drive the Europeans and Americans from their spheres of influence in China, for until this was done—until this daily functioning system of white supremacy and Asian inferiority was ended—all Asian peoples would be held up in everlasting shame. All kinds of negotiations had been going on between the two countries aimed at ending foreign domination. They never succeeded, and China appeared, in the eyes of Japan at least, to be hopelessly resigned to her fate.

To put it bluntly then, Japan decided that if Big Brother persisted in humble submission to the white West, and could not be persuaded to co-operate in the emancipation of Asia, then the only thing left to do was to give Big Brother a thrashing, take control of the country, and thereby end Western domination. There is some evidence that Western leaders, though accusing Japan of aggression and imperialism, understood the Pan-Asian aspect of the Sino-Japanese war and what the outcome might mean to the Open Door policy.

Pearl Harbor was Japan's last desperate effort to strike the final blow for an Asia for Asians. She had been steadily consolidating her position since her victory over Imperial Russia, becoming a greater and greater industrial, military and naval power, and now had to be recognized as a great power and welcomed, with misgivings, to the exclusive community of Big Powers' politics and alliances.

There was the possibility that this added recognition and prestige might divert Japan from her threatening course in attempting to unify Asia, especially the Far East, under the Rising Sun. The Anglo-Japanese Alliance, the Four Power Pact, the Five Power Treaty and the Nine Power Pact were all failures. Japan played the game of power politics Western style and, by seeming to assent to treaty provisions that were clearly against her program, she outsmarted the other great powers. At the moment it was expedient for her to agree, for example, to the Open Door provision in Article I of the Nine Power Pact.[12] This should have fooled no one, but it did. She entered World War I on the side of the Allies "in principle," moving only when Asian interests were involved, but steadfastly refraining from joining what she regarded as a white man's war of mutual extermination. And this is what she wanted, while biding her own time and growing stronger meanwhile.

We are not unaware of Japanese jingoism and the fanatics who dreamed of Japanese conquest, not only of China and Asia, but of the world. But a study of the Far East history since European and Ameri-pan penetration of the area leads us to the conclusion that Japanese imperialism was a diversion from Pan-Asianism to cope with the pressing exigencies raised by foreign domination. It can be argued that Western policies and practices or, in short, Western imperialism created Japanese imperialism, and that Japan's seemingly hostile relations with China were far from the course she really wanted to pursue.

The real Japanese purpose is not so much reflected in the role played in international diplomacy with the West as in the almost countless Pan-Asiatic societies, such as Count Okuma's "'Pan-Asiatic Association," the "Pacific Ocean Society," the "Indo-Japanese Association," etc., the special efforts to establish friendly relations with other Asiatic countries, the drive to cement fraternal bonds through education and, to this end, inviting thousands of students from all Asia to study in Japan and, above all, her avowed purpose to achieve racial equality by first driving the white man out of Asia.[13]

THE RACE AND SPIRITUAL FACTOR

By the very nature of the East-West situation, the racial factor was and is at the heart of the problem. Nothing has been gained by overlooking or trying to minimize this central fact. Much will be lost by continuing to do so. This rising racism is the dynamic force behind Asian nationalism, and the pan movements are very largely efforts to assure success for racial equality through the union of oppressed forces in the non-white world. And this is the great danger. That nationalism and the pan movements accompanying it are not developing, as in Europe and the Americas, as the normal aspirations of peoples geographically situated, expected, and therefore posing no threat one way or another to the rest of the world—that this is not happening is a danger that can hardly be overstressed, because the future of life on this planet may be involved. For what the Pan-Afro-Asian movements mean, actually, is defensive consolidation against the white world.

Strangely enough, it is the white world that evokes and furthers this "rising tide of color" against itself. The Asians and Africans are more spiritual in outlook and, therefore, have an urge toward brotherhood with all mankind. But the trouble with the idea of brotherhood is that it also means racial equality. Up to the year of our Lord, 1960, the white races were unable to accept this except in principle; and this fact was not only reflected in interpersonal relations, but in international policies also. The non-whites have no "scientific" theory of yellow, brown or black superiority, no doctrine of non-white supremacy. Their race prejudice, which is just as real as that of the whites, is, nevertheless, retaliatory. It is a reaction against the prejudice of the whites.

This point is important. For the fact is that even now there is little hostility to the white man as such or to his leadership. The opposition is to his racial ideology. If he could somehow honestly rid himself of this, the problem of his leadership, in contradistinction to his domination, would be largely solved.

The difficulty in doing this is the same difficulty that enshackles the West in meeting the Communist threat. The West is caught on the sharp prongs of its own rampant individualism, its own idea of liberty and freedom. Its fears of "regimentation" are carried to such an extreme that unity of policies and of action cannot be achieved within a single nation or between a group of nations even in the face of imminent peril. In allied warfare it requires the increasing threat of actual extermination to bring about the appointment of a generalissimo or a supreme commander over all. The traditional bogey of dictatorship appears to make Western man unable to understand the true nature of leadership, or how the powers required for positive action may be structured to safeguard the very liberties about which there is so much emotional concern.

This means that the need for a positive leadership role in a democracy, with full powers of action assigned, is not appreciated. Hence the West, clearly seeing the trend of contemporary history, is unable to declare new policies and a new relationship with the colored peoples in any unified, positive or reassuring way. The colonial powers, for example, still seem unable to understand that even from a strictly economic viewpoint, they themselves should have assumed positive and very articulate leadership in ending colonialism and in establishing new economic relationships on the basis of equality. Had this been done, does anyone think that "Red China" would be Red today? For China, more traditionally friendly to the West than any other Oriental country in spite of all the indignities suffered, was seeking not Communism but freedom from Western domination and equality in the comity of nations. Failing to achieve this, she turned to Communism; and the point here is that she would have turned to any ism whatsoever that would enable her to lift her head as a free and equal nation among the other nations. "Red China" is a creation of Western stupidity.

Furthermore, the West, having lost its spiritual force in the triumphs of its technological civilization, has left the door wide-open for Communism to enter in a spiritual-moral guise. For the Communists, while basing their ideology on a materialistic conception of history, have nevertheless been wise enough to apprehend the spiritual force that moves men, and have made their approach with the evangelistic zeal of a great religion. Everywhere it is "comrades," brothers. This is saying to a non-white world yearning for respect and equal dignity, "Come, we are brothers!" No matter about the hypocrisy, seen or hidden. The fact that Communism has made such tremendous sweeps despite its obvious defects as a way of life only points up the transcending power of a spiritual appeal over all others. Men do not live by bread alone, an important fact that the West apparently has forgotten. We may have the "second chance" in Asia about which Michener writes.[14] But we have always had all the chances one could wish. The question is, are we able to avail ourselves of the opportunities?

THE BROWN PEOPLE AND THE MOSLEM SPIRITUAL FORCE

The other part of colored Asia is the homeland of its brown people, stretching all the way across southern Asia in a grand wide screen from the Pacific to the Atlantic and spilling over across the whole of North Africa. Thus brown and black men meet in the latter's continent, and this fact is now beginning to have universal significance, as we shall later see.

The Near and Middle Eastern peoples are of many types and shades of color, ranging from white or near-white to jet black. Equally diverse are their cultures and traditions. Rivalries and enternecine strife have characterized their history. Yet, like the white world, they quickly close ranks before a non-Asiatic common foe.[15] They are bound together with the two ties of instinctive Asiatic feeling and Islam. Where the latter is weak and insufficient, as in India, the former replaces it with almost equal force.

Mohammedanism is in fact a form of Pan-Asianism and has much to do with Pan-Asia becoming Pan-Afro-Asia. Mohammedanism is a practicing brotherhood without reference to race, and herein lies its effective power over Christianity in Asia. Christianity preaches brotherhood, the Moslems practice it. We think this accounts for the Moslem hold in Asia and Africa more than anything else. Religion, racism and nationalism combine and become inseparable in Mohammedanism. When the Moslem speaks of the millions of our brothers "under Christian rule and struggling to shake off its fetters," he is talking as much about the race of the rulers as he is their religion. We have talked to Moslems who feel that to be a "true Asiatic" is to be a Moslem and vice versa. Their missionary work is carried on quietly and persistently, in sharp contrast with the publicity and fanfare of Christian missionary work. One hardly knows it is going on. One reason is that almost every Moslem is a missionary.

The Moslem system of brotherhoods, scattered everywhere in Asia and North Africa, is the more active form of Pan-Asianism which is, as we have pointed out, also Pan-Asianism incorporating Africa. The Senussiyah Brotherhood doubtless is the strongest and best organized, and may still be regarded as the leader in the expansion and unification of the Moslem world.

And Mohammedanism is as flexible as it is non-racial. It can extend the hand of fellowship to Asian Buddhists and Hindus alike, even though Moslem India might resist being overwhelmed by Hindu India because of fundamental differences in religion and social outlook. Happily, we shall not have occasion to see how quickly the current hostility between Pakistan and India would disappear if a non-Asiatic power attacked either. Stoddard's assumption that the growing solidarity in the brown world during the first quarter of the twentieth century was a wholly negative phenomenon is wrong, we think. This alliance against a common foe, the white man, was the only occasion for unity, he thought; remove the white man, and mutual extermination would set in again. This assumes, of course, that non-white peoples are incapable of anything else and, what is more, can never be expected to learn to live without endless internecine wars. And this is said with as straight a face as if the West had achieved this happy state of perpetual peace.

There are Pan-Asian movements that one would hardly suspect as such. Pan-Islam, as we have said, is one of the most powerful. But the significance of the great pilgrimages to Mecca in this connection is also important. Mecca could be called the capital city of Pan-Asia and Africa, for here the great congress of Asians and Africans, high and low, assemble—Arabs, Indians, Negroes, Burmese, Iranians, Chinese, Egyptians, Indonesians, Malayans, *et al.*—a united family of groups as diverse as anyone could conceive. Here is where the groundwork for what the West regards as a sudden outbreak of nationalistic movements, occasioned by the world wars, was being quietly and patiently laid during the past sixty years.

RED CHINA AND PAN-ASIANISM

What the two suicidal world wars did was to so weaken Europe that it could no longer hold Asia and Africa against their will. The new nations had been planning for the event before either occurred. The movements of the colonial powers began to operate on the level of independent nationhood as rapidly as a new nation was born after the Second World War. Those that became free and independent states immediately began to help every Asian and African country that was also struggling to throw off the colonial yoke. The powerful effects of this active moral support from the new nations should not be minimized.

"The solidarity first sought by the new nations of Asia," Straight writes, "was on a basis of common faith rather than common background and color."[16] Asian solidarity was further promoted by the West, this writer suggests, not only by its support of colonialism, but also by its exclusion of Communist China from the World community and the "white-dominated military network to hold the region."

Here again it should be noted that the non-Communist nations, formally crystallizing Pan-Asianism at Bandung, were moved more by the fact of China being Asiatic than of China being Communist. Hence, India's persevering insistence that Red China be admitted to the United Nations, backed by other independent Asian states.

On the other hand, Chou En-lai dropped Communist extremist tactics at Bandung and was the soul of modesty. No one was berated as a benighted Western stooge—not even the very pro-Western Philippines. No effort was made to win anyone over to Communism, nor was there the usual pose of Communist self-righteous mightiness. Red China had a single purpose at Bandung. That purpose was to escape from the isolation that the United States was imposing and become one with her non-Communist and neutral Asian brethren. All else could wait. To be welcomed to the community of Afro-Asian nations was important to China. It was a partial offset to the indignity of being barred from the U.N. and, therefore, lowered in prestige below the Soviet Union. And since the Russian ruling classes are all white notwithstanding the fact that they are a minority in the Soviet Union, Red China may not be sure that Red Russia really wants her in the U. N.

American theorists, eagerly and hopefully looking for some signs of cracks in the Sino-Russian Communist wall, overlook, as they naturally would, the Pan-Asian factor. For if a break between the Chinese Peoples Republic and the Soviet Union ever occurs, this will be the important factor. It is quite clear that (1) Communism as it has developed under Russian leadership is itself colonialism in a different guise; (2) that this guise does not deceive penetrating Asiatic eyes; (3) that China embraced Communism as a means of escaping from colonialism; (4) that she does not intend to submit to this new imperialism at all; (5) that the millions of submerged Asiatics in the Soviet Union are not forgotten; (6) and that as long as she is kept out of the United Nations and, therefore, unable to function as a world power equal with the Soviet Union, her dependence on Moscow remains the most trying experience.

For one thing, China is forced to play along with the Soviet Union for reasons of expediency—even to the extent of denouncing Tito, whose policies are nearest to her heart. Americans have allowed themselves to become so frightened by Communism that they appear unable to cope with it effectively or even think clearly and dispassionately about it. But to those who have studied basic Oriental philosophy and trends over the past fifty years, Red China's denunciation of Titoism was amusingly hollow, and so much so that one wonders if the equally sharp Kremlin was deceived by it.

The United States, of course, has missed the boat in its relations with both China and Yugoslavia. In the case of China we could have modified the racial aspect of Pan-Asianism by forthrightly disavowing colonialism, proposing a timetable for its steady elimination, seeing Chinese Communism as something our policies helped to bring about, ignoring it insofar as the Chinese people were concerned, and grasping their proffered hands of friendship in a new program of mutual collaboration on terms of equality. Failing to do this, we have actually promoted and strengthened Communism in China.

In the case of Tito, the millions of American dollars poured into Yugoslavia are millions poured down a drain insofar as the objective is concerned. Foreign aid is useless there, as it is throughout the world, and it will continue to be so just as long as we proclaim its only purpose to be the defeat of Communism or even, as in the case of Tito, to weaken a country's relations with the Soviet Union. If the American dollar cannot carry the spiritual message of brotherhood, now trying to help the peoples to help themselves, it might just as well remain at home. This is the idea superior to Communism and the only kind of shot that can affect it.

PAN-ASIAN PROGRAMS

We have paid little attention to the formal arrangements between the new nation-states of Asia, such as the Colombo Plan of 1950, the Manila Treaty of 1954 and the Southeast Asia Treaty Organization. But they are the practical application of the Pan-Asian spirit to a program of action in a regional framework that is approved by the United Nations. SEATO, though actively supported by the United States, is in a very real sense a reaction to NATO, which is looked upon in many Asian quarters as an exclusive white man's club for the defense of American and European interests — interests which may not be wholly aimed at meeting the Communist threat. The adoption of the Pacific Charter may have indicated the underlying feeling.

The Colombo Plan is more significant, we think, than any Asian imitation of NATO. The Plan provides for co-operation of nine Asian countries on economic development in South and Southeast Asia.

These include India, Pakistan, Ceylon, Laos, Burma, Cambodia, Viet-Nam, Nepal and Indonesia. The United States is a co-operating member.

The organizational structure is weak. There is no central machinery, secretariat, permanent headquarters or budget. But the program is important.[17] There has been a series of projects. The agricultural projects have included irrigation, improved seedings, fertilizers, extension service and village community improvement projects. Better credit and marketing facilities have been introduced and new capital and technical assistance have been channeled into such industrial projects as transportation and communications, steel manufacture, cement, locomotives and better educational and medical facilities.[18]

These are Western contributions and they have been spread far and wide all over Asia. Why are we losing then? Why do so many influential Asians still feel convinced that Communism must be used as a lever against the capitalistic West and that "to nationalists communism means liberation of the oppressed, and it also means a dynamic view of history just the opposite of their own teaching of resignation"?[19] We have already given the answer several times in the course of this chapter: There is no over-all, positive Western program of salvation for the East. What is done, no matter on what gigantic scale, appears to be piecemeal, only anti-something, and it is always lacking in the most powerful thing Communism offers — not money, but the spiritual promise of equality among the nations of the world. *With this, Communism can win without spending a single ruble; without it we lose even though we may spend billions.*

We have stressed the spiritual factor as the dominant one in Pan-Asianism. The term "spiritual" is so generally limited to supernatural phenomena that its practical, everyday meaning is often misunderstood. The minute we enter the realm of brotherhood and good will, however, we are in the realm of the spiritual, civilization's higher ground. Calculating expediency has no place here. Justice, freedom and equality arrived at under this heading are cold and miss the mark at which mankind at its best is aiming. These must be the basic elements in a way of life characterized by feelings of fellowship and good will coming straight from the heart. This is spiritual. It finds expression in many ways — in religion, in art, in literature, in drama, in dance and song, in the search for knowledge, in concern for the sick and in tears for the dying — it is love in search for the art of living, and of a way of life that gives some sense to existence as it widens the gap that separates man from beast.

East and West have not yet met, except physically. This is the trouble. The gulf that separates them is still spiritual, and since the spiritual side is the direction of a civilization higher than that of materialism, it is the West that must make the stride. For the "backward" peoples, with all of their faults and failures, have the essential qualities of genuine friendship and good will that place them on the side of the angels. And if Asia now draws more closely to her still darker brethren in Africa, the reasons run deeper than color or even the common suffering from colonialism. They are the unseen yet deeply felt bonds of a spiritual outlook on life.

THE EMERGENCE OF PAN-AFRICANISM

The underlying ideology of the Pan-African movement is essentially the same as that of Asia. It differs only in the degree of its intensity, sense of urgency and drive. It is as though a people, having been asleep a thousand years, suddenly awoke to find that the whole world has passed them by and was far ahead, and determined to catch up even if it means telescoping the progress it took others a millennium to make into a fraction of that time. For they have become painfully aware that not only are the whites at the top in almost everything, but the colored races of Asia are also far in advance of themselves. Hence the intensity, the urgency, and the self-impelling drive.

Yet the awakening began outside of Africa and among the descendants of African slaves in the West. The spirit of the movement can be caught here in its first organized expression under the leadership of a West Indian Negro, Marcus Garvey in 1914. His movement, known as the Universal Negro Improvement Association, was introduced into the United States two years later and began to spread like a prairie fire, to the increasing concern of both white Americans and Negro intellectual leaders.

For Garvey's paper, the *Negro World,* was perhaps the most radical appearing on American newsstands. Its blasts against the whole white world were ceaseless, relentless and bitter. He was a great orator, and could bring audiences to tears with his dramatic recital of the sufferings of the black race and he could turn tears to laughter in ridiculing the mulatto leadership of the race, believing as he did that lighter-skinned Negroes hated blacks as much as the whites did, and aimed at "integrating" with whites, not blacks. This tactic was effective.

American Negro intellectuals regarded the whole thing as a passing joke and Garvey as the rankest of demagogues. He was ridiculed and made the object of puns and laughter among the elite circles of his race. And he had supplied them amply with fuel with his fantastic regalia, titles of nobility, etc.[20] Yet the movement continued to grow amazingly in membership and in so much wealth and power that it called for a second look. The United States Government became interested, because the "Back-to-Africa" movement and its avowed purpose to drive the white man out had become something more than a joke when Garvey organized the Universal African Legion "to drive the white usurpers out," the Universal Black Cross Nurses, the Universal African Motor Corps, the Black Eagle Flying Corps and the Black Star Steamship Line.[21] Since ships were actually being purchased and launched, the movement could no longer be a joke. The Colonial powers were clearly disturbed, and this made the organization of later Pan-African movements difficult in Europe.[22]

The Government, meanwhile, had been carrying on exhaustive investigations of the movement quietly in an effort to find some legal grounds for stopping it. They found none. So the Government decided that the Black Star Steamship Line was a fraud, just as though it did not actually exist, and as though over a million dollars had not already been invested in it. "Using the mails to defraud" was the charge, and upon this charge Garvey was convicted in 1925 and thrown into a Federal penitentiary to serve five years. Two years later he was pardoned by President Coolidge for the purpose of deportation as an "undesirable alien." Garvey died in 1940, but his central idea did not.

John Hope Franklin, eminent American historian, thought of the movement as "Negro Zionism" that was doomed to failure. Many others also viewed it as nothing more than a visionary "back-to-Africa" movement for American and West Indian Negroes, and fantastic because American Negroes generally seemed to have the same low view of Africans as the whites, knew nothing about Africa and cared less. Garveyism, however, appeared to be more far-reaching than this limited view, for it aimed at uniting black men everywhere in an effort to drive the whites out of Africa. The pages of the *Negro World* proclaimed this purpose repeatedly, and perhaps nothing is better known about the movement than this. This was the angle of the movement that aroused the colonial powers and the American Government, not its "Negro Zionism" — which white Americans generally would have welcomed. The Garvey movement then, though having its own peculiar rough-and-ready approach, was, we think, a Pan-African movement. Kwame Nkrumah said, "But I think that of all the literature I studied, the book that did more than any other to fire my enthusiasm was *Philosophy and Opinions of Marcus Garvey*."[23]

ORGANIZING FOR ACTION

The five Pan-African Congresses were far more sophisticated, founded and promoted as they were by the eminent American scholar, W. E. B. DuBois. The first Pan-African Congress met in Paris in 1919 to present the case of the Negro peoples before the peace Conference. Its membership was small, having only fifty-seven delegates. Only twelve of these were Africans. The significance of this Congress was not in its immediate results, which were meager, but in the fact of a Pan-African concept at all, the fact of American, West Indian and African Negroes forming a union and planning to make it permanent through subsequent Congresses.

The three Congresses that followed served mainly to keep the Pan-African ideal alive. But with the meeting of the Fifth Pan-African Congress at Manchester, England in 1945, Pan-Africanism became a burning reality. DuBois' dream came to life when two hundred delegates from all over the world assembled in October of that year in the Manchester Town Hall. There was a reason. Kwame Nkrumah and George Padmore were the joint secretaries of the Organization Committee, and this fact alone meant a relentless, unceasing drive for its success.

Working night and day in London with a typewriter in Padmore's small kitchen, they sent hundreds of letters to organizations all over Africa and the West Indies, "explaining the aims of the Congress and the political tactics that should be adopted to achieve liberation in the colonies." "And it was the Fifth Pan-African Congress that provided the outlet for African nationalism and brought about the awakening of African political consciousness. It became, in fact, a mass movement of Africa for Africans."[24]

Dr. W. E. B. DuBois and Dr. Peter Milliard of British Guiana served as co-chairmen. Other leaders of the Congress were Jomo Kenyatta of Kenya, Peter Abrams of South Africa, and T. K. Makonnen, Ethiopia.[25]

The Congress, after prolonged discussions, rejected capitalist and other reformist proposals for the solution of colonial problems and adopted an African revised version of Marxist socialism, in contradistinction to Soviet Communism. Manifestoes were drafted for the Colonial Powers and the world, in which the determination to be free was declared, monopoly capitalism and the system of economic life for personal profits *alone* condemned, and economic democracy declared to be the only real democracy.

The Congress, unlike the others, then proceeded to institute a permanent and continuing program of action from day to day. The Pan-African Federation was formed and a Working Committee set up to carry through the action program that had been developed by the Congress. Kwame Nkrumah became the general secretary, and headquarters for the Congress was to be set up in London to serve as a stimulus and clearing house for all colonial movements for freedom.

In order to get something more definitely underway by narrowing the continent-wide field to a limited area as a beginning, Kojo Botsio and others met with Nkrumah to form a West African National Secretariat. The first major project was to be the calling of a West African National Congress to spearhead a liberation movement for both British and French West Africa. Everything was thrown upon Nkrumah's shoulders to carry on — everything, that is, except the money with which to carry on. It was not only work without pay, but it was more often work without either food or heat during one of England's very cold winters. A donation here and there, now and then, enabled Nkrumah and a small group of dedicated assistants to carry on.

Two papers appeared, *The New African,* published in London by the West African National Secretariat, and *Pan-Africa,* a magazine published in Manchester by the Pan-African Federation.

The African members of the French National Assembly were active in supporting the plans for a great West African congress to which, however, representatives from all over Africa were to be invited. It was to meet at Lagos, Nigeria in October, 1948 and was to be called as the West African National Conference. The conference was never held, because Nkrumah, to whom all the work of arranging the conference

229

had been assigned, was summoned home to take direction of a concrete nationalist uprising in his own country.

Nkrumah became the living symbol of Pan-Africanism and its most outspoken advocate. But it was not something that began in London with the fifth Pan-African Congress, but began much earlier — how much earlier it is doubtful if he himself knows. But what is known is that back in his student days in America he was an ardent Pan-Africanist and argued for a united action movement by Africans in the colonies not only *before* independence, but as the direct means of achieving it. Some of his hottest debates with other students, particularly the Nigerians who favored a separate and more cautious approach, were concerned with the question of pan-action as a means to liberation. It appears that the Gold Coast Africans generally, and not only Nkrumah, always think in all-Africa terms.[26]

The opposition of the Nigerian students should be clarified. They were strongly in favor of a pan-African movement *after* independence, but not before a few of the colonies had achieved it. They felt that any widespread inter-colony movement for independence would only serve to alarm the Colonial Powers and delay the very thing they sought to achieve. They therefore insisted that any concrete pan-African movement was premature at the time, and that each dependent territory should work out its own separate program for achieving independence. Moreover, many of the Nigerian students were apprehensive about the Marxist approach of the Gold Coasters. They regarded Communism as another form of colonialism, feared it just as much, and appeared to be in full agreement with a South African Negro leader who had declared that the African people would be fools to "replace their white masters with Red masters." And while the Gold Coasters insisted that they were Marxian socialists and not Communists at all in the Soviet sense, the distinction seemed not to be clear enough for the Nigerians.

THE BROWN-BLACK TIES OF BROTHERHOOD

It has been noted that brown Asia has spilled over into black Africa, and that it is mainly Moslem, and occupies the northeast portion of the continent. This Moslem influence on native Africans, while far-reaching, has not been an unmixed blessing. The over-all brotherhood approach of Mohammedanism has made it far more appealing to Africans than Christianity. An additional favorable factor in this connection is the dark color of the Arab missionaries, along with the fact of similar customs, such as polygamy and the inferior status of women. Therefore the stride from paganism to Islam is much shorter and easier than it is to Christianity.[27]

On the other hand, traditional Mohammedanism does not meet the present-day requirements of native Africans and, indeed, it does not meet its own requirements. It has been opposed to general, universal education, the upper classes thriving on mass ignorance. The Moslem schools we saw were nothing more than Koran catechism classes.[28] The other alarming fact is slavery. We are not aware that the Arab slave-trading into Africa has been stopped since the relatively recent U.N. report on the subject. Now since the slaves are always Africans seized in Africa, the genuineness of the Moslem brotherhood approach may be questioned.

The fact that Pan-African leadership has been kept native African notwithstanding the stature and maneuvering of Nasser may not be without significance.

Yet there is no question about the Moslem tie between Africa and Asia, and the importance of this factor in understanding the rather quick development of a Pan-Afro-Asian movement. It is not suggested, however, that Islam is the only important explanation. Just the fact of being colored is, as we have stated, an important factor. The people of India, for example, follow almost every incident involving American Negroes with the closest attention. They appear to be far better informed on race relations in the U.S.A. than many of the American visitors whom they badger with questions. White Americans, traveling as spokesmen for American democracy in Asia and trying to spread good-will, report being embarrassed everywhere by these racial questions and are surprised at their persistence. Occasionally a prominent American Negro is sent over to present the brighter side of Negro life in America, only to be ridiculed or laughed down as a paid stooge. The significance of all this seems to be that while the Indians know that they have been theoretically classed as members of the white race, they feel a closer kinship with Africans, not so much because of color *per se* as of their common racial experience in relations with the white world. This means, very simply, that regardless of what white men say, their attitude toward the Negro is taken as the index of their *real* attitude toward all colored peoples.

THE LEADERSHIP OF GHANA

The mainsprings of the pan movements of course are in nationalism

231

and, more particularly, in the ideology from which they gather their force. In this connection the role of Ghana is unique. It has become the leader of Pan-Africa, not so much by deliberate choice, it appears, as by common expectation and common consent. It is no overstatement to say that all of black Africa looks to Ghana for leadership. It is expected to be the pace-setter, and every move made there is followed anxiously and uneasily. For if she fails? . . . . If she fails, the feeling is that the whole black race shall have failed, and thus justified the ideology of racial inferiority that is still more widely believed than one would like to admit.

Ghana's role is not an enviable one, for she is kept under a glaring searchlight and anything that even seems to be an error is quickly spotted and decried. Yet the leadership role has been assumed forthrightly.

African nationalists from all over the continent converge on Accra, the capital city. They come for inspiration, consultations about strategy, to observe progress made, and to discuss plans for possible union of forces. The West appears to be somewhat confounded by this widespread and, apparently, spontaneous movement toward African unity. For it is contrary to all presuppositions regarding the internecine disposition of "backward peoples," the much harped on cultural differences, and the eternal "language barrier." Colonial power rested its security on these divisive tendencies as though they were innate, permanent.

But the Pan-African movement is strikingly different from the Pan-Asian movement in still another important respect. It aims at a "United States of Africa," beginning with West Africa. This is the meaning of the proposed union of Ghana and Guinea, agreed to at Accra, November 23, 1958. Moreover, the proposed union envisions something more than a loose confederation of independent states. The approach rather is toward single nationhood through parliamentary action for a common constitution and a common flag.[29] On that date November 23, 1958, the Government of Ghana and the Republic of Guinea, acting through their respective prime ministers, Kwame Nkrumah and Sékou Touré, issued the following historic Declaration:

> Inspired by the example of the thirteen American colonies which, on the attainment of their independence, constituted themselves into a confederacy which ultimately developed into the United States of America; inspired also by the tendencies among

the peoples of Europe, Asia and the Middle East to organize in a rational manner; and inspired further by the declaration of the Accra Conference regarding the African Personality,

We, the Prime Ministers of Ghana and Guinea, on behalf of our respective Governments and subject to ratification of our respective National Assemblies, have agreed to constitute our two States as a nucleus of a Union of West African States.

Conscious of the fact that an aspiration for closer union is shared by all the peoples of our continent, we appeal to the Governments of the Independent States of Africa, as well as to the leaders and peoples of the territories still under foreign rule, to support us in our action. In the same spirit, we would welcome the adherence to this Union of the other West African States . . . .[30]

The Declaration then states the adoption of a Union flag is to be the first step, and the working out of a Constitution "giving effect to the establishment of the Union" is the second step.

In presenting the Declaration to the Ghana Parliament on December 12, 1958 for ratification, Dr. Nkrumah continued,

I must confess a deep sense of pride and satisfaction in that I have been an instrument in this move, as I look upon it as the first step in the fulfillment of a dream long held by those who have carried high the banner of African freedom. I am, moreover, firmly convinced that it represents the will of the peoples all over this Continent unable to speak for themselves, who today are searching after some form of African Union which will give purpose and expression to their desire for freedom and independence and the resultant task of building up a re-constituted Africa along the lines of unity and interdependence.

This new Africa of ours is emerging into a world of great combinations — a world where the weak and small are pushed aside unless they unite forces. It is time for us in this part of the world to realize that our individual national freedoms can only be safeguarded within a structural inter-dependence of our countries and States. . . . Whether we like it or not, history has assigned to us a great responsibility, and we shall fail all the millions on this continent who look to us as a symbol of their hopes in Africa, if we do not rise to this responsibility and meet it seriously and unitedly. The presence in Accra of so many African Freedom Fighters from all parts of this vast continent at the All-African People's Conference is testimony enough that, despite all of our shortcomings and limitations, our brothers still languishing under colonialism and imperialism look to this free independent land of Ghana as their mecca — their hope and inspiration.[31]

233

We have quoted at some length because there is hardly a better spokesman for the ideology of Pan-Africa than the original Pan-Africanist, Kwame Nkrumah.

The Parliamentary Opposition, while enthusiastically hailing the idea of an All-African Union of States, were critical of the procedure and the haste. As to the procedure, they objected to the Ghana-Guinea nucleus proposal, claiming that this would lessen the chances of a wider union unless the other countries had a direct hand in developing the Union Constitution, and that this should be done at an All-African Constitutional Convention, called for that purpose before any further steps are taken toward the Ghana-Guinea Union. As to haste, they criticized both the speed and particularly the secrecy surrounding the negotiations between the two countries, insisting that this was not calculated to inspire confidence either at home or among the other African territories or states.

THE RAPID TREND AND ITS MEANING TO THE WEST

The Pan-African movement reached its height in two gatherings in the capital of Ghana in 1958. The first was the Conference of Independent African States which met in April. Representatives of Ghana, Libya, Liberia, Morocco, the Sudan, Tunisia, Ethiopia and the United Arab Republic attended. Warm greetings were sent by many of the world's statesmen and others. Inter-African co-operation and brotherhood were stressed. The central theme of the conference was centered around the problem of how to maintain the "hard-won independence, sovereignty and territorial integrity." The problem of colonialism and racialism was explored in detail. The Conference pledged its wholehearted support of the U.N. Charter, the five principles of peaceful coexistence of the Bandung Conference, and the people of dependent territories still struggling for freedom. "Arab Africa," "Black Africa," "Islamic Africa," "Non-Islamic Africa," "Mediterranean Africa," and "Tropical Africa," etc., no longer existed. "Today the Sahara is a bridge uniting us. We are one."[32]

The other significant meeting was not on the high government level of the Conference of Independent African States. It was the All-African Peoples' Conference which met in November, 1958, at Accra. This Conference was more widely representative of all Africa than the Independent States Conference because delegates came from almost everywhere, representing organized bodies of all kinds, including trade unions, political parties, etc.

Both Conferences reflected the increasing solidarity of Africans, and both set up permanent machinery to continue their work of mutual aid and co-operation. And both Conferences brought the world press to Accra.

The picture presented to the Western world, stark and clear, is an Africa that is to be ruled in the future by native Africans — all of Africa. To this end the determination is grim and real. They do not intend to "drive the white man out of Africa," although this expression is often heard in the speeches of the most fiery of the nationalists. What they mean is that the white man will be driven from his seat of power and control. They hate the white man's superior attitude, but not the white man. Africans everywhere seem to be demanding nothing more than *equality with the whites, and on that basis, sincere friendship and political and economic relationships which are equally beneficial to all.* This, on the basis of available evidence, is the gist of the African position. This is what African nationalism is all about. This is what Pan-Africanism is all about.

The problem then becomes the white man's problem. The West's responsibility for leadership arises from its long domination and control of the two non-Western continents and the countless island communities spread over the world. Its too-little-too-late policies have made it a convenient scapegoat for everything wrong. White men, obviously, were not responsible for the backward conditions they found among the peoples of Asia and Africa. Some of the great civilizations in both continents had declined, while others had disappeared almost completely. In other vast areas it appeared that the people were in the same savage state they had been from the beginning, and there were no signs that it would ever be otherwise. Yet nature had especially favored them with the economic basis for great civilizations — almost limitless natural resources. These were little used. The people were asleep, and white men did not put them in that state.

The theory that without the coming of white men they never would have awakened is an important issue. There had been great civilizations in Africa before the advent of the West. The new Ghana, for example, draws its nationalist inspiration from medieval Ghana. The most that white men did, we think, was to speed up the processes of progress. Having done so, they erred in trying to establish a line beyond which the non-whites were forbidden to pass. The ideology in

235

support of this color line is the ideology against which Pan-Afro-Asianism aims its attacks.

The American Southerners and the South African Boers drown out the voices of fair-minded and reasonable white men everywhere; and not even their governments, struggling for the best road to adjustment, can be heard above the Southerner's mighty din. To the non-white world they appear to represent the true feelings of the majority of white men everywhere. If there is violence in Africa and elsewhere, it will stem very largely from this feeling that the whites will not willingly accept any role short of domination, one way or another, even in the homeland of the peoples concerned. For central in the Pan-African movement is the Gandhi ideology of non-violence.

At this writing, February 28, 1959, violence is spreading over Africa from the Belgian Congo[33] to Central and Southeast Africa. This could occur only where the white leadership indicate determination of permanent supremacy or, what amounts to the same thing, there is not even an unclear timetable for the realization of basic native aspirations. In short, there is violence where there is no hope.

The present position, uncertain policies and practices by the West are untenable. Since Western co-operation and even its position of world leadership are nowhere decried, self-preservation would seem to demand a new Pan-Euro-American ideology designed expressly to meet the challenge of Asia and Africa. For that challenge is first of all a spiritual challenge. Somehow a unified and convincing Western policy must be evolved out of the distressing disunities which characterize our idea of individual liberty and independent (and separate) sovereign policies and actions.

A new Western Declaration of Faith and Action, more powerful and sincere than the Communist Manifesto, is called for; a new Afro-Asian relations program must be developed, and highly trained task forces should be spread out over the Afro-Asian field. The great work that the white race has done in Asia and Africa will be without sufficient reward to the West unless the self-interest basis for it is quickly superseded by a spiritual-moral basis.

And, again, what, precisely, do we mean by "spiritual-moral" basis? If we invested first in people instead of investing only in immediate self-liquidating projects, it would be a spiritual-moral investment. If we were more concerned with human improvement than industrial improvement, it would be a spiritual concern. Note that

236

this is only a shift in emphasis, and that the economic advantages of investing in people would be far greater than huge capital investments in areas of mass illiteracy. A single, simple Western school in such an area with a single, simple Western message: "We're here only to help," would be far more effective than any military pact, air base, or even a factory.

The Pan-Afro-Asian movements, we have been saying, are essentially spiritual movements. As such they can become a real danger only if the West continues to force the movements into a racial pattern. They are at once a great challenge and a great opportunity.

SELECTED BIBLIOGRAPHY

Achmed Abdullah, "Seen Through Mohammedan Spectacles," FORUM, LII:4 (October, 1914), 484-497. This article aims attack primarily at Christianity for what the writer calls its false pretenses and practices. He holds Christianity responsible for widespread racial prejudice.

Takaaki Aikawa, "Thoughts on New Asia," THE CHRISTIAN CENTURY, LXXII (October, 1955), 1172-1174. Communism found useful lever for Nationalist leaders, according to Aikawa, and a more effective liberating force than capitalism.

"The Asian-African Conference," UNITED ASIA, VII (June, 1955), 178-182. A report on proceedings and the significance of the First Asian-African Conference at Bandung.

Lawrence H. Battistini, THE BACKGROUND OF ASIA, 2nd edition (Tokyo: Sophia University Press, 1953), 289. A good background approach to the Orient. Useful as a short study beginning.

George W. Carpenter, "The Role of Christianity and Islam in Contemporary Africa," Chapter 2, 90-113, in C. Grove Haines, Ed., AFRICA TODAY (Baltimore: Johns Hopkins University Press, 1955), 510. Traces the penetration of Africa by two great religions, and undertakes to assess their significance and relative strength. See also the follow-up commentary by Dr. G. M. Wysne, 113-117.

E. J. Dillon, "The Asiatic Problem," THE CONTEMPORARY REVIEW, CCCCCVI (February, 1908), 241-248. This article appears in the "Foreign Affairs" section of the magazine and reflects the traditional American view of the Orient. It might be described as "tolerant paternalism."

John Hope Franklin, FROM SLAVERY TO FREEDOM, Chapters XXIV, XXV, XXX, 462, 481, 482, 588. (New York: Alfred A. Knopf, 1950), 622. A standard history of the American Negro. It includes study of the African background and current Pan-African connections.

K. M. Gould, "Asia for Asians," SCHOLASTIC, XLVI, (February, 1955), 11. Another presentation of the ideology of Pan-Asia. Not very different from the rising mass of books and articles on the subject.

J. Liddell Kelly, "What Is the Matter with the Asiatic?," THE WESTMINSTER REVIEW, CLXXIV (September, 1910), 292-299. This article, like so many others appearing during the first decade of the twentieth century, in attempting to interpret Asia for the West, does a much better job in revealing the Western mind to Asia.

Max Lerner, AMERICA AS A CIVILIZATION, Chapters II, IV, V, IX, X, XII, 53-73, 209-352, 621-775, 869-950 (New York: Simon and Schuster, 1957), 1036. Our own appraisal of the dominant characteristics and trends of Western civilizations under the American influence was based on this remarkable recent study of American life and culture. We differ in our interpretation of the significance of American civilization, and our points of emphasis present the nation as less unique and more typical of Western culture as a whole.

Franz H. Michael and George E. Taylor, THE FAR EAST AND THE MODERN WORLD, Chapters VI-XV, 119-688 (New York: Henry Holt & Co., 1956), 724. We drew heavily on this work for most of the materials on Sino-Japanese relations, impact of the West on the Far East, and Japan as leading force in the rise of Pan-Asiatic spirit.

James A. Michener, THE VOICE OF ASIA, 237-242 (New York: Random House, 1951), 388. The changing scene in Asia is evaluated in the much-needed human terms by a close student of Asian life. The Asiatic attitude toward the West is of particular interest.

M. R. Mosani, "The Mind of Asia," FOREIGN AFFAIRS, XXXIII (January, 1955), 540-565. This article presents certain aspects of Asian psychology as an aid to better Western understanding.

Ryutaro Nagai, "The White Peril" (in Japan Magazine), quoted in AMERICAN REVIEW OF REVIEWS, XLVIII,: I, (July, 1913), 107-108. Professor Nagai reviews the injustices and oppressive acts perpetrated by the white race on other branches of the human family.

Kwame Nkrumah, GHANA, The Autobiography of Kwame Nkrumah, Chapters 4 and 5, 35-63 (Edinburgh: Thomas Nelson and Sons, 1957), 310. A close-up view of Pan-Africanism and its basic ideology by the foremost Pan-African leader of the day. This work also indicates the direction of Pan-Africa toward a United States of Africa.

Yone Noguchi, "The Downfall of Western Civilization," THE NATION, (October 8, 1914), 4320. Great Western wars seen as unmasking the deceptive character of a Western civilization that seems glorious but rests on the institutionalization of the "avaricious instincts of primitive barbarism."

George Padmore, "Pan-Africanism and Ghana," UNITED ASIA, LX, 1 (February, 1957), 50-54. The article is more about Ghana Nationalist movements than Pan-Africanism.

Lothrop Stoddard, THE RISING TIDE OF COLOR (New York: Charles Scribner's Sons, 1920), 320. This was one of the earliest warnings to the West about the pan movements in Asia and Africa. Stoddard drew on many earlier documentary sources to support his thesis, and thus led us to some of the same sources. And while we arrived at quite different conclusions from the same facts, we feel more indebted to this work than any other for help in tracing the history of the Pan-Afro-Asian movements.

————, THE CLASHING TIDES OF COLOR (New York: Charles Scribner's Sons, 1935), 414. In this work, thirty years after his original "Tides," the author saw his original thesis as confirmed, and his predictions taking concrete form. Western civilization was disintegrating, due in large measure to Western disunity at home and unwise policies in Asia and Africa.

M. Straight, "Do We Want Asian Unity," NEW REPUBLIC, CXXXII (April 25, 1955), 5-6. Writer stresses "common faith" as basic ideology of Pan-Asia and the tie with Africa. The "common faith" has to do with the common objective rather than religion.

W. L. Thompson, "Bandung Shows Spirit of Unity," CHRISTIAN CENTURY, LXXII (April 20, 1950), 470-471. A commentary on social phenomena of so many diverse cultural groups forming a united front in a common cause.

Meredith Townsend, ASIA AND EUROPE, 17-19 (London: A Constable and Co., 1905), 388. A series of studies based on the author's many years of study of European-Asian relations up to the turn of the century. Excellent for background and interesting forecasts of things to come. Very comprehensive, including treatment of Negro problems in America.

Max Yergan, "The Communist Threat in Africa," Chapter 3, 262-280, in G. Grove Haines, Ed., AFRICA TODAY (Baltimore: Johns Hopkins University Press, 1954), 510. Points up reasons for Communist successes, a leading one being their well-organized, well-trained "missionaries," in Africa and elsewhere, with a definite program of action with an emotional appeal.

CURRICULUM VITAE

CHANCELLOR WILLIAMS (1905-   ) was born in South Carolina and attended the elementary school there before moving to Washington, D.C., where he graduated from Howard University, B.A., 1930; M.A., (1935); Ph.D., American University (1940). While Visiting Research Scholar, Lincoln College, Oxford University (1953-1954) he continued studies of sociological and educational problems of Africa; in 1956-1957, attached to the University College of Ghana, he carried out field studies in the country, which included a community study, a national opinion poll, in 143 schools and colleges. A member of the faculty of Howard University since 1945, he also serves as Visiting Professor of Sociology and Education. Tuskegee Institute

(Summer Sessions). Author of such works as THE RAVEN (historical work on Poe, 1943), HAVE YOU BEEN TO THE RIVER? (novelized version of doctoral dissertation: THE SOCIO-ECONOMIC STATUS OF STORE-FRONT CHURCH MOVEMENT IN THE UNITED STATES). He edited THE NEW CHALLENGE, and THE PRINCIPALS ANALYZE THEIR TASK (a research publication), and has contributed to JOURNAL OF NEGRO EDUCATION, THE SOCIAL STUDIES, etc.

CHAPTER TWELVE

LATIN AMERICA

STEPHEN S. GOODSPEED

*University of California,
Santa Barbara, California*

Frequently, North Americans have to be reminded of a certain fundamental difference between their method of thinking and the methods of thought in Latin America. We tend to be pragmatic, dealing with problems as they arise, and subsequently inventing reasons. To Latin Americans, ideas and currents of thought have a vivid reality and are considered to be the matrix of forces which ultimately shape destiny. It may be that the Latin-American mentality, being older and in many ways more disciplined and subtle, merely gives conscious expression to considerations which North Americans indulge unconsciously. In any event, the recent course of history, concerned as it is with the fundamental challenge to the West of Soviet imperialism following closely on the heels of Fascist and Nazi expansionism, makes it imperative that the North American understand the developing position of the Americas to the South. Latin America is no longer an uncharted area on the fringe of civilization, merely a source of raw materials for industry, and a stage for *opéra bouffe* governments, bandits, and sleepy-eyed peasants. This is not to say that all the peoples of Latin America have solved their problems or achieved the degree of political and economic development or social dignity and equality enjoyed generally in North America or in Western Europe. It does mean, however, that the Latin peoples of America, for some decades now and in increasing tempo, have been demanding and achieving an ever greater freedom from the imperialisms and oligarchichal systems which characterized their past.

THE CHANGING SCENE IN LATIN AMERICA

The twenty republics of Latin America actually form a much larger area than the United States and Europe combined. All of them passed through a similar colonial experience and share, except for French-speaking Haiti and Portuguese-speaking Brazil, a common language. Common elements can also be seen in religious preference, in social structure and political and economic development. But it would be extremely dangerous to conclude that these and other identifying features represent what has been often and inaccurately described as a Latin-American community. If one considers geography, it is by no means certain whether Latin America is a single community or a series of communities. From the standpoint of a feeling of unity or a consensus of belief among Latin Americans, despite linguistic, cultural, historic and religious ties, there are very marked differences. With respect to the peaceful adjustment of problems, there is a history of traditional rivalry and deep-seated animosities in certain regions represented by border strife and conflicting national ambitions.

At the same time, while there are great differences and disparities between them Latin-American countries in the twentieth century have all been subjected to various growing, dynamic forces which have had increasingly profound effects upon their way of life. These forces are reflected in an expanding social revolution which is characterized primarily by a rising spirit of nationalism accompanied by economic development designed to permit greater freedom from the traditional foreign ownership of major elements in the economy. In ever increasing degree the state is employed as a means for fostering this feeling of "anti-imperialism" and bringing about social and economic progress. Associated with these developments are a number of strong political movements frequently rooted firmly in well-developed and strongly argued indigenous political, economic and social thought. An understanding of the contemporary scene, therefore, requires first of all a cursory examination of the major forces which are at work in a setting without a truly enlightened public opinion, an adequate standard of living, or a positive maturing of the fruits of democracy. But light is beginning to relieve the dark shadow of the past, sometimes only faintly and perhaps not at all in some instances but here and there brightly.

The population of the entire Latin-American region is expanding at a phenomenal and even alarming rate. The rate of growth is at least as fast as that of any other area of the world and may well provide Latin America with the problem of feeding as many as China, i.e., about 600 million, by the end of this century. Although the death rate is still high, especially when compared to the United States, a number of Latin-American countries in the last decade reveal a sharp increase in life expectancy. Infant mortality shows a notable decline. Increased interest in public health and new discoveries in the control of tropical diseases point in the direction of a continuing trend downward in the death rate. The twin problems of feeding and employing the greatly increasing population become evident immediately.

While population grows rapidly, the towns and cities tend to drain the countryside. Urban and rural expansion do not keep pace and certain areas of the continent are virtually uninhabited. The urban birth rate is much lower than that of the rural areas but the constant stream of people to the cities results in a relatively greater growth of the urban population since over 50 per cent of the increase is due to rural migrants. With the growth of urbanization one can expect a progressive trend toward modernization since the cities are in the van of social change. At the same time, the growth of the cities, while accompanied by a lower illiteracy rate, has certain attendant evils in the form of housing shortages and slum areas, school overcrowding and unemployment. As urbanization tends to develop further the already predominant position of the cities in the political life of the Latin-American states, the drift to the cities raises many questions for the rural areas. For instance, serious attention must be directed toward discovering means of expanding agricultural output and retaining manpower to work the fields.

The racial composition of Latin America is extremely varied. The economic and political life of the region reflects this differentiation. Countries with large Indian populations, notably in Mexico, Central America and in the Andean areas, have wrestled constantly with the problem of assimilating these peoples. What developed in the nineteenth century with regard to the Indian, the Negro and the mestizo was the cultural and social isolation of these groups from the full life of their countries. They became prey to disease, economic displacement and political exploitation. In recent years, however, the barriers separating these peoples from national life have steadily been weakening. The absorption of the Negro in Brazil, long a country of racial

243

tolerance, has progressed rapidly. No longer is the Indian the forgotten man of Latin America. All of the countries with large Indian populations provide special services and even separate government agencies to deal with Indian affairs. In part responsible for this are the archaeologists and anthropologists who have awakened interest and pride in the native background. There is also an increased social conscience which has been growing in these countries. The development of public health services, the expansion of education into rural areas and a determined effort to raise standards of living have brought the Indian and mestizo into closer partnership with the national community. The end-product of this process may well be the development of greater political stability in the Indian countries. The Mexican revolution of 1910 ushered in an era of improving the lot of the Indian and today, all careers are open to him. The Aprista movement in Peru represents another facet of strong and determined Indo-Americanism. Contemporary Latin Americanists, among them notably the brilliant Mexican philosopher José Vasconcelos,[1] view the mestizo as potentially the most important factor in virtually all Latin-American populations.

Industrialization has been a slogan of nearly all Latin-American economic and political leaders for many years. The wonders that industrialization is expected to accomplish are impressive indeed. It is considered to be a panacea to cure all economic ills, the best way of obtaining diversification and thereby eliminating the traditional economic one-sidedness of so many countries. Wealth, prestige and high standards of living are guaranteed if only industrialization can be pushed as rapidly and widely as possible.

In spite of the greatly exaggerated role designed for industrialization, unquestionably the speed with which it is being pursued is one of the most fundamental elements of the contemporary scene. Its effects are bound to be far-reaching, primarily in the challenge to the ancient economic policies of colonialism, the rise of a new industrialist class, the significant progress made by organized labor as a factor in the political life of many countries, and the growth of social legislation. Closely associated are such controversial issues as the role of government in the promotion of national economies, heavy or basic industries versus light or secondary industries, the source of needed capital investments, the barriers to the investment of foreign capital, self-sufficiency in food production, the limits of technical assistance, and the foreign aid policy of the United States.[2]

One of the most basic conditioning factors of government in Latin America involves the ownership of land and how it is worked. Any study of the causes of upheaval and revolt on this continent during most of the preceding century would reveal that a high percentage of this violence was associated with demands for land reform or by opposition to any change. Of primary concern is the ancient institution of the large estate or *latifundio* system.[3] The problem of the accumulation of rural property by the few is a phenomenon which has existed for centuries. With the encouragement of the *latifundio* in the nineteenth century, the course of economic development tended to strengthen and solidify the economic power of the landed aristocracy. Political oligarchy was also strengthened since those who governed were closely connected with the large landowners.

Beginning dramatically with the Mexican revolution and continuing with increasing intensity has been the attack upon this system and such associated issues as peonage, monoculture, rural disenfranchisement, political isolation, and agricultural export policies. While neither the industrial nor agricultural change can guarantee the full development of democratic institutions, in the opinion of a number of observers, the "most active agents of democracy in Latin America — land reform and industralization — are clearly related developments, for a gain in the one is reflected in a better environment for the other."[4]

A prominent Catholic layman has observed: "Latin America is what it is because Catholicism is what it is. Its culture, its expression, its art and its thought bear the unmistakable imprint of the Church. Customs, habits and daily living are a faithful reflection of Catholic life."[5] This statement reflects the influence of the Church over several centuries. However, while the Catholic hierarchy actively engaged in politics in the nineteenth century, usually on the side of conservatism and reaction, and hence found itself on the defensive against reform elements seeking to divest it of its preeminent political and economic position, such is rarely the case today. The Church has become increasingly concerned with socioeconomic problems and can now be found in many countries supporting agrarian reform, labor unions and legislation in the realm of social welfare. Certainly in Mexico, the scene of the most bitter Church-State conflict of all in Latin America in the 1920's and 1930's, the Church has accepted the reform

245

program of the Mexican revolution and removed itself from partisan politics.

Progress has been made, even if painfully slow in some countries, in extending educational facilities to the lower economic and social classes in Latin America. In Mexico, there has been a particular effort made to extend these facilities to the Indian. Each year in a growing number of countries, larger number of students with the necessary prerequisites seek admission to universities and to new and broadened professional and technical schools. Most countries now provide financial support for programs to reduce illiteracy. In some, financial aid is granted to needy or exceptionally qualified students. Women are also enrolling in professional schools and universities in increasing numbers.

What has been developing in the field of education is in part, at least, a reflection of the changing patterns of the class structure in Latin America. While the situation varies from country to country, the former rigidity of stratification is weakening. In Mexico, Uruguay, Argentina, Costa Rica and Chile and to a lesser extent in several other countries, a middle class is rising to assert increasing importance in national life. A powerful labor movement is in evidence in these and some other countries where influence is asserted through political parties frequently oriented to represent the needs and desires of labor.

Much of what has been discussed above is reflected in what might be called "the new constitutionalism" in Latin America. Nineteenth-century constitution-making was primarily artificial and imitative. Influences came chiefly from the United States, France, Spain, and in lesser degree from the British but occasional experimentation in no real sense made any successful break with the past.

However, as World War I was approaching a climax, the most significant of all constitutional developments in Latin America took place. This was the Mexican Constitution of 1917, which indicated that the period of imitation had come to a close, that the "Latin American states were now ready, a century after independence had been won, to write constitutions that would be more inherently national than any that had gone before. . . . In the respect that the Querétaro Constitution introduced this new era it may be regarded as symbolically Latin American rather than narrowly Mexican."[6] The most outstanding characteristic of this document is its strident and positive nationalism, especially in the economic sphere. The nineteenth-century emphasis upon economic individualism gave way to the principle laid down in the famous Article 27 which asserted national ownership of subsoil wealth which heretofore had been benefiting foreign interests. The absolute right of private property was denied. In its stead, there was outright encouragement of government regulation in behalf of the general welfare.

The profound changes introduced in the Querétaro document have been incorporated in varying degree in virtually every Latin-American document subsequently adopted. Great interest in experimentation and innovation can be seen in a number of constitutions drafted since 1917. In almost every instance, the increased authority and responsibility of the state in every sphere of activity is evident. The expansion of governmental functions invariably is seen in the hitherto unknown or untouched areas of the general welfare. In some instances, such as in Mexico, these provisions might be labeled anticipatory in that labor and agrarian movements appeared after the constitutions came into effect. In others, new political alignments and political and economic theory have been the precursors of constitutional change. The result has been, although it varies from country to country, a concerted challenge to the old order in the form of new movements, parties and ideas.

No single perspective could possibly cover the entire Latin-American scene, since so many elements enter the picture, so many countries, racial groups, diverse geographical regions, economic and cultural extremes, customs and traditions. It will be necessary, therefore, to cover some countries and regions separately where particularly unique and relatively independent political movements strive for recognition and accomplishment. Yet there are some currents of thought which cross frontiers and, at times, and in some circumstances, seem to approach a major trend.

ANTI-AMERICANISM

If any one sport, other than bull-fighting or soccer could be selected as being the most popular in Latin America, it would have to be that of baiting the United States. Anti-Americanism stems from a number of sources and takes a variety of forms. Economic anti-Americanism has existed for some years. Few aspects of United States culture have been more bitterly attacked in Latin America than capitalism. Opposition is expressed against the private investments of the United States

247

in Latin America and the activities of individuals associated with such enterprises as are customarily referred to as "exploitive." Capitalism is also denounced in theoretical terms while the appeal of various approaches to collectivism is viewed in most intellectual circles with enthusiasm. What appears to be the strongest trend away from capitalism in the North American sense is the move from semi-feudalism to centralized economic planning while by-passing the capitalistic stage. The desired aims are to be accomplished by a rigid centralized governmental control over property and resources. Contemporary constitutions lend increasing support to this position. In recent decades a number of ideological and political movements have all expressed varying degrees of collectivism in the economic portions of their program — *Aprismo* in Peru, the Mexican Revolution, *Peronismo* in Argentina, the *Estado Novo* in Brazil, *Acción Democratica* in Venezuela, the *Movimiento Nationalista Revolucionario* in Bolivia, *Liberación National* in Costa Rica, to mention some of the more important examples. Marxist and especially Communist movements represent strong economic and political anti-Americanism and will be treated separately later.

Less understood but equally important has been a positive anti-Americanism reflected in the views of a large number of *pensadores* — novelists, essayists, poets, professional people and artists who exert a most important influence among those who govern in Latin-American countries. Inherent in the attitude of this significant group is the conviction of the superiority of Hispanic cultural values to those of the United States. The Good Neighbor Policy has done comparatively little to weaken this trend. The influence upon contemporary writers of Rodó, Araquistain, Vasconcelos, Garcia Calderon, Altamira y Crevea and others is obvious from even a cursory examination of their output. There is a stated or implied assumption that there are "two Americas" in the Western Hemisphere, that *"nuestra America"* means the America with a common historical experience, religion and language—items which form the basis for common values assumed to be unknown in the area of Anglo-Saxon influence. What is essential is the preservation of the values inherited from Spain and Portugal and a constant alert against the cultural imperialism from the north. Frequently suggested is an informal cultural union of Spanish-speaking peoples in the New World and the development of *hispanoamericanism* through cultural exchange programs, the establishment of literary and professional societies and similar activities devoted to the defense of the values of Hispanic culture, past and present.

MARXISM

The Latin-American setting has been ideally suited to the introduction of Marxian ideology since its primary concern with the labor movement has led to an emphasis upon industrialization and economic planning. Several of the more prominent political movements in the twentieth century reflect Socialist thought: in the Mexican Revolution, in the Aprista movement in Peru, in the reforms of José Battle in Uruguay, and in similar movements in Venezuela, Cuba and Bolivia.[7] While Socialist ideas have received considerable support in reforming and liberal circles, Socialist parties have been singularly weak. The oldest and strongest has been the Socialist Party in Argentina which achieved some electoral victories and was a major force in the labor movement until the Perón era. Generally speaking, the weakness has been the result of their being too doctrinaire and intellectualized and lacking in practical common sense. Thus, while possessing articulate leaders, Socialist parties in Latin America have had little genuine influence over the masses and have allowed that role to be pre-empted by the Communists and other activist movements.

Communist thought and action have made definite inroads in Latin America and have cleverly employed the increasing tempo of social revolution as a means of obtaining power.[8] Quick to cloak themselves with the mantle of nationalism, Communists pose as anti-imperialists and enjoy considerable success in attacking the "designs" of the United States. They have also taken the lead in weakening traditional class relationships, in making use of the strong drive for economic development, and in portraying themselves as defenders of democracy. The largest single group is in Brazil where Luis Carlos Prestes, its leader, has been the most prominent Communist in Latin America. Elsewhere Communism has made some progress in Chile, Cuba, Argentina, Bolivia and Venezuela.

While possessing some strong weapons in the great appeal of economic nationalism to peoples still believing themselves to be victims of foreign exploitation and in the desperate poverty of miners and peasants, it is surprising that Communism has not achieved greater success. However, where there are strong mass movements of

249

native Latin-American origin responsive to the requirements for social progress, such as in Peru, Costa Rica, Venezuela and Chile, Communist appeals evoke minor responses. Strong Catholic sentiments of the majority as well as an inherent hostility to regimentation are added checks to Communism. Finally, despite their attempts to perform as true nationalists, it is obvious frequently that the Communist orientation is not Chilean or Brazilian but Russian, since there is little originality in Communist thought, which tends to mirror the position of the Kremlin on most basic issues.

CATHOLIC SOCIAL ACTION

The neo-Catholic Christian Democratic movements are comparative recent arrivals in Latin America. Based upon the ideas of encyclical *Rerum Novarum* of Pope Leo XIII, there has developed an anti-Marxist Christian labor movement in addition to a lay movement for social action within the Church.[9] Interest in Catholic liberalism is perhaps strongest in Brazil and Chile. In Argentina, strong opposition to Perón came from a Christian Democratic movement formed in Cordoba in 1954. Unión Cívica in Uruguay, originally representing an orthodox, conservative Catholic point of view, more recently has veered toward the political and social philosophy of Jacques Maritain. The *Falange Nacional* of Chile (in no way connected with Franco's Falange in Spain) is a group of intellectuals with some labor backing, supporting a program and philosophy similar to Christian Socialism in Europe. It gives some promise of future influence in Chilean politics. Catholic labor groups in Ecuador, Costa Rica and Colombia have also been gaining power and prestige in recent years.

While these movements are in their infant stage, the religious renaissance which has been developing in Latin America in the past two decades reveals a strong emergence of Catholic social thought. Strong in their opposition to Marxism, this neo-Thomist thinking has had considerable influence through such able spokesmen as Clarence Finlayson of Chile, Oswaldo Robles of Mexico, Nicolás Derisi of Argentina, and Alceu Amoroso Lima of Brazil.[10]

THE MEXICAN REVOLUTION

Francisco I. Madero began the armed movement in 1910 which signaled the close of an era and the introduction of a deep-seated social and political revolution which has continued with varying emphasis until the present. His political and military action set in motion the forces of discontent which were to push the Mexican Revolution far beyond what he contemplated or even desired. Madero's *Plan de San Luis Potosí* was formulated to serve as the ideological banner of the Revolution but it did not correspond to the needs of Mexico in 1910. No detailed economic and social program was suggested to replace the outmoded Díaz pattern of national life. Only one paragraph was devoted to the agrarian problem — the crucial question in the country — and not a word on the explosive item of labor reform. Thus at the start, the Mexican Revolution had no clearly defined goal beyond political reform nor did it have any recognized body of theorists, no statesmen-philosophers. Explosive forces existed, however, which would have provided a revolution with or without a program. Madero became the symbol of a profound desire for change in all quarters. From his election as president in 1911 until his treacherous assassination in 1913, Madero indicated his awareness of the needs of his people but believed that remedies should be evolutionary, a long-range consequence of a more pressing task of political readjustments.

The chaotic years of civil war following 1913, however, were to produce a significant ideological development which culminated in the Constitution of 1917. Emiliano Zapata, a peasant born in a little village in the state of Morelos, provided the spark which ignited further demands for land reform. Others gave military and political assistance to the movement which was forming behind Venustiano Carranza, Governor of Coahuila. The self-appointed First Chief of the Revolution and actual leader of the "constitutional army," Carranza promised "all laws and measures necessary to satisfy the economic, social and political needs of the nation, effecting thereby such reforms as public opinion believes indispensable, to establish a regime which will guarantee the equality of all Mexicans."[11] Gradually obtaining labor and agrarian support, and a strong backing from the *pensadores* led by Luis Cabrera, the *constitucionalistas* issued a formidable list of decrees which provided substance to the social and economic revolution in the making. The legal basis for Carranza's power and the full content of the reforms in progress were established by the constitutional convention meeting late in 1916 at Querétaro.

This remarkable document contains two contradictory conceptions of the role of the state and of the relation of the individual to the government. Virtually all of the ideals relating to personal freedom found in the French and American Revolutions are restated. But these are in conflict with provisions which seek to ensure social betterment. Article 27, which is concerned with agrarian reform, national subsoil rights and the place of private property; the labor and welfare stipulations in Article 123; and the strict limitations upon the Church in Article 130 all reflect the philosophy of Querétaro that the social interest shall have precedence over the individual. It is entirely probable that this "ideological conflict within the Constitution was recognized for what it was, and much of the contradictory policy of Mexican governments since has stemmed from this fact. Different governments have emphasized one rather than the other of these commitments."[12]

Following from provisions of the Constitution and the views of the *constitucionalistas* has been the development of a strong and conscious nationalism which has had a profound influence upon other Latin-American countries. Evidence of this can be seen clearly from provisions which require Mexican birth for important office holders, the declaration of national ownership of subsoil wealth, close restrictions on alien land ownership, and the granting of advanced status to labor — since large employers were primarily foreigners. Laid down also were principles against foreign intervention for any reason, belief in the equality of all countries under international law, and the provision for equal legal treatment alike for citizens and aliens.

The changes in the economic and social structure of Mexico which have proceeded from the days of Carranza have not come evenly nor have they been instituted without internal contest or external pressure. Under Presidents Alvaro Obregón (1920-1924) and Plutarco Elías Calles (1922-1928), land distribution was pushed slowly accompanied by the institution of the *ejido* or semi-collective land holding community, labor organization was supported, and educational reforms were instituted giving an impetus to the regeneration of the Mexican Indian. The bitter conflict between Church and State erupted under Calles and was to continue for nearly two decades. Also under Calles came the birth of the political movement known today as the Institutional Revolutionary Party (PRI) which has been the primary vehicle for bringing into being the provisions of the 1917 Constitution and solidifying the political careers of those who at least have professed support for the ideas of the Revolution.

Reform reached its apogee under Lázaro Cárdenas (1934-1940)

who came into office following a series of provisional presidents functioning under the dictate of Calles. Cárdenas was convinced that the solution for Mexico's economic, social and political problems lay in expanding greatly the program of agrarian reform begun earlier on a modest scale. He also characterized a popular demand for greater implementation of the goals of the Revolution and the Constitution of 1917. Consequently, land distribution and the strengthening of the *ejido* program developed rapidly, together with strong support for labor organization, education and public health. Foreign investment was discouraged, especially following the expropriation of foreign oil holdings and railroads. Nationalization of sugar and textile mills and of electricity was also accomplished.

But with the administrations of Manuel Avila Camacho (1940-1946), Miguel Alemán (1946-1952), Adolfo Ruiz Cortines (1952-1958) and Adolfo López Mateos (1958-   ) , the course of reform has reflected the appearance of a new political generation. The old forces opposing change no longer actively oppose the tenets of the Revolution and have been reconciled to the development of a New Mexico. At the same time, the direction given the Revolution under Cárdenas has been modified considerably. Beginning late in the war, a rapid industrial expansion has been taking place. Foreign investors have quietly been invited back with capital, machinery and ideas to feed the boom that López Mateos inherited as President in 1958. A vigorous new middle class has come where nothing like it existed before — and a new rich to take the place of the old-time aristocracy. Caught up in their careers like middle class people the world over, these Mexicans are obviously not revolutionaries in the old Latin-American sense. With their stake in society, they are rather a new bulwark against the succession of rebellions of the past. They are, nevertheless, the products of a struggle that took the lives of some one and a half million Mexicans a generation or so ago.

Finally, mention should be made of the emergence of a strong Indianist-mestizo social force which has been a product of the Revolution. It was the first real step forward for these millions toward a new social consciousness. Brought into being was a new realism, and fused with it was the indigenous folk feeling which generated the leading artistic current in contemporary Latin-American life. Furthermore, in Mexico, the sons of the Revolution appreciate their Indian heritage. It has become fashionable to collect pre-Colombian art, to dabble in archaeology, to wear Indian costumes, and to study Indian customs. Interest is increasingly directed toward the evolution of a new nationality, the mestizo, a joining of races for a new one moving toward cultural maturity. Other Indianist nations, viewing the results of the Mexican Revolution, have been stirred to action by this example.

APRISMO IN PERU

Latin-American *pensadores* in the twentieth century have devoted increasing attention to their own people and society. Much of this activity has been centered around anthropological and archaeological studies of native cultures and indigenous history. It has just been noted that concentration upon *indigenismo* has been strong in the ideas and values of the expanding Mexican Revolution and is to be seen in other countries possessing a deeply rooted Indian base. Most powerful, in many respects, however, has been the movement originated in Peru in the early 1920's by the brilliant Víctor Raul Haya de la Torre called *Alianza Popular Revolucionaria Americana*. As a political party, APRA has enjoyed only sporadic success at the polls, reaching the height of its political power in 1945 when it obtained a majority of seats in congress and supported the victorious candidacy of a non-Aprista for president. APRA's limited electoral victories do not provide the true picture of a broad mass following which has usually been unable to make its strength felt at the polls because the party has been officially declared illegal for most of its life.

An analysis of the ideology and program of the Aprista movement reveals that it is not a totally new political thought since Aprista leaders have embraced a number of Marxist principles. However, these leaders "have combined certain ideas about the unique character of Latin America with the general ideas of democratic socialism in such a way that they comprise a doctrine which is a distinctive contribution to the political theory of Latin America."[13] One of the major Aprista contributions is the plan for the future organization of Latin America. Visualized is a continent democratized and industrialized which has assimilated its Indian population. It would be a unified nation-state strong enough to play a dominant role in world affairs. Repeated emphasis is placed upon the repudiation of "foreign" ideas, not because they are foreign "but because in many cases the attempt is made to introduce copied ideas and methods without trying to fit them into the rhythm of Latin American life."[14] Recognizing that foreign capital is needed to develop the continent, the Apristas nevertheless express a typical nationalistic bias against the predominant role of such capital, demanding that it be subordinated to the desire of the people. As an example of this view, they advocate joint ownership of the Panama Canal with the United States. Above all, they believe that what is needed for the continent is political and economic unification based upon a kind of overall planning that would rule out a highly competitive, unplanned industrial society.

Aprista thought reflects the social revolution under way in Latin America in its discussion of the specific social, economic and political reforms believed necessary for Peru. Prominent is the cry for agrarian reform and the suggestions for state control of basic industries. In addition, similar to the Mexican Revolution, APRA has given birth to an intense artistic movement which has led writers, musicians and painters to turn to indigenous themes for inspiration.

PERONISMO IN ARGENTINA

On June 4, 1943, President Ramon Castillo was overthrown by a military *coup d'état* which made possible the rise to power of a new *caudillo* in the person of Juan Domingo Perón, who was to govern Argentina with a firm grip until 1955. Ruling first behind the scenes until his election in 1945, Perón as president created a strong political movement based upon a demogogic appeal to the working and under-privileged classes. The *Partido Peronista,* assisted by a full-fledged distaff counterpart, the Peronist Feminist Party, more than any other political movement in Latin American history, developed a dialectic which sought to undergird it philosophically.

While there was much that was purely opportunistic, unscrupu-lously calculating and evil in *peronismo,* it did reflect, nevertheless, the drive for social and economic reform which has been so charac-teristic of contemporary Latin America. Workers were rewarded with wages, bonuses and social legislation such as Argentina had never known before. The constitutional revision of 1949 repeated a number of the major provisions of the Mexican Constitution of 1917. All property was to have a social function; capital was placed "at the service of the national economy" with "social welfare as its principal object," and the state given the right to intervene "in the economy and monopolize certain activities to protect the general welfare."

While it has been common to label *peronismo* as a quasi-fascist movement, it might more properly be called nationalistic. Explosive nationalism was perhaps the keynote of the Perón regime. A campaign of "economic independence" resulted in the reservation of all subsoil rights for the nation, nationalization of foreign-owned properties and state control of foreign trade among other things. Definite attempts were made to foster anti-foreign sentiment. A prominent slogan of the 1943 revolutionists was "Argentina for the Argentines, because only they created it, defended it, and are worthy of it."

Justicialismo was the official philosophy through which Perón sought to justify his regime. A peculiar hodge-podge of theories and catch phrases designed to glorify Perón and Argentina, *justicialismo* purported to be a middle ground between the capitalism of the United States and Soviet Communism. Through the doctrine, social justice was to be assured for all. Four basically conflicting forces were supposed to operate in society—idealism, materialism, individualism and collectivism—each had an appropriate and legitimate role to play in human affairs. However, similar to Marxist and Hegelian systems, *justicialismo* was a theory of conflict. It follows that "injustice, evil, and tyranny arise whenever any of the four elements is subdued and not permitted to exercise its proper role in society."[15] As might be expected from such a doctrine, it gave rise to a series of slogans such as "Elevation of Social Culture," "Signification of Labor," "Faith in God," "Humanization of Capital," and "Solidarity among Argentines." There is much in this and the policies of *peronismo* which resembles recent European totalitarianism. However, as one observer has stated: "I don't think you can pin standard labels on present-day Argentina. General Perón uses parts of the program of Mussolini, techniques of Hitler . . . the vocabulary of Marx and a legalistic framework of democracy. You can't call it conventional fascism . . . communism or socialism. . . . You have to use the name its followers use."[16]

BATTLISMO IN URUGUAY

José Battle y Ordóñez has made "Uruguay the foremost political laboratory in all of Latin America for social and economic experimentation."[17] Although he died in 1929, Battle's ideals and program while president (1903-1907 and 1911-1915) culminated in profound constitutional changes in 1919 and have retained influence in the eyes

256

of his followers in the powerful Colorado Party. The chief contribution politically has been the adoption of the unique plural or collegiate executive, first established in a modified form in 1919, abolished in the 1930's, but recreated fully in 1951 with the elimination of the presidency and its replacement with the nine-member National Council of Government. The present leading party, the Blancos (who in 1958 defeated the Colorados for the first time in ninety-three years) is permitted six of the nine seats and the second highest party is allowed the remaining three. It is possible for any minority within these major factions to obtain membership provided it polls more than one-sixth of the vote.

Largely through the original efforts of Battle, Uruguay has progressed far in becoming a model welfare state. Most of his ideas have been incorporated into fundamental social and economic reforms. In addition to his firm belief in the democratic process, Battle was convinced that a modified state socialism would free Uruguay from foreign economic exploitation. His faith in state ownership has become a feature of the Colorado ideology and today the government operates a large number of industrial and commercial undertakings. Battle's convictions can be summed up in his own words: "There is great injustice in the enormous gap between the rich and the poor. . . . But this does not mean that a man is either exploited or an exploiter. The inequality is not deliberate on the part of the more fortunate. The real source of inequality is in the difficulty of arriving at a just distribution. The gap must be narrowed and it is the duty of the State to attempt that task."[18]

BRAZIL AND VARGAS

The broadening social revolution and the forces of notionalism have not by-passed Brazil, thanks largely to the efforts of the most prominent Brazilian in recent decades, Getulio Vargas. From 1930 until 1944 and again from 1950 until his suicide in 1954, Vargas left a deep imprint upon his country and chartered a course which his recent successors have had to follow. Governing as an autocrat in the first period and as a democrat in the second, he early sought and obtained support for his regime from the working classes. He can be credited with a genuine and almost pathetic desire to help and hold the affection of ordinary people. The *Trabalhista* (workers) Party which he formed in 1946 was the means of returning him to power in 1950 though he had governed his *Estado Novo* without any parties after 1937.

A firm believer in economic and social reform and convinced of the need for industrialization for Brazil, Vargas in the 1930's put into effect a series of decrees embodying the main features of a comprehensive social security system. Minimum wages were established and syndicates of workers and also of employers were created along with special labor courts to handle labor problems. Foreign capital was still welcome but was subjected to strict regulation. Struggling Brazilian industries were assisted in every way. Under Dutra (1946-1950) and Café Filho and Kubitschek after 1954, much of this has been continued without, however, the Vargas flamboyance and demagoguery.

OTHER NATIONAL AND REFORM MOVEMENTS

The political, social and economic thought behind the movements already discussed applies in some degree to several other Latin-American countries. Chile, in particular, can boast of economic and social developments similar to those in Uruguay, thanks to the beginning made under Arturo Alessandri (1920-1925). The high level of Chilean intellectual productivity has been reflected in the evolution of a fully developed and frequently turbulent multi-party system. In the mid-1930's, a coalition of left of center parties under the leadership of Pedro Aguirre Cerda greatly expanded the work begun by Allessandri. These developments have continued in the postwar years, especially under the able tutorship of Gabriel González Videla and a former dictator turned democrat, Carlos Ibáñez. Similarly, under Galo Plaza and José María Velasco since 1948, Ecuador has leaned in the direction of ever-increasing state intervention in the economy.

With strong undertones of the Mexican Revolution, the *Movimiento Nationalista Revolucionario* in Bolivia has been a powerful force in that country since 1952. With a strong Marxist influence and an emphasis upon a concept of democracy more social-economic than political, the MNR has similar counterparts in such movements as Democratic Action (Venezuela) and National Liberation (Costa Rica). While it is too early to make more than a tentative comment, Cuba under the followers of Fidel Castro may well be classified in this group.

Much of what has been labeled fascism in Latin America has been, in reality, a homespun authoritarianism with strong militaristic tendencies. Dictatorships in Latin America rarely have sought to establish totalitarian control over the cultural and economic life of a country. They usually lack mass support, drawing strength from the military and certain oligarchical elements and do not engage in much interference in the private lives of the people. Rarely is there an economic basis for such regimes.

However, several countries in the 1930's had small neo-fascist movements which have now disappeared or declined rapidly in importance with the world-wide repression of fascism itself. In Brazil, the *Integralistas* denounced democracy, favored a corporative state and sported the slogan "God, Country, and Family." The *Nacistas* in Chile had a number of German and Italian nationals as leaders and displayed a marked resemblance to German and Italian fascism. *Hispanidad*, the philosophy of the Spanish Falange of Franco, found some support among conservative classes and occasional interest by elements of the Church. Although still in existence the *Sinarquista* movement in Mexico, created in 1937, lacks any great following. Its goal has been to restore Mexico to its traditional patterns—Spanish traditions, Catholic faith, home, village, and Christian political order. Strongly anti-foreign and nationalistic, the *Sinarquistas,* made some headway in rural areas and found Church support in its opposition to the constitutional restrictions against the Church

GENERAL CURRENTS AND CONCLUSIONS

The foregoing analysis reveals immediately an intense desire on the part of Latin-American peoples to shake off the dead hand of the past, to exhibit pride in their indigenous as well as their Hispanic origins, and to develop political and economic systems which they believe will be more responsive to their needs. The influence of Marxism, directly or indirectly, can be seen clearly in the economic and political movements of at least a score of countries. Newer but meriting close attention in the future is the rise of anti-Marxist Christian labor movements reflecting the influence of neo-Thomist ideas. Above all, the repercussions of the Mexican Revolution, the only true Latin-American revolution in the sense that it gave expression to profound social and economic change, can be seen in the continent-wide trend away from the controlling ideas and institutions of earlier years.

Certain individuals and movements have been singled out for special attention since they have had more than passing influence in their particular setting. All have in common the belief that the state must be employed increasingly as the instrument to provide the better life. In several states this attitude is receiving added support by a rising urban working class which employs essentially a European-type social democratic or labor party as an outlet for its views.

Possibly the only full statement of a political and social theory has come from Haya de la Torre and the Aprista movement. While the literature on the Mexican Revolution is extensive, virtually all of it, with the exception of Vasconcelos, does not form a systematic whole. Much of is is repetitive and strongly Marxian. Political writers in Mexico and elsewhere tend to produce polemics in favor of democracy as an ideal. The major contribution of the Apristas is the systematic proposal for the future organization of Latin America. Probably the most fundamental weakness in Aprista theory is its inability to describe how the movement might obtain power.[19] Education on a broad scale through the spread of *Aprismo* is thought to be sufficient but considering the problems to be encountered by an oppositionist force trying to unseat the traditional sources of power, this is not a realistic approach. At the same time, as Francisco Madero observed: "The only way to make a people strong is to educate it and to elevate its material, intellectual, and moral level."[20] American humanism, which has been built around the concepts of freedom and justice, is founded on a philosophy of law, order and peace. If it is to be operative fully throughout the continent, all the peoples of America must be truly free and skilled in the techniques of modern civilization.

SELECTED BIBLIOGRAPHY

Robert J. Alexander, COMMUNISM IN LATIN AMERICA (New Brunswick, N. J.: Rutgers University Press, 1957). A definitive analysis of Communist thought and action in Latin America.

———, THE PERON ERA (New York: Columbia University Press, 1951). A useful study of *peronismo*.

George I. Blanksten, PERON'S ARGENTINA (Chicago: University of Chicago Press, 1953), The best presentation of *justicialismo* in English.

W. Rex Crawford, A CENTURY OF LATIN AMERICAN THOUGHT (Cambridge, Mass.: Harvard University Press, 1944). A stimulating study of a large number of writers.

Harold E. Davis, LATIN AMERICAN LEADERS (New York: H. W. Wilson Co., 1949). The ideas of selected political leaders and leaders of thought.

Russell H. Fitzgibbon, URUGUAY: PORTRAIT OF A DEMOCRACY (New Brunswick, N. J.: Rutgers University Press, 1954). The best treatment of *battlismo*.

Simon G. Hanson, ECONOMIC DEVELOPMENT IN LATIN AMERICA (Washington: Inter American Affairs Press, 1951). A brief but good survey of economic thought.

Harry Kantor, THE IDEOLOGY AND PROGRAM OF THE PERUVIAN APRISTA MOVEMENT (Berkeley, Calif.: University of California Press, 1953). An excellent examination of *aprismo*.

Stanley Ross, FRANCISCO I. MADERO, APOSTLE OF MEXICAN DEMOCRACY (New York: Columbia University Press, 1955). The most recent study of the origins and meaning of the Mexican revolution.

William L. Schurz, LATIN AMERICA (rev. ed.; New York: E. P. Dutton and Co., 1949). A good general survey.

T. L. Smith, BRAZIL: PEOPLE AND INSTITUTIONS (Baton Rouge: Louisiana State University Press, 1946). A satisfactory introduction to Brazilian thought.

Frank Tannenbaum, MEXICO: THE STRUGGLE FOR PEACE AND BREAD (New York: Alfred A. Knopf, 1950). An interesting analysis of the course of the Mexican revolution.

Walter S. Washington, A STUDY OF CAUSES OF HOSTILITY TOWARD THE UNITED STATES IN LATIN AMERICA: BRAZIL (Washington, D.C.: U. S. Department of State, External Research Paper 126, February 24, 1956). One of three useful studies on anti-Americanism in Latin America. See also Research Paper 126.1 (Chile) and 126.2 (Argentina), issued in 1956 and 1957 respectively.

CURRICULUM VITAE

STEPHEN S. GOODSPEED is Associate Professor of Political Science, Special Assistant to the Chancellor, University of California, Santa Barbara; on the Santa Barbara campus since 1946; taught also on Berkeley and Los Angeles campuses of the University of California. Received A.B. and Ph.D. from University of California, Berkeley; studied also in Germany, England, Sweden and Mexico; extensive travel in Europe and Latin America.

Author: *The Nature and Function of International Organization* (Oxford University Press, 1959); *El Papel del Jefe del Ejecutivo en Mexico* (Mexico: Problemas Agricolas e Industriales de Mexico, 1955), and a number of articles in scholarly journals.

Member: Pan American Institute of History and Geography, American Political Science Association, Western Political Science Association.

New Democracies

CHAPTER THIRTEEN

FRANCE'S FIFTH REPUBLIC: "UNITY, TRUTH, AUSTERITY"

JOHN T. EVERETT, JR.

Texas Christian University

"The destiny of France: these words bring to mind the heritage of the past, the duties of the present and the hopes of the future. Since, here in Paris, almost a thousand years ago, France took her name and the State began to function, our country has lived through many things. Now in sorrow, now in glory, it has vigorously surmounted innumerable vicissitudes from within and without. During the last half century, it has been more gravely wounded and sorely rent than at any previous time in its history. But now, it has suddenly been offered an opportunity to emerge from doubt, from dissensions, from humiliations. And now our country wants to seize this opportunity by giving general interest precedence over all individual interests and prejudices. Now, by the grace of God, a better life is available to the French people provided they remain true to effort and unity . . . *Vive la République! Vive la France!*"[1]

Through the dark days of the Second World War, from the Fall of France to the Liberation, General Charles de Gaulle represented the French people's will to resist. As charismatic leader and embodiment of their hope for the future, he issued ringing calls to unity and sacrifice, that France might once again take her rightful place among the great, independent nations of the world.

As President of the Fifth Republic, General de Gaulle is once again engaged in the task of rallying his people. Again he is exhorting them to unity and sacrifice, that France may realize her potentialities and live up to his vision of her greatness.

The difference in the appeals lies in the different situations in which they were uttered. Whereas during the war he sought to marshal the French for opposition to an alien conqueror, he now faces the more difficult task of inducing them to forget old differences and to live and work together as a nation. Why should this be such a difficult task? The answer lies in the history of France, in the bitter conflicts and unresolved disputes, in the entire legacy of frustration and mistrust which have plagued the French since 1789. It is this legacy, with its historic associations and deeply rooted attitudes, that de Gaulle must overcome. His success will be measured in terms of his achievements in resolving basic conflicts and inducing consensus where only antagonisms have hitherto existed.

THE LEGACY

The political organization and *modus operandi* of any country find their roots in the national environment. Physical and geographic elements, intellectual and cultural evolution, and historic patterns and developments interact upon each other over time to produce the regime under which the nation will live. Of undoubted importance in modern France has been the influence of physical and geographic factors in determining the patterns and directions of economic progression, or lack thereof, and in influencing attitudes based on economic considerations.[2] Of equal importance has been the impact of history in molding the political culture, the conceptions of authority, and the uses to which it should be put.

France is a country haunted by revolution and the threat of revolution, each of which adds a new thread to the tangled skein of French ideology. No revolution has succeeded to the point where it could command the loyalties of all, or even a great majority of the populace over any length of time.[3] Rather, each attempt has exacerbated existing differences and compounded the difficulties of reaching agreed solutions.

History has left France a legacy of contradictions, the foremost of which juxtapose political stability with instability, and economic dynamism with *immobilisme*. Taken together, these elements are the main sources of ideological and political conflict, though the total picture is complicated by additional conflicts over religious questions (e.g., the position of the Roman Catholic Church, particularly in the field of education), the requirements of foreign policy (e.g., nationalism versus internationalism, militarism versus pacifism), and relations with the colonies.

The most obvious feature of France in the modern era has been the tragic divisions which separate the French people. So deep have been the schisms that they have prevented the development of even a minimum of consensus as to the proper organization of the

266

state, agreed objectives, or an acceptable relationship between the government and the citizens. So bitter has been the struggle that France for 170 years has undergone a succession of changing regimes, wavering between more or less ineffectual republicanism and authoritarianism, as Frenchmen have sought a form of government on which they could agree and which could cope with the increasingly complex problems posed by modern economics and international conditions.[4]

A contradictory, but less obvious feature of France is the basic stability of certain aspects of her governmental apparatus, notably the administration. Inherited from the monarchy and greatly strengthened by Napoleon I, the administrative structure has shown remarkable resiliency. Through all the vicissitudes of modern history it has been the anchor of the French state, providing a chain of orderly continuity. It has proved indispensable to each new regime, and it has permeated every aspect of life to the point that "France is not ruled, but administered, and it is her apparent political instability which guarantees the stability and permanence of her administration."[5]

The economic situation is similarly confused and contradictory. Uneven development has created a crazy-quilt of varying interests, one composed of modern and ancient, efficient and inefficient elements. The economic inheritance embraces a traditional peasant agricultural system, an artisan and small-shop sector of considerable proportions, and an inefficient family-managed type of industry. The modern sector includes a mechanized, up-to-date agriculture and dynamic, efficient industries and businesses. Anomalously, a great industrial laboring class has developed quite apart from the other segments of French society.

Unfortunately, these groups view their various interests as being basically opposed and incapable of reconciliation. The politically powerful traditionalists maintain themselves by virtue of legal privileges and governmental subsidies, and oppose any move which might upset the *status quo*. The modernists are resentful of traditional restrictions regarding them as the primary barriers to further economic development, while the working class insists upon a revolutionary overturning of existing forms, in accordance with their own historical approach. And, intensifying the differences are the age-old French dislike for large, powerful organizations, a sympatheic interest in the small, independent producer, and a pronounced tendency to oppose rather than to support positive policies.

267

France's legacy also includes a significant paradox, a stable instability; that is, the persistence not only of old conflicts but also of traditional attitudes and proposed solutions. Despite the succession of political regimes, actual experience with possible alternative forms of government has been limited.[6] Rather than experiment with bold new concepts, Frenchmen have been content to reiterate time-worn formulae regardless of the circumstances confronting them. In other words, each generation has sought to solve its problems by looking to the past. In such circumstances, however, the range of possible solutions has been predetermined. Formulations ostensibly designed to break the impasse have in fact blinded the French to the complete range of alternatives.

Since 1789 French politics has been dominated by the disjunction between two major political orientations, the Left and the Right,[7] These orientations are ideological in nature and provide "fixed" theoretical reference points for a variety of political parties and associations. As such, they establish the principal foci and delineate the avenues of approach to the problems of each age.

In terms of the major issues, the Left basically supports republicanism, defining it in terms of parliamentary democracy and the Rights of Man. The Right tends toward authoritarian government in which individual rights are secondary to the needs of the state. The Left favors modernization of the economy under governmental control and direction, while the Right defends free enterprise but splits on the question of modernization versus maintenance of the *status quo*. In matters of religion the Left, although upholding freedom of belief, opposes the Roman Catholic Church as an institution because of its past record of political activity; the Right supports it as an important instrument of social control.

Finally, in foreign affairs and colonial relations the Left is broadly internationalist, pacifist and anticolonialist in contrast to the nationalism, militarism and colonialism of the Right.

IDEOLOGY, PARTIES, AND THE FAILURE
OF THE FOURTH REPUBLIC

Despite the persistence of the Left-Right ideological orientation in French political thought, the prevailing system in the realm of practice is multi-party rather than bi-party. In 1935 as many as twenty parties had representatives in *Parlement*. In November, 1958, twelve parties and two coalitions supported candidates for election to the first National Assembly of the Fifth Republic.[8]

Although the various parties are generally classified as Leftist or Rightist, such assertions often confuse more than they enlighten because of the existence of several "tendencies" or major schools of thought. On this basis the fundamental breakdown reveals two principal political positions, one anti-democratic and the other pro-democratic. These provide the cores of the party philosophies.

The anti-democratic parties occupy the extreme positions on the political spectrum. Farthest to the Left are the Communists, who draw their inspiration from revolutionary Marxist sources and are closely tied to the Soviet Union. Nevertheless, they couch their appeals in terms of the French tradition of anti-clericalism, humanism, and revolutionary Jacobinism. Other extreme Leftists include some Syndicalists and Left-wing Socialists, plus a few Trotskyites.[9] Farthest to the Right are the dictatorial-minded neo-Fascists who are also dedicated to the overthrow of democracy. They differ from the Communists in their relative disorganization, clericalism and colonial attachment.[10] Nor do they posit any definite political and economic program.

Between the extremes lie four distinctly observable shades of opinion. First is the evolutionary-Marxist, anti-clerical, social-democratic Left which adheres mainly to the Socialist Party (SFIO). In the middle are the Christian Democrats represented by the Popular Republican Movement (MRP). Although a non-Marxist, Catholic party, the MRP normally co-operates with other moderates on social and economic questions. It has, however, moved slightly to the Right over the last decade, and its stand on colonialism has been equivocal.[11]

Radicalism constitutes a third traditional current of thought. It finds expression through the Radical Socialists and other small Center groups. Strongly republican, the Radical Socialists historically headed the anti-clerical movement and became the defenders of small, independent economic interests. Since World War II they have moved slightly to the Left in economic outlook,[12] and the termination of the Indochinese War was effected by a Radical Socialist Premier, Pierre Mendès-France.

Finally, to the Right is a more or less democratic, economically conservative, nationalistic, strongly Catholic school of thought which is represented by a group of small, undisciplined *assemblements*.

The common focal point of the Centrist parties is their willingness

269

to operate within a framework of political democracy. These groups provided the principal support for the Fourth Republic. The debacle of that regime signifies the failure of the democratic elements, particularly of the Left, to produce a viable regime, operating as they did within the limits of their traditional philosophies.[13] On the basis of an overwhelming mandate following the Second World War,[14] the Left had a unique opportunity to establish a new form of government, reform the economy, and redefine France's relations with her colonies. Blinded by their preconceptions, however, most of them did not see that modern conditions require strong leadership.[15] Consequently they failed to establish effective governmental institutions although creating the need for them by initiating a broad program of nationalization.[16] In defining the relationships with the colonies, they paid lip service to the ideal of equality but set up a system ensuring the dominance of the mother country. Again, however, the governing institutions were too weak either to maintain their control or to abandon it in the face of opposition.

Not only traditional philosophies, but also traditional forms contributed heavily to the expiration of the Fourth Republic. Regardless of the nearly unanimous electoral demand for a new regime, the product of the Constituent Assembly was little more than a resurrection of the Third Republic. Practically stillborn, it never commanded the loyalties of the bulk of the French people. In the constitutional referendum of October, 1946, which brought it into existence, 31 per cent of the potential voters abstained from casting a ballot, while another 31 per cent voted in opposition. Thus the new regime was launched with the approval of less than 40 per cent of the electorate. The pattern of abstention and opposition continued throughout its life.

Popular apathy, impotent institutions, and inability to resolve old conflicts or to agree on positive approaches to overwhelming problems—these factors contributed most heavily to the failure of the postwar system and provided the backdrop to what followed.

DE GAULLE AND THE FIFTH REPUBLIC

The Algerian explosion of May 13, 1958, signaled the demise of the Fourth Republic. It did not, however, ensure the birth of the Fifth. This achievement was the work of one man, General Charles de Gaulle.

De Gaulle's spectacular rise to power was not without precedent in French history. Periods of extremity have often produced strong leaders —men such as Henry IV, the two Napoleons, Clemenceau, and de Gaulle himself during World War II—*réconciliateurs,* capable of submerging old differences and rallying the nation to spiritual unity in the name of *la patrie.* The accession of de Gaulle, therefore, while by no means inevitable, was one of a number of predictable eventualities in terms of French historical experience.

Ideologically speaking, de Gaulle is a man of neither the Left nor the Right.[17] He views himself as a symbol of national unity, synthesizing in his person all of the contradictory traditions of the French. The people share this view, seeing in him "the monarchic order and the republican dream, Catholic discipline and social prog- ress, feudal chivalry and popular revolt."[18] In accepting him as head of the government, the French performed an act of faith rather than opting for a particular creed or policy.

Nevertheless, de Gaulle entered office with discernible precon- ceptions. A casual reading of his works will reveal an exaggerated, often irrational feeling for the *"destiné éminente et exceptionnele"* of France.[19] *Grandeur,* the desire for France once again to assume "front rank" among the nations of the world, these are the ardent desires of the "man of destiny." Moreover, he believes he is suited by tempera- ment, by training and experience, and by his "sense of mission" to be her leader.

On assuming office, de Gaulle saw the existence of certain major problems: to re-establish order in the state, to solve the Algerian prob- lem, and to restore unity to the nation. Rejecting temporary solutions, he sought and received full powers for a period of six months[20] in order "to eradicate the deep-seated cause of our troubles . . . the confusion and, by the same token, the helplessness of constituted authority."[21]

As early as 1945 de Gaulle viewed with alarm the proposal to revert to the traditional French parliamentary system. Following the electorate's approval of the Constitution of the Fourth Republic in May, 1946, he retired from public life, only to emerge partially in 1947 as leader of an extreme Right-wing "non-party coalition," the *Ras- semblement du Peuple Français* (RPF). Five years later he categori- cally withdrew his support from this group and returned to self- imposed solitude.

Until de Gaulle's accession there was considerable speculation

271

regarding the nature of his views concerning proper governmental organization. His statements on the subject were vague, except in their insistence on strong executive power, while the admitted anti-parliamentarianism of the RPF roused fear that he aspired to dictatorship. In his policy statement of June 1, however, he pledged himself "to lead the country, the State and the *Republic* to safety";[22] he also laid down three basic principles for a republican regime; (1) universal suffrage, (2) separation of the executive and legislative branches, and (3) Governmental (i.e., Cabinet) responsibility to the parliament. These principles were reiterated, and judicial independence promised, in the Constitutional Law of June 3, 1958, which actually authorized reformation of the government.[23]

The Constitution of the Fifth Republic proclaims France to be "a Republic, indivisible, secular, democratic and social" (Art. 2). It ensures the Rights of Man (Preamble), guarantees the equality of all citizens before the law (Art. 2), asserts the right of universal suffrage (Art. 3), and says that "political parties and groups . . . shall be formed freely and shall carry on their activities freely," though with due respect for national sovereignty and democracy (Art. 4). It thus incorporates the major elements of Leftist political ideology, although departing from their traditional form of parliamentary organization, as will be discussed.

The Constitution is a long (15 Titles and 92 Articles), complex, cumbersome document. The governmental structure which it authorizes includes: the President of the Republic (Title II) a Government (Title III), a bicameral Parliament (Title IV), a Constitutional Council to ensure regularity of elections and to offer declaratory judgments as to the constitutionality of organic laws (Title VII), a High Council of the Judiciary to nominate certain judges and to oversee the judicial branch (Title VIII), a High Court of Justice to try impeachments of the President and members of the Government (Title IX), and an Economic and Social Council to act as consultant on economic and social problems at the request of the Government, and to present its opinions to the Parliament (Title X). Title XI affirms the traditional centralized administration of local government,[24] and authorizes Overseas Territories to maintain their status, become Overseas Departments, or change into Member States of the Community. Titles XII and XIII contain provisions concerning the Community, while Title XIV specifies procedures for amendment.

272

The most notable feature of the new constitution is the power given to the President. Instead of being a figurehead as under the Third and Fourth Republics, the President is now the strongest figure in France. A special electoral college elects him to a seven-year term (Arts. 6 and 7) with no specified limitation on the number of terms permissible. His duties include the appointment of the Premier, the appointment of other members of the Government upon proposal of the Premier, presiding over the Council of Ministers, and terminating the functions of these officials upon resignation of the Government (Arts. 8 and 9). He also signs "the ordinances and decrees decided upon in the Council of Ministers," and makes civil and military appointments (Art. 13).

Although Article 34 specifies that "All laws shall be passed by Parliament," the President also figures largely in the legislative process. In the first place, he may take the initiative by sending messages to be read to each assembly, presumably for their guidance; these communications, however, are not subject to debate (Art. 18). It is the duty of the President to promulgate newly adopted laws within fifteen days following their transmission to the Government, but within this period he may order a reconsideration of all or part of the law in question (Art. 10). On proposal of the Government during Parliamentary sessions, or on joint motion of the two assemblies, he may submit to referendum any bill dealing with certain specified matters (Art. 11). After consultation with the Premier and the Presidents of the assemblies, he may dissolve the National Assembly (but not the Senate) and force new elections, though he may not take such action oftener than once a year (Art. 12). His ultimate power may be exercised in the event of a threat "to the institutions of the Republic, the independence of the nation, the integrity of its territory or the fulfillment of its international commitments," or "when the regular functioning of the constitutional governmental authorities is interrupted." Thereupon, the President "shall take the measures commanded by these circumstances" after consulting with the Premier, the Presidents of the assemblies, and the Constitutional Council (Art. 16).

Finally, the President is in charge of foreign relations (Arts. 14 and 52). as well as being commander-in-chief of the armed forces and presiding over the higher councils and committees of national defense (Art. 15).

Theoretically, in terms of Article 5, the President is supposed to ensure "the regular functioning of the governmental authorities" by means of arbitration. In actuality, the sum of his powers and prerogatives places him in a position where he may dominate both the executive and the legislative branches. However, the Constitution also provides *separately* for a Premier and a Government to be appointed by the President but responsible to the National Assembly of the Parliament. The Constitution charges this Government with the determination and direction of policy, and places the administration and the armed forces at its disposal (Art. 20). The Premier is made responsible for directing "the operation of the Government" and for national defense. He is to ensure the execution of the laws; he has certain regulatory powers; and he makes civil and military appointments "subject" to the power of the President. (Art. 21). "Should occasion arise," he may replace the President as chairman of the defense councils and committees, and "in exceptional circumstances" replace him as chairman of a meeting of the Council of Ministers. In such case he must be explicitly delegated and provided with a specific agenda (Art. 21). The powers and prerogatives of the Premier thus overlap those of the President in hazy, indeterminate fashion.

Article 24 establishes a bicameral Parliament consisting of a National assembly and a Senate. The former is directly elected, while the latter is indirectly elected and represents territorial units. The terms of office are not specified, but will be determined by organic law.[25] Regular sessions are held twice a year but are restricted to five and one-half months' duration annually. The Premier or a majority of the National Assembly may call a special session to consider a specific agenda (Art. 29), but Presidential decree actually opens and closes it (Art. 30). Although the houses are supposedly of equal significance, the National Assembly can override the Senate if there is disagreement on a bill (Art. 45).

The powers of the Parliament are considerably restricted when compared with the situation in the Fourth Republic.[26] Although the Parliament alone has the authority to pass all laws, the "domain of law" is specifically listed (Art. 34). All other matters are considered to be "of a regulatory character" and are dealt with by decree (Art. 37). Even measures normally within the "domain of law" may be enacted by decree for a limited period if the Parliament so authorizes (Art. 38). While all members of Parliament, as well as the Premier, have the right to initiate legislation (Art. 39), Government bills take

274

priority. On proposed amendments the Government has the prerogative of acceptance or rejection (Art. 44). Bills and amendments introduced by members of Parliament cannot be considered if they reduce taxes or increase expenditures (Art. 40). Subject to appeal to the Constitutional Council, the Government may declare inadmissable bills or amendments which it considers outside the "domain of law" or contrary to a grant of power under Article 38 (Art. 41). Parliament alone may authorize a declaration of war (Art. 35), but the Council of Ministers decrees martial law for a period not exceeding twelve days (Art. 36).

Potentially the most important power of the National Assembly is its prerogative to censure the Government and force its resignation (Art. 50). Under Article 49 the Premier, after deliberation with the Council of Ministers, may "pledge the responsibility" of the Government with regard to its program or a declaration of general policy. If a motion of censure is signed by one-tenth of the membership of the house, a vote of confidence will ensue after forty-eight hours. Adoption of the motion by a majority will cause the Government to resign. Failure to adopt debars the signatories from introducing another such motion during the same session.

The Premier may also pledge the responsibility of the Government on the vote on a specific bill. In such case, the text will be considered adopted unless a motion of censure is introduced within twenty-four hours and receives a majority after forty-eight hours, as above. The Parliament votes as a matter of right only on questions of confidence and texts of bills.

Unquestionably the position of the executive *vis-à-vis* the legislature is one of great strength. There are, nevertheless, a number of points of potential friction though the full implications of the dicephalous executive and its relations with the legislature are not fully apparent as yet.

The first point of possible controversy lies in the overlapping authorities of the President and the Premier. Since the lines of authority are not clearly drawn, disagreement between these two officials is bound to cause confusion eventually. The Premier certainly cannot force the President to accept his position, nor can the President directly coerce the Premier because of the latter's primary responsibility to the National Assembly. In the event of dispute, recourse would seem to be to Parliament, and the resolution might well enhance the authority of that body at the expense of both executive leaders.

Contention may also arise between the executive on the one hand and the legislature on the other. Already disagreement has arisen over the question of the National Assembly's voting rights. The Deputies are trying to broaden their prerogatives, while the executive is attempting to maintain the constitutional restrictions.[27]

On a broader plane, what if the President insists on a Premier or a program which the National Assembly censures? Two courses seem to be open: (1) the President might dissolve the Assembly and force elections hoping that the new body would be more amenable, or (2) he might declare that "the regular functioning" of the Government has been interrupted and institute rule by decree under Article 16. It is not certain that the former course would settle the impasse, while the latter is filled with hazards for democracy.

CONCLUSION

The die is not yet cast. Politically, France has moved to the Right in terms of strengthening the government, but democracy still exists since authority is based on the electoral process and individual rights are preserved. It is a far cry, nevertheless, from the ideal formula of the Left, and some Leftist leaders find cause for concern in its concentration of executive power atop the centralized administrative structure.[28] Moreover, the actual seats of power in the executive are not directly responsible to the electorate.

Anxiety also arises because of the Electoral Law of 1958 and the distorted representative picture produced by its implementation in the first election to the new National Assembly. This law rejects the system of voting by list with proportional representation used by the Fourth Republic and establishes a two-phase system of balloting with the second vote following the first by one week, with its basic unit the single-member district. To be elected on the first ballot a candidate must receive an absolute majority, "as well as a number of votes equal to one-fourth of the number of registered voters." On the second ballot a relative majority is sufficient.[29]

The results of the first election held under this system were startling. For example, in the first round of voting which occurred on November 23, 1958, 17.6 per cent of the electorate cast ballots for the de Gaullist Union for the New Republic (UNR), 15.5 per cent voted

Socialist, and 18.9 per cent voted Communist. The second ballot a week later, however, resulted in the election of the following: 189 Deputies affiliated with the Union for the New Republic, 66 affiliated with the Socialists and allied parties, and 10 Communists.[30]

The extremity of the misproportion emphasizes the dilemma of democracy in France.

Aside from direct issues such as economic and fiscal policy and the seemingly endless war in Algeria,[31] the basic governmental problem facing France is to grant the authorities sufficient power to enable them to govern with reasonable effectiveness and efficiency, while establishing procedures to ensure that the wishes of the people are respected and their liberties protected. Such a formula assumes, however, that the wishes of the people and the needs of the state are in some measure commensurable. Unfortunately, the fragmentation of French society, ideologically, economically and socially indicates the difficult nature of the problem.

The present constitution grants the government sufficient power for effective government. But, it is effective because of de Gaulle's strength and because of the depth of the French crisis — not because the French desire it. The unhappy paradox is that each positive step the government takes in terms of the general interest increases rather than diminishes opposition. Does it modernize the tax structure? This wins support from the laboring classes but alienates the commercial and industrial groups. Does it hold the line against inflation? This wins the applause of the modern economic sector but estranges the low-paid working class and the traditionalists who depend on government subsidies for their subsistence.

And what about the Algerian War? This is the most immediately pressing problem the government faces. Again, however, clashing interests and uncompromising attitudes render reasonable solutions on the basis of the general interest difficult, if not impossible.

What, then, are the alternatives? One might be to return to parliamentarianism and lapse back into *immobilisme* in the hope that matters will work themselves out. Current legislative impatience denotes the presence of this as a possibility, but recent history indicates the probable consequences. On the other hand, a greater slide to the Right, perhaps even a dictatorship based on the all-pervasive administration with the support of the conservatives, is a second potentiality.

Thirdly, the Communists might assume control, a contingency not

277

to be taken lightly in view of their powerful organization and the extent of their electoral support. Even a return to the Popular Front would almost inevitably be Communist-dominated today.[32]

Then, there is always the chance of civil war, particularly if an extremist group should attempt a *coup*.

The final possibility is that de Gaulle may succeed where others have failed. The present regime is tailored to correspond to his conceptions, and it has received the overwhelming endorsement of the French people. Despite its shortcomings, it provides an alternative to, or at least a modification of, traditional formulations. In long-run terms, though, it cannot remain under the domination of one man, however dedicated, if it is to continue as a democracy. The essential requirement is the development of a loyal opposition, democratically oriented, with a broad base of popular support. The moderate Left provides the logical locus for the evolution of such a group.

France has been given another chance. In the progressive unfolding of the Fifth Republic may lie her best hope for democratic government.

In January, 1960, since the above was written, an unsuccessful rebellion took place in Algeria as the extreme Right-wing *colons* attempted to repeat their *coup* of May, 1958—this time against General de Gaulle and his government. The failure of this uprising demonstrated the power of de Gaulle, as well as possibly clearing the way for a settlement of the Algerian question. It also led the Government in Paris to obtain from the legislature special ordinance powers for a one-year period as authorized by Article 38 of the Constitution.

Despite de Gaulle's success in overcoming the radical Right in this instance, however, the basic questions remain: Can de Gaulle achieve sufficient consensus among Frenchmen to provide the basis for a stable regime? Will the regime be democratic in nature?

SELECTED BIBLIOGRAPHY

Richard Barron, PARTIES AND POLITICS IN MODERN FRANCE (Washington, D.C.: Public Affairs Press, 1959). A brilliant study of the major parties.

Samuel H. Beer and Adam B. Ulam (eds.), PATTERNS OF GOVERNMENT (New York: Random House, 1958). Professor Nicholas Wahl's chapter on France is a penetrating analysis of the background and functioning of the Fourth Republic.

Léon Blum, FOR ALL MANKIND, Trans. by W. Pickles (New York: Viking Press, 1946). A major statement of principle and a broadly humanistic appeal for political and social democracy by a leading French Socialist.

William C. Buthman, THE RISE OF INTEGRAL NATIONALISM IN FRANCE (New York: Columbia University Press, 1939). An important study of both the rise and nature of French nationalism. Concentrates especially on the life and influence of Charles Maurras.

Elizabeth Davey (ed.), FRANCE IN CRISIS (New York: The H. W. Wilson Company, 1957). A symposium. Many of the articles are excellent though some are not too good.

Jean-Marie Domenach, "Democratic Paralysis in France," FOREIGN AFFAIRS, Vol. 37, No. 1 (October, 1958). Analysis of de Gaulle's rise to power and the weakness of the non-Communist Left from the point of view of a leading Leftist.

"France and the Fifth Republic," CURRENT HISTORY, Vol. 36, No. 213 (May, 1959). Contains articles on the "Rightist revolution," the Third and the Fourth Republics, French policy in 1959, the Community, finance and industrial relations. Authoritative and up-to-date.

"France: Education at Mid-Century," CURRENT HISTORY, Vol. 35, No. 204 (August, 1958). Good articles on most major aspects of the French educational scene, though nothing specifically on the influence of Catholicism. Has documents on the crisis of May and June, 1958.

"France in Africa," CURRENT HISTORY, Vol. 34, No. 198 (February. 1958). Symposium of first-rate articles by recognized scholars.

Charles de Gaulle, THE ARMY OF THE FUTURE (Philadelphia: J. B. Lippincott Company, 1941). Provides insight into General de Gaulle's thinking. Note particularly Part VI, "The High Command."

Charles de Gaulle, WAR MEMOIRS: THE CALL TO HONOUR, 1940-1942, Vol. I; UNITY, 1942-1944, Vol. II (New York: Viking Press, 1955 and 1959). Highly important for their revealing self-portrait, as well as for literary merit and historical information.

E. Drexel Godfrey, Jr., THE FATE OF THE FRENCH NON-COMMUNIST LEFT, Doubleday Short Study in Political Science (Garden City, New York: Doubleday, 1955). A brief, but penetrating study of the Left in terms of both history and theory.

Francois Goguel-Nyegaard, FRANCE UNDER THE FOURTH REPUBLIC (Ithaca, New York: Cornell University Press, 1952). An outstanding analysis.

Herbert Luethy, FRANCE AGAINST HERSELF, Trans. by Eric Mosbacher (New York: Frederick A. Praeger, 1955). One of the best analytical histories of the Fourth Republic.

Jacques Maritain, LES DROITS DE L'HOMME ET LA LOI NATURELLE (New York: *Editions de la Maison Française*, 1942). An important work by the leading spokesman of liberal French Catholicism.

Kingsley Martin, THE RISE OF FRENCH LIBERAL THOUGHT, ed. by J. P. Mayer (New York: New York University Press, 1954). A solid study of the eighteenth-century *philosophes* showing their impact on Leftist thought.

J. P. Mayer, POLITICAL THOUGHT IN FRANCE (London: Routledge & Kegan Paul Limited, 1949). Short survey from the Revolution of 1789 to the Fourth Republic. Concise but good.

Constantin Melnick and Nathan Leites, THE HOUSE WITHOUT WINDOWS: FRANCE ELECTS A PRESIDENT, Trans. by Ralph Mannheim, (Evanston, Illinois: Row, Peterson & Co., 1958). Provides insight into French politics through an analysis of the presidential election of December, 1953. A RAND Corporation research study.

Charles Morazé, THE FRENCH AND THE REPUBLIC (Ithaca, New York: Cornell University Press, 1958). An economic interpretation exhibiting bias. Contains useful information particularly on the development of the economy.

René Remond, LA DROITE EN FRANCE DE 1815 A NOS JOURS (Paris: Aubier, 1954). The major study of the Right by an astute scholar.

CURRICULUM VITAE

JOHN T. EVERETT, JR., Associate Professor of Government, Texas Christian University (Fort Worth Texas), received his Bachelor of Arts from Princeton University and Master of Arts and Doctor of Philosophy from University of Cincinnati. He has attended summer session at the University of Paris (Sorbonne), and made two study tours to England, Low Countries, France and Germany. In 1958 he participated in Cultural Exchange Program at the invitation of the West German Federal Government. Is the author of "The Bricker Amendment and United States Foreign Affairs," University of Cincinnati Law Review, XXIII, 2, Spring, 1954. He served as Instructor of Political Science, 1952-1955, University of Cincinnati, Cincinnati, Ohio; Associate Professor of Political Science and Acting Chairman, 1955-1956, The Western College for Women, Oxford, Ohio; and Assistant Professor, Ohio University, 1956-1959.

CHAPTER FOURTEEN

GERMANY'S RECONSTRUCTION

Eric Waldman

Marquette University

CHAOS — 1945

About twenty-two hours after General Jodl and Admiral von Friedeburg signed early in the morning of May 7, 1945, at the Allied Headquarters at Reims, the document providing for Germany's unconditional surrender, the thunder of heavy guns, the roar of Allied bombers in the fire-red sky, and the deafening explosions of bombs and shells ceased. The survivors of Hitler's *Goetterdaemmerung* dug themselves out of the rubble of their destroyed cities. A belated spring hesitatingly moved through the wounded and devasted land.

The eastern parts of the country had been overrun by the Red Army. A trail of senseless destruction, violent death, and raped women was left behind by the Red soldiers. The devil's seed sown by Hitler and his cohorts in the East when large areas of Russia were occupied and millions of people were mistreated and ruthlessly exploited, had germinated and was bearing fruit. The Red soldiers were taking revenge on the German people for the crimes inflicted by the Nazis upon their country and they were paying it back with cruel and devastating interest.

The cynical remark heard frequently near the end of the war among the desperate population combined a grim humor (*Galgenhumor*) with the uncertainty of the future and the possibility of violent death: "Friends, better enjoy the war while it lasts; the peace will be terrible!"

Six years of total war had forced Germany to employ eventually all her human and material resources and reserves. Almost all of her territory became part of the combat zone. Gradually the entire country was transformed into a vast heap of rubble by Allied ground and air operations. A great part of the industry was destroyed. Transportation was wrecked. The entire administrative machinery disintegrated. A great many government and party officials attempted to submerge among the millions of homeless and wandering about masses.

The intensity and totality of the German collapse and of the seemingly unsurmountable difficulties which the surviving people faced can best be illustrated by a few revealing figures. The population of the cities was greatly reduced as a result of the evacuation of nonessential civilians from the heavily bombed urban and industrial centers and of the heavy casualties caused by the war. Berlin, for example, had only slightly over half of its former 4½ million people at the end of the war. Cologne which in 1939 was a city with 750,000 inhabitants had only 40,000 left in 1945. Twenty-five million people were uprooted; five or six million had been killed; and at least five million former soldiers were prisoners of war.[1]

The over-all situation was further aggravated by the fact that since the fall of 1944 millions of refugees from the eastern areas were on the move trying to escape the horrifying grasp of the advancing units of the Red Army. Furthermore, the Nazi government had brought over five million foreign workers and prisoners of war to Germany in order to utilize them in the war industries or to replace German manpower needed to fill the decimated ranks of the military machine. Many of these former slave laborers, their human dignity violated during years of extreme hardship and merciless exploitations, were adding to the confusion by their acts of revenge and violence.

Industrial production was at a standstill. Money rapidly lost its value. People resorted increasingly to trading their meager possessions for essential foodstuff. Aimless masses milled in the streets with but one determination left — the will to survive. Many were ready to pay any price for this.

The only existing sources of authority which attempted to maintain order within the defeated land were the military commands of the victorious Allies. The government of Admiral Doenitz was of short duration because the Allies refused to recognize it. Hitler had appointed Doenitz as his successor on April 30, 1945. Probably this was his last political act before he ended his own life in the depth of the crumbling *Fuehrerbunker* at the beleaguered Reich Chancellory in Berlin. Admiral Doenitz and most of the other members of his "government" at Flensburg were arrested by British troops on May 10, 1945 and became prisoners of war. Germany as a state had ceased to exist. Its last remnants of administrative organization and bureaucracy had disappeared. The Allies assumed supreme authority and commenced with the realization and implementation of their predetermined plans designed to eliminate once and forever Germany from becoming again a menace to the peace of the world.

Within one month after the unconditional surrender and preceding the Potsdam Agreement by two months, the supreme military commanders of the United States, Great Britain, France and the Soviet Union signed on June 5, 1945 the "Arrangements for Control of Germany by Allied Representatives." This document set the basic pattern for the civil administration of occupied Germany and it also determined the machinery of control and the division of a truncated Germany into four occupation zones. Her eastern areas were placed "temporarily" under Polish and Soviet administrations. The commanders-in-chief of the four powers were the supreme authorities in their respective zones of occupation. In matters affecting Germany as a whole they were supposed to act jointly through an Allied Four Power Command.[2] While combat operations were still in progress the future zonal boundaries were originally drawn up as lines of military demarcation. Eventually, they became the political boundaries between the different zones. Those which separated the three western zones from the Soviet zone of occupation even became part of the Iron Curtain.

In spite of strong disagreements among the Allies about the economic reconstruction of Germany and about the amount of reparations in kind to be extracted from Germany, the Four Powers agreed during the early phase of the occupation at least in political matters. The Potsdam Agreement of August 2, 1945, while leaving the question of the final settlement of Germany's eastern boundaries undecided, stated the Allies' common over-all plans and main objectives. First on the agenda was the determination of eliminating any future possibility for Germany to violate the peace and security of other countries. Secondly, there was the intention "to prepare for the eventual reconstruction of German political life on a democratic basis" although the Allies failed to clarify what they understood under the concept "democratic basis." There is a great difference between Western and Soviet interpretations of democracy. Finally, there was the reference to the utilization of German resources for reparation, especially to be rendered to those countries which suffered most under the German occupation.[3] This agreement served during the initial phase of the Allied occupation as the blueprint for the establishment of military government, occupation policies, basis for indigenous co-operation, and most important for the attitude toward the conquered. The American basic directive (JSC 1067) was squarely based on the same concepts as those contained in the Potsdam Agreement.[4] Thus under the control and supervision of the occupation powers, local German governments were set up and "reliable" German personnel, recruited from among former anti-Nazis recommended by priests and pastors, former trade union officials and members of political parties that had been prohibited by Hitler, were appointed to various local positions.[5]

One still unexplained and seldom mentioned phenomenon of World War II was the negative attitude of the Allies toward the German anti-Nazi resistance. These forces operated under the most difficult conditions. Many of the courageous underground fighters were apprehended and executed by Hitler's Secret Police. The German underground was comprised of people who came from all walks of life. Social Democrats, former members of the Catholic Center Party, priests, professors, officers and government officials joined in actions and planning for a happier future political life in a new Germany.[6]

The negative position taken by the Allies toward the German resistance forces might have been based on a general distrust against anything *German*. This outlook might well have been the outgrowth of the unconditional surrender attitude. However, a far more Machiavellian scheme played cleverly by the Soviet Union should also be considered as a possible explanation of the policy of non-co-operation with the German resistance. Contrary to experiences in France and elsewhere, the German Communists played only a minor part in the German underground. The overwhelming majority of the anti-Nazis were anti-totalitarian as well. The Soviet leaders realized that they could not utilize the German resistance to further their objectives. They stressed, therefore, the necessity to come to a complete break with the past. At the same time they proceeded to implement their plan of building up a new Communist movement around a core of Russian-trained German Communists, such as Wilhelm Pieck and Walter Ulbricht, who could be fully trusted from the Soviet Union's point of view.

ALLIED OCCUPATION — THE BEGINNINGS OF
POLITICAL RECONSTRUCTION

Still during the chaotic and unsettled period which immediately followed the German collapse, political groups made their appearance. These groups remained, however, under strict control and supervision of the occupation forces. The Soviet Military Administration (SMA) appeared quite eager in activating so-called "anti-fascist" groups which were to serve as Communist front organizations. As early as June 10, 1945, SMA Order No. 2 permitted the founding of political parties. On the following day, June 11, the Communist Party (*Kommunistische Partei Deutschlands* — KPD) was officially founded in Berlin. The Socialist Party (*Sozialistische Partei Deutschlands* — SPD) became activated on June 16. The Christian Democratic Union (*Christlich-Demokratische Union* — CDU) followed on June 22. The fourth political party to receive its license from the Soviets was the Liberal-Democratic Party (*Liberal-Demokratische Partei* — LDP) at the beginning of July, 1945.

Judging from their actions, the Western Allies were not interested in encouraging the formation of political parties at that time. In fact, they did not issue any licenses until after the Potsdam Agreement and then to local political groups only. This restriction was supposed to be one of the methods of keeping most aspects of German life decentralized. In the British Zone, after September 15, 1945, political organizations were permitted to operate on a district (*Kreis*) level. British military government insisted that these groups were "democratic in spirit" and were willing to co-operate with the occupation authorities. At this time the Communists were included together with the Christian-Democrats, the Socialists and the Liberals in the category of "democratically oriented groups." Also in the United States Zone local organization was stressed. For example, until November 30, 1945, military government granted sixty-two licenses to political *Kreis* parties in Bavaria. Twenty-three of them were socialist, twenty-one Communist, and fifteen had different names. The latter group eventually consolidated in the Christian-Social Union (*Christlich-Soziale Union* — CSU), the Bavarian version of the Christian-Democrats.

In order to qualify for a license, a number of Allied restrictions had to be met. A political party was prohibited to praise German militarism and war, to attempt the re-establishment of a Nazi government, to discriminate against people of different color, race or religion and to undermine the authority of military government or to create disharmony among the Allies.

Some of the main difficulties the new political parties had to overcome were: (1) the organizational limitations which prevented activities above the *Kreis* level; (2) the non-existing or poor communication and transportation facilities of the postwar period which handicapped the co-operation among similarly oriented groups; (3) the political apathy found by party organizers among their fellow countrymen; and finally (4) the large number of Germans, between six and eight millions, disqualified from participating in any political organization as a result of their own past Nazi affiliations.

Political apathy probably was one of the many symptoms of the intense individual and group insecurity prevalent in postwar Germany. The Germans believed that their destroyed country was nothing but an *object* of foreign power politics with no chance left for the population to influence their own destiny. Furthermore, most people had no time for politics. They were preoccupied with gathering of food and finding housing facilities.[7]

Most of the political organizations were able to adapt themselves to work under these difficult conditions. For example, voluntary associations (*Arbeitsgemeinschaften*) co-ordinated the "decentralized" political groups and successfully circumvented the official military government directives restricting organized political activities to the local level.

These postwar political groupings were supposed to be "new beginnings." In actuality, most of them were revivals of political parties dating back to the Weimar period. The Communist Party, for example, showed hardly any differences from the KPD of the Weimar era. Also the SPD followed the old pattern. The Christian Democratic Union and the Free Democratic Party (*Freie Demokratische Partei —* FDP, an analogous organization to the Liberal-Democrats in the Soviet zone) represented in contrast a conglomeration of political forces which before 1933 were organized in several political parties.

As a result of prior planning by their Soviet masters, the German Communists had in terms of organization and programming an original advantage. Following the pattern which proved successful in the "liberated" East European area, the German Communists wished to obtain the leadership in a "democratic, anti-fascist bloc" comprised of several political parties. They hoped that in the chaotic postwar conditions and through the support of the Red Army, they would eventually be able to seize control. The Communist "action program" of June 11, 1945, can be interpreted as a means toward establishing a common platform for all truly "democratic" parties. Overtly, the Communists tried to appear as a moderate group, dedicated to fight together with the Allies and the other "democratic and anti-fascist" Germans to eliminate the last remnants of the Nazi regime and to rebuild a new and democratic Germany.

The German Communists were apparently so confident that their efforts would succeed — counting heavily on the active direction and support of the SMA — that early approaches made by Social Democratic leaders (e.g., Max Fechner and Otto Grotewohl) in favor of a united workers' party were turned down. When the Communists realized that their "front tactics" could only be used effectively in the Soviet zone, they took up the drive to unite all workers in one party. In April of 1946, in the Soviet zone, their effort led to the founding of the Socialist Unity Party (*Sozialistische Einheitspartei* — SED), a merger of the KPD and SPD, forced upon the Socialists by the Soviet authorities.

In the Western zones the Communists failed to bring about the merger of the Social Democrats with the small groups of Communists. In order to increase their influence, Communists then tried to convince the people that they were genuine democrats and ready to co-operate with all anti-Nazi forces. Communists eagerly participated in the work of local governments and special agencies founded by the Western occupation authorities.[8]

Neither the memories of the Nazi concentration camps nor the experience with a divided labor movement during the Weimar Republic were sufficient reasons for the Social Democrats to forget their ideological differences with the Communists. This development was most important for the later reconstruction period because the Socialist Party emerged as one of the main pillars of the new German democracy.[9]

A unity movement of an entire different kind, aiming at the founding of a German "labor party" comprised of Social Democrats and certain groups of the former Christian labor unions, also failed to materialize. Dissensions about a German labor party were held already prior to Hitler's ascent to power among Socialists and Christian labor representatives. Of the latter, Jakob Kaiser and Ernst Lemmer participated in these discussions prior to 1933. They were among those who survived the Nazi regime. Still in 1945, they approached officials of the former Social Democratic Party with the proposal to organize a political party modeled after the British example. Their efforts failed.

The concept of an organization representing the interest of labor succeeded, however, in the trade union field. Non-partisan trade unions were formed comprised of Socialists and members of the Christian labor unions of the pre-Hitler era. In October 1949, a single parent organization for the six million trade unionists (i.e., one-third of the entire German labor force) was formed, the German Trade Union Federation (*Deutscher Gewerkschaftsbund* — DGB). The DGB consisted of sixteen national industrial unions.[10]

While the Socialists and Communists were unable to unite in a common party because of their incompatible ideologies — Communist totalitarianism versus Democratic Socialism — the Christians of both major denominations drew the logical consequences from their common suffering under the Nazis and from a realistic evaluation of the impact their combined strength could have. It was indeed of major importance for the future development of democracy in Germany that Catholics and Protestants formed an interdenominational party which consciously based its policies on Christian principles.

In Berlin the leading personality in the founding of the CDU was Dr. Andreas Hermes of the former Catholic Center Party who was appointed Second Mayor of Berlin after the end of hostilities. The first official statement published by the CDU in Berlin on June 26, 1945, bears the signature of thirty-five people, Catholics and Protestants. Many of the founders were freed only a short time before from Nazi concentration camps or jails.

Interdenominational political organizations were founded simultaneously in many other localities. While the founding of the CDU at Cologne in July, 1945 — one of the major centers of Christian Democratic activities — was primarily the result of the work of former Center Party members, such as Dr. Schwering, in other areas, especially in the North, the Protestant element had the initiative. In spite of the fact that hardly any communications existed between such main centers, as Berlin and Cologne, their respective programs contained strikingly similar provisions.[11]

RE-EVALUATION OF WESTERN POLICIES

Within a short period of time, it became apparent that the wartime unity of the Allies gave way to a serious power struggle for the future control of Germany. The dissimilar concepts the Allies had concerning Germany's reconstruction heavily taxed the agreed-upon policies. The ensuing breakdown of Allied co-operation was really the *result* and not the cause of the over-all power struggle which still engulfs the entire world. Soviet leaders successfully sabotaged combined Allied actions and in general disregarded existing agreements which demanded uniform policies and procedures for all of occupied Germany. By fall of 1946, the East-West split compelled the United States, Britain and France to re-evaluate their entire occupation policies.

The current power contest between the Soviet Union and the Free Nations constitutes a most dangerous situation for all the world. On the other hand, it is asserted that this split became the most decisive factor of Germany's recovery. If the wartime alliance had remained intact and operational, it is highly doubtful if either the spirit of Potsdam or the occupation rules within the Western zones would have been replaced so quickly by new directives. Co-operation with the Germans and the early return of self-government and sovereignty to the German people became the elements of the new policies. Germany's price for this development is the unfortunate division of the country into an eastern part, ruled in Soviet fashion by a militant Communist minority, and into a democratic western part, the Federal Republic.

One of the outstanding landmarks of the policy change of the United States was the address delivered by Secretary of State James F. Byrnes on September 6, 1946, at Stuttgart, Germany. He stated the new official position of the United States government and announced the determination of the Americans and British to unite the economies of their respective zones in order to facilitate German economic rehabilitation. The address ended with a promise for American help to the Germans:

> The American people want to return the government of Germany to the German people. The American people want to help the German people to win their way back to an honorable place among the free and peace-loving nations of the world.[12]

The new British attitude toward Germany was reflected in the famous Churchill speech in Zurich on September 19, 1946, in which he demanded that Germany again be accepted in the European family of nations.

As expected, the Soviet Union refused to participate in the U.S.-British economic unification plan. Also the French declined to cooperate. The first step toward German economic unity and eventual rehabilitation was, therefore, a Bizonial Agreement signed in London in December, 1946 by representatives of the United States and Great Britain. German Bizonial agencies commenced operations on January 1, 1947.

The French did not show any change in attitude until the Foreign Minister Conference in London in December of 1947 again failed to agree on a common approach to solve the German question. French co-operation, as a matter of fact, came only after it had become quite certain that the Soviet Union was persistent in her policy of blocking the eventual economic and political reunification of Germany except on her terms. The French also realized that the United States and Britain decided to go ahead with their plans with or without the French zone.[13] The three Western Powers finally agreed to meet and to consider trizonal economic fusion and the establishment of a West German government. At the London Six-Power Conference (two sessions: February 26 until March 5, 1948, and April 20 until June 1, 1948), representatives of the Benelux countries and of the Western Powers clarified the conditions a future German governmental system would have to meet in order to obtain Allied approval. It was emphasized that a German constitution would have to include provisions for a federal structure and for the protection of substantial civil rights. The Allies also agreed that for reasons of mutual advantages, Germany was to be included in the European Recovery Program.[14]

The Minister Presidents of the eleven West German *Laender* received from the military governors the authorization to appoint a constituent assembly and to instruct its members to prepare a constitution for the future German state. Due to the fact that not all of the four occupation zones were able to participate, the Germans felt that it would be more appropriate to elect a "Parliamentary Council" and to draft a "Basic Law" (*Grundgesetz*) which, after the approval by the Western Allies and ratification by the West German *Laender*, would become the governmental basis for a unified political

290

and economic administration of the area comprised of the Western occupation zones. The drafting of a "constitution" remained reserved for the time when all of Germany could be included.[15]

THE CONSTITUTIONAL FOUNDATION OF
GERMAN RECONSTRUCTION

The Parliamentary Council adopted the Basic Law on May 8, 1949. The text was submitted to the military governors and received approval on May 12. In the week of May 16 to 22, the Basic Law was ratified by the legislatures of more than two-thirds of the West German *Laender* and became the "temporary constitution" of the Federal Republic of Germany officially on May 23, 1949.

On August 14 of the same year, the first free elections for the Federal Diet (*Bundestag*) were held. During the following month the federal offices were established. The university city of Bonn was selected as the temporary federal capital.

Although the new German government had wide powers, an "Occupation Statute," promulgated simultaneously by the Western Allies, staked out certain reservations retained by the former military occupants. These reservations included items directly related to the security of Allied forces stationed in the territory of the Federal Republic and to problems concerning restitution and reparation. The Allies also reserved for themselves the right to invalidate German laws when these laws were detrimental to Allied interest or to the functioning of democratic government in Germany. These rights were gradually trimmed down in the "deoccupation" process. Germany was restored to full sovereignty at the time when the Federal Republic joined the Western European Union and also became a member in the North Atlantic Treaty Organization on May 5, 1955.

According to the Preamble, the Basic Law was adopted only for a "transitional period." At the time of this evaluation, it has been in operation for ten years. The Basic Law constitutes a marked improvement over all of its constitutional forerunners starting with the proposed constitution of March 23, 1849, the work of the Constituent National Assembly which met at the *Paulskirche* in Frankfurt, the first Reich Constitution of April 16, 1871, and the Weimar Constitution of August 11, 1919. The Third Reich (1933-1945), a period during which "the will of the Fuehrer" took the place of a constitution, contributed to the constitutional development inasmuch as it serves as a vivid warning of the unavoidable effects of a totalitarian political system.

Partly as a result of the legalistic German tradition, but also partly as a reaction to the recent experience with unlimited and arbitrary government, the Basic Law attempts to provide a detailed pattern for the political, social and economic life within the Federal Republic. An examination of its provisions, therefore, reveals not only the conceptual background, but also the actual operations of the German political system.

The sixty-three members of the Parliamentary Council, most of them experienced parliamentarians and constitutional lawyers, were still strongly under the impact of the crimes the Hitler regime had committed against the dignity and freedom of man. In order to impress the people with the significance of the basic rights, they placed them at the very beginning (Articles 1 to 19) of the Constitution. Article 1 reads:

> The dignity of man is inviolable. To respect and protect it is the duty of all state authority.
> The German people therefore acknowledge inviolable and inalienable human rights as the basis of every community, of peace and of justice in the world.
> The following basic rights bind the legislature, the executive and the judiciary as directly enforceable laws.

The enumeration of the basic rights is an impressive one. Possibly the framers committed an oversight when they failed to remind the citizen of his duties to the community. Nothing is said about subordination to the common good or about the duty to participate actively in public life.

In the Weimar Republic so-called "democratic" rights were misused by totalitarian demagogues to undermine the political order. Therefore, the Basic Law "prohibits" activities "directed against the constitutional order or the concept of international understanding." (Article 9) These limitations apply not only to individuals but also to political organizations and parties. Article 21 provides the provision for the outlawing of anti-constitutional parties:

> Parties which, by reason of their aims or the behavior of their adherents, seek to impair or destroy the free democratic basic order or to endanger the existence of the Federal Republic of Germany are unconstitutional. The Federal Constitutional Court decides on the question of unconstitutionality.

The Federal Constitutional Court in its short history has used this Article twice to declare a political party unconstitutional. In both cases, the court's decision led to the prompt dissolution of the party concerned. In 1956, the small but articulate neo-Nazi Socialist Reich Party and the Soviet-dominated Communist Party were thus effectively eliminated from the German political scene.

In order to provide the best possible protection to the basic rights, the framers made it "inadmissible" to amend Articles 1 to 20. Thereby, they made these articles an unchangeable part of the Basic Law.

Article 20 does not deal directly with individual rights and their protection. It contains, however, some of the most fundamental provisions of the constitutional arrangement:

> The Federal Republic of Germany is a democratic and social federal state.
> All state authority emanates from the people. It is exercised by the people by means of elections and voting and by separate legislative, executive and judicial organs.
> Legislation is subject to the constitutional order; the executive and the judiciary are bound by the law.

A federal arrangement as part of the governmental structure for Germany was not an undisputed issue. The United States and France, supported by most Christian Democrats within the Parliamentary Council, were in favor of a federal system. The British government and the German Social Democrats preferred a unitary state organization. When the Basic Law finally was promulgated, it provided for a rather strong federal arrangement. The Federal Council (*Bundesrat*), the German equivalent to the U.S. Senate, has substantially greater powers than the former *Reichsrat* of the Weimar Republic.

As could be expected, many provisions of the Basic Law are the result of specific experiences made under the Weimar Constitution and of the conscious efforts made by the Parliamentary Council to correct alleged constitutional shortcomings. There are, for example, no "emergency powers" vested in the Federal government like the often misused Article 48 of the Weimar Republic.

The framers also were much concerned to create a constitution which could provide favorable conditions for the development of a stable political system. The division of legislative powers between the Federal government and the *Laender* governments (Articles 71 to 74) is one important aspect of this effort. Probably the most ingenious single constitutional device is the arrangement affecting the tenure of office of the Federal Chancellor, the most powerful individual position within the government.

> The *Bundestag* can express its lack of confidence in the Federal Chancellor only by electing a successor by the majority of its members and by requesting the Federal President to dismiss the Federal Chancellor. The Federal President must comply with the request and appoint the person elected.
> Forty-eight hours must elapse between the motion and the election. (Article 67)

This Article eliminates the practice used frequently in the Weimar Republic of ousting a Chancellor by a vote of non-confidence without having a majority to elect his successor.

The method of electing by direct popular vote a president who is vested with strong powers was also considered an important constitutional shortcoming which contributed to the eventual destruction of the Weimar Constitution. Therefore, the Basic Law provides for the election of the Federal President by a special Federal Convention (*Bundesversammlung*). This convention is comprised of the members of the Federal Diet plus an equal number of electors who are appointed for this occasion on the basis of proportional representation by the *Laender* legislatures. The President's functions are essentially restricted to those exercised by a representative head of state.[16]

The direct popular participation in the Federal election process is now restricted to the elections for the Federal Diet. There are no provisions for plebiscites which during the Weimar Republic were frequently misused by effective demagogues.

In spite of the fact that the present election law, together with a number of constitutional innovations and provisions, has received a large share of the credit for the contemporary political stability, it still might be considered as one of the weakest parts of the new governmental system. The Basic Law leaves it up to the Federal legislature to devise rules for the next elections for the Federal Diet. The party in power could, if it desired, use its influence to have election rules enacted which would perpetuate its dominant position. The effects of the election laws so far enacted have been intentionally designed to discourage the development of small splinter parties and, thereby, are responsible that a *de-facto* two-party system has emerged. The use of the plural when discussing the election laws is justified because for each of the three elections for the Federal Diet, a new law has been enacted. Proportional representation in the Weimar Republic had aimed at "electoral justice." This was achieved, but the price was governmental instability and a multi-party system with all its inherent difficulties.

The new electoral approach used in the Federal Republic is a combination of the single-member district system and elections by simple plurality with proportional representation. The latter is restricted, however, to those parties which either are able to obtain 5 per cent or more of the total vote cast or at least one single-member district seat within a particular *Land*. The elections for the first Federal Diet used this compromise solution with a ratio of 60 per cent of single-member district seats and 40 per cent of seats obtained from *Land* lists based on proportional representation. For the second Federal elections the proportion was changed to half and half with each voter having two ballots, one to elect a deputy within the single-member districts and the second for a deputy from the *Land* list of the political party of his choice. The election law for the third Federal Diet made it even more difficult for certain minor parties to obtain legislative representation. In order to benefit from proportional representation the party either had to receive at least 5 per cent of the total popular vote cast in the entire Federal Republic or three single-member seats instead of only one as required previously. By this manipulation of the election law for the third Federal Diet, the German Party (*Deutsche Partei*), a coalition party of the CDU, was able to obtain seventeen deputies (six were elected in single-member districts) with only 3.4 per cent of the popular vote. In contrast the Refugee Party with 4.6 per cent of the popular vote failed to receive even one seat. (In the second Federal Diet this party still had twenty-seven seats.)

The Basic Law as adopted in 1949 made no provisions for a military establishment. When the Federal Republic joined the Western defense alliance, a whole series of amendments were necessary to enable German participation. These defense amendments came into force in March, 1956. An interesting illustration of the break with certain German traditional concepts is the incorporation into the defense amendments—upon the insistence of the SPD—of a provision for non-military service for conscientious objectors.

The Basic Law appears to have provided the Federal Republic with the kind of constitutional arrangement best suited for the present

German situation. The genesis of the Basic Law reflects influences from the Western powers, retrospective evaluations of shortcomings of the Weimar Constitution, and last but not least the frightful experience with Nazi totalitarianism.

THE "IDEOLOGICAL" FOUNDATION OF GERMAN RECONSTRUCTION

The Western Allies, especially the United States and Britain, facilitated the German postwar political revival and the establishment of a free, democratic and sovereign state. Their influence was also quite evident in the economic field. Through some of their economic policies and measures, such as the currency reform of June 1948, the continuous strong support for free markets and liberalization of foreign trade, channeling of counterpart funds into critical areas of the economy, stopping of the dismantling of German industries, reappraisal of German reparations, and the inclusion of the Federal Republic into the European Recovery Program, they helped directly and indirectly in paving the way for Germany's "economic miracle."[17]

The improvement of living conditions provided a favorable climate for the new political life to develop. Elections were held more frequently. New political parties, often representing some special interest, made their appearance. Without exception, they failed to capture a large electorate in federal elections. Two of the early political parties, the CDU/CSU and the SPD, had become the major political forces in an unprecedented de-facto two-party system in Germany. The Christian Democrats have been in effective control of policy-making and policy administration on the federal level since the founding of the Federal Republic. An examination of their concepts, actions and reactions to challenges, especially those from the Socialist opposition, reveals the dynamic factors of Germany's reconstruction.[18]

The CDU became a "national party" when its different local organizations merged at the first Party Congress at Goslar in October, 1950. The Bavarian organization preferred to retain its separate identity although agreeing to form with the CDU a parliamentary working arrangement. The major concepts and ideas of the German Christian Democratic movement had by then been formulated and even to some degree translated into practice.

As indicated above, Berlin was the first place where Christians of both denominations, based on their wartime pledge, formed one party.

Common Christian ethical values provided the basis on which the Berlin CDU was established. Probably one of the most remarkable documents of the history of the CDU is the proclamation of the Berlin group, dated June 26, 1945, which was announced when the dust had hardly settled upon their devastated city. The thirty-five individuals who signed their names to this document thought not only of the long-range mission of their party, but also of the need for an immediate emergency program. They were also aware of many of the difficulties faced by the German people as a result of the liabilities inherited from the Nazi period. They were convinced that only actions based on genuine Christian principles could succeed in pulling Germany out of her moral and material decay. A few passages from this proclamation may serve to illustrate this attitude of the Berlin founders.

> ... From the chaos of guilt and shame, into which the deification of a criminal adventurer has plunged us, an order based on democratic freedom can emerge only when we return to the cultural, moral, and spiritual forces of Christianity and make these sources of strength ever more available to our people. ...
>
> Today ... we stand in front of a terrible legacy, in front of a rubble heap of moral and material values. . . . Great is the guilt of wide circles of our population because they were only too eager to lower themselves and serve as Hitler's helpers. . . . Every guilt calls for atonement. . . . Fighters of genuine democratic convictions, Protestant and Catholic Christians, countless Jewish fellow citizens, men and women from all levels of society suffered and died under the terror. ... A truly democratic state based on the people's duty to faithfulness, sacrifice, and service to the common good as well as on the respect for the individual personality, its honor, freedom, and human dignity must replace the distorted concept of Hitler's state.
>
> Law must again become the basis of the entire public life. The law: "lawful is what is good for the people," must be replaced by the eternal truth: "Only what is lawful is also good for the people." ...
>
> The parents' right concerning the children's education must be respected; the youth must be educated to respect God, [their] elders, and life experience. Church directed religious instructions must be an organic part of education. ...

In regard to the emergency situation, the proclamation contained the approaches proposed by the Berlin group of the Christian Democratic movement.

297

The emergency program, intended to provide food, shelter and work has top priority.

In order to protect once and for all the state authority from unlawful influences resulting from the concentrations of economic power, it will be necessary that natural resources will be brought under state ownership. The mining industry and other key enterprises of our economy with the character of a monopoly, must clearly be subordinated to the state authority.

We endorse private property which secures the development of the individual personality but it must remain responsible to the general welfare....

The voluntary alliance of all working people corresponds to the Christian and democratic basic laws of state and society. Therefore, we endorse the united trade movement of workers and employees [as an instrument] to guard their economic and social rights. We recognize the power which the workers contribute to the entire nation....

For the conduct of foreign relations we demand that the same basic principles of freedom and justice as they apply to our personal and domestic lives must be used....

We are standing deeply moved at the graves of our dead. We shall not forget our prisoners of war. Looking at the ruins of our houses, of our villages and cities, we remember with deep human and Christian feeling that nations around us suffered the same. And we solemnly promise to eliminate absolutely everything which caused this horrible sacrifice in blood and terrible misery and we will see to it that nothing remains undone which in the future could save mankind from this kind of a catastrophe.[19]

Also the program of March 1, 1946 of the CDU in the British zone relied strongly upon the common Christian values as a basis for political actions for the reconstruction of a new Germany.

The CDU wishes to build a new and different Germany. The era during which the materialistic way of life became in Germany the intellectual basis and ruled over the state, the economy, and cultural lives must come to an end. . . . A moral renewal is necessary. . . . The Christian way of life must replace the materialistic views and basic Christian ethical principles must replace doctrines based on materialism. . . . The Christian concepts of world order alone guarantee a system of law, order and moderation, dignity and freedom of the individual person and thereby assure a truly and genuine democracy. . . . We regard the high principles which Christians have concerning human dignity, the value of every individual human being, as the basis and direction for our work within the political, economic and cultural life of our nation.[20]

298

This program included in addition to the statement of principles also concrete proposals for the reconstruction of Germany. The past experiences with Nazi totalitarianism led to a strong emphasis of *limited* state authority and to the stress of individual civil rights such as religious and political freedom for all citizens.

The economic views of the CDU were in content considerably more along lines of the political Left than the later accepted principles of the Social Market Economy. The CDU was strongly concerned with the social functions of the economy and with the need for a new economic order, which would justly distribute the profit and thereby eliminate the "spirit of the class struggle." The CDU was from the beginning against large trusts and monopolies because it was thought that these economic concentrations could endanger the economic and political freedom within a nation.

While the Christian Democrats believed that the nationalization of segments of the country's economy was not an opportune undertaking, they thought, however, many of their belief that coal was the decisive product of the entire German economy, that the mining industry should be socialized.

The Christian evaluation of the value of the individual was and still is the basis of the CDU's cultural program. The latter includes the concern for adequate education and the rights of the parents to decide on the "ideological contents" of their children's education. The program demanded the co-operation among the different churches and with the state authority.[21]

As early as December, 1946, the "basic program" of the Christian Social Union of Bavaria contained in addition to the application of the same principles discussed above, the demand for the "reconstruction of Germany on a federal basis." The CSU made it abundantly clear that it was highly opposed to any individual, party or class dictatorship. The CSU promised to fight against state bureaucratism, against a too powerful state, and against militarism and centralism. The party advocated the greatest possible degree of independence for the individual *Laender* from the central government. For a second legislative chamber the CSU preferred a corporate system.

"We demand the compliance with Natural Law principles in law making." In other words, Christian ethics and moral law were to form the basis for the new legal political, social and economic order.[22]

The social part of the program stressed the importance of the family for society and, therefore, demanded far-reaching state support for family life. In the educational field, the CSU proposed public assistance for the talented youth. The traditional German arrangement which gave preferential treatment to the children of the well-to-do classes was strongly opposed.

The CSU also expressed belief in the equal moral value of any type of honest work; it therefore demanded adequate living wages and profit sharing. An adequate welfare program, as a result of the social conditions of the postwar situation, was believed essential. "Help for the needy is a nation's common obligation."[23]

The economic aspects of the program were especially significant because they reflected the concepts which went into the making of the official economic policies. As a matter of fact, the application of the social teachings of the Churches in the economic field resulted in the Christian Democrats continuing to receive support from people of all social and economic groups including workers who in the past endorsed the policies of the SPD.

The economic order proposed a compromise solution between economic *laissez-faire* and state intervention to safeguard the common good.

> 1. The economy is not an end in itself; it must serve the well-being of society as a whole and of the individual:
> We recognize that the state has the right to direct the economy according to the interest of all!
> We reject the planned economy as an outcome of collective ideas. We fight economic liberalism and are in favor of the free development of the individual personality within the framework of his social obligations.
> 2. Employers and employees are of equal importance for the economy:
> We demand a suitable right of codetermination for the employers and employees concerning the direction of the economy, codetermination for the employees for setting up working conditions and production methods. . . .
> We are opposed to any arbitrariness and one-sided interest group pressure within the economy.
> 3. For Bavaria, the middle size enterprise is the basis for a healthy economy. . . .
> 4. The right to property is a natural right. . . .
> We reject the liquidation of property through collectivization or general socialization.

We are for transfer of private property into community property with proper compensation when this step is demanded for the general welfare. . . .[24]

A European confederation and economic union were proposed as means toward pacification of Europe and of the world.[25]

Even though individual Christian Democratic groups had announced their programs and platforms, the voluntary association of the CDU/CSU units announced in January of 1950 (the official merger of these groups into the party did not take place until October of that year) their *basic principles*. These "principles" incorporated practical experiences the Christian Democratic movement already had accumulated at that time as a result of its work in the economic administration of Bizonia and of its participation in several *Laender* governments.

By January of 1950, the so-called Social Market Economy had become one of the main aspects of Christian Democratic policy. It was Professor Ludwig Erhard's blueprint for the economic rehabilitation of Germany and for maintaining thereafter a healthy German economy. Professor Erhard is a proponent, like the economists Walter Eucken and Wilhelm Roepke, of an economic philosophy usually referred to as neo-liberalism. The neo-liberal approach attempts to solve the main economic problems within a free society, such as the co-ordination of a multitude of private economic activities, through limited state action. The state is to establish and to enforce the degree of competition needed for maximum production and for free market activities. In contrast to the economists of the classic *laissez-faire* tradition and the socialists' concepts of a completely and centrally controlled economy, the solution offered by the neo-liberals stands somewhere between these two extreme positions. The state has a most important function; its authority is used to support and preserve the free market system by establishing the standards of competition. But the state does not interfere with the day-to-day economic transactions. In its final analysis, the roots of the Social Market Economy are to be found in the Christian basis of Christian Democracy.[26]

The "basic principles" of the CDU/CSU of January, 1950 also discussed the governmental activities needed to perpetuate the "free" interplay of economic forces without controlling every last economic activity. It is considered that governmental control over monopolies is

301

needed in order to safeguard economic competition. The state is supposed to deepen the sense of responsibility within the economy through proper legislation. The country's currency must be protected through central control of monetary or fiscal policies. In spite of the fact that the neo-liberal rejects officially price fixing through private or public agencies, he still supports the concept that the state must "organically influence" the basic structure. The state, through its taxing, credit and fiscal policies, can see that prices correspond to market conditions.

In order to make German products more competitive on the world market, the "basic principles" proposed the lowering of the German price level.

The final point made in the "basic principles" is the belief that the Social Market Economy as a policy can only then succeed when all people, entrepreneurs, workers, employees and consumers have confidence in it and are willing to participate actively in its realization.[27] This last point deserves some additional comment since it refers to a psychological factor rather than to an economic one. Professor Erhard strongly believes that the psychological aspect is an integral and indispensable part of his entire economic policy.[28]

When, after the first elections held for the Federal Diet *(Bundestag),* the Christian Democrats came into the position of the governing party —a position they still are holding in 1959—and Konrad Adenauer was elected as Federal Chancellor, Professor Erhard became Federal Minister of Economics. In this position and with the strong support of his party and the other coalition parties, he was able to continue with the implementation of his policies on the federal level. He had made a start with them in Bizonia as director of the economic administration.

THE "ECONOMIC MIRACLE"

Probably there are no better examples to illustrate more convincingly the interrelation of theory and practice than the example offered by the so-called German "economic miracle." Germany's speedy economic rehabilitation was greatly the upshot of daring economic theories. The economic success did much more than just raise the living standard and provide for more material well-being for Germany's population. It also facilitated the return of self-respect among the people and it created a healthy climate for the development of political stability expressed for example, in a strong pro-constitutional attitude among the overwhelming majority of the people. In general the economic boom supplied the material means for an expanding social and cultural program of the new Germany.

A brief analysis of the contemporary economic situation may prove the validity of the economic theories and policies carried out under the auspices of Germany's Christian Democrats.

Between 1949, the year when the Social Market Economy became the economic policy of the first elected government of the Federal Republic, and 1956, the gross national income went up from about 11.8 billion dollars to about 23 billions (as compared with a gross national income of about 12 billions in 1936 and expressed in 1936 prices). Private consumption increased by 75 per cent from 1949 to 1955.[29] This remarkable increase was only possible because of the steadily increasing production and greater output by the individual worker as a result of the modernization of the production process. Thus the hourly worker's productivity rose by 58 per cent in the period from 1950 until 1958. During the same length of time, the output of the individual worker increased only 41 per cent because of a shorter working week. The hourly wages between 1950 and 1959 went up by 83.1 per cent. The individual income improved by 69.5 per cent.[30] These wage increases have been real improvements because they were not offset by raising prices. While German wages between 1950 and 1958 rose 70 per cent for men and 77 per cent for women, living cost went up only by 19 per cent.[31] However, this situation was even further improved by subsequent developments. In his opening speech at the Frankfurt Spring Fair in 1959, Minister of Economics Professor Erhard appealed to the manufacturers to lower prices as an effective means to stimulate mass production which in turn would provide new avenues for economic expansion. Most of the industries exhibiting at this fair and at the industrial exhibition at Cologne followed Erhard's suggestion. Prices were going down already before. Plastic articles, household articles dropped as much at 25 per cent. Within one year prices of industrial goods have been lowered by about 1.5 per cent, consumer goods by 4 per cent, textiles by 10 per cent. In general, prices in January of 1959 were 20 per cent below those of 1951.[32]

The labor market also indicates the high degree of stability of the German economy. In July, 1959, it was reported that the number of job openings exceeded the number of unemployed. (Of a labor force of about twenty millions, 255,000 were reported unemployed as of the end of June, 1959.) [33] Actually, in spite of the continuous influx of manpower from East Germany and of foreign labor (e.g., 10,000 Italians), Germany is experiencing a shortage of skilled labor.

The year 1958 gave evidence of a general slowdown in the economy. However, Germany experienced neither a recession like the United States nor an economic stagnation like the other West European countries. Germany's industrial production rose in 1958 by 2.8 per cent, the gross national product increased by 3 per cent. (In 1957 it was 5 per cent.)

The striking economic stability is in all probability the result of the government's economic policies discussed before. Prices remained stable or even decreased because competition became more intensified. Governmental actions were mainly responsible for a sharp increase in the building industry. The yearly construction of about 500,000 dwellings receives governmental financial support. The automobile industry, highly competitive in the world market, showed a 20 per cent production rise. The electrical industry turned out 1,100,000 television sets; that is twice as many sets as it produced in 1957.[34]

Most impressive to the world is Germany's comeback in the field of foreign trade. Presently Germany is the third largest exporter, following only the United States and Canada. Professor Erhard believes that the success in the foreign trade field was greatly influenced by a new trade policy adopted in 1949 which gave Germany's economy the means to compete effectively on the international markets. On September 19, 1949, the new German currency, the *Deutsche Mark*, was devaluated by 20 per cent. This changed the dollar exchange rate from DM 3.33 to DM 4.20. The results were overwhelming. Between October, 1949 and December, 1950 German exports trebled. Exports increased from about 121.3 million dollars in December, 1949 to about 162.9 million in June, 1950. The import surplus during these six months went down from about 133.2 million dollars in January, 1950 to about 34.65 million in June, 1950. In 1950 Germany still had an unfavorable foreign trade balance of about 750 million dollars. In 1958, German exports exceeded imports by about 1.5 billion dollars.[35] In the first half of 1959, Germany's imports were close to 4 billion dollars and her exports amounted to 4.8 billion dollars. Both of these figures represent 8 per cent increases over the first half of 1958. However, as a result of lower prices in comparison with 1958, the actual import volume constitutes a gain of 15 per cent and the actual export an increase of 11 per cent over last year.[36] As a result of her considerable reserves of gold and foreign currency—at the end of 1958 it amounted to 6.1 billion dollars—Germany is greatly interested in foreign investments and during 1958 at least 200 million dollars in loans and credits were granted by public and private institutions to foreign countries.[37]

THE IMPLEMENTATION OF THE SOCIAL PROGRAM

The Christian Democrats, stressing the fact that the economy is not an end in itself, utilized the economic situation to pursue effectively their various social policies. For example, social service payments went up from about 2.29 billion dollars in 1949 to about 5 billion in 1955.[38] In 1957, this type of governmental expenditure was about 7.66 billion dollars, or 23.2 per cent higher than in the preceding year 1956. It was the largest single increase within a one-year period since 1950 and primarily the result of the reform of the old age pension plan. Also accident insurance benefits rose considerably. Other important areas of governmental aid include unemployment insurance, health insurance (which is required for all persons employed), equalization of wartime losses, payments to war victims such as disabled veterans, war widows and war orphans. The social service payments for the 1958-59 fiscal year are expected to amount to about 8.75 billion dollars, a figure which will exceed roughly by 500 million dollars the governmental estimate.[39]

The Christian Democrats as the governing party were justified in claiming the major share of credit for the economic and social achievements. The party's program, adopted at its Fourth Congress on April 22, 1953 in Hamburg, had a dual purpose. In view of the coming election campaign for the September 6, 1953 federal elections, the program gave an account of the advancements made under the leadership of Konrad Adenauer; it also attempted to provide an outline for future activities—provided that the party was kept in power. The program stated that the successes of Germany's reconstruction were only possible because of the co-operation of the entire nation and of the help received from abroad. It categorically declared that "it is an historic merit of the CDU that under its leadership the domestic and foreign conditions for the German reconstruction were provided."

With a striving economy serving as a solid foundation, the Christian Democrats could proceed to propose future improvements in the direction of higher living standards for the masses and increased mass participation in the economy. One of the most challenging single items is the concept of "broadening the basis of ownership" especially that of industrial property. "Combining codetermination with co-ownership is the best method to realize the principle of the division of power in the domestic economy."

The aim of the Christian Democrats to maintain and secure social peace was also strongly emphasized. ". . . Social policies are not an appendix to the Social Market Economy but rather its final aim."[40] The fact that German labor had displayed throughout the years of reconstruction a highly co-operative attitude toward management is believed to be largely the result of the system of codetermination granted to the employees. This effective means of participation by the workers was originally demanded by the Socialists but adopted and actually carried through by a coalition of Christian Democrats and SPD. The restraint exercised by labor in wage demand can effectively be illustrated by the fact that Germany had not a single really critical labor conflict throughout this period. The labor unions after the war showed the highest degree of co-operation. This attitude was partly caused by the frequent common experience mäde by management and labor of clearing together the rubble before the actual rebuilding could be undertaken. On the other hand, there is still much room for improvements in regard to German wages and to working hours. Up to a few years ago, the forty-eight hour week has been the rule. In general, however, workers are satisfied, especially since they are confident that further improvements are forthcoming.[41]

TOWARD GREATER ECONOMIC AND SOCIAL JUSTICE

The great victory of the Christian Democrats in September, 1953, indicated the popular approval of the work of the government of the First Federal Diet. It also placed the party in the position to continue with the responsibilities of government.

At the Fifth Party Congress in Cologne (May 28-30, 1954), the "Hamburg Program" was officially announced as the blueprint for the period of the second Federal Diet (1953-57). The over-all aim was to make "Germany a social state under the law in a united Europe."[42]

The program is a consequent continuation of the earlier "Ahlen Plan" (February 9, 1947) and the "Duesseldorf Statement of Principles" (July 5, 1949) although it reflects a more conservative approach than those in the proclamations and basic programs of 1945 and 1946. Much of the original radical influences from former leaders of the

Christian trade unions, considered the "left wing" of the Christian Democrats, had to give way to the conservative influences of the neo-liberals of Professor Erhard's school.[43]

Probably one of the most challenging economic programs with a great potential impact upon the social and economic structure of the Federal Republic, is the government's plan for a wider *distribution of private property* and the *denationalization* of federally owned industrial property. Both of these policies, complementary to a considerable extent, are in their early development stages and, therefore, long-range effects still remain to be seen.

The denationalization of government industrial property and the realization of the concept of broadening the basis of ownership have become matters of the immediate action program of the Christian Democrats. It is believed that ownership of land and homes, monetary savings, and industrial investments will create a stronger sense of security and a feeling of independence of a more contented and increasing new middle class.

The Federal government recently commenced with the execution of a plan liquidating government-owned industrial holdings by selling inexpensive shares in large numbers to people from the lower income group. These federal holdings at present are quite substantial and probably when liquidated can actually create an entirely new strata of "people's stock holders."[44] Furthermore, under the concepts of the Social Market Economy it is most difficult to justify the state as a competitor to private industry. So far, that is within the last few years, thirty-three state enterprises valued at about 21.2 million dollars have been sold;[45] however, with the denationalization of *PREUSSAG* (a joint stock company comprised of mining and foundry corporations formerly owned by the Prussian State in March of 1959, the real beginning was made with the execution of the plan to create thousands of people's stockholders.[46] This project turned out to be a tremendous success. Earlier fears that people of the lower income groups who never possessed shares before might not be interested proved unfounded. At the end of March, three times as many applicants registered their intentions to buy shares as the minimum of 60,000 needed to sell the 300,000 shares made available. Therefore, the government decided to offer additional shares in the value of 20 million dollars and to keep only 26 per cent of the company shares under government ownership.[47] Reports received at the end of July, 1959 indicate that the

307

people's shares program had passed its ultimate test. After a moratorium, the *PREUSSAG* shares are again listed and stand 30 per cent higher than when they were sold a few months ago—as a result of recent advances made on the German market. Only a small fraction of the share holders resold their shares in order to make a quick profit. The overwhelming majority kept their shares.[48]

The next large denationalization project is supposed to be the *Volkswagen* works. However, there is still a property question to be settled between the *Land* government of Lower Saxony and the Federal Republic. Both of them claim to be the legal owner of this property formerly owned by the Labor Front and the Nazi state. Presumably, the Federal government will succeed in this contest and then will proceed in due time to sell hundreds of thousands people's shares of this most lucrative and prosperous enterprise.

Thus one of the main social and economic objectives of the Christian Democrats becomes more and more reality, the large group of property owners. With a large number of people participating in the economic undertakings and sharing also in the profits, the class war in West Germany can be considered a thing of the past. The so-called "class-conscious worker" is replaced by the new social ideal of the *Wirtschaftsbuerger,* i.e., the citizen with economic property and interest.[49]

There are many voices in Germany which express confidence in the social policies of the Christian Democrats. They maintain that in our modern mass society 80 per cent of the people are wage and salary earners and that wage policies can lead only to limited increases in income. Therefore, they believe that the people's share idea might provide a far more promising new source of income and security in our capitalist economy. However, in order to be really effective, the selling of government-owned industries will not be enough. An appropriate tax reform could provide the incentive for private industries also to sell people's shares. Only then would it be possible to institute a wider distribution of property and not remain restricted to the "ideologically-burdened people's shares."[50] The Federal government has so far shown the initiative; however, in order to create a substantial group of small property holders the process of distributing property must be followed by private industries.

The combination of denationalization and wider distribution of property still has to prove that it can achieve the goals set forth in the Christian Democratic platform. It might be of interest to note that in Austria a similar undertaking or experiment failed. Instead of regarding the shares as a permanent investment, the initial share buyers resold them as soon as a profit could be realized above the purchasing price.[51]

The Federal government in its attempt to create a large middle class utilizes also other methods than those discussed above. For example, substantial tax advantages are offered to people who save for various purposes such as the future acquisition of private homes. And indeed, the number of privately owned family dwellings and savings accounts earmarked for home building have increased appreciatively.

In 1958 the Federal Republic experienced also a tax reform sponsored by the Christian Democrats. The new tax law favors the lower income groups, freeing about three million citizens from paying income taxes at all.[52] Also this step was intended to increase the purchasing power of the broad masses.

Summing up it is possible to say that throughout the Federal Republic there are convincing signs that her prosperity is becoming more and more as Professor Erhard intended it to be, a "prosperity for all."

ECONOMIC PROBLEMS—1959

The general consensus is that Germany's economic rehabilitation and her social policies are among the most impressive postwar developments. Germans usually receive recognition for their diligence and dedication to hard work. The German people overcame obstacles of a magnitude not experienced in modern times by any other nation. Even the problems related to the approximate twelve million refugees who came from the eastern territories were successfully solved. These problems could have become a devastating drain on the country's economic resources. However, the great majority of these people were not only incorporated into the economic process but actually through their skills, basic needs and attitudes contributed considerably to the over-all reconstruction.[53]

But opinions are also voiced which take exception to the "economic miracle." For example, there is the opposition of the SPD and trade unions. This is primarily the result of their adverse position toward denationalization of government-owned industrial property and toward the social policies of the Christian Democrats. Even after some of the effects of the government's economic policies have become apparent, the Socialists still insist that the effort to broaden the basis of property ownership through denationalization is bound to be a failure. They claim that the workers have no interest in "people's shares" and, furthermore, they predict that within a short period of time strong financial interests will buy up the shares from the original buyers. In place of the policies carried out by the government, the SPD advocates the use of government-owned industrial enterprises to influence the price structure, that is to lower the market prices, a development from which the entire population would benefit.[54]

As late as June, 1959, the government's economic policies were strongly attacked in the Federal Diet by the SPD because of their alleged preferential treatment of the wealthy industrialists. The Socialists question the effectiveness of the German anti-trust law *(Kartellgesetz)* and refer to it as a "dull sword" in use against dictatorial entrepreneurs. Professor Erhard is attacked by the SPD as a "troubadour of freedom" floating through the countryside while Chancellor Adenauer is making all the decisions.[55]

Aside from the Socialist opposition there are other critics who either believe that they can discover danger signs in the present German boom or who challenge some of the government's policies. There is, for example, concern about the observed tendency of "economic concentration" because of its inherent threat against the economic security of small and middle-sized industries. This development is also in sharp contrast with the principles of the Social Market Economy and the policy designed to broaden the basis of ownership. There are, of course, also those who defend a certain measure of concentration as a by-product of improved technological production methods. They also justify economic concentration as an argument needed in order to stand up favorably against stiff international competition. The need to support smaller industrial enterprises is recognized. Suggestions are made to secure their position by improving their credit supply, fixing raw material prices and finally through changing the tax policies.[56]

At the occasion of the Economic Conference of the CDU/CSU on April 16, 1959, at Hanover, Professor Erhard expressed his confidence in the economic policies of the government in spite of the fact that occasional difficulties are bound to appear in a free economy. In the recent past, difficulties in the coal and textile industry have presented problems. According to Professor Erhard the task of the government is not merely to "react" to economic problems on a case-to-case basis but rather to give impulses, influence the development of the economy, and to point out general aims.[57]

But even the greatest admirers of Professor Erhard's work will have to admit that there are at least two important sectors of the German economy which are hardly affected by the concepts of the Social Market Economy. These sectors are agriculture and housing control (*Wohnungswirtschaft*). Prices for agricultural products are fixed and not determined by the free play of forces on the open market. In order to make up for this price control and to provide an incentive for greater productivity, the farmers received subventions from public funds, a method quite in contradiction to the principles of the Social Market Economy. The situation has become further complicated as a result of agricultural overproduction and it is difficult to envisage how the two million farmers will eventually become a part of the free market economy.[58] The present Minister of Food, Agriculture, and Forestry, Heinrich Luebke (the newly elected Federal President), announced at the occasion of the Economic Conference of the CDU, mentioned above, that public aid to the farmers will gradually be discontinued in order also to integrate agriculture into the Social Market Economy.[59]

In housing affairs the situation is even worse in spite of the highly intensified building activities. The postwar housing shortage necessitated rent control. However, in order to stimulate private construction for additional housing, rent control was limited to apartments in old houses. With the end of the housing shortage in sight, plans are made to abolish rent control altogether.[60] By 1962-63 it is envisaged that a new social rent law will replace rent control. This contemplated law is intended to help the low income group with its housing problem. The government plans to provide minimum housing at low cost with the monthly rent not to exceed 15 per cent of the family's income.[61]

The annual report of the Federal Bank for 1958 is most optimistic in its evaluation of the German economic situation. According to this report the German economy has come nearer than ever before to fulfilling the monetary and economic objectives of the "magic triangle": maximum employment, price stability and a balance of payments.[62]

311

POLITICAL STABILITY—EVALUATION AND PROSPECTS

An evaluation of the contemporary political situation in the Federal Republic would do wisely not to approach the task in terms of "reconstruction," because neither the Western Allies nor a substantial part of the German population wished or intended to "reconstruct" many of the past political institutions. Opinions about Germany's political "achievements" during the postwar period vary greatly and range from highly optimistic to rather pessimistic views. However, there might be agreement among most observers that for the first time Germany has a constitutional basis upon which democratic institutions can develop.

The Basic Law has succeeded so far in preventing a repetition of the political fragmentation of the electorate and the legislature. The emergence of a *de-facto* two-party system has contributed to a kind of political stability which Germany had never experienced before. The two major parties, the CDU/CSU and the SPD, represent together 82 per cent of the German electorate. Both parties stand squarely on the provisions of the Basic Law and are determined to defend the constitutional arrangements against any Left or Right wing extremists.

A second important contributing factor to the political stability is the strong and purposeful leadership of the Federal Chancellor, Konrad Adenauer. There has been and still is from time to time criticism about the alleged authoritarian type of rule exercised by the Federal Chancellor. His recent conflict with the Minister of Economics, Professor Erhard, about the succession to the presidency and the chancellory has been used to point out—and apparently with certain justification—that Adenauer is a most determined personality who is controlling his party with an iron hand. If the political stability should actually depend on a strong individual leader and on a patriarchal concept of government, hidden under democratic trimmings, a decisive change in top personnel could be disastrous for the further development of German democracy.

Possibly the greatest influence working in favor of political stability is the fact that during the formative phase of the new political system, Germany experienced a period marked by the absence of any really strong conflicts. During this period which lasted at least until 1949, only the occupation authorities were in a position to make important decisions. When eventually dividing issues, such as rearmament, atomic weapons for the new German army, participation in

NATO, and approaches to German reunification, made their appearance and brought Socialists into intense opposition to the Christian Democratic government, the constitutional foundation of German political life remained unaffected.[63]

On the Federal level, the SPD has been in the role of the opposition from the beginning of the Federal Republic in 1949. This situation has given rise to fears that the Socialists might develop into a kind of permanent opposition. Not only do they fail to discover a "key" political issue with which to win a Federal election, but they are not able to improve their relative power position in spite of their strenuous efforts to appeal to a broader electorate than the former "class-conscious" SPD ever attempted.[64]

The high percentage of election participation—88.2 per cent at the last Federal election in September, 1957—is occasionally cited as proof of the active political role played by the German people. On the other hand there are convincing indications that a widespread political apathy is prevalent in spite of the high participation in elections. The election phenomenon is explained as nothing but an expression of a German sense of duty and orderliness. Low party memberships—even the highly orgainzed SPD has according to the latest report only 623,817 members[65]—and very little active participation in politics are typical features of the contemporary political scene. It appears to some observers that the average German since the Second World War is far more interested in his economic betterment than in political issues which apparently fail to arouse his interest and enthusiasm.[66] Charges are even made that the democratic reorientation, the de-Nazification, and political re-education were nothing but failures. The liberal-democratic group of the early phase has decreased in importance as time goes on and German society in the Federal Republic has produced a very small anti-Nazi minority and a large pragmatic majority.[67] To some extent the decrease in the use of traditional German "ideological" justification for every political action might be a healthy development and it has been pointed out that the present parties with few exceptions have no programs in the traditional sense of the term but rather directives and policy statements. Present political parties in Germany appear to be less doctrinaire than their precursors of the Weimar era.[68]

Even prior to their official dissolution as anti-constitutional parties, neither the Communists nor the neo-Nazi Socialist Reich Party had

313

succeeded in making much of an impact execpt among the relatively small number of political extremists which most societies contain. For example, the pronounced nationalistic German Party *(Deutsche Reichspartei*—DRP)*, which presently occupies the position on the extreme Right received in the last Federal elections only 1 per cent of the vote.[69]

Anti-Semitism is probably even less of an issue in contemporary Germany than extreme nationalism. However, it is not entirely eliminated. Isolated incidents are at times overdramatized and the publicity they received in the world press goes far beyond their real significance. All political parties, with probably one exception, are strongly opposed to anti-Semitic attitudes. The official views of the German government are too well known to be discussed here. The Federal Republic has attempted to make up at least to some extent for the crimes committed by the Nazis. Over 1.4 billion dollars have been paid out so far for restitution to persons who were persecuted during the Nazi regime because of race or political affiliation,[70] the largest amount went to the surviving Jewish people within and outside Germany.

Probably one of the weakest points in the present political climate in the Federal Republic is the lack of a thorough examination and awareness of the implications of the recent Nazi era. Unfortunately, there is little knowledge among the youth about Hitler or about the true nature of the Nazi dictatorship. Topics concerning the era from 1933 to 1945 received insufficient attention in schools as well as in private and public discussions. Many Germans who achieved their economic "reconstruction," have failed to recognize their responsibility to work out their own "personal" reconstruction. It took the German government until July of 1959 to have its new army officially recognize the heroic deeds of the German resistance leaders—many of them military personnel—who lost their lives in the ill-fated attempt against Hitler on July 20, 1944.

The future of the Federal Republic in its political and economic aspects is as uncertain as the future of the relations of the Free World to the Soviet Union and her satellites. Much will depend upon the Germans; upon their basic convictions and aspirations, however, there might also be influences from without which could prove inimical to a continuation of democratic political practices and institutions in Germany.

SELECTED BIBLIOGRAPHY

PERIODICALS AND NEWSPAPERS

BULLETIN DES PRESS- UND INFORMATIONSAMTES DER BUNDESREGIERUNG, Bonn. (Official information bulletin of the Federal Government; appears several times each week.)

CIVIS, Zeitschrift fuer Christlich-Demokratische Politik, Bonn. (Monthly periodical of the Christian-Democratic Students.)

DAS PARLIAMENT, Bonn. (Weekly paper published by the *Bundeszentrale fuer Heimatdienst.*)

DEUTSCHE KORRESPONDENZ, Bonn. (Official information bulletin issued weekly in English and German.)

DEUTSCHES MONATSBLATT, Bonn. (Official monthly publication of the Christian-Democratic Union.)

DIE WELT, Hamburg. (One of the three leading German daily newspapers.)

DIE ZEIT, Hamburg. (An independent weekly newspaper.)

FRANKFURTER HEFTE, Frankfurt a.M. (A monthly periodical with strong sympathies for the labor wing of the Christian-Democratic movement.)

GERMAN BUSINESS WEEKLY, New York. (Weekly publication of the German-American Chamber of Commerce, Inc.)

GERMAN INTERNATIONAL, Bonn. (An English language bimonthly periodical for finance, industry and business.)

NEWS FROM THE GERMAN EMBASSY, Washington, D. C. (Issued by the German Embassy at *irregular* intervals.)

SCHNELLDIENST DES DEUTSCHEN INDUSTRIENINSTITUTS, Cologne. (Appears several times per month; the *Deutsche Industrieninstitut* also publishes at irregular intervals important lectures within the general field of economics, the VORTRAGSREIHE DES DEUTSCHEN INDUSTRIENINSTITUTS.)

THE BULLETIN, Bonn. (A weekly survey of German affairs issued by the Press and Information Office of the German Federal Government.)

BOOKS

Ludwig Bergstraesser, GESCHICHTE DER POLITISCHEN PARTEIEN IN DEUTSCHLAND (Munich: Isar Verlag, 1955). An excellent handbook of the history of the German political parties.

Karl Buchheim, GESCHICHTE DER CHRISTLICHEN PARTEIEN IN DEUTSCHLAND (Munich: Koesel-Verlag, 1953). A history of the Christian parties in Germany covering the period from the early nineteenth century up to the realization of the concept of the Christian union.

Department of State, GERMANY 1947-1949, THE STORY IN DOCUMENTS (Washington, D. C.: U. S. Government Printing Office, 1950). A collection of all official documents pertinent to political and economic developments of Germany for the 1947-49 period.

Ernst Deuerlein, CDU/CSU 1945-1957, BEITRAEGE ZUR ZEIT-GESCHICHTE (Cologne: Verlag J. P. Bachem, 1957). Background analysis and genesis of the CDU/CSU.

Ludwig Erhard, PROSPERITY THROUGH COMPETITION (New York: Frederick A. Praeger, 1958). Discussion of the economic concepts and policies which are greatly responsible for Germany's economic reconstruction.

John Ford Golay, THE FOUNDING OF THE FEDERAL RE-PUBLIC OF GERMANY (Chicago: University of Chicago Press, 1958). An excellent and thorough discussion of the emergence and contents of the new German constitutional system.

Alfred Grosser, THE COLOSSUS AGAIN, WESTERN GER-MANY FROM DEFEAT TO REARMAMENT (New York: Freder-ick A. Praeger, 1955). A lucid account of Germany's postwar developments.

John H. Herz, "The Government oi Germany," MAJOR FOR-EIGN POWERS (3rd edit., New York: Harcourt, Brace & Co., 1957). A scholarly and most informative study of the contemporary German situation, with occasional pessimistic comments concerning German democratic institutions.

Gustav E. Kafka, Ed., DIE KATHOLIKEN VOR DER POLITIK (Freiburg, Germany: Verlag Herder, 1958). A symposium containing outstanding contributions by leading German Catholic political thinkers and academicians.

Edward H. Litchfield, Ed., GOVERNING POST-WAR GER-MANY (Ithaca, N. Y.: Cornell University Press, 1953). A critical and scholarly symposium covering the German postwar developments; contributions by outstanding American experts on German political and social affairs.

Wilhelm Mommsen, DEUTSCHE PARTEIPROGRAMME, EINE AUSWAHL VOM VORMAERZ BIS ZUR GEGENWART (Munich: Isar Verlag, 1952). A collection of the most important political pro-grams and comments by Professor Mommsen.

John D. Montgomery, FORCED TO BE FREE, THE ARTIFI-CIAL REVOLUTION IN GERMANY AND JAPAN (Chicago: Uni-versity of Chicago Press, 1957). The result of a military-government research program conducted in the Operations Research Office of the Johns Hopkins University. The study investigates the impact made by Allied occupation programs and policies upon Germany and Japan.

James K. Pollock, Ed., GERMAN DEMOCRACY AT WORK (Ann

Arbor, Mich.: University of Michigan Press, 1955). An evaluation of the status of German democracy and democratic institutions by four well-qualified American political scientists.

James K. Pollock, James H. Meisel, & Henry L. Bretton, GERMANY UNDER OCCUPATION, ILLUSTRATIVE MATERIALS AND DOCUMENTS (Revised edit., Ann Arbor, Mich.: George Wahr Publishing Co., 1949). A valuable collection of documentary material concerning the occupation of Germany.

Press- und Informationsamt der Bundesregierung. DEUTSCHLAND IM WIEDERAUFBAU, TAETIGEKEITSBERICHT DER BUNDESREGIERUNG FUER DAS JAHR 1958 (Bonn, 1959). A detailed report by the government of the Federal Republic about government organization and personnel, activities and achievements.

Herbert J. Spiro, "The German Political System," PATTERNS OF GOVERNMENT (edit. by Samuel H. Beer & Adam B. Ulam, New York: Random House, 1958). An excellent and provocative analysis of the contemporary German political situation.

Norbert Toennis, DER STAAT AUS DEM NICHTS: ZEHN JAHRE DEUTSCHER GESCHICHTE (Stuttgart: Constantin-Verlag, 1954). A lucid account of the first ten postwar years in Germany by a German journalist.

Wolfgang Treue, DEUTSCHE PARTEIPROGRAMME 1861-1956 (Goettingen: Musterschmidt-Verlag, 1956). This collection of party programs contains also important proclamations, action programs, and manifestoes of the post-World War II political parties in Germany.

Eric Waldman, THE SPARTACIST UPRISING OF 1919 AND THE CRISIS OF THE GERMAN SOCIALIST MOVEMENT (Milwaukee: Marquette University Press, 1958). An analysis of the ideological background and effects of the divided German labor movement.

Henry C. Wallich, MAINSPRINGS OF THE GERMAN REVIVAL (New Haven: Yale University Press, 1955). A splendid analysis of German postwar economic developments.

Hans Georg Wieck, DIE ENTSTEHUNG DER CDU UND DIE WIEDERGRUENDUNG DES ZENTRUMS IN JAHRE 1945 (Duesseldorf: Droste-Verlag, 1953). A very detailed and complete account of the founding of the Christian Democratic groups and of the Catholic Center Party.

CURRICULUM VITAE

ERIC WALDMAN, Chairman of the Department of Political Science and Director of the Institute of German Affairs at Marquette University, was educated at the University of Vienna, Austria and at the George Washington University at Washington, D. C., where he

317

received his Ph.D. Prior to his coming to Marquette University in 1955, he taught at the George Washington University and worked as a research analyst for the War Documentation Project of Columbia University. He utilized captured German military documents for a number of published though classified monographs which deal with German occupation administration and related subjects.

During World War II, he served as intelligence officer, first as an instructor in the military intelligence school, later as a research analyst in the War Department General Staff, G-2, and finally as an operations officer in Germany from 1946 until 1949. He is a member of the boards of directors of the Phi Beta Kappa Association of Greater Milwaukee, of the World Affairs Council of Milwaukee, and of Goethe House, Inc., of Milwaukee. He is a member of the Sovereign and Military Order of Malta. His most recent publication is THE SPARTACIST UPRISING OF 1919 AND THE CRISIS OF THE GERMAN SOCIALIST MOVEMENT, (Milwaukee: Marquette University Press, 1958).

CHAPTER FIFTEEN

REJUVENATED ITALY

TIBOR KEREKES

Georgetown University

BACKGROUND

Early on July 25, 1943, after an all-night sitting, the Fascist Grand Council deposed Mussolini. The preceding months, which saw the final defeat of the Axis troops in North Africa and the constant bombings of Sardinia, Southern Italy and Sicily, had been marked by feverish Party manifestations in the form of disputes, orders and changes in personnel.

In the background were Mussolini's policies since 1922. His policy was to suppress all rival political parties and make everyone who wanted to get on join his own Fascist Party which ran the whole country. A network of magnificent modern roads was built throughout the country; new railways were opened up in mountainous parts; electrification was carried through on a grand scale. Some parts of Italy used to suffer from the terrible scourage of malaria, spread by mosquitoes living in stagnant water; this disease was largely prevented by draining the marshy areas and settling peasants from the more crowded districts to cultivate the reclaimed lands. These improvements did affect the lives of ordinary people. But they did not convince the many political opponents of Fascism which were driven underground or exiled. They opposed the helplessness of a country under a single-party dictatorship.[1]

Apparently even the restrictions on personality might have been tolerated by many Italians as being necessary, though unpleasant, while they were seeing some tangible benefits. But there was a darker side to Fascism. Mussolini wanted to make the nation proud and efficient in order to prepare it for a new war of conquest, and certified to this in his writings and speeches. In the schools, boys and girls were taught that the young Italian generation had a mission to re-establish the might of the Roman Empire.

In 1935 the Italian Army invaded Abyssinia (Ethiopia). The League acted only halfheartedly, and Hitler was quick to take advantage of this by making an Axis alliance with Mussolini. In 1940, when it looked as though Britain and France were already as good as beaten by the Nazis, Mussolini joined the war on Hitler's side.

This proved to be the biggest mistake on Mussolini's part. Although France collapsed, Britain fought on. The invasion of Greece proved to be a fiasco, and Mussolini had to be saved by Hitler. The war suffering was soon apparent in Italy, and the Germans soon ruled the roost. The Italians were driven out of North Africa; Sicily was invaded, and on July 25, 1943, even the old supporters of Mussolini in the Grand Council deserted the dictator. The King asked Marshal Badoglio, a professional soldier who had never been an active supporter of Il Duce, to form a new government. His first act was to ask for an armistice with the United Nations in which he agreed to help them drive the Germans out of Italy. Italy suffered terribly from the war; there was a terrible starvation; the Germans, gradually driven northward, bought up or requisitioned what little food was left. Mussolini was "rescued" by Nazi paratroops and set up a new Fascist regime at Bologna, but it was only a cat's-paw of Germany. It collapsed when the German Army withdrew and Mussolini was shot by Italian partisans in April, 1945.[2]

POLITICS SINCE WORLD WAR II

Marshal Badoglio, who had signed the Armistice, became Prime Minister of that part of Italy which the Allies had occupied; he soon retired to be succeeded first by Signor Bonomi, then by Signor Parri. In fact, six governments had taken office between that Sunday afternoon when King Emmanuel informed an incredulous Mussolini that his twenty-five year dictatorship had come to an end — end 1945. On June 5. 1944, King Emmanuel resigned and appointed his son, Prince Umberto, Lieutenant of the Realm. The King abdicated on May 9, 1946, and Umberto succeeded him — for only a month. At the beginning of June a referendum was held to decide the form of the state. Twelve and a half million people voted in favor of a Republic, ten and a half million voted in favor of the Monarchy. King Umberto and his family said farewell on June 13 and took refuge in Portugal.

At the same time as the referendum, a general election was held. On July 14, 1946, Signor Alcide de Gasperi became Prime Minister. Soviet Russia had not yet openly quarreled with the United States and Britain and the Communists were admitted to the Government as well as Signor de Gasperi's Christian Democrats — the largest party — the Socialists and Liberals (Republicans). But the unreal union did not last long. It was soon plain that Italy had to choose between the democratic world of the West and Communist Russia. The Peace Treaty was signed on May 11, 1946; Italy lost all her colonies in Africa; Venezia Giulia was annexed by Yugoslavia, and Trieste became an international zone partly occupied by the British and the Americans, and partly by the Yugoslavs. This was resented by many Italians; the Communists were becoming increasingly violent on orders from Moscow; and a new government was formed in July, 1947, without them and without the left-wing Socialists, led by Signor Nenni (who took the Soviet side). But the Communist Party, led by Signor Togliatti, was the strongest in Europe and Moscow thought it could extend its control over the country.

This was the great issue of the General Election of April, 1948. On the one side were the Communists and the fellow-travelers exploiting the grievances of the unemployed, the underpaid and the peasantry. On the other side were the promises of Marshall aid (soon to have a decisive effect in restoring the life of Italy) and the proposal of the Western Powers that Trieste be restored to Italy. The Pope and the Bishops proclaimed that it was the strict duty of every man and woman to vote and support only candidates standing for Christian principles.

The overwhelming victory for the Christian Democrats was the result. Italy became a member of the Council of Europe and signed the Schuman Plan (with France, Western Germany, Belgium, Holland and Luxembourg).

Italy's President is elected for a seven-year term by a two-thirds majority by a joint session of the legislature, sitting with delegates from each of the nineteen regions of Italy. In the June, 1953 election the Christian Democrats won (a Roman Catholic Party, with some extreme right-wing members, led by Antonio Segni, coalition Premier until 1955, Giuseppe Pella, a former Premier, and Amintore Fanfani, a former Premier and leader of Democratic initiative, a militant Christian and land-reforming group); Communists (the largest Com-

321

munist Party in Western Europe, with 2,000,000 members) were next in the number of seats won. In July, 1955 Antonio Segni became Prime Minister of a coalition government of Christian Democrats, Italian Socialist Democrats and Liberals, with Republican support. The new electoral law restoring full proportional representation was passed by the Chamber on March 21, 1956; on April 23, 1956, a new Constitutional High Court, modeled upon the United States Supreme Court, was formally inaugurated.

Save for continued soul-searching and unsuccessful realignment on the left, the political scene continued hazy under President Giovanni Gronchi (elected on April 29, 1955) ; the Cabinet of Premier Segni carried on until May, 1958 (supported by the Republicans, Liberals and Right Socialists — and opposed by Neo-Fascists, Monarchists, Left Socialists and Communists).

Italy's Communists, led by Palmiro Togliatti, continued to suffer defections and electoral losses as a result of Soviet suppression of Hungary's revolution (1956) and renewed feuds between Stalinists and anti-Stalinists. But despite reverses and dissensions, the party (like the French counterpart) continued to command the support of a quarter or more of the electorate and in some areas had begun to regain strength. But the Communist support, stemming from attitudes of protest against the *status quo* in domestic and foreign affairs, remained formidably large and tended to grow with the advent of the Soviet sputnik and the diminished prestige of the United States.

Italian Socialists (split in 1947 over the issue of collaboration with the Communists into a minority faction) remained divided into a small anti-Communist faction and a large mass party willing to co-operate with Togliatti's followers. The Christian Democrats, precariously poised in power over popular opponents to left and to right in parliament, have been not of one mind as to how the Italian interests could best be served in the troubled world.

At any rate, in May, 1957, Premier Antonio Segni and his twenty-two-month-old cabinet resigned in the face of a decision by Saragat's Right Socialists to quit the government. On May 15, 1957, Gronchi entrusted cabinet-making to Adone Zoli, a sixty-nine-year-old Florentine lawyer and left-wing Christian Democrat, who formed an exclusively Christian Democrat Cabinet.

Among the few surprises in the 1958 Italian election was the sharp decline of the Monarchists and the failure of the new Communist

Party to elect any of its candidates other than Olivetti. Popular votes cast and percentages of the total, with corresponding percentages in 1953 in parentheses, were: Christian Democrats, 42.4% (40.1%); Communists, 22.7% (22.6%); Left Socialist, 14.2% (12.7%); Monarchist, 4.7% (6.9%); Neo-Fascist, 4.7% (5.8%); Right Socialist, 4.6% (4.5%); Liberals, 3.5% (3.0%). In the New Chamber, Christian Democrats won 273 seats (261 in 1953); Communists 140 (143); Left Socialists 84 (75); Monarchists 23 (40); Neo-Fascists 25 (29); Right Socialists 23 (19); Liberals 16 (14); and Republicans 7 (5). Of the 246 elective seats in the Senate, the Center parties won 133, of which 122 were Christian Democrats; the two Left parties won 98; and the Right 15.

The general elections gave the four moderate, pro-Western Center parties (Christian Democrats, Democrat Socialists, Liberals and Republicans) a firm majority in the Senate and a slight but sufficient working majority in the Chamber of Deputies.

So far as the popular vote was concerned, the elections brought out three important points: (1) Since the 1953 elections, the extreme Left had advanced very little if at all. The Communists gained only a small fraction of one percentage point in the five years. Their friends and associates, the Left-wing Socialists, gained a little more if allowances are made for their two small groups of Socialists who ran independently in 1953 and threw their votes to the Left-wing Socialists this time. (2) The extreme Right, composed of two rival Monarchist parties and of the Neo-Fascists, suffered a near collapse. As compared to the votes obtained five years ago by the only Monarchist party then existing and by the Neo-Fascists, they lost by a good 900,000 votes. (3) The votes lost by the extreme Right were gained by the Center, and particularly by the dominant Christian Democrats, who were the only party that can be said to have triumphed.

In 1953, 27,092,000 Italian men and women voted. In 1958, the number of voters who went to the polls was almost exactly 9 per cent greater. If the figures for 1953 are increased by 9 per cent, in order to make them comparable with the 1958 figures, one finds that the following parties list the following number of votes:

National Monarchist Party	1,366,000
Neo-Fascists	320,000
Republicans	72,000
Others	365,000
	2,123,000

It must be noted that the Republicans were the only party that lost votes.

The following parties gained the following number of votes:

Christian Democrats	697,000
Democratic Socialists	19,000
Liberals	157,000
Total Center	**873,000**
Communists	27,000
Left-wing Socialists	447,000
	474,000

The Popular Monarchist Party, the party of shipping magnate Achille Lauro, which did not exist in 1953, received 776,000 votes.

In 1953, the two small Socialist parties which ran independently polled 380,000 votes. When allowances are made for the growth of the electorate, this corresponds to about 414,000 votes. Deducting this number of votes from the Left-wing Socialist gains of 447,000, the net gain amounted to only 33,000 votes. This compared with gains of 27,000 by the Communists.

One outstanding aspect about the Communist vote was that it showed a tendency to decrease in the industrial north. Sometimes the decrease was accompanied by an increase of the Left-wing Socialist vote, but not always. Another remarkable thing about the Communist vote was that it showed a tendency to decrease in the great Communist strongholds. In 1953 the highest Communist vote was registered in Siena, Leghorn and Modena. In 1958 the Communist vote dropped: Siena — from 48.7% to 47.7% of the total; Leghorn — from 43.2% to 41%; Modena — from 42.3% to 40.9%. The Communist vote decreased also in Ferrara, but increased slightly in Bologna and Florence.

The Christian Democrats retained almost the whole of their very high vote in the regions which are traditionally Roman Catholic (the Upper Adige, some parts of Lombardy, and Venetia). In the province of Vicenza, they actually improved their vote from 62.3% to 66.7% of the total. But where the Christian Democrats registered their greatest gains was throughout southern Italy — in those same parts, in other words, where enormous sums had been spent in the previous eight years to make land available to the landless laborers and to create the structures for future industrial development. These were the parts, also, where the Monarchists, and to some extent the Neo-Fascists, lost heavily.

On the whole, the electorate of Italy thus endorsed the middle-of-the-road policies that had been followed by the Center parties during the previous decade. The campaign was fought largely on matters of foreign policy, and the electorate thus approved NATO and the possibility of an integrated Europe, which all the Center parties specifically had upheld during the campaign.

POLITICAL PARTIES

The political spectrum of Italy can be divided into two major and two minor sectors. The two major ones are the Marxist parties (which polled 35.3% of the vote in the 1953 elections and 36.9% in 1958) and the Christian Democratic Party (40.1% votes in 1953 and 42.4% in 1958); the two minor sectors are the lay liberal and republican parties and the fascist and monarchical right. The programs of the parties are the most definite expressions of the ideological cross-currents agitating the Italian political scene; on this point the bibliography is immense.[4]

Christian Democracy. The Christian Democracy Party includes many shades of political opinions in its ranks from left to right, cemented together by its Catholic ideology, mirroring the social principles of the church. Born at the end of World War I, it polled one-fifth of the votes in 1919, reached 48% in 1948, and fell back to a very large 40.7% in 1953. In order to satisfy its many factions, the party uses compromises as its technique, and has the advantage in Italian politics as, formally, it is a united party — while the Left is divided. It has only one thing in common with the Marxist parties — its opposition to the bourgeois capitalistic world, and, historically, represents a reaction in the name of certain communal and collective theories of economic organization against the extreme individualistic utilitarianism of the Industrial Revolution. But while Marxism attacks the contemporary society from a materialistic point of view, Christian Democracy does this from the opposite point of view of the need of the restoration of certain moral and supernatural values which eighteenth-century thought had destroyed. The basic difficulty of the party has been how to promote these spiritual values of the Christian religion without, at the same time, subjecting itself to the Catholic Church.[5]

Its distinguished leaders included such great personalities as Don Luigi Sturzo, who showed that it was possible to have a political party inspired by Christian ideology yet free from Church controls. Under the contemporary leader, Alcide de Gasperi (whose anti-Fascism landed him in jail for sixteen months in the 1930's), the party has sheltered many of the conservative elements of the country, fearful of, or opposed to change. But the struggle between the right and left wings has frequently paralyzed the party. In the eyes of the Marxist critics, the party is a clerical and reactionary tool of the Vatican.

It is necessary to deal here with the ideological ramifications of the "Democratic" aspects of the Christian Democratic Party. The explanation is rooted in Pope Leo XIII, who, responsible for the revival of political Catholicism, made clear (in 1903) that for a Christian Democrat "democracy means to govern for the people, to do good to the people; it does *not* mean government *by* the people."[6] This benevolent paternalism explains the political creed of Catholicism, and allows Catholics to be "good" democrats when they are in a minority and want to use civil rights to resist the oppression of a non-Catholic minority, or, when in power, to take away the liberty from the citizens when they could be subjected to an inducement to abandon The True Faith.

But these have not been the main issues within the Italian Christian Democratic Party, which has been agitated, mainly, by economic policies. A small group, headed especially by former Premier Pella, favors free enterprise, while a larger group favors a semi-socialist economy (under Gronchi, the President of the Republic, and Pastore, the leader of the Catholic labor unions); but the majority (whose spokesman is the economist Fanfani) favors a corporate economy based on private ownership of property, state regulation of the uses of property and abolition of competition. Politically, this means, from an over-all point of view, the authoritarian and semi-authoritarian Christian Democrats, while the deputies, thanks to historical circumstances, sit in the center of the House of Deputies (while, actually, they should sit on the right).

The strength of this group is derived from the traditional conservatism of the Italian people, and this trend has been helped by political and economic recovery.

Socialism. Socialism became a force in Italy at the end of the last century. Its stronghold can be found in the factory towns of northern

Italy.[7] The party opposed Italy's participation in World War I, and Mussolini, editor of the *Avanti*, resigned and eventually became a bitter opponent of the party. In 1920, the metal workers seized numerous factories; this led to a reaction against radicalism in general and the result was the victory of Mussolini's followers and the ruthless persecution of the Socialists (as well as trade unionists and cooperators). Following the Soviet revolution, the Communists split from the Socialists and formed their own party. Following an attack on Mussolini's life in the fall of 1925, the Socialists were thrown out of Parliament. In 1947, left-wing Socialists, under Pietro Nenni, sided with the Soviets in the ideological struggle between East and West. Nenni's Partito Socialista Italiano (PSI) remains unrecognized by the Soviet International.

Under the leadership of Giuseppe Saragat, the strongly anti-Communist right-wing Socialist group formed the Partito Socialista Democratico Italiano (PSDI); although basically anti-clerical, the Italian Democratic Socialist Party has been also able to collaborate with the Christian Democrats.

Premier Alcide de Gasperi set up a Cabinet in May, 1947, which excluded both the Nenni Socialists and the Communists; these together proceeded to form an opposition. (By the following December, De Gasperi's Cabinet was composed of Christian Democrats, Liberals, Republicans and Social Democrats.) In the elections of April, 1948, Nenni's Socialists presented a "Popular Front" list in partnership with the Communists (his group receiving forty-eight seats, and Social Democrats thirty-three).

The disagreements of the two Socialist parties meanwhile were promoted by conditions abroad. The Social Democrats accused the Nenni Socialists of serving as proponents of international Communism, while, in turn, they were attacked for the support of the all-powerful and clerically oriented Christian Democrats and the interests of the Capitalist West.[8]

In 1953 Nenni started to change his views on the political setup. His party abandoned the Popular Front platform of the 1948 elections and adopted the slogan, "Socialist alternative," which implied the willingness to participate in the give-and-take of the democratic process independently of the Communist Party. The agreement for "joint action" remained but the Socialists had taken a measure of initiative. This independent stand helped to increase the number of Nenni's

Socialists from forty-eight to seventy-five in the Chamber of Deputies in the 1953 elections. This showed that the Italian electorate was looking for an opposition party to the Christian Democrats but which would not be allied to Communism. Nenni's group started to support occasionally the government.

The real turn came after the Twentieth Party Congress in Moscow (February, 1956) and the publication of the famous Khrushchev report. Nenni proclaimed himself more frequently on Soviet policies. This induced the young secretary of the Social Democratic Party, Matteo Matteotti, to issue, in June, 1955, an appeal to all Socialists to join forces, independently of Communism.

Just at the time of these events, local elections were held in Italy and their results gave a further impetus to unification. The Socialist Party made gains, while the Social Democrats recovered several hundred thousand votes lost in 1953. For the first time, the Communists suffered a loss. Especially important was one result: the Social Democrats polled 400,000 more votes in the provincial elections, where the Socialists and Communists presented a joint ticket, than they did in the municipal elections, where the Nenni Socialists presented a list of their own. "It was plain that many people voted for the Socialists only on condition that they were fully independent."[9]

On June 1, 1955 the leaders of the Social Democratic Party voted in favor of including Nenni Socialists in executive bodies at the municipal and provincial level.

In an editorial in L'UNITA in December, 1957, in which Signor Amendola, a member of the Politbureau, acknowledged the Communist losses in members, particularly deplored the "confused and equivocal" conduct of Pietro Nenni's left-wing Socialists, although recently the left-wing Socialists have been again drawn closer to the Communists, evidently under the psychological impact of Soviet rocketry.[10]

Communism. The Italian Communist Party is the largest this side of the Iron Curtain. In its heyday it claimed more than two million dues-paying members and, together with its left-wing Socialist allies, commanded more than one out of every three votes at election time. The party has skillfully managed to penetrate important segments of Italy's structure; this penetration extends to the armed forces, the pseudo-independent left-wing Socialist Party and even the administrative apparatus of the Vatican.

Italian workers have been faithful to the Communist Party longer

328

than any others in Europe. Its yearly income amounted to, in its peak years, $40 million, perhaps $50 million; it had 365,000 employees — one to every six members — on its payroll; and it numbered among its thousands of publications the newspaper L'UNITA, with the largest daily circulation in Italy. The organization had, until recently, good leadership, ample funds (derived from local collections, profits from Communist-sponsored East-West trade, and Moscow's help). At every level there are party schools: cell schools for elementary propaganda; correspondence courses with test papers to be filled out and returned; national schools for the higher party ranks.

The party got a good start after World War II by seizing Mussolini's private fortune and a great deal of Fascist property. From the beginning the Communists made millions by extortion from rich Fascists or from manufacturers who would pay bribes to avoid strikes. The Communist-dominated commercial companies monopolized trade between Italy and the Soviet empire and paid percentage cuts to the party (the Societa Importazioni-Esportazioni, Nord Export, Tecno-Export, Compagnia Centra Orientale, Compagnia Europeo Balcanacio, Neos, Unione Rappresentanze Estere, Societa Commerciale Finanziaria and Impresse Mercantili Commerciale).[11]

The strength of the Communist Party is one of the strangest phenomena in modern history, since Italy is the predominantly Catholic country. According to Salvadori the paradox is due to the existence and governing of the Christian Democratic Party, since its proponents, although resenting certain aspects of Communist policies, believe that the path to economic salvation can be laid down by the Communist Party; and there are many who are neither Communists nor Socialists but who also are convinced that Communism is the only ideology and a movement which can save Italy from becoming the new Papal state. "There are relatively few real communists in Italy — maybe only the few tens of thousands of activists. The communist vote comes mainly from the millions convinced that, to oppose clericalism, something firmer, more substantial and more determined than democrats or socialists is needed. Most Italians are skeptical about liberty and find democratic procedure tedious and unproductive. . . . Those who want a change, a different class structure, more equality and more solidarity among the citizens, and who believe in the need for a powerful collective effort in order to abolish poverty and to abandon intellectual and moral stagnation, vote communist — again, without too many illusions."[12] After all, "clerical activists preach about salvation in heaven and believe in it; communist activists preach about salvation on earth and believe in it; the bulk of Italians of all classes have little confidence in any kind of salvation."

The party has inherited Fascism's techniques and position in mass propaganda. The propaganda promises everything to everyone: "a lessening of international tensions . . . action in favor of the popular masses, the small and middle producers, the rural population . . . extension of the home market, increasing of capital investments, stepping up or full production activity. . . ."

The main theater of operations of the party has been the industrial north and central Italy (until recently); in recent years the Communists have been showing the greatest gains in the south (until recently); the gain of the party there has materialized not in a vacuum but as a result of an early decision by the party's leadership to concentrate its electoral agents in that area. Large numbers of agricultural day laborers and tenant farmers, long and notoriously ignored by Italy's privileged classes, have received their first political education from Communist agitators. The southern Italian may not be a convert to the ideological tenets of international Communism. But his support of the Italian Communist Party and of its various trade unions, youth, women's and co-operative auxiliaries is anything but negatively determined.

The Communists retain a firm grip on the party machinery of Pietro Nenni's left-wing Socialists — an important factor. It is widely known that the Communists pay the Nenni Socialists' organizing expenses and make up the deficit of their party press. Signor Nenni is emotionally pro-Soviet rather than intellectually pro-Communist. Paradoxically, he was one of the earliest Fascists in Italy and set up the first Fascist organization in Bologna.

Until the middle of 1947, the Communists had held posts in the Italian Government. Their agents were carefully placed all over; despite all the subsequent efforts to ferret them out, it is believed the party still has access to secret orders of the Interior Ministry. The Communists built up a strong espionage and sabotage organization. The Communist military apparatus, headed by Luigi Longo, who directed the International Brigades of the Spanish Civil War, has a series of secret armaments caches throughout Italy.

The top leadership is efficient. At the top is Secretary General

Palmiro Togliatti, who used to broadcast from Moscow and became a Soviet citizen. He had spent eighteen years in the USSR and was at one time a member of the Presidium of the Executive Committee of the Comintern; he also served as an adviser to the Soviet Foreign Commissariat in Moscow.[13]

Ironically enough, the Communist Party fulfills, according to Italian intellectuals, a "liberal function," since it represents a guarantee for the liberties enjoyed by Italian citizens in post-Fascist years. This opinion is even acknowledged by convinced anti-Communists like the leaders of the small but influential Republican Party and numerous former resistance fighters; for, without the Communist Party's check there would be a clerical dictatorship in Italy and Italy's Constitutional Republic would be transformed into a "stato pontifico" (a Papal State) ; "Salazarismo" (derived from Portugal's dictator's name) would be inaugurated. As long as the Communists command one-third of the electorate (including the fellow-travelers), controls the administration of a third or so of Italy's municipalities, and are supported by powerful labor unions like the General Confederation of Labor (CGIL), clericalism has to follow democratic procedures and respect the basic liberties of citizens.

It was expected, in the anti-Communist circles, that the Twentieth Party Congress in the USSR and the Hungarian anti-Communist revolt would weaken the Italian Communist Party. There was something like a crisis between April, 1956 and January, 1957 among the Italian Communists, but the Party Congress in Rome did not fulfill the expectations. There were some resignations among the intellectuals — but not among the working people.[14] The leaders considered the Soviet action "to be perfectly consistent with the ultimate goal of 'the triumph of socialism'." In fact, the party was "far from being weakened," reports Salvadori. Yet, the party has been losing what Italians call "mordente," or bite.[15] "Not long ago, an organizer for an anti-Communist union couldn't even walk into Fiat without running the risk of a beating," but "neither in Modena nor in Bologna nor anywhere in Emilia do the landowners any longer need police protection." All union activities on factory premises are not tolerated any more in such Communist strongholds as Bologna, Turin and Milan's industrial suburb of Sesto San Giovanni.

The losses were especially glaring in 1957 when Antonio Giolitti, one of the most intellectually influential members and the bearer of a famous name in politics, resigned from the party. Grandson of Giovanni Giolitti, great Italian pre-World War I statesman, Antonio Giolitti announced not only his resignation from the party but also his resignation as a Communist Deputy in Parliament; he gave as his reason that he finally had given up hope of being able to initiate within the party any discussion on political and ideological problems that now face Italian Communism.

Resignation was seen as proof that Palmiro Togliatti, Communist Party leader, had been unable to discipline rebels within the party who had been pressing for a measure of democratization in party organization and in policy decisions. (Signor Giolitti had been a rebel since the twentieth Congress of the Soviet Communist Party in February, 1956, which opened up new vistas with its decisions on de-Stalinization and its attack on the personality cult.)

Signor Giolitti's resignation produced rumblings among the party rank and file in Piedmont, his home province where he enjoys great popularity and a wide following. More important still, it is an event which had psychological impact upon the younger elite of the Communist Party. Signor Giolitti was, in one way, a Communist Party showpiece.

In addition to bearing a great name in Italian politics, he had taken an active and prominent part in the wartime resistance movement. He was also a young man of ability and of idealistic devotion to the cause of Socialism. He was, in fact, the epitome of a large group of young intellectuals who, after World War II, were attracted toward the Communist Party in the belief that it was the only force capable of bringing their political ideals to fulfillment.

There were other blows suffered by the party during this period. In the financial field it was significant that there were no longer sufficient funds available for continuation of the Turin and Genoa editions of the party's official newspaper L'UNITA, the Free World's biggest Communist newspaper and second biggest daily in Italy (after Milan's conservative CORRIERE DELLA SERA). In August, 1957, L'UNITA folded its once-thriving editions in industrial Turin and Genoa, and announced that its sole surviving regional edition in Milan would now serve all three cities; beyond that, the paper was reduced to running a page-one jeremiad by Party Boss Palmiro Togliatti, imploring the faithful to dig deep in their pockets to save L'UNITA from "extermination." Money-losing, with an annual deficit of more than $1,000,000, L'UNITA's financial crisis was brought on by sharp cutbacks in its subsidies from Moscow and from the financially pressed Italian Communist Party. But its most serious problem was shriveling circulation, then well below 300,000 from a 1953 peak of 1,574,000.

Then, in 1957, the Communist-controlled Confederazione Generale Italiana del Lovaro (CGIL), Italy's biggest union, lost another round in its fight with the country's free trade unions. The latest defeat occurred in the April shop-steward elections at Fiat's twenty factory production complex in Turin. The Red union ran a poor third behind a Christian Democratic Union (CISL) and its Democratic Socialist ally (UIL), polled a measly 21.1% of the ballots cast vs. over 70% in elections in the late forties. All of this was quite a switch from the early postwar years when the CGIL controlled 90% of Italian labor. What has happened to deplete Red labor strength? For one thing, the Italian gross national product has more than doubled since World War II. Meanwhile, some prominent Italian executives have adopted a hard line toward Communists (isolation from non-Red workers, special security checks) while making material concessions to workers in general. (Most generous of these concessions have been those granted by Fiat's chairman and managing director Vittorio Valletta, Italy's foremost business statesman. Valletta has upped his workers' pay roughly 80% above the minimum required by national work contracts and has installed an intricate system of individual bonuses and prizes.)

But perhaps the biggest reason for the weakening of Communist power in Italian labor lies within the Communist-run CGIL itself. Although the union claims to be a Communist-Socialist coalition, Socialist members are poorly represented; CGIL is, consequently, vulnerable to the charge that it serves only the interests of the Communist Party; then, too, CGIL abuses of union power have soured many an Italian worker, especially on strikes called by CGIL purely for party-line purposes.

All in all, Italian Communism had lost 15 per cent of its organized strength in 1957; this was nearly half a million fewer than in 1954 when the party membership reached its peak. Still the strongest in the West, the party said it has 1,700,000 card-holding members. Acknowledgment of the losses was made by Giorgio Amendola, a member of the party's seven-men Secretariat (Politbureau); in an editorial in

L'UNITA, Communist Party organ, Signor Amendola said that those who had deserted were the "weaklings" and "traitors."[16]

Amendola's article expresses confidence that Italian Communism was through the worst and that the time had come to stage a formidable comeback—the hope, apparently, being based on the Soviet earth satellites. (L'UNITA and all other Communist publications had been dwelling for weeks on Soviet successes in the East-West scientific rivalry and sneered at the disappointments of the United States.)

At the Communist National Congress in 1956 the party membership was given at 2,035,353. In September, 1957, Signor Amendola reported that the membership had shrunk to 1,817,229. On the strength of the late disclosures it appeared that in the previous three months 100,000 had quit the party.

Signor Amendola particularly deplored the "confused and equivocal" conduct of Pietro Nenni's left-wing Socialists.

In 1959, the anti-Communist front in Italy was strengthened by two political moves. The first was the unification of the two hitherto quarreling Monarchist groups into a new party with the title of the Italian Democratic Party; the second was the Papal interdict forbidding Roman Catholics to give their support or aid to the Communist cause. Together, these two events consolidated the democratic front against Communism.

Minor parties. The Movimiento Sociale Italiano (MSI), the Neo-Fascist Party, was founded in 1947 by the leaders of the dissolved Fascist Party, and the proponents of "Mussolini's Social Republic," sponsored by the Nazis in northern Italy in 1943. Die-hard Fascists and youth for the most part compose the following of this ultra-nationalistic party that aims to establish a corporate state.

"It is plain that the many laws designed to bar a return to Fascism have been next to impotent."[17] By avoiding calling themselves Fascists and advocating what they cryptically call their "idea," MSI followers, with few exceptions, have escaped prosecution; but they advocate a return to something barely short of Mussolini's dictatorship. The MSI has no "Duce" but its leaders and prospective candidates are: Giorgio Almirante, a MSI official and Parliamentary member, who was with Mussolini's government, set up behind German lines after the King's surrender in 1943. There is Marshal Rudolfo Graziani, the former Italian Army Chief of Staff who agreed to form a new Italian army and navy behind German lines in 1943; he was found guilty of treason by a postwar military court but the death sentence was suspended in Italy's postwar "pacification"—so he served only five years. Prince Valerio Borghese, commander of the tiny navy of Mussolini's post-1943 rump government, who sent torpedo boats into Alexandria harbor and managed to sink major British warships. The brains of the organization is Augusto de Marsanich, a sunken-cheeked, white-haired veteran of Mussolini's "march" on Rome; he is executive manager of the MSI, apes Mussolini's hand-on-hip speaking technique, and is able to keep modern Fascism's clashing wings together. Behind these three, there are some lesser lights: Filippo Anfuso, the last-ditch Mussolini government's ambassador to Hitler; Roberto Mieville, a former tank officer who was a prisoner of war in Texas, and became a MSI member of Parliament; Ezio Maria Gray, editor of a MSI paper. There are a few others, who are not party members, but support it: Achille Lauro, a shipping line operator, one of the wealthiest men in southern Italy and Mayor of Naples, and Vittorio Mussolini, the eldest son of the late dictator (now living in Argentina).

The reason that no "Duce" has emerged has been due to the score of different political tendencies among them, characterized by the Monarchists and fierce enemies of royalty, ardent supporters of the Church and implacable anti-clerics, backers of big business and advocates of doctrines only a step short of Communism. The latter, "neo-Communists," are assembled around a publication called NATIONAL THOUGHT. The Communists think so highly of it that they advertise it in their own press. Another neo-Fascist fringe group is Fernando Gori's, whose band gives membership to anybody who had volunteered for the Ethiopian war or for Graziani's North Italian Army. On the other side are those who are denounced by extremists as the "Americanizers" of the neo-Fascist movement, especially Borghese, who rejects Communism and hints that the United States should support the MSI against Italy's democrats because the virile martial type of the MSI members might be useful to Washington in a war. A similar faction is the Ezio Gray group. But if all these factions agree on anything, then it is their hate of Alcide de Gasperi, the ex-Austrian, Christian Democrat Premier of the postwar republic who took wind from the neo-Fascist sails by allowing the police necessary measures to put down Fascist and Communist uprisings.

The Monarchist Party (The Partito Nazionale Monarchico—PNM) showed considerable increase in strength in the 1953 elections; it wants a new referendum on the question of republic or monarchy. It agreed with the Neo-Fascist Party on most national issues—with the exception of the Atlantic Pact. But the National Monarchists, the Popular Monarchists and the big-business and landowner Liberals have lay traditions which make them disliked by the good Catholics. At any rate, these three groups have ample funds at their disposal and the support of much of the "independent" press, but obviously neither money nor newspaper helped them to win an election.

In 1959, the two hitherto quarelling Monarchist groups formed a new party with the title of the Italian Democratic Party. The Monarchist initiative was more than a device to mend a split that divided the Monarchist Party in 1954 into two bickering groups. It was, in fact, noticed that the Monarchists, under their new name, had decided to play a more active and realistic role in the political arena.

Ever since the postwar plebiscite which favored a republican constitution and sent King Umberto into exile in Portugal, the Monarchists have lived in a nostalgic nimbus on the fringes of Italian political life. This made it almost inevitable that they should line up, although loosely, with the neo-Fascists. As a party dedicated to the restoration of the monarchy, there was little constructive political contribution they could make under a republican regime. Because of the unreality of their position their appeal to the electorate steadily has dwindled. In the May, 1958 election they suffered greater losses than any other party. With the merger of the two Monarchist groups, the old ties with the neo-Fascists have been severed and a practical political program, answering some of the needs of the electorate, has been adopted. This was summed up in general in terms of a communiqué which had the full approval of ex-King Umberto.

The new party now advocates democratic principles and promotes practical measures for greater social and economic progress. While it remains devoted to the ideal of monarchy, it promises loyal service to the republic. In practical politics this means that the Monarchists have become respectable members of a democratic community, have moved their position from extreme right to the center. They cease to be a sort of fifth column working for the overthrow of the present Constitution in favor of the restoration of the monarchy. This automatically gives added weight to the democratic alignment as against the Communists and the extreme left.

The Partito Liberale Italiano (PLI) is a center party, conservative and predominantly monarchist in its right wing, liberal only in its left. It advocates free trade and enterprise and the separation of Church and State.

The Republican Party (the Partito Republicano Italiano—PRI) advocates the republic form of government and the separation of Church and State; its moderate left-of-center economic and social program is rather vague.

THE CONSTITUTION

A set of ideological compromises characterizes the Italian Constitution passed by the Constituent Assembly, after prolonged consideration, and which came into effect January 1, 1948. It formed a bicameral legislature comprising a Senate of 237 members elected for six years on a regional basis and a Chamber of Deputies of 590 members for five years by universal suffrage. The Republic was proclaimed for all time and this article is declared unamendable. Concessions to the radicals were made in an electorate Bill of Rights which limits the rights of property, grants workers an unlimited right to strike, and makes it obligatory upon the state to provide work for the unemployed. On the other hand, the dominance of religious and conservative elements in the Constituent Assembly appeared in the provisions recognizing freedom of religion but making the Catholic Church the established religion. (The Lateran Accord of 1929 was made part of the Constitution, thus conferring special privileges upon the Catholic Church.)

The President of the Republic (chosen by the National Assembly for seven-year term by a two-thirds majority on the first two ballots or by an absolute majority if more ballots are required) may be removed by the National Assembly by a majority vote for treason or violation of the Constitution or laws of the Republic. No extraordinary powers were granted him except the rights to refer bills in dispute between the two houses to a popular referendum.

Both houses have equal powers, and when sitting together they constitute the National Assembly. Members of the Chamber of Deputies are elected by universal suffrage on the basis of one from each province; in addition, three senators are chosen from each of the twenty-two newly created regions by the regional councils thereof. Members of both houses hold office for five years—unless Parliament is dissolved sooner by executive decree. Bills must be passed by both Houses.

The Premier is chosen by the President of the Republic, and the other members of the Cabinet by the Premier and confirmed by the President. The Cabinet must be approved by a majority of the National Assembly and can be removed in the same way.

The Constitution created a Constitutional Court on the order of the United States Supreme Court and has the power to pass upon all questions of constitutionality of laws and conflicts of power between different branches of government. It sits also as a Court of Impeachment for the President and ministers; judges are appointed for nine years by the National Assembly.

Among interesting features was included the popular initiative and referendum. An attempt was made to provide some regional autonomy through the creation of twenty-two regions with substantial administrative powers under Regional Councils whose acts are subject to review by the National Assembly.

The attempt to provide more stability was shown in the creation of a powerful upper house and in making the Ministry responsible to the National Assembly; this was an effort to avoid the ministerial crises characteristic of the French Cabinet which, under the Third Republic, was responsible to each of the Houses; and to place checks upon overhasty public opinion as represented in the lower house. The same purpose is to be served by the Constitutional Court.[18]

CROSS-CURRENTS IN POLITICAL SOCIOLOGY

According to LaPalombara, "Adequate knowledge of Italian social, economic, and political institutions has been . . . inhibited by the retarded state of the social sciences in Italy . . ."[19] With the exception of economics (the field not considered a social science in Italy), such disciplines as political science, sociology, psychology and anthropology "are today at primitive levels of development." This is, indeed, a paradoxical situation, as Italy has contributed great names in the field of social sciences which are considered great names in the evolution of this discipline everywhere: Lombroso, Ferri, Mosca, Galiani, Pareto, Vico and others. The difficulty can be traced to the late nineteenth century, when Italian scholars fought against the nascent social diseases. As pointed out by Giannini of the University of Perugia: "A culture that prized clarity and acumen above all could not respect research so tendentiously obscure and so abounding in banalities as that engaged in by the new social sciences, not only in Italy but in France, Germany, England and the United States as well."[20]

While Professor Giannini objected to the foundation of sociology as a respectable academic field because of its effort to emulate the methodologies of the more exact sciences, other Italian critics made their objections because of the goals which had little, if anything, to do with advancing the condition of man's knowledge of his social institutions, opposing them dialectically. They represented the idealistic reaction against positivism which took place at the turn of the present century (for instance, Benedetto Croce once dismissed the work of Pareto as so much "nonsense").

Fascism only completed this trend and when the curricula were being retrenched, the social sciences were the first to go, and the universities were made the instruments of the "organic state." Writings about Fascism and its history were nearly all, if not all, violently partisan.

A last blow was handed out to the social sciences in 1944 when faculties of Political Science (of which there existed a few) were suppressed as the mere creatures of Fascism.

Social Sciences after Fascism. The downfall of Fascism, the upholder of a definite ideology, had important effects on the ideological atmosphere in Italy. Above all, "the liberal point of view seemed to have received a decisive confirmation in events, a solemn response from history, and that victory extended from political philosophy to the entire domain of the social sciences."[21] The leaders here, the representatives of the liberal tendencies, were Croce and Einaudi—the first representing the speculative and the other the economic level.[22]

On the other hand, the problem of social justice, left unresolved by Fascism, reappeared again in all its urgency and gave weight to the opposite theory, the position of socialists and planners. Both of these opposites have been trying to reach a synthesis, but in vain. The "third force" (the formula adopted quite successfully in Italy) has been promoted by numerous men of good will who try to reach a compromise between liberty and authority by propounding the ideology of liberal socialism (C. Rosselli, SOCIALISMO LIBERALE, 1945; Calogero, IL LIBERALSOCIALISMO, 1946, etc.).

Notwithstanding these many barriers, the social sciences have made a little headway in the postwar era in Italy. Of definite help here was the flooding of the literary markets, after Mussolini's downfall, with an enormous amount of documents, testimonies, accusations and defenses of those responsible for Fascist policy who deny or attenuate their responsibility, of anti-Fascists claiming the reward of their past record, and, ever more boldly, of the Fascists themselves, who sometimes acknowledge the consequences of their mistakes but also stress that this is not sufficient to condemn all Mussolini's policy.[23] Above all, much has been written about Mussolini's policies and his personal life.

In this respect the available summary of the literature in English can be found in Noether,[24] and a rather critical re-evaluation provided by Smith.[25] Monelli portrays rather fully the story of *Il Duce's* career, his passionate hatreds, jealousies and vendettas, of boldness alternating with timid indecision, of disease and delusion and petty vanity, of tumultuous love affairs and bitter family squabbles—all told against a background of world events.[26] Dombrowski has reconstructed the two strange last years of Mussolini's life, from his unexpected deposition in July, 1943 to his violent death in 1945.[27] A singular, repellent defense of Mussolini's foreign policy is Villari's volume.[28]

Since Count Ciano played a leading part in Italy's foreign policy after 1935, especially in the Abyssinian and Spanish adventures, his memoirs rank high; as one of the leading actors in the world drama, his testimony cannot be but important, although it is only one of the pieces of evidence, many more of which will have to be forthcoming before we can get a satisfactory picture of the drama and its participants.[29]

No small part of Mussolini's title to a place in history arises from the malign example he set for Hitler, who in the years of his struggle for power looked upon "the great man south of the Alps" as his mentor and idol, "a genius second only to himself." Firsthand acquaintance with Il Duce and the blundering conduct of military affairs caused Hitler to revise his estimate; Mussolini's downfall in July of 1943 disillusioned the Fuehrer more than anything else in his career to that point, while in the twenties the Italian had only contempt for his prototype in Bavaria, and flatly declined to accede to Hitler's request for a signed photograph.

At that time Mussolini dismissed Hitler as unrevolutionary and pro-bourgeois, almost exactly Hitler's ultimate verdict on the Duce. After the blood bath of 1934, Mussolini reviled the Fuehrer as a "dangerous fool," whose Nazi fanaticism diverged radically from Fascism, as brilliantly shown by Wiskemann, [30] although she insists that Mussolini never held any clear-cut objectives, never rose above the level of a journalist and orator. The commonplace opportunism of the Italian is contrasted, in a manner not entirely convincing, with the superman ferocity of the Austro-German. Hitler's "clumsy and treacherous courtship" won Il Duce over and together they hammered out one of the most hideous plunderbunds in history, though Italian army officers, the bourgeoisie and highly placed diplomats heartily and always disliked the tie-up with Germany. In all, the two dictators, fellow pupils of Nietzsche, conferred on sixteen occasions, three of them after Mussolini had been toppled from his pedestal. Certain of the meetings, the visit of Mussolini to Germany in 1937, notably, are now reconstructed with dramatic intensity; never did anything akin to genuine intimacy or trustfulness develop between the two men.

Wiskemann is primarily concerned "with the extraordinary manner in which Hitler advanced inexorably towards the subjugation of Italy independently of his romantic hero-worship for the Duce and yet— using this sentimental devotion . . . to complete his political mastery" (p. 20). The main acts in the melodrama were fierce controversies over Austria until the Anschluss, the forging of diplomatic and military partnerships, Italian "neutrality" in 1939, then intervention, the overthrow of Mussolini, the neo-Fascist episode, and the resounding collapse of the Axis confederacy.

Then the preparatory works and speeches stirred up by the Constituent Assembly produced a mass of literature. The government sponsored a study by jurists and economists, and published a series of volumes containing the reports of commissions (on the reorganization of the state, the problems of economics and finance, labor) ; these were presided over by Professor Forti, Demaria and Presenti. The government also published two large collections, one on TESTI E DOCU-MENTI CONSTITUZIONALI edited by G. Perticone, and the STUDI STORICI, edited by A. M. Ghisalberti; at the same time, the General Secretariat of the Assembly published the acts of the parliamentary commission for the Constituent Assembly.

Progress has been more slow in the strictly academic field, as seen in the field of sociology. "Despite the strong support sociology received from prominent personalities, like L. Sturzo, the Universities were still inhibited by old preconceptions which, which was still worse, suffered from almost complete lack of qualified teachers and institutes."[31] In fact, it has had too many arguments even to establish a regular chair of sociology in the Faculty of Political Science in Florence University—and it still remains the only one in Italy. According to LaPalombara, "historicism, legalism, formalism are still the germs which best describe Italian scholarship. The influence of Hegelianism and neo-Hegelianism is ever present; modern social science is compelled to develop largely outside the accepted university curriculum."[32]

CONCLUSIONS

Italy's first decade as a republic presents a picture of amazing recovery from the political and economic ravages of Fascism and war. But there remain important sources of tension and instability in the society.[33] The fact that the political center has successfully warded off threats from the extreme is no reason for concluding that democratic institutions are now firmly established; Communism is still a menace; a democratic alternative to a Christian democracy that grows paternalistic because the security of its tenure is still wanting; unemployment and underemployment remain extensive; and the socioeconomic differences between the north and south continue to be immense and politically unsettling. The future demands more systematic changes in the interest of securing democratic institutions. The situation is further complicated by the glaring evidence that changes themselves cannot be wholly realized without the economic and political co-operation of other nations.

SELECTED BIBLIOGRAPHY

V. M. Barnett, Jr., " 'Competitive Coexistence' and the Communist Challenge in Italy," POLITICAL SCIENCE QUARTERLY, LXX, 2 (June, 1951), 230-257.

V. D. Bornet, "The Communist Party in the Presidential Election of 1958," WESTERN POLITICAL QUARTERLY, XI, 3 (September, 1958), 514-538.

Jane Perry Carey and A. G. Carey, "The Varying Seasons of Italian Politics, 1956-57," POLITICAL SCIENCE QUARTERLY, LXXII, 2 (June, 1957), 200-223.

Margaret Carlyle, MODERN ITALY (New York: Rinehart, 1957). Examines the political and economic scene in present day Italy.

Robert Eric Dickinson, THE POPULATION PROBLEM OF SOUTHERN ITALY: AN ESSAY IN SOCIAL GEOGRAPHY (Syracuse, New York: Syracuse University Press, 1956). A study of the geographic incident, of poverty and unemployment in rural southern Italy in terms of the conditions and possibilities of agricultural production and the quantity of labor and the ways in which it can be used most effectively for the increase of production. The thesis is summarized in: Dickinson, "Land Reform in Southern Italy," ECONOMIC GEOGRAPHY, XXX, 2 (April, 1954), 157-176.

Mario Einaudi, "The Italian Land: Men, Nature, and Government," SOCIAL RESEARCH, XVII, 1 (March, 1960), 8-34. By the son of the former Italian Premier.

Dante L. Germino, THE ITALIAN FASCIST PARTY IN POWER: A STUDY IN TOTALITARIAN RULE (Minneapolis, Minnesota: University of Minnesota Press, 1959). A study of the structure, activities, leaders, effects on youth, relationship to other institutions, and military alliances of the Italian Fascist Party.

H. Hilton-Young, THE ITALIAN LEFT. A SHORT HISTORY OF POLITICAL SOCIALISM IN ITALY (New York: Longmans, Green, 1950). A history of the Italian left-wing from the middle of the eighteenth century to the present, focusing on the Italian Socialist Party but covering also such movements as anarchism and Communism.

H. Stuart Hughes, THE UNITED STATES AND ITALY (Cambridge: Harvard University Press, 1953). A condensed survey discussing the land and the people, the recent history, the legacies of Mussolini, the consequences of war, the struggle with social, economic, and political problems since 1945, and, in conclusion, the election of June, 1953.

Norman Kogan, ITALY AND THE ALLIES (Cambridge: Harvard University Press, 1956). Italy since World War II; and the role of United States, British and Soviet policies in the Italian story.

Joseph La Palombara, "A Decade of Political and Economic Change in Italy," WORLD POLITICS, IX, 3 (April, 1957), 422-432; THE ITALIAN LABOR MOVEMENT: PROBLEMS AND PROSPECTS (Ithaca, New York: Cornell University Press, 1958). A substantial and documented story.

Admiral Franco Maugeri, THE ASHES OF DISGRACE (New York: Reynal and Hitchcock, 1958). An account of Fascism by the former Director of Italian Naval Intelligence.

L. Minio-Paluello, EDUCATION IN FASCIST ITALY (New York: Oxford University Press, 1946). After first reviewing the evolution of Italian educational policy from 1859 to the March on Rome, the author describes the processes by which the Fascists sought to "reform" the schools into instruments for party indoctrination.

Leonardo Olschki, THE GENIUS OF ITALY (Ithaca, New York: Cornell University Press, 1954). Italian cultural and intellectual life, as it developed in the context of the social and political situation; a fascinating guide to the spirit and thought of Italy as they have evolved since the Middle Ages.

343

Roy Pryce, THE ITALIAN LOCAL ELECTIONS, 1956 (New York: St. Martin's Press, 1958). This third volume of St. Anthony's Papers applied to an Italian local election, the methods used in the Nuffield studies of British general elections.

Count Carlo Sforza, ITALY AND ITALIANS (New York: E. P. Dutton, 1949). Chapters, originally delivered as lectures at the University of California, on the history and culture of his country, by the Foreign Minister of Italy.

L. C. Webb, CHURCH AND STATE IN ITALY, 1857-1957 (New York: Cambridge University Press, 1959). With excellent bibliographical footnotes.

Gerardo Zampaglione, ITALY (New York: Praeger, 1958). Traces the forces and men which have shaped the past one hundred years of Italian history and discusses Italy's probable future course.

CURRICULUM VITAE

TIBOR KEREKES, Executive Director of the Institute of Ethnic Studies, Georgetown University, received his Ph.D. from University of Budapest (1921), L.H.D. (Honoris Causa) from Georgetown University (1955). After service in World War I he became tutor in the Imperial House of Habsburg; he emigrated to the United States (October, 1922) and joined the faculty of Georgetown University (1927) and became the Head of the Department of History (1941); lectured at Fordham University and at the California, Iowa and Texas branches of the Catholic University of America; also at the University of Vienna and the National War College in Washington, as well as before a great many religious and civic groups throughout the United States. During World War II was a special consultant in Hungarian matters to the Department of State, also Executive Director of the American Hungarian Federation, Co-ordinator of the American Hungarian Relief, and National lay representative of the Hungarian Catholic League; during the Korean War, was a member of the Advisory Committee of Historians to the Secretary of the Navy. In 1953 was appointed by the Congressional Select Committee on Communist Aggression, Director of Special Research, in which capacity was responsible for the publication by the Government Printing Office (during 1954) of fourteen studies on the Communist takeover of the European satellite countries; in 1956 was made consultant to the Internal Security Subcommittee of the Senate Judiciary Committee on Hungarian Refugee problems and was elected Trustee of the American Military Institute (publisher of MILITARY AFFAIRS). Is the author of MODERN EUROPEAN HISTORY, co-author of CONTEMPORARY EUROPE, contributor to AMERICANA ANNUAL (1948, 1949, 1950, 1951), member of the Editorial Board of THE HISTORIAN, official publication of Phi Alpha Theta, National Honor Society in History. Received the honor of the Knighthood in the Order of St. Sylvester from Pope John XXIII (1958).

CHAPTER SIXTEEN

AUSTRIA'S SURVIVAL

HERBERT P. SECHER

Western Reserve University

THE BACKGROUND

Among the peoples that at one time were ruled by the Hapsburgs, only the Germans living in the remnant of the old Austro-Hungarian Empire—the former Crownlands of the monarchy now constituting the Second Republic of Austria—have not been absorbed into the Russian sphere of influence. The failure of both threats and blandishments by Communism to cause in Austria a repetition of events that brought about the downfall of non-Communist governments in other Central and East European countries after the war is due to a number of factors. Of great importance in this respect were undoubtedly the stringent policies pursued by the Soviets themselves in that part of Austria under their control; these policies contrasted sharply with the conciliatory and constructive measures associated with Allied policy in their sector and were, later, enhanced considerably by the positive impact of American financial and material aid. But most significant in creating an inhospitable climate for further Communist penetration was the immediate collaboration in the new government of the Second Republic of two parties that had once been at opposite ideological poles. These are the Socialist Party of Austria *(Sozialistische Partei Oesterreichs, SPoe)* , known as the Social Democrats in the First Republic and in 1945 still considered the party of radical Austro-Marxism and the People's Party of Austria, *(Oesterreichische Volkspartei, OeVP),* successor to the Christian Social Party of pre-1934 days and as such identified mainly with ultra-conservative political Catholicism.

Under the stress of the post World War II occupation period these parties were able to develop a contractual system of joint policy-making under which no major piece of legislation may be introduced, no major administrative decision or appointments made by one coalition partner without the consent of the other. Neither majority nor minority are any longer very meaningful terms as used in this Austrian system. Depending on the proportion of votes cast for either one of the two major parties, the distribution of power within the government is merely readjusted to favor one or the other party. Under the circumstances the party in the minority is not especially desirous of reaching a majority but prefers instead to exploit a momentary electoral advantage by insisting on individual personnel changes within the power complex of the state in order to increase the party's patronage. In other words, the "arithmetical accident" of an election result has to a large extent been replaced by a weighted index of votes which are used to fix quantitatively the position of either party within a controlled framework of political collaboration.[1] Since electoral landslides have been unknown in either the First or Second Republic of Austria the system thus evolved has worked fruitfully to keep either party from ensconcing itself securely in the seat of government power while forcing the other one into the frustrating wilderness of "permanent opposition."

In this manner the coalition government has dealt successfully with most issues that in the countries to the East were considered major obstacles in the path of stable, democratic governments prior to and since World War II. Dominant among the problems that faced the Austrian as well as other East-Central European governments after the war was the task of achieving an advanced stage of industrialization in the presence of pressures exercised largely by two major groups. One was the large contingent of well-organized, tradition-bound small landholders and shopkeepers; the other was the equally militant and aggressive force of a dissatisfied urban, industrial proletariat. Ideologically these groups were oriented, respectively, toward corporatist doctrines mixed with Catholic Social reformism and toward the original adaptations of Marxist doctrine — known as Austro-Marxism—introduced by early twentieth-century Social Democratic theoreticians. Both ideologies represented the polarization of major political forces in Austria during the late nineteenth and early twentieth centuries, with the Roman Catholic Church, the monarchy and its affiliated groups as one center and the Social Democracy of workers, lower-middle-classes and Jewish intellectual circles as the other. However, a minor group has oscillated between these two centers of power from the days of the monarchy up to the present time. This is a small group of mainly Protestant intellectuals, businessmen and professional militarists who, ever since the middle of the nineteenth century have championed a "folkish" nationalism with the object of establishing an indissoluble tie with the greater German neighbor.

It is possible therefore to identify three major political movements in Austria that have perpetuated themselves through over half a century and which have survived, in effect, three major changes in regime. Political Catholicism, Democratic Socialism and German Nationalism represented, respectively, in the First Republic by the Christian Socials, the Social Democrats and the Pan-Germans, and during the Second Republic by the Austrian People's Party, the Socialist Party and the so-called "Independents." A successful reconciliation of the demands issuing from these groups—peasants, industrial workers, organized Catholic laity and former National Socialists—has been, in fact, the major objective to which the Austrian coalition policies have addressed themselves since the inception of the Second Republic in April, 1945.

In order to gain the proper perspective on the political viability of the Second Austrian Republic it is proposed to examine here the current ideological orientation of the political parties and relate it to the changes that have occurred in the economic life and social structure of the country. It should be recalled that the revival of the Austrian state in 1945 was greeted with considerable skepticism. Since the existence of an "Austrian" nationality was itself subject to debate it followed that the re-establishment of governmental authority would depend heavily on the ability of the several political movements to compromise those doctrines which had spelled the downfall of the First Republic. The search for a common ideological denominator and its acceptance by all forces of the political community is thus an essential requirement for the survival of the Austrian state.

1. POLITICAL CATHOLICISM AND THE NEW CONSERVATISM: THE AUSTRIAN PEOPLE'S PARTY

The senior partner of the coalition government introduced a new concept in Austrian politics when it was first organized in 1945. Unlike their predecessors in the First Republic, the Christian Socials, the

People's Party conservatives spurned too close an identification with the Church and aimed at a much more diversified social and economic electoral base.

To achieve this goal the party adopted a double structure; it was divided vertically into territorial districts and horizontally along the lines of the dominant economic interests of the country—Business, Agriculture and Labor. These interests were organized in the form of Leagues—a Business League (*Wirtschaftsbund*), a Farmers League (*Bauernbund*) and a Workers and Employees League (*Arbeiter und Angestelltenbund*) —each of which exercised control over its own separate local organization, usually running parallel to the territorial divisions of the national party.[2] The vertical, i.e., territorial organization was to serve as an integrating structure in order to overcome the latent separatist tendencies of the leagues; though it is possible to join the OeVP directly via any of its territorial units, the number of members acquired in this way is hardly significant, the party having constantly refused to give a separate accounting of the size of this membership. Currently the over-all membership is given at approximately 600,000. There are also several auxiliary organizations such as the League of Austrian University Students, the Austrian Women's Movement, the Austrian Youth Movement, the Social Aid Society, the Children Aid Society, the League of Political Persecutees and many other smaller organizations. The structure thus is intended to reflect the major voting contingents of the party, namely the peasants, the self-employed in business and industry, the traditionally conservative groups of secondary schoolteachers and bureaucrats, and the strongly anti-Marxist groups of Catholic workers, mostly skilled.

The dominance of the League over the national party organization is reflected in the fact that direct membership dues play only an insignificant role in the financing of the party's activities. The party organizational statute recognizes the financial autonomy of the Leagues and makes the national organization dependent on contributions from them. Only a small share of these contributions goes to the National Executive Committee of the OeVP, by far the largest part going to the local and provincial units of the party which then channel it upward to the executive. This leaves the national executive with little control over local organization and activities and makes the local units more responsive to pressure and influence by the Leagues. Of course, as do conservative parties everywhere, the OeVP must expect to have the greater part of its expenses defrayed through sizable contributions raised by subscriptions from its more affluent members. That would also explain why the OeVP is much more sensitive to charges of receiving bribes than is its Socialist partner.

Of the three leagues, that of the Farmers commands the strongest political backing. Prior to 1945 the *Bauernbund* was organized along federal lines with the farmers of Lower Austria furnishing the largest contingent as well as the leadership of both Bund and party. After 1945 the *Bauernbund* was reorganized into a highly centralized system under which the previously federated units were now absorbed by the Lower Austrian organization. The Business League follows next in importance, depending for its support primarily on the ranks of small business, artisans, tradesmen and the crafts. It is however, also closely identified with industry, and the large commercial and banking interests. The Workers and Employees League runs far behind the other two leagues in either size or importance, representing primarily the militantly Catholic elements among labor and the civil service.

Both business and Catholic labor circles are not unaware of the massive political strength of the Farmers League, and the revamping of the old Christian Social party along centralized, territorial lines must be interpreted as an attempt to assure *both* business and labor permanently of the disciplined voting bloc of the Agrarians. The value of this integration became apparent when Ing. Raab replaced Dr. Figl as prime minister. As the former head of the Farmers League Dr. Figl had favored the protectionist-minded policies of the Agrarians; Ing. Raab, as the President of the Business League, favored a liberalization of the hitherto stringently regulated economy. When he introduced his new policies the Farmers League yielded only reluctantly to the entreaties of the OeVP leaders to support the new program. They let it be known that such support would be had only if the OeVP could be counted upon to initiate legislation in the near future that would assure the privileged position of agriculture.

Though the OeVP readily enough agreed to such a promise its realization was and still is a matter of profound political difficulty since it would involve some basic realignments of the coalition partnership. Consequently the relation between the Agrarians, and their almost solid voting bloc of 20 per cent of the population, and the other Leagues has remained strained. The strain reached occasionally such proportions that veiled threats emanated from the Agrarians, warning of their possible joining of forces with the Socialists—the feared "red-green" coalition. Such a move is premised on the supposition that in the kind of regulated economy envisaged by the Socialists a bargain could be entered into that would preserve at least some of agriculture's privileges. Though this is still a very remote possibility it underlines the desire of part of the OeVP to escape the confines of the "unified party command" when it feels itself put at a disadvantage by any of the coalition policies. And under the compromises necessary to keep the coalition going the current business leadership of the OeVP is only apt to reach agreements at the expense of either the Farmers League, the Workers and Employees League or both.

Of the three leagues only the AAB is really concerned with ideological purity. Basic to the AAB's ideological position is a strongly Church-oriented program and, in consequence, its insistence that the party take a stronger stand regarding education and marriage. The AAB feels constrained to remind the party on occasion that it also represents the interests of the economically less favored groups of the population, and that, indeed, the founding of the AAB as a separate group within the OeVP was a serious bid by the new party for workers' votes. Though this in accord with the party's general principles, the OVP does not want to have the AAB's militant Catholicism identified as the sole voice of the party. The dogmatic social reformism of the AAB recommended itself much less to the sophisticated OeVP's business leaders than did the "unprincipled" diluted Marxism and even anti-clericalism of the Socialists. Most of the current leaders of the AAB are products of the militant Catholic youth movement of the First Republic, and in contrast to any of the other Leagues the AAB does not permit among its members any national-liberal, Protestant or anti-clerical elements. In consequence the original plan of giving the AAB a permanent voice in the party councils by appointing an AAB man as minister without portfolio was shelved after a short period of experimentation following the 1949 election. Ever since then the AAB has been the neglected part of the OeVP and occasionally its *enfant terrible*. The working-class character of its following permits it to take a much more radical line on social welfare legislation where it finds itself occasionally close to the Socialist position. As a matter of fact in certain strongly Catholic provincial areas, industrial pockets where the SPOe has hardly any following at all, the AAB presents a separate slate of candidates at election time in competition with the regular

OeVP. In 1955 the OeVP made some concessions to AAB pressures by appointing an AAB man to the Office of Education Advisor and putting another one in charge of some industrial enterprises that had not been fully nationalized and are under the trusteeship of the Finance ministry. But neither position is one of great moment in the sphere of major policy decisions.

Despite its somewhat "crowded" position within the OeVP the AAB is most appreciative of the backing that a large party organization affords. In the face of the mammoth organization of the Socialists, the AAB would have little opportunity to make its influence felt independently. The AAB is already laboring under great recruitment difficulties, since its ideological dogmatism tends to discourage younger men who recognize that membership in the AAB is hardly conducive to advancement in either OeVP or the government. Its new members therefore derive primarily from those with strong Catholic ideals, usually former members of the Catholic youth movement. But even the Catholic youth movement is not entirely without reservation concerning the AAB as long as the over-all position of the OeVP toward the church remains ill defined.

Thus the idea of corporatism—or estatism—can be seen to linger even in the present organizational setup of the conservative mass party. It is significant in this respect to recall that at the time of the OeVP's founding all three chairmen of the then autonomous leagues—Ing. Raab for the Austrian Business League, Dr. Figl for the Farmers League and Herr Kunschak the venerated leader of the Catholic Workers and Employees—issued statements to the effect that they were "ready to *join* the OeVP." What was formed then, despite the ostensible adherence to the mass party concept was really a coalition of powerful economic interest groups whose solidarity was based primarily on their religious tie (Roman Catholicism) and on their political anti-Marxism. This became especially apparent in the initial choice of party doctrine which was intended to provide a meaningful and all-embracing ideology for the divergent social and economic interests. The Christian reform doctrine of "Solidarism" exhorted the harmonious co-operation of all classes within a somewhat modified corporative system and condemned "atomistic competition" for bringing about an intensified class struggle. Solidarism approved governmental intervention and the regulation of the economy, accepted governmental responsibility for social welfare and scorned unbridled laissez

351

faire for having brought about periodic economic crises. The rights of private property were to be recognized by the corporations who acted as the representative organs of the social interest groups. The corporations were also charged with jurisdiction over the industrial sector of the economy.[3]

Despite this strong corporatist flavor the recognition of the social welfare state presented a substantial concession to the Socialist forces. That corporatism was still considered a working concept in the years from 1945 to 1952 was due to the leadership of the Agrarians within the OeVP. As the strongest and most conservative of the three groups it was not surprising that they tried to fashion the party in their own image. It was under agrarian leadership for example that the so-called wage-price pacts came into being, setting maximum agricultural and food prices with only very inadequate compensatory increases in wages enabling the workers to barely maintain the same standard of living. The agreements were a kind of holding action, considered necessary evils at best, that reflected the inability of Agriculture and the consequent unwillingness of Business and Labor seriously to increase production.[4] It was only after Marshall Aid had released new productive energies and after the decisive defeat suffered by the Agrarian-nominated OeVP candidate for the presidency in 1951 that the Farmers League had to hand over controls to the Business League and the whole OeVP program underwent a corresponding modernization. Under Ing. Raab of the Business League the wage-price pacts were discontinued since he rightfully recognized that their unpopularity was based on the open protection they granted to agrarian interests at the expense of business and labor. Internally, the damage wrought by the cavalier leadership of the agrarians to the relations between Leagues and party was to be repaired by a new policy concept, the "Primacy of the party over the Leagues" and which adopted an intensified unified command structure to counteract the separatist tendencies of the Leagues.[5] A new set of principles was issued in January, 1952, which still constitutes the basic political platform of the OeVP.[6] The new program — popularized as the Raab-Kamitz course, in honor of the Premier and his Finance Minister — provided for new measures designed to bring about, on the one hand, a reduction in governmental controls over the economy and on the other, strong governmental intervention in the areas of social welfare. In essence the program leaned heavily on the "Social Market" economy of the West German

CDU though it did not come out as forcefully against all planning as did that program. It constituted the acceptance by a Catholic party of the principle of the modern welfare state, and impressed with its lack of ideological exegesis. The program omitted mention of the party's Church ties, and did not single out any of the leagues for a favored role within the party. Though the program preferred co-operative housing schemes over public housing projects it promised substantial government aid to the former; and it accepted without argument all schemes for improvements in the workers' standard of living. There were no demands for denationalization and the reference to "corporatism" even in the guise of solidarism was omitted.

Sociologically then, the OeVP, similar to conservative parties else-where, presents a more comprehensive structure than its coalition partner. But a *sine qua non* of its political effectiveness is continuous agreement on major policy issues among the three leagues — no issue must reach the point where it might conceivably lead to the splitting off of one of the leagues. Yet today it is generally recognized that only the adherence to the common faith acts as a bulwark against truly autonomous tendencies, a bulwark that becomes weaker as the agnos-ticism of the Socialists loses in political significance. It is for this reason that the OeVP watches with apprehension all attempts of the coalition partner to establish a more viable relationship with the Church. Con-cerning its own relations to the Church, the OeVP is torn between the pressures of the dominantly devout Catholic character of the party's stable following and the knowledge, that its absolute majority can be maintained only by inviting the support of either religiously indifferent Socialists or of the Protestant "national-liberals." In 1949 the OeVP had issued a statement declaring that the party wanted "to provide a political and spiritual haven for all *liberals, nationalists* and *cleri-cals.*" What had motivated this statement was the reappearance by 1949 of another conservative, middle-class party with a predominately Protestant or anti-clerical orientation which threatened to undermine the absolute popular majority won by the People's Party in the 1945 election. The Church reaction to this declaration was one of general disapproval. The OeVP was given a sharp reminder that such a variegated composition would deprive the party of its right to consider itself the representative of the true Catholic sector of Austrian society. It was intimated that the political development since 1945 had been a great disappointment to Church authorities insofar as the OeVP had failed to correct the absolute separation of Church and State that had been inherited from the Hitler regime. The Church expressed willingness to achieve a new synthesis in its relationship to the second Republic but it put the OeVP on notice that it expected more than tacit support from the conservative Catholic party.[7]

So far, despite continued insistence by the episcopate, the OeVP — and in effect the coalition government — has been able to maintain its show of reserve toward the solutions of outstanding church-state problems. The OeVP is aided in this unquestionably difficult maneuver by the appointment of Bishop Koenig to the Archdiocese left vacant by the death of Cardinal Innitzer in 1955. The selection of Bishop Koenig — elevated to the cardinalcy in 1958 — a man of well-known moderate views, indicated that at least for the time being Vatican policy was going along with those circles in the Austrian church that wanted to free the Church from its anti-labor stigma. As a result it also discouraged any further moves designed to reduce the People's Party to a mere appendage to Church power. Koenig had been known even in prewar Austria for his determined opposition to the unholy alliance of the clergy with Dollfuss' Fascist regime. In the Second Republic, Koenig was equally opposed to any tieup of Church and party, which he repeatedly denounced as detrimental to the long term interests of the Church. It is known that he is very much aware of the fact that, given the current constellation of political forces in Austria, any settlement, of, for example, the still pending Concordat question (i.e., the recognition by the Second Republic of the Concordat entered into with the Vatican by the Dollfus government in 1934) can only be achieved via the co-operation of the Socialist Party. The conciliatory policy of the Church under the influence of Cardinal Koenig has made it possible for the OeVP to avoid any open conflict over the issues of marriage and education within its ranks. At a party conference in 1955 concerned with shaping future policies "cultural" problems were not even put on the agenda; and at the last parliamentary election of 1956 the party conveniently overlooked an earlier promise to put a Church sympathizer on the list of candidates. On the other hand the OeVP in co-operation with the SPOe has been able to make some progress toward the settlement of the sensitive Concordat question. Although the Vatican has neither accepted nor rejected the proposals brought forward by the Austrian government in an exchange of notes during the past year, the fact remains that both parties have been able to agree on a vital aspect of the problem, namely the non-enforcement but not the unilateral abrogation of the 1934 Concordat pending further adjustments of its provisions.[8] Politically this amounts to a victory by the liberal forces within the Oevp, and by the Socialists. Both groups have surmised correctly that the pattern of Church-State relations in Austria is determined primarily by the existence of a largely homogeneous Catholic population and that militant anti-clericalism or its opposite, the identification of Socialism with "atheistic bolshevism," have ceased to be very useful slogans for political exploitation. Both major parties recognize that they must depend for support on an electorate consisting in its great majority of professing Catholics. And the Church too, having become much more conscious of the Catholicism of *all* voters, is not anxious to repeat the folly of the First Republic and commit itself exclusively to the support of just one political party.[9] This situation tips the balance somewhat in favor of the Socialists, who are anxious to gain the "respectability" they so urgently need to penetrate doubtful areas of the Catholic middle-class and peasant vote. Probably no moves can be expected within the near future that will bring about radical changes in the policy of either side. Both the Vatican and the Austrian coalition of Socialists and Conservatives have stated their position and so far there are no pressures that would call for an immediate settlement of outstanding Church-State issues. But given the continuation of the coalition, the areas of compromise mapped out so far are not likely to be abandoned and can even be expected to undergo a very gradual expansion.

II. AUSTRO-MARXISM REPENTANT: THE SOCIALIST PARTY OF AUSTRIA

In the post-World War I era, the Austrian Social Democracy had often been regarded as the theoretical as well as political link between Western Socialism and Soviet Communism. At that time, having foresworn all participation in the national government by retiring into "permanent opposition," the party, through the capture of the city government of Vienna, could there engage in the most extensive and beneficial practices of peaceful economic and social changes as well as cultural uplift, while pursuing nationally an orthodox Marxist-revolutionary line. Through the application of sound financial policies, it created a standard of living for the workers of Vienna almost unequaled anywhere else in Europe. The consolidation of these social achievements provided a fertile field of activity for the moderates among the leadership, while to the radicals fell the mapping out of a national ideological line which, generally, regarded the dictatorship of the proletariat as the ultimate goal of the party.

The theory and organization of pre-1934 Austro-Marxism had patterned itself in many respects on the "closed" nature of the old monarchical system of the Empire. Then the dynasty had occupied a "neutral" center around which were grouped, according to their importance, the social and economic classes. Similarly, the Social Democracy became the focal point for divergent interests of the lower middle classes, the small artisans and the industrial proletariat. Its internal politics were for the most part an attempt to achieve compromise solutions on economic issues between these forces.[10]

In order to carry this out, the party needed a determined leadership structure with great emphasis on the personality of these leaders. That the organization of the party was highly centralized and its ideology only very little short of totalitarian was further conditioned by the fact that it knew itself to be on probation: Vienna was the first city anywhere in Europe, outside of Russia, that came under Socialist control. Viennese Marxism (rather than Austro-Marxism) of the twenties became a political instrument as well as a social ideal. It represented itself as a science, transmitted a new culture and consequently a new educational model. It stressed the release of new energies by its emphasis on physical training which gave the working-class youth especially a sense of importance that had been denied to it in the rigidly stratified monarchy. But in its dedication to social uplift, the party also undermined its own revolutionary socialism.[11]

The contradictory and haphazard measures of a divided party leadership during the short but bitter fighting in 1934 led not only to the defeat of the party but also to the defeat of the Austrian labor movement. Part of the radical element found their way to the Communist Party, while the others, after a highly confused and desultory period of illegality, gave up finally in resignation. The former moderate Vienna leadership deliberately kept its distance from the attempts to organize an underground party and, without the sanction of their prestige and respectability, the efforts of the remaining young men met with failure. For practical purposes, the Austrian Social Democracy ceased to exist after 1934.[12] After the *Anschluss,* Hitler shrewdly exploited the grievances of the Austrian workers against the former government as well as against the old leadership of the Austrian Social Democracy — many of them Jewish — thereby eliminating almost all serious opposition to his regime.

The complete hiatus that existed in the Hitler period predicated an utterly new reconstitution of "Social Democracy" in 1945. The leading personnel of the party was composed of men who had remained largely untainted by contact with the former discredited radicals. To be sure, the link with Austro-Marxism was acknowledged, but more from a sense of historical courtesy than from a real desire to continue in this ideological direction.

Socioeconomically, the SPOe ceased to be the party of the urban industrial proletariat or even of the so-called proletarianized middle class. Its voter distribution soon showed that the party was successfully penetrating other strata of society. The party presented its new political face by declaring from the start its intention of becoming a "people's (mass) party" in which everyone would feel at home and it toned down its class conflict ideology accordingly. In part this was made possible by the respectability which the party gained through its participation in the government. But it can also be considered as the result of certain fundamental changes that had occurred in the nature of the Austrian worker. The Austrian worker, on the basis of a recent survey, is fast losing that closed socioeconomic unity as a group that had marked him during the First Republic.[13] At a much slower pace, but not a little due to the reformist component of the old SPD, the Austrian worker has turned from oppressed revolutionary to self-assured member of society.

The reactivation of the economy brought the newly prospering labor elements as well as the prospering middle classes within the party influence, and for these groups the party became primarily the guardian of the higher standard of living and the defender of the welfare state. To the niceties of the Marxist theology these groups were largely indifferent. Those who actually joined the party considered membership primarily in terms of its usefulness to their careers. In this connection the most important aspect of the party's attractiveness to new members is its controlling position in certain vital sectors of the economy. Among the leadership of the SPOe, it is an open secret that only its continued role as partner in the coalition acts as guarantor of a large part of its following, a fact that may be partly responsible for the party's reluctance to go into opposition during

357

the last two years when such an act would have contributed greatly to the shaping of a more consistent party policy.

The unexpected defeat of the party at the election of 1956 on the issue of more stringent nationalization measures provided the impetus for a rejuvenation of the top leadership and for plans to subject the party program to a thorough reappraisal. The impending presidential election was to prove opportune for the injection of younger blood into the top echelons of the party. If Dr. Schaerf the vice-chancellor and chairman of the SPOe could be made to run successfully for the presidency the way would be opened for an organizational and ideological face-lifting. Though Schaerf was a man of decidedly moderate political views his anti-clericalism and known enmity to political Catholicism made him unsuitable to lead an ideological reorientation toward better Church relations. Already, following the May, 1956 defeat, the authority to make party policy was transferred from the cabinet level, where Schaerf as vice-chancellor and party chairman exercised dominance, to the parliamentary level of the SPOe club under leadership of Dr. Pitterman. This transfer was made official at the party congress in November, 1956 with the formation by the Central Committee of a Subcommittee of Ten charged with the "preparation and execution of decisions made by the Party Executive and the Party Control Council." The members of the committee were the younger men in the party bureaucracy.[14]

As planned, Schaerf's victory at the Presidential election in May, 1957 made it possible for Dr. Pitterman to succeed to the party chairmanship and the office of vice-chancellor. He did not, however, fall heir to the great authority exercised by Dr. Schaerf before him and the Committee of Ten continued to act as advisory and control organ. One of the first decisions of this new leadership was to conduct a survey among young men in responsible party positions to ascertain their views on questions of ideology as well as on organization. Virtually all of them expressed their dissatisfaction with either the remnants of Marxist ideology or with the oligarchical character of the party leadership, or both. Using this survey as a guide, a committee was constituted and charged with the task of drafting a preliminary program for submission to the 1957 November party congress. This preliminary party program came close to removing even the last vestiges of Marxist ideology.[15] It is probable that this was done deliberately so that in succeeding discussions and debates the program planners could simulate a strategic retreat on certain less important theoretical points. In its over-all effect the draft program differed little from the program finally adopted in May, 1958.[16] Although some stylistic changes were made to satisfy the old die-hards, there is no question that the new program proceeds in the direction outlined at the 1956 Party Congress by Pitterman's declaration that, "the SPOe is a political action group and not an ideological community."

The program represents the culmination of an ideological transformation already apparent in two important areas of practical governmental policy: the financing of the reconstruction of the Austrian economy and the establishment of sound Church-State relations.

Even before revising its ideological program, the SPOe, upon entering the coalition government, accepted the principle of private savings by agreeing to OeVP-sponsored measures to stimulate such savings. Thus the Socialists recognized, by implication, the social function of private capital. They thereby abandoned the advocacy of an inflationary policy which would have undermined the slowly but steadily rising standard of living enjoyed by the Austrian worker. They also proscribed a program of deficit spending by voting for a balanced budget and accepted the principle of investment financing as largely a function of private savings by acquiescing eventually to the issuance of so-called "People's Shares" in the nationalized banks.

Originally the Socialists favored the adoption of both income and inheritance taxes at confiscatory rates, or, failing that, at least of some very selective "luxury" taxes, of the kind that had once earned the Viennese Socialists of the First Republic the epithet "Tax Bolsheviks." Though they continued to press for reforms of the income tax progressions, the law which was eventually adopted provided for an across-the-board percentage increase, in flat contradiction to the announced Socialist program. In 1954, the SPOe agreed to a 10 per cent cut in income taxes starting with an across-the-board reduction and later moving into a sliding scale. Three more tax reductions were enacted with SPOe approval between 1954 and 1958. Since 1955, the revenues derived from indirect taxes have in fact risen more than those from income taxes.[17]

This departure by the Socialists from their original concept of the "cold" social revolution reflects, on the one hand, the general economic stability of the country and, on the other, the changing income pattern within the SPOe membership itself and on the part of the party's voter contingent. The greater part of the SPOe supporters and the majority of its bureaucratic apparatus, including trade union officials, have experienced such substantial increases in their incomes that they have actually moved into the tax brackets once occupied by middle-class groups. Consequently, negotiations over tax policies have long since lost their ideological flavor and have become instead attempts to determine the upper limit at which the term "middle income" can be applied.

The position of the SPOe on the delicate problems affecting Church-State relations have been influenced by equally practical consideration. Thus the new party program recognizes explicitly the mutual dependence of Socialism and Christianity and rules out categorically the possibility of conflicting interests between them.

This significant action by the SPOe is in fact the culmination of a series of rapprochements initiated by the Austrian Catholic Church itself and beginning with its decision, early in the life of the Second Republic, to prohibit the clergy from becoming in any way politically involved.[18] Once that decision had been made, mutual distrust began to wane, helped along considerably by the fact that the SPOe's participation in the government made outright hostility to the Church quite difficult. To gain the "respectability" needed to penetrate the doubtful areas of Catholic middle-class and peasant voters, the Socialists recognized realistically that they must arrive at a permanent *modus vivendi* with the Church. This was forcefully advocated by Dr. Pitterman upon his elevation to the chairmanship of the party and assumption of the post of vice-chancellor. He let it be known that the SPOe was no longer fundamentally opposed to signing a Concordat with the Vatican — provided only that it was not that of 1934.

Since then both parties were able to work out an acceptable formula on the basis of which the Austrian government could approach the Vatican for a reopening of the negotiations in the 1934 Concordat.[19] The Socialists could thus claim for themselves an open-mindedness and willingness to compromise on an issue which had once been regarded as the greatest potential danger to the coalition government and even to the stability of the republic. Publicly, at least, the burden of shifting from a too rigid position now lies with the Vatican and/or the ultramontane wing of the People's Party. This is a political victory that should not be minimized; moreover the Socialist policy of either a new version of the Concordat, or, at least, a very broad interpretation of existing clauses amounting to virtual renegotiations, appears to be much more in accord with the trend of popular feelings on religious issues generally.

The adoption of the 1958 program by the SPOe merely underwrites a long since completed departure from radical Marxist ideology whose perpetuation, according to some critics, had only served to prevent the Socialists from reaping the full benefits of their continued participation in government since 1945. The new program is not the result of intense competition between rival factions but represents, rather, a general and official acknowledgment of the party's transformation from Marxist radicalism to conciliatory laborism. Austrian Socialists no longer insist on an over-all planned economy, are vague on a rigid separation of Church and State and display considerable reserve in their statements on agrarian reform. The program thus confirms what has long been party policy, namely its willingness, induced by its partnership in the government since 1945, to adjust its policies to those of the peasant, middle-class bloc represented by the Austrian People's Party. Yet the very fact that the SPOe has been able to maintain a firm hold on its share of the Austrian government has contributed to the development of a much more sustained form of political power and a much wider dissemination of the party's influence. It is to be hoped that this latest official modification in the views of a once doctrinaire party will continue to have a positive impact on Austrian governmental affairs, whose stability has been one of the outstanding political phenomena of post-World War II Europe.

III. AUSTRO-MARXISM UNREPENTANT:
THE COMMUNIST PARTY OF AUSTRIA

From the beginning of the Second Republic the Communist Party of Austria (*Kommunistische Partei Oesterreichs, KPOe*), was conspicuous among Western European Communist parties because of its poor showing in early postwar elections. This was due partially to the distinctive tradition of Austro-Marxism which had pre-empted doctrinaire radicalism, as well as to the immediate contact with Russian troops on the part of the Austrians. Nevertheless the small size of the Communist vote — it fluctuated around 5 per cent — was not a satisfactory index of Communist strength in Austria. At a time when neither of the two large parties had reached even its pre-1934 size, the KPOe had actually reached enormous proportions when compared with its pre-1934 following. The concentration of the party in one small area of the country assured the party of at least one basic mandate in the National Assembly and since 1945 the Communists have always had at least three parliamentary representatives compared to none in the First Republic. Furthermore, the party's concentration in the country's vital industrial center where it can call crippling strikes provides the Communists with a political significance that is far out of proportion to their electoral showing. Until today Communist voting strength has coincided nearly always with this area: the KPOe basic mandate continues to be located in the industrial city of Wiener Neustadt in Lower Austria.

In 1945 the party announced its membership at 174,257 — a figure that was only slightly less than the actual support at the polls. In 1947 the party published for the last time a separate membership figure; it was given at 155,000.[20] Since then the party has maintained that its membership is identical with its voting support. From 1949 to 1953 the voting strength of the party rose from 213,066 to 228,159, an increase that can be accounted for primarily by the expansion of the then Russian controlled USIA industries where employment was dependent to a large extent on KPOe membership. Before the Russian withdrawal from these plants they contained a well-organized network of Communist Party cells which dominated the workers' representative institutions, the so-called work councils. In 1955 the Communists still elected 45 per cent of the shop stewards in 335 plants located in Lower Austria. In the iron and steel industry 28 per cent of the shop stewards ran under Communist sponsorship. On the basis of this distribution the party was able to exercise pressure on trade union policy quite out of proportion to its popular strength and it repeatedly called strikes without prior approval by the Austrian Trade Union Federation.[21] Until 1951 the KPOe disposed over an effective para-military organization, the *Werkschutz,* whose nominal job it was to watch over the Russian holdings (USIA). These guards were heavily armed, uniformed and subjected to regular drills and maneuvers; its size was unofficially estimated at 12,000.[22]

The party soon realized that unless it took advantage of the presence of the Russians its chances of gaining power by legitimate means were slim. It was for this reason that the KPOe decided in October, 1950 to exploit the popular dissatisfaction with coalition economic policies and issue a call for a general strike. Though the strike call failed the ensuing four-day riots were quelled by the police — under orders of the Socialist Minister of the Interior — and only due to the unexpected passivity of Russian occupation forces. Nevertheless, KPOe could take satisfaction in the knowledge that its organization was at least eminently capable of disabling major parts of the country's economy *until* outside intervention was assured.[23] However, as it turned out, the 1950 *Putsch* attempt was the last show of extra-parliamentary force engaged in by the KPOe. The steadily improving domestic economic situation no longer supplied the Communists with the pretexts needed to arouse the population and the unpredictable course of the Korean War discouraged any similar ventures in Europe under Russian auspices for the time being.

The era of international good feeling fostered by the Russians in the wake of Stalin's death further reduced the threat of the KPOe as an instrument of indirect Russian aggression. The focusing of Russian attention on Austria as an example of Russian diplomatic good will hinted strongly at the expendability of Austrian Communists, and the news of the impending state treaty caused an inordinate amount of confusion and conflict in Austrian Communist circles. Since the KPOe had never been more than the most pliable of all non-Russian Communist parties — not excepting the East German Communist Party — it was struck completely silent by the Twentieth Soviet Party Congress announcements. Having previously been left to sink or swim as they pleased by the withdrawing Red Army after the ratification of the Austrian state treaty in October, 1955, the leadership soon recognized that absolutely nothing could save them except a convincing domonstration of their being at least the *Austrian* branch of the Communist International and not some errand boys left behind by the Russians. Fortunately the state treaty stipulated strict observance of a non-discriminatory clause promising immunity to all employees of an occupation power, thereby enabling the KPOe to save its cells and functionaries into the post-treaty area.

With alacrity, therefore, the KPOe went about mending its fences with the Socialist neighbor. On the same day that the final signatures were being affixed to the treaty document a statement was issued by the KPOe executive endorsing objections by pacifist groups in the SPOe to the re-establishment of an Austrian army. Later the KPOe also declared its solidarity with Socialist demands for nationalization of the oil and industrial complexes which the treaty had delivered into Austrian hands. However this kind of shirt-tail politics did not have the desired effect in the 1956 election, the first one following the signing of the treaty. The KPOe lost one seat, reducing its parliamentary representation to three. Nevertheless, local results indicated that the KPOe disposed over enough local organization which, by attracting the dissidents and disgruntled among the SPOe, could still endanger the Socialist majority.

That Communist organization remained so surprisingly intact even after the Russian withdrawal was due largely to a rather far-sighted reorganization scheme that had gone into effect following the *Putsch* attempt of 1950. Recognizing that the party might have to face another long pull before such an opportunity again presented itself, the organizational emphasis was shifted from militancy and immediate striking power to long-term political effectiveness and dependability. The *Werkschutz* was dissolved and in its place the party established new centers for the training of politically adept functionaries. New organs of supervision and control saw to it that the unreliable elements were dropped. A rotating training schedule provided every functionary with regular periods of intensive political schooling. The training schools were arranged hierarchically and a functionary was either promoted to the next higher one or expelled from the party. Organizational soft spots were thus detected in time to take preventive action and, as events proved, the loss of face after 1955 was not accompanied by any appreciable weakening of the organization.[24] Not until after the Hungarian catastrophe did the Austrian KPOe find it necessary to engage in some personnel changes in its top leadership, and in a corresponding shift in the party line.

At the January, 1957 meeting of the Central Committee two documents were issued for party discussion prior to the general session of the party Congress in April of that year. One was a "guiding concept" for Austria's way to Socialism and the other one listed specific "points for discussion" to be submitted later as resolutions to the Seventeenth Congress of the KPOe.[25] Both documents showed recognition of the changed world situation after the Hungarian episode and indicated the necessity for the adoption of different methods now that the chance of Austria's entering the camp of the People's Democracies was no longer a realistic policy premise. The party admitted that the conditions in Austria were so utterly different from those prevailing in the other East European countries that entirely new methods must be tried to achieve the ultimate revolutionary goal. The "guiding concepts" mapped out an alliance with the middle classes rather than with the peasants and workers. They avoided any mention of violent revolutionary means but instead recommended a "painless" transfer to Socialism, permitting the continuance of other parties, provided they were led by progressive elements. The nationalization of trades and small businesses was openly disavowed since, in the words of the program, "they will continue to be of great importance in a socialized Austria." There is no mention of the socialization of agriculture but instead a strongly worded guarantee for the protection of religious worship. The points for discussion by the Congress, after some perfunctory bows to Moscow, went on to stress the equality of status of all Communist parties and rejected any claims to infallibility by the Russian Communist Party. The document also urged the revision of all Communist international organizations as no longer serving their original purpose. Finally, the party admitted that previous mistakes had made it easy for opponents to stigmatize the KPOe as a "Russian" party. However, the document did not go as far as an earlier resolution by the Central Committee which openly blamed the behavior of Russian troops for the estrangement of the party from the masses.

The result of the discussions engendered by these two policy documents was, as could be expected, the adoption by the party Congress of a new policy that was designed to find points of contact with the SPOe, and bring about the establishment eventually, of a popular front. Organizationally the Congress approved the establishment of "contact committees" of the type that had existed in the immediate postwar period. In order to effectuate this new policy several members of the old guard were relieved of specific administrative functions though they retained their positions in the Central Committee. If there was any inner conflict in the party hierarchy it manifested itself in the lack of a unanimous vote by which some old leaders were re-elected and others dropped from the party councils.

The most important new appointment was that of Erwin Scharf to the editorship of the party newspaper, VOLKSSTIMME. A former Democrat and Member of the SPOe's Central Committee, Scharf in 1947 had published a pamphlet in which he stigmatized the SPOe as a traitor to its original program because of the continued adherence to the policies of the coalition.[26]. He documented this "working-class treason" by publishing secret proceedings of the SPOe executive committee, urging the Socialist Party leadership to turn back from its path of co-operation with the OeVP and instead make common cause with the KPOe. The result of this public exhortation was Scharf's trial before a party honor court which summarily but not unanimously expelled him from the SPOe. Scharf remained in parliament as the representative of the *"linksbloc"* which of course was joined to the KPOe. Eventually, in 1950, Scharf succeeded in founding his own party, the *Sozialistische Arbeiter Partei,* (SAP), undoubtedly with considerable financial aid from the Communists. Scharf's "independent" political existence was of considerable value to the KPOe, which regarded him as a kind of clearing house for information on the inner workings of the SPOe leadership where supposedly loyal Scharf followers were presumably still keeping him abreast of the trend of Socialist opinions and policies. Scharf never attracted more than a handful of followers to his party and after its insignificant showing at the 1956 election — but more likely as a result of the drying up of Soviet funds after the signing of the state treaty — the SAP was officially dissolved and Scharf formally joined the KPOe. It became known that out of the approximate 2,500 members of his party not quite one hundred followed his example. Scharf himself, after joining the KPOe, was elected immediately to the Central Committee and soon after to the Politbureau.

Scharf's appointment to the VOLKSSTIMME editorship merely brought out into the open a change of policy that was begun even while the Stalinist leadership was still in complete control of the party. It would be erroneous to interpret his appointment, therefore, as a defeat of the Old Guard or possibly as a victory of "revisionism." Neither Titoism nor anti-Stalinism ever played an important role in the goals and policies of the Austrian Communists. "Revisionism," if such it can be called for want of any better term, simply connotes closer co-operation with the SPOe and a temporary moving into the background of the Old Guard. No far-reaching changes in personnel were made that would indicate that the former Stalinists had really been discredited and removed from positions of power. It is indeed a matter of speculation whether Scharf's appointment could actually have been expected to provide a suitable basis for a closer link to the SPOe. Judging by his failure to take with him into the KPOe even so small a contingent as composed the SAP, there seemed to be sufficient doubt even in the minds of crypto-Communists of the worth of an open alliance with the Kpoe: and it is equally doubtful that in the Socialist rank and file, Scharf is considered anything more, by now, than a renegade.

The new turn in the Kpoe's policy took the form of an official endorsement by the central committee of vice-chancellor Dr. Adolf Schaerf as candidate for the Presidency. During the 1951 presidential election no such official pronouncement had been issued, the party having merely refrained from taking a stand against the Socialist candidate. The Kpoe's support of Schaerf was particularly surprising in view of the long history of attacks on the vice-chancellor by the VOLKSSTIMME as a completely un-trustworthy reactionary and traitor to the working class. At least in the case of General Korner's candidacy in 1951 the party had not found it necessary to reverse itself since the General had always been fairly popular. In 1957, however, there was, according to reliable reports, considerable dissatisfaction among the rank and file with the party's endorsement though this did not have any visible effect on the election. Communist voters did not go contrary to the party's orders and the Schaerf victory was exploited fully by the Kpoe leadership as proof of the wisdom of their decision. Actually the electoral results of the Schaerf victory were not at all indicative of the decisiveness of Kpoe support. On the contrary, Schaerf's election led if not to an eclipse then at least to a further reduction in the Kpoe chances of rapprochement with the Socialists. Now that the SPOe was assured of continued support by the Kpoe, the Socialists had even less reason to undertake a radicalization of their program and instead could double their efforts to penetrate the wavering "independents" or Catholic voters. The above-mentioned changes in Socialist principles certainly can be interpreted as evidence of the SPOE's unwillingness to make a direct play for Kpoe support.

That the Kpoe did not escape entirely unscathed from the conflicts and debates that engaged it after the Hungarian revolution was indicated by a rather surprising revelation about the party's shrunken membership. If the last official claim of the party's real membership is to be believed — 155,000 in 1947 — the party lost approximately 95,000 since then. The current membership figure of 63,000 was never given out officially but can be arrived at rather elementarily by counting 150 members per each of the 402 delegated who attended the 1957 Congress. This key for delegate representation was published in an issue of the VOLKSSTIMME shortly before the party congress.[27]

Financially, too the party is experiencing its difficulties. Prior to the Soviet withdrawal the KPOe quickly received subsidies in the amount of approximately 15-20 million A.S. Most of this money was used to build and equip a modern printing and publishing house — the Verlag Globus — whose orders were to come not only from the local KPOe but also from all the international front organizations which then had their headquarters in Vienna, e.g., WFTU, World Peace Council, etc. Most of these organizations have since left Vienna and the Globus plant is working under a continuous deficit that is only slightly reduced by orders for German textbooks from the DDR.[28]

The party has naturally lost the "voluntary" contributions collected from the workers in the formerly Russian-managed industries. As another consequence of the signing of the treaty the party no longer collects commissions on engineering projects and other export deals between Austria and the satellite countries. This task is performed now by a special division of the Austro-Soviet Society which maintains direct contact with the Soviet Trade Missions and the Soviet Export Trust, promoting especially the trade of embargoed goods. The role of the KPOe as middleman was performed in the person of Professor Dobretsberger, one of the few if not the only fully accredited university professor — he teaches economics at the University of Graz — with outspoken Communist sympathies. At first the KPOe promoted its association with him for the propaganda value to be derived from having a former "national-liberal" (rather than Jewish) middle-class intellectual in the party's ranks. But later on it became apparent that Professor Dobretsberger's business training was of greater value than any of his ideological pronouncements. And it may possibly be that Dobretsberger's shrewd sense of business turned him to the KPOe in the first place. The professor built a fairly well-run organization that arranged contacts for Austrian firms interested in export to the satellites. It enabled legitimate Austrian businessmen to enter into trade relations without being compromised by direct KPOe or Soviet contact. The commissions which Dobretsberger received for this middleman function constituted an important source of income for the KPOe. With the coming into force of the state treaty, Dobretsberger's function was of course taken over by the Austrian-Soviet society. He managed to survive however, by transferring his activities to that of unofficial mediator for business deals with the Far East. Of course here the profits are much smaller and though the good professor now publishes his own newspaper, apparently without any subsidization, it is highly questionable that his organization makes enough now to provide a significant source of income for the KPOe. The financial instability of the KPOe became already known at the time of the folding of Scharf's paper DER NEUE VORWAERTS which had been heavily subsidized by the KPOe. It was followed shortly thereafter by the dissolution of Scharf's party, the SAP. This in turn was accompanied by a series of internal economy measures by the KPOe, the most important of which included the dismissal on very short notice of personnel in the secretariat and other administrative organs. With the exception of the VOLKSTIMME all KPOe papers have either ceased publication or have been changed into weeklies.

The KPOe is currently going through its most difficult period since the founding of the Second Republic. The party cannot expect to reach ever again even the limited eminence it enjoyed during the Russian occupation. Nevertheless it would be highly premature to write off the KPOe as an influential factor in Austrian politics. Though its ambitions to hold the popular balance of power between the two parties is not likely to be realized, the party may, via a tightly controlled remaining core of loyal voters, still make its weight felt in certain local areas and thereby reward or punish the SPOe. On the plant level, within the lower echelons of the trade union organization the KPOe undoubtedly will continue to act as a disturbing factor. But the slogans of "workers' unity" and "popular front" will lose much of their drawing power even with those who until recently saw in the KPOe only another legitimate organ of working-class representation rather than the willing instrument of Russian influence in Central Europe. The party will continue to draw the votes of the most dissatisfied and in a sense most reactionary elements of Austrian politics. Though these will be hardly ever sufficient to increase the parliamentary representation of the Austrian Communists they may easily continue to provide the KPOe with at least one seat. In view of the rapidly disintegrating FPOe this could lead to the possibly exaggerated but nevertheless probable situation where two equally strong coalition partners are faced by one lone KPOe deputy who then could really hold the balance of power. This would be a bizarre development but it can be assumed to exist somewhere in the planning of the KPOe leaders.

IV. THE "THIRD FORCE" IN AUSTRIA

The fourth party in Austria represents, somewhat paradoxically, the "third force" among the electorate. Wedged between political Catholicism and Marxism is the group of mainly Protestant and middle-class voters which until recently had been the chief target of the political efforts by the coalition partners to assure themselves of an absolute majority. Numerically this segment of the population is estimated at about 600,000, which far outweighs the voter potential of the Communist Party. However, it was also from this group that the Nazi movement in Austria had recruited most of its followers, a fact which led the Allied Council in 1945 to prohibit the formation of any other parties except those of the OeVP, SPOe and the KPOe. The People's Party welcomed this decision since it ruled out competition from another middle-class party, thereby assuring the OeVP's absolute majority over the Marxist parties. For the very same reason, of course, the Socialists were hardly in sympathy with this early Allied decision. At the time of the second parliamentary election in 1949 therefore, strong pressure was brought on the Allied Council to rescind its earlier prohibition, and, eventually the Council relented. The result was the introduction to the voters of a new party, the League of Independents (*Verein der Unabhängigen,* VdU), thus opening up another and possibly final chapter in the history of Austria's "Nationalist" movement.

It is one of the peculiarities of Austrian politics that a *Nationaler* is not a person imbued with a high sense of Austrian nationalism, but one who, on the contrary, denies the existence of just such patriotic feelings. Instead, his emotional attachments are those of German, indeed, Pan-German nationalism which he views as the only respectable sentiment for one who speaks the German language. Generally, a *Nationaler* thinks of himself as a *Liberaler,* which, in turn, does not refer to an attitude of tolerance and belief in the perfectibility of man. A *Liberaler* is in fact one who has "liberated" himself from the dogma of Catholicism as well as from the insidious influence of a "Jewish" progressivism. Militant anti-Catholicism together with an inflexible anti-Semitism, both linked to a belief in the superiority of Prussian culture and society, are the ideological hallmarks of this group. Economically, it favors the classical tenets of free enterprise, thus completing its contrast to the Anglo-American variety of liberalism.

370

Since the middle-class complexion of this group brought it inevitably into opposition to the Marxism of the Social Democracy during the First Republic, the Christian Social Party did its best to persuade this group of the necessity of a permanent anti-Marxist front. But the economic conservatism of this part of the population proved not quite sufficient to overcome its distrust of the strongly Church-dominated leadership of the OeVP and coalitions between the two parties during the First Republic were never of long duration. With the deterioration of the Austrian economy and the advent of Hitler in Germany, this group turned increasingly hopeful eyes toward the "great neighbor to the north" and eventually provided the mainstay of the National Socialist movement in Austria.

In the second republic the VdU could be expected to represent core elements of the Protestant middle classes which now included, in addition to former Nazi Party activists, former career officers in the German *Wehrmacht,* technical specialists who had held managerial position in the giant *Reich* economic enterprises, journalists who had worked for the Nazi press, teaching personnel at all school levels that had been picked for purity of their Nazi views and, last but not least, *Volksdeutsche,* i.e., German D.P.s who had fled into Austria from German-settled areas in Eastern Europe. The large majority of the latter were small businessmen, artisans and craftsmen, the rest professional people and a few farmers, all of whom were resentful over the restrictive practices in the trades and professions which were assiduously maintained by Austrian interest groups against the newcomers, and who therefore did not see in the OeVP, as the political representative of these groups, a champion of their immediate interests.

The program of the VdU in the main reflected the desires of these groups quite accurately. The new party offered as its chief programmatic points the eventual complete removal of the National Socialist disabling legislation, the rehabilitation of soldiers and officers who had served in the *Wehrmacht* and the compensation of former owners of German assets who were citizens of Austria rather than Germany. The VdU was on much less solid ground when it came to the formulation of principles. Here its stand was negative rather than positive. The party opposed nationalization, it was heavily critical of the wage-price pacts and of course it condemned the whole theory and practice of the *Proporz.* The VdU stressed its apolitical attitude and

371

generally affected a show of non-partisanship which, it said, was needed to overcome the increasing "politization" of public life.[29] If there still was a yearning for *Anschluss,* it could no longer be admitted to publicly, as indeed the whole complex of Pan-German phraseology no longer proved to be a body of useful political ideas.

It is not unreasonable, consequently, to ascribe to the VdU characteristics of a pressure group — albeit one with parliamentary representation — rather than those of a political party. It moved into parliament not in order to act as a possible responsible opposition but to be able to bargain with the coalition partners for concessions on specific pieces of legislation. However, since the VdU commanded only a very loosely organized and haphazardly constructed party apparatus — it was based chiefly on former minor Nazi officials and their families — the solidarity and efficiency of concerted political action among its heterogeneous following was put in doubt from the beginning. The lack of either a dominant economic interest or an inspiring idea soon made itself felt among the voter potential of this group. It was recognized by them that the precision with which the coalition operated made their chances of being heard much better within than outside one of the major parties. And the ideological welcome mat set out by either one of the big parties made these groups turn increasingly to them for support.

Only once was the VdU able to show the full strength of its voter potential and that was on the occasion of the presidential election of 1951. This, the first popular election of a president in either the First or the Second Republic, provided the "independents" with the opportunity of showing themselves as the true holders of the balance of power. Under the provisions of the presidential election law a run-off election was called if none of the candidates received an absolute majority on the first ballot. The law permitted parties to substitute different candidates on the second ballot. In 1951 all four parties presented candidates on the first ballot. The results showed conclusively that the People's Party had lost ground since 1949, all of which had been picked up by the VdU. The SPOe registered only nominal gains while the KPOe support remained approximately the same. In view of the unexpected gain shown by the VdU candidate, this party tried to prevail upon the OeVP to substitute him for the original candidate presented by the People's Party. The VdU pointed to the simple arithmetic of the first ballot to prove the soundness of their reasoning:

OeVP + VdU by far outvoted SPOe + KPOe. But the price they were asking — acceptance as partners in the coalition against the objections of the SPOe — was still too high a price to pay for the People's Party. This refusal incensed the VdU, which now issued instructions to the "independent" voters to abstain from voting, or, since voting is compulsory, to turn in empty ballots. Although these instructions were not followed uniformly, enough people heeded them to provide the SPOe-KPOe combination with a safe margin. But with this gesture of defiance the VdU had also underwritten its gradual dissolution since its political ineffectiveness had now become clear to most of its adherents.

The party began to be plagued by serious conflicts which were reflected in a split among the leadership. A moderate and radical faction emerged, the former advocating continued emphasis on a policy that would make possible an eventual coalition with one of the larger parties and consequently the espousal of any and all political issues that would promise popular support, the latter insisting on a further elaboration of a nationalist line together with an unwavering opposition to the evils of coalition politics. Quarrels, intrigue and general distrust soon marked the further course of party councils and conferences. Walk-outs from conferences, resignations from the executive committee as well as reconciliations followed each other in rapid succession.[30]

The disunity within party councils had its impact on the 1953 parliamentary elections in which the VdU lost two seats, and in the provincial elections of the succeeding year when the defeat amounted to a rout. This caused renewed arguments and further splits that eventually led to the formation of small groups whose racist and Fascist views could no longer be concealed. The remaining VdU leadership to a certain extent welcomed these defections since they could be assumed to purify the party. Indeed, with another parliamentary election in the offing it was decided to make the most of these defections and reorganize the party from the ground up. Accordingly, steps were taken to provide the party with a more positive attitude toward parliamentary government. But now the party ran into an unexpected obstacle — and that was that without the structural support provided by former Nazi Party members there was little chance of maintaining an effective organization. Yet with their support and that of others with strong national views the plan to fashion the party into

373

a really liberal, i.e., middle-of-the-road party was bound to fail. The denouement came at the 1956 party congress, one month prior to the parliamentary elections in May of that year. At that congress the remaining moderates were forced out of the executive committee, the party was rechristened *"Freiheitliche Partei Oesterreichs,"* FPOe (Liberal Party of Austria), and an economic program adopted that echoed in many ways the "Social Market Economy" principles of the German CDU.[31] But except for this slight change in economic principle the rest of the platform reiterated the party's previous anti-collectivism and its distrust of the religious de-emphasis of the conservative coalition partner. The party's principled declaration against any kind of coalition government and its insistence instead on the introduction of plebiscitary devices in order to strengthen direct democracy showed fairly conclusively that the "national" elements had carried the day. The result of the May, 1956 election confirmed what many circles had already begun to suspect — that the FPOe as a party was merely the last holdout, not necessarily of unreconstructed Nazis, but of unreconstructed anti-parliamentarians, Prussophiles and discontented expelee elements: the FPOe moved into parliament with only six representatives.

In view of this result the strategy displayed by both the FPOe and the OeVP in the presidential elections of 1957 appears naïve if not indeed ill-advised. Despite its poor showing in the parliamentary election of the preceding year the FPOe was able to persuade the OeVP that its victory depended on presenting a candidate whose political past was untainted by close association with either the party or the coalition and whose religious connections to the Church were purely nominal. If the OeVP were to do that, the FPOe would refrain from offering a competing candidate and instead throw all its organizational support behind the People's Party candidate. The OeVP accepted this offer and nominated as its candidate Professor Denk, a complete political unknown, but one whose scientific career — he was a surgeon and cancer specialist — supposedly would make him more acceptable to the anti-clerical, nationalist intelligentsia. He proved to be a poor match for the tactics of such a seasoned politician as Dr. Schaerf, the Socialist candidate. The defeat of the People's Party candidate by a safe margin proved fairly conclusively that the FPOe's voting contingent was no longer a solidly united bloc of votes that could be delivered as it once might have been back in 1951. It was being slowly ground down between the two large millstones of the coalition partners.

The permanent nature of the coalition can, in fact, be held primarily responsible for the steady loss of influence of the so-called nationalist element. Since the coalition pact automatically ruled out any agreements with third parties except at the risk of the dissolution of the coalition, the avenues of access for the fourth party as a representative of divergent social and economic elements were severely restricted, if not indeed barred altogether. The inability to penetrate the bastiои of decision-making — the cabinet and/or the parliamentary coalition committee — could not but nullify most of the originally purported "balancer function" of the "third" force.

The doctrinal flexibility of the two major parties together with the discreditation of the body of ideology surrounding both *Anschluss* and the idea of an all-German national community have deprived this group of their hitherto most effective political platform. However, this must not be interpreted to mean that this group has lost completely its former volatility. On the contrary, it can be expected that any changes in the popular margins of either one of the coalition partners will still be the result of a shift in voting support by the small but comparatively compact group of unorganized "independents" (i.e., nationalists). Consequently the political appeal of either one of the major parties will continue to be made for some time with an eye toward the ideas and attitudes held by the "national camp" in Austria. The parliamentary representation of this camp can be expected to be further reduced, but its function as the chief reservoir of floating voters will continue to be a primary characteristic of the political process in Austria.

CONCLUSION

Much like the rest of Western Europe the new climate of Austrian democracy is producing a trend away from *Weltanschauungsparteien*. Neither the youthful idealism of the Austro-Marxist tradition, nor its counterpart, the universalism and neo-romanticism of the estatist school of thought have been able to survive intact in the much more pragmatic political atmosphere of the Second Republic. The stability of the coalition equally reduced the supporters of "non-partisanship" and/or "direct democracy" to a mere handful. The drawing power of a Nineteenth-century economic liberalism as well as of anti-clericalism

375

finds itself seriously impaired by the success of the coalition's economic policies and its reluctance to enter upon any changes in the prevailing Church-State relations. Last, but not least, the neutralization of Austria as a condition of the state treaty has made it incumbent upon Austria's political leaders not to turn to either the revival of the Greater German *Anschluss* idea or to the old Hapsburg dream of the supranational Danubian Empire as reliable guides for Austria's future. Continuous ideological de-emphasis together with Austria's special international role as mediator between East and West will function as the best guarantees for the maintenance of its present political viability.

SELECTED BIBLIOGRAPHY

No book that deals exclusively with government and politics of the Second Austrian Republic has been published so far. The following selections will serve as a useful guide to understanding the complexities of the Austrian prewar and postwar political experience.

Heinrich Benedikt, Ed., GESCHICHTE DER REPUBLIC OESTERREICH (Munich: R. Oldenburg, 1954). A descriptive account of the First Republic with few references to the Second. Emphasis is on chronology, economics and culture. An exception is the contribution by Adam Wandruszka, "Oesterreichs politische Struktur," providing a novel if somewhat prejudicial theory to account for the ideological divisions of the last years of the Empire, which were prepetuated into the First Republic. The blame is put on the secularizing influence of the enlightenment which destroyed the comfortable harmony of the Empire's political community.

Joseph Buttinger, AM BEISPIEL OESTERREICHS (Cologne: Verlag fuer Wirtschaft und Politik, 1953); English translation: THE TWILIGHT OF SOCIALISM (New York: F. A. Praeger, 1953). A highly personal but nevertheless penetrating analysis of the declining years of the Austrian Social Democracy by a former leading figure in that movement.

Ulrich Eichstaedt, VON DOLLFUSS ZU HITLER (Wiesbaden: Franz Steiner Verlag, 1955). A chronologically very detailed account of the period leading up to the *Anschluss*. No interpretation.

Albert Fuchs, GEISTIGE STROEMUNGEN IN OESTERREICH 1867-1918 (Vienna: Globus, 1949). A thoughtful interpretation, albeit by a Marxist historian, of the intellectual currents that were uppermost in the social and economic climate of the Hapsburg Empire. His thesis of the common origin of these movements is strikingly similar to that held by the Catholic historian Wandruszka (OP. CIT.)

though they arrive at different conclusions concerning their fate following the collapse of the Empire.

Karl Gruber, ZWISCHEN BEFREIUNG UND FREIHEIT (Vienna: Ullstein Verlag, 1953); English translation: BETWEEN LIBERATION AND LIBERTY (New York: F. A. Praeger, 1955). Memoirs by the first Foreign Minister of the Second Republic and later its Ambassador to Washington. Has some revealing comments on the early period of collaboration between the parties.

Charles A. Gulick, AUSTRIA FROM HABSBURG TO HITLER (Berkeley: University of California Press, 1948), 2 vols. The chief virtue of this work is its voluminous, encyclopedic accumulation of facts, its main defect the uncritical Marxian analysis of these facts. This is the only historical account (by an economist) in English which covers the full twenty-year period of post-St. Germain Austria. No bibliography.

Richard Hiscocks, THE REBIRTH OF AUSTRIA (London: Oxford University Press, 1953). A readable account, couched in somewhat eulogistic terms, of the trying first years of the Second Republic under Allied and Russian occupation. Very useful on economic and cultural data.

Ludwig Jedlicka, EIN HEER IM SCHATTEN DER PARTEIEN (Graz: Böhlaus Verlag, 1955). A truly excellent study of the politics of the Austrian Army between 1918 and 1934.

H. M. Jolles, WIEN-STADT OHNE NACHWUCHS (Assen: Van Gorcum & Co., 1957). A demographic analysis of the steady decline in the birth rate in Vienna from the 1890's to the present with some observations on political causes and consequences.

Mary Macdonald, THE REPUBLIC OF AUSTRIA, 1918-34 (London: Oxford U. Press, 1946). A very brief analysis of the causes responsible for the breakdown of democratic government in Austria. The Constitution is the villain of the piece.

Kurt W. Rothchild, THE AUSTRIAN ECONOMY SINCE 1945 (London: Royal Inst. of International Affairs, 1950). An explanation of the problems facing the truncated Austrian economy in the period of reconstruction immediately following its formal separation from the Reich.

Rudolph Schlesinger, FEDERALISM IN EASTERN AND CENTRAL EUROPE (London: Kegan Paul, Ltd., 1945). A very sophisticated and at times brilliant account by a Marxian sociologist of the social forces that dominate Central Europe. The First Republic of Austria is treated incidentally to the larger theme of creating a federal solution to the political problems of this area.

———, CENTRAL EUROPEAN DEMOCRACY AND ITS BACKGROUND (London: Kegan, Paul Ltd., 1954). An investigation of the development of social mass parties in Central Europe and their attitude toward democratic institutions. Austrian parties during the

377

First Republic are used to illustrate the thesis that the defeat of democracy was *not* brought about by a split in the labor movement but was due to the unwavering inimical attitude of the conservative forces.

Otto Schulmeister, Ed., SPECTRUM AUSTRIAE (Vienna: Verlag Herder, 1957). A luxuriously printed collector's item that runs the spectrum of Austria's achievements in culture, history, art, economics and politics. In German.

Gordon Shepherd, THE AUSTRIAN ODYSSEY (London: Macmillan, 1957). A narrative and highly colored account of Austria's "mission in Europe."

ARTICLES

Murray Edelman, "The Austrian Wage-Price Agreements," THE MONTHLY LABOR REVIEW, LXXVII, 6 (June 1945).

E. L. Erickson, "The Zoning of Austria," THE ANNALS OF THE AMERICAN ACADEMY OF POLITICAL AND SOCIAL SCIENCE, CCLXVII, (1950), 106-13.

A. J. Fischer, "Austria's Oil and the Soviet Union," CONTEMPORARY REVIEW, CLXXVI (1954), 224-27.

Frederick Hertz, "Karl Renner: Statesman and Political Thinker," CONTEMPORARY REVIEW, CLXXIX (1951), 142-45.

Hans, Kohn, "Independent Austria," CURRENT HISTORY, XVIII (1950), 12-15.

Herbert P. Secher, "Coalition Government: The Case of the Second Austrian Republic" AMERICAN POLITICAL SCIENCE REVIEW, LII (September, 1958), 791-809.

——"The Socialist Party of Austria: Principles, Organization, and Policies," MIDWEST JOURNAL OF POLITICAL SCIENCE, III (August 1959), 277-299.

Robert Strausz-Hupé, "Austria's Dilemna," YALE REVIEW, XXXIX (1949), 311-24.

CURRICULUM VITAE

HERBERT P. SECHER (1924-   ), Assistant Professor in Political Science, Western Reserve University, was born in Vienna: he received his B.A. degree from the University of Wisconsin in 1947, M.A. in 1949, and Ph.D. (Honors) in 1954. His thesis was THE PROBLEM OF THE AUSTRIAN STATE—THE POST WORLD WAR II EXPERIENCE, and was awarded the Genevieve Gort-Herfurth Prize for Outstanding Research in Social Studies at the University of Wisconsin for 1953-54. He was part-time Instructor at the University of Maryland (1952-1954), Instructor at Western Reserve University (1954-1955), and Assistant Professor in the same institution since 1955. On leave of absence in 1956-57, he was U. S. Fulbright Research Scholar at the University of Vienna, and lectured, by invitation, for the Free University of Berlin, Bonn University and University of Innsbruck.

CHAPTER SEVENTEEN

JAPAN'S REFORMS

DAVID HENRY KORNHAUSER

State University Teachers College
New Paltz, N.Y.

INTRODUCTION

In the six years following the surrender in the Pacific the United States became one of the missionary-minded conquerors of history and attempted to remake Japanese society. New in this role, the Americans of the Occupation went about the task with a radical, crusading zeal that has been attributed to two broad assumptions, both of which in light of subsequent events appear erroneous, at least in degree. The first of these was that the defeat and reform of our adversaries would cure the world's ills, and the second was that practically everything about Japan needed changing.[1]

At this writing, only a decade since the height of this imposed reformation, it would appear unwise to pass final judgment on the outcome even of its outward manifestations, let alone of its more subtle ramification, the reshaping of the Japanese mind and spirit. To do so with any certainty would earn, for one, the scorn of no less an authority on the Japanese than Sir George Sansom, who in speaking of many of the recent histories of Japan, has said:

> Understandably, but regrettably, they belonged to that class of historical work . . . of which the purpose is not to discover or expound truth but to promote those perversions of systematic thought which are known by the suitably ill-sounding name of "ideologies."[2]

What follows, then, contains a generous sprinkling of conjecture, though generally the conclusions are based on trained observation, including my own.

IDEOLOGICAL HERITAGE

To trace the origins of current Japanese ideology it is necessary to turn to their earliest historical records. The Japanese were fortunate in their early history to be situated close to the most dazzling culture in the world of that day—that of China in the T'ang Period. Recorded history for the Japanese dates from their first contact with this great civilization, but the Chinese by this time had already seen several thousand years of development. The Japanese were quick to recognize the superiority of things Chinese and it is largely from this very early infusion of what initially was purely Chinese culture that the Japanese constructed their first and most significant ideological foundations. The product of this experience has comprised the essence of Japanese religious and social ideology to this day and although a great many influences have since been introduced, it is doubtful in so short a time as is encompassed by modern history that this original structure could have been fundamentally undermined.

The religion of modern Japan is chiefly a broad amalgam of two ancient beliefs, native Shinto, originally a nature cult with overtones of ancestor worship, and Buddhism, of Indian origin but imported from China in the sixth century, a spiritual system of great profundity. The former was peculiarly suited to a relatively simple, agrarian people living in a beautiful but disaster-prone land, but as these people became more sophisticated and Shinto failed to answer the need for a more intellectually satisfying faith, the Japanese turned to Buddhism. The two have existed as correlative beliefs since this early point in Japanese history.

Social ideology is also based on a combination of Chinese and Japanese influences. The native, tribal-kinship system, with its cult of clan loyalties, bravery and general stoicism, was joined with the stabilizing force of Confucianism so that to the glorification of the warrior was added the prestige of the scholar, the male, the elderly, and above all, the family, as the irrefutable foundation of society.

The modern Japanese has been forced to adjust this ideological heritage to the requirements of a competitive, yet interdependent world, and the adjustment has engendered stresses that have seemed to shake the ancient structure. It is the objective of this paper to reveal some of these stresses and perhaps to indicate the direction in which the old order is moving.

Beginning after the Meiji Restoration of 1868, the Japanese, mainly through their voracious appetite for the printed word, acquainted themselves with the ideological notions of the West and some of these acquired a significant audience. Usually the official climate was hostile to alien ideology, but there were times of some leniency. In the 1920's, for example, despite a prodigious system of checks that would seem to have precluded free expression entirely, the moderates gained a voice in practical politics and it was then that representative government received a short but important trial. This was Japan's early "liberal" era, and although hesitant and ephemeral, it helped to provide a basis for the sweeping changes that took place in the apparatus of government after 1945.

But the ruling oligarchy[3] that dominated Japanese prewar politics and government was careful never to allow much latitude to any but its own particular brand of radicalism. Beginning as early as 1925 with the Peace Preservation Law, elements that would have threatened the *status quo* were increasingly hard-pressed by the authorities. And after 1931, when a decade of military adventure began in Manchuria, all ideologies, including even moderate liberalism, were black-listed. All ideologies, that is, except one, *kokutai* or "national entity," the theme that accompanied Japanese dreams of Far Eastern hegemony and the ideological force behind the Fascist experiment. Many intellectuals were thus faced with a paradox. They were obliged to accept *kokutai* yet they could not fail to be attracted by Western notions of freedom and democracy.

Nationalism, then, became the prevailing spirit of the 1930's, and the militarists, in whose hand the direction of the nation had become entrusted, made the most of whatever mythical or otherwise flimsy pretext they were able, to create in the minds of their people an image of divine origin and mission.[4] Various forces, including those of religion, were enlisted in this effort. State Shinto[5] was strengthened as a national cult, with all citizens as its adherents and the emperor as the symbol of God. A powerfully centralized school system became an especially effective propaganda mechanism, for public education, although universal at the primary level and in many ways admirable, was limited after this to the privileged and almost exclusively to males. Thereby, children in the formative years were satisfactorily indoctrinated and the gifted few that went further in their education were either too few or too technically specialized to cause trouble, or, most likely, were "safe" in the first place. Under such a system, it is not surprising that most Japanese were politically docile. There were, of course, geographical differences in the popular acceptance of *kokutai* between the two poles of society, the stolidly conservative rural element and the urban public, which in the 1930's was increasing rapidly in size and influence, and which tended to be more skeptical. But an omnipresent and terroristic national police as the proconsuls of an elaborate "thought-control" program, effectively squelched any deviation whether real or imagined.

Rarely has a nation been so successful in the support of its people. The Japanese toiled under increasingly stringent circumstances and later fought bravely and often fanatically, and although there was disillusion at the failure of the plan, there seems relatively little complaint or regret. It is absurd to think that defeat in war and less than a decade of occupation, despite its efforts to the contrary, could have erased the spirit of *kokutai* entirely. The emphasis of the 1930's was only the reiteration of a national consciousness that has punctuated Japanese history from time to time since the middle of the seventeenth century.[6]

Although there is little doubt that it has survived to the present day, it is also true that nationalism in postwar Japan has undergone a distinct change of direction. One authority seems to see it as a kind of latent force, neither good nor evil, that could work for the betterment of the Japanese if (largely external) circumstances contrive to prevent its adoption either by the old or the new forces of reaction.[7] Both forces have made attempts in the last fourteen years to enlist its services, but so far neither seems to have been successful, mainly because economic conditions at home and abroad have allowed one to block the aspirations of the other to the benefit, happily, of the man in the street. Since the surrender and especially since the end of the Occupation in 1952, nationalism often appears to have been directed—as perhaps it should be—toward the improvement of living conditions for the individual.

Nor have only the extremes of the Japanese political spectrum attempted to harness the power of historic nationalism. It went to work immediately after the surrender as a primary means of insuring the co-operation of the Japanese in carrying out the objectives of the

Occupation. The decision to perpetuate the emperor system had come about before the surrender through the influence of persons who, knowing the Japanese, were convinced that the acceptance of certain nationalistic proclivities would greatly facilitate the enactment of the postwar rehabilitation program. History has endorsed the wisdom of this policy, for whatever the ultimate judgment of the Occupation— and there are vastly conflicting opinions about this—there is little doubt that it was carried out with a minimum of friction.

Although one of the initial tasks of the Occupation was to remove from the emperor the aura of divinity, it was not the intention of the conquerors to remove him as a person. On the contrary, as a now mortal figure, he became one of the most important means of further-ing their ends. Vital Occcupation "directives" were frequently given the imperial sanction that assured their acceptance by the Japanese public. The relationship between SCAP[8] and the emperor has been likened to the ancient one between emperor and *shogun* (military chief) and the Occupation has been termed a modern *bakufu* (feudal military government).[9] The similarity is unmistakable and many of the Occcupation procedures were thus perhaps quite in context with Japanese history. The importance in the eyes of the Occupation of the imperial tradition is emphasized, furthermore, in the first chapter of the postwar constitution, whose eight articles carefully define the emperor's role as a constitutional monarch. In this way after 1945, nationalism was continued, and in a sense became a major force for internal stability.

CONSTITUTIONAL CHANGES

The legal cornerstone for the contemporary ideology and the single most important legacy of the Occupation is the postwar constitution. It provides the basic guarantees of freedom for the individual, but for reasons to be noted, it has also become the chief bone of political contention.

Obviously modeled on the leading constitutional concepts of his-tory the postwar constitution is designed to establish in Japan a thoroughly democratic society. Essentially, however, the Japanese regard it as a foreign instrument, for there is now very little doubt that it was drawn up by the Occupation, although the Japanese were later allowed a few minor changes.[10] For this reason, as will be explained later, it is and probably will remain in constant danger of revision or outright replacement.

Chief among its many innovations is the transfer of sovereignty from the emperor to the people, who are guaranteed freedom in great detail. Governmental power, formerly the main providence of the executive organs, is now shifted to the entirely elective Diet (congress). An independent judiciary modeled on the American system is established and elaborate provisions are made for the strengthening of the legislative process at the local level. War is renounced forever and, as previously mentioned, the emperor is "humanized." This last provision goes especially against the Japanese grain and has aroused a good deal of resentment which, of course, has strengthened the argument of those who wish to see the constitution changed or even replaced.[11]

As is the case with any monarchists of long standing, and the Japanese are probably able to boast the longest rule by a single family of any country in the world, there is a deep, unshakable base of conservatism in their collective personality. For a nation with no such background at all, this is especially hard to rationalize. Our brashness in abruptly substituting our own ideas of individual freedom for their system of hereditary leadership with a veneer of democratic machinery, may ultimately see the frustration of our basic design. For the moment, however, as will be indicated subsequently, most Japanese are yet unwilling to make major changes let alone to abandon wholly their newly inherited, ready-made democracy.

RIGHTIST REACTION

There are, nonetheless, many who are appalled at the "humanizing" of the emperor as well as at other aspects of the new democratization. Adverse reaction, as might be expected, is felt generally by the elderly, by those in rural areas and particularly by factions in remote places where rightist sentiment has always been strongest. Not long after the surrender, organizations arose to voice familiar nationalistic pronouncements and, with the newly given constitutional freedoms, some of these were disseminated in private publications that after 1949 were free of any restraint of Occupation censorship. In general, however, these forces were without much effect, but recently they seem to be gaining in strength and some have apparently acquired national scope. Typical of these is the resurgence of a wartime organization with the nostalgic name Toa Remmei (The East Asia Federation Society), whose leader Tsuji Masanobu, an outspoken ex-colonel of unmistakably nationalistic sentiments, demonstrated his popularity by being elected to the Diet in 1952.[12] Another, and probably more consequential rightist organization is a newly federated society of ex-service people, the Nihon Go-yu Remmei (The Hometown Friendship Society of Japan), which claims a national membership of well over one million and which has already pressured the government into a budget appropriation of around eighty million dollars in pensions. According to their own statements, the principal aims of this group are the general glorification of militarism and a return to traditional nationalistic behavior in order to improve the moral fiber of the younger generation.[13]

Despite the ominous tone of these developments, it seems improbable that as long as the present constitutional guarantees remain effective, the power of these extremist organizations will get out of hand. Certain events in very recent years, however, indicate that the maintenance of constitutional guarantees as they are now established is open to serious question. No sooner had the Japanese been delivered from the technical jurisdiction of the Allied Occupation than demands arose to review the constitution with the objective of revising those aspects that were not in accord with current conditions or were otherwise inappropriate. The most obvious weakness of the original document, denounced by Americans and Japanese long before the peace settlement, was Article 9, the famous renunciation-of-war clause which was optimistically inserted by the victory-flushed Americans and gratefully received by the Japanese who, at the time, were weary of war and of the disaster it had brought them. Events after 1945 quickly emphasized the impracticability of such a rule and even its original champion, General MacArthur, had come to admit the fact before his removal from the supreme commandership in 1951. Urged by the American government and certain Japanese, an embryonic Japanese army had, in fact, already been established, but since Article 9, which still had wide appeal despite world conditions, remained intact, in a thin effort at disguise, these were called at first the "National Police Reserve" (Keisatsu Yobi-tai) and then after 1956, enlarged and more fully equipped, they became the "Self-Defense Forces" (Jiei-tai) .

Left after 1952 to pursue their own affairs, the issue of constitutional revision with the specific aim of changing Article 9 soon became a political football and it was in this regard that a curious paradox arose between the two leading political forces of the present day in Japan, the Socialist minority and the controlling Liberal-Democrats. Normally the most critical of United States policy, the Socialists became the staunch supporters of the constitution as originally drawn, while the Liberal-Democrats, whose policies are usually acceptable to this country—especially to the current administration in Washington—became the champions of revision. Consideration of present political ideologies must be deferred at this point, however, to allow for an attempt to review the ideological currents of society in general.

SOCIAL IDEOLOGY

As already mentioned, Confucian ethics are the basis of Japanese family and other interpersonal relations, but in recent years, especially since 1945, this doctrine has been heavily influenced by Western concepts of individualism. An ideological vacuum was created by the collapse of the country's military ambitions and for a while the reaction was one of utter bewilderment and chaos. The American Occupation forces did their best to fill the gap, but notions of democracy from this immediate source were frequently apt to mislead rather than edify the Japanese. These were years of total confusion physically, as well as of the mind. The country was in ruins, millions of unrepatriated husbands were still abroad and the women at home were often in routine association with other men. Food was the shortest supply in modern times and householders, particularly in the cities, were forced into humiliating daily foraging expeditions to the countryside. These conditions seemed often to bring out the worst in everybody as old patterns of behavior were forgotten in the exciting agony of the new era. The term "democracy" became a by-word to almost every situation but usually the idea of license was mistaken for the concept of liberty. Japanese, who, with their strict ethical training, would never have considered such behavior, found themselves involved in all sorts of anomalous and unprecedented situations in the name of democracy. Infidelity of wives, a practice virtually unknown in prewar times, became a common occurrence and women often, in the desire to reap immediate profit from their new equality, neglected their families, sought spurious "careers," obtained quick divorces and behaved widely in a most unaccustomed way. The men, meanwhile, were robbed temporarily of their virility. For several years, countless thousands were unable to find jobs in their hopelessly burned-out, stagnant and defeated land and either they gravitated in desperation to questionable enterprises, accepted employment from their conquerors, or perhaps at worst, drifted aimlessly and suffered the supreme humiliation of being supported by their wives. This situation, coupled with the decentralization and consequent emasculation of the once-feared police, opened the door to crime, thievery and illegalities of all sorts, often committed in broad daylight in the midst of heavily traveled areas. The emptiness and moral lapse of this proud people is aptly typified by the rise, shortly after the war, of the pinball (*pachinko*) parlor to national prominence. Though fairly harmless in themselves, these establishments seemed to spring up overnight in every city and town block, some of them multiple-storied and lavishly decorated, and quickly they became a refuge for millions. The addiction of Japanese men and women of all ages to this pastime became a national problem. In this case, as was true of most social developments in this chaotic period, it was not the action or activity itself that was surprising, but the excessiveness of it. Countless examples of this could be cited. Nudity, to which the Japanese male had been traditionally indifferent, became a chief form of entertainment in the postwar world, and one is able to read in the press pleas from the irate and scandalized to quell the emphasis on sex. Although these extremes now seem to be a thing of the past, as late as 1955 mothers were complaining to Tokyo producers about a televised "strip-tease" program, and certain widely-circulated newspapers were featuring a "nude of the week" on the front page. Recent history, of course, helped to prolong the postwar ideological turmoil, for no sooner had the Japanese begun to recover their natural dignity of mind than the Korean War brought additional psychological upset.

It would be strange indeed if there were no reaction to this era of upheaval and here we are not disappointed. The forces of reaction are busy in every quarter. But the surprising thing is that there has been no violent move toward any extreme in the process. To be sure, the success of moderation so far is attributable in part to the balance of political forces, but perhaps a more important reason lies in the innate stability of Japanese society.

Reaction to postwar ferment will probably continue indefinitely and in the end certain social patterns are bound to be affected. Even at the moment we can see the results of these stresses on various elements of society. Youths in their teens are particularly influenced and although it is very doubtful that their behavior is as anti-social as is the case in the West, the problem of delinquency is regarded in some circles with concern. It became a political issue, for example, when Prime Minister Kishi used it recently to back his attempt to rush through a bill to vastly strengthen the powers of the national police. Opposition to the plan (or perhaps mostly to Mr. Kishi's tactics) was so strong, however, that the proposal was withdrawn and the factor of juvenile delinquency was belittled by many as a red herring. But notwithstanding, there is a good deal of talk about the changing attitude of youth.

Public education was completely revised by the Occupation to the American system and the youth today are apparently, despite the technical shortcomings of the new arrangement, getting a more pragmatic introduction to life. Higher education, although it is often regarded as not being of very high caliber, is now available to the majority and thousands are even traveling abroad for a year or more. The freely outspoken and largely unbiased public information media are also helping to provide a balanced view of their contemporary surroundings. There is no doubt that this is all leading to a greater awareness of world problems and of Japan's true role in international affairs. The sociological consequences of these developments are obvious. Youth are more critical of themselves and of others in their associations, including those who formerly were considered beyond reproach. Old family relationships, while perhaps fundamentally unchanged, have at least tended to become less rigid. The extended family is still predominant, but love marriages are no longer uncommon and the general relaxation of Confucian dogma is the rule rather than the exception.[14] It is perhaps too optimistic to view all this as beneficial, but the happy effects of the swing to naturalism in human relations is everywhere seen in the openness of youth in contrast to traditional patterns of indirectness and perfunctory politeness.[15]

Reaction to the supposed loose behavior of the young has seen the reintroduction of "moral education" (*dotoku kyoiku*) into the public school curriculum. Such teaching was used for chauvinistic purposes before the war and so fell prey to the ax of Occupation reform, but concern for the demoralizing effects of postwar conditions, resulting in a long period of noisy debate in the Diet, has seen its revival. Much of the pressure for a return to prewar ethics has been exerted from the usual conservative circles, but it can be imagined that indications of the passing of traditional values might be cause for general alarm.

Unprecedently elevated living standards and wider distribution of the wealth have had a great affect on the revision of ideological patterns in the postwar world. This has probably been felt most strongly in rural areas where, for the first time in their long history, the farmer occupies an economic status equivalent to the rest of the citizenry. Thanks to the most successful of Occupation reforms, he now generally owns his own property and these gains have given him greater dignity and a higher status in society than he has known in the past. As has been the case in the United States in the past twenty years, the concept of the country person as inferior to the city-dweller seems to be losing force. A far wider distribution of the wealth, with its consequent reduction of social tensions, has also helped to create in postwar Japan an atmosphere favorable to the retention of the democratic ideal. These hopeful signs must be balanced, of course, by an awareness of the forces that threaten a return to absolutism, but it should be remembered that the Japanese, along with many of the world's people, are not the masters of their own fate. The vulnerability of Japan to the vagaries of world power politics and to fluctuations of world economics is an especially salient factor in any evaluation of the future. Before a final summation, however, it will be well to assess the contemporary political beliefs insofar as their effect on the national psyche is concerned.

The subject of political ideology has been sectioned, rather arbitrarily, into three parts: conservatism, liberalism and Communism. This has been done merely for the sake of orderly discussion, however, and is not meant to be definitive.

CONSERVATISM

It has been remarked previously that the Japanese are basically conservative people—a tendency not unexpected in a nation so recently descended from authoritarian rule and whose population, despite government statistics to the contrary, is still mostly rural and agrarian. Perhaps moderate would be a more appropriate term, for conservatism in the sense of postwar ideologies here means chiefly the avoidance of extremes—a sort of middle-of-the-road approach to the last decade and a half of governmental affairs. This has been the tone except for a brief period in the late 1940's when there were signs of political polarization, but since then the pendulum has swung back to its usual position, slightly to the right of center.

The political manifestation of the Japanese conservative bent is embodied today in the Liberal-Democratic Party which has held the largest number of Diet seats since its formation, four years ago. At that time, the multi-party organization that had characterized Japanese politics since the surrender was ended when a series of mergers created for the first time in modern history a two-party system. At the same time on the other side of the fence, a parallel coalition joined most liberal and ultra-liberal forces into the present opposition party, the Socialists. These events do not imply, however, a high degree of party unity, for both remain so ideologically factionalized that the present consolidation is in constant jeopardy. Nonetheless, both have managed to stay together and to preserve, at least outwardly, the impression of stability. On the other hand, national issues have served to maintain this situation, for the two parties have struggled rather consistently for opposite objectives and the public has thereby been allowed a clear choice of the two alternatives. The struggle has been vastly uneven, for the conservatives have won all elections except that of 1947, yet the Socialists have usually had the strength to thwart, if they so desired, the majority's aims, and this is especially true of the issue of constitutional revision.

Ever since their formation, the Liberal-Democrats have been faced with a series of seeming ideological contradictions. While openly conservative in their views to the point of being generally in favor of a return to certain prewar conditions, they are also the leaders of the pro-American camp.[16] Moreover, while philosophically drawn to support a doctrine of nationalism and Japanism, they are also strongly inclined toward internationalism. These are only apparent paradoxes, however, for as leaders of big business at home, the Liberal-Democrats realize that salvation for Japan lies in as favorable a balance of trade as can be obtained abroad, and thus they are obliged to pursue internationalism. This leads them inevitably into friendship with the United States, Japan's chief supplier of raw materials and her biggest single customer for manufactured goods—not to mention the demands and opportunities of cold war politics. This policy, it should be noted, has enjoyed marked success in helping to elevate per capita incomes and in promoting the general welfare, but the basic problems of economics remain to haunt the politicians and to threaten the well-being of the nation.

The public, meanwhile, has accepted the leadership of the Liberal-Democrats, but at the same time on certain key issues (such as the aforementioned attempt to strengthen the national police, or generally on the question of constitutional revision) they have shifted their support to the opposition. One therefore gets the impression, judging by their postwar voting habits, that most Japanese currently prefer moderately conservative political direction, but that once this leadership seems to be taking them along the all-too-familiar path toward extremism and possible absolutism, they are quick to resist. The postwar Japanese in this way seems to have gained a good measure of political maturity, although it must be admitted that world economic and political conditions have contrived to create and maintain this situation. A world war or a depression might easily upset these delicately balanced politics and send the Japanese off on another, less hopeful tangent.

LIBERALISM

Many, perhaps, would not accept the premise that Japanese politics has liberal roots very much deeper than those established by the postwar constitution. Yet, we cannot ignore certain signs, again evident mostly in the cities, of liberal development at a much earlier time. The "liberal" era of the 1920's has already been recalled, but even in the 1930's when all overtly democratic institutions were stifled by the tide of reaction, the spirit of liberalism was kept faintly alive in certain urban, intellectual circles. In Japan, as in the West, the liberal ideology has appealed to the intellectual, but unlike the situation in the West, the Japanese intellectual, as a result of centuries of Confucian teaching, has enjoyed an especially preferred position in society. This condition produced another paradox, for it forced the militarists of the 1930's to act contrary to their ideological heritage in suppressing the intellectuals, and perhaps for this basic reason, some of the liberal elite survived this dark period to provide a continuity to the democratic ideal that is often overlooked.

In the realm of current practical politics, most liberal elements are represented by the Socialist Party, the product of a merger in 1955 of its right and left wings. The Socialists of contemporary Japan adhere to the usual precepts of Socialism and in local affairs espouse a policy

391

that is almost directly opposed to that of their opponents on most important issues. Among other things, this policy advocates the maintenance of the constitution, whatever its origin, and including the controversial Article 9—an attitude that contributes to a major confrontation between the two parties. Both sides are obstinate on this issue and much heat is generated especially in the Diet where, much to the embarrassment of the Japanese people, several disreputable brawls have occurred. Paradoxically, while advocating the retention of the American-drafted constitution, the Socialists are also predominantly against their country's present involvement with the United States. They emphasize, instead, a condition of "normal" relations with mainland China and with the Communist bloc in general.

Support for the Socialist cause comes from several rather clear-cut segments of society. Because of their stand on relations with the Communist world and particularly with China, which many believe is Japan's natural trade partner, the Socialists enjoy the backing of ultra-leftist and often of pro-Communist elements.[17] Their main support, however, comes from the intellectuals and mostly from organized labor, headed by Zenro, the Japan Labor Union Congress, with a membership of over half a million.[18] White collar workers are also known Socialist Party supporters, as are urban women, according to the 1955 election results.[19]

In this way, the Socialists have developed since 1955 into a promising opposition party and their strength seems to be growing. It remains to be seen whether this growth will produce a greater stability in Japanese politics, but for the time being their strength allows them to perform a valuable service for the public by acting as a means to prevent the attainment of immoderate goals by the majority.

COMMUNISM

Little has been said in this report of the Communists, mainly because it has been the desire to accord them their proper place in the ideological hierarchy. Indeed, a whole section devoted to this topic may be too much emphasis, but since a twist of history might vastly improve their chances for success, it is perhaps wise to mention their status in the present ideological pattern of Japan.

Communism attained some relatively spectacular success in the 1920's, chiefly among the intellectuals and labor. A small, well-knit party organization was formed then under the leadership of Moscow-trained Japanese, but ruthless suppression, backed by the Peace Preservation Law, soon reduced the movement to a state of dormancy, in which it remained until 1945.[20] The postwar atmosphere of ideological vacuum was especially inviting and quickly, and sometimes blatantly, the Communists struggled to win popular support. Their campaign was not without success, but with a return to stability in the post-Occupation period, the electorate has tended to shun them for the majority parties.

Thus, with their public appeal at a low ebb, the Communists await future opportunity by supporting the Socialists or by trying to woo certain minority elements within society. Their audience today is small but not insignificant, for theoretical Marxism has long been a favorite ideology for intellectuals, particularly for certain politically aware college and university people. So-hyo, the General Council of Trade Unions, also tended toward Communist support and especially its affiliate, the Japan Teachers Union (Nikkyo-so). Another friendly force is the Labor-Farmer faction of the Socialist Party which the Communists view as a bridge to the Socialist camp and as a possible aid, when the time is ripe, in establishing a popular front.

CONCLUSION

Little atempt has been made in this report to exhaust the topic of ideological reform and change. It has been the purpose here merely to point out what appears to be a few general characteristics and trends. In the final analysis, the ideologies of the modern Japanese turn out to be not unlike those of many other of the world's people, and the more recent the history of this development, the truer this seems. That the Japanese are sometimes immature in our eyes, as far as certain aspects of political and social behavior are concerned, is hardly surprising considering their brief association with Western ideas and aspirations. The really striking thing is their stability in the face of conditions that might have upset another people a great deal more. Six years of occupation, with its consequent humiliations, and several more years of close contact on a day-to-day, wholesale basis between our two people, might have been expected to produce a mutual enmity that would take centuries to erase. But such has not occurred. After this experience, it is a great tribute to the over-all soberness of both people, but especially of the Japanese, that relations between us are still overwhelmingly dignified and cordial.

All things considered, the postwar gains toward individual freedom and mass participation in government appear to be appreciated by the majority, and therefore, the gains seem to outweigh the reverses. Insofar as the future history will allow, and it must be reiterated that the Japanese are probably among the least able to control their exact role in this process, democracy—Japanese style perhaps, and not quite what we envisioned—has a reasonable chance for survival.

SELECTED BIBLIOGRAPHY

George C. Allen, JAPAN'S ECONOMIC RECOVERY (London: Oxford University Press, 1958). As the title connotes, an analysis of postwar economic conditions by the renowned British economist, this work is brief but well written and highly informative.

Thomas A. Bisson, PROSPECTS FOR DEMOCRACY IN JAPAN (New York; Macmillan, 1949). An interesting prognostication about prospects for the success of the Occupation reforms, written when the reform movement was at its height.

Lawrence A. Battistini, JAPAN AND AMERICA (New York; John Day, 1954). The last two chapters of this book contain an evaluation of the Occupation and a summary view of Japan's major problems. Otherwise, little of this brief work is directly pertinent to the problem encompassed by this paper.

Hugh Borton, Ed., JAPAN BETWEEN EAST AND WEST (New York; Harper, 1957). This is a most valuable symposium by a group of Japan specialists. The first two chapters on Japanese politics and on Communism in Japan are especially timely for a current view of conditions.

Hugh Borton, JAPAN'S MODERN CENTURY (New York: The Ronald Press, 1955). A political and historical survey of Japan since 1850, this definitive volume contains helpful information on the bulk of the American Occupation and of Japanese government and politics since 1945.

Delmer M. Brown, NATIONALISM IN JAPAN (Berkeley: University of California Press, 1955). This is the only book-length study of this subject and as such it forms the basic reference for the initial chapters of this paper.

Jerome B. Cohen, JAPAN'S POSTWAR ECONOMY (Bloomington: Indiana University Press, 1958). Another contemporary view of the Japanese economic scene, this time by an American scholar. This is an introspective but essentially sympathetic analysis of Japan's weighty economic problems and is built around the thesis that Japan's hope for future stability lies in the world's willingness to accept Japanese goods. Dr. Cohen, in a handsome set of statistics and tables, sets out to prove that the principal party in this affair is the United States as Japan's chief market and source of supply. The idea of mainland China being the normal customer and supplier for Japan is effectively countered.

R. P. Dore, CITY LIFE IN JAPAN (Berkeley: University of California Press, 1958). This is a recently published account of life in Tokyo in the period immediately preceding the peace treaty. It contains insights into Japanese postwar opinions and ideals that are appropriate background material to the section on social ideologies in this paper. It is a very interesting and quite remarkable study of present-day city life in Japan and as such is a relatively unique work in this field.

Robert A. Fearey, THE OCCUPATION OF JAPAN, SECOND PHASE, 1948-1950 (New York: Macmillan, 1950). A detailed account of the aims, aspirations and conduct of the American occupation of Japan in its later stages.

Douglas G. Haring, Ed., JAPAN'S PROSPECTS (Cambridge: Harvard University Press, 1946). A symposium on Japan written immediately after the surrender. One chapter, a product of the editor, concerns Japanese ideology as it appeared at that time.

Nobutaka Ike, JAPANESE POLITICS, AN INTRODUCTORY SURVEY (New York: Knopf, 1957). This highly informative but compact account of Japanese politics deals more with the background to the political scene rather than with political happenings. And so it provides some valuable understanding of the behavior of the electorate and of politicians in general.

Edwin O. Reischauer, JAPAN, PAST AND PRESENT (New York: Knopf, 1952). This and the work that follows provide the most important background for this paper. These books succinctly explore nearly every aspect of Japanese society, with especial attention to the contemporary scene.

Edwin O. Reischauer, THE UNITED STATES AND JAPAN (Cambridge: Harvard University Press, 1957). Similar to the above, this work concentrates on Japan's relations with the United States and is somewhat more recent than that previously cited.

Jean Stoetzel, WITHOUT THE CHRYSANTHEMUM AND THE SWORD (New York: UNESCO, 1955). This is an attempt to reveal aspects of the Japanese postwar personality and is obviously meant to contrast this view with that of Ruth Benedict's famous work. Largely by means of analyzing public opinion polls and similar media, the author suggests recent changes in Japanese behavior.

Rodger Swearingen and Paul Langer, RED FLAG IN JAPAN (Cambridge: Harvard University Press, 1952). As stated in the text, this is the most comprehensive view of Communism in Japan from its inception to the peace treaty that has been written.

Robert B. Textor, FAILURE IN JAPAN (New York: John Day,

1951). An interesting and highly critical evaluation of the Occupation, written before the end of that era by a former Occupationnaire and graduate of the U. S. Army language training program.

THE UNITED STATES AND THE FAR EAST (New York: The American Assembly, 1956). A symposium on the Far East containing certain insights into the nature of the Occupation.

CURRICULUM VITAE

DAVID HENRY KORNHAUSER was born in Philadelphia, Pennsylvania, March 17, 1918. Attended Bucknell University, Lewisburg, Pa., 1937-41 (A.B., 1941 in English). Graduate student at University of Michigan, Ann Arbor, 1950 to 1955 and received his M.A. degree in Far Eastern Studies, 1951, and Ph.D. in Geography, 1956. In 1952-53 was awarded Metropolitan Community Seminar Fellowship, University of Michigan, and studied characteristics of central business district of Flint, Michigan. In 1953-54 was awarded a fellowship by the Center for Japanese Studies, University of Michigan, and spent one year at the Center in Japan at Okayama. During World War II was an area and language student in Japanese of the ASTP program of the Army and also of the Military Intelligence Language Program. As such, spent three years at Yale University, University of Michigan and the Presidio of Monterey, California, 1943-1946. Was resident in Japan, 1946-1950 as army officer in GHQ, SCAP, as civilian employee of the army (both as a press censor and as a self-employed civilian). Writings include: THE INFLUENCE AND RELATED FACTORS ON THE RISE OF JAPANESE CITIES, University of Michigan, Ann Arbor, 1955; "Urbanization and Population Pressure in Modern Japan," PACIFIC AFFAIRS, September, 1958; "The Japanese 'Medium City,' 1888 to 1950," OCCASIONAL PAPERS, Center for Japanese Studies, University of Michigan Professional experience includes three years as a Teaching Fellow in Geography, University of Michigan, one and a half years as Assistant Professor of Geography, Pennsylvania State University and three years as Associate Professor of Geography at the State University Teachers College, New Paltz, N. Y. In the summers of 1957 to 1959, directed the Seminar on Asia which is partly sponsored by the Japan Society, Asia Society and the Asia Foundation. Married on November 8, 1949 at U. S. Consulate, Yokohama, Japan to Kyoko Nakamura of Hyogo Prefecture, Japan.

CHAPTER EIGHTEEN

INDIA'S GANDHISM

HOWARD BOONE JACOBSON

University of Bridgeport

and

DANA RAPHAEL

Columbia University

Any assessment of what India stands for in the mainstream of contemporary ideologies would be incomplete if it did not include the inspiring principles of freedom, democracy, nationalism and socialism, yet one can hardly say that these concepts are uniquely "Indian" since most of the nations of the world would claim these very same ideals as their own.

What is distinctly "Indian" lies not so much with what Indian leaders have embraced of Western social and political philosophy for a better society, but with what is emerging because of the amalgamation of these Judeo-Christian ideals with the great and local Sanskritic traditions of India. These Hindu values supply the day-to-day nourishment that sustains her people's spiritual and cultural life, as it has for centuries.

India's great architect of national freedom, Mahatma Gandhi, was the first to give age-old Indian values a continuity and unity with modern Western social and political ideas.

Said Gandhi: "Some friends have told me that truth and nonviolence have no place in politics and worldly affairs. I do not agree. I have no use for them as a means of individual salvation. Their introduction and application in everyday life has been my experiment all along. . . . For me, politics bereft of religion are absolute dirt, ever to be shunned. Politics concerns nations and that which concerns the welfare of nations must be one of the concerns of a man who is religiously inclined, in other words, a seeker after God and Truth. For me, God and Truth are controvertible terms, and if any one told me that God was a God of untruth or a God of torture I would decline to worship Him. Therefore, in politics also we have to establish the Kingdom of Heaven."[1]

The ethico-political acts which Gandhi prescribed in his nation's struggle with the British for self-rule were remarkable for their ideological duality.

He asked his people to practice passive resistance through non-violence (*ahimsa*) and non-co-operation (*satyagraha*), and they listened. He explained: "In the application of *satyagraha*, I discovered in the earliest stages that pursuit of Truth did not admit of violence being inflicted on one's opponent but that he must be weaned from error by patience and sympathy. For what appears to be Truth to the one may be error to the other. And patience means self-suffering. So the doctrine came to mean the vindication of Truth, not by infliction of suffering on the opponent, but on one's self."[2]

The idea unified millions of his followers in a mass movement for freedom's cause. It taught the virtue of self-discipline (*sanyam*).

But it was directed against the British as well. Thousands of volunteers staged sit-down strikes, paralyzing an economy. Other thousands, proclaiming their belief in civil resistance, offered themselves up for arrest. The British jail soon became the unusual qualification for the role of civil resister. The colonial government was frustrated by all this confusion.

He held up the spinning wheel to the masses and asked them to spin daily and dress only in homespun cloth, *khadi*. Even at the most important party meetings, Gandhi could be seen spinning quietly. The act brought upper caste and lower caste together in the common task. It dignified hand labor. It also gave millions of unemployed something to do.

What was its impact on the British: It was an open boycott of British goods, a direct signal for resistance to exploitation. It dealt a heavy blow to the cloth industries in England. When Gandhi visited them later, humbly he told the disgruntled, unemployed mill workers that he had come to apologize and to ask them to understand that where their plight only concerned several thousand, India's affected millions.

He declared to the Indian masses that he was going to make salt from the free ocean in defiance of the salt tax imposed by the Viceroy on the home-mined product. Many thousands joined him as he walked across India in his march to the sea. The entire mass was pledged to passive resistance if the British retaliated. The deed awakened the country to the evils of colonial rule. It symbolized the need for self-government.

As for the British, it weakened their legislative hold over the masses. It degraded the colonial government's policies. It created civil resistance to law while yet maintaining a high regard for law and order—that law and order which Gandhi knew the British would respect despite the fact that the Indian tactics threatened the very existence of colonial rule. Such was the greatness of the act.

From prison he announced a fast until death which stirred the conscience of the nation against the injustices practiced by Indian against Indian. With this method of deliberate, personal sacrifice he taught shame, self-respect and human dignity.

But he was speaking to the British too, as proof of his sincerity and his dedication. It led one English journalist to write: "I have never met any man more utterly honest, more transparently sincere, less given to egotism, self-conscience pride, opportunism and ambition, which are found in greater or lesser degree in all the other great political figures of the world."

He was teacher, spiritual leader, revolutionist, father and son to his people, reaching out for their minds and hearts with love and service and quietly preaching non-violence, which became the powerful force in the nation's struggle for freedom.

What does it take to find truth (satya)? As early as 1906 Gandhi took the classical holy vows of brahmacharya (celibacy) because he firmly believed that chastity is one of the greatest disciplines without which the mind cannot attain requisite firmness. He remarked that to be a teacher in India the vows of aparigraha (non-possession) and sunyasa (renunciation) were essential. This gave him a magic influence over India's spiritually rooted millions.

His home became the villages of India. He walked the path that Buddha trod. He often spoke of the Rama Rajya, the golden days which had been and which would return, much like the "guru" (teacher) had done for centuries in the memory life of Hindus.

Gandhi offered advice. There was no subject he did not touch

399

upon. Every local problem was his personal concern. He talked about vitamins in food, mudpacks to use for certain diseases, the habits of tobacco and opium, and the need for recreation for adults and children.

He stiffened the backbone of the country. He made poverty and tilling of the soil a virtue, ennobling the poor. He gave them shame by pointing out how cruel they were to their brothers, the outcasts, whom he renamed *harijans*, children of God.

But if he showed them shame, he also gave them pride. He demanded that one should not take "leftovers" and that starvation was no excuse for accepting food which was not offered nicely, gently and with kindness. Consider the attitude behind the giving of food, he said, before accepting it.

He told the *harijans* not to drink liquor so that the upper-caste Hindu would not despise them. He advised the middle-road Hindu to give up exploitation by not becoming lawyers and doctors. He implored the students to give up the British schools that were imprisoning their minds, and he begged the intellectual to be an example to the British of the finest that was Indian.

Bapu (the father, as he was called) spiritualized everything he touched. He demanded a rigid discipline of himself which far outdistanced what he demanded of his followers. He assumed their burdens on his own shoulders, freeing others from the heavy responsibilities and the hard privations. His complete selflessness led Gandhi's political heir, Jawaharlal Nehru, to say: "To us he has represented the spirit and honor of India, the yearning of her sorrowing millions to be rid of their innumerable burdens, and an insult to him by the British government or others has been an insult to India and her people."

Thus to millions, he was the prodigal son who needed protection, but he was more than that, much more. He was the "revolutionary," out for big changes, and a born rebel, defiant and unyielding. Neither his quiet tone nor his simple words and passive actions covered the fire of indignation, the sincere determination to reach his goal.

The path was quite clear. He rejected the power motivation of politics and substituted instead the service motive. He believed in conversion of an enemy, not his defeat. He stood for conquest by love, and he chose mass action based upon passive resistance. What evolved was a powerfully new ideological force—ethical politics.

To add "resistance" to his peoples' centuries-old passivity portrays

400

the genius of its originator. The national inertia was transformed into action in a manner which spoke of the glory of turning the other cheek. In Gandhi's own words: "Passive resistance is an all-sided sword; it can be used anyhow; it blesses him who uses it and him against whom it is used. . . . Wherein is courage required—in blowing others to pieces from behind a cannon or with a smiling face to approach a cannon and be blown to pieces? Who is the true warrior—he who keeps death always as a bosom friend or he who controls the death of others? Believe me that any man devoid of courage and manhood can never be a passive resister."[3]

Once these ideals were established, a series of tangible actions, all invented and instigated by Gandhi, followed and each, one after the other, became the visible symbols of the new ethical politics. The spinning wheel, salt, jail, fasting and prayer meetings—these were the "revolutionary" acts and symbols in the name of self-rule.

At times his followers seethed with indigation to think that he could choose as an expression of civil disobedience what they considered unimportant and inadequate. When he chose the British plan for separate electorates for "untouchables" as the reason for his first fast, it seemed, according to Nehru, "an extraordinarily trivial matter for such a tremendous step. It was quite impossible to understand his decision, even though he might be completely right in his argument with the government. We could do nothing, and we looked on, bewildered."[4]

Gandhi had a supersensitivity to India's needs as they became manifest. Later on Nehru admitted that the Mahatma knew his India well, reacted to her slightest tremor, gauged a situation accurately and almost instinctively, and had a knack for acting at the right psychological moment.

The rest is history. Eventually the British yielded and granted independence. But in victory Gandhi found defeat. India was partitioned. Forty years of teaching and preparing could not prevent the bloodshed which followed. He had prepared his people to tolerate the British by non-violence, but their sudden departure coupled with decades of humiliation and personal degradation at their hands left Moslem facing Hindu, with no one upon whom to vent the deepseated antagonisms of one for the other. Personal hatred exploded into a religious war, an ideological war.

The outbreaks hurt him deeply. They represented a violent rejec-

401

tion of non-violence. He seemed disillusioned but he did not falter. At the end of his life, he could be seen walking from village to village in the midst of the riots, with no protection, crying for a cessation of the atrocities and the hate, doing penance for what had failed.

Gandhi left this forceful ideological heritage with his people, but the events which followed his death beclouded them. The country quickly became preoccupied with national elections and the first five-year development plan. In the drive for increased productivity and industrialization, the Gandhian revolution seemed to fade from the national scene.

THE BHOODAN MOVEMENT

Ideologically, a split occurred among Gandhi's successors. There were those who felt that the new India should accept capitalistic values that went along with the country's commitment to the democratic ideals of the West; others saw the indigenous culture and the Gandhian ideology as the proper foundation for any social or economic change. However, the proponents of a mixture of modern Western liberalism and British Fabian Socialism seemed to prevail among the numerous plans put forth to inspire the nation.

There arose from among Gandhi's closest followers, however, one who felt that the new government had too quickly forgotten its Gandhian heritage, and who seems determined to make the new political leaders realize that Gandhism is not outdated.

Vinoba Bhave has attempted to apply the concept of non-violence in the economic sphere—particularly to the problem of land, an issue long linked to conflict and violence. Moving from village to village in land-hungry areas, Bhave exhorts the landowners, land tenants and the landless to mutually work out a solution to the land shortage based on love and non-violence. He has prophesied to them that if a proper atmosphere for land reform is not created then bloody revolution will certainly follow.

The *bhoodan* or land-gift movement evolved out of Bhave's need to find some field for experiment with non-violence after Gandhi's death, for he was convinced that the whole fabric of Gandhism was in danger of destruction.

Walking through Telangana, Hyderabad State, in 1951, where Communists had seized the property of landholders with murderous violence, Bhave stopped in the village of Pachampalle to address a prayer meeting, as was Gandhi's custom also. Asking the people about their needs and hardships, a group of low-caste villagers snapped back: "We want some land." Surprised by this frank request, Bhave reports that he just as suddenly turned to the assembled and asked if there was anybody who had some spare land to give away. When an offer of a hundred acres was made by a landlord, the Bhoodan idea had its birth. Bhave writes:

> I was not confident of the result. How can a few drips of nectar sweeten a sea? But God put strength into my words. Somehow people understood the spirit. They realized that the events that were happening would bring a revolution in their life, which was beyond the capacity of Governments. They began to give free gifts of land, at times beyond my expectation.[5]

Tens of thousands of donors, big and small, have heeded his quiet words at prayer meetings. He has told the people that land, like air, sun and water is a free gift of God. With approximately 300 million acres of cultivated land in India and the average family having five members, he has asked that every family give away one-sixth of its land holdings and accept the poor landless man as the sixth member of the family.

One Indian economist has called the *bhoodan* movement "an ideological revolution and where there is an ideological revolution life marches toward progress. India has produced men who have renounced large kingdoms as if they were worthless straw. The bhoodan movement is born of the same ideology. The ethical and spiritual basis of the movement is based on the Hindu view of life and thinking. . . ."[6]

Bhave's appeal is spiritual, not political, yet he has found that politics is necessary. He once told a lifelong friend, now director of the Gandhi Memorial Fund in New Delhi, that his motive in life was to find God, but because the situation compelled him to come out into public life, he would have to find God in the next life.

As one Indian writer has analyzed the *bhoodan* phenomenon: "Like the Vaman of Hindu mythology, asking for three feet of land from King Bali, Vinoba is asking for three simple gifts from the Indian *demos*: land, cash donations and labor-gift sacrifice. Once these ideals take root, the whole face of India can and will be transformed."[7]

Even Prime Minister Jawaharlal Nehru, Gandhi's political heir, whose progressive policies of modern development schemes and industrialization have been in conflict with Bhave's conviction that India's villagers must grow their own food and make their own cloth, has remarked that "This movement may be beyond the understanding of the economic *pundits* [wise men] but it reaches the minds and hearts of the people."[8]

The full-scale land reform legislation which was hoped for when the land-gift movement became widespread has not yet come. Although Nehru pledged full legal co-operation to Bhave (despite Vinoba's opposition to Western materialism) and although several state governments enacted their own legislation, the dominant Congress party is obliged to support its own program of land reform which includes the payment of compensation for any land taken from the landlords. But the rapid depletion of India's sterling balance has deterred action by the government on this scheme now. This, in turn, has curbed the action of state governments in pushing for further land legislation on their own beyond ceilings on existing holdings.

Because of the snail's pace with which land expropriation has occurred, the Indian Communists have capitalized on the situation with the impoverished village peasantry and landless, preaching Marxist ideology mixed with promises of several acres of land for all, a plow and a bullock cart.

Recent victories at the polls in Kerala State, where population density is as high as seven thousand per square mile in some areas and where 50 per cent of the land holdings are less than an acre in size, indicate the hard fact that ideological battle will be waged over the issue of land reform and how it is to be accomplished. The Communist regime in Kerala has managed to push through a new land reform law which limits holdings to fifteen acres and gives added tenure rights to small tenants as well as the prospect of land to till for many landless agricultural workers. There is no information yet available as to how this legislation will be enforced.

The Planning Commission of the Indian government now recognizes "what Gandhi called India's 'problem of problems'—how India can, by democratic means, organize a system which can use land, rural capital and rural labor to secure higher production, higher incomes, higher employment."[9]

> On this issue there is little experience in the history of the democratic nations to draw upon for guidance. Indeed, no democracy has ever before faced a similar problem. Western nations

by and large have not had the excessive, densely crowded, rural populations common in much of Asia. Although China's own political and economic systems differ, India has studied with considerable interest the agrarian organization methods used in China, where the pressure on land is similar to India's. Since India has deliberately chosen the democratic process, it remains for India to evolve its own agrarian system, which would conform to Indian principles and traditions.[10]

The land problem represents only a beginning for Bhave and his followers. He has asked the people in the villages to accept more. He has asked for a virtual transformation in Indian life itself, consistent with orthodox Sanskritic and Gandhian ideals, based on sacrifice (*yajna*), charity (*dana*) and austerity (*tapasaya*).

Of the new social order, Bhave has said:

> The days of kings are past; and so are those of the *zamindars*. The present age has no use either for the kings or the *zamindars*. The world-to-be belongs to the people whose voice will henceforth be supreme. The rise of the people in the affairs of the world signifies that the present age demands equality — equality as between friends. The relationship among different individuals constituting society must be based on comradely love. . . . Not service, but comradeship is its ideal. It does not mean that those who deserve respect will not receive it. Excellence will certainly receive due respect, but the relationship between individuals will be that of comradely equality.[11]

He would transfer virtually all powers to the village leadership, so that the necessary reforms would come about not only by legislation from Delhi but from the village itself. With decentralized rule, reforms would happen only when local conditions necessitated it, and with the full consent of the villagers.

Says Bhave:

> We want an order of society which will be free not only from exploitation but also from every governmental authority. The power of government will be decentralized and distributed among the villages. Every village will be the State in itself; the center will have only nominal authority over them. In this way, gradually, we will reach a stage when authority in every form will have become unnecessary and will therefore, fade away giving rise to a perfectly free society.[12]

405

The land-gifts mission and its extensions, co-operative-yet-individual cultivation of land, the trusteeship or socialization of land and co-operative village management are in tune with the cultural ideals of India. They compound the spiritual past with a modern Gandhian interpretation of that past. They ask for a change in the psychology of the masses by looking at social and economic change from an entirely Indian point of view, that of non-possession or *aparigraha,* and one which is quite compatible with the pronounced aims of India's leaders for a socialist pattern of society.

What Bhave seems to be advocating is a kind of ethical socialism. His ideal is that of a non-possessing society. He has made it quite clear that his brand of common-property-for-all socialism is not to be achieved by divestment or *apaharana,* the doctrine of a good many countries in the world today. Rather he implies an ideology of non-possession or *aparigraha;* all one has, his land, his property and his intelligence, is to be an offering to society.

And finally he makes it quite clear that what he propounds is the ethical idea of *sanyasa* (asceticism) on a mass scale, where *all* the people, rich and poor alike, voluntarily sacrifice everything for the benefit of all and for the common good *(sarvahit sampatidan)*.

Although the movement's greatest "success" to date has been with the redistribution of land (more than four million acres of land and some two thousand gifts of whole villages), the fact that it emphasizes the responsibility of the privileged to the underprivileged and the need for peaceful and orderly social justice has unquestionably produced a climate for indigenous reform. This is most clearly seen in India's Second Five-Year Plan which outlines the steps to be taken to achieve co-operative farming and co-operative village management along the lines advocated by Vinoba Bhave.

In the Gandhian tradition, Bhave picked up the old Hindu words and patterns to propagate the novel reforms he has introduced. Much like Gandhi, he has the habit of wearing the loincloth and sitting at prayer meetings in the crouched position of the teacher, priest and wise man. He is thereby able to catch the imagination of the masses in terms of their own religious experience and mentality and at the same time to create an atmosphere for social reform.

NEHRU'S CONTRIBUTION

Yet, in a sense, India's Prime Minister Nehru has been as important for India ideologically at this time in her history as is Bhave. Although he does not seem to succeed himself in the villages except through the enormous prestige his Congress party has built up around him, he does, with his proper dress and his English training, get his response from the classes in India which are like him — the people who seem to be most responsible now for planning India's future.

Nehru's British background and his acquired mixture of Western liberalism and Fabian Socialism when combined with indigenous Gandhism produce a new ideological rhythm which does not fit any of the old categories.

In internal affairs, Nehru approaches the problems of democratic government in a somewhat experimental manner, modifying, changing and contradicting himself when delineating the social and economic rights of individuals and groups, primarily because he must consider this tremendous latent force of Gandhism which affects each and every one of his progressive policies.

And Bhave, as the leading spirit behind Gandhism in India today, indicates by his words the pressures that confront the present Indian government:

> . . . We must continue to go ahead in our own direction. People ask me how far they should cooperate with the Government plans. I say to them, we should certainly cooperate in those plans which we approve of, but we must keep ourselves free. We cannot accept any of these plans and projects as our own and get entangled in them. We may give to Government our advice if and when it is sought and may occasionally help it when there is need, but it will be a mistake to make its plans any of our responsibilities. This is my view.[13]

But it is Nehru's unique ethico-political position in international affairs where the essence of Gandhism and classical Hindu ideals have been most evident and where he has carved out a new genus of leadership for Asia in world politics and has increased his own personal stature and that of India as well.

Nehru has asked all nations to heed the concepts of non-alignment and unlimited mediation as an important contribution to international peace when disjunctive ideological forces are at work in the world.

407

He has maintained that "Taking sides would lessen our capacity to serve as a bridge between the opposing blocs."[14] He firmly believes that ethico-political relativity will develop a greater capacity for adjustment on both sides, even for coexistence, in a world where to the Indian leader circumstances keep changing and where absolute commitment only makes it harder to sit down with the other side and work out differences.

Moreover, such a policy seems to make good sense in her present condition of nationhood. Because of her low sterling balance, India must have the support economically of both the Western and Communist blocs. Because of her rivalry with Pakistan over Kashmir — knowing full well that Pakistan has behind her the entire Moslem bloc (a major reason for not recognizing the state of Israel) — India is forced to cultivate the political support of her Chinese neighbors to the north as well as the major world power blocs. That such a policy of non-alignment seems to work in the face of these potential crisis situations is testimony to its rightness for India and its moral force in preventing disputes.

India's role as leader of the non-alignment bloc of Asian-African nations in the United Nations Assembly and her active role as mediator in the small wars in Korea and Indochina, as well as sideline participation in many other between-nations disputes, indicate quite dramatically how other nations have come to accept Nehru's ideas about the conduct of nations during disputes and in times of peace.

Chester Bowles wrote of Nehru and his non-alignment policy: "When Nehru refuses to answer Russian insults with equally violent replies, when he insists that negotiations should always be attempted even when the outlook is forbidding, when he suggests that mutual fear feeds the Cold War conflict, he and all India believe that he is following in the footsteps of Mahatma Gandhi. And like Gandhi, he becomes angry when anyone implies that such a course means passive neutrality, or a refusal to resist evil."[15]

In accordance with Gandhian tradition, non-alignment does not mean non-resistance to evil. Nehru and India would have all the nations of the world commit themselves to active resistance to evil with the moral force of justice and the spiritual force of non-violence.

Nehru's non-dualistic attitude (*advaita*) about conflicting political ideologies is consistent with the great Sanskritic teachings. The concept of *brahman* intimates that reality is the logically indeterminate basis of apparently conflicting determinate forms. Ideally, any intelligent Hindu has for centuries been able to accept the other great religions of the world as different manifestations of the same universal God, or view different systems of moral and social training as leading to man's ultimate fulfillment.

The Hindu mythological story of the transformation of the serpent power from an ever-threatening enemy into a friend by mediation with love, sympathy and understanding applies here. Historically too, during nearly six hundred years of Moslem rule in India, the village Hindu went to his own village court because of the severity of Moslem law. These courts were concerned with arbitration rather than justice. The village elders felt that in the interests of the village, it was their job to pacify both parties and to settle the quarrel. Knowing full well that both parties had to go on living together, they insisted upon arbitration. The attitude of the village *panchayat* or elders was to try to get neighbors to live peacefully together.

Similarly, Nehru has tried to use the ideological forces of non-violence and mediation to persuade the great powers to renounce force and threats of war as a means of solving international or nation-to-nation political or economic problems. He asks that they replace this attitude with a desire for collective living, respect for the views and feelings of other peoples and nations, mutual accommodation and brotherly love.

Says Nehru: "As we get used to living together as neighbors and as the fear of war recedes, both the Soviet nations and the democratic nations will modify their policies. In China and the Soviet Union, the patterns that now seem so rigid may well be altered. The areas of agreement will grow and the areas of conflict will shrink. And eventually, I think, both sides will see that there was not so much to fight about as they thought. The cold war will be just a phrase in our history books."[16]

It has been the expressed purpose of this paper not to deal with the contradictions in modern Indian history and affairs which seem to negate these ideals. There have been events and actions by her leaders which apparently do. Nonetheless,, this paper has only attempted to demonstrate how, through the actions and thoughts of recent leadership, the pivotal ancient Sanskritic concept of *ahimsa* developed into the modern Indian creeds of service, love and non-violence or Gandhism. Even at this moment these values are finding application. They form the ideological base upon which the Indian democracy will build and plan for the future.

SELECTED BIBLIOGRAPHY

Swami Akhilananda, HINDU PSYCHOLOGY (New York: Harper & Brothers, 1946). A non-technical introduction to the thought of India and the East and the basic facts about the Hindu religion and the direction of mental life compared with the current theories of Western thought.

ALL MEN ARE BROTHERS: LIFE AND THOUGHTS OF MAHATMA GANDHI AS TOLD IN HIS OWN WORDS (New York: UNESCO, 1958). UNESCO pays homage to the person and the writings of a man whose spiritual influence extended throughout the world. The text selections are intended to appeal to a wide public and to make better known the different aspects of Gandhi's personality and writings. The Vice-President of India has written the introduction.

Vinoba Bhave, BHOODAN YAJNA (Ahmedabad: Navajivan Publishing House, 1953). The only authoritative collection of articles by the author, most of which originally appeared in the Indian paper, HARIJAN. It attempts to present the case for the *bhoodan* movement through Bhave's letters, speeches and prayer meetings. There is a cheap English edition available from the publisher.

G. D. Birla, IN THE SHADOW OF THE MAHATMA (Calcutta: Orient Longmans Ltd., 1953). A collection of the letters written to the author, one of India's leading industrialists, by Gandhi and other pre-independence leaders, and in turn answered by him. The letters give intimate glimpses of English personalities during the Gandhian era.

Chester Bowles, AMBASSADOR'S REPORT (New York: Harper & Brothers, 1954). The former Ambassador to India describes his diplomatic mission from 1951-53. He describes U.S. cooperation in India, offers a closeup of Nehru and analyzes the tactics of the Chinese and Russians in Asia.

Mahatma Gandhi, AN AUTOBIOGRAPHY, OR THE STORY OF MY EXPERIMENTS WITH TRUTH (Ahmedabad: Navajivan Publishing House, 1940).

————, DELHI DIARY (Ahmedabad: Navajivan Publishing House, 1948).

————, INDIAN HOME RULE (Madras: Ganesh & Co., 1922).

————, YOUNG INDIA (New York: B. W. Huebsch, 1923).

————, SERMON ON THE SEA (Chicago: Universal Publications, 1924).

These books cover the most significant aspects of Gandhi's political and emotional life. They range from his autobiography to religious sermons to his practical social and political treatises. Covering a wide range of feelings and style regarding the ethico-political method of non-violence, the books contain the "stuff" with which Gandhi led his people to national freedom and instituted his indigenous reforms.

B. R. Misra, V FOR VINOBA (Calcutta: Orient Longmans Ltd., 1956). The author, a leading Indian economist, attempts to examine the significance of the *bhoodan* movement in the context of India's agrarian problems. The land-gift movement is seen as an important economic mechanism to help achieve the objectives of a socialistic economy. Former Ambassador Chester Bowles has written the foreword to the English edition.

Jawaharlal Nehru, GLIMPSES OF WORLD HISTORY (New York: John Day, 1942).

————, MAHATMA GANDHI (Calcutta: Signet Press, 1949).

————, NEHRU ON GANDHI (New York: John Day, 1948).

————, THE UNITY OF INDIA (New York: John Day, 1948).

————, TOWARD FREEDOM (New York: John Day, 1941).

GLIMPSES is a unique history of India written in letter form to his daughter by Nehru while in prison as a political offender. His writings on Gandhi are forceful interpretations of Gandhian philosophy and politics and a personal tribute to his mentor. His views on Indian freedom are an amplification of Gandhi's as well as Western ideals.

Jawaharlal Nehru and Norman Cousins, TALKS WITH NEHRU (New York: John Day, 1951). Tape-recorded conversations between a magazine editor and India's Prime Minister on democracy, Communism, Russia, China, the U.S. and the United Nations. The talks first appeared in two issues of the SATURDAY REVIEW OF LITERATURE.

Dana Raphael, THE AURA THAT WAS GANDHI (Patna: United Press Ltd., 1953). An analysis of the symbolism emanating from Gandhi, through his person and public behavior, and how it caught the imagination of the masses in terms of their own religious experience and mentality and at the same time instigated political action.

Vincent Sheehan, LEAD KINDLY LIGHT (New York: Random House, 1949). A clear, sympathetic explanation of Hindu philosophy, Gandhi's own beliefs and how he applied them, the story of his rise to leader of India's masses, the author's meetings with Gandhi, and a vivid description of the assassination and funeral of the Mahatma. The title of the book is taken from Gandhi's favorite hymn.

THE NEW INDIA: PROGRESS THROUGH DEMOCRACY (New York: The Macmillan Co., 1958). This book by the Planning Commission of the Indian government, sets forth the underlying approach and main features of India's economic and social programs embodied in her Second Five-Year Plan.

CURRICULUM VITAE

HOWARD BOONE JACOBSON attended the School of Journalism of the University of Missouri, where he received his Bachelor of Journalism and M.A. degrees. He has worked on both the editorial and advertising sides of several newspapers, in public relations and product merchandising, as an industrial editor, and for some years has been a consultant to management on communicating with employees. Professor Jacobson became associated with the University of Bridgeport (Conn.) in 1948, where he pioneered the development of one of the first degree programs in industrial journalism. He is chairman of the Department of Journalism and director of the Connecticut High School Journalism Workshop. He is a frequent contributor to magazines and research journals on current problems in education for journalism and is a member of the editorial board of THE JOURNALISM EDUCATOR. He is author of INDIA NOTEBOOK, a syndicated newspaper series on modern India, through which he traveled and lectured in 1953-54. He has published several reports in journals which analyze press treatment of India in the U.S. He is co-editor with Joseph S. Roucek of the recently published book, AUTOMATION AND SOCIETY.

DANA RAPHAEL, who is the wife of Professor Jacobson, is currently completing her doctoral studies in anthropology at Columbia University. She accompanied her husband to India in 1953-54, where she also lectured in several universities. She has written, THE AURA THAT WAS GANDHI, published in India in 1953.

Cross Currents

CHAPTER NINETEEN

THE AMERICAN WELFARE STATE: NEITHER IDEOLOGY NOR UTOPIA

Heinz Eulau

Stanford University

The New Deal of Franklin D. Roosevelt, just as the New Freedom of Woodrow Wilson before, and the Fair Deal of Harry Truman later, had its quota of ideologues, but was not an ideology; it had its following of true believers, but was not a chiliastic faith; it produced far-ranging reforms, but was not a crusade; it was rich in inventions, but was not an experiment; it mobilized huge majorities, but was not a revolt of the masses; it generated forceful national leadership, but was not a charismatic surrender. It is possible to see the New Deal as the fulfillment of the promise of American life — Herbert Croly's dream in the years before the First World War;[1] or as an exercise in instrumental pragmatism which John Dewey had celebrated in the years following that war.[2] But if it was the realization of the liberal promise or the application of the pragmatic philosophy, it was so by way of improvisation rather than design. All of these elements were present, but they do not express the dynamics of the New Deal. If it was anything, the New Deal between 1932 and 1940 was, simply and foremost, evidence of the viability of democratic politics in an age of crisis.

Ardently defended by its admirers, and bitterly denounced by its enemies,[3] the New Deal came to make a lasting impression on the American experience — an impression, I venture to say, which in the long run can only be compared with the birth of the nation itself and the fratricidal blood-letting of the Civil War. The New Deal fascinated and continues to fascinate the national consciousness, not only because it was an intense and dramatic political episode, but also because it was, like the birth of the United States and the Civil War, a national event. By comparison, the earlier New Freedom and the later Fair Deal were merely incidents—the former a pale prospectus, the latter a faded postscript, to the politically most exciting period in American history.[4]

NOT AN IDEOLOGY

Though the New Deal was non-ideological, this does not mean that it was anti-ideological. In fact, it was shot through with ideologies, or utopias, whichever emphasis one may prefer. Total planners and piecemeal planners, budget-balancers and deficit-spenders, trust-regulators and trust-busters, protectionists and free traders, "sound money" proponents and inflationists — all vied with each other under the hospitable tent that was the New Deal. Wall Street bankers, Midwest farmers, Harvard economists, Columbia lawyers, labor intellectuals, old-time progressives, new liberals, social workers — men of the Right, Left and Middle — supplied ideas and programs, if not panaceas. Theories were welcome as they had never been welcome before; and never before, or thereafter, did so many blueprints of a better order reach the citadel of influence. Ideas were, indeed, the true coins of the realm.[5]

But, for precisely these reasons, there was little of the ideological in the New Deal — if by ideology one means a coherent and consistent set of beliefs, values, opinions and aspirations. To attempt to construct out of the welter of these beliefs and values, opinions and aspirations an internally congruent system of thought is to do violence to history and to the meaning of the New Deal.[6] Not that such attempts have not been made, or will not be made in the future. But they can be made only at the risk of great distortion. For the New Deal was an ideologically much too elusive phenomenon to be squeezed into the convenient categories of ideological analysis. In fact, insofar as it responded to ideological pressures at all, the New Deal was engaged in a continuous effort to disengage itself from ideological commitments.[7]

The difficulty of ideological analysis is that it cannot easily free itself from the Aristotelian mode of thinking, with its neat and even aesthetically satisfying dichotomies. This is the mode of thought which pitches liberty against security, private property against public ownership, national regulation against decentralization, monopoly against competition.[8] Granted, the New Deal emphasized the positive role of national government and strong federal action. But, granted too, the consequences of such action, as in the federal grants-in-aid programs, were an enormous expansion and strengthening of both state and

416

municipal activities.[9] Granted, the Tennessee Valley Authority represented as "socialist" an undertaking as had ever been devised in the United States. But, granted too, one of its consequences was the flowering of private enterprise in an area where previously it had great trouble flowering.[10] Granted, the New Deal promoted social and economic security in manifold ways. But, granted too, it did not do so at the expense of liberty: there was hardly a period in American history in which public discussion of public issues and the freedom to speak freely had been practiced with as much abandon as under the New Deal.[11] The New Deal simply defies ideological classification.

All this does not mean that the New Deal was not anchored in a cultural milieu of attitudes and predispositions which was congenial to its operation. This milieu was the liberal tradition in America. As Louis Hartz has suggested, in one sense the whole American political tradition is liberal.[12] In this perspective, the New Deal, non-ideological though it was, was clearly an indication, if not a vindication, of liberalism. Without this tradition, there would have been no New Deal. But, in the American context, the liberal tradition as such has rarely been experienced as an ideology. Rather, it appears as a cultural given which, like the air we breathe, is so close, so natural, so much a part of our daily life that we fail to notice it. The liberal tradition explains, I suspect, why its many contradictions and inconsistencies were "built in" New Deal programs, plans and policies. For liberalism, unlike other isms, has never been a set of dogmas, but a state of mind.[13] It represents an attitude which insists on questioning self-evident propositions, partly to find out what evidence there is to support them, partly to discover possible alternatives. It follows that liberalism is not bound to any particular social or economic system. No wonder that so many different ideologues, theoreticians, administrators and politicians could find the New Deal a congenial environment in which to work. Indeed, they shaped that environment. And the New Deal reflected, in varying degrees and at varying times, the varying enthusiasms and different approaches to the national problems.[14]

NOT A FAITH

That the New Deal gave new hope to millions, that it brought new confidence into government, that it ultimately became a testament of national courage, there is little doubt. Where there had been drift, the New Deal offered mastery. Just as Hoover's "We are at the end of our string" had symbolized the old order,[15] so Roosevelt's "firm belief that the only thing we have to fear is fear itself" symbolized the new approach.[16] But at no time did the New Deal assume that man does not live by bread alone. It generated fresh expectations in the hearts of people who had recently experienced little but misery, and a new spirit came about the land. But it was a hope and a spirit nourished not by promises and good intentions, but by governmental action. The New Deal was a reconfirmation of the old American assumption that action is its own reward. What the New Deal articulated was not a faith in a better morrow, but a call for action now.[17]

And the people were captivated, not because they were asked to be true believers, but because action gave them a new sense of dignity. The dole had given them the minimum means of subsistence, and charity had made them loathe a humility to which they were not accustomed. Now they found their way into public works, conservation corps, rural settlements and, as the economy began to grind again, back into jobs in industry, transportation and commerce. They were grateful. But even if the New Deal had tried to take the role of the savior, it is doubtful that it could have saved many souls. What generated the new spirit that made the thirties so exciting was not government action alone. True, the government played a role as it had never played one in the lives of Americans before. But what sustained the popular drive and confidence that came with the New Deal was the old faith that man can control his destiny — given the conditions that make action and self-help possible.[18]

Much nonsense has been written to the effect that the New Deal made of Americans unthinking and faithful dependents of a "welfare state," so-called — a people which has lost initiative and entrusts its fate to the benevolence of an all-powerful government.[19] The welfare state, it is alleged, is the new dispensation — man's reward on this earth for conformity and compliance based on faith and political suicide. But the New Deal was not a sacred mission, but a most secular, indeed profane, manifestation of modern man's quest for security— not the security that comes from an anticipation of heavenly bliss, but the security that comes from an ability to make this earth one's home.[20]

The New Deal, then, was not an "escape from freedom," a surrender of the intellectual faculties. Rather than calling for faith, it was an enormous educational effort. Perhaps never before in the history of

418

the republic was it necessary to re-educate the preferences and redirect the energies of the people. Whatever one may wish to call it — propaganda or education — the American people were exposed to a flow of information about the activities of the government unexcelled in the past. And the people responded. There was new understanding of the difficulties besetting the nation, a new tolerance of innovations, and a new commitment to creative intelligence in politics. Rarely has there been so much knowledgeable participation of the people in public affairs. Letters poured into Washington, and the newspaper columns reflected popular interest. Rather than escaping from freedom, people once more had a genuine sense of being part of the governmental enterprise. Not submission to authority, but a lively feeling of one's efficacy, one's ability to influence the course of events characterized the popular response. It has been said that if the New Deal had wanted to assume totalitarian forms, it could have done so without much difficulty, for the people were ready to accept almost anything that would give them a better deal. Nothing could be further from reality. The New Deal was what it was, and became what it became, precisely because it did not promise a millennium, but because it confronted the American people with the harsh realities of the present, first at home, and then abroad.[21]

NOT A CRUSADE

To think of the New Deal as a unified program, a plan or a policy is as mistaken as to think of it as a movement or a crusade. There were many programs and policies, and there was more than a movement. What made the New Deal the phenomenon it was — a new deal in American life, a fresh start — was not a zest for reform, but the need to respond to national problems, as they were dictated by the exigencies of the moment, not as they may have been preconceived by reformers. Whatever preferences for reform may have motivated individual New Dealers as they found themselves in the seats of power and influence after the politically lean years of normalcy, the task at hand was to revive the economy, not to translate long-cherished proposals for reform into reality.

Reforms, of course, there were.[22] Some were successful and became permanent features of American life. Industrial violence, long the scourge of labor-management relations, gave way to the peaceful method of collective bargaining. Unemployment and old-age insurance programs remedied long-standing ills among the socially and economi-

419

cally most disadvantaged sector of the population. Securities legislation brought discipline and responsibility into the disorderly state of banking and investment practices. But other reforms were doomed to failure. Rural resettlement was a temporary stop-gap. and fell victim to its own idealism. The National Resources Planning Board never got off the ground. Other programs were conceived as self-liquidating and were liquidated, though some of them, like the Civilian Conservation Corps or Public Works Administration, left a rich heritage of national accomplishment. Still other programs represented *ad hoc* inventions to cope with pressing problems which had hardly been envisaged by the reformers. They were, in fact, determined efforts by the government to maintain the *status quo*. Programs such as agricultural adjustment or bank deposit insurance were not so much acts of reform as of preservation.

The one attempt made to conduct a crusade — the National Recovery Administration under Hugh Johnson — resembled more an Alice-in-Wonderland grotesque than a viable governmental structure and policy. NRA had important successes — abolishing child labor, setting maximum hours and minimum wages, removing unfair trade practices, and so forth — which, once re-enacted after NRA's demise, became monuments of social progress. But, on the whole, NRA was a fiasco because it tried to do too much in too little time within a single institutional setting which, at its roots, sought to reconcile business regulation by business itself with protection of free-market mechanisms by the government. The effort often led to an atmosphere of histrionics much at variance with that kind of earnestness that is the hallmark of reform. The Blue Eagle campaign was more a circus, really, than a crusade, and few tears were shed when the whole enterprise was declared unconstitutional.[23]

It is only in the perspective of history that the New Deal can possibly be conceived as a political or social movement. But even in this perspective it was only a new phase, a most intensive phase perhaps, forced by the great depression to heroic exertion, in the long-range national development which is the promise of American life. It was directly related — not only in ideas it shared, but also in some of its older personnel — to both the Square Deal and the New Freedom, to the historical trend to achieve Jeffersonian ends by Hamiltonian means.[24] That the Square Deal had been Republican and the New Freedom Democratic made the national character of the New Deal all the more poignant. Of all the deals in American history, the New Deal was truly national in scope, liberal in purpose, and effective in action.

NOT AN EXPERIMENT

The New Deal has come to be cited as the prize exhibit of the success of the experimental method in the making of public policy and the development of administrative techniques. The New Deal's willingness and capacity to chart new social and political paths is seen as an expression of John Dewey's philosophy of instrumentalism.[25] But this interpretation represents a tendency to overintellectualize the political process. It is more often in the nature of an apologia than of analysis. By calling anything new that is done an "experiment," success of the experiment is heralded as proof of the uses of experimentation, while failure is explained away as inconsequential. The analogy between social efforts to create new alternatives and scientific experimentation ignores more than it explains. In fact, when the metaphor becomes a myth, it may be detrimental to a genuine understanding of the New Deal.

Roosevelt himself gave credence to the experimental metaphor when he declared that what the country needed was "bold, persistent experimentation." Yet, one may doubt that his call for experimentation was intended to make experimental pragmatism into a political formula. His notion hardly included the scientist's image of the carefully designed and controlled experiment. As he suggested, "It is common sense to take a method and try it: if it fails, admit it frankly and try another. But above all, try something."[26] But an experiment is the very opposite of common sense. Quite clearly, Roosevelt's accent was less on the nature of the method used than on the injunction to "try something." Roosevelt was prepared to try things, not to test theoretical propositions or to follow hunches — his mind was much too untheoretical for that — but to meet urgent social needs and pressures. Indeed, many potential New Deal proposals never left the drafting boards, not because they might not have worked, but because they were politically unfeasible. And not a few others were prematurely terminated long before their success or failure could be demonstrated.[27]

Though the New Deal was not an experiment or a series of experiments, it was admittedly an experience in social inventiveness. There was, again in Roosevelt's words, no room for "foolish traditions." Innovation, not experiment, was the trade-mark of the New Deal. The

421

proliferation of administrative agencies came with the suspicion that the old-line departments would not or could not aggressively pursue the new policies; balancing the budget no longer meant what it had traditionally meant — social values defied accounting in terms of dollars and cents, and it was the national economy, not the government budget, that was thought to be at stake; an agriculture of abundance was to be realized, paradoxically, through promoting programs of scarcity, like killing pigs or sowing under the crops which could not be marketed at adequate price;[28] and on the political front, from Roosevelt's personal appearance at the 1932 Chicago convention to his breaking of the two-term tradition eight years later, the New Deal defied conventions.[29] Yet, it is interesting to note that in politics proper this proved most difficult, as the ill-fated "court-packing plan" or the President's abortive attempt to purge his opponents in the 1938 Democratic primaries demonstrated.[30]

But, paradoxically too, the New Deal with all its inventions was in the great American political and social tradition. For that tradition meant innovation: free religious worship, free public education, free public lands, a chance at economic betterment and social mobility, a broad democratic franchise and many other social gains had at first been innovations — inventions which at one time had made the difference between the Old World and the New. The New Deal was in the mainstream of that tradition, but again with a difference.

NOT A REVOLT

Easy comparison can be made between the New Deal's success in mobilizing great electoral majorities and the plebiscitary mirages performed by totalitarian regimes. Both, it has been claimed, represented that revolt of the masses which José Ortega y Gasset had so somberly described only a few years earlier.[31] Increased popular participation in the most far-reaching decision a national community can make — the election of its government — has been said to be a sign not of social health, but of social tension; an index of cleavage rather than consensus; evidence of despair rather than creative involvement.[32]

Whatever the veracity of this argument in regard to totalitarian mass behavior, it lacks relevance to the New Deal as a political event. The New Deal elections were not plebiscites, but hard-fought, free battles of the ballot. Even in the landslide election of 1936 almost seventeen million people, or about 38 per cent of the total electorate, voted for the Republican candidate. In spite of the personal attractiveness of the Democratic candidate, few campaigns in twentieth-century America have been as genuinely democratic as the early New Deal elections.[33] Although the press was predominantly anti-New Deal, rarely has there been so much discussion of the real issues facing the nation.[34] What moved the New Deal majorities was not a sense of revolt, but a renewed spirit of confidence in the willingness and ability of the government to carry out the popular mandate.

In organizing its electoral majorities, the New Deal restructured the political map. Its political techniques were anything but the contrived plebiscitarian technology of mass manipulation. That the New Deal succeeded in harnessing to its wagon the forces of labor, the young as well as the old, the socially underprivileged ethnic groups, farmers and urbanites, former Republicans as well as former Socialists, was not the result of hidden persuasion or silent threat, but its sensitivity to popular needs and demands.[35] In doing so, the New Deal was an almost perfect system of political feedback. Rarely in a modern democracy has the politics of democracy been equally conducive to the strengthening of democracy as a viable political system.

Had the New Deal been an ideology, a faith or a crusade, it might have been otherwise. But because it was none of these things, the New Deal could engage in its support the great electoral majorities which it needed in order to cope forcefully with the tasks of the nation. Nevertheless, impressive as the New Deal majorities were, it would be to simplify the situation if one elevated the New Deal into a flowering of the majoritarian principle as a "general will." The New Deal majority was, above all, a product of the political process as it had developed its particular flavor in the American culture. In the abstract, one might say that the majority demanded "something be done," or that it approved of what was done. Yet, that something was invariably done, sooner or later, does not mean that the majority, so-called, was agreed on what should be done, or that it endorsed what was done for the same reasons. To assume that the New Deal majorities were united in purposes and goals is not only naïve, but incorrect. The New Deal majorities were, in reality, only evidence of the complex processes of group adjustment and compromise that had preceded the electoral majorities; proof that these processes were reasonably efficient in generating the electoral power that was needed to continue the processes of adjustment and compromise.[36] Like all American majorities, the New

Deal majorities were the products of a salient coalition politics, only more so. No ideological or militant politics, no revolt of the masses, could have been equally successful — at least not in a free democracy.

NOT A CHARISMA

If ever the right man came to occupy the right office at the right time, Franklin D. Roosevelt was that man. Indeed, so close was the contemporary identification of New Deal and FDR, and so close does it continue to be in the perspective of history, that it is difficult to think of the one without the other. Both FDR's most devoted supporters and his most vociferous critics, as well as the historians of whatever persuasion, are agreed that it was the President who symbolized the New Deal. But to acknowledge that FDR was the chief architect of the New Deal, its most convincing spokesman, its forceful leader and also its most tangible target, is not to imply that he was a charismatic personality.[37] Undoubtedly, there were people who ascribed to him the qualities of charisma — infallibility, omniscience, omnipotence. And some of his most bitter opponents were equally intent on seeing in him the very incarnation of the charismatic opportunist. But neither orientation is correct. FDR was unduly loved by some and unduly hated by others, but to the vast majority of the American people he was Mr. President — the legally chosen head of a government whose function it was to represent and execute the power of the nation in time of crisis. This role FDR was superbly fitted and able to carry out.[38]

While it is facile to interpret the New Deal in terms of the President's role and personality, one wonders what FDR would have been like as chief executive without the New Deal? Was it because FDR was not an ideologue, a reformer or a prophet that the New Deal was not an ideology, a faith or a crusade for reform? Or was it because the New Deal was none of these things that FDR came to play the role he did? A categorical answer is impossible. The President's personality and the character of the New Deal, if it is permissible to speak of character, were admirably blended to produce the kind of strong governmental leadership which the nation required in the moment of crisis.[39] But this makes it all the more necessary not to exaggerate, yet also not to minimize, the role of the President in the total configuration of the New Deal. Because the tendency to exaggerate has probably been the dominant one, it seems desirable to point to some less frequently noticed features of the New Deal's personnel.

While Roosevelt never allowed the impression to prevail that he was not boss and master of the situation, his effectiveness as a leader did not derive from an unqualified loyalty that he may have been able to extract from his "subordinates." Rather, it derived from his ability to allow his lieutenants enough free-wheeling initiative to work out programs and policies — and it was one of his favorite images to see himself as the quarterback who was merely called upon to call the signals. The forceful leadership provided by the New Deal was not just Roosevelt's, but truly the product of teamwork. Leadership under the New Deal was both concentrated, in the White House, and decentralized, in the many departments and agencies of the federal government, most of them headed by able men who themselves were leaders, not henchmen or yes-men.[40]

Moreover, the spirit of leadership under the New Deal was not only pervasive in the executive branch, but also in the legislative branch, and, after the mandate of 1936, in the judicial branch as well. There has been a tendency to neglect the part played by Congress in providing political leadership. There were the "Hundred Days," it is true, when the new Congress had little choice but to go along with the President's "must" programs. But the New Deal Congresses were not simply "rubber-stamp" legislatures. They included men of vision, wisdom and sagacity, progressives who often succeeded in moving the White House in directions in which it would not have moved on its own initiative.[41] Similarly, once the Supreme Court — or rather two of its members, including the Chief Justice — had realized that it could not set itself up against the wishes of the great majority of the people, the representative Congress and the popular President, it produced decisions which themselves were important ingredients of New Deal policies.[42]

It is in this larger context of "collective leadership" shared by all the branches of the federal government that the President's role must be located. Economic policies and social programs came from many sources — braintrusters, interest groups, administrators, Congressmen and finally Justices. It was Roosevelt's genius that he could pick men with ideas, and it was his glory that he encouraged ideas; it was his skill that he could articulate both popular needs and governmental responses; it was his confidence that he could transmit similar confidence to his associates; it was his power that he could humor, persuade and, if necessary, threaten those who sat on the sidelines; it was his personality that he could make charm and courage instruments of government; above all, it was his spirit that he could convey his own idealism to the people as well as to those who worked with him and for him.[43]

But Roosevelt was not an ideologue — for he did not work with theoretical preconceptions, but with presuppositions. He was not a prophet—for his faith was terrestrial, not celestial. He was not a crusader — for he did not do many things he might have done by way of reform. He was not an agitator — for he was not driven by frustration, but committed to the proposition that common problems are best solved by common efforts. He was not a charismatic leader — for his own self-image as a politician forbade a charismatic image to be held by others. Roosevelt was a politician who saw that the business of government was politics, and who came to the business of government as a politician.

A MATURE POLITICS

If the New Deal was not an ideology, a faith, a crusade, an experiment, a revolt or a charisma, what was it? In retrospect, what makes the New Deal so memorable, so significant an event in the history of the United States is that it is both a symbol and evidence of the nation's political maturity, its ability to solve its problems through politics rather than through ideology or violence. Politicians though they were, the Founding Fathers essentially distrusted politics. Whatever their real commitments, they believed in the cult of reason and natural law. In the Civil War, ideological intransigence — Lincoln, who came too late and passed away too early, excepted — underlined the poverty of politics, so largely responsible for both the violence and its unfortunate aftermath. By way of contrast, the New Deal was neither distrustful of politics nor poor in political strategies. If a commitment there was, it was a commitment to a mature politics.

A mature politics cannot afford to be either ideological or utopian. Ideologists and utopians are essentially apolitical. They are, in many respects, like children who are preoccupied almost exclusively with what they want when they want it, for whom their little selves are the center of the cosmos.[44] Preoccupied with their own diagnoses and therapies, ideologists and utopians are, paradoxically, "thoughtless," in the literal sense of the word — blind to the needs of others and unconcerned with the consequences of their self-centered aspirations for others. Responsibility is a concept alien to both children and ideo-

426

logues alike. Maturity, on the other hand, is the capacity to respond to others without making the demands of the self the sole criterion of perception and behavior. Real and necessary as the demands of the mature person are, maturity involves recognition of the legitimate interests of others. A mature politics involves adjustment, compromise, integration. It can never be a purely ideological politics which exaggerates the importance of the self at the expense of the other, or which may even mean the destruction of the other.[45]

The New Deal was a politics of maturity in this sense, for it brought to the problems it faced political, not ideological solutions. This is often not understood by its ideological critics or ideological defenders. The very debate which the New Deal aroused, and continues to arouse, is the best evidence. The New Deal is "incomprehensible" to the ideologues of the Right and Left because it was so unideological, because it was not a "scheme" but a "deal" so different from the political solitaire which the ideologue likes to play. The New Deal was a search for acceptable solutions to problems rather than an imposition of preconceived solutions on problems. The ideologues and theoreticians were necessary to the New Deal, vital in its growth and development, but they could not be its conductors. Some were disgusted, others despaired, unable to fathom the rationale of a program which was no program and had no rationale that fitted their ideological preconceptions. Those who stayed with the New Deal — men as different in their interests as Harold Ickes, the old progressive, or Jesse Jones, the financier, or Henry Wallace, the Republican farmer — served the New Deal for what it was: not a return to an ideological yesteryear, or a road to a utopian tomorrow, but a political enterprise which harnessed political forces in the spirit of political maturity.

It was not so much a characteristic of the New Deal's political maturity that many ideas and interests found expression in the hurly-burly of politics, but that politics took these ideas and interests seriously, that it encouraged their expression, that it took it for granted that these ideas and interests would clash, and that it was ready to give, but also to take away. The New Deal represented, on the level of national politics, a tough-mindedness that allowed for little ideological self-indulgence. Ideological thinking, however camouflaged, is tender-minded because it is self-indulgent. But in politics self-indulgence means bargaining from a position of weakness rather than strength. It represents an escape from a politics of maturity, not a recognition

427

of the potentialities as well as limitations of political life. The New Deal was politically tough and mature, for it accepted the limits of the possible.

Too much emphasis has been placed on the role of the "brain trust" and the intellectuals who joined the New Deal.[46] That they played an enormous and desirable role in orienting the public policies of the New Deal cannot be denied. But to assume that they operated with the single-mindedness of an idealized high command is to ignore the great diversity of backgrounds and opinions that they brought to bear on the common effort. Rarely did New Deal measures represent clear-cut ideological preferences. Programs were proposed, adjustments were made, compromises were negotiated, and the new syntheses only remotely resembled the original proposals. The New Deal was a governmental process which reflected the necessities and obstacles of a mature democratic politics.

Only when the shadow of war had become a specter worse than depression, and when the New Deal had remedied much of what sickened American life, did politics give way to defense and apologia as well as to surrender of the political imagination. There appeared the bandwagon mentality—what Morris Cohen has called "the vile habit of thinking that the latest is always the best"—and the convenient belief that present trends will continue indefinitely into the future. It was then that the New Deal tended to become an affair of pronunciamento and magic formula. But this, in fact, meant the end of the New Deal. Yet, it is against this later phase that the New Deal can be best assessed—as a flowering of sensitivity to the paradoxes, ambiguities, complications, compromises and adventures of politics. To live with these characteristics, not only to tolerate them, but to thrive on them, was the mark of that political maturity which distinguished the New Deal as a national event.

SELECTED BIBLIOGRAPHY

Daniel Aaron, MEN OF GOOD HOPE: A STORY OF AMERICAN PROGRESSIVES (New York: Oxford University Press, 1951). An attempt to rehabilitate the progressive tradition through a reappraisal of such thinkers as Emerson, Parker, George, Bellamy, Lloyd, Howells and Veblen. Progressivism fails "when it permits a respect for power to become an admiration for *power* qua power."

Max Ascoli, INTELLIGENCE IN POLITICS (New York: W. W. Norton and Company, 1936). A much neglected book by the founder and editor of THE REPORTER. Democracy is not incompatible with intellectual activities. An adjustment is needed between intelligence, conscious of social responsibility, and political reality.

Daniel J. Boorstin, THE GENIUS OF AMERICAN POLITICS (Chicago: University of Chicago Press, 1953). America has not produced "grand" political theories. Rather, there is a broad consensus and acceptance of "givens." American political thinking should not be forced into ideological straitjackets.

Henry Steele Commager, THE AMERICAN MIND (New Haven: Yale University Press, 1950). An interpretation of American thought and character since the 1880's. Particular emphasis is put on what distinguishes American thought from English and European sources. An excellent introduction to the literature.

Merle Curti, THE GROWTH OF AMERICAN THOUGHT (New York: Harper & Brothers, 1943). The best and most comprehensive survey of social and political ideas in America from colonial times to the New Deal, a magisterial compendium and handy reference book which, nevertheless, makes good reading.

Arthur A. Ekirch, Jr., THE DECLINE OF AMERICAN LIBERALISM (New York: Longmans, Green and Company, 1955). A nostalgic celebration of Jeffersonian liberalism, in comparison with which later developments, from Jacksonian democracy to Progressivism and New Deal, are deemed deteriorations, if not betrayals, of the liberal tradition.

Carl J. Friedrich, THE NEW IMAGE OF THE COMMON MAN (Boston: The Beacon Press, 1950). A reaffirmation of the democratic and humanistic ethic and its institutional foundations, especially majority rule and representative government. Even if man is not as rational as classical theory assumed, he is yet politically capable to run his own affairs.

Harry K. Girvetz, FROM WEALTH TO WELFARE (Stanford: Stanford University Press, 1950). A perspicacious dissection of the changing contents of liberalism in evolution, cast in a broad psychological, political and economic frame of reference. The problem of individualism and collectivism is discussed dispassionately and lucidly.

Eric F. Goldman, RENDEZVOUS WITH DESTINY (New York: Alfred A. Knopf, 1952). An assessment in historical perspective of the tradition of dissent and of the difficulties of reform in a plural society like the American. Skillfully combines the discussion of ideas with human portraits.

Louis Hartz, THE LIBERAL TRADITION IN AMERICA (New York: Harcourt, Brace and Company, 1955). A superb study of the development of liberalism in America, really the only "ism" that has ever been successful. The source of American liberalism is found in the absence of feudal institutions. Includes an interesting chapter on the New Deal.

Richard Hofstadter, THE AMERICAN POLITICAL TRADITION AND THE MEN WHO MADE IT (New York: Alfred A. Knopf, 1948). An interpretation of American politics by way of twelve biographical portraits of American Presidents. Includes a perceptive chapter on Franklin Roosevelt.

Murray Kempton, PART OF OUR TIME: SOME MONUMENTS AND RUINS OF THE THIRTIES (New York: Simon and Schuster, 1955). A first-class account of the Communist movement in the thirties and of some of the men and women who succumbed to it, by a well-known journalist. Makes exciting reading.

Harold J. Laski, THE AMERICAN DEMOCRACY (New York: The Viking Press, 1948). In spite of many shortcomings in interpretation and factual errors, Laski's diagnosis of American politics and social life from the point of view of an English Socialist makes rewarding reading for acquisition of a wider perspective.

Max Lerner, AMERICA AS CIVILIZATION (New York: Simon and Schuster, 1957). This compendious review of many facets of American life and thought by a former militant liberal who has come to accept the viewpoint of pluralistic realism serves to provide a broad perspective of the context of American politics.

Walter Lippmann, THE PUBLIC PHILOSOPHY (Boston: Little, Brown and Company, 1955). The latest statement of the natural law interpretation of liberalism by America's most restless and perhaps most creative political thinker of the twentieth century. The decline of liberalism is ascribed to loss of faith in natural law and the illegitimate rise of executive power.

Francis M. Myers, THE WARFARE OF DEMOCRATIC IDEALS (Yellow Springs, Ohio: The Antioch Press, 1956). The impact of various schools of formal philosophy — empiricism, logical positivism, neo-Thomism, idealism and instrumentalism — on the operation of the democratic ideals.

J. Roland Pennock, LIBERAL DEMOCRACY: ITS MERITS AND PROSPECTS (New York: Rinehart and Company, 1950). A solid, scholarly discussion of liberal and democratic ideas in relationship to their institutional contexts and policy alternatives.

Clinton Rossiter, CONSERVATISM IN AMERICA (New York: Alfred A. Knopf, 1955). An attempt to discover a "conservative tradition" in America. The author finds it evidently difficult to distinguish conservatism from liberalism. Includes a chapter on conservatism in the age of Roosevelt and Eisenhower.

Arthur M. Schlesinger, Jr., THE VITAL CENTER (Boston: Houghton Mifflin Company, 1949). A spirited discussion of the problems confronting American liberalism in the face of the Communist challenge. Progressives are criticized for their failure to take responsibility.

David Spitz, PATTERNS OF ANTI-DEMOCRATIC THOUGHT (New York: The Macmillan Company, 1949). A lucid analysis and criticism of such anti-democratic theorists as Burnham, Dennis, Santayana, Babbit and others, from the point of view of democratic liberalism.

Morton G. White, SOCIAL THOUGHT IN AMERICA: THE REVOLT AGAINST FORMALISM (New York: The Viking Press, 1949). An appraisal of the men whose ideas shaped much of New Deal thinking — Dewey, Holmes, Veblen, Beard and Robinson —from the standpoint of professional philosophy.

CURRICULUM VITAE

HEINZ EULAU, Professor of Political Science at Stanford University, received his Ph.D. from the University of California (Berkeley) in 1941. He served as an Organizations and Propaganda Analyst, Special War Policies Unit, Department of Justice, 1941-1943, and as an Assistant Editor, THE NEW REPUBLIC, 1943-1947. From 1947 to 1957 he taught at Antioch College. He was a Ford Foundation Fellow, 1951-1952, and a Social Science Research Council Fellow, 1956-1957. During 1957-1958 he was a Fellow at the Center for Advanced Study in the Behavioral Sciences. He is editor (with Samuel J. Eldersveld and Morris Janowitz) of POLITICAL BEHAVIOR (The Free Press, 1956) and (with John C. Wahlke) of LEGISLATIVE BEHAVIOR (The Free Press, 1959). He has contributed numerous articles on political theory, public policy and political behavior to both learned and other journals.

NOTES

NOTES TO CHAPTER ONE

[1] See Carle C. Zimmerman and M. E. Frampton, *FAMILY AND SOCIETY* (New York, Van Nostrand Co., 1935), v.

[2] On this problem of the state of sociology, which applies in a considerable degree and similarly to the other social sciences, see Carle C. Zimmerman, PATTERNS OF SOCIAL CHANGE (Washington, D. C.: Public Affairs Press, 195), all; Carle C. Zimmerman, "Contemporary Trends in Sociology in America and Abroad," in Joseph S. Roucek, Ed., CONTEMPORARY SOCIOLOGY (New York: Philosophical Library, 1959), 3-25.

NOTES TO CHAPTER TWO

[1] THE OXFORD UNIVERSAL DICTIONARY ON HISTORICAL PRINCIPLES, 3rd edition, revised with addenda, revised and edited by C. T. Onions (Oxford: The Clarendon Press, 1955), 1954.

[2] As quoted in R. N. Carew Hunt, THE THEORY AND PRACTICE OF COMMUNISM (New York: The Macmillan Co., 1951), 151.

[3] Lenin, "Our Tasks and the Soviet of Workingmen's Deputies," SOCHINENIYA (Fourth edition, Moscow 1949), X, 3, as quoted by Merle Fainsod, HOW RUSSIA IS RULED (Cambridge: Harvard University Press, 1953), 51.

[4] Lenin, SELECTED WORKS, Volume VI, 23, as quoted in Gwendolen M. Carter, John H. Herz, John C. Ranney, MAJOR FOREIGN POWERS, 3rd edition, (New York: Harcourt Brace & Co., 1957), 594.

[5] Philip Selznick, THE ORGANIZATIONAL WEAPON (New York: McGraw-Hill Book Company, 1952), 92.

[6] Carter, Herz, Ranney, *op. cit.*, 595.

[7] *LOC. CIT.*

[8] "The Role of the Party in the Proletarian Revolution," THESES OF THE SECOND CONGRESS OF THE COMMUNIST INTERNATIONAL, (1920) as quoted in Selznick, *op. cit.*, p. 88.

[9] As quoted in W. W. Kulski, THE SOVIET REGIME (Syracuse: Syracuse University Press, 1959), 207.

[10] S. S. Studenikin, SOVETSKOW ADMINISTRATIVNOE PRAVO, All-Union Institute of Juristic Sciences of the Ministry of Justice of the USSR (Moscow, 1949), 11 and 12, as quoted in Kulski, 207.

[11] A. A. Askerov, et al., SOVETSKOE GOSUDARSTVENNOE PRAVO, Institute of Law of the Academy of Sciences of the USSR (Moscow) 1948, 429, as quoted in Kulski, 208.

[12] Peter S. H. Tang, COMMUNIST CHINA TODAY (New York: Frederick A. Praeger, 1957), 384.

[13] W. W. Kulski, OP. CIT., 812.

[14] U.S. Senate, Committee of the Judiciary, Internal Security Sub-Committee, THE REVIVAL OF THE COMMUNIST INTERNATIONAL AND ITS SIGNIFICANCE FOR THE UNITED STATES (Washington: Government Printing Office, 1959), 31.

[15] IBID., 30.

[16] U.S. Congress, House of Representatives, Committee of Un-American Activi-

ties, LANGUAGE AS A COMMUNIST WEAPON, Consultation with Dr. Stefan T. Possony, (Washington Government Printing Office, March 2, 1959), 14 and 15.

[17] IBID., 15.

[18] LOC. CIT.

NOTES TO CHAPTER THREE

[1] Mao Tse-tung, ON PEOPLE'S DEMOCRATIC DICTATORSHIP (1949).

[2] IBID.

[3] Mao Tse-tung, KAT-TSAO WO-MEN TI HSUEH-HSI (TO REFORM OUR LEARNING).

[4] HONQUI (Red Flag) editorial, September 1, 1958.

[5] JEN MIN JIH PAO editorial, September 3, 1958.

[6] See the Communiqué and Resolutions of the Sixth Plenary Session of the Central Committee of the Communist Party of China in PEKING REVIEW, December 23, 1958.

[7] For a summary of the various forms of state capitalism as transitional stages in the transformation of industry and commerce, see Chien Chia-chu, "State Capitalism in China," PEOPLE'S CHINA, December 1, 1954. For a summary of steps in the liquidation of private enterprise, see Theodore H. E. Chen, "The Liquidation of Private Business in Communist China," FAR EASTERN SURVEY, June, 1955.

[8] Mao Tse-tung, THE CHINESE REVOLUTION AND THE COMMUNIST PARTY OF CHINA (1939).

[9] Liu Shao-ch'i, INTERNATIONALISM AND NATIONALISM (1948).

[10] IBID.

[11] Mao Tse-tung, ON THE NEW DEMOCRACY.

[12] Mao Tse-tung, ON PEOPLE'S DEMOCRATIC DICTATORSHIP.

[13] Mao Tse-tung, "INTRODUCTORY REMARKS TO THE COMMUNIST" (1939).

[14] JEN MIN JIH PAO (Peking: People's Daily), June 26, 1958.

[15] Fang Ching-hsin, "The Flourishing Socialist Camp," PEKING REVIEW, January 6, 1959, 18.

[16] PEKING REVIEW, October 28, 1958, 17.

[17] JEN MIN JIH PAO, August 20, 1958.

[18] Mao Tse-tung, RECTIFY THE PARTY'S STYLE IN WORK (1942).

[19] See quotations in Lu Ting-yi, "Education Must Be Combined with Productive Labor," JEN MIN JIH PAO, September 2, 1958. English translation in PEKING REVIEW September 9, 1959, 5-12.

[20] IBID. (PEKING REVIEW), September 9, 1958, 11.

NOTES TO CHAPTER FOUR

[1] "Collective Leadership," NEWS FROM BEHIND THE IRON CURTAIN, III, 7 (July, 1954), 21-33.

[2] See, for instance SCINTEIA (Bucharest), February 26, 1956; NEUES DEUTSCHLAND (East Berlin), March 4, 1956; TRYBUNA L'UDU (Warsaw), March 10, 1956; RUDE PRAVO (Prague), April 10, 1956; also, NEWS FROM

BEHIND THE IRON CURTAIN, 5, 4 and 5 (April and May, 1956), 46-48 and 42-45, respectively.

³ See, for instance, RUDE PRAVO (Prague), January 29 and June 19, 1957.

⁴. See, for instance, SZABAD NEP (Budapest), May 30, 1956; SCINTEIA (Bucharest), June 23, 1956; RUDE PRAVO (Prague), June 12, 1956; also, NEWS FROM BEHIND THE IRON CURTAIN, IV, 9 (September, 1955), 49-50, and V, 11 (November, 1956), 54-56.

⁵ RUDE PRAVO (Prague), December 8, 1956, and June 19-23, 1958; RABOTNICHESKO DELO (Sofia), December 6, 1956; SCINTEIA (Bucharest), March 3, 1957; Moscow Declaration of the Twelve Communist Parties of November, 1957.

⁶ For a few samples see: RUDE PRAVO (Prague), February 27, March 4, and April 10, 1956; SCINTEIA (Bucharest), February 26, 1956; NEUES DEUTSCHLAND (East Berlin), March 4, 1956; TRYBUNA L'UDU (Warsaw), March 10, 23, 26, and April 9, 1956; RABOTNICHESKO DELO (Sofia), April 9, 1956; EAST EUROPE, 8, 3 (March, 1959), 36-38 and 51-56.

⁷ The text of the dissertation, whose authenticity is beyond any doubt, was smuggled out of Hungary and published in New York: IMRE NAGY ON COMMUNISM: IN DEFENSE OF THE "NEW COURSE" (New York: Frederick A. Praeger, 1957). Extensive excerpts are reprinted in EAST EUROPE, VI, 7 (July, 1957), 3-16.

⁸ For a comprehensive review of the course of the uprising as reflected by the Hungarian broadcasts see THE REVOLT IN HUNGARY, A DOCUMENTARY CHRONOLOGY OF EVENTS (New York: Free Europe Committee, 1956), 112.

⁹ IBID., 7-8.

¹⁰ Italics added.

¹¹ IBID., 14.

¹² Published in TRYBUNA L'UDU (Warsaw), October 21, 1956. Excerpts in English may be found in NEWS FROM BEHIND THE IRON CURTAIN, V, 11 (November, 1956), 4-5 and 42.

¹³ TRYBUNA L'UDU, May 16, 1957. For excerpts in English see EAST EUROPE, VI, 7, (July, 1957), 38-42.

¹⁴ TRYBUNA L'UDU, October 26 and 29, 1957.

¹⁵ TRYBUNA L'UDU, March 11, 1959. Excerpts in English may be found in EAST EUROPE, VIII, 5, (May, 1959), 3-12.

¹⁶ See, for instance, L. B., "Revisionist Poland," THE WORLD TODAY, XIV, 6, (June, 1958), 247-259.

¹⁷ PRAVDA and IZVESTIA (Moscow), November 22, 1957.

¹⁸ See, for instance: Leszek Kolakowski, "Responsibility and History," NOWA KULTURA, September 1, 8 and 15, 1957; English excerpts in EAST EUROPE, VI, 12 (December, 1957), 12-15, 7, 2 (February, 1958), 17-21, and 7, 3 (March, 1958), 24-28 VII, 5 (May 1958), 12-16; Jerzy Szacki, "Some Remarks About Contemporary Marxism," PRZEGLAD KULTURALNY, 16 (1957); Leszek Kolakowski, "Valid and Outdated Conceptions of Marxism," NOWA KULTURA, January 27, 1957; S. Brodzski, "Which Democracy?" TRYBUNA L'UDU, December 2, 1956; also, "Ferment in Poland," NEWS FROM BEHIND THE IRON CURTAIN, IV, 3 (March, 1956), 3-14; "The Revolt of the Intellectuals", IBID, V, 6 (June, 1956), 3-10; "Poland's October Revolution," EAST EUROPE, VI, 1 and 2 (January and February, 1957), 3-15 and 3-15, respectively; L. B., "Revisionist Poland," THE WORLD TODAY, XIV, 6 (June, 1958), 247-259.

¹⁹ This has been apparent, in particular, at and around various post-Stalin congresses and conferences of writers, artists, educators, student, youth and other groups. See, for instance, Edward Taborsky, "The Revolt of the Communist Intellec-

437

tuals," THE REVIEW OF POLITICS, XIX, 3 (July, 1957), 308-329; "The Revolt of Intellectuals," NEWS FROM BEHIND THE IRON CURTAIN, 5, 6 and 7 (June and July, 1956), 3-17 and 3-14, respectively; a rich documentation in English may also be found in many issues of EAST EUROPE and PROBLEMS OF COMMUNISM.

20 IBID.

21 RUDE PRAVO, January 9, 1958.

22 In "Responsibility and History", OP. CIT.

23 "Polish Intelligentsia Clubs," EAST EUROPE, VI, 9 (September, 1957), 15-26; "Studijní krouzky v C SR", CESKOSLOVENSKY ZPRAVODAJ, 216 (October 9, 1958), 1-2; "Current Trends in Czechoslovak Culture," EAST EUROPE, VII, 12 (December, 1958), 26-32.

NOTES TO CHAPTER FIVE

1 Quoted in Vladimir Dedijer, TITO (New York, Simon and Schuster, 1953), 418.

2 YUGOSLAVIA'S WAY: THE PROGRAM OF THE LEAGUE OF THE COMMUNISTS OF YUGOSLAVIA, Stoyan Pribechevich, Trans. (New York: All Nations Press, 1958), 71.

3 IBID., 13.

4 Edvard Kardelj, quoted in the NEW YORK TIMES, May 6, 1959.

5 YUGOSLAVIA'S WAY, OP. CIT., 212.

6 Vladimir Velibit, "Yugoslavia on Her Way Toward a Socialist Democracy," INTERNATIONAL AFFAIRS, XXX (April, 1954), 160.

7 Vladimer Dedijer, OP. CIT., 422-423.

8 Edvard Kardelj, in intro. to NEW FUNDAMENTAL LAW OF YUGOSLAVIA (Belgrade: Union of Jurists' Association of Yugoslavia, 1953), 9.

9 Edvard Kardelj, in a speech before the Federal People's Assembly of Yugosalvia, December 6, 1956, in THE SOVIET-YUGOSLAV CONTROVERSY, 1948-1958, A DOCUMENTARY RECORD, Robert Bass and Elizabeth Marbury, Eds. (New York: Prospect Books. 1959), 99.

10 Quoted in Vladimir Dedijer, OP. CIT., 427.

11 YUGOSLAVIA'S WAY, OP. CIT., 13.

12 Milovan Djilas, THE NEW CLASS (New York: Frederick A. Praeger, 1957), 49-55 PASSIM.

13 YUGOSLAVIA'S WAY, OP. CIT., 29-31 PASSIM.

14 Milovan Djilas, "Yugoslavia-Soviet Relations", INTERNATIONAL AFFAIRS, XXVII (April, 1951), 172.

15 There is still no workers' control in the electric power industry and in communications.

16 FUNDAMENTAL LAW OF YUGOSLAVIA, Art. 25.

17 Edvard Kardelj, in intro. to THE NEW FUNDAMENTAL LAW OF YUGOSLAVIA, OP. CIT., 23.

18 Tito, quoted in Vladimir Dedijer, OP. CIT., 431.

19 Edvard Kardelj, in speech of December 6, 1956, OP. CIT., 88.

20 YUGOSLAVIA'S WAY, OP. CIT., 122.

21 John Kenneth Galbraith, JOURNEY TO POLAND AND YUGOSLAVIA (Cambridge, Massachusetts: Harvard University Press, 1958), 76.

22 Vladimir Velibit, OP. CIT., 165.

23 YUGOSLAVIA'S WAY, OP. CIT., 24.
24 PRAVDA, January 28, 1959.
25 YUGOSLAVIA'S WAY, OP. CIT., 64.
26 Vladimir Dedijer, OP. CIT., 432.
27 NEW YORK TIMES, January 20, 1959.
28 IBID., November 10, 1958.
29 Edvard Kardelj, intro. to THE NEW FUNDAMENTAL LAW OF YUGO-
SLAVIA, OP. CIT., 50.
30 YUGOSLAVIA'S WAY, OP. CIT., 22.
31 YUGOSLAVIA'S WAY, OP. CIT., 39.
32 YUGOSLAVIA'S WAY, OP. CIT., 120.

NOTES TO CHAPTER SIX

1 Quoted in Hans Gerth, THE FIRST INTERNATIONAL: MINUTES OF
THE HAGUE CONGRESS OF 1872 WITH RELATED DOCUMENTS (Madison,
Wisc.; The University of Wisconsin Press, 1958), 259.

2 G. D. H. Cole, THE SECOND INTERNATIONAL 1889-1914, Volume III,
Part II of A HISTORY OF SOCIALIST THOUGHT (London: Macmillan & Co.,
Ltd., 1956), 962-976.

3 James Joll, THE SECOND INTERNATIONAL 1889-1914 (New York:
Praeger, 1956), 105.

4 G. D. H. Cole, COMMUNISM AND SOCIAL DEMOCRACY 1914-1931,
Volume IV, Part I of A HISTORY OF SOCIALIST THOUGHT (London: Macmillan & Co., Ltd., 1956), 329.

5 Adolf Sturmthal, "Democratic Socialism in Europe," WORLD POLITICS,
III (October, 1950), 109.

6 IBID., 109 ff.

7 The structure of the Socialist International resembles earlier models. The
typical organs consist of a Congress, the supreme body, proclaiming basic principles
and admitting new members, to be convened every two years; a smaller Council
of two delegates from each member party, formulating policy toward current
political issues and electing the officers, to meet at least once yearly; the Bureau,
dealing with organizational matters; and the Secretariat. See Julius Braunthal,
Ed., YEARBOOK OF THE INTERNATIONAL SOCIALIST LABOUR MOVE-
MENT, 1956-1957 (London: Lincolns-Prager International Yearbook Publishing
Co., Ltd., 1956), 15-16.

8 IBID, 39 ff. The quotations to follow are from the Declaration. Also see
Julius Braunthal, "The Socialist International in World Affairs," a lecture sponsored
by the Social Science Foundation, Univ. of Denver, Denver, Colo., Nov. 28, 1958
(mimeographed), 1-12.

9 Space limitations preclude treating the Swiss, Belgian, Dutch and Finnish
parties. They too have played a significant role in their own countries and in the
Internationals. Not to be forgotten are the contributions made by socialist parties
in Eastern Europe, now outlawed but active in varying degrees before World War
II.

10 Klaus Schütz, "Die Sozialdemokratie im Nachkriegsdeutschland," Section
II, 157-271, in PARTEIEN IN DER BUNDESREPUBLIK (Stuttgart: Ring Verlag,
1955), 170.

11 F. R. Allemann, "German Socialists Reorganize", THE NEW LEADER, XLI

(June 16, 1958), 18-19. See also Klaus-Peter Schulz, OPPOSITION ALS POL-ITISCHES SCHICKSAL (Köln : Verlag für Politik und Wirtschaft, 1958).

[12] Walter F. Hahn, "The Socialist Party of Austria: Retreat from Marx," JOURNAL OF CENTRAL EUROPEAN AFFAIRS, XV (July, 1955), 115-133.

[13] Karl Czernetz, "Nur keine Selbstzufriedenheit," DIE ZUKUNFT, Nos. 5, 6 (May-June, 1956), 128-131.

[14] Josef Hindels, "Kann der Sozialismus den Mensch ändern?," DIE ZUKUNFT, Nos. 5/6 (May-June, 1956), 123-127.

[15] W. Hilton-Young, THE ITALIAN LEFT: A SHORT HISTORY OF POLITI-CAL SOCIALISM IN ITALY (London: Longmans, Green and Co., 1949), 207.

[16] IBID., 150.

[17] Saragat's secession from the PSI was the forerunner of others. Giuseppa Romita left in 1949, and Carlo Matteotti in 1951. A United Socialist Party (PSU) was formed by Romita, Silone, Mondolfo and Matteo Matteotti, but remained a small splinter group. In May, 1951, it united with the Saragat faction to form the PSDI. Raphael Zariski, "Problems and Prospects of Democratic Socialism in France and Italy," JOURNAL OF POLITICS, XVIII (May, 1956), 254-280.

[18] Giuseppe Saragat, "Italy's New Government," THE NEW LEADER, XLI (August 18-25, 1958), 18.

[19] Leo Valiani, "Die ideologische Entwicklung des demokratischen Sozialismus in Italien," Chapter X, 161-181, in Julius Braunthal, Ed., SOZIALISTISCHE WELTSTIMMEN (Berlin and Hannover: J. H. W. Dietz, 1958), 179-181.

[20] E. Drexel Godfrey, Jr., THE FATE OF THE FRENCH NON-COMMUNIST LEFT (Garden City, N.Y.: Doubleday & Co., 1955), 1-11.

[21] See his, FOR ALL MANKIND (New York, N.Y.: The Viking Press, 1946).

[22] Henry W. Ehrmann, "The Decline of the Socialist Party," CHAPTER XI, 181-199, in Edward M. Earle, Ed., MODERN FRANCE: PROBLEMS OF THE THIRD AND FOURTH REPUBLICS (Princeton, N.J.: Princeton Univ. Press, 1951), 186.

[23] Maurice Duverger, "S.F.I.O.: Mort ou Transfiguration?," LES TEMPS MODERNES, X (May, 1955), 1863-1885.

[24] Philip Williams, POLITICS IN POST-WAR FRANCE; PARTIES AND THE CONSTITUTION IN THE FOURTH REPUBLIC (London: Longmans, Green and Co., 1954), 69-70.

[25] Torolf Elster, "The Ideological Development of Democratic Socialism in Norway," SOCIALIST INTERNATIONAL INFORMATION, V (November 5, 1955), mimeographed reprint, 3.

[26] Dankwart A. Rüstow, "Scandinavia: Working Multiparty Systems," Chapter V, 169-193, in Sigmund Neumann, Ed., MODERN POLITICAL PARTIES (Chicago: the University of Chicago Press, 1956), passim.

[27] Ernst Christianson, "The Ideological Development of Democratic Socialism in Denmark," SOCIALIST INTERNATIONAL INFORMATION, VIII (January 4, 1958), 1-16.

[28] THE NEW YORK TIMES, April 17, 1959.

[29] Elster, OP. CIT., 21-25.

[30] Quoted in C. A. R. Crosland, "Socialist Parties of the Future," CONFLU-ENCE, VII (Summer, 1956), 160.

[31] Paul Ramadier, "Socialist Ideas — Theory and Practice," SOCIALIST IN-TERNATIONAL INFORMATION, VIII (May 24, 1958), 325.

[32] The writer is indebted to Professor Albert Lauterbach (Sarah Lawrence College) for permission to see the manuscript of his forthcoming book, BEYOND CAPITALISM AND SOCIALISM, which deals with this theme.

NOTES TO CHAPTER SEVEN

1 The terms England and Britain (as well as English and British) will be used interchangeably to refer to England, Wales, Scotland and Northern Ireland.

2 For an examination of American political thought and action, in the context of European, which makes many of the points which follow, see Louis Hartz, THE LIBERAL TRADITION IN AMERICA (New York: Harcourt, Brace and Co., 1955).

3 I refer, of course, to the impact of the specifically Calvinist ethic. See Max Weber, THE PROTESTANT ETHIC AND THE SPIRIT OF CAPITALISM, trans. Talcott Parsons (London: George Allen and Unwin Ltd., 1930).

4 For a discussion of the transition see Dorothy George, ENGLAND IN TRANSITION (London: Penguin Books Ltd., 1953).

5 See Elie Halévy, THE GROWTH OF PHILOSOPHIC RADICALISM, trans. Mary Morris (London: Faber and Faber, 1934).

6 For comprehensive histories of the developments see the following standard texts: E. L. Woodward, THE AGE OF REFORM (Oxford: Oxford University Press, 1938), and R. C. K. Ensor, ENGLAND, 1870-1914 (Oxford University Press, 1936).

7 For summaries of the thought of the early Socialists see G. D. H. Cole, SOCIALIST THOUGHT: THE FORERUNNERS (1789-1850) (London: Macmillan and Co. Ltd., 1955), 86-158; and M. Beer, A HISTORY OF BRITISH SOCIALISM (London, 1940), 160-271.

8 Henry Pelling, THE ORIGINS OF THE LABOR PARTY (London: Macmillan and Co. Ltd., 1954), 13-34.

9 Philip P. Poirier, THE ADVENT OF THE BRITISH LABOUR PARTY (New York: Columbia University Press, 1958), 44-61.

10 For T. H. Green and the idealists see Adam Ulam, PHILOSOPHICAL FOUNDATIONS OF ENGLISH SOCIALISM (Cambridge: Harvard University Press, 1951). For the Fabians see Edward R. Pease, THE HISTORY OF THE FABIAN SOCIETY (New York: E. P. Dutton & Co., 1916). The egalitarianism of at least some of the Fabians is open to question. The Webbs, for example, seemed to see Socialism in terms of an administrative elite governing a Socialist society in the general interest.

11 The classic history of the British trade union movement is that of Beatrice and Sidney Webb, THE HISTORY OF TRADE UNIONISM (1920 ed.; New York: Longmans, Green and Co., 1920). See also Francis Williams, MAGNIFICENT JOURNEY (London: Odhams Press, Ltd., 1954).

12 Note these remarks of a not untypical employer, made somewhat later in the century.

"He wished to express his entire concurrence in the remarks of Mr. Potter that Labour ought to be considered a commodity to be regulated like every other commodity . . . every one who has read a passage of political economy must be aware that the existence of political economy depended upon the supposition that Labour in all questions of demand and supply was to be treated the same as any other commodity." Mr. H. Fawcett, speaking at the Fourth Annual Meeting of the National Association for the Promotion of Social Science held in 1860.

13 For a discussion of these events and the condition of the working class see J. L. and Barbara Hammond, THE TOWN LABOURER (2 vols. London: The British Publishers Guild, Ltd., 1949); and J. L. and Barbara Hammond, THE VILLAGE LABOURER (2 vols. London: The British Publishers Guild, Ltd., 1948).

441

14Note the remarks of Mr. Henry Ashworth at the Fourth Annual Meeting of the National Association for the Promotion of Social Science: ". . . he appeared before them as a manufacturer. . . . He believed . . . that the existence of organized bodies is essential in the condition of society in which we lived. . . . The men took care that the masters did not trench on their interests; and the masters . . . took care that the men did not trench upon their interests.

15 S. and B. Webb, OP. CIT., 327.

16 R. F. Wearmouth, METHODISM AND THE WORKING-CLASS MOVEMENT OF ENGLAND, 1800-1850 (London; The Epworth Press, 1937); and R. F. Wearmouth, METHODISM AND THE STRUGGLE OF THE WORKING CLASSES (Leicester, England: E. Backus, 1954).

17 B. C. Roberts, TRADE UNION GOVERNMENT AND ADMINISTRATION IN GREAT BRITAIN (Cambridge: Harvard University Press, 1956), 474.

18 D. H. Cole, BRITISH WORKING CLASS POLITICS, 1832-1914 (London: Routledge and Kegan Paul Ltd., 1941), 213-15.

19 Francis Williams, ERNEST BEVIN: PORTRAIT OF A GREAT ENGLISHMAN (London: Hutchinson, 1952). V. L. Allen, POWER IN TRADE UNIONS (London: Longmans, Green and Co., 1954).

20 For example, see Trades Union Congress, ANNUAL REPORT, 1933, 262.

21 For the early years of the Party and for a discussion of the I. L. P.. see Henry Pelling, THE ORIGINS OF THE LABOUR PARTY (London: Macmillan and Co. Ltd., 1954), and Henry Pelling and Frank Bealey, LABOUR AND POLITICS (London: Macmillan and Co. Ltd., 1958).

22 G. D. H. Cole, OP. CIT., 142-52.

23 IBID., 237.

24 For a discussion of the I. L. P. during this period see Fenner Brockway, INSIDE THE LEFT: THIRTY YEARS OF PLATFORM, PRESS, PRISON AND PARLIAMENT (London: Allen and Unwin. 1947).

25 As George Orwell describes the situation in INSIDE THE WHALE (London: Victor Gollancz, Ltd., 1940), 162:

"But quite suddenly in the years 1930-1935 something happens. The literary climate changes.

"As early as 1934 or 1935 it was considered eccentric in literary circles not to be more or less 'left', and in another year or two there had grown up a left wing orthodoxy that made a certain set of attitudes de rigeur on certain subjects. . . . Between 1935 and 1939 the Communist Party exercised an almost irresistible fascination for any writer under 40."

26 Trades Union Congress, ANNUAL REPORT, 1933, 337.

27 The Labour Party, FOR SOCIALISM AND PEACE, 8.

28 For a typical view see Clement R. Attlee, THE LABOUR PARTY IN PERSPECTIVE—AND TWELVE YEARS LATER (London: Longmans, Green and Co., 1949). The book was originally written in 1937. The only change in the 1949 edition is the addition of an introduction by Francis Williams.

29 Hugh Dalton, THE FATEFUL YEARS: MEMOIRS, 1931-1945 (London: Frederick Muller, Ltd., 1957), 131-41.

30 For a history of Labour Party attitudes on foreign policy in the 1930's see Elaine Windrich, BRITISH LABOUR'S FOREIGN POLICY (Stanford: Stanford University Press, 1952).

31 It should be noted that the record of the Conservative Party in the 1930's, was probably an important factor in the 1945 victory of the Labour Party.

32 G. D. N. Worswick and P. H. Ady, THE BRITISH ECONOMY, 1945-50 (Oxford: Oxford University Press, 1949).

[33] Harry Eckstein, THE ENGLISH HEALTH SERVICE (Cambridge: Harvard University Press, 1958). To be sure it did convert doctors into quasi-civil servants.
[34] Leon D. Epstein, "The Politics of British Conservatism," THE AMERICAN POLITICAL SCIENCE REVIEW, XLVIII (March, 1954), 27-48.
[35] Leon D. Epstein, GREAT BRITAIN: UNEASY ALLY (Chicago: University of Chicago Press, 1954).
[36] See Aneurin Bevan, IN PLACE OF FEAR (New York: Simon & Schuster, Inc., 1952).
[37] Epstein, OP. CIT., gives a summary of the position of the left until 1954. More recent material will be found in the pages of the NEW STATESMAN AND NATION (London), and the TRIBUNE (London), both of which represent a left wing point of view.
[38] See, for example, the most recent party statement on the H-Bomb as reported in the NEW YORK TIMES, June 25, 1959, 4.
[39] A summary of this thinking will be found in Gerard Loewenberg, "The Transformation of British Labor Party Policy Since 1945," THE JOURNAL OF POLITICS, 21 (May, 1959), 234-258.
[40] G. D. H. Cole, THE POSTWAR CONDITION OF BRITAIN (New York: Frederick A. Praeger, Inc., 1957), 41, 42.
[41] C. A. R. Crosland, THE FUTURE OF SOCIALISM (London: Jonathan Cape Ltd., 1956).
[42] For the changes occurring in traditional working class culture see Richard Hoggart, THE USES OF LITERACY (New Jersey: Essential Books, 1957).
[43] Kenneth Allsop, THE ANGRY DECADE (London: Peter Owen Ltd., 1958).

NOTES TO CHAPTER EIGHT

[1] Paul van Zeeland, THE SACRED MISSION OF CIVILIZATION (New York: Belgian Government Information Center, 1953), 7-8.
[2] Eric A. Walker, COLONIES (Cambridge: University Press, 1944), 162.
[3] Dr. Kwame Nkrumah, "Independence and Sovereignty of the African Peoples," WESTERN WORLD (October, 1958), 32.
[4] Stefan T. Possony, "Colonial Problems in Perspective," Ch. 2, 17-43, in Robert Strausz-Hupé and Henry W. Hazard. ed., THE IDEA OF COLONIALISM (New York: Frederick A. Praeger, Inc., 1958).
[5] IBID., 29.
[6] IBID., 42.
[7] IBID., 25.
[8] E. W. Evans, THE BRITISH YOKE (London: William Hodge and Co., Ltd., 1949), 194.
[9] IBID., 198.
[10] Sir Alan C. Burns, IN DEFENCE OF COLONIES (London: George Allen and Unwin Ltd.. 1957), 293.
[11] IBID., 294.
[12] IBID., 300.
[13] IBID., 302.
[14] Nikolai Lenin, IMPERIALISM (New York: The Vanguard Press, 1929), 71-2. (First published in 1916).
[15] V. I. Lenin, IMPERIALISM AND THE SPLIT IN SOCIALISM (Moscow: Foreign Languages Publishing House, 1954 (written in 1916).

[16] Demetrio Boersner, THE BOLSHEVIKS AND THE NATIONAL AND COLONIAL QUESTION, 1917-28, (Geneva: Librairie E. Droz, 1957), 25-6.

[17] V. I. Lenin, THE RIGHT OF NATIONS TO SELF-DETERMINATION (Moscow: Foreign Languages Publishing House, 1951), 110, (written in 1914).

[18] The NEW YORK TIMES, October 5, 1958.

NOTES TO CHAPTER NINE

[1] Budget is used in the broadest possible sense; the millions referred to would include the funds directly and indirectly used to aid in the achievement of Israel whatever their source.

[2] Talcott Parsons, THE SOCIAL SYSTEM (Glencoe, Illinois: The Free Press, 1951), 349.

[3] Israel Cohen, A SHORT HISTORY OF ZIONISM (London: Frederic Muller Ltd., 1951), 13.

[4] Genesis 15:18. THE HOLY BIBLE (New York: Oxford University Press, 1938), King James Version, 21.

[5] IBID., Ezekial 33:24, 924.

[6] IBID., Isaiah 2:3, 751.

[7] I. Epstein (ed.), THE BABYLONIAN TALMUD (London: Loncino Press, 1938), MO-ED V, Yoma, 546, 257.

[8] IBID., MO-ED IV, Pesahim 113a, 582.

[9] IBID., Nashim IV, Kethuboth II, 111a, 117.

[10] A. Cohen, EVERYMAN'S TALMUD (New York: E. P. Dutton & Co., Inc., 1949), 362.

[11] Nahum Glatzer (ed.), THE LANGUAGE OF FAITH (New York: Schocken Books, 1947), 70.

[12] IBID.

[13] Israel Cohen, OP. CIT., 20. See also Rufus Learsi, FULFILLMENT (Cleveland: World Book Co., 1951), 30.

[14] Moses Hess, ROME AND JERUSALEM, trans, by Meyer Waxman (New York: Block Publishing Co., 1943).

[15] Jacob S. Raisin, THE HASKALAH MOVEMENT IN RUSSIA (Philadelphia: the Jewish Pub. Society of America, 1913), 13.

[16] Leon Pinsker, AUTO-EMANCIPATION, trans. by D. S. Blondheim (New York: Zionist Organization of America, 1944).

[17] In his AUTO-EMANCIPATION Pinsker did not specify Palestine as the homeland although subsequently he bent his efforts in that direction.

[18] For a discussion of the BILU see Maurice Samuel, HARVEST IN THE DESERT (Philadelphia: The Jewish Publication Society of America, 1948), Chapter 6.

[19] IBID., 60.

[20] Leon Simon (trans.), AHAD HA-AM (London: East and West Library, 1946).

[21] Theodor Herzel, THE JEWISH STATE, trans. by Sylvie D'Avigdor (New York: Scopus Pub. Co., 1943).

[22] Nahum Sokolow, HISTORY OF ZIONISM 1600-1918 (London: Longmans, Green and Co., 1919), Vol. I, 268-269.

[23] IBID., Vol. II, 83.

[24] Under conditions of the British mandate the Zionist Organization func-

tioned through the Jewish Agency in its relationship with the British Administration. It represented both Zionists and non-Zionist Jews in its advisory, co-operative and administrative capacity.

[25] Alan R. Taylor, PRELUDE TO ISRAEL (New York: Philosophical Library, 1959), 58-60.

[26] David Ben Gurion, "Words and Values," FORUM FOR THE PROBLEMS OF ZIONISM, WORLD JEWRY, AND THE STATE OF ISRAEL, III (August, 1957), 9.

[27] IBID., 8.

[28] IBID., "Towards a Further Clarification of the Subject," 20.

[29] IBID., 33.

[30] IBID., 33.

[31] IBID., 32.

[32] IBID., 33.

NOTES TO CHAPTER TEN

[1] All percentages are rounded and based upon the population estimates for 1959.

[2] In 1946 72.5% of the European population was urban; in 1951 74%; and in 1954 78.4%; giving a curve easily projected over the 80% mark in 1959. In 1954 77.5% of the Colored and 64.5% of the Indian population was urban. The largest shift came in the Bantu, who were only 10.4% urban in 1904 but 27.6% in 1951. Or to put the matter another way: in 1904 the Bantu were less than 30% of the urban population; in 1954 they were 43% of it. What this means is that all of the major metropolitan areas of the Union have a non-white (Bantu, Colored and Indian) majority with the exception of East London. UNION OF SOUTH AFRICA POPULATION CENSUS, 1946 (Pretoria: Government Printer, 1950), I. 6-7; SUMMARY OF THE REPORT FOR THE SOCIO-ECONOMIC DEVELOPMENT OF THE BANTU AREAS, U. G. 61/1955 (Pretoria: Government Printer, 1955), 27.

[3] The Dutch Reformed Church (Nederduits Gereformeerde Kerk) is by far the largest of the three "Reformed" Churches, with a membership embracing half of the European population, all Afrikaners. Much smaller are the Nederduits Hervormde Kerk and the Gereformeerde Kerk van Suid-Afrika. All have a basic Calvinistic theology.

[4] A good summary of this statement is in Leo Marquard, THE PEOPLES AND POLICIES OF SOUTH AFRICA (London: Oxford University Press, 1952), 211-215.

[5] A good expression of this argument is by Dr. John E. Holloway, THE PROBLEMS OF RACE RELATIONS IN SOUTH AFRICA (New York: Union of South Africa Government Information Office, 1954).

[6] A good example of this second argument may be found in the pamphlet by Professor N. J. J. Olivier, APARTHEID—A SLOGAN OR A SOLUTION (Stellenbosch: South African Bureau of Racial Affairs, 1954).

[7] An excellent example of such an "official" view is that by Wentzel C. du Plessis, South African Ambassador to the United States, in an address before the Harvard Law School Forum in 1958, subsequently printed as a brochure under the title, HIGHWAY TO HARMONY (New York: Union of South Africa Government Information Office, 1958).

[8] Not to be confused with Professor A. W. Hoernlé, also interested in racial matters, but with a different orientation.

[9] Notably in his SOUTH AFRICAN NATIVE POLICY AND THE LIBERAL SPIRIT (Johannesburg: Witwatersrand Univ. Press, 1945).

[10] Hoernlé regarded this absorption as less a gradual than as an accelerating process.

[11] The most important native reserves are the Ciskei and the Transkei, created in the Cape Colony prior to the unification of South Africa.

[12] Genesis IX, 22-25.

[13] The conflict between the two types of apartheid is as old as European settlement in South Africa, dating back to the effort by Governor Jan van Riebeeck in 1651 to separate settlers from Hottentots by a wild orange hedge, which the settlers trampled down to impose their own functional apartheid upon the Hottentots.

[14] The Orange Free State and the South African (Transvaal) Republic gave the franchise only to white males and employed a system of indentured and apprenticed non-white labor. The British colony of Natal, with rigid territorial apartheid for its Zulu population, in theory gave the vote to all "civilized" non-Europeans; but the tests were so onerous that few of them reached the polls in that colony. In contrast, the Cape had a color-blind franchise after 1854, and Cape Afrikaners insisted on its continuation in the new Union, although in 1936 its native aspect was greatly modified and twenty years later also its Colored phase.

[15] Act 27 of 1913 (Statutes of the Union of South Africa).

[16] Act 12 of 1936.

[17] Technically the "Mines and Works (1911) Amendment Act," No. 25 of 1926, the law closed specific jobs except to persons holding certificates of competence in them, and then barred granting of such certificates to non-Europeans. The measure also permitted the government to extend the list of such jobs.

[18] But not in pay rates, thereby throwing the fat into the fire. In addition, the close of World War I saw the beginning of Afrikaner migration into urban industry, where they continued their frontier attitudes toward non-whites.

[19] All South African churches, particularly the Dutch Reformed Church, carry on missionary programs among the non-whites, especially the Bantu, aiming at both their conversion and their acceptance of European ways of living. Government activity among non-whites has until recently been concentrated upon improving native agriculture. In the past decade government welfare policy has included industrial and urban aspects in its native program.

[20] Act 55 of 1949.

[21] Act 21 of 1950.

[22] Act 5 of 1927.

[23] In this connection Alan Paton's novel, TOO LATE THE PHALAROPE, an excellent study of the various groups and types in a modern Afrikaner dorp, is quite revealing.

[24] Professor Gwendolen M. Carter in her excellent study, THE POLITICS OF INEQUALITY (New York: Praeger, 1958), using a cautious formula to calculate party strength in uncontested seats, estimates that in the 1953 elections the Nationalists won 45.5% of the popular vote (pp. 158-159). An application of the Carter formula to the 1958 election results indicates Nationalist popular strength as being 49.6%. This percentage corresponds closely to the percentage of Europeans belonging to the Dutch Reformed Church, although it would be erroneous to assume that all of its members are Nationalists.

[25] The Eiselen appointment represented a particular triumph for SABRA, inasmuch as he was not a member of the civil service, hitherto the source of such appointments to permanent heads of departments.

[26] Carter, POLITICS OF INEQUALITY, 267.

[27] Eric A. Walker, A HISTORY OF SOUTHERN AFRICA (London: Longmans, Green and Co., 1957), 906.

[28] Three Europeans represent Cape natives able to meet certain property qualifications in the Assembly. Four indirectly elected white Senators represent other natives. In addition, four nominated European Senators are supposed to be experts in native affairs, but no South African government has ever honored this qualification. Since 1956 four Europeans also represent Cape Coloreds, meeting a property franchise, in the lower house. In contrast to the European franchise, since 1930, the various non-European suffrages are for males only.

[29] Act 47 of 1953.

[30] Calculated on the basis of Bantu children actually in school the figure was £7 per child; on the basis of all Bantu children of elementary school age the per capita figure was £2 13/4 (Walker, HISTORY OF SOUTHERN AFRICA, 899). Even the lower figure, however, left South Africa with the highest per capita expenditure on African education of any country on the continent.

[31] For a summary of the arguments for and against the law see THE BANTU EDUCATION ACT (Stellenbosch: South African Bureau for Racial Affairs, 1954). The SAIRR report by A. W. Hoernlé, REPORT ON THE WORKING OF THE BANTU EDUCATION ACT (Johannesburg: South African Institute of Race Relations, 1955), is more significant as SAIRR has generally been critical of Nationalist racial policy. This writer, after seeing the Bantu Education Act in actual operation on the back veld of the Transvaal in 1955, admits that he was impressed.

[32] Act 41 of 1950.

[33] Native (Urban Areas) Act, 21 of 1923.

[34] Act 30 of 1950.

[35] SUMMARY OF THE REPORT OF THE COMMISSION FOR THE SOCIO-ECONOMIC DEVELOPMENT OF THE BANTU AREAS WITHIN THE UNION OF SOUTH AFRICA, (Pretoria: Government Printer, 1955). U. G. 61, xviii (to be cited henceforth as U.G. 61/55).

[36] IBID., xvii.

[37] IBID., 208.

[38] IBID., 207.

[39] Remarks to American Women's Club, Pretoria, August, 1955.

[40] For the constitutional issues raised see Colin Rhys Lovell, "Afrikaner Nationalism and Apartheid," AMERICAN HISTORICAL REVIEW, LXI, No. 2 (January, 1956), 308-330, espec. 327-330.

[41] Act 44 of 1950.

[42] Numerous examples of this socioeconomic isolation of the two white elements can be given. A typical example is the Afrikaner attitude toward banks, which makes Volkas "national" and Barclays "English" and "foreign." So serious was this Afrikaner attitude's effects for Barclays that it made N. C. Havenga, long associated with Afrikaner Antinationalism, a director shortly before his death.

[43] This policy has been implemented on the provincial, rather than the national level, although "mother-tongue instruction" is a Nationalist party principle.

[44] Notably Leo Marquard, the product of a Dutch Reformed predikant's family, and Mrs. Margaret Ballinger, leader of the tiny Parliamentary Liberal Party.

[45] THE POLICIES OF THE LIBERAL PARTY OF SOUTH AFRICA (Rondebosch: South African Liberal Party, 1955), 2-8. It is important to notice that the Liberal Party does not advocate racial mixing, although calling for the repeal of

447

such laws as the Mixed Marriages and Immorality Acts as insulting to personal ethics.

⁴⁶ The government plans to substitute regional Bantu councils for this Parliamentary representation became law in 1959.

⁴⁷ Reported to this writer by an observer at the meeting.

NOTES TO CHAPTER ELEVEN

¹ Franz H. Michael and George E. Taylor, THE FAR EAST IN THE MODERN WORLD, Chapters VI-XV, 119-688, (New York: Henry Holt and Co., 1956) 724.

² J. Liddell Kelly, "What is the Matter with the Asiatic?" WESTMINISTER REVIEW," CLXXIV (September 1910), 292-299.

³ Lathrop Stoddard, THE RISING TIDE OF COLOR (New York: Charles Scribner's Sons, 1920), 3.

⁴ IBID., 97.

⁵ Michael, OP. CIT., 167.

⁶ Achmed Abdullah, "Seen Through Mohammedan Spectacles," FORUM, LII, 4 (October, 1914), 484-497.

⁷ Ryutaro Nagai, "The White Peril," THE AMERICAN REVIEW OF REVIEWS, XLVII 1 (July, 1913), 107-108.

⁸ Yone Noguchi, "The Downfall of Western Civilization," THE NATION, (October 8, 1914), 432.

⁹ Meredith Townsend, ASIA AND EUROPE, 17-19 (London: A. Constable and Co., 1905). 388.

¹⁰ To compare Taiping social reform program with the present-day Chinese efforts at communal organizations may be highly significant. The latter may have its ideological origin in China's own history, not Soviet Communism. This may also explain why the Soviets have not been enthusiastic about the communes. See Michael, OP. CIT., 185.

¹¹ IBID., 223-224 and 627.

¹² IBID., 617-620.

¹³ Stoddard, OP. CIT., 31, 32 et seq.

¹⁴ James A. Michener, THE VOICE OF ASIA (New York: Random House, 1951), 241.

¹⁵ Stoddard, OP. CIT., 54-60.

¹⁶ M. Straight, "Do We Want Asian Unity," NEW REPUBLIC, CXXXII (April 25, 1955), 56.

¹⁷ William Costello, "What Asia Needs," THE NEW REPUBLIC, CXXXII, 4 (January 24, 1955), 11, 12.

¹⁸ IBID., 12.

¹⁹ Takaaki Aikawa, "Thoughts on the New Asia," THE CHRISTIAN CENTURY, LXXII (October 12, 1955), 1172-4.

²⁰ There were such titles as "Knights of the Nile," "Dukes of Uganda," etc. See John Hope Franklin, FROM SLAVERY TO FREEDOM, Chapter XXV (New York: Alfred A. Knopf, 1947), 481-2.

²¹ IBID., 482.

²² IBID.

²³ Kwame Nkrumah, GHANA (Edinburgh: Thomas Nelson & Sons, 1957), 45.

²⁴ IBID., 52-54.

²⁵ Fifth Congress also differed radically from the previous four in the overall

composition of its membership. Instead of being made up mainly of Negro intellectuals, the delegates were workers, farmers, unionists, African students, etc.

[26] In a three-year survey of African opinion in the Gold Coast (1954-57), we found that people in all walks of life seemed to think of Ghana's forthcoming independence only as a first step. There was a marked concern about Africa. For example, one question had to do with one's choice for a national language as a medium of instruction from the seventy Gold Coast languages. We had feared that everyone was going to vote for the language of his own tribe. But, to our great surprise, not only was one's own tongue passed over in an overwhelming vote for the most widely spoken language in the Gold Coast, but an astonishing number chose what they thought to be the most widely spoken language on the African continent as a whole, and gave unity of all Africans as reason for choice.

[27] Stoddard's interpretation is different. According to him, Mohammedanism appeals to Africans because of its "fierce, warlike spirit" in contrast with the "gentle, peace-loving, high moral standard of Christianity." See Stoddard, *op. cit.*, 95.

[28] George W. Carpenter, "The Role of Christianity and Islam in Contemporary Africa," Chapter 2, 90-113, in C. Grove Haines, Ed., AFRICA TODAY (Baltimore: Johns Hopkins Univeristy Press, 1955), 510.

[29] GHANA PARLIAMENTARY DEBATES, OFFICIAL REPORT, Vol. 12, No. 10 (Accra, December 12, 1958), 387-88.

[30] IBID., 388-89.

[31] IBID., 389-91.

[32] From speech of the Prime Minister of Ghana at final Conference sessions, April 22, 1958.

[33] In a previous study we noted that the Belgian Government's program was to check native political aspirations in the Congo by stepping up economic and social welfare programs and by giving some kind of special status to its few educated Africans in such a way that the masses will not be disturbed. "It would seem to be obvious," it was stated, "that this latter expectation can hardly be realized, and time alone will tell whether the educated classes can be kept permanently satisfied by a scheme of preferential treatment." See Chancellor Williams, "Sociological Trends in Africa South of the Sahara," in Joseph S. Roucek, Ed., CONTEMPORARY SOCIOLOGY (New York: Philosophical Library, 1958), 1087.

NOTES TO CHAPTER TWELVE

[1] See particularly his LA RAZA COSMICA: MISION DE LA RAZA IBERO-AMERICANA (Paris: N.D.).

[2] For example, see the discussion of the controversial Prebisch thesis by Benjamin A. Rogge, "Economic Development in Latin America: The Prebisch Thesis," INTER AMERICAN ECONOMIC AFFAIRS, IX (Spring, 1956), 24-29.

[3] Sanford A. Mosk, "An Economist's Point of View," in W. W. Pierson, Ed., "Pathology of Democracy in Latin America: A Symposium," AMERICAN POLITICAL SCIENCE REVIEW, XLIV (March, 1950), 129-142.

[4] Mosk, OP. CIT., 142.

[5] Richard Pattee, CATHOLICISM IN LATIN AMERICA (Washington, D.C.: National Catholic Welfare Conference, Part I, 1949), 9.

[6] Russell H. Fitzgibbon, "Constitutional Development in Latin America: A Synthesis," AMERICAN POLITICAL SCIENCE REVIEW, XXXIX (June, 1945), 519.

[7] Harold E. Davis, "Trends in Social Thought in Twentieth Century Latin America," JOURNAL OF LATIN AMERICAN STUDIES, I (January, 1959), 59.

[8] Robert J. Alexander, COMMUNISM IN LATIN AMERICA (Rutgers, N. J.: Rutgers University Press, 1957), 9-12.

[9] Davis, OP. CIT., 63.

[10] IBID., 63-64.

[11] Stephen S. Goodspeed, EL PAPEL DEL JEFE DEL EJECUTIVO EN MEXICO (Problemas Agricolas e Industriales de Mexico, 1955), 44.

[12] Frank Tannenbaum, MEXICO: THE STRUGGGLE FOR PEACE AND BREAD (New York: Alfred A. Knopf, 1920), 60-61.

[13] Harry Kantor, THE IDEOLOGY AND PROGRAM OF THE PERUVIAN APRISTA MOVEMENT (Berkeley, Calif.: University of California Press. 1953), 115.

[14] IBID., 118.

[15] George I. Blanksten, PERON'S ARGENTINA (Chicago, Ill.: University of Chicago Press, 1953), 285.

[16] Quoted in Blanksten. OP. CIT., 305.

[17] Russell H. Fitzgibbon, URUGUAY: PORTRAIT OF A DEMOCRACY (Rutgers, N. J.: Rutgers University Press, 1954), 134.

[18] Quoted in Simon Hanson, UTOPIA IN URUGUAY (New York: Oxford Univeristy Press, 1938), 22.

[19] Kantor, OP. CIT., 129.

[20] Quoted in Stanley Ross, FRANCISCO I. MADERO, APOSTLE OF MEXICAN DEMOCRACY (New York: Columbia University Press, 1955) 192.

NOTES TO CHAPTER THIRTEEN

[1] General Charles De Gaulle, "Inaugural Address," FRENCH AFFAIRS, No. 77 (New York: Ambassade de France, Service de Presse et D'Information, January 8, 1959), 2.

[2] On this point see Charles Morazé, THE FRENCH AND THE REPUBLIC, trans. by Jean-Jacques Demorest (Ithaca, New York: Cornell University Press, 1958), 35-43.

[3] Of course, it remains to be seen whether or not the Fifth Republic, itself the product of quasi-revolution, can gain long-run acceptance.

[4] For excellent accounts of modern French history to the Second World War, see D. W. Brogan, FRANCE UNDER THE REPUBLIC: THE DEVELOPMENT OF MODERN FRANCE 1870-1939 (New York and London: Harper and Bros., 1940); and Jean Jacques Chevallier, HISTOIRE DES INSTITUTIONS DE LA FRANCE (Paris: Dalloz, 1952). For the period following the war, see Herbert Luethy, FRANCE AGAINST HERSELF (New York: Frederick A. Praeger, 1955), and André Siegfried, DE LA TROISIEME A LA QUATRIEME REPUBLIQUE (Paris: B. Grasset, 1956).

[5] Herbert Luethy, OP. CIT., 40.

[6] France has been governed by absolute monarchs and emperors, a constitutional monarch for a short period, and four republics. All republican governments have been dominated by the legislatures.

[7] The literature on French political thought is extensive. A useful bibliography may be found in R. S. Schermerhorn, "French Political Thought," in Joseph S. Roucek (ed.), TWENTIETH CENTURY POLITICAL THOUGHT (New York: Philosophical Library, 1946), 464-466.

8 For listing see "Procedure for the Election of Deputies from Metropolitan France and the Overseas Departments to the National Assembly," FRENCH AFFAIRS, No. 72 (New York: Ambassade de France, Service de Presse et D'Information, November, 1958), 6-7.

9 The best recent work in English on the major French parties is Richard Barron, PARTIES AND POLITICS IN MODERN FRANCE (Washington, D.C.: Public Affairs Press, 1959). Much of the following material derives from this source.

10 Some neo-Fascists are to be found among the *colons* of Algeria, See Henry Giniger, "Solution for Algeria de Gaulle's Big Task," NEW YORK TIMES, Section 4, p. 4b, May 10, 1959.

11 Professor Nicholas Wahl classifiies the MRP as a conservative party. See his section, "The French Political System," in S. H. Beer and A. B. Ulam (eds.), PATTERNS OF GOVERNMENT (New York: Random House, 1958), 243.

12 Professor Wahl categorizes the Radical Socialists as a reformist-liberal party. IBID., 248.

13 For various points of view as to the causes of France's difficulties under the Fourth Republic, see Elizabeth Davey (ed.), FRANCE IN CRISIS (New York: The Reference Shelf, H. W. Wilson Company, 1957).

14 On October 21, 1945, by a vote of 18½ million to 700,000, the electorate registered its desire for a new constitution in preference to a return to the Third Republic. In the Constituent Assembly the three great Leftist parties, the Communists, the Socialists, and the MRP, shared about 80 per cent of the seats in approximately equal numbers.

15 The MRP favored a strong executive but could not impose their viewpoint.

16 Despite the *immobilisme* of the government, the economy as a whole made great advances. See the United Nations BULLETIN OF MONTHLY STATISTICS (New York: April, 1959), 24.

17 This is true despite his temporary leadership of the RPF. See below.

18 Jean-Marie Domenach, "Democratic Paralysis in France," in FOREIGN AFFAIRS, XXXVII, No. 1, October, 1958), 35.

19 Charles de Gaulle, MEMOIRS DE GUERRE, L'APPEL, 1940-1942 (Paris: Librairie Plon, 1954), I, 1.

20 This was extended by another four months in the case of the Republic, and six months in the case of the Community, by Articles 91 and 92 of the Constitution of the Fifth Republic. For full text of the Constitution in both French and English, see THE FRENCH CONSTITUTION (New York: Ambassade de France, Service de Presse et D'Information, 1958).

21 "Premier Charles de Gaulle Outlines His Governmental Program," SPEECHES AND PRESS CONFERENCES, No. 108 (New York: Ambassade de France, Service de Presse et D'Information, June 1, 1958). This is the full text of de Gaulle's policy statement before the National Assembly.

22 IBID., (Author's italics.)

23 For text of this law, see CURRENT HISTORY, XXXV, No. 204, August, 1958, 115-116.

24 Compare with Title X of the Constitution of 1946.

25 An organic law deals with the organization and regulation of governmental authorities.

26 An important point to note is the separation of executive and legislative personnel. No member of the Government may be at the same time a member of Parliament (Art. 23), though the former may appear in the assemblies to "be heard" (Art. 31) and to answer questions (Art. 48).

27 NEW YORK TIMES, May 17, 1959, 3.

451

[28] Domenach, OP. CIT., 43.

[29] "Procedure," OP. CIT., 2.

[30] For complete listing see "The New National Assembly Elected November 23 and 30, 1958," FRENCH AFFAIRS, No. 73 (New York: Ambassade de France, Service de Presse et D'Information, December, 1958).

[31] Unfortunately limitations of space preclude discussion of these issues. For excellent recent articles on them, see "France and the Fifth Republic," CURRENT HISTORY, XXXVI, No. 213. May, 1959. For an official survey of the de Gaulle government's accomplishments, see "Balance Sheet of the de Gaulle Administration, June 3, 1958 - February 5, 1959," FRENCH AFFAIRS, No. 84 (New York: Ambascade de France, Service de Presse et D'Information, May, 1959).

[32] Dr. Richard Barron feels the Communists to be the greatest menace to any democratic regime in France. Barron, OP. CIT., 90. The gains registered in the municipal elections of March 8, 1959, in which the Communists garnered 27.7 per cent of the votes, give evidence of their continuing support. NEW YORK TIMES, March 10, 1959, 13.

NOTES TO CHAPTER FOURTEEN

[1] Hans Georg Wieck, DIE ENTSTEHUNG DER CDU UND DIE WIEDER-GRUENDUNG DES ZENTRUMS IM JAHRE 1945 (Dusseldorf: Droste-Verlag, 1953), 28. See also Gabriel Almond, Ed., STRUGGLE FOR DEMOCRACY IN GERMANY (Chapel Hill, N.C.: University of North Carolina Press, 1949), 111 f, 134 f.

[2] James K. Pollock, James H. Meisel, Henry L. Bretton, GERMANY UNDER OCCUPATION. ILLUSTRATIVE MATERIALS AND DOCUMENTS (Ann Arbor, Mich.: George Wahr Publishing Co., 1949, rev. edit.), 7-16.

[3] IBID., 17-23. Wieck, OP. CIT., 25-26.

[4] Pollock, OP. CIT., 76-91.

[5] Wieck, OP. CIT., 33-34. There are a number of excellent sources for the study of Allied and U.S. occupation experiences: Harold Zink, AMERICAN MILITARY GOVERNMENT IN GERMANY (New York: Macmillan Co., 1947); Carl J. Friedrich, et al., AMERICAN EXPERIENCES IN MILITARY GOVERNMENT IN WORLD WAR II (New York: Rinehart & Co., 1948); Harold Zink, THE UNITED STATES IN GERMANY, 1945-1955 (New York; D. Van Nostrand Co., 1957); Edward H. Litchfield, Ed., GOVERNING POST-WAR GERMANY (Ithaca, N. Y.: Cornell University Press, 1953); John D. Montgomery, FORCED TO BE FREE. THE ARTIFICIAL REVOLUTION IN GERMANY AND JAPAN (Chicago: University of Chicago Press, 1957). A collection of most of the important documents can be found in Pollock, *op. cit.*

[6] Wieck, OP.CIT., 20-24. There are many reliable publications available about the German resistance movement, such as Hans Rothfels, THE GERMAN OPPO-SITION TO HITLER (Chicago: Regnery, 1948); Rudolf Pechel, DEUTSCHER WIDERSTAND (Erlenbach-Zuerich: E. Rentsch Verlag, 1947); Erich Kosthorst, DIE DEUTSCHE OPPOSITION GEGEN HITLER ZWISCHEN POLEN— UND FRANKREICH FELDZUG (Bonn: Bundeszentrale fuer Heimatdienst, 1957); Gerhard Ritter, CARL GOERDELER UND DIE DEUTSCHE WIDERSTANDBEWE-GUNG (Stuttgart: Deutsche Verlagsanstalt, 1954). Ludwig Bergstraesses, GE-SCHICHTE DER POLITISCHEN PARTEIEN IN DEUTSCHLAND (Muenchen: Isar Verlag, 1955) contains a brief discussion of German political resistance groups by a highly qualified German authority on political parties.

[7] Wieck, OP. CIT., 27, 29, 38, 44-45.

[8] Bergstraesser, OP. CIT., 322-26.

[9] For a discussion of the effects of a divided labor movement see Eric Waldman, THE SPARTACIST UPRISING OF 1919 AND THE CRISIS OF THE GERMAN SOCIALIST MOVEMENT (Milwaukee: Marquette University Press, 1958), 200-09, 222.

[10] Karl Buchheim, GESCHICHTE DER CHRISTLICHEN PARTEIEN IN DEUTSCHLAND (Muenchen: Koesel-Verlag, 1953), 415-17.

[11] IBID., 419-20, 427, 429-31. Bergstraesser, OP. CIT., 333.
The emergence of a Christian-democratic movement in postwar Germany was a parallel development to the founding of Christian-Democratic Parties in other West European countries. Professor Fogarty defines Christian Democracy as follows:
. . . that aspect of the ecumenical or catholic movement in modern Christianity which is concerned with the application of Christian principles in the areas of political, economic, and social life for which the Christian laity has independent responsibility. (Michael P. Fogarty, CHRISTIAN DEMOCRACY IN WESTERN EUROPE, 1820-1953 [London: Routledge & Kegan Paul Ltd., 1957], 435.)
Since Catholics have a strong influence within the CDU, the concept of "political Catholicism" deserves attention. It indicates specially organized activities of a country's Catholics for the purpose of realizing Christian state principles and Christian social concepts. There is no inherent dependence of these activities with the Church organization and as a matter of fact Pope Leo XIII officially stated that political Catholicism must be free of "church tutelage." (Joseph N. Moody, Ed., CHURCH AND SOCIETY, CATHOLIC POLITICAL THOUGHT AND MOVEMENTS, 1789-1950 [New York: Arts, Inc., 1953], 435-36.)

[12] Department of State, GERMANY 1947-1949. THE STORY IN DOCUMENTS (Washington, D.C.: U.S. Government Printing Office, 1950), 8.

[13] John Ford Golay, THE FOUNDING OF THE FEDERAL REPUBLIC OF GERMANY (Chicago: The University of Chicago Press, 1958), 1-6.

[14] Department of State, OP. CIT., 75-84. After the establishment of the Federal Republic of Germany (Bundesrepublik Deutschland), the German government signed on January 2, 1950 the first Marshall Plan agreement. The economic aid which Germany received from the United States amounted to more than $3\frac{1}{2}$ billion dollars. The United Kingdom provided about 800 million dollars and France 15 million dollars. (Henry C. Wallich, MAINSPRINGS OF THE GERMAN REVIVAL [New Haven: Yale University Press, 1955], 354-57.)

[15] Golay, OP. CIT., 6-26 discusses the events leading to the final draft of the Basic Law.

[16] In 1949, Professor Theodor Heuss was elected by a small majority as the first Federal President. In 1954 he was elected almost by a unanimous vote. On July 1, 1959, Heinrich Luebke was elected to succeed President Heuss on September 15, 1959.

[17] Wallich, OP. CIT., 344, 371-73.

[18] A comprehensive discussion of Socialist thought can be found in the "Socialist Internationals and Continental Socialism," by Gerhard Braunthal.

[19] Wolfgang Treue, DEUTSCHE PARTEIPROGRAMME 1861-1956 (Goettingen: Musterschmidt-Verlag, 1956), 178-81.

[20] IBID., 181-82.

[21] IBID., 182-83.

[22] IBID., 187.

[23] IBID., 188.

[24] IBID., 188-89.

25 IBID., 190.

26 Patrick M. Boarman, LUDWIG ERHARD'S ACHIEVEMENT (Manuscript, University of Wisconsin, Milwaukee, May, 1959), 5-7, 15-16.

27 Wilhelm Mommsen, DEUTSCHE PARTEIPROGRAMME, EINE AUSWAHL VOM VORMAERZ BIS ZUR GEGENWART (Munich: Isar Verlag, 1952), 150-52.

28 Ludwig Erhard, PROSPERITY THROUGH COMPETITION (New York: Frederick A. Praeger, 1958), 179.

29 IBID., 3, 164. From 1950 until 1955 private consumption rose from 7.25 billion dollars to 12.75 billion dollars (using again the 1936 price level as a basis for comparison). German living standards improved percentage-wise more than those of other European countries and of the United States. For comparative figures see IBID., 4.

30 "Lohnentwicklung und Produktionsergebnis," SCHNELLDIENST DES DEUTSCHEN INDUSTRIEINSTITUTS, No. 45 (June 9, 1959), 2-3.

31 "Smoothing the Path of German Labor Peace," GERMAN BUSINESS WEEKLY (July 3, 1959). Compare U.S. figures for the same period: wages increased 45 per cent; living cost went up 20 per cent.

32 "Whither German Prices?" GERMAN BUSINESS WEEKLY (March 11, 1959).

33 DIE WELT (July 7, 1959). In May, 1959, the number of unemployed was 320,000. At the same time, there were over 293,000 job vacancies. (IBID.)

34 Sidney Gruson, "Boom in West Germany Slows a Bit; Prices Stable Amid High Employment," NEW YORK TIMES (January 13, 1959).

35 Erhard, OP.CIT., 31-32, 36, 63. Arthur J. Olsen, "Bonn Trade Rises for the 10th Year," NEW YORK TIMES (January 13, 1959).

36 GERMAN BUSINESS WEEKLY (July 29, 1959).

37 Olsen, OP. CIT.

38 Erhard, OP. CIT., 5.

39 "Der Beitrag fuer die soziale Sicherheit," DEUTSCHES INDUSTRIE-INSTITUT, Material zum Zeitgeschehen, No. 4 (April 9, 1959), 1-3, 6, 11.

In July, 1959 it was announced by the Federal Ministry of Labor that in the period from 1949 until 1958 within the territory of the Federal Republic (since 1953 including West Berlin) about 58 billion dollars were paid for various social services and benefits. A breakdown of this figure reveals the major items of the widespread governmental social services which are evaluated by some people as unmistakable signs of a development toward the social "welfare state."

19 billion dollars various social security payments (old age included)

8.5 billion dollars health insurance

3 billion dollars unemployment insurance

2.3 billion dollars accident insurance

0.6 billion dollars family assistance

8.1 billion dollars aid to unemployed, social services, equalization of burden

6.9 billion dollars aid to war victims (disabled veterans, war widows and orphans)

9.1 billion dollars civil service pensions

0.6 billion dollars administrative expenses

(DIE WELT, July 22, 1959.)

40 Treue, OP. CIT., 240, 246, 249. See pp, 240-52 for the entire program.

41 The relatively few strikes also indicate that the workers are in general satisfied. For example in 1958, a total of 202,437 workers were involved in strikes with a loss of only 780,559 work days. (GERMAN BUSINESS WEEKLY [July 3, 1959].)

As a result of increasing friction within the German Trade Union Federation (DGB) between the Socialist members who openly sided and supported the SPD and the minority of "Christian-Social" workers, the latter started in 1955 to form

454

again their own Christian unions. On June 28, 1959, they combined in a Christian Trade Union Federation (*Christliche Gewerkschaftsbund Deutschlands* — CGB). The CGB is comprised of 14 Christian unions with about 200,000 members. In comparison with the present membership of 6.3 million of the DGB, the Christian unions still represent a relatively small minority. However, the trade union unity is destroyed. The CGB is supported by both the CDU and the Christian Democratic government and the upshot of the development will be the existence of two "ideologically" oriented federations: the DGB co-operating with the SPD and the CGB backing the policies of the Christian Democrats. ("Spaltung — DGB und CGB," DER SPIEGEL, Vol. 13, No. 28 [July 8, 1959], 25-26. "Konkurrenz fuer den DGB," DIE ZEIT, Vol. 14, No. 27 [July 3, 1959]. DIE WELT [June 29, 1959].

42 Ernst Deuerlein, CDU/CSU 1945-1957, BEITRAEGE ZUR ZEITGE-SCHICHTE (Cologne: Verlag J. P. Bachem, 1957), 176.

43 In 1957, the Christian Democrats succeeded again in the Federal elections and Konrad Adenauer was able to continue as Chancellor. At the September 15, 1957, elections the CDU obtained 11,865,798 or 39.7 per cent and the CSU 3,132,956 votes or 10.5 per cent of the total vote. Thus the combined CDU/CSU received 50.2 per cent of the popular vote. It was the first time in German history that a political party obtained a majority in a free election. (BULLETIN DES PRESSE-UND INFORMATIONSAMTES DER BUNDESREGIERUNG, No. 172 [September 17, 1957], 1597.)

44 In June of 1959, the Federal government owned among other things 42 per cent of the West German automobile industry, 29 per cent of the hard coal mining, and 72 per cent of the aluminum production. It is estimated that the real value of the enterprises owned by the Federal Republic — excluding the *Volkswagen* works — is close to one billion dollars. (Herman Lindrath, "Keine Freiheit ohne Eigentum," BULLETIN DES PRESS- UND INFORMATIONSAMTES DER BUN-DESREGIERUNG, No. 102 [June 10, 1959], 1008. "People's Shares in Preussag," GERMAN INTERNATIONAL, Vol. II, No. 6 [December, 1958—January, 1959], 40.)

45 "Die Privatisierung des Bundesvermoegens," BULLETIN DES PRESS- UND INFORMATIONSAMTES DER BUNDESREGIERUNG, No. 36 (February 24, 1959), 338.

46 300,000 shares of common stock of PREUSSAG were sold to its 22,000 employees and other people in the lower income bracket (i.e., a maximum yearly income of $4,000). The shares were sold at an intentionally low price. In order to obtain a broad distribution, the sale was restricted to five shares per person. (Hermann Lindrath, "The First People's Shares," THE BULLETIN, Vol. 7, No. 11 [March 17, 1959], 4. GERMAN INTERNATIONAL, Vol. II, No. 6 [December, 1958—January, 1959], 39.)

47 "Nun weiter privatisieren!" SCHNELLDIENST DES DEUTSCHEN INDUS-TRIEINSTITUTS, No. 26 (April 3, 1959), 2. GERMAN BUSINESS WEEKLY (April 8, 1959), 2.

48 GERMAN BUSINESS WEEKLY (July 29, 1959).

49 Lindrath, "Keine Freiheit," OP. CIT., 1005.

50 Rudolf Herlt, "Der Mythos der Volksaktie," DIE WELT (July 4, 1959).

51 GERMAN INTERNATIONAL, Vol. II, No. 6 (December, 1958 — January, 1959), 40.

52 Lindrath, "Keine Freiheit," OP. CIT., 1008.

53 Wallich, OP.CIT., 263-87.

Refugees comprise 20 per cent of the population of the Federal Republic. Refugees, especially from the Soviet zone, are still arriving. During the first six months of 1959, 74,367 persons have fled the so-called German Democratic Republic. In comparison, 98,389 individuals left East Germany during the first six months of 1958 (DIE WELT, [July 6, 1959].)

The costs of the government's refugee program were enormous between 1948 and 1957. Almost 14 billion dollars were spent in support of the refugees. As a result of these and other social expenditures the tax rate in the Federal Republic is very high. For example, during 1957-58, tax revenues amounted to 33 per cent of the gross national product. ("Refugees in the Federal Republic, the Financial Problem," NEWS FROM THE GERMAN EMBASSY, Vol. III, No. 4 [March 19, 1959], 1-2.)

54 BULLETIN, No. 36 (February 2, 1959), 339. GERMAN INTERNATIONAL, Vol. II, No. 6 (December 1958—January 1959), 40. SCHNELLDIENST, No. 26 (April 3, 1959), 3.

55 "Unser Ziel: Der Wirtschaftsbuerger," DIE WELT (June 13. 1959).

56 Guenter Henle, "Konzentration und soziale Marktwirtschaft," VORTRAGS-REIHE DES DEUTSCHEN INDUSTRIEINSTITUTS, No. 4 (January 26, 1959), 1.

57 "Vor Schwierigkeiten nicht kapitulieren, Appell Erhards an die Unternehmer," DIE WELT (April 11, 1959).

58 Theodor Sonnemann, "Ueberproduktion im Agrarbereich?" DEUTSCHE KORRESPONDENZ, Vol. 9, No. 10 (July 3, 1959), 4-5.

The Federal Ministry of Finance announced that the yearly subvention for Agriculture is about 450 million dollars. (DIE WELT [July 31, 1959].)

59 "Etzel fordert Streuung des Eigentums," DIE WELT (April 11, 1959).

60 Since the end of the war over 4½ million new apartments have been built. In 1958 alone 500,000 new units have been added. The yearly government subvention to housing is about 88 million dollars. (DIE WELT [July 31, 1959].)

61 Paul Luecke, "Soziales Mietrecht in der sozialen Marktwirtschaft," DEUTSCHE KORRESPONDENZ, Vol. 9, No. 9 (February 2, 1959), 4-5.

62 "Economy Moves Toward Consolidation," THE BULLETIN, Vol. 7, No. 23 (June 16, 1959), 5.

63 Wallich, OP. CIT., 317-21.

64 George Bailey, "The Permanent Opposition," THE REPORTER (June 11, 1959).

65 Reported at the Congress of the Socialist International in Hamburg, July 1959. (DIE WELT [July 15, 1959].)

66 Wallich, OP. CIT., 321-22.

67 John H. Herz, "The Government of Germany," MAJOR FOREIGN POWERS (3rd edit., New York: Harcourt, Brace & Co., 1957), 438-41.

68 IBID., 449-51. Mommsen, OP. CIT., 149.

69 Federal elections—September 15, 1957: DRP 307,310 votes—1.0 per cent. The DRP demands the withdrawal of all "occupation troops" from East and West Germany and is for the neutrality of a reconstructed German Reich.

70 DIE WELT (July 18, 1959).

NOTES TO CHAPTER FIFTEEN

1 The literature on the ideology of Fascism is rich; see such works as: Gunther Reiman, "Fascism," Chapter XVIII, 695-710, in Feliks Gross, Ed., EUROPEAN IDEOLOGIES: A SURVEY OF 20TH CENTURY POLITICAL IDEAS (New York: Philosophical Library, 1948); Floyd A. Cave, "Italy," Chapter 5, 229-265, in Joseph

S. Roucek, Ed., GOVERNMENTS AND POLITICS ABROAD (New York: Funk and Wagnalls, 1948),and bibliography, 264-5; Marian D. Erish, "Fascism," Chapter— 7, 83-104, in Joseph S. Roucek, Ed., TWENTIETH CENTURY POLITICAL THOUGHT (New York: Philosophical Library, 1946); etc. Fascist doctrine was authoritatively propounded by Mussolini himself in his article, "The Doctrine of Fascism," which appeared in Vol. XIV of the ITALIAN ENCYCLOPEDIA, translated and distributed by the Italian government; his ideas may be studied more extensively in the official SCRITTI E DISCORSI DI B. MUSSOLINI, ed. V. Piccoli, 11 vols. (Milan, 1934-1939); see also the apologia by Alfred Rocco, "The Political Doctrine of Fascism," INTERNATIONAL CONCILIATION, No. 223 (October, 1926), and the discussion by Mario Palmieri, THE PHILOSOPHY OF FASCISM (University of Chicago Press, 1936).

2 For the most recent re-evaluation of Mussolini, see: Denis Mach Smith, "Mussolini, Artist in Propaganda, The Downfall of Fascism," HISTORY TODAY, IX, 4 (April, 1959), 223-232.

4 For the Italian literature, see: Giacomo Perticone, "Political Science in Italy," 249-261, in UNESCO, CONTEMPORARY POLITICAL SCIENCE: A SURVEY OF METHODS, RESEARCH AND TEACHING (Paris: UNESCO, 1950), 258. For the studies in English see: Mario Einaudi, ITALY IN CRISIS, Vol. XIII, 3 (August, 1953), BEHIND THE HEADLINES (Toronto: Canadian Institute of International Affairs); Gabriel Almond, "The Christian Parties of Western Europe," WORLD POLITICS, I (1948), 30-58; Mario Einaudi, "Christian Democracy in Italy," REVIEW OF POLITICS, IX (1947), 16-33; "The Italian Elections of 1948," REVIEW OF POLITICS, X (1948), 346-361; Mario Einaudi, COMMUNISM IN WESTERN EUROPE (Ithaca, New York: Syracuse University Press, 1951); M. Einaudi and F. Goguel, CHRISTIAN DEMOCRACY IN ITALY AND FRANCE (Notre Dame, Indiana: University of Indiana Press, 1952).

5 Mario Einaudi and Francois Goguel, CHRISTIAN DEMOCRACY IN ITALY AND FRANCE (Notre Dame, Indiana: Notre Dame University Press, 1952); Renzo Sereno, "Italy," in Taylor Cole, Ed., EUROPEAN POLITICAL SYSTEMS (New York: A. A. Knopf, 1953).

6 Massimo Salvadori, "Italian Democracy in 1957," ORBIS, I, 3 (February, 1957), pp. 269-277.

7 For details, see: G. D. H. Cole, THE SECOND INTERNATIONAL 1889-1914 (London: Macmillan, 1956), Chapter XIX, "Italy," 709-745; Harry W. Laidler, A HISTORY OF SOCIALIST THOUGHT (New York: T. T. Crowell, 1927), 565-566.

8 Ugo La Malfa, "The Socialist Alternative in Italy," FOREIGN AFFAIRS, XXXV, 2 (January, 1957), 311-318.

9 Ugo La Malfa, OP. CIT., 315.

10 Paul Hofmann, "Red Membership in Italy Off 15%," NEW YORK TIMES (December 9, 1957).

11 C. L. Sulzberger, "All Life in Italy Infested by Reds," NEW YORK TIMES (March 17, 1954). See also: Ugo La Malfa, "The Socialist Alternative in Italy," FOREIGN AFFAIRS, XXXV, 2 (January, 1957), 311-318; Legislative Reference Service of the Library of Congress, WHO ARE THEY?, Part 7, MAURICE THOREZ AND ALMIRO TOGLIATTI (FRANCE-ITALY) (Washington, D.C.: Government Printing Ogce, 1957); Emmet John Hughes, "The Red Specter That Haunts Italy," LIFE, XXXVII, 9 (August 30, 1954), 92-105; Vincent M. Barnett, Jr., "Competitive Coexistence and the Communist Challenge in Italy," THE WESTERN POLITICAL QUARTERLY, LXX, 2 (June, 1954), 202-226; Enzo Tiberti, "The Italian Ex-Communists," PROBLEMS OF COMMUNISM, VIII, 1 (January-February, 1959), 52-56; etc.

[12] Massimo Salvadori, "Italian Democracy in 1957," ORBIS, I, 3 (Fall, 1957), 269-277.

[13] For more details, see: Legislative Reference Service of the Library of Congress, WHO ARE THEY?, Part 7; MAURICE THOREZ AND ALMIRO TOGLIATTI (FRANCE-ITALY) (Washington, D.C.: Government Printing Office, 1957), 4-8.

[14] Enzo Tiberti, "The Italian Ex-Communists," PROBLEMS OF COMMUNISM, VIII, 1 (January-February, 1959), 52-56.

[15] Claire Sterling, "The Crucial Hour for Italian Democracy," 291-299, in Max Ascoli, Ed., THE REPORTER READER, Garden City, New York: Doubleday, 1956).

[16] Paul Hofmann, "Red Membership in Italy Off 15%," NEW YORK TIMES (December 9, 1957).

[17] Barrett McGurn, "Mussolini's Dead—Fascism Isn't," NEW YORK HERALD TRIBUNE MAGAZINE (April 26, 1953), 7 ff.

[18] For more details, see: Mario Einaudi, "The Constitution of the Italian Republic," AMERICAN POLITICAL SCIENCE REVIEW, XLII, 4 (August, 1948), 661-676; J. C. Adams and Paulo Barile, "The Implementation of the Italian Constitution," IBID., XLVI (March, 1953); M. Ruini and others, LA NUOVA CONSTITUZIONE ITALIANA (Rome: 1947); Paoli Biscaretti di Ruffia, "The Italian Constitution on the Tenth Anniverasy of Its Enactment," IL POLITICO, XXIII, 1 (March, 1958), 59-71.

[19] Joseph LaPalombara, "A Decade of Political and Economic Change in Italy," WORLD POLITICS, IX, 3 (April, 1957), 423-432, reviewing Muriel Grindrod, THE REBUILDING OF ITALY: POLITICS AND ECONOMICS, 1945-1959 (London: Royal Institute of International Affairs, 1955); see also: Camillo Pellizzi, "Italy," 851-872, in Joseph S. Roucek, Ed., CONTEMPORARY SOCIOLOGY (New York: Philosophical Library, 1958); Franco Ferrarotti, "Sociology in Italy: Problems and Perspectives," chapter 24, 695-710, in Howard Becker and Alvin Boskoff, Eds., MODERN SOCIOLOGICAL THEORY: IN CONTINUITY AND CHANGE (New York: The Dryden Press, 1957); Charles E. Nowell, "Twentieth Century Trends in Italian, Spanish, and Portuguese Historiography, ITALY, Chapter 27, 367-373, in Matthew A. Fitzsimons, Alfred G. Pundt, and Charles E. Nowell, Eds., THE DEVELOPMENT OF HISTORIOGRAPHY (Harrisburg, Penna.: The Stackpole Company, 1954); Max Salvadori, Italy," Chapter IV, 140-183, in Max Salvadori, Joseph S. Roucek, George B. de Huszar, and Julia Bond, Eds., CONTEMPORARY SOCIAL SCIENCE, II: EASTERN HEMISPHERE (Harrisburg, Penna.: The Stackpole Company, 1954); Howard Becker and Harry Elmer Barnes, SOCIAL THOUGHT FROM LORE TO SCIENCE: II: SOCIOLOGICAL TRENDS THROUGHOUT THE WORLD (Washington, D.C.: Harren Press, 1952), Chapter XXV, "Sociology in Italy," 1002-1028.

[20] Massimo S. Giannini, "On the Development of the Social Sciences in Italy," INTERNATIONAL SOCIAL SCIENCE BULLETIN, II (Summer, 1950), 226.

[21] Giacomo Perticone, "Political Science in Italy," 249-261, in UNESCO, CONTEMPORARY POLITICAL SCIENCE: A SURVEY OF METHODS, RESEARCH AND TEACHING (Paris: UNESCO, 1950), 256.

[22] Internationally, the name of Benedetto Croce (1866-1952) stands out; in a series of volumes beginning with AESTHETIC AS SCIENCE OF EXPERIENCE AND UNIVERSAL LINGUISTIC (1902), Croce, Italian Senator and Minister of Education, advocated the revived doctrine of idealism. He repeated Hegel's phrase, "Philosophy is history," but reinterpreted it to give more emphasis to change and to progress. His theory of history regards all history as contemporaneous (WHAT IS LIVING AND WHAT IS DEAD OF HEGEL, 1915, HISTORICAL MATERIALISM AND ECONOMICS OF KARL MARX, 1922, HISTORY AS THE STORY OF

LIBERTY, 1941). For the relation of Croce to Fascism, see: Chester Macarthur Destler, "Benedetto Croce and Italian Fascism: A Note on Historical Reliability," THE JOURNAL OF MODERN HISTORY, XXIV, 4 (December, 1952), 382-390.

[23] For the works in Italian, see: Perticone, OP. CIT., 256.

[24] Emiliana P. Noether, "Italy Reviews its Fascist Past: A Bibliographical Essay," AMERICAN HISTORICAL REVIEW, LXI, 4 (July, 1956), 877-899.

[25] Denis Mach Smith, "Mussolini, Artist in Propaganda, The Downfall of Fascism," HISTORY TODAY, IX, 4 (April, 1959), 223-232.

[26] Paolo Monelli, MUSSOLINI: THE INTIMATE LIFE OF A DEMAGOGUE (New York: Vanguard Press, 1954).

[27] Roman Dombrowski, MUSSOLINI: TWILIGHT AND FALL (New York: Roy, 1956).

[28] Luigi Villari, ITALIAN FOREIGN POLICY UNDER MUSSOLINI (New York: Devin-Adair, 1956).

[29] Hugh Gibson, Ed., THE CIANO DIARIES 1939-1943, introduction by Summer Welles (New York: Doubleday and Company, 1946).

[30] Elizabeth Wiskemann, THE ROME-BERLIN AXIS: A HISTORY OF THE RELATIONS BETWEEN HITLER AND MUSSOLINI (New York: Oxford University Press, 1949).

[31] Pellizzi OP. CIT., 870.

[32] LaPalombara, OP. CIT., 425-426.

[33] Muriel Grindrod, THE REBUILDING OF ITALY: POLITICS AND ECONOMICS, 1945-1955) (London: Royal Institute of International Affairs, 1955).

NOTES TO CHAPTER SIXTEEN

[1] This practice, popularly known as the *Proporz,* is discussed in Herbert P. Secher, "Coalition Government: The Case of the Second Austrian Republic," AMERICAN POLITICAL SCIENCE REVIEW, LII (September, 1958), 791.

[2] On the origin of the Oevp see Felix Hurdles, "Wie die Oesterreichische Volkspartei entstand," OESTERREICHISCHE MONATSHEFTE, No. 10 (1945), 9. Also, BUNDESORGANISATIONSSTATUT DER OEVP. (Besshluss der Bundesparteileitung vom 19. 5. 1948 zufolge Weisung des 1. Bundesparteitages und Stellungnahme der Delegiertentagung vom 5. 12. 1947 in der Fassung des Beschlusses des 3. Bundesparteitages vom 3. März 1951 Mimeog); and Appendix: DIE OESTERREICHISCHE VOLKSPARTEI: WERDEN, WESEN UND ZIELE (also Mimeogs).

[3] Alfred Kasamas, PROGRAM OESTERREICH (Vienna: Oesterreichischer Verlag, 1949), Part III; see also Felix Hurdes, "Unser Solidarismus," OESTERREICHE MONATSHEFTE, No. 3 (1951) 133; N. Paunovic, "Organische Gesellschafsbetrachtung und Solidaritaet," IBID., No. 3 (1947 and Rudolf Pauker, "Gedanken ueber den Solidarismus," IBID., No. 9 (1948), 385.

[4] Murray Edelman, "The Austrian Wage-Price Agreements," MONTHLY LABOR REVIEW, June, 1954 LXXVII, No. 6. See also Herbert P. Secher, THE PROBLEM OF THE AUSTRIAN STATE: THE POST-WORLD WAR II EXPERIENCE (unpubl. Ph.D. diss., Univ. of Wisconsin, 1958), ch. 6.

[5] O. Dobrowlynski, "Partei und Buende," OESTERREICHISCHE MONATSHEFTE, No. 2 (1950) 78. Von besonderer Seite, "Primate der Partei," IBID., No. 3 (1950). 129. A. Maleta, "Noch einmal: Partei und Buende," IBID., No. 5 (1950). 299.

[6] DIE PROGRAMMATISCHEN LEITSATZEDER OEVP, Beschlossen am aus-

serordentlichen Bundesparteitag der OVP am 28. und 29. Jänner 1952 (Vienna: OEVP, 1952).

[7] "Pastoral Letter of the Austrian Archdiocese, "DIE FURCHE, March 1, 1949, 1.

[8] DIE WOCHEN-PRESSE, February 15, 1958.

[9] This position becomes apparent on reading the White Book of the Austrian Episcopate, KIRCHE UND STAAT IN OESTERREICH (Herausgegeben im Auftrage der oesterreichischen Bischofkonferenz, Vienna, 1955); cf. also DER SOZIAL-HIRTENBRIEF DER OESTERREICHISCHEN BISCHOFFE (Herausgegeben im Auftrage der Bischofskonferenz und mit Kommentar versehen von Dr. Paul Rusch, Innsbruck, 1957).

[10] Charles A. Gulick, AUSTRIA FROM HABSBURG TO HITLER (Berkeley: University of California Press, 1948), Vol. V.

[11] Rudolf Schlesinger, FEDERALISM IN CENTRAL AND EASTERN EUROPE (London: Kegan Paul, Ltd., 1945) ch. XI.

[12] Joseph Buttinger, AM BEISPIEL OESTERREICHS (Cologne: Verlag fuer Politik und Wirtschaft, 1953).

[13] Karl Bednarik, DER JUNGE ARBEITER VON HEUTE (Stuttgart: Gustav Kilpper Verlag. 1953). For a more detailed exposition of the internal structure and social composition of the Socialist Party, see Herbert P. Secher, "The Socialist Party of Austria: Principles, Organization, and Policies," MIDWEST JOURNAL OF POLITICAL SCIENCE, Vol. III, (August, 1959), 277.

[14] PROTOKOLL DES 12. PARTEITAGS DER SPOe (Vienna: Hrsgbn vom Zentralsekratariat im Auftrag des Parteivorstandes der SPOe, 1956).

[15] SPOE—Vertrauensman, Sondernummer, "Vorentwurf fuer ein neues Programm der SPOe" (nd.).

[16] DAS NEUE PROGRAM DER SPOE, beschlossen 14 Mai 1958 (Vienna: Zentralsekretariat der SPOe. 1958).

[17] DIE WOCHEN-PRESSE- November 30, 1957, 2.

[18] WIENER DIOZESANBLATT, (1945), 9.

[19] DIE WOCHEN-PRESSE, January 25, 1958, 3.

[20] WEG UND ZIEL, April 15, 1947.

[21] DIE SOLIDARITAET, No. 166, 1952 (Monthly of the Austrian Trade Union Federation), 2.

[22] Based on information in U.S. Dept. of State (Legation-report) MEMORANDUM NO. 146, March 22, 1949. Also, in 1951, the KPOe still listed 28,105 active organizers and party stewards, PROTOKOLL, KPOe Parteitag, 1951, 82. Assuming these to work in cells of five to ten persons each, roughly about 200,000 members can be estimated.

[23] Fritz Klenner, Ed., PUTSCHVERSUCH ODER NICHT? (Vienna: Verlag des OeGB, 1951).

[24] This is according to information gained by the author in interviews with former KPOe members during his residence as U.S. Fulbright Scholar at the University of Vienna.

[25] DIE VOLKSTIMME, January 26, 1957.

[26] Erwin Schaerf, ICH KANN NICHT SCHWEIGEN (Vienna: Privatdruck, 1947).

[27] DIE VOLKSTIMME, March 21, 1957.

[28] The information of this and the following paragraph is also based on interviews with several former KPOe members.

[29] "Das Programm der Vdu—52 Punkte," DIE NEUE FRONT, July 30, 1949.

[30] Herbert Kraus, "Ein aufschlussreiches Wahlergebnis," BERICHTE & INFOR-

MATIONEN (1951), Vol. V, 3718.
³¹ "Die Bedeutung der Freiheitlichen Partei Oesterreichs," BERICHTE UND
INFORMATIONEN (1956), Vol. II, 510.

NOTES TO CHAPTER SEVENTEEN

¹ Edwin O. Reischauer, JAPAN, PAST AND PRESENT (New York: Knopf,
1953), viii.

² George B. Sansom, in the foreword to JAPAN, PAST AND PRESENT (New
York: Knopf, 1953), 210.

³ Thomas A. Bisson, PROSPECTS FOR DEMOCRACY IN JAPAN (New York:
Macmillan, 1949), 3, states that Japan in its modern history has been controlled by
a "dictatorial oligarchy" composed of the military-naval leaders, the zaibatsu
(financial-industrial combines), the top bureaucrats, political leaders, and the big
landlords. Although not always united in their methods, all were solidly behind the
expansionism of the 1930's.

⁴ Of the many references to nationalism, probably the most exhaustive is
Delmer M. Brown's NATIONALISM IN JAPAN (Berkeley, Calif.: University of
California, 1955).

⁵ The Meiji oligarchs had recognized the potentially unifying force of Shinto
by bifurcating it into popular (everyday) and state (official) cults.

⁶ Brown, OP. CIT., 50-51.

⁷ Brown, OP. CIT., 278.

⁸ SCAP—Supreme Commander for the Allied Powers.

⁹ Robert A. Scalapino, "The United States and Japan," 11-75, in the American
Assembly's THE UNITED STATES AND THE FAR EAST (New York: Columbia
University, 1956), 45.

¹⁰ For a thorough review of the background to the so-called "MacArthur Constitution," see Robert E. Ward, "Origins of the Present Japanese Constitution,"
AMERICAN POLITICAL SCIENCE REVIEW, Vol. 50 (December, 1956), 980-1010.

¹¹ A sympathetic acount of the question of constitutional revision and the posi-
tion of the emperor is presented in K. Kawai, "Sovereignty and Democracy in the
Japanese onstitution," AMERICAN POLITICAL SCIENCE REVIEW, Vol. 49
(September, 1955), 663-672.

¹² Brown, OP. CIT., 267-268.

¹³ Murakami Hyoe, "Activities and Ideologies of an Ex-Service Organization,"
CHOU-KORON (Central Opinion) (Tokyo: May, 1958), 109-115.

¹⁴ R. P. Dore, CITY LIFE IN JAPAN (Berkeley, Calif.: University of California,
1958), 166.

¹⁵ It is interesting that the Japanese language has been enriched since 1945 by
terms describing prewar and postwar conditions. A traditionalist, for example, is a
"wet" (uetto) type, while an enlightened person is a "dry" (orai) type.

¹⁶ According to Nobutaka Ike in JAPANESE POLITICS, AN INTRODUCTORY
SURVEY (New York: Knopf, 1957), the Liberal-Democrats enjoy the support particularly of business executives, owners of business enterprises, bureaucrats and ex-
landowners, 203. It is also apparent that the rural vote is also largely conservative,
204-210.

¹⁷ Jerome B. Cohen, JAPAN'S POSTWAR ECONOMY (Bloomington, Ind.:
Indiana University, 1958), argues convincingly that it is largely an illusion to
consider China as Japan's most likely prospect for future trade. See especially
Chapter I.

[18] Hugh Borton, JAPAN BETWEEN EAST AND WEST (New York: Harper, 1957), 21.

[19] Taguchi Fukuji "A Treatise on the Japanese Socialist Party," CHOU-KORON (September, 1958), 137.

[20] The most complete account of Communism in Japan is that of Rodger Swearingen and Paul Langer in their RED FLAG IN JAPAN (Cambridge, Mass.: Harvard University, 1952), but for post-Occupation developments, see Paul F. Langer, "Communism in Independent Japan," Chapter II, in Hugh Borton, Ed., JAPAN BETWEEN EAST AND WEST (New York: Harper, 1957).

NOTES TO CHAPTER EIGHTEEN

[1] ALL MEN ARE MY BROTHERS: LIFE AND THOUGHTS OF MAHATMA GANDHI AS TOLD IN HIS OWN WORDS (New York: UNESCO, 1958), Introduction.

[2] Mahatma Gandhi, YOUNG INDIA (New York: B. W. Huebsch, Inc., 1923), 12.

[3] M. Gandhi, INDIAN HOME RULE (Madras: Ganesh & Co., 1922), 5th edition, 96-101.

[4] J. Nehru, NEHRU ON GANDHI (New York: John Day & Co., 1948), 84.

[5] Vinoba Bhave, BHOODAN YAJNA (Ahmedabad: Navajian Publishing House, 1953), 14.

[6] B. R. Misra, V FOR VINOBA (Calcutta: Orient Longmans Ltd., 1956), 36.

[7] Feature in *The Hindustan Times,* September 11, 1953, by A. V. Barve.

[8] S. N. Agarwal, "Economics of Boomidan," ECONOMIC REVIEW, IV 12, (April 1, 1953), 1.

[9] THE NEW INDIA: PROGRESS THROUGH DEMOCRACY (New York: The Macmillan Co., 1958), 196.

[10] LOC. CIT.

[11] Misra, OP. CIT., 55.

[12] Suresh Ramabhai, VINOBA AND HIS MISSION (Wardha: Sevagram, 1954), 208.

[13] Bhave, OP. CIT., 106.

[14] William Atwood, "Nehru Talks," LOOK, Vol. XVIII, No. 22 (November, 1954), 32.

[15] Chester Bowles, AMBASSADOR'S REPORT (New York: Harper & Brothers, 1954), 235-36.

[16] Atwood, OP. CIT., 35.

NOTES TO CHAPTER NINETEEN

[1] Herbert Croly, THE PROMISE OF AMERICAN LIFE (New York: The Macmillan Company, 1909).

[2] John Dewey, THE PUBLIC AND ITS PROBLEMS (New York: Henry Holt and Company, 1927); INDIVIDUALISM OLD AND NEW (New York: Minton, Balch and Company, 1930).

[3] Much of the polemical literature was more directed against Roosevelt, as a symbol, than against the New Deal as such. For a caustic left-wing critique, see

Mauritz A. Hallgren, THE GAY REFORMER (New York: Alfred A. Knopf, 1935); for a more virulent right-wing attack, see John T. Flynn, COUNTRY SQUIRE IN THE WHITE HOUSE (New York: Doubleday, Doran and Company, 1940); for a friendly appraisal, see Ernest K. Lindley, HALF WAY WITH ROOSEVELT (New York: The Viking Press, 1936).

4 For a broad interpretation of American liberalism since 1900, see Eric F. Goldman, RENDEVOUS WITH DESTINY (New York: Alfred A. Knopf, 1952).

5 Some of the intellectual vitality of the early New Deal is well caught in Hugh S. Johnson, THE BLUE EAGLE FROM EGG TO EARTH (New York: Doubleday, Doran and Company, 1935), and Francis Perkins, THE ROOSEVELT I KNEW (New York: The Viking Press, 1946).

6 For this reason, an ideological critique like Walter Lippmann, AN INQUIRY INTO THE PRINCIPLES OF THE GOOD SOCIETY (Boston: Little, Brown and Company, 1937), really missed its target.

7 This, at least, is my reading of Edgar Kemler, THE DEFLATION OF AMERICAN IDEALS (Washington: American Council on Public Affairs, 1941).

8 The best-known example of this genre of writing probably is Friedrich A. Hayek, THE ROAD TO SERFDOM (Chicago: University of Chicago Press, 1944).

9 Jane P. Clark, THE RISE OF A NEW FEDERALISM (New York: Columbia University Press, 1938).

10 David E. Lilienthal, TVA—DEMOCRACY ON THE MARCH (New York: Harper Brothers, 1944).

11 For a broad description of the intellectual ferment, see Merle Curti, THE GROWTH OF AMERICAN THOUGHT (New York: Harper & Brothers, 1943), 717-53. For a spirited discussion, see Leo Gurko, THE ANGRY DECADE (New York: Dodd, Mead and Company, 1947).

12 Louis Hartz, THE LIBERAL TRADITION IN AMERICA (New York: Harcourt, Brace and Company, 1955).

13 For a lucid statement of this position, see Morris Cohen, THE FAITH OF A LIBERAL (New York: Henry Holt and Company, 1946), 437-69.

14 The best and most comprehensive description of New Deal currents and cross-currents now available is Arthur M. Schlesinger, Jr., THE COMING OF THE NEW DEAL (Boston: Houghton Mifflin Company, 1959).

15 Quoted in Claire Leighton, Ed., THE ASPIRIN AGE (New York: Simon and Schuster, 1949), 275.

16 Samuel I. Rosenman, Ed., THE PUBLIC PAPERS AND ADDRESSES OF FRANKLIN D. ROOSEVELT (New York: Random House, 1938), II:11.

17 See James M. Burns, ROOSEVELT: THE LION AND THE FOX (New York: Harcourt, Brace and Company, 1956), 165-71.

18 Carl J. Friedrich, THE NEW BELIEF IN THE COMMON MAN (Boston: Little, Brown and Company, 1942).

19 For an attack of this sort, see Jules Abels, THE WELFARE STATE (New York: Duell and Pearce, 1951).

20 For a broad theoretical view, see Harry K. Girvetz, FROM WEALTH TO WELFARE (Stanford: Stanford University Press, 1950), 230-78.

21 For the "inside story" of New Deal informational campaigns, see Stanley H. High, ROOSEVELT—AND THEN? (New York: Harper & Brothers, 1937); for a scholarly account, see James L. McCamy, GOVERNMENT PUBLICITY: ITS PRACTICE IN FEDERAL ADMINISTRATION (Chicago: University of Chicago Press, 1939).

22 For a convenient, short history of the New Deal from the point of view

of social and economic reform, see Dixon Wecter, THE AGE OF THE GREAT DEPRESSION, 1929-1941 (New York: The Macmillan Company, 1948).

23 See Schecter *v.* United States, 295 U.S. 495.

24 A superb interpretation is offered by T. V. Smith, "The New Deal as a Cultural Phenomenon," Chapter X, 208-28, in F. S. C. Northrop, Ed., IDEO-LOGICAL DIFFERENCES AND WORLD ORDER (New Haven: Yale University Press, 1949).

25 For this interpretation, see Alan P. Grimes, AMERICAN POLITICAL THOUGHT (New York: Henry Holt and Company, 1955), 436-58.

26 Rosenman, OP. CIT., II:165.

27 The relationship between programs and Roosevelt's personality is well presented by Rexford G. Tugwell, THE DEMOCRATIC ROOSEVELT: A BIOG-RAPHY OF FRANKLIN D. ROOSEVELT (Garden City, N. Y.; Doubleday and Company, 1957).

28 For background and development of these New Deal measures, see Charles A. Beard and G. H. E. Smith, THE OLD DEAL AND THE NEW ((New York: The Macmillan Company, 1940).

29 Harold F. Gosnell, CHAMPION CAMPAIGNER: FRANKLIN D. ROOSE-VELT (New York: The Macmillan Company, 1952).

30 On the "court-packing plan," see Joseph Alsop and Turner Catledge, THE 168 DAYS (New York: Doubleday, Doran and Company, 1938); or Robert Jackson, THE STRUGGLE FOR JUDICIAL SUPREMACY (New York: Alfred A. Knopf, 1941). For the "purge" of 1938, see James Farley, JIM FARLEY'S STORY: THE ROOSEVELT YEARS (New York: McGraw-Hill Book Company, 1940); or Alben W. Barclay, THAT REMINDS ME (Garden City, N. Y.: Doubleday and Company, 1954).

31 José Ortega y Gasset, THE REVOLT OF THE MASSES (New York: W. W. Norton and Company, 1932).

32 See Francis G. Wilson, "The Inactive Electorate and Social Revolution," SOUTHWESTERN SOCIAL SCIENCE QUARTERLY, VI, No. 4 (1936), 73-84.

33 Edgar E. Robinson, THEY VOTED FOR ROOSEVELT (Stanford: Stanford University Press, 1947); Eugene H. Rosenbloom, A HISTORY OF PRESIDENTIAL ELECTIONS (New York: The Macmillan Company, 1957), 430-76.

34 For a New Dealer's view of the American press in the New Deal period, see Harold L. Ickes, AMERICA'S HOUSE OF LORDS: AN INQUIRY INTO THE FREEDOM OF THE PRESS (New York: Harcourt, Brace and Company, 1939).

35 William A. Lydgate, WHAT AMERICA THINKS (New York: Thomas Y. Crowell Company, 1944).

36 For this "realistic" interpretation of politics, see E. Pendleton Herring, THE POLITICS OF DEMOCRACY (New York: Rinehart and Company, 1940).

37 The concept of "charisma" as used by Max Weber refers to "the absolutely personal devotion and personal confidence in revelation, heroism, or other qualities of individual leadership." H. H. Gerth and C. Wright Mills, Eds., FROM MAX WEBER: ESSAYS IN SOCIOLOGY (New York: Oxford University Press, 1946), 79.

38 For a contemporary, balanced portrait, see Gerald W. Johnson, ROOSE-VELT: DICTATOR OR DEMOCRAT? (New York: Harper & Brothers, 1941).

39 For suggestive speculation along this line, see Robert E. Sherwood, ROOSE-VELT AND HOPKINS (New York: Harper & Brothers, 1948).

40 The best evidence comes, perhaps, from the autobiographies of Roosevelt's associates. The number of these works is great, but these are especially noteworthy: Harold L. Ickes, THE SECRET DIARY OF HAROLD L. ICKES (New York: Simon and Schuster, 1953-4), 3 vols.; Samuel I. Rosenman, WORKING WITH ROOSEVELT

(New York: Harper & Brothers, 1954); Marriner Eccles, BECKONING FRONTIERS (New York: Alfred A. Knopf, 1951); Cordell Hull, THE MEMOIRS OF CORDELL HULL (New York: The Macmillan Company, 1948).

[41] Wilfred E. Binkley, PRE3IDENT AND CONGRESS (New York: Alfred A. Knopf, 1947), 235-60.

[42] For a non-technical discussion of the decision process of the Supreme Court, see Charles P. Curtis, LIONS UNDER THE THRONE (Boston: Houghton Mifflin Company, 1947); for an appraisal of the post-1937 Court, see C. Herman Pritchett, THE ROOSEVELT COURT (New York: The Macmillan Company, 1948).

[43] Eleanor Roosevelt, THIS I REMEMBER (New York: Harper & Brothers, 1949).

[44] This formulation is indebted to George H. Mead, MIND, SELF AND SOCIETY (Chicago: University of Chicago Press, 1934).

[45] See Harold D. Lasswell, "Democratic Character," in THE POLITICAL WRITINGS OF HAROLD D. LASSWEL (Glencoe, Illinois: The Free Press, 1951), 465-525.

[46] For a close-up, see Joseph Alsop and Robert Kintner, MEN AROUND THE PRESIDENT (New York: Doubleday, Doran and Company, 1939).

INDEX

Abendroth, Wolfgang, 121
Abraham, 179
Abrams, Peter, 220
Adenauer, Konrad, 302, 305, 310, 312
Adler, Victor, 122
Alemán, Miguel, 253
Alessandri, Arturo, 258
Alexander II, Czar, 183
Almirante, Giorgio, 334
Amendola, Giorgio, 328, 333, 334
Anfuso, Filippo, 335
Araquistain, 248
Aristotle, 4, 25
Aron, Raymond, 132
Arzhanov, M. A., 36
Attlee, Clement, 151

Babeuf, Francis N., 127
Bacon, Francis, 6
Badoglio, Pietro, 320
Bakunin, Mikhail, 113
Balfour, Arthur James, 187
Bauer, Otto, 122
Bebel, August, 113, 118
Ben Gurion, David, 189, 190, 191
Bentham, Jeremy, 142
Beria, Laurenty D., 37, 38
Bernstein, Eduard, 102, 114, 119
Bevan, Aneurin, 150, 153
Bevin, Ernest, 145, 151, 153
Bhave, Vinoba, 402, 403, 404, 405, 406, 407
Bismarck, Otto Eduard, 113, 118
Blanc, Louis, 113
Blum, Leon, 127, 128
Boersner, Demetrio, 170
Bonomi, Ivanoe, 320
Borghese, Valerio, 335
Botsio, Kojo, 229
Bowles, Chester, 408
Breitner, 122
Brockway, Fenner, 148
Bukharin, Nikolai, 92, 102
Bulganin, Nicholas A., 39
Burns, Alan, 168, 169
Byrnes, James F., 289

Cabrera, Luis, 251
Calderón, Garcia, 248
Calles, Plutarco Elís, 252, 253
Camacho, Manuel Avila, 253
Cárdenas, Lázaro, 252, 253
Carlyle, Thomas, 214
Carranza, Venustiano, 251, 252
Castillo, Ramon, 255

Castro, Fidel, 258
Cerda, Pedro Aguirre, 258
Chalasinski, 78
Chamberlain, Joseph, 163
Chamberlain, Neville, 151
Chou En-lai, 41, 223
Churchill, Winston, 151
Ciano, Galeazzo, 340
Clausewitz, Karl von, 22
Clemenceau, Georges, 271
Clementis, Vlado, 66
Cohen, Morris, 428
Cole, G. D. H., 142, 155
Comte, Auguste, 23, 25
Coolidge, Calvin, 227
Cortines, Adolfo Ruiz, 253
Crevea, Altamira, 248
Croce, Benedetto, 339
Croly, Herbert, 415
Cyrankiewicz, 39

Dalton, Hugh, 142, 151
Dedijer, Vladimir, 95
Deist, Heinrich, 121
Demaria, 341
Denk, 374
Depreux, Edward, 129
Derisi, Nicholás, 250
Dewey, John, 415, 421
Díaz, Porfirio, 251
Dimitrov, G. M., 89
Dijilas, Milovan, 89, 96, 100, 103
Dobretsberger, 368
Doenitz, Karl, 282
Dollfuss, Engelbert, 122, 354
Dombrowski, 340
Dreyfus, Alfred, 184
DuBois, W. E. B., 228
Dutra, Eurico, 258

Einaudi, Luigi, 339
Eiselen, Werner, 201
Elizabeth I, Queen, 6
Emmanuel, King, 320
Engels, Friedrich, 47, 62, 63, 97, 111, 113, 118, 127, 170
Erasmus, Desiderius, 6,
Erhard, Ludwig, 301, 302, 303, 304, 307, 309, 310, 311, 312
Erlander, Tage, 131
Eucken, Walter, 301
Evans, F. W., 167

Fanfani, Amintore, 321, 326
Ferri, Enrico, 338
Figl, 349, 351
Filho, Café, 258
Finlayson, Clarence, 250
Flinders-Petrie, W. E., 7
Forti, 341
Fourier, Francois, 127
Franco, Francisco, 250
Franklin, Benjamin, 3, 5
Franklin, Johno Hope, 227
Friedeburg, von, 281
Fulbright, 25

Gaitskell, Hugh, 117
Galbraith, John Kenneth, 100
Galiani, 338
Gandhi, Mahatma, 163, 236, 397, 398, 399, 400, 401, 402, 403, 404, 406, 408
Garcia-Calderón, Francisco, 214
Garvey, Marcus, 226, 226
Gasperi, Alcide de, 321, 326, 327, 335
Gaulle, Charles de, 129, 265, 266, 270, 271, 277, 278
George, Henry, 142
Gero, Erno, 40
Ghisalberti, A. M., 341
Giannini, 338, 339
Ginsberg, Asher, 184, 185
Giolitti, Antonio, 332
Giolitti, Giovanni, 332
Gobineau, Joseph, 214
Gomulka, Wladyslaw, 40, 41, 65, 66, 69, 72, 73, 74, 75, 76, 77, 78, 79
Gori, Fernando, 335
Grant, Madison, 214, 215
Graziani, Rudolfo, 334, 335
Green, T. H., 142
Gregory of Tours, 8
Gronchi, Giovanni, 322, 326
Guesde, Jules, 127

Hanusch, 122,
Hardie, Keir, 141, 142, 146
Harz, Louis, 417
Haya de la Torre, Victor Raul, 254, 260
Hegel, G. W. F., 23
Henry VIII, King, 6
Hermes, Andreas, 288
Hertzog, J. B. M., 204
Herzl, Theodor, 184, 185, 186, 187
Hilferding, Rudolphfi 119, 122
Hess, Moses, 182, 183, 184
Hitler, Adolf, 4, 11, 120, 256, 281, 284, 286, 292, 297, 320, 335, 340, 341, 356, 357, 371

Hoernlé, R. F., 197, 203
Hoover, Herbert, 417
Hoxha, Enver, 89
Hyndman, H. M., 142

Ibáñez, Carlos, 258
Ickes, Harold, 427
Innitzer, Cardinal, 354

Jansen, Ernest George, 201
Jerome, 8
Jodl, Alfred, 281
John of Salisbury, 8, 16
Johnson, Hugh, 420
Jones, Jesse, 427
Juarés, Jean, 114, 127, 128

Kadár, János, 40, 41, 71
Kaganovich, Lazar, 40
Kaiser, Jakob, 288
Kalischer, Zebi Hirsch, 181, 182
Kardelj, Eduard, 93, 103
Kautsky, Karl, 102, 113, 119, 130
Kennan, George, 163
Kerensky, Alexander, 9, 33
Khrushchev, Nikita, 38, 39, 40, 41, 43, 44, 53, 67, 68, 69, 73, 76, 101, 102, 165, 328
Kipling, Rudyard, 161
Kishi, 388
Knoeringen, Waldemar von, 12
Koenig, Bishop, 354
Kolakowski, Leszek, 75, 78, 81
Kostov, T. D., 66
Kott, 78
Kubitschek, Juscelino, 258
Kulski, W. W., 41
Kun, Béla, 33
Kunschak, 351

Landa, Bishop, 7
Lassalle, Ferdinand, 118
Lauro, Achille, 324, 335
Lemmer, Ernst, 286
Lenin, Nikolai, 31, 32, 33, 43, 47, 48, 54, 69, 88, 95, 97, 162, 165, 167, 169, 170, 17
Leo XIII, Pope, 250, 326
Liebknecht, Wilhelm, 113, 118, 119
Lima, Alceu Amoroso, 250
Lincoln, Abraham, 426
Liu, Shao-chi, 54, 59
Locke, John, 141
Lombroso, Cesare, 338
Long, Huey, 3
Longo, Luigi, 330
Luebke, Heinrich, 311
Luther, Martin, 6

Luxemburg, Rosa, 113, 119

MacArthur, Douglas, 386
MacDonald, Ramsay, 142, 148, 149
Machiavelli, Nicollo, 6
Madero, Francisco, 251, 260
Makonnen, T. I., 229
Malater, Pal, 41
Malenkov, Georgy, 37, 38, 40
Malthus, Thomas, 141
Mann, Tom, 145
Mao Tse-tung, 41, 44, 47, 48, 54, 55, 57, 58, 61
Maritain, Jacques, 250
Marsanich, Augusto de, 335
Marx, Karl, 47, 62, 63, 69, 80, 96, 104, 105, 111, 112, 113, 114, 116, 117, 118, 123, 127, 128, 130, 141, 170, 256
Masanobu, Tsuji, 385
Mateos, Adolfo López, 253
Matteotti, Matteo, 126, 328
Maxton, James, 148
McGuffery, William Holmes, 3, 5
Mendelssohn, Moses, 182
Mendés-France, Pierre, 129, 269
Mieville, Roberto, 335
Mihailovich, Draza, 89
Mikoyan, Anastas, 69, 172
Milliard, Peter, 228
Mollet, Guy, 117, 128, 129
Molotov, Vyacheslav, 40
Monroe, James, 11
Mosca, Gaetano, 338
Mussolini, Benito, 125, 256, 319, 320, 317, 334, 335, 340, 341
Mussolini, Vittorio, 335
Myrdal, Gunnar, 172

Nagai, 215
Nágy, Imre, 40, 41, 69, 70, 71, 72
Napoleon I, Emperor, 267
Nasser, Gamal Abdel, 4, 167
Nehru, Jawaharlal, 400, 401, 403, 407, 408, 409
Nenni, Pietro, 125, 126, 321, 327, 328, 330, 334
Newton, Isaac, 6
Nietzsche, Friedrich, 341
Nkrumah, Kwame, 166, 228, 229, 230, 232, 233, 234
Noether, 340
Noguchi, Yone, 215

Obregón, Alvaro, 252
Okuma, 218
Olivier, N. J. J., 208

Ortega y Gasset, José, 421
Orwell, George, 76
Ollenhauer, Erich, 120, 121
Ordóñez, José Battle y, 248, 256
Owen, Robert, 141, 142

Padmore, George, 228
Pareto, Vilfredo, 338
Parri, 320
Pastore, 326
Paton, John, 148
Pella, Giuşeppe, 321, 326
Perón, Juan, 249, 250, 255, 256
Perticone, G., 341
Philip, André, 129
Pieck, Wilhelm, 284
Pijade, 89
Pinsker, Leon, 183, 184, 185, 186
Pitterman, 358, 359, 360
Plaza, Galo, 258
Poskrebyshev, Alexander, 37
Possony, Stephan T., 166, 167
Presenti, 341
Proudhon, Pierre Joseph, 113, 127

Queretaro, 252

Raab, Ing., 349, 351, 352
Rajk, Laszlo, 40, 66
Rákosi, Jeno, 40, 89
Ramadier, Paul, 133
Renner, Karl, 122
Rhodes, Cecil, 163, 207
Ricardo, David, 141
Robles, Oswaldo, 250
Rodó, José, 248
Roepke, Wilhelm, 301
Roosevelt, Franklin D., 3, 22, 415, 418, 421, 424, 425, 426
Roosevelt, Theodore, 215

Saladin, 213
Salvadori, 329, 331
Samuel, Viscount, 184
Sansom, George, 379
Saragat, Giuseppe, 125, 126, 322, 327
Schaerf, Adolf, 358, 366, 374
Scharf, Edwin, 365, 366, 367, 369
Schumacher, Kurt, 120
Schuman, 321
Schumpeter, Joseph, 163
Schuschnigg, Kurt von, 122
Schutz, Alfred, 214
Schweitzer, Albert, 14
Schwering, 286

469

Seeger, Heinz, 120
Segni, Antonio, 321, 322
Shaw, George Bernard, 142
Shepilov, 40
Simmel, Georg, 25
Slansky, Rudolph, 37, 66
Smith, 340
Smith, Adam, 141
Snowden, Philip, 149
Sorokin, P. A., 7
Spencer, Herbert, 23, 25
Spengler, Oswald, 7, 15, 25
Stalin, Joseph, 22, 31, 37, 38, 39, 41, 47,
   48, 66, 67, 68, 69, 77, 88, 89, 90, 91, 97,
   101, 102, 103
   101, 102, 363
Stallard, Charles Frampton, 197
Stoddard, Lothrop, 214, 222
Srijdom, J. G., 198, 202
Sturzo, Don Luigi, 326, 341
Sun Yat-sen, 164

Tito, Josip Broz, 39, 40, 56, 67, 68, 89, 90,
   91, 93, 95, 96, 101, 102, 224
Togliatti, Palmiro, 321, 322, 332
Tomlinson, F. R., 202, 203
Tourè, Sèkou, 232
Townsend, 215
Toynbee, Arnold, J., 7, 25, 161
Trotsky, Leon, 32, 88, 96, 102
Truman, Harry S., 415

Ulbricht, Walter, 284
Umberto, King, 320, 336

Vaillant, Edouard, 127
Valletta, Vittorio, 333
Vandervelde, Emile, 114
Vargas, Getulio, 257, 258
Vasconcelos, José, 244 248
Veblen, Thorstein, 13
Velasco, José Maria, 258
Verwoerd, Henrik, 201, 208
Vico, G., 338
Videla, Gabriel Goonzález, 258
Villari, L., 340
Vukmanovic-Tempo, 103

Walker, Eric, 165
Wallace, Henry, 427
Wazyk, 78
Weizman, Chaim, 187
Wells, H. G., 142, 161
Wilson, Woodrow, 3, 20, 163, 415
Winslow, E. M., 163
Woroszylski, 78

Zaisser, Wilhelm, 38
Zapata, Emiliano, 251
Zeeland, Paul van, 164
Zhdanov, Andrei, 37, 69
Zhukov, Georgy, K., 39, 40
Zimand, 78
Zoli, Adone, 322

470